HISTORY OF KERALA

HISTORY OF KERALA

WRITTEN IN THE FORM OF NOTES ON VISSCHER'S LETTERS FROM MALABAR

K. P. PADMANABHA MENON

EDITED BY
T. K. KRISHNA MENON

IN FOUR VOLUMES
VOLUME ONE

GYAN

Published by

Gyan Publishing House
5, Ansari Road
Daryaganj, New Delhi-110002
Phone: 011-47034999, 9811692060
E-mail: books@gyanbooks.com

Distribution Network
gyanbooks.com
India, USA, Canada, UK, Australia, France

ISBN : 978-81-212-3526-6 (Set)
ISBN : 978-81-212-4663-7 (HB)
First Published, 1929

2nd Impression 2020

Printed at: Gyan Press, Delhi.

History of Kerala Vol. I
Author: K. P. Padmanabha Menon

DEDICATION

TO

MRS. K. P. PADMANABHA MENON.

CONTENTS.

NOTES

LIST OF ILLUSTRATIONS.

FOREWORD

BY THE EDITOR

Mr. K. P. Paḍmanābha Mēnōn (1857—1919), the author of these 'Notes', came of an ancient and respected Nāyar family. His mother, Śrīmaṭi Pārvaṭi Amma, had a very generous heart and a religious turn of mind. Mr. Paḍmanābha Mēnōn was greatly devoted to her, and dedicated to her his monumental *History of Cochin.* His father, Mr. P. Śaṃkuṇṇi Mēnōn, rose from the humble estate of a petty writer to the proud position of the Senior Dewan Peishkar in the model State of Ṭrāvancōre; and 'Ruler after Ruler, Dewan after Dewan, and Resident after Resident praised and petted him' not alone for the diligent discharge of his official duties under trying conditions, but also 'for services unselfishly rendered in various walks of life'. Rājā Sir T. Māḍhava Rāo, with whom Mr. Śaṃkuṇṇi Mēnōn had to enter the lists many a time, entertained the highest regard for him; and, when he retired from the Prime Ministership of Ṭrāvancōre, presented Mr. Mēnōn with a memento, and referred in graceful terms to 'his patriotic devotion to his adopted country' and, in particular, to 'the freedom and independence' with which he had always submitted his counsels to his sovereign. "His *History of Travancore* is the only connected, complete and authoritative work on the subject that we possess at the present day, even after so many decades of research, and it is an added testimony to the capaciousness of his genius that he should have found time in the midst of his arduous official work to collect the materials for it and to write it."

Mr. Paḍmanābha Mēnōn was the last of the three children born to this couple; and heredity bestowed on the son in full measure the admirable qualities of his parents.

His career as a student was smooth and sunny, promising and successful. His masters and professors always spoke in terms of praise of his ability, industry and general good conduct. He attained considerable proficiency in English and Malayāḷam, History and Law. After his graduation in law, he served his apprenticeship under Sir H. H. Sheppard, who was then the Advocate-General to the Government of Madras, and who afterwards became a Judge of the Madras High Court and then the Legal Advisor to the Secretary of State for India. Before he settled down in life, he went on an extensive all-India tour which served to widen his intellectual horizon and to put, as it were, the finishing touches to his education at school and college. And, then, to be with his mother in her old age, and to enable him to look after her affairs, he settled down, in 1885, at Eṟṇākulam to practise before the Appeal Court of the Cochin State. With his deep legal erudition and general culture, his patient study of cases and his warm but calm and courtly advocacy, his accessibility and his affable though dignified manners, he easily won the confidence of an increasing number of liberal and respectable clients. But he set his face against unnecessary litigation, and had no partiality for rich parties whose payments were problematical. He soon topped the profession, and, what is more commendable, also began to lead public opinion in Cochin. The people of Cochin were, therefore, very sorry to let him go when, in 1899, he left Eṟṇākuḷam for Ṭṟivāndṟuṃ, where he thought he could find a wider field for his activities and better facilities for carrying on his researches into the early history of Kēraḷa, a subject on which he had set his heart for a long time. On that occasion, he was presented with an address by the prominent citizens of the State, including Dewan Gōvinda Mēnōn and Pāliyaṭṭ Valiya Achhan, the premier noble of the State. Let me quote a few sentences from that document :

> "Allow us to take advantage of this occasion to convey to you our feelings of extreme sorrow at your separation from us, and also of our appreciation of the several sterling qualities by which you have not merely distinguished yourself as the head of your profession here, but also made yourself alike dear to us all in your private capacity as well. * * * . You have now rightly come to occupy the first and foremost position amongst them. Your sound knowledge of law, your independence and honesty, above all your perseverance and thoroughness in the discharge of your duties cannot but furnish an example worthy of imitation not merely by those practising along with you, but by every student of law aspiring to rise and distinguish in the profession. Not less exemplary has been your conduct all along as a true, loyal and public-spirited citizen. * * * * . Your readiness and capacity to give sound and sensible advice in matters public and professional have been taken advantage of not merely by your large clientele, your numerous friends and the helpless poor, but also by the Darbar which has chosen you as a member of its Legislative Committee."

Equally pertinent are the remarks contained in the address which, in 1917, the Eṙṇākuḷaṃ Bar Association presented to him on the completion of his sixtieth year.

> "In so doing, it is tempted to look back on the long vista of your past life of supreme usefulness, and to hold up your manly independence, many-sided scholarship, the almost religious fervour with which you maintained the high traditions of the bar, the purity and greatness of your character, and the enthusiasm you have displayed in legal and historical researches as models of imitation for the present generation and for generations yet to come."

These are not conventional platitudes pressed out of servile flatterers, but the grateful offerings of reverential appreciation spontaneously paid to him by individuals, well-known and independent.

But I am anticipating incidents.

At Ṭṙivāṇḍṙuṃ too, he had very good practice ; the Judges also were pleased with his dignified address, his 'complete mastery' over his cases and his 'lucid presentation' which, they said, 'betokened superior attainments in law, and hard and patient labour in the preparation of his cases.' The Government of Ṭrāvancōre recognised his ability by nominating him as a non-official member of its Legislative Council, and the public by electing him as one of the members of the Marumakkaṭṭāyaṃ Committee, appointed to consider important changes in the law and custom that affected the Nāyars.

The memorandum that he prepared on the various questions referred to that Committee is, in the opinion of competent critics, a masterpiece. It contains a critical examination of the origin of the Marumakkaṭṭāyaṃ system, an accurate account of the existing state of Malayāli society and practical suggestions for reforming it, so as to satisfy the growing needs of the time. When a piece of similar legislation was found necessary in Cochin, its Government appointed Mr. Mēnōn as one of the members of the Committee whose labours resulted in the passing of the 'Nāyar Regulation' in the State. His report is a learned treatise on the social conditions of the Nāyars, and an effective and convincing reply to those who opposed all legislative attempts to reform them, and particularly on the lines suggested by that Committee.

It should have been stated before this that, in 1902, domestic affairs, considerations of health and repeated calls from old clients forced Mr. Mēnōn to come back to Cochin, and once again to settle down in Erṇākuḷaṃ.

He liked his profession; he took to it seriously; he did not flirt with Law like a dilettante, nor did he try to win her favours with the mere fading glories of a gown; but he courted that 'jealous mistress' like a devout votary, gained her good graces and succeeded in keeping them to the last day of his life. The arduous struggle, the blows and bruises he took in good part, and spoke with pride of the ties of comradeship at the bar which were rarely found in other walks of life. He always stood for the traditions and the dignity of his profession. On a memorable occasion, when he had to espouse the cause of a poor client against persons in position, the special First Class Magistrate not only convicted his party, but passed certain adverse remarks on the conduct of the counsel. The Sessions Judge upheld the conviction, and did not question the propriety of the irrelevant remarks of the Magistrate ; but a Full Bench of the Appeal Court acquitted the accused and completely exculpated the lawyer from the charge of professional misconduct. Being a member of the High Court Bar of Madras, Mr. Mēnōn placed all the papers, together with the written arguments he had prepared for the Appeal Court, before Sir Arnold White, the Advocate-General, who afterwards became the Chief Justice of the Madras High Court. Sir White remarked that 'the written argument showed great ability and erudition', and expressed his opinion that there was 'no foundation or justification for the charges', and said that the Magistrate committed 'a serious error of judgment in taking upon himself to rebuke Mr. P. Mēnōn in connection with his conduct.' 'On the facts of the case as disclosed on the record, one fails to see how any impartial tribunal dealing with the question of alleged misconduct could come to any other conclusion than that which was arrived at by the Judges of the Appeal Court.'

This question was fought out with no malice, at least on the side of Mr. Paḍmanābha Mēnōn. 'He was never wrath except with wrong'. And he was indignant only with an exertion when actuated by a sense of duty. It was in a spirit of charity that he always judged his fellows. His was no sunless creed. He was a deeply religious man. That he was generous, that he had a rare feel for his fellows will be seen from the numerous liberal benefactions he made in his last will and testament to temples, asylums, watersheds, educational institutions and to the Bar Association. Special reference must be made at least to one of these gifts. It is the handsome endowment, which now amounts to Rs. 17,200, in favour of the Madras University to encourage post-graduate research work in the History of Ancient India. Here we find the man who not only dwells on the past but also 'reaches a hand through time' into the future.

President Wilson once remarked that "the world never needed lawyers who are also statesmen more than it needs them now." True; and it is so not only in America but also in every part of the civilised world. And in this small State of Cochin, Mr. Mēnōn has considerably helped 'to swell that common tide, on the force and set of whose currents depend the prosperous voyaging of humanity'. On every page of his *History of Cochin* will be seen the temper and the vision of the seer who wants his countrymen to read the past to benefit the present and the future. Of this book, H. H. Kērala Varma, the late Valiya Kōil Ṭampurān, a great scholar, poet and politician wrote in these appreciative terms:

> "The work is of absorbing interest, of immense educative value, and unique in the annals of Malayalam Literature. You have laid all available resources under contribution, and produced a colossal work which does the highest credit to your task, culture, judgment and perseverance. The major portion of the information contained in it is thoroughly new in the sense that it has hitherto been a sealed book even to the student of history. What prodigious industry you must have brought to bear on this self-imposed task of yours, the world will appreciate, though it can never adequately gauge. I hope that this great work will be preserved as an invaluable treasure in every household."

Thus it will be seen that Mr. Paḍmanābha Mēnōn was not only a lawyer and statesman, but also a scholar and historian. Lord Bryce remarks that "for the highest sort of historical work, four gifts are needed: unwearied diligence in investigation, a penetrating judgment which can fasten essential points, an imagination which can vivify the past, and the power over language which we call style" He had the full equipment for a historian: thirst for truth, mental training and unflagging patience.

The present work is another striking illustration of these qualities of our author. The form of the work and the delay in its publication are entirely due to his pious solicitude for historical accuracy. He knew that, if he were to write a connected and complete history of ancient Malabar, there would be breaks which he could not very well fill up with authentic materials. So he took Visscher for his aid and prepared cameos on many of the important events and institutions, customs and manners and the salient features of the country, and of its social, political and economic conditions based, as far as possible, on contemporary records. The work was completed long before 1910; and well-known works and papers have laid it under contribution; yet, he went on investigating matters over which there could possibly be any doubt or dispute, or which could be viewed from different standpoints, so that he might present a front of unassailable veracity. His scrupulous regard for truth and the strenuous efforts to attain high standards of scholarship must remind one of the ideals which Lord Acton was never tired of preaching.

He remained a student, a systematic, diligent student, from start to finish. With him rest meant only change of work. A certain scrupulous austerity streaked his tastes. He refused to be drawn to the dissipations of social or civic life ; and his circle of friends too was select and solid. His health was not robust ; and his sedentary habits, mental strain and absence of physical exercise did not leave much room for improving it. And but for his wife, that tireless nurse, who dedicated her married life to preserve that of her dear husband, it would not have been possible for him to turn out the prodigious work that he did.

The present work was the great undertaking of his life. His numerous and valuable contributions to Indian and English journals, even his *History of Cochin* may be considered as mere bouquets he prepared from the superfluous flowers he gathered for this rare garland. Visscher's book he has used as the thread on which to string the ancient history of Kērala.

Jacobus Canter Visscher, at the time he wrote these letters to his friends at home, was Chaplain at Cochin. He lived there five whole years (1717-1723). " I have been induced to write these memoirs, " says he, " by the desire to relate the veracious circumstances of which I have either myself been an eye-witness, or which I have heard from trustworthy persons. * * My observations will bear only upon the manners and customs of the people, their laws, rites and ceremonies, the description of their kingdoms, as well as their origin and their modes of government, and other similar subjects. "

Even the educated people in Malabar know very little about the early history of their own country. They may have been fortunate enough to study a little of the history of India ; they may be on familiar ground in the histories of Europe and of America. But of their own land they know very little ; and of the particular part of the country from which they come, they know much less, in spite of their great inheritance from its past which has enriched every moment of their lives. The fault is not entirely theirs. No books are extant that treat of the civilisation of ancient Kērala, of its Maṭhaṃs and Pāṭhaṡālās for advanced study, of its culture in the fine arts, of the military prowess and maritime enterprise. That brilliant and fascinating chapter is closed for them. They think that the tide of their national history set in only with the advent of the English. The period anterior to that is to them dark, unrelieved by any achievement, either martial or intellectual, and puzzling alike to the historian and to the student of history.

Mr. Paḍmaṅābha Mēnōn has lighted up with a flood of light a part of that region shrouded in dense darkness, and has displayed in an orderly fashion a few of those wonderful events and institutions, manners and customs which will give one an idea of the eminent position to which Kēraḷa had arisen even in those early days of her social and political evolution. In this, he has done a service not alone to Kēraḷa but also to India as a whole. For, as a great historian rightly remarks, "The attempt to find the basic element of Hindu civilisation by a study of Sanskrit and of the history of Sanskrit in Upper India is to begin the problem at its worst and most complicated point. The scientific historian of India ought to begin his study with the basin of the great rivers of the south, and not with the Gangetic plain". Another seconds him and says that "a variety of causes has tended to the belittlement of Peninsular India's contribution to the history of India and of the world at large," and asserts that the time is ripe for South India "to champion her cause and to assert her claims to recognition." This book, it is hoped, would serve to promote a comprehension of that contribution and of its recognition, and to stimulate in others a spirit for further study and research. Of the merits of this work, I shall not presume to speak. It will remain as a standing reproach to those who float in the placid stream of idleness, with the dreamy consolation that a busy officer or practitioner has only time to make money and, perhaps, to try to save it. The work has come to stay; let it remain with its sphere of ever-increasing usefulness—that is my wish, that my prayer.

I edit this because of the direction in the author's will: "I appoint Mr. T. K. Kṛṣhṇa Mēnōn my literary executor. I request him to see my *Notes on*

Visscher's Letters from Malabar through the press after full and satisfactory revision at his hands." On my own account, I am glad to be connected with this production. For, it is a privilege to me to be of service to my friend and guide whose help was sure and whose word was clear in all the trials of my life. Further, the editing, I find, is at once a discipline no less than a delight to me. I have endeavoured to the best of my ability to execute the sacred trust imposed on me by the confidence of my friend. In the performanee of my work, Mrs. Paḍmanābha Mēnōn has extended to me a kindness and confidence which has considerably enhanced the delight I feel in the discharge of my duty. To one who is more than a sister to me, an offer of thanks must be out of place.

It is but proper to gratefully record here that the early pages of this book had the benefit of revision by Messrs. D. M. Cruickshank and Glyn Barlow, two former Principals of the Mahārājāh's College at Eṛṇākuḷaṃ. For the index and for aid in revising the proofs, I am obliged to Mr. M. Achyuṭa Mēnōn, B. A., B. L. To him they were a labour of love for the memory of his brother-in-law. I am also indebted to my friend, Mr. P. Ḍāmōḍara Mēnōn, B. A., the Secretary to the Diwan, for the support he ungrudgingly gave me on various occasions. The task of preparing the manuscript for the press was cheerfully undertaken by Messrs. N. M. Kṛṣhṇa Ayyar and P. Achyuṭa Mēnōn, two quondum clerks of the author. Their work I remember, and record with pleasure. But for the willing and efficient co-operation of Mr. C. P. Nārāyaṇa Mēnōn, B. A., F. L., the Superintendent of the Government Press, and of Mr. N. M. Paramēśwara Ayyar, the Head Examiner, and the staff under them, it would not have been possible for me to bring out the book so soon or in such good form. To them my very best thanks are due. I have great pleasure to add that a few of the blocks that illustrate the work are prepared by Brother Leo of the local Industrial Press. Most of the rest were kindly lent to me by the Cochin Darbar. The author's will states that " the Cochin Darbar has, in the time of Mr. A. R. Banerji, M. A., I. C. S., C. I. E., kindly permitted me to use for my work the blocks prepared to illustrate the volumes of ' Cochin Castes and Tribes '. My warmest thanks are due to Diwan Mr. Banerji for this. "

If there are defects, I am prepared to bear the blame till the book is relieved of them by the kind attention of discerning critics. The future of the book I safely leave in the hands of the lovers of this land and to the GRACE of GOD.

Kumārālayaṃ,
Eṛṇakulaṃ ;
7th November 1924.

T. K. KṚṢHṆA MĒNŌN.

Visscher's
LETTERS FROM MALABAR.

LETTER I.

Situation of Malabar—Signification of the name—First colonization according to the Native legends—Difference between the Highlands and Lowlands—The stone found in Highlands—Cheapness of provisions—Neither volcanoes to be found nor earthquakes ever experienced here.

Though the broad ocean which rolls between the Netherlands and Malabar presents a barrier to my personal enjoyment of your delightful society, it can neither extinguish my affection nor prevent me from holding communication with you by letter. I, therefore, despatch this, as the first tribute of our constant friendship, in which I propose to relate the origin of Malabar according to the tradition of the natives.

This country of Malàbar[1] is situated about 10 degrees north of the Equator, stretching from Cape Comorin[2] in the south to Mount Delli[3] in the north. The inhabitants are called by us Malabaris, by the Portuguese, Malavares, and by themselves Mallealler. This word properly signifies mountaineers, not that the inhabitants dwell amid lofty mountains, for the greater part of the country, stretching along the sea coast, is flat and marshy; but the name must be derived from the original colonists, who were a mountain race.

Their legend,[4] doubtless embellished by fiction, is as follows:—In by-gone ages, the sea washed the foot of a mountain range, which now lies 7 or 8 miles inland. The men who dwelt in the neighbourhood gained their subsistence by fishing along the mountain shores. Now it happened that there dwelt at Gocarna near Goa, a certain prophet universally renowned for sanctity whose name was Paroese Raman. Discovering to his sorrow that his aged mother had acquired an evil notoriety in the neighbourhood for her misdeeds, he felt unable to endure the public shame she had brought upon him. At length, inspired by a divine impulse, he seized a rice-winnow, and hurled it with tremendous

1. Note 1, pp. 1 — 7.
2. Note 2, pp. 7 —13.
3. Note 3, pp. 13—16.
4. Note 4, pp. 17—20.

force from Gocarna right over the sea: by a wonderful miracle, it was carried onward as far as Cape Comorin, upon which all the sea between the two places immediately dried up, and was transformed into that tract of level land, to which we now give the name of Malabar. The prophet resolved to take up his abode with his mother in this strange land, hoping here to find a hiding place for her disgrace. Meantime, the fishermen of the mountains, hearing of the miracle, flocked into these lowlands and made for the seashore. The prophet met them, and, knowing that a land without inhabitants is waste and desolate, persuaded them to remain and settle there; and in order the more to attract them, he invested them with the dignity of Brahmins, promising at the same time to support them according to his custom, by which he was pledged to provide food daily for 3,000 of that caste. He then took the fishing nets with which they were laden, and tore them into stıands, which he twisted together, to make the three cords which the Brahmins wear as a sign of their dignity tied in a knot on the shoulder, and falling down below the waist. These Brahmins of Malabar are called Namboories and are reproached by the other Brahmins for their descent from fishermen.[1]

You will agree with me in treating this story as a mere fiction, but there is probably some foundation in fact for it,[2] as there is for most fables: and any one who carefully examines these lowlands, will grant that formerly they must have been submerged under the sea. Not only do they lie so low that, like the coast of Holland, they are under water in the rainy season,

1. Note 5, pp. 20—22.

(Another account of this tradition is as follows:—When Parasuraman was doing penance on the mountain Mahandra, where, after having gained twenty-one victories over the Kchettries, he had laid up all his arms, the chief *Munees* or saints came to see him, and, having saluted him, advised him to cause the sea to recede, and to bring to light the land of Kerala,[3] which had been submerged under the ocean in a former age. Parasuraman immediately went to the neighbourhood of Gokarnam and, hurling an axe, recovered the land from the sea as far as to where the weapon fell. The limits are Cape Comorin on one side, and Gokarnam on the other. There are three divisions, that of Kerala, Tulu and Heiga. From Cape Comorin to the river Kanyirota is the Kerala division. The middle portion from thence is the Tulu division. The last part is the Heiga division, the boundary of which is the river Bashpasetu. These three divisions embrace what is now called Malayalim. Parasuraman, having thus created the land of Kerala, summoned the Brahmins from a foreign country,[4] and made over the country to them, and giving chief authority to them over the employments and occupations of the four castes, namely. the Brahmin, the Kchettry, Veyshya and the Sudra, he rested from his work.—H. D.)

2. Note 6, pp. 22—28.

3. Note 7, pp. 28—42.

4. Note 8, pp. 42—76.

but they are in many parts broken up into islets by the waters of the sea, which flow in channels[1] between them, and into which the rivers from the mountains empty themselves. May we not then suppose that this low and broken land is washed over entirely from time to time? We know that, in some European countries, the sea encroaches on the land, and in other places recedes. It is true, no doubt, that many parts of the shore are elevated. Nearly the whole coast from Kully Quilon to Ponnani is low and broken up by numerous water-courses but the coast of Quilon[2] is steep and rocky, or rather it is merely a rock covered with a stratum of soil, so that here it would seem the land can never have been under water. While I am on the subject of this rocky district, I must add that the local stone is very well adapted for building. There are quarries here from which the stone is hewn; and I have seen a piece of this stone when being cut from the rock, split like wood under the stroke of the axe. The stone is reddish yellow and spotted,[3] very porous and full of holes, in which the lime used in building, gets mixed up, and the whole becomes so well consolidated, that old stone is often preferred to new.

The East India Company find this stone very serviceable for erecting their fortresses and factories, and the inhabitants use it in building their houses.[4]

But to return from this digression. I must inform you that the variety of soil here causes a marked variation in the fertility of different districts. It is true, generally speaking, that the pleasant champaigns and sweet clover fields with which Holland abounds are not to be found here, nor is it the case that the fields are clothed with many coloured flowers, breathing sweet fragrance, as the poet Antonides has it, in his poem on the river Y.[5]

"Fruitful Cochin, where sweet blossoming May.
"For ever decks the earth with livery gay."

This is a poetical license deviating far from the real truth, as, commonly, the vegetation is but thin and scanty, and the fields are anything but rich in flowers. It is true, indeed, that the low sandy tracts are more fertile than the more elevated and rocky districts, for, while these yield nothing but trees and tree-fruits,

1. Note 9, pp. 76—83.
2. Note 10, p 83.
3. (Laterite, below which is found limestone6 and lignite. The cliffs rise to nearly 250 feet in some places.—H. D.)
4. Note 11, p. 83.
5. (Antonides van der Goes, a Dutch poet who flourished in the seventeenth century. His principal work was a poem on the river Y, or the "Ystroom". See Foreign Quarterly Review, Vol. IV, p. 57.)
6. Note 12, pp. 83—85.]

the former contain vast expanses of rice fields, which are so productive that they suffice to furnish rice not only for the whole of Malabar but also for exportation. It is curious that so dry a plant as rice grows in the water. In fact, the natives sow the *nely* in the low lying meadows, at the time when they are a foot or two under water, scattering the seed in the water, through which it sinks to the earth, and there takes root; when about a foot high, the seedlings must be transplanted.[1]

Provisions are all cheap here, especially rice and meat. A pig can be brought for a dollar, a good calf for half a dollar, a fowl for ten cents.[2] This must be attributed to the habits of the natives, among whom it would be considered a sacrilege to eat beef—merely to kill a cow being a crime punished by death without mercy. Some castes are permitted to eat other meats, but it is little done ; the Brahmins have a mortal abhorrence of animal food, and make use of nothing that has had life.[3]

Upper Malabar is very elevated, and contains many mountain ranges rising one behind the other.[4] It boasts few mineral productions,[5] except iron, which is beaten out in small bars and exported to Mocha. There are no volcanoes in this part of the world, nor are any serious convulsions of the earth known. Indeed there has never been an earthquake within the memory of man,[6] while, in the countries lying further to the East, both volcanoes and earthquakes are more common.

LETTER II.

On some disorders indigenous to the country and the causes of them—The distinction of seasons, and the effects thence arising.

The great respect I entertain for your judgment causes me to take up my pen with diffidence, being aware that my letters are not worthy to meet your eye; but I trust your kindness to overlook their deficiencies, and to be satisfied with my desire to inform you of all that I have observed in these distant lands.

I remember to have read in certain books of travels that there are men to be met with in the Alps whose necks are covered with swellings, and that the inhabitants look upon them as

1. Note 13, pp. 85—100.
2. Note 14, pp. 100—101.
3. Note 15, pp. 101—109.
4. Note 16, pp. 109—110.
5. Note 17, pp 110—120.
6. Note 18, pp. 120—122.

ornamental.[1] Similar swellings are often to be seen on persons in this country ; but here the disorder generally attacks the legs, and other parts of the body besides.[2] The disorder always begins with a fever, which they here call the raging fever, which sometimes causes delirium, and, as the strength of the malady increases, great pain is felt in the legs or in other parts attacked : the fever then settling in the suffering part, causes it to swell in a frightful manner. In the commencement of the disorder, the swellings subside again, but, as the fever returns, at intervals of one or two months, or a longer period, they reappear and become permanent ; so that men have been found with legs as thick as my waist and with other frightful swellings.[3]

This malady cannot be ascribed to any particular nation or race of men. I remember to have read that it attacks only the St. Thomas' Christians, and that they may be known by this mark ; but nothing can be more absurd than such a notion, for we see every day people of all kinds, men and women, Mahometans, Heathens, and Christians, and even Europeans who reside here, attacked by it. You, who have given your mind to the investigation of the mysteries of nature, will, no doubt, be able to give a sufficient reason for these facts ; but I trust you will have the goodness to weigh my opinion, which may possibly assist in the explanation.

I believe that the cause of the disorder is in the water and the soil, and partly also in the air, which is filled with vapour drawn up from the water. It appears that in the low parts of Malabar in the neighbourhood of Cochin, the earth is full of saltpetre or some other substances, which mingle with the water of the pools or rivers near the sea coast ; and the people who constantly drink this water acquire a disorder and fever which causes at first shivering, and then drives the particles which occasion the fever into a certain part of the system. These particles, being sharp

1. (The author alludes to the goitre or bronchocele. The classical reader will recollect the line in Juvenal (Sat. XIII, 162) *Quis tumidum guttur miratur in Alpibus?* The sufferers were called ' Gutturosi '. It was formerly supposed that this glandular swelling only appeared in certain countries, such as Switzerland and Savoy, and that its origin arose from drinking snow-water. It is, however, found in certain districts of South America , Sumatra, and even in Great Britain, especially in Derbyshire, from whence it has been called the " Derbyshire Neck. " Its origin is very obscure, but as it prevails in countries, both where snow exists and where it does not, drinking snow-water can no longer be asserted as the cause of its appearance.—H. D.)

2. (Elephantiasis. This prevails to a great extent among the inhabitants of the Western Coast ; nor has any certain remedy hitherto been discovered for the disease, short of amputation of the diseased part. It is more than probable that bad water and bad diet, are its remote causes.—H.D.

3. Note 1, pp. 123—130.

pungent, cause great pain, and at last distend the small vessels in the afflicted region, which after the first access of the complaint, subside again, but after fresh particles have been driven in by fresh fevers, the enlargements not only remain fixed but increase in size. On the legs thus deformed, the flesh becomes loose and spongy, but this makes them light also, so that, however enlarged they may be in size, the patients can walk with ease.

These remarks of mine seem to be strengthened not only by the taste of the water of these lowlands, which is brackish and unpleasant, but by actual experience; for the people who are in better circumstances, and can afford to bring their water from a distance, from the river Mangatti, are seldom visited by the disease, while on the other hand, those who drink the water of the neighbourhood suffer therefrom. On this account, the East India Company has wisely ordered that this water should no longer be given out to the garrison, but water from the Mangatti instead; and it has been observed that the malady has been much less prevalent among the troops since that time. I must add that the juice of the young cocoanuts is also very deleterious; and my neighbour said that he himself had caught the disorder from that cause. The reason is plain: for we know that the vessels of the cocoanut palm are of great width, so that it imbibes water from the earth just as it is, without detaching it from the particles of saltpetre; and in this state the fluid enters the young nut, the interior of which contains nothing but a sort of water, rather sweet in taste, and consequently it gives rise to the same disorder as the water of the wells.

I am so fortunate as never to have suffered this disease; though I could not escape another, which the natives term *Mal-de-terre*,[1] which attacked me almost every month, beginning with great uneasiness and pain in the bowels, and ending with violent sickness and diarrhoea. The Indians have a curious remedy for it, which is to take a hot iron and burn the soles of the feet with it. This often has a good effect.

Not to detain any longer with these painful topics[2], I shall now turn to descriptions of other natural phenomena and proceed to relate briefly the courses of the seasons in this part of the world.

One hardly finds here that difference of seasons[3] which is experienced in Europe: for neither are heavy hailstorms,[4] nor

1. Note 2, pp. 130—133.
2. Note 3, pp. 134—157.
3. Note 4, pp. 157—160.
4. (Hailstorms have occasionally occured in these districts, though they are of very rare occurrence. One of unusual severity occurred only last month (April 1862) in the Town of Cochin itself.—H. D.)

thick falls of snow, nor hard frosts, ever seen or felt in these parts. One must divide the year into two *Monsoons*,[1] or seasons, the one being the period of dry weather, the other the period of rain. The dry season may be divided again, first into a temperate season, when the air is tolerably cool: this begins in November, when the atmosphere is bright and clear; the S. E. landwinds then begin to blow, attaining their greatest force in January and subsiding again in February. They blow every morning during this period, and are found by experience to be prejudicial. After this follows the hot season, when the wind ceasing, the air becomes exceedingly sultry, especially in the forenoon and at night, because there is not the slightest breeze to cool it; whereas, in the afternoon, there is often a wind from the sea. In the month of May, the season begins to change. The heavens become overspread with the heavy clouds, and violent storms of thunder and lightning occur. I cannot find that these storms cause so much damage as among us in Holland, the cause of which I take to be the rarefaction of the air through the continued heat of the sun; so that the thunder and lightning, finding less obstruction, become more easily diffused and fall to the earth with diminished force. The rainy season sets in at the end of May or beginning of June, and lasts till October, bringing perpetual storms of rain, often accompanied by violent winds. It would be well-worth the trouble of any philosopher to enquire into the cause of this rainy season, and I consider it my duty to speculate upon it, because the phenomena afford some clue to the decision of the question.

In the hot season we find that the wind blows entirely from the North and West—on which account ships then coming from Persia and Surat have a speedy voyage. It is also certain that as, during that time, the powerful action of the sun causes a quantity of vapours to accumulate in those regions, and rain falls

1. (A knowledge of the monsoons may be traced from very early ages. Humboldt says that Alexander's companions were not ignorant of the existence of the monsoons, by which navigation was so greatly favoured between the Eastern Coasts of Africa and the North and Western parts of India. After having spent ten months in navigating the Indus between Nicaea on the Hydaspes and Pattala, with a view of opening the river to a universal traffic, Nearchus hastened to sail from Stura, at the mouth of the Indus at the beginning of October, since he knew that his passage would be favoured by the N E. and Eastern Monsoons in the same parallel of latitude. The knowledge of this remarkable local direction of the winds, subsequently emboldened navigators to attempt to sail from Ocelis on the Straits of Babelmandeb, cross the open sea to Muziris (south of Mangalore), the great Malabar emporium of trade, to which products from the Eastern shores of the Indian peninsula, and even gold from the distant Chryse (Borneo?) were brought by inland trade—Cosmos.)

there as little as it does here, therefore the north-west wind must drive those vapours in a south-easterly direction, till they meet the mountain ranges which are a barrier to their further progress. These mountains are the same which stretch from Cape Comorin through Asia. Now the vapours, as they approach these mountains, get more and more condensed, till at length, in the month of May, they are forced down by violent winds, then rebound again, and finally descend in rain on all places situated west of the chain. That these mountains are the true cause of the rainy season appears from the circumstance that when the rainy season sets in on this side of the chain, on the other side, just at the same time, the dry season begins. Hence we are frequently astonished to find that in two places on opposite slopes of the same mountain, one has the rainy and the other the dry weather at the same time : and when, on our side, the rains leave off and the south-east winds begin to blow, just then the rains commence of the Coromandel Coast.

And while we are on the subject of the weather, I must observe that, in these countries, storms do not last so long as with us in Holland; for, while, there, we often know them continue without intermission for two or three days, here, on the contrary, high-winds never maintain their violence beyond an hour or two, when a calm ensues, after which the wind rises again : resembling in this circumstance the sudden whirlwinds (*Travades*) which navigators encounter in the tropics, and chiefly near the Equator. These storms come on very quickly, and generally end as suddenly. First, a small cloud is seen, which increases rapidly, and then, whirled onwards by a strong wind, bursts in heavy rain. It is very curious to observe how suddenly the clouds gather in the midst of a clear and hot atmosphere. It would seem that some vapours in the lower portion of the atmosphere are prevented by the powerful action of the sun's rays from collecting together ; then driven up higher than usual, they encounter a cooler stratum of air, by which they are condensed together with all the other vapours that meet them by the way (like the steam condensed on the lid of a tea-kettle) ; then, urged forward like an ever-increasing snow-ball, by the force of the wind and the heat of the sun, they become over charged with weight, and finally precipitate themselves to the earth. A description of this kind of storm or something like it seems to be given us in 1st King's XVIII, 44, 45 .—"Behold a little cloud no bigger than a man's hand rose out of the sea * * * and it came to pass in the meanwhile that the heavens were black with clouds and wind, and there came a great rain."

In conclusion, I will note the effects of the rainy season on our roadstead. This it closes up entirely and chokes with sandbanks, on which the repelled waves break with violence. These sandbanks begin to form in the month of May and are washed away in September and October. Their formation and their destruction are owing partly to the action of the river, and partly to that of the sea; for, at the commencement of the season the river empties itself with great impetuosity into the sea, dragging with it a quantity of sand: on the other hand, the waves of the sea acting in the opposite direction, stop the progress of the sand just where the two bodies of water break upon each other. This is the reason why the sandbanks at that time are constantly augmenting; but, when the force of the sea subsides, and the river has still a vast weight of water to carry down, then the sandbanks are washed away again.

LETTER III.

Description of Cochin and Calicut—Conduct of the English there.

I must now give you a description of Cochin,[1] the place where I am settled. It was wrested, as you are no doubt aware, together with other forts, from the Portuguese, by the arms of our East India Company. During the war with that nation, in the year 1662, the Admiral, Ryklof van Reede, was despatched from Batavia with a fleet to besiege this town; but the Governor defended it with so much resolution that the attempts of the Admiral were foiled, and the mortality among his men compelled him to retreat. The courage of the gallant sailor was not cooled by this failure. At the close of the same year, he returned with a fleet, and, after some conflicts, a Captain named Pierre du Pont succeeded in making himself master of one of the gates; upon which the Governor, Ignatio Sarmento, capitulated, being allowed to march out with his troops and baggage, and with all the Portuguese inhabitants with their false gods and images.[2] This conquest took place on the 8th of January 1663; and the anniversary is still celebrated by a sermon in the morning, and in the evening by the display of banners and discharge of guns from the walls.

The principal founders of Cochin were Francisco and Alphonso Albuquerque, who visited this country in 1504, in the reign of king Emanuel of Portugal.[3] It was afterwards much enlarged and beautified under Vasco, so that it became one of the wealthiest

1. Note 1, pp. 161—183.
2. Note 2, pp. 183—207.
3. Note 3, pp. 207—210.

commercial towns in the Indies, and was erected into an Episcopal See by the Roman Pontiff.[1] The Portuguese have still a titular Bishop of Cochin, whose residence is at Goa or near Quilon; but he does not possess the slightest authority here. This town formerly contained handsome churches, but they have been either demolished, or converted into magazines. The Church of St. Francisco alone remains, and is used for our reformed service; while the Roman Catholics perform their services outside the city, having several churches scattered over the country. Before it fell into the hands of the East India Company, Cochin must have been a considerable town, as is proved by the remains of buildings which are everywhere to be seen; but, since that time, it has become much less prosperous, in consequence of the restrictions imposed by the Company upon its commerce,[2] which, under the Portuguese, had been entirely free, with the exception of the titles due to the Raja. The town is situated at the mouth of a noble river abounding in fish, with pleasant well-wooded banks, and studded with many islets which are planted with cocoanut palms. If wealthy persons ever settled here, as they do in Batavia, they might lay out very pretty villa residences and gardens upon these shores.[3]

As regards the fortifications,[4] they are sufficient to protect the town against the natives, who do not understand the science of besieging, the methods of bombarding, etc., but they would not be strong enough to resist a large European force, especially as the garrison, consisting of only 300 men, is inadequate to man the walls.

The circumference of the town is tolerably extensive. It would take a man a good half hour to walk round the walls. but the space enclosed by them contains several unoccupied portions. The streets are regular enough, but the houses are quaint, and built after the old Portuguese fashion. Each apartment has a separate roof. The dwelling rooms are not level with the ground, but you mount several steps to reach the hall, which is the first apartment of the house: underneath are empty chambers, in which probably the Portuguese lodged their slaves, or stowed away their goods. Most of the rooms in the common houses are plastered after the Hindoo custom, with cow dung, which serves for paving, and is renewed every week. They say here that such floors are much more wholesome than stone ones; it is certain at least that they retain the dampness in the rainy season.

The town of Cochin is inhabited by Christians, for the Heathens are not allowed by their own laws to dwell in it.[5] The

1. Note 4, p. 210.
2. Note 5, pp. 210—212.
3. Note 6, pp. 212—213.
4. Note 7, pp. 213—215.
5. Note 8, p. 215.

inhabitants comprise, however, different classes: there are the native Christians, the Topasses, and the Europeans; the last, who form the most considerable portion of them, comprising also the mixed race, sprung from European fathers and native mothers. This is the class chiefly employed in the service of the East India Company, though they seldom rise to higher offices than that of book-keeper.

There is a very commodious roadstead at Cochin, in which several ships from all parts of the world annually cast anchor; as Malabar, situated as it were in the centre of the East Indies, is a convenient station for vessels to refit and take in water, fuel, and provisions (which articles are good and plentiful here) before continuing their voyage, vessels from Batavia to Mocha, or from Persia and Surat to Batavia, touch here, as well as French and English ships on their way to and from their Indian settlements. It is also frequented by Moorish vessels. It is true that none but small craft can enter the river, on account of the sandbanks, above which are not more than eleven or twelve feet of water; and in the rainy season, large ships cannot remain in the roadstead: but about four leagues from Cochin is a bay called Muddy Bay,[1] where they may lie securely in the mud.[2]

Next to Cochin I shall place the capital of Malabar, Calicut,[3] which has been made famous by Portuguese books of travels,

1. (Mud Bay or Muddy Bay, is the commercial port of Alleppie in the kingdom of Travancore, 36 miles south of Cochin, remarkable for the singular natural break-water formed in the open sea, consisting of a long and wide bank of mud, the effect of which is so completely to break the waves, that ships of all sizes can securely anchor even at the stormiest season of the year in the open roads, where the water is perfectly calm. The origin of this deposition of mud, has never been satisfactorily accounted for. It imparts a dirty colour to the water and makes it thick and slimy. It has shifted more or less within the last century, but not to any great extent. A similar deposit exists at Narakkal about 20 miles north of Cochin, and the advantage of this latter place, as a natural open harbour for shipping, has recently been brought to the notice of the British Government —H. D.)

2. Note 9, pp. 215—227

3. Note 10, pp. 227—239.

(The well-known city of Calicut, which has experienced such a variegated fate, lies on the sea-coast, in the latitude of 11° 15′ north. It consists partly of houses constructed of teakwood, and partly of huts composed of palm branches interwoven through each other, and covered with palm leaves. Of stone buildings there are very few. The fortress of Calicut is of much greater antiquity than the city to which it has given its name. The natives of Malabar believe that it was built by *Cheramperumal* from whom all the petty Malabar princes are descended. This city was raised almost to the ground by Tippoo Sultan, who destroyed its flourishing trade expelled from the country the merchants and factors of the foreign commercial houses; caused all the cocoanut and sandal trees to be cut down, and

and also by its being the seat of Government of the Zamorin. This town is called by the natives *Karrekovre*, which signifies *hencoop*. The reason they give for this name is that when Cheramperumal divided his kingdom, he gave to the Zamorin for his share only so much land as the sound of a cock crowing from its perch could be heard over. You must not suppose that this town is in any way to be compared with those of Europe, or that it comes up to the exaggerated descriptions of the old Portuguese travellers. It possesses neither walls nor fortifications of any sort, but is built irregularly along the shore. In the bazaar or market place alone is there any order in the arrangement of the houses. These, which are mostly built of stone and covered with the dried leaves of the palmyra tree, are of so miserable a description that they can be compared to nothing one sees anywhere else. Being a free port, Calicut is frequented by various races. Among the Europeans, the English and French have factories there, the former being the most influential.[1] The Moors also are in great force, and form the majority of the inhabitants.[2] They are not very favourable to the English, whom the fear of the Zamorin alone prevents them from attempting to expel from the city. Mr. Adams, the head of the English in these parts, never ventures into the streets unarmed, which is a plain proof of the fear he entertains of the inhabitants. The English, depending on the favour of the Zamorin, do not refrain from injuring the Mahometans in underhand ways. They will inform the bandits who lurk in the vicinity, some seven or eight leagues from the town, when the Moorish *Almadcs* (or small vessels used for trading along the coast) are about to depart with merchandize, so that they may take the opportunity to pillage them.

Calicut, though still a commercial town, is falling into decay. Many ships, both English, French and Moorish, however, keep up their trade with it, because there are no restrictions on commerce, with the exception of a duty of 5 per cent paid to the Zamorin on all imports, to enforce which he keeps officers stationed here. As the English have the largest business, they are the most favoured by the Zamorin, whom also they often supply with money when he is in want of it.

ordered the pepper plants in the whole surrounding district to be torn up by the roots, and even to be hacked to pieces, because these plants, as he said, brought riches to the Europeans and enabled them to carry on war against the Indians.—*Bartolomeo's Voyage to the East Indies.*

1. Note 11, pp. 239—248.
2. Note 12, pp. 248—249.

Mr. Adams, the head of the English in this place, was brought up there from a child, and having, from his youth, traded with the people of Malabar, he acquired a familiarity with their language which gained for him much influence among them. In consequence of this advantage, he was chosen by the English as their Governor. Being an enemy to our Company, [1] he incited the Zamorin to the late war, himself lending, in order to promote it, 100,000 rix dollars, with which that Prince defrayed the expenses of the war. We have no reason to doubt this story, since he even sent English officers to assist the Zamorin, to defend Fort Paponette against our arms. Nay more, when Chetwa was conquered by the Zamorin, and our people expelled, the English immediately erected a factory there, in order to secure the pepper-trade; this factory was destroyed when the fort was re-taken. From all this, it is evident that the Dutch have but little good to expect from the English, and that they cannot prevent that people from playing their game slyly whenever it is in their power. The English cannot but look with envious eyes upon the great influence our Company possesses in India, and the confidence they inspire among the nations with whom they trade. It would be better if our neighbours would examine more closely into their own behaviour, and see whether their arrogance is not the cause of the mistrust and dislike with which they are regarded.

I will relate an instance of this sort of conduct which took place at Calicut in the year 1720. The English officer, Second-in-Command there, went out one day to drive in his carriage. It happened to be a day when the great national assembly of the Malabars[2] was collected in the open air to deliberate on the affairs of the State. The Englishman, in order to show his contempt for them, instead of making a circuit, drove right through the multitude, in spite of their entreaties that he should desist from such unbecoming conduct, which threw the whole assembly into the utmost confusion. On the following day, when the assembly met again at the same place, the Englishman chose to shew his courage by driving through it again with some ladies who were in his carriage. This time the people were so incensed at the repetition of the outrage, that they struck their hands to their weapons and cut the carriage to pieces, and the hero and his amazons had to escape wounded to their homes. Though this was no more than the miscreant deserved, yet Mr. Adams, declaring that the conduct of the natives was cruel and inhuman, left Calicut and threatened to set the bazaar on fire. The Zamorin, who reaped so much

1. Note 13, pp. 249—250.
2. Note 14, pp. 250—269.

profit from the English trade, managed to pacify him and to recall him to Calicut, but as the bad feeling of the natives towards the English still exists, he distrusts them and spends most of his time at Tellicherry.

LETTER IV.

Description of Quilon, Aiwike, Kully Quilon, Porcad, Cranganur, Paliport, Chetwa—Dutch fortresses in Malabar—Narrative of the late war—Cannanore, Anjengo, and Tellicherry belonging to the English—Eddawa, formerly a possession of the Danes, but not abandoned.

Your laborious but honourable office being connected with military affairs, it seems fitting, in writing to you, to blow the trumpet of war, and I shall therefore proceed to relate the history of the last which occurred in Malabar. I will give you also a description of the forts situated in that country, that you may conceive a clearer idea of the whole.

About 30 leagues south of the town of Cochin, is the Fortress of Quilon,[1] which was conquered by the Company from the Portuguese. It was formerly a town,[2] but is now only a petty fort, and as the sea washes, and has been undermined, a portion of the walls, it has now been resolved to reduce it on that side, so that some of the inhabitants will be forced to break up their houses, and take up their abode outside the walls. This fort is of use in vesting the power of the Rajahs of Travancore and of Signati,[3] in whose domains it is situated; and as an outpost against the foreigners, especially the English, whose fort at Anjengo is at no great distance. The Fortress of Quilon commands the bay of the same name: tolls are levied from the native traders, and licenses (*passen*) issued to them. It possesses little territory inland, besides the plain: on the sea side the boundary is marked by a gate with four stone pillars. There are certain stations in this province, such as Tengapatnam in the south near Cape Comorin, which serve principally as places for the despatch of letters, and for cutting millstones and other stones used in the service of the East India Company. A good deal of linen also is woven here, though the trade belongs to Tutacorin. North of Quilon are

1. (Collam, Coilon, Coulon, or Quilon, signifies, in Malayalim, a tank. It was built, A. D. 825; and was at one time a place of considerable importance. The natives of the country begin their era from its foundation, in the same manner as the natives of Cochin begin theirs from the origin of the island of Vaipeen. In former days there were a great many weaving looms, and manufactures of cotton and stoneware here. Alexius Menezes, the first Archbishop of Goa, built an excellent fortress here, which afterwards fell into ruins, being neglected by the Dutch.—H. D.)

2. Note 1, pp. 270—292.

3. Note 2, p. 292.

some other factories, among which are the great and little Aiwike,[1] situated at the mouths of rivers, where the Company stations corporals with some coloured soldiers to prevent the smuggling trade in pepper.

The factory of Kully Quilon is especially noteworthy, being the first which the East India Company possessed in Malabar. The Rajah of Kully Quilon was the first sovereign who admitted the Company into his territories, though he would not grant them permission to erect a fort. About 400,000 lbs. of pepper are annually purchased by the Company in this place.[2]

Poracad[3] is a second factory, situated nearer to Cochin. This also bears the name of the kingdom in which it is situated, A considerable quantity of rice is produced here owing to the fertility of the low-lands. The Company obtain the same amount o pepper here as in Kully Quilon.

There are three forts belonging to the Company to the north of Cochin, where more danger is to be apprehended from hostile powers. Cranganoor is about fifteen miles from Cochin in this direction, situated at a bend of the river of the same name. It was once, as the Portuguese travellers tell us, a considerable town,[4] but it is now merely a small, though strong, fortress, and it formerly served as a restraint upon the power of the Zamorin; but this object has ceased to exist, since that prince has withdrawn from the neighbourhood, and the Company's territories have been extended particularly during the late war. The fort serves now as an outpost against the Raja of Cranganoor, a very feeble potentate, and yet more against the Raja of Porcad, whose territories lie on the opposite side of the river.[5] It is also of use as a preventive station and against the smuggling trade, and the transit of prohibited goods; as well as in levying certain tolls for the East India Company. The station of Palliport [6] is in the same province; it is situated at the mouth of the river Cranganoor, which falls into the sea three miles from the town of the same name, and takes its name from a *strong quay* which was formerly garrisoned, but is now abandoned, as there is no enemy to be feared in the neighbourhood; and the place is only tenanted by a corporal and a few black soildiers. Like other forts it is used as a preventive station.

1. Note 3 pp. 292—293.
2. Note 4, pp. 293—294.
3. Note 5, pp. 294—297.
4. Note 6, pp. 297—328.
5. Note 7, pp. 328—329.
6. Note 7 (a), pp. 329—330.

Chetwa is another fort about twelve leagues from Cochin, serving partly to protect commerce, and partly as a defence against the Zamorin, whose dominions lie contiguous. It stands at the mouth of the river, and is, at the present moment, the strongest fortress in Malabar. Its erection, seven or eight years ago, cost us a severe war which lasted several years, and the history of which is worth relating.[1]

The East India Company having resolved to build a new fort[2] gave oders to B. Ketel, the Commandant of Malabar, to finish it as speedily as possible. This alarmed the Zamorin, who knew it was intended to curb his power on this coast. He accordingly left no means untried to impede its progress; and not succeeding by fair methods, he determined to try force. The fort was now almost completed; and he saw that the time for his attempt was come. He was encouraged by learning that the garrison, consisting of 48 men, were lodged outside the half finished fortress, and that none of the requisites had been provided for its defence. This shewed the greatest want of foresight in the Commandant, who had received intelligence of the intended attack, and ought therefore to have increased his garrison, to have made convenient places for artillery, and ordered his men to keep within the walls, and be on the alert. The Zamorin perceiving his advantage, crossed the river at night with 600 men, who were soon followed by more: and all was effected so quietly, that about 4 o'clock in the morning of Jan. 22nd, 1715, they surprised the soldiers who were sleeping in their huts before the fort. They took to flight in great alarm, and the Zamorin obtained possession of the place without striking a blow. Near the fort was a *pagger*[3] of the East India Company built of palm trees,

1. Note 8, pp. 330—331.

2. The following account of this transaction is given by Captain Alexander Hamilton, who travelled among the East Indies between the years 1688 and 1723:— 'The Dutch were building the fort of Chetwa, and the Zamorin got some of his men under the disguise of labourers to be employed by them, and to take an opportunity of surprising the Dutch. The two lieutenants who had the overseering of the work were one evening diverting themselves with a game at tables in a guard room about half a mile from the fort. They had let some of their soldiers go straggling about, and the disguised natives took the opportunity to kill the sentinels, signal to the ambuscade, and take the half built fort. One of the lieutenants, in attempting to retake it, was killed; the other, thinking it impracticable to attack greater forces within than he had without, embarked for Cochin with his men. I was fortuned to be at Cochin when he and his men arrived, and by a Court Martial he was sentenced to be shot, which sentence I saw executed. The Zamorin caused the English flag to be hoisted, and the fort was destroyed.'' —Trans.

3. Note 9, pp. 331—332. A *pagger* appears to be a small fortified village or hamlet.

the interstices filled with earth and rubbish so as to make a breastwork to which the fugitives hastened announcing their misfortune. Ensign Stock, who was in command of the place, received the tidings with consternation, and having but a very weak garrison, while the enemy's force was continually increasing, he made no attempt to expel them. For this neglect, capital sentence was pronounced against him by the Council of Justice sitting at Ceylon, God knows with what right, and he was shot, only a few weeks after he had been elevated to the rank of lieutenant. When the tidings of this disaster reached Cochin, it caused a universal panic among the Dutch, and gave rise to a spirit of indolence among the natives, who thought that we were ruined. Commandant Ketel resolved to march out of the city with three companies, which formed the greater portion of the garrison, leaving orders that the artificers, sailors and scribes should man the walls. He advanced rapidly, taking with him three pieces of artillery, and two mortars, and hastened to Chetwa. Mangatatya,[1] the Zamorin's general, stationed himself with his troops to obstruct his passage, but as soon as they felt the power of our cannons and musketry, they took to their heels; many were cut down, others drowned in the river, and others took refuge in the fort at Chetwa, where their defeat caused a great panic; and there is no doubt that, if the Commandant had followed up his victory by attacking the fort, the enemy would then have abandoned it in alarm. But instead of this, he marched with his troops into our neighbouring *pagger*, and thus gave time to the enemy, who were totally unprovided, to supply themselves with necessaries by aid of the English at Calicut, and to barricade the entrances to the fort; proving themselves in this last measure wiser than our people, who had left the gateways unprovided with doors. At length, on the 1st February, the Commandant resolved to assault the place, and scale the walls; but oh folly! when the troops reached the walls, they found that they had neglected to bring scaling ladders, and were consequently forced to retire foiled, with the loss of eighty men. The Zamorin took advantage of this opportunity, to build a fort called Paponetti, between Chetwa and Cranganoor, which he fortified with three trenches, and manned with a troop of soldiers, among whom were some Portuguese deserters, and even some English officers.

Towards the end of 1715, three Captains arrived from Batavia with a reinforcement; they attacked this building on the 11th January, 1716, but, owing partly to some misunderstanding among the officers, and partly to the faint heartedness of Captain Pluis,

1. Note 10, p. 332.

the second-in-command, who trembled at the sound of cannon, the attempt failed. For, when the besieged beheld our men advancing they were so terrified at their numbers that they rushed out of the fort on the opposite side; and those of our troops who were stationed there, mistaking the cause of the sally, and imagining it was an assault upon themselves, were seized with a sudden panic, and fled in disorder. The enemy, beholding this unexpected diversion, mustered courage and returned to the forsaken fortress: and there is no doubt that, had they understood how to follow up their advantage, they might have completely routed our army, by cutting off their passage and obstructing their retreat, as there is no beaten road or path through the forest which surrounds the fort. This fruitless result of the expedition created universal consternation, which was increased by the rumours which began to fly about, mostly originating in an apprehension that the allied princes were about to desert us; the Rajah of Parvel[1] in particular who, it was reported, was about to attack the fort of Cranganoor. Hearing this, the Commandant resolved to abandon our *pagger* at Chetwa, in order that the garrison might not be cut off, and to remove it in order to assist in strengthening Cranganoor.

Things remained in this state till the end of the year 1716, when William Bakker Jacobz was despatched from Batavia as Admiral and Commander-in-Chief. He had served in his youth as Lieutenant in the Navy, and had never been engaged in any other campaign. With him were associated Major Hans Frederic Berkman. who was experienced in the Military affairs of Malabar, having passed many years here; and Commander Johannes Hertenberg, who was to supersede Ketel in the management of mercantile affairs. They brought with them a splendid army composed of Europeans, Javanese, Balinese and others, to whom were joined the troops of the Rajah of Cochin, so that they were well-prepared to carry on a compaign. Their first attempt was upon the stronghold of Paponetti. When they reached the anchorage up the river called Caro, about a quarter of a league distant from the enemy's *pagger*, the General gave notice of his approach by discharging three pieces of artillery. This was answered by three shots from the enemy within the fort, who meant by this to shew that they were prepared to await the attack of the General and his army. The latter advanced as soon as it was morning, resolving to attack the *pagger* on three points at once; which was achieved with such good effect that before 10'o clock the enemy displayed a flag of truce. Owing either to the state of intoxication into which most of the principal officers (except the Major) were plunged, or to some other cause, no regard

1. Paroor.

was paid to this signal; and as our army had by this time made itself master of the two first trenches, the enemy perceiving that their flag of truce was disregarded, retreated within the third entrenchment, which was very strong, and now well-supplied with men. Here they defended themselves with great courage, inflicting considerable loss upon our troops; and when at length they again hoisted the flag of truce, it met with more attention, and a treaty was concluded by which they agreed to evacuate the fort with arms in their hands. But an unfortunate accident occurred, caused, it was said, by the Europeans who were within the fort. The powder magazine was set on fire, that it might not fall into the hands of our army, whilst the Zamorin's troops were in the act of leaving the fort; many were burnt, and several others rushed so violently on our ladders in order to escape, that some of our soldiers were pushed off and fell to the ground, which infuriated them so that they struck at the heathen multitude with the butt-ends of their fire-arms; and the more the poor wretches attempted to defend themselves, the more violent they became, and they cut down such numbers, that, according to one reckoning, three thousand of the enemy were killed within and without the fort—others say one thousand. The fort was afterwards destroyed, and completely razed to the ground. The bones of the dead remained for many years in the surrounding fields, a memorial of this great defeat.

The heathens received a great shock by the result of this battle. In order to follow it up, some of our vessels were sent to attack Chetwa by sea. On arriving there, no enemy was to be found. At first, it was supposed that they were in concealment, and we did not venture to approach too near, lest they should fall upon us; but at length on receiving certain intelligence that they had deserted the fort, our men entered and found out a soul there. Our General afterwards captured several *Paggers*, Mapowvane,[1] Towtamburi, Avatorti, and Ourganoor in the land of the Paliat; and gained a decisive victory over the Zamorin's army near Ourganoor. The Balinese pikemen did him great service in this battle, rushing furiously on the foe, and terrifying them so much that they dreaded them more than the Europeans, as men from whom no quarter was to be expected. If the General had chosen to advance his victorious banners, he could no doubt have made himself master of the Zamorin's Court at Ponnany, and of Calicut itself; but whether private reasons of his own induced him not to do this, and therefore not to conclude peace that year (which he might have done on advantageous terms) and thus have spared

1. Note 11, p. 332.

the Company costly preparations for the ensuing campaign), or whether other considerations weighed with him, we will not now pause to enquire. Nothing was done in the rainy season, (which is not adapted for carrying on warlike operation): but at the close of the year, Patricotti[1] was taken, and a noble pagoda of the Poenetoar Namboori was pillaged by the Balinese and other coloured soldiers, although the General, for reasons of his own, had issued a strict prohibition. The Javanese soldiers, attracted by the booty, broke this prohibition, and obtained a quantity of gold and silver articles and precious stones, which the Europeans, not daring to disobey, could not share. I have obtained many heathen idols from these spoils which I keep as relics. Shortly after this followed the peace concluded in 1717,[2] so that the reinforcements sent from Batavia were not wanted.

In conclusion, I shall add that thirty-six leagues to the north in the kingdom of Colastri[3] is the fort of Cannanore, which on one side is washed by the sea, and consequently could not be easily blockaded. This fort serves as a bulwark, not only against the power of the native monarch, but also against the Moors, who have a prince there called Ali Raja.[4] The latter has up to this time been a good friend of the Company,[5] transacting business with them, and supplying them with cardamoms and turmeric.

From all this history, you can form a good idea of the power and means of the East India Company in Malabar. Other European nations have great possessions here. The English have a

1. Note 12, p. 332.
2. Note 13, p. 332.
3. Note 14, p. 332.

3. ("Proceeding along the sea coast" says Bartolomeo, "you then arrive at Cannanore, a town with a castle, and subject to the government of Queen Collatiri, by the Europeans called Collastri. This city is of great antiquity, and the kings of Collatiri belonging to the first class of the Indian princes.

"The capital of the kingdom of Cannanore, called also Colanada, lies in the latitude of 11° 50′, and is distinguished by the same name. The whole surrounding district, which extends towards the north as far as Mount Delly, is inhabited by the *Molandis*, who live merely by piracy. These sea-robbers are mentioned by Pliny, Arrian, Ptolemy and other ancient authors. They unite themselves to other pirates, who reside on the Angedib islands, near Goa, and capture all the small vessels, which sail from Goa to Cochin. The huts in which their wives and children live, stand on the eastern side of Mount Delly. This mountain, which forms a cape or head-land, lies in the latitude of 12° 5′, and here Malabar or Malayala, properly so-called, ends."—*Voyage to E. Indies.*)

4. Note 15, pp. 332—334
5. Note 16, p. 334.

fort called Anjengo.[1] south of Quilon; it is tolerably strong, as it has need to be; for there are many enemies in the neighbourhood, and it has often been attacked. In the north they have a fort called Tellicherry,[2] between Calicut and Cannanore, which of late years they have considerably strengthened.

The poor Danes have also a residence in Malabar, called Eddawa, resembling a miserable hut, rather than the dwelling of a commercial officer. It is situated three leagues south of Quilon. This nation has fallen quite into obscurity in these parts, from its want of money and influence; so that the natives last year (1722) refused them lodging, there; upon which their Superintendent repaired to Quilon to dwell for a time under our protection, and in the sequel to Tranquebar, a factory of theirs on the Coromandal Coast.[3]

Here then you have a sketch of the European settlements in Malabar, together with an account of the late war. I hope you will not take it amiss that I have related all the circumstances without keeping back anything and without sparing the managers of the war, for it seems to me that the whole truth of such things should be related without disguise, though this rule is but little regarded by historians of the present age.

LETTER V.

Description of Canara, Vingorila, Goa—and the Customs of the Portuguese in these parts.

The pleasure you have always taken in the study of history, and of its sister science geography, induces me to give you an account of some countries lying to the north of Malabar, and in some measure belonging to it: as it contains factories fortified in ancient times by the company, which are under the management of its officer, who bears the title of Commandant of Malabar, Canara, and Vingorla.

Canara is a kingdom adjoining Malabar on the north, subject to an independent prince, who is much more magnificent and

1. Note 17, pp. 334—354.

(Anjengo or Angintenga, a corruption of the two Tamil words unjee taynkul or five cocoa trees, was for many years an English factory and a place of some note in former days. It is now desolate and deserted. The ruins of the Portuguese Church and fort, still exist. Orme, the Historian, was born at Anjengo. For further accounts of this interesting spot, see Forbes' *Orienta. Memoirs*, and Abbe Raynal's *History of the Indies*.—H. D.)

2. Note 18, pp. 354—356.

3. Note 19, pp. 356—357.

powerful than those of Malabar, though the religion of the inhabitants of the two countries is nearly identical. The East India Company possess no jurisdiction whatever in this place, and are only tolerated there as merchants, driving a good business in spices, sugar, etc.

This kingdom produces many peculiar commodities, such as sandal wood, which is found there in great abundance, as well as rice. We might call it the granary of all Northern India; indeed the East India Company are often obliged to get rice from here for the consumption of Malabar and Ceylon. The Portuguese send a fleet annually to occupy the seaport of Canara, not only for the purpose of supplying themselves with rice for Goa, and other parts of India, but in order also to prevent their enemies, the Arabs, from obtaining any provisions there.

The city of Canara, where the Raja holds his Court, lies some leagues inland, and is connected with the seaport by a fine road, planted with trees, which the inhabitants are obliged to keep in excellent order. This road is so secure that any stranger might go and sleep there with bags full of money, and nobody would molest or rob him; for, if such a thing occurred, the people in the neighbourhood would be not only severely punished, but would be forced to make good the money to the owner. Indeed the laws of the Hindoos to prevent robbery are admirable. At Surat itself, a city with so many thousand inhabitants, the merchandize lies out under open tents, as safe as if it were locked up in our storehouses.

Vingorla, lying some miles behind Goa, was formerly also a factory of the East India Company, where a considerable trade was carried on, but they were lately forced to abandon it on account of the continued attacks of the Mogul Governor, and the Marasyn robbers under Mara Rogia, a rebel who devastates the empire of the Mogul with fire and sword. The Mahometans have indeed, since that time, proposed to restore this place to the company, but the offer has been refused, the more so as the trade has been transferred to Surat.

While I am occupied with this part of the country, I must add some description of Goa,[1] as it lies between Canara and Vingorla.

1. There is a legend that the old city of Goa was overwhelmed by a sudden rush of the sea, and that its houses may still be seen in calm weather below the waters. The following lines in allusion to this tradition may fitly be inserted in this place :—

> There was a city, glorious and free,
> Built on the shore of the dark blue sea.
> Where towers and spires of gilded hue.
> Shone over the waves of the ocean blue.

It is considered by the Portuguese, as you know the capital of the Indies, and here a Viceroy sent from Portugal has his seat of Government and holds his Court. It is sufficiently strong on the seaside and the moles are protected by forts and dykes: but it has nearly fallen into decay within, and is destitute of inhabitants, excepting the ecclesiastics, who have a convent here, the artizans, and the poor people. The upper classes have retreated to the

And palace and cottage smiling told
How fair was that city in days of old!
Far, far above was the glowing sky
Where the sun shone bright o'er the turrets high,
While the cocoa shade and the graceful palm
Hung o'er the waters so lovely and calm,
Thick and numberless, side by side,
Drinking the stream of the onward tide.
But, now, from that spot where the glad sun shone,
That glorious city of palms is gone,
Gone with its pride and people so brave,
Whelmed by the tide of the salt sea wave.
Yes! there below the surging deep
Fair Goa's sunken towers sleep,
All, all that once was glad and bright,
Reposing there in ceaseless night!
Swift the remorseless billows roar
Rose wildly o'er that fated shore,
Nor human power availed to stem
The tide that rolled o'er the ocean's gem·
The wild surge broke—the rising foam
Dashed furious o'er each hall and home
Sweeping the happy and the fair
'Neath the deep wave unburied there!
'Tis thus that olden annals tell
How Goa's beauteous city fell!
And, now, 'tis said, in midnight clear
When the boatmen o'er those waters steer
From sunset's tranquil hour until
The waves are hushed and winds are still,
Deep, deep below the water shining
They see the turrets still reclining
And the dim outline, lingering yet,
Of many a glittering minaret,
And groves and gardens, and the wall
That, still unharmed, surrounds them all;
And silent streets, so drear and dread
O'er which no living beings tread—
A city wrapt by envious fate
In darkest gloom, most desolate!
Not the fair mistress of the world [1]
Was thus to pitiless ruin hurled,
Tho' famine's waste, and sword and fire,

1. Rome.

environs of the town on account of the insalubrity of the climate: and the river banks and islets are adorned with flourishing farms and plantations of cocoa and other fruit trees, on the profits of which they subsist. The whole island of Goa is furnished with such like farms, as is also the case with

Combined to make her life expire,
Tho' floods and tempests, and the tide
Of wild Barbarian crushed her pride,
And superstition's furious zeal.
Hath rent her more than savage steel;
Yet, still her palaces deny
The wrath of man, and time defy
And many a ruin can yet unfold
Where warriors stood and spoke of old.
Nor has worse fate that [1] town befel,
Which felt the burning mountain's power
Which, flaming like an earthly hell,
Enwrapt it in its lava shower.
Ages swept by, none knew the spot,
Almost the thrilling tale forgot,
For, vineyards rose and blossomed where
Was once a town so stately and fair
Yet now uncovered it stands alone,
As once it stood in the days that are gone,
And the bright sun shines on the marble floor
As it shone there a thousand years before.
And, still more famed for wealth and pride,
Where kings and prophets lived and died,
Was that great city [2] whose dread power
Survived not o'er its destined hour.
The "mighty city"—ere it fell
Where earth's proud princes loved to dwell,
And gorgeous monuments upreared
To those they honoured and they feared.
Yet seers foretold the threatened doom,
And, darker than the sculptured tomb.
All pomp and pride for ages lay
In heaps beneath the mouldering clay.
Yet though deserted in despair.
The ruined city still is there!
But thou, fair Goa! not again
Shall rise from out the boundless main.
In all thy beauty buried deep
Beneath the wave for ever sleep!
No falling rock, no lighnting's blast,
Thy sea-girt towers to earth have cast,
Nor cruel foe with sword and flame,
Thy self won power e'er overcame,
The water swept thy pride away,
To lifeless doom, but not decay.—H. D.)

1. Pompeii.
2. Babylon.

Salsette in the north, where the Jesuits play the master, and other places.

It would be considered a disgrace by the Portuguese Fidalgos, to follow any trade, but the Jesuits look on such employments as honorable, and they are in fact the chief traders of these parts. We need be under no apprehension that the Portuguese will cause any injury to our commerce here, for they are devoid of any knowledge of business, ,and what with their indigence, of their fraudulent conduct which has destroyed all confidence in them, they are held very low in public estimation throughout the Indies. But they are great lovers of fine titles. High offices and generals are all the talk among them. An office which with us would be filled by a small tradesman, must needs require a general with them. For each ship of war, they have a *Capitano di Marre Guerre*, and a levy of captains, lieutenants and ensigns besides. It would be a great mistake, however, to suppose that their pay is proportionate to their titles. A captain receives less than one of our serjeants, and the Resident of Panoor assured me that he had only twenty golden *fanams* or shillings per month from the king, for his maintenance; yet these gentlemen like to cut a figure. Not satisfied with having one umbrella carried over his head, a man of high rank requires two or three, ornamented with hanging fringes and silver buttons. The bearers must be Kaffres, clothed in red coats, and these are accompanied by other Kaffres bearing long swords called *Espingardes*, who act as bravoes of their masters. For, as their incomes are so slender and their state so imposing, these signors often betake themselves to schemes of plunder and assassination; and every year they despatch an expedition against their hereditary enemies, the Arabs, in the hope of obtaining booty, of which, however, in these days, they do not gain much.

There is no place in the world where law is less regarded than here. Scarcely any enquiry is instituted into cases of murder; moreover the Fidalgos or noblemen cannot be punished for crime in the Indies, but must be sent to Portugal for trial; and this is rarely done. Their vice and dissipation are excessive; they surround themselves with troops of *Bayaderes* or dancing girls, row with them in their *Oranbaien* on the rivers, and spend their time with them in all sorts of amusements. These *Bayaderes* are, for Hindus, very pretty. In their dances, they move not their feet alone, but all their limbs. They attire themselves very gaily, with bracelets and golden ornaments, and exercise great fascination over the pleasure-loving Portuguese.

d.

The Portuguese ladies are not better conducted than their husbands. When a man of any rank travels abroad, he does not leave his wife at home, but takes care to shut her up in a convent. Indeed the jealousy of the husbands goes so far that they remark, if any man speaks to their wives, and not unfrequently death is the penalty he incurs.

The Viceroy here is the highest in command; he remains for three years only, unless the Portuguese sovereign should prolong the term. He has two residences, one in the city, called the *Casa di Pulvere*, and the other, where he commonly sojourns, outside the walls. He holds audience every morning; standing under a canopy; and takes his meals alone. His Court circle is considerable: and he makes a good sum out of the presents which the inhabitants, according to custom, must offer at his coming and going. In the interregnums between the departure of a Viceroy and the arrival of his successor, the Archbishop or Primate takes the reins of government, and then the clergy have their turn in the appointment to offices.

The ecclesiastics here are innumerable; Hindus and natives of Canara as well as Europeans—so that there are much fewer soldiers than priests. The reason why so many natives enter the priesthood, is that they may be spared the insults of the Portuguese, who treat all black men as if they were slaves.

The Portuguese trade in the Indies is of little value. It makes a great noise when two ships from the mother country arrive together in the year at Goa: and these come more for the purpose of providing the inhabitants with necessaries than for commercial enterprise. Each has on board more than forty ecclesiastics of various orders. Tobacco is charged with heavy imposts, the produce of which is assigned especially to the queen for her private purse. It is nevertheless an article of great consumption; being not only used by the Portuguese in all parts of India, but exported also to foreign nations in Europe, the Dutch taking no small share of it.

The most profitable trading voyage of the Portuguese is that to Mozambique. Here they sell linen and other commodities, and purchase in exchange many slaves or Kaffres, whom they convey to Goa, where they fetch a good price. They carry on commercial transactions with China likewise, where they possess an island called Macao. The Macao merchants have for some years kept up a brisk intercourse with Batavia, the Chinese junks having kept aloof. But not more than one or two ships visit Goa during the course of the year, and these part with most of their cargo, consisting principally of Chinese luxuries, as silks, tea, sweetmeats and sugar, at Cochin and Ceylon. There is no nation in the world so fond of sweetmeats as the Portuguese. They always hand them about on their social visits. But, for wine, beer, and strong liquors in general, they have no taste: intoxication is of rare occurrence among them. The Dutch, on the contrary, drink to such an extent as to expose themselves to the reproaches of the Portuguese and the natives, who commonly call us *Hollandeses bebidos* or Dutch drunkards. The English are liable to the same imputation : they are greatly attracted by the Persian wines, and by Punch, which is made of the arrack of Goa. I must remark, by the way, that though in England they talk a great deal about the Protestant religion, the English in India allow themselves to be very much mixed up with members of the Romish communion, generally having their children baptized by the Priests, and marrying Roman Catholic wives.

Having thus far extended my account of the Europeans at Malabar and the neighbouring places, which I trust you will not find tedious;

I shall now conclude, etc.

LETTER VI.

Malabar an expensive settlement to the Dutch East India Company—Its importance—Remarks on the duties incumbent on our Commandants—Encomiums on Joh: Hertenberg—Administration of the East India Company—Landed estates belonging to them.

As the welfare of our State and the prosperity of commerce have always concerned you deeply, I have no doubt that you will peruse with pleasure the account of the Company's trade in Malabar, and the importance it has attained on this coast ; the methods of maintaining it, and its vast wealth, which influence in a peculiar manner the welfare of our country.[1]

1. (In 1602, the Dutch East India Company was formed by the amalgamation of several different companies into one united body. The members were invested with authority to conclude peace or make war with oriental potentates, to build forts and garrison them according to discretion. For many years, this new Company acquired considerable authority and power in the East. Its commercial relations were very extensive, and for its better protection, the Company despatched a fleet of fourteen vessels, as a support to their numerous colonies. It was not long before they came in contact with their jealous rivals, the Portuguese, and the hostile fleets of both nations frequently encountered each other in the Indian seas. It was not till after many conflicts that the superiority of the Dutch was maintained. In less than half a century, they had taken or destroyed upwards of 300 Portuguese vessels, and thus made themselves masters of the sea. Upon

Malabar is considered by the East India Company as an expensive settlement, for the profits obtained on the goods which are here sold are far from defraying the expenses required for its support. You will easily understand this, when you learn that a ship of 145 feet is sufficient to provide the settlement not only with merchandize, consisting chiefly of arrack, sugar, spices, tin, copper etc., but also with all the provisions requisite for a year. But, on the other hand, the maintenance of the garrison, its munition, and its servants, who may be reckoned at present at 1,200 souls, costs a large sum of money, and, if to this we add the extraordinary expenses which have been incurred by the Company for some years past, by the erection of a new dispensary, rice-warehouse, hospital and powder magazine, a new fort at Chetwa, and a smith's shop, which are now almost completed—and also the expenses they have still before them in the establishment of a new factory at Porcad, and the occupation of the two forts of Cannanore and Quilon—it is evident that their outlay must far exceed their profits here, without mentioning their expensive wars, the last of which cost nearly two millions.[1]

You must not, however, conclude from this statement is a useless position to the Company, and that it were better to abandon it; for there are weighty reasons for its retention. The first is that we may remain masters of the pepper-trade in Malabar,[2] for it is certain that if the Company were to quit this place, the Portuguese would endeavour to obtain possession of it. They already affect to have claims upon it, and say arrogantly enough that "the Company are keeping it for their king."[3] Still more would the English strive to get hold of it; for they have no commercial station in all Malabar that can at all be compared with this, for abundance both of pepper and of other goods.

the destruction of the maritime power of the Portuguese, the Dutch found no difficulty in attacking and capturing their settlements on land, and the booty of military stores and ammunition which they seized in their several conquets, turned greatly to their advantage, as the magazines and fortresses contained every thing necessary both for themselves and the prosecution of their commercial projects. Such was the origin of the great prosperity of the Dutch East India Company. Last, after the lapse of a hundred and fifty years, the Company began to decline owing to many concurring circumstances, chiefly from the speculation and avarice of the Government and merchants, and partially from the innumerable wars in which they became engaged Settlement after settlement becoming a prey to internal faction, or the attack of the natives, fell from their grasp, and the English soon supplanted a power which was unable to maintain itself either by land or sea.—H. D.)

1. Note 1, pp. 358—365.
2. Note 2, pp. 365—368.
3. Note 3, pp. 368—369.

In the second place, Cochin is very useful as a provisioning station for vessels sailing from Batavia to Mocha, or returning from Surat and Persia to Batavia. They can obtain here not only very good water (fetched from the river Mangatti), but also abundance of victuals at a cheap rate, such as poultry, pigs, cattle, fish and fruit. For this reason, European vessels visiting the Indian coasts always put in at Cochin for provisions.

In the last place, we may add that Cochin serves as an outpost to protect Ceylon against the attempts of other European nations, especially the English, who we have most cause to fear; for if they were masters of this place, they might use it as a rendezvous for their fleets. This they could do even in the rainy season: for light vessels of less than twelve feet might be brought over the sand bank into the river, while the larger ones might lie securely in the Muddy Bay, three leagues distant.

Thus, you see the importance of this settlement, which requires a man of ability to manage it with discretion; for though, like the Company's other settlements, it is governed by the Political Council, the chief responsibility rests with the head of that assembly, who is the Commandant; and it behoves him to be very ready-witted when he converses with the native Rajahs, who are most difficult to deal with. For, if he hesitates, they deem it a sign of fear and confusion, and immediately assume a contempt for him. The Commandant must cultivate, also, a figurative and metaphorical mode of expression, which, besides being considered a proof of wisdom, enables him to throw a cloak over subjects which are disagreeable to them, and to carry out measures which they would not take so easily if they were expressed in plain words.[1]

Having made close observations on all the commercial affairs of Malabar, my belief is that the following rules[2] should be observed in order to a successful management of this country :—

I. The Commandant must effectually defend the kingdom of Cochin against the future attacks of its enemies, to which end the Company have declared themselves the protector of that kingdom. If this were not done, the Zamorin would soon weaken the power of the Rajah of Cochin, and would allow other nations to establish themselves in the territories he might gain. It is, therefore, clearly for the Rajah's interest to keep on good terms with the East India Company.

1. Note 4, p. 369.
2. Note 5, pp. 369—372.

II. The Commandant must especially endeavour to prevent the Rajah of Cochin from making aggressions on the Zamorin or others, or provoking them to war; which he would be very ready to do, relying on the Company's arms, and hoping by their assistance to regain some lands to which he lays claim.

III. He must enquire narrowly into the justice of the claims the Rajahs make mutually on each other, as he is often called on to arbitrate between them. This is the more necessary as their claims are very obscure and are seldom settled, so that they have continual pretexts for the wars which perpetually arise between them. A wise Commandant will take care not to involve himself in these disputes, unless they immediately affect the interests of the Company.

IV. He must be thoroughly acquainted with the laws and customs of the natives, who cling very much to them, making them a part of their religion. They carry these feelings to such an extent that if a Commandant were unwittingly to infringe their laws in passing sentence, it would arouse a general spirit of murmuring and disatisfaction.

V. He must undertake no wars without great deliberation, and with a good prospect of success, as the Company might otherwise be placed in great danger; the character of the natives then to grow insolent and daring at the slightest misfortune that happens to us, and in such cases, their numbers swell like a snowball. An instance of this occurred in 1715—16, when we lost the fort of Chetwa, on which occasion the natives broke out into all manner of extravagance, using most insolent language; their spirit was quelled, however, in the following year by our arms.

The Commandant, Johannes Hertenberg, has extorted from the Rajah of Cochin two stipulations which are very conducive to the welfare and tranquillity of the Company. The first is that all the Rajahs, Princes and Nobles of the kingdom shall lay their complaints and disputes before him, so that he is constituted arbitrator between them, by which means he becomes acquainted with the grounds of their difference, and is thus enabled to hinder many illegal enterprises of the Rajah of Cochin, which occasioned great annoyances to the former Commandants. The second stipulation is that the Rajah shall undertake no hostilities against the Zamorin or any other Prince without the previous knowledge and consent of the Commandant; without which agreement he could frequently plunge us into war merely to advance his own interests.[1]

1. Note 7, p. 372.

As we are engaged on the subject of the administration, it will be as well to describe how this settlement is managed.[1] The East India Company having received by patent, from the States General, supreme jurisdiction in their own settlements, this power is vested in the chief place of each great settlement, of which Malabar is one. All the native Christians dwelling in the lowlands are under the authority of the Company, and neither the Rajah of Cochin nor any of his princes have the power of putting them to death or punishing them; if they did so, satisfaction would be demanded. The Jewish, Moorish, and Canarese inhabitants are partly under the authority of the Rajah, and partly under that of the Company.[2]

Crimes are punished here, as they are in Europe, by fines, imprisonment, flogging, branding, hanging and shooting.[3] Criminals are sometimes sent in chains to labour on the public works, as there are no jails here. The assemblies, as in the other Indian settlements, are either political, where the Company's affairs are discussed; judicial, where criminals are tried and judgment passed in important causes; and civil, where disputes of less amount than 100 rix dollars between the native townspeople are decided, and before which the ceremony of betrothal takes place.[4] There are also an Orphan-chamber,[5] whose business it is to take care of the property of orphans, and the College of Aldermen, who have the superintendence of the streets, houses and canals.

In the last place, it will be as well to notice here the various landed properties which the Company possess in this place, and the rents they receive. They consist of estates and islands which the Company have acquired from time to time either by gift or by treaty. I must premise that the islands are situated not in the sea but in the rivers, or else are detached pieces of land washed over by the sea and rivers. They are let on leases of ten or fifteen years, in order by this length of possession to encourage the tenants to make new plantations, hoping in the interval to receive the fruits of them; and the rents consequently rise at each new lease. Indeed, it is made a condition of the lease that the tenant shall make plantations of cocoanut palms; and a person is appointed to number the trees in all the estates every year, in order to ascertain how much the plantations have increased. The islands contain not only cocoa palms, but also arable fields and saltpans, for this country produces an abundance

1. Note 8, pp. 372—374
2. Note 9, pp. 374—378.
3. Note 10, pp. 378—380.
4. Note 11, p. 380.
5. Note 12, p. 380.

of salt, which is exported to other places. The following is a list of these arable lands and fields, with the years in which they were acquired :—[1]

Lands		Year
The lands of Edourtien Paponetti	...	1666.
Muskieten island, gardens, and arable field	...	1708.
Gardens in the island of Caddemata	...	1689.
Do. at Arkotte	...	1712.
Saltpans in the island of Bollogatti	...	1670.
Arable fields and gardens in the island of St. Domingo	...	1718.
Do. do. do. Poul or Hosser's Island	...	1665.
Arable fields and gardens in the island Ilha Perdido	...	1664.
Arable fields in Cruz de Milagre	...	1620.
Do. the island of Guassini	...	1692.
Do. at Antje Caimal	...	1692.
Do. at Castelle	...	1663.
Do. in the island of Bindverti	...	1663.
Do. at Aroe	...	1683.
Gardens and lands behind the Company's garden	...	1663.
Arable fields at Senhora Saude	...	1687.
Do. St. Iago	...	1687.
Do. St. Lovys	...	1687.
Do. Belijoor de Fonseka	...	1667.
Arable fields at Mondanbelli	...	1681.
Do. Perperangerre	...	1690.
Do. Maincorde or Muddy Bay	...	1668.
Do. St. Andre	...	1665.
Do. Chermagellam	...	1667.
The lands of Rajah Marta, called Banbasse	...	1673.
Calicatte or Marenbal	...	1669.
Kully Quilon's strand	...	1717.

The East India Company has also bestowed on the Deaconry some gardens and lands in the island of Vypeen, behind the Canarese bazaar, in order that the revenues thence derived should be devoted to the use of the poor.

1. Note 13, pp. 380—383.

LETTER VII.

Trade of the English in Malabar, and the disasters they have experienced.

You are doubtless aware that the trade of the East India Company, so famous throughout the world, one of the main stays of our country, and the resource of thousands of poor creatures who make their livelihood by the employment it affords them, has been greatly undermined by the English, not so much by the English Company and their vessels, as by the private traders, who are much more numerous, and who besiege the Coast of Bengal, Coromandel, Malabar and Surat. At Cochin we see at least thirty English vessels, large and small, in the course of the year, which perform the transit between the neighbouring regions, and put in here chiefly for the sake of provisions. Three or four of the English Company's ships have also been here lately. It is certain that their trade in these places is less considerable than that of the Dutch Company who despatch three or four vessels annually to Surat, on account of the spices which are brought there in large quantities, and of which they monopolize the trade.[1]

The character of the English is, as you are aware, proud, domineering, and selfish, and, when combined with a disposition to cruelty, has been the cause of many sad events in India. For, as they always oppress the natives, the English gain from them little in return but hatred and curses, and the feeling thus engendered often results in deeds of violence and murder. There was an instance of this some years ago at Bencoolen on the coast of Sumatra, where the natives were so much irritated by the outrages committed upon them, that they at length resolved to destroy the English fort, a purpose which they accomplished with the slaughter of every one they could lay hands on.

Not long afterwards a similar occurrence took place at Anjengo, a fort belonging to the English in the country of Travancore, about sixteen miles from Quilon. It is said to have originated in some misconduct of the English on Shrove Tuesday, in the year 1720. Their interpreter, who was a native Christian, and consequently a Roman Catholic, was preparing for the approaching fast, as the members of his church are wont to do, by an ebullition of unusual license, and among other things he slily instigated some lads to pelt, with eggs and filth, the Moors, always a peculiarly sensitive race, together with some heathens who happened to be passing by. The Moors, whose habit it is to go about armed, instantly clapped their hands on their weapons and

1. Note 1, pp. 384—393.

threatened not to leave this insult unavenged. The interpreter upon this, quieted the tumult, and secretly informed the Commandant of what had taken place; and that officer, instead of punishing the oppressors, caused the Moors to be apprehended and imprisoned, while the English remained perfectly indifferent to the exasperation which this transaction excited among the rest of the Moors around them.

But another crime ensued, attended by more serious consequences, arousing the anger of the whole nation. The English seized a heathen medicine master, called a *Pandyt*, who is always a Brahmin, and compelled him to shave the beards of their slaves, which is an act that Brahmins cannot perform without losing caste. This insult to an order of men so highly honoured, was deeply felt, and vengeance was resolved upon.

Accordingly the natives proceeded to blockade the English fort all round on the land side, preventing the ingress of supplies in this direction. They could not however prevent communication by sea, and as long as the fine weather lasted, the English obtained their supplies by that means. But from June till October the rainy season prevailed, and navigation was rendered impossible by the violence of the winds, and then, accordingly they suffered from great scarcity of provisions. At length after the sea was again open, and some English vessels had made their way to the fort, in February 1721, a peace was nominally concluded with the natives, who however reserved a secret intention of wreaking dire vengeance on their foes as soon as a fitting opportunity should occur. An occasion for the execution of their design presented itself that same year, at the beginning of the rainy season.

With the view of conciliating the Queen of Attingal, mother of the royal race, whose authority was great in that country, the English Commandant determined to offer her some splendid presents; and to make them the more acceptable he brought them in person, accompanied by a numerous retinue, leaving within the fort none but the sick and infirm. His escort consisted altogether of 140 persons. Troubled by no misgivings, they advanced with much pomp, with sound of trumpet and drums, to the Court of the Queen, who gave them a most friendly reception, and appeared to derive extreme gratification from their arrival and the gifts they brought, though for certain reasons she said she must defer receiving the latter until the following day. Meanwhile she pressed them to pass the night at her court, and the Commandant, utterly unsuspicious of danger, assented. Pretending that she was unable to accommodate the whole party in one place, the artful Princess assigned different lodgings for them, so that they should be too much scattered to assist each other in case of need. Then, in the course of the night, the inhabitants fell upon their unfortunate guests and massacred them, and this so thoroughly, that not a single European escaped, though, being armed, they made an energetic resistance. Some coolies managed to get away, and brought the dreadful intelligence to the fort.

Great was the consternation there. The women, whose husbands were slain, in grief and terror got into a sloop which chanced to be at the spot, and fled to Coromandel. Those who remained in the fort, weak and unarmed as they were, expected certain death. The next day came however, and no foe was seen approaching ; so their courage began to revive : they shut the gates, took some native Christians into their ranks, and as well as they could, put themselves into a state of defence, and when shortly afterwards the hostile natives did indeed come to the attack, they were repulsed without difficulty, being altogether without knowledge of the art of seige. Thus it appears that both parties made a mistake : the Commandant in leaving the fort without a garrison, and the natives in not immediately attacking ; when they could have captured it without a blow.[1]

Since this time, no hostilities of any consequence have been exchanged, but the ill-feeling still smoulders on, and there is a consciousness of mutual distrust. It was generally expected that the English would have taken dire revenge for the massacre last described, but the event has proved otherwise : nothing has been attempted by their ships of war that have lately arrived, though nothing could have been easier than to lay waste the country or inflict punishment of some sort.[2]

The ships in question—consisting of three English men of war, and three frigates, fitted out something like galleys with oars—were sent by the sovereign to sweep the sea of pirates and of illicit traders, but up to this time they have performed little worthy of note. When the fleet arrived at Madagascar with the intent of extirpating the European robbers, who have a stronghold there and have been extremely mischievous in the Indies, all its efforts were frustrated in consequence of the favour shewn to the outlaws by the natives of the island.[3] Nor has the expedition been more successful in other parts, as, for instance, against the pirates of Angria, who constantly capture English vessels. These pirates

1. Note 2, pp. 393—406.
2. Note 3, pp. 406—407.
3. Note 4, pp. 407—408.

occupy the shores of Sevajee, a revolted subject of the Mogul in the regions near Surat, and they maintain themselves by robbery, which, owing to the barreness of the land, is their only means of support. They possess three forts, and a good many vessels furnished with oars, which hold several men and pedereros. They endeavour to surprise and board other vessels, and generally choose the night for their time of attack. The English and Portuguese having been the greatest sufferers from their depredations, formed a close alliance against them, and the Portuguese even granted the English, in the year 1721, a factory surmounted by their own flag, within the city of Goa. The two fleets then set out, commanded respectively by the Portuguese Viceroy and the English Commandant, with the intention of routing out this pirate's nest: but the scheme soon vanished in smoke, for, while, on the one hand, Sevajee came forward to render his assistance to the marauders of Angria, on the other hand, the Portuguese entered into a secret compact with them, for a sum of money and just as the fight was about to begin, treacherously deserted the English, who accordingly were compelled to re-embark as quickly as possible, not without the loss of some men.[1]

Since then, these ships have done nothing except to levy contributions on English privateers under pretext of conveying them, and to such an extent, that they are more dreaded than even the pirates themselves. They have committed all kinds of malpractices in our roadsteads, forbidding all privateers to seek shelter there under the company's flag. Captain Brandwit of the *Salisbury* even went so far as to attack two foreign vessels, the one carrying the English, and the other the Portuguese flag. One managed to escape by means of a stratagem: but the other was compelled to pay money, like the English privateers, in order to satisfy the rapacity of the Captain, who had thus shamefully perverted the orders of his master.

Here I conclude my account of English affairs, etc.

LETTER VIII.

Divisions among the royal houses, and wars thence arising—Character and manners of Rajah Wierlam.—Customs at the decease of the Rajahs—Observations on the conduct which ought to be observed by the Dutch Government in its intercourse with these princes.

Not only is the whole of Malabar occupied by a multiplicity of kings and potentates, a circumstance causing in itself endless dissension, but these again are broadly ranged into two parties,

1. Note 5, pp. 408—414.

whose hatred is the more effectual, and probably the more interminable seeing that it arises from the unfair distinctions introduced by the original laws of this kingdom.[1]

The adherents of the two parties are called the Pandelakoers and the Chodderakoers:[2] and just as Italy was formerly torn by the two rival factions of the Guelp and Ghibelliner, and England distracted by the wars of the white and red Roses, and the Netherlands had to shed tears of blood owing to the ravages of the Kaa beljancos[3] and Flocks, so has the trumpet of war blown by the Pandelakoers and Chodderakoers often summoned the princes of Malabar to mutual hostilities. Regarding the origin of these two parties, I find two different accounts, which are not unworthy of record.[4] Some will have it that the great Cheramperoumal who partitioned Malabar[5] and made laws for it which are still observed, instituted them, for two important reasons, the first of which was to confirm the distribution of kingdoms that he had made; for being about to undertake a journey, either to the Ganges in fulfilment of a vow, or, as the Moors say, to visit Mahomet in Arabia for the purpose of embracing his religion,[6] he divided among his favourites the whole of Malabar. Now, he assigned the kingdom of the Zamorin to his illegitimate children,[7] who according to the law could not inherit, and it was natural to suppose that this would cause umbrage to his nephews who were the lawful heirs of the crown and to whom he had only given the kingdom of Cochin. They would probably use every endeavour to recover their rights when opportunity offered. For this reason he originated these two parties, and he regulated the number of princes, noblemen, etc., who should belong to each, with the express command that if a king, prince or landowner should be attacked by one of the opposite faction, he should be assisted by all the members of his own party, under

1. Note 1, pp. 415—418.
2. Note 2, pp. 418—419.
3. (Kaabeljancos and Flocks—two parties which in the 14th and 15th centuries divided and agitated the whole population of Holland and Zealand. The origin of this burlesque denomination was a dispute between two parties at a feast, as to whether the codfish took the hook, or the hook the codfish? This was made the pretext for a serious quarrel, and the partisans of the towns and of the nobles ranged themselves on either side, the former, the Flocks, wore red caps and the latter, the Kaabeljancos, grey ones. Jacqueline of Holland was supported by the former in her quarrel with Philip of Burgundy, and in the year 1492 the extinction of the faction struck a final blow to the dissension. See History of Netherlands by T. Colley Grattan—(Trans).)
4. Note 3, pp. 419—420,
5. Note 4, pp. 420—431:
6. Note 5, pp. 431—467.
7. Note 6, pp. 467—468.

pain or loss of privileges. The Zamorin king was appointed chief of the Pandelakoer, and received a sword[1] in token of his authority: and the king of Cochin as chief of the Chodderakoers received a shield.[2] Cheramperoumal's second reason for establishing these factions was to create a martial spirit: lest, living in perpetual peace, the Malabar people should sink into effeminacy and thus become a prey to the surrounding nations.

There are a kind of sham combats still held in many kingdoms of Malabar, which probably owe their origin to this institution. In these jousts or combats, many hundred, perhaps a thousand, persons attack each other, armed with sword and shield, and inflict mutual wounds, sometimes indeed death, as happened at Cully Quilon when I was there last October.[3]

From this account of the rival factions you perceive that the Zamorin is no Emperor of Malabar, as the Portuguese used to tell us in their books, for he is no greater than three other chief princes of Colastri, Cochin and Travancore, and inferior in dignity, indeed, to the Rajah of Cochin as being of inferior race. Nevertheless, the opinion has always held ground that he is the most powerful and possesses the best army of them all.[4]

But to return from this digression. I said before that there are *two* traditions regarding these parties. The other tradition is that there were formerly two families, possessors of two pagodas.[5] The name of the one was *Pandel*, that of the other *Choddar*, and the former being the strongest and most powerful, attacked the latter and plundered them, until the Choddars implored help from the prince of Walwonatti in order to revenge themselves on the Pandels. These now being unable to withstand their enemies alone, conspired with the Zamorin against them: and thus drove them to apply in their turn to the king of Cochin, who consequently became the head of the Choddar party, while the Zamorin assumed the character of protector of that of the Pandels. Each of these monarchs enticed others to espouse their causes, and the dissensions thus originating have descended to posterity.

Most serious consequences have arisen from these divisions. In the first place, it was inculcated by law upon the principal States (Stenden) or each of these kingdoms that they must always espouse the faction of the supreme Rajah: Cochin has four of

1. Note 7, pp. 468—469.
2. Note 8, p. 469.
3. Note 9, pp. 469—476.
4. Note 10, pp. 476—478.
5. Note 11, pp. 478—479.

these States, which are called the pillars of the kingdom. They are Porcad and Paroe, the Rajahs of which belong to the spiritual order, and Berkenkoer and Mangatti, having temporal Rajahs.[1] Though there are other princes in the kingdom of Cochin even more powerful than some of these Stenden, yet these are bound as Chodderakoers to assist the Cochin monarch in his wars against the Zamorin, and in return have a voice in the election of the new prince to the succession of the Cochin throne.[2]

Secondly, to this division may be attributed the continual warfare which exists between the kingdoms of the Zamorin and Cochin. No firm or lasting peace is ever made, but merely, so to speak, a cessation of hostilities, invariably followed by a renewal of war.[3] The irreconcilable hatred arising from the violence of these party feelings, was rendered more inveterate by the murderous deed of a Zamorin prince of bygone times, who caused three Cochin princes to be killed.[4] Animosity was exasperated by this to such an extent that even to this day members of the rival factions will never meet voluntarily or speak to each other. A reconciliation will never be effected until the law of retaliation be satisfied, which, according to their customs, demands the death of an equal number of princes of the murderer's family.[5]

You have read in the Portuguese narratives of their voyages published by Vander Aa, (accounts no doubt containing many fictions and exaggerations, after the wont of these masters of the sea as they style themselves) how, when rejected by the Zamorin, they were received with open arms by the Rajah of Cochin : and now you can understand his motive for the kind reception he gave them ; he hoped with their assistance to accomplish his revenge upon his enemy, which he had not sufficient strength to do unaided, and he immediately plunged into hostilities.

The East India Company who established themselves as protectors of the kingdom of Cochin, were consequently also involved in these interminable wars.

It is the duty of a wise and prudent Commandant to take care that the Rajah of Cochin is not the aggressor, which, influenced by the noted hatred he bears his enemy, he is always ready to be, in the hopes of being able, assisted by the Company's arms, to acquire from the Zamorin certain territories to which he lays claim. Had this rule always been observed, the Company

1. Note 12, pp. 479—480.
2. Note 13, pp. 480—483.
3. Notes 14 & 15, pp. 483—508.
4. Note 16, pp. 508—509.
5. Note 17, pp. 509—510.

might have been spared many of the expensive wars they have been engaged in, and of which they had sad experience during the reign of the late Rajah.

This Rajah was a man of average height, dark and ugly, for which reason he was commonly called by the towns people, the charcoal burner; he was crafty and designing, and was in the habit of clandestinely injuring other princes in order to provoke them to hostilities against each other.

He delighted in wars, though with his own soldiers he did but little execution, and laid the chief burden of prosecuting it upon the Company. His private interests occupied all his thoughts; he paid his soldiers so badly that they were sometimes forced when garrisoning a place to make a sortie to provide themselves with food. This was the case at Eunemakke. His extortions were unrivalled; he was always devising fresh means of levying funds, so that from being one of the poorest he became the richest of the Cochin Rajahs. Confiding in no one, he would shut up his money in the pagoda, or bury it under ground, or carry it about with him in boxes. He condescended to traffic in the commonest commodities; thus, he sold to his court rice and cocoanut shells both burnt and raw; and by keeping the monopoly of these things in his own hands he enhanced the price of them. He lived on bad terms with Commandant Hertenberg, who did not relish his rogueries and refused to co-operate in his artful and underhand practices. He died after a long and painful illness. It is said that on his death-bed he enjoined upon his successor to live on good terms with the company, though he had neglected to do so himself latterly. Death carried him off on the 9th October of last year (1732); he had reigned 20 years, and had nearly attained the 70th year of his age. He was little known by his own name, Wierlam, among his subjects; for their custom is never to call the Rajahs by their names but by their titles, as the Rajah of Cochin, Cranganur and so forth. The individuals in the line of succession are not named after the properties of which they are sometimes the owners, but according to the order in which they stand with respect to the succession, as the first prince (that is the Rajah) the second, third, fourth,[1] etc. The private territorial lords (landsheren) or grandees are called after their estates, dignities, or offices, as Kaimal, Ragiadoor, etc. The Rajah does not put his name as a signature to his letters (which are called Olas)[2] but a mark, each kingdom having its own peculiar mark, which never varies; so that on merely seeing

1. Note 18, p. 511.
2. Note 19, p. 511.

these letters one can tell at once from what kingdom or monarch they come, though the Rajah's name does not appear.

The successor to the late rajah was, up to the time of his accession to the throne, the second prince, and thus by his elevation all the others below him attained a step in the order of succession; and to keep the number full, a new prince, chosen from the legitimate royal family was incorporated among them[1]. From this constitution it is apparent that a prince seldom attains the throne in his youth, unless in case of some extraordinary mortality. All who are above him, sometimes seven or eight, must precede him, before he can hope to enjoy the crown.

These princes either live on their own estates or on incomes allowed them by the Rajah. As these are but small, they often live in a very impoverished condition, and are for State reasons excluded generally by the Rajahs from the administration of affairs.[2] The present Rajah is a man of little or no judgment, and was despised by his predecessor. His whole bearing and conduct betoken his inferiority; he is rude and unpolished, extravagant in his conversation, irresolute in counsel, and violent in behaviour: not only do his courtiers and grandees esteem him but lightly, the Company too have little hope of getting any good out of him; and perhaps they have as little reason to fear mischief, as he has not sense enough to injure them in any underhand manner. Yet they had better keep on good terms with him, in order to detach him from uniting against them with those who bear them no good will, of whom the most to be dreaded is the Paliat with his family. He is the General-in-Chief of the kingdom at this time. Hitherto this dignity has belonged to another family. His vast estates, and his excellent army combine to make him a dangerous neighbour, even to his sovereign, in the island of Vypeen, where he resides and a great portion of which belongs to him. His enterprising spirit was manifested four years ago, when he had the effrontery to slay a wealthy and influential Canarese called Malpa, one of of the Company's merchants, and to boast of the deed; and, as the Company, probably fearing more serious consequences, let the crime go unpunished, his arrogance increases. Time will shew how far his turbulent spirit will carry him; at present, he is occupied with endeavours to foment angry feelings against the Rajah and the Company.[3]

1 Note 20, p. 511.

2. Note 21, pp. 511—512.

3. Note 22, pp. 512—522

I must return to the accounts of the Rajahs and the customs observed at their deaths and accessions.[1] On his death-bed a Rajah presents 200 or 300 cows to the Brahmins, and other gifts: he also distributes among his relations, money, jewels, etc., for all that he dies possessed of devolves on his successor. At his decease, the grandees assemble and prepare all the necessaries for the burning of his remains, which ceremony must take place within 36 hours, and is performed, as is the custom among the Brahmins, with but little pomp. Money and other alms are distributed in the interval; and the Olas are made out, which are circulated to notify the Rajah's decease. It is not a matter of indifference to the Rajahs at what place they expire: when they find themselves dangerously ill they retire to certain spots which are especially sanctified for the purpose. These are Trichore (where the late Rajah died) Kankanoer[2] and Tripontorah. The first twelve days are the days of great mourning, when all the subjects manifest their grief by tearing their hair and letting their beards grow; no business may be transacted, not even buying and selling provisions, throughout the country. For the first three days the successor is bound to furnish food for all the Brahmins present, and to give them money: this is repeated on the 40th day, and again at the expiration of three months. He wears mourning for a whole year, and during that period must submit to certain restrictions, such as not being allowed to shave his beard, chew betel, eat more than once a day, sleep on anything but a mat, etc. Neither may he enter any of the Company's factories or forts, or any other unholy place where cows are killed or eaten, so that the Commandant is obliged to wait upon him, at his Court or elsewhere if he wish to see him. After the first twelve days are ended, his principal subjects must pay their court to him occasionally and offer him presents. First comes the head of the fishermen, who, after making his obeisance, lays before him a golden fish, a silver net, and an earthen dish containing sand and salt. On the anniversary of his predecessor's death, the Rajah gives a great feast to his court, for which preparations are made on a grand scale. I have been assured that sometimes as many as 14,000 or 15,000 of the venerated caste flock to these banquets, and these must be all regaled for three days with rice, butter, sugar, milk, piesang, etc., which, not being much used to such good cheer, they devour with voracity, and, besides furnishing all this, the host is bound to give all his guests money according to their rank, so that the amount of money spent at these ceremonies, is enough to maintain them for years if they

1. Note 23. pp. 522—539.
2. Note 24. p. 539.

are not rich. Similar feasts, but attended with less pomp, are given in memory of the Queen mother and the Princes of the kingdom.

The people of high caste also celebrate the memory of their deceased parents, wives, 'etc. They give a banquet on the first anniversary, and in the following anniversaries they double each time the triple cord they wear as the badge of their rank, so that they who, in the beginning of the year, wear one triple cord, in the sequel wear three or four of them :—which mode of wearing the cords is peculiar to the Brahmins, Chetties and Vaysias.

On the birth of a royal child in the line of succession, he is laid on earth brought from Vanneri,[1] near Baliancotte, whence the royal family sprang, in the regal house of Chetria Gouron.

The Chettriahs in ancient times came here from the country of Hindustan in the north. There they might have lawful wives, but here they are not permitted to have them.

I must add a few remarks on the finances of the Rajah of Cochin. Some time ago the authorities in Batavia thought good to give him a grant of the Alfandigos, pepper customs, and 500 kandies of pepper, together with other privileges. Their object was to enrich him, as to enable him to make head against the Zamorin. This policy seems to me nugatory, because in the first place their avaricious dispositions induces these Rajahs to appropriate all that they can get to their private use; we saw a specimen of this in the late Rajah, who from the poorest became one of the wealthiest of his race, whilst no one ever paid his troops so poorly, and his army was consequently in a wretched condition; and as his wealth increased his spite and enmity towards the Company augmented. In the second place, a Rajah is generally poor on his accession to the throne, though he is heir to all the property and wealth that his predecesser died possessed of, for they generally distribute before their death all the wealth they have amassed together, consisting principally of jewels and money, among their nearest relatives (excluding the next heir). Thus the late sovereign made his nephew the third prince his heir in these things, so that he can afford to laugh at the new king who is poor: and so the kingdom is no gainer by the wealth of the king.

And to this, thirdly, the dread of the Zamorin's arms which has taken deep root in the hearts of the remaining princes. I believe it would have been better had the East India Company from the beginning reserved for themselves all that they have conquered from the Zamorin, and therewith made a fund to defray the expenses of the succeeding wars.

1. Note 25, pp. 539—540.

NOTES ON

VISSCHER'S

LETTERS FROM MALABAR.

LETTER I.

1. **Malabar.** Al Biruni (A. D. 970-1039) appears to have been the first to call the country by its proper name Malabar. Before him, Kosmos Indikopleustus, the Egyptian merchant, who, for purposes of trade, made some voyages to India, mentions a port named Māle, "where the pepper grows", on the West Coast, which, he says, was most frequented on account of its extensive trade in that spice. Dr. Robertson, the historian, is disposed to derive the word Malabar from Māle. He says that Malabar means the country of pepper[1]. On the other hand, Padre Paolino da San Bartolomeo, the learned Carmelite, who was for long a resident in Malabar, points out that the country was known as *Malanadu*, (Malanādu) and says that from the latter has been formed, by various contortions, the word Malabar. He further assures us that the opinion of Fr. Raulin, who contends that Malabar is of Arabic extraction, being compounded of Māle and Bārr, has no foundation[2]. Both Al Idrisi, the Muhammadan geographer at the court of Roger II of Sicily (A. D. 1153 to 1154), and Abulfeda (A. D. 1273 to 1331) have al-Manibar, while Al Kazwini (A. D. 1263 to 1275) and Ibn Batuta (A. D. 1324 to 1347) write it as al-Malibar. Similar variations occur also in the works of early European travellers.

1. Historical Disquisition concerning Ancient India.
2. A Voyage to the East Indies, p. 102.

The following are a few of the various forms in which the word Malabar was written by the old geographers and travellers:—

Al Biruni (A. D. 970--1039) Melibar.
Al Idrisi (A. D. 1153) Manibar.
Rashidu'ddin (A. D. 1247-1381) Manibar.
Al Kazwini (A. D. 1263--1275) Malibar.
Abulfeda (A. D. 1273--1381) Manibar.
Ibn Batuta (A. D. 1342--1347) Malibar.
Bakui (date not ascertained) Malibar.

The Turkish work translated by Von Hammer for the Bengal Asiatic Society's Journal calls it Moueber [Mu'abar] (date not ascertained).

Marco Polo. (A. D. 1271—1294) Melibar.
Friar Odoric (A. D. 1286—1330) Minibar.
Marignolli (A. D. 1290—1355) Mynibar.
John of Monte Corvino (A. D. 1291) Minabar.
Friar Jordanus (A. D. 1320) Molebar.
Nicolo Conti (A. D. 1419) Melibaria.
Fra Mouro (A. D. 1440) Melibar.

According to Abulfeda, the country of al-Manibar extended from Honawar to Kumahri. Rashidu'-ddin, however, includes Sindabur, *i. e.*, Goa also. Al Biruni says that it extended from Karoha, the identity of which it is difficult to make out, to Kaulam or Quilon, three hundred parasangs[1] in length. Al Idrisi's Manibar extended from Honore to Kwalam, while Ibn Batuta says that its length is a journey of two months along the shore from Sindabur to Kaulam. At a later date, a point between Mt. D' Ely and Mangalore on the north and Kaulam on the south was the usual limit assigned to Malabar. It may be noticed here that the country between Quilon and Comorin, known once as *Mushaka*, (Mūshaka) is left out, as not forming part of Malabar during the mediaeval period.

1. A Persian measure of length equal to 3¾ miles.

General Cunningham, in his Geography of Ancient India, identifies Malabar with the Mo-lo-kiu-cha, Malakūta or Malayakūta of the Chinese traveller, Hiuen Tsiang (A. D. 629 to 645). "The first half of the name Mo-lo-kiu-cha is," says Dr. Hulzsch, "no doubt the well-known Dravidian word *mala*, a hill, (mala in Malayālam) and the second may be connected with Kurram, which means a division, or more probably with Kottam, which means a district in Tamil inscriptions. Thus Mo-lo-kiu-cha or Mala-kōtta would be a synonym of Malanādu or Malai-nādu, the hill country. But as Hiuen Tsiang places Malakōtta to the south of the Dravida country, and attributes to it a circuit of 5000 li,—(the li may be reckoned at the full value 1079·12 ft.), General Cunningham is, doubtless, right in supposing that it must have included, besides Malabar, the whole southern part of the Madras Presidency beyond the Kāveri."[1] The Chinese traveller has noticed the fact that sandalwood and a camphor-bearing tree (cinnamon) grew on the mountains of Malaya. In Sanskrit and Malayālam the term Malaya is applied to the Western Ghats, and the sandal is called *Malayaja*, *i. e.*, the produce of Malaya.

Hiuen Tsiang places the capital of Malakōtta 3000 li to the south of Kānchīpura (Conjeevaram). If that is so, General Cunningham points out that that distance would take us out to the sea beyond Cape Comorin. Mr. Beal identifies Chimola (which the Chinese editor of Hiuen Tsiang remarks in a note as another name for Malakōtta) with the Tamil Kumāri, *i. e.*, Cape Comorin.[2] There is nothing improbable about it, if we keep in mind that the coast-line extended at one time to a long distance south of the present Cape. In the Chino-Japanese map of India, the alter-

1. Indian Antiquary, Vol. VIII, p. 239.

2. Ancient Geography of India Vol. I p. 559, *et seq*. See also p. 552.

native name for Malayakūta is Hai-an-mew which suggests a connection with Ptolemy's country of the Aioi. Professor Wilson thinks that the Aioi may stand for the Sanskrit *ahi*, a serpent, the reference embodying, no doubt, the local tradition, mentioned in the Kēralōtpaṭṭi of the Nāgas or serpents driving the Brahmans out of Kērala.

Mr. C. P. Brown, in the third volume of the Journal of the Royal Asiatic Society, says that the Arabs and Africans, who first visited the West Coast of India, came to "Muabbar from beyond the sea." He conjectures that the name Malabar might be the product of a slight change or variation, perhaps unconsciously made in transcribing the original name in the Syrian character. He proceeds to observe that the eastern shore of India was also visited by men from "beyond the sea", and the name Malabar has been wrongly applied to the Coromandel Coast also. Orme, the historian of India, calls the Tamil people, inhabiting the Coromandel Coast, the Malabars,[1] and styles the Tamil language Malabārēsa. Dr. Caldwell has fully discussed the circumstances which led the Portuguese originally to make the mistake. The Portuguese apply the term Malabar not only to the language and people of the country so called, but also to the Tamil language and the people speaking Tamil. Says Dr. Caldwell, "The Portuguese * * sailing from Malabar on voyages of exploration * * made their acquaintance with various places on the eastern or Coromandel Coast * * , and finding the language spoken by the fishing and sea-faring classes on the eastern coast similar to that spoken on the western, they came to the conclusion that it

1. By "Malabars" early European travellers always meant the fishermen inhabiting both the Malabar and Coromandel Coasts. It was a sailor's error and was almost universal.

was identical with it, and called it in consequence by the same name, viz., Malabar * * . A circumstance which naturally confirmed the Portuguese in their notion of the identity of the people and language of the Coromandel Coast with those of Malabar was that, when they arrived at Coel, in Tinnevelly, on the Coromandel Coast * * , they found the King of Quilon (one of the most important places on the Malabar Coast) residing there."[1] Yule and Burnell, in Hobson Jobson, have collected a number of passages from various authors illustrating the use and misuse of the term. This mistake of using the name Malabar to mean part of the Coromandel Coast has led some to believe that the West Coast fell a prey to the invasion of the Muhammadans from the north under Malik Kafur (A. D. 1310) The name applied to the East Coast by Marco Polo and by Ibn Batuta about this time was Ma'abar, meaning literally "the passage", and it is not unlikely that this gave occasion to the belief of the Muhammadan conquest of Malabar under Malik Kafur. According to Rashidu'ddin, Al Biruni, and others, Ma'abar extended from Quilon on the western coast to Nellore on the eastern coast, including both the Chola and Pandya Kingdoms.[2] Ritter places Ma'abar on the west coast, and Lassen says with Ibn Batuta that the name signifies the southernmost part of the Malabar Coast. But Col. Yule has noted the error into which both these learned scholars have fallen. Professor Kuntsman of Munich thinks that the name applies neither specially to the south-west coast, nor to the south-east coast, but to the whole apex of the Peninsula. This again is erroneous. There is no evidence whatever to show that the term Ma'abar was

1. Comp: Grammar of the Dravidian Languages, 2nd Ed., pp. 10-12.

2. Cathay. p. 219.

ever used to denote the whole southern apex of the peninsula. "All use of it that I have seen" says Col. Yule, "is clear of its being the south-eastern coast, as Abulfeda precisely says, commencing from Cape Comorin."[1]

The indigenous word used by the people of Malabar to denote the country is Malayālam, which some take to be a compound of *Mala*=hill and *ala*=wave, meaning the country of the hills and waves.[2] Others derive it from *mala* (maḷa)=rain.[3] Mr. Logan thinks that Malabar is probably, in part, at least, of foreign origin. "The first two syllables are almost certainly the ordinary Dravidian Mala (hill, mountain), and bar is probably the Arabic barr (continent), or Persian bar (country)."[4] The native name of the country is suggestive enough. It is *Mala+alam* (āḷam)=Malayāḷam, *Mala* meaning mountain, and *alam* (āḷam) depth; land at the foot, declivity or valley, the whole signifying the land at the foot of the mountain, Malabar being precisely the Piedmont of the Indians. *Malavaram* (Malavāram) is another term signifying the same thing, and the transition from Malayālam or Malayāḷam (the *am* being but the terminal half letter peculiar to the Malayāḷam language) to Malabar is more easy and less open to objection than the transition from Manibar or Malibar or Malangara to Malabar. Under the well-known rule of grammar *Bavayorabheda*, (Bāvayōrabhēda) the letters *ba* and *va*, are interchangeable. Grimm's Law also points in the same direction. The natives themselves might have used the words Malabar and Malavar

1, Cathay, Vol. 1, p. 81 note. See Gildmeister, pp. 56 to 185.

2. Comp. the title of the Zamorin, Raja of Calicut: Kuṅṅalakkōnāṭiri, i. e., Kuṅṅu=Hill, ala=wave, Kōn=King ṭiri=an honorofic; the term on the whole meaning King of the hills and of the waves.

3. Sewell's List of Antiquities in S. India, Vol. II, p. 110.

4. Malabar, Vol. I, p. 1.

CAPE COMORIN.

To face page 7.]

indifferently, and foreigners, coming into the country, may reasonably be expected to call it by the name by which they heard the natives themselves call it, if not exactly in its accurate form, still with some modification or verbal variation.

2. **Cape Comorin.** Cape Comorin is the southernmost point of Malabar and of India. It was well-known to the ancients. It belonged to the Pandyan Kingdom, and as such is noticed by the Greek geographers. It is called Kumāria Akron, Cape Kumāria by Ptolemy, and Kumāri or simple Komar by the author of the Periplus. The latter says, "After Bakāre occurs the mountain called Pyrhos (or the Red) towards the south near another district of the country called Paralia (where the pearl fisheries are, which belong to King Pandion), and a city called Kolkhoi. In this tract the first place met with is called Balita, which has a good harbour and a village on its shore. Next to this is another place called Komar, where is the Cape of the same name and a haven. Those who wish to consecrate the closing part of their lives to religion, come hither and engage themselves to celibacy. This is also done by women, since it is related that the Goddess Kumāri once on a time resided at the place and bathed."[1]

The natives call the place *Kanya-Kumari*, (Kañyā-Kumāri) the virgin Goddess. No doubt it derived its name from the Sanskrit *Kumari*, (Kumāri) a virgin, one of the names of the goddess Durga, the presiding deity of the place. The monthly bathing in the sea in honour of the goddess Durga is still continued by her devotees, but not to the same extent as formerly. In 1864 the late Bishop Cotton visited Cape Comorin in company with two of his clergy. Having bathed at Haridwar, one of the most sacred Hindu bathing-places in the north, he expressed a wish to bathe at

1. Mc'Crindle, The Periplus, p. 139.

Cape Comorin as well, one of the most sacred bathing-places in the south. Hand in hand the Bishop and his Chaplains entered the surf, which was so heavy that his right-hand aid was violently separated from him from time to time. Had not the other been able to hold fast, the Bishop could hardly have escaped drowning.

Mr. Talboys Wheeler in his History of India considers that the virgin worshipped at Comorin is "The infant babe who had been exchanged for Krishna and ascended to heaven at the approach of Kamsa,"[1] and points out that the Temple of Kumāri was erected by Krishna Rajà of Narasinga (Vijayanagar), a zealous patron of the Vaishnavas. Mr. Wheeler's authority is the Portuguese historian Faria-y-Souza, who says, "The Pagod called Comori from which that famous point of land takes its name is also remarkable. Comori Pagod signifies 'The Church of the virgin'. It is like the other in structure, but not in riches, because they trust them not there, since our fleets sail upon those coasts (a sad confession of the nature of the Portuguese rule in India). The Pagod is dedicated to a virgin daughter to a shepherdess, that was changed for a son of Davagni (Dēvaki) sister to the giant Māveli (Kamsa, not Mahābali or Māveli) who killed all her children, because he was told that one of them would be the cause of his death. He thought to kill this virgin, and she giving him a kick flew through the air into the desert to the place where the Pagod now stands on the shore, having been formerly 60 leagues from the sea. She after slew a great giant by the help of the God Vishnu, and set his head on a rock that now appears in the sea, and is above 1000 fathoms round. In the very place where the virgin sate after victory was erected the Pagod."[2]

1. Vol. III, p. 386.
2. The Portuguese Asia, Vol. II, p. 394.

From whatever source Faria obtained this account, it has no foundation either in the Purāṇās or in local tradition. Col. Yule remarks that the "application of the virgin title connected with the name of the place may probably have varied with the ages," and goes on to observe that "Krishna Raja of whom Mr. Wheeler speaks reigned after the Portuguese were established in India, but it is not probable that the Krishna stories of that class were even known in the Peninsula (or perhaps anywhere else) in the time of the author of the Periplus 1450 years before: and 'tis as little likely that the locality owed its name to Yaśōda's Infant, as that it owed it to the Madonna in St. Francis Xavier's Church that overlooks the Cape."[1] There is indeed the excellent authority of the learned Bishop Caldwell to identify the virgin with Durga. Lassen too at first identified the virgin of the Cape with Pārvaṭi, wife of Śiva,[2] though he afterwards connected the name with the story in the Mahābhāraṭa about certain Apsarases changed into crocodiles.[3] The verdict of Col. Yule is "that, on the whole, there does not appear sufficient ground to deny that Pārvaṭi was the original object of worship at Kumāri, though the name may have lent itself to various legends." It is, perhaps, not difficult to reconcile the two theories thus put forward. In the Hindu Pantheon, Durga assumes different forms. While she is once incarnate as Pārvaṭi, wife of Śiva, at another time she comes into the world as Kāṭyāyani, the daughter of Yaśōda. She has even different forms such as Vanadurga, Śānṭidurga, etc. She was the wife of Śiva as Saṭi, daughter of Daksha; she afterwards occupied the same position as Pārvaṭi, the daughter of Himavaṭ. Hence the virgin worshipped at Comorin may be

1. Marco Polo, Vol. II, p. 388.
2. Ind. Alt. 1st Ed. 1. 158.
3. Ibid. 564 and 2nd Ed. 1. 193.

taken to be Kāṭyāyani, daughter of Yaśōda, as well as Pārvaṭi, wfe of Śiva, the one a Vaishnava and the other a Saiva Goddess. And it is very probable that the existing temple was built or rather rebuilt by Krishna Raja of Vijayanagra, a devout Vaishnava. So far as the Malayālīs are concerned, they have never been known to be Dvaiṭīs, that is, those who differentiate between Siva and Vishnu as a point of religious dogma.

In the early years of the Christian Era, the *Regio Pandionis*, of which Madura was the capital, seems to have comprehended the greater part of the southern portion of the Coromandel Coast, and to have extended across the Peninsula westward to Canara and Malabar. Professor Wilson observes, "that the author of the Periplus of the Erythrian Sea particularises Nīlcynada or Nīlīswaraṁ, Paralia, Malabar or Travancore, Comari, Cape Comorin under King Pandyan. Dr. Vincent conjuctures that the King of Madura had extended his power from the eastern to the western side of the Peninsula and was master of Malabar when the fleets from Europe first visited the Coast."[1] He also thinks it likely that the power of the Pandyan had been superseded in Malabar between the age of the Periplus and of Ptolemy, for Ptolemy reckons the Avi next to Limyrike on the south, and takes no notice of Pandyan till he is past Cape Comorin.[2]

Through the continued encroachment of the sea, the harbour which the Greek mariners found and the fort have completely disappeared; all that is left is a fresh-water well in the centre of a rock a little way out at sea. It is, however, interesting to note that the

1. Vol. II, p. 401.

2. Vol. III, R. A. S. Journal. p. 200, Note.

enlightened Government of His Highness the Maharaja of Travancore is endeavouring to restore the long-lost haven. The attention of the Darbār has been drawn recently to the advantages offered by a small bay situated within two miles of Comorin near Sīpuram, as it is said that this sea-board inlet possesses all the requirements of a first-rate harbour for all classes of ships plying between Calcutta and Bombay, Ceylon and S. India. The sea here is sufficently deep to admit of even large vessels riding at anchor about a mile from the land, and it affords sufficient protection against the severity of the South-west and North-east monsoons. The Travancore Government have established a custom-house at the port; and a flagstaff and a light-post, perhaps to be replaced before long by a regular light-house, are under construction. Altogether, there is every prospect that Comorin will once more take it's place, after centuries of obscurity, among the important harbours of India.

Marco Polo speaks not only of the Cape but also of the country called Comari. He says, "Comari is a country belonging to India, and there you can see something of the Northern Star, which we had not been able to see from the Lesser Java thus far. In order to see it, you must go some thirty miles out to Sea, and you see it about a cubit above the water. This is a very wild country, and there are beasts of all kinds there, especially monkeys of such peculiar fashion that you would take them for men! There are also gatpaulo (a kind of ape) in wonderful diversity, with bears, lions and leopards in abundance."[1]

Abulfeda speaks of Ras Kumhari as the parting point between Malabar and Ma' abar. He says, "The country called Ma' abar is said to commence at the

1. Bk. III, Ch. 23.

Cape Kumhari, a name applied both to a town and a mountain."[1]

Old geographers have sometimes confounded Kumāri with Khmer or Kambōja.[2] Similarly, geographers of the 16th century have confounded Cape Comorin with the Kory of the Greek geographers. Purchas remarks that, "Malabar extendeth itself from the river Cangeroees to Cape Comori, which some take to be the promontory Kori in Ptolemy. Magnius doubteth whether it be that which he calleth Commario Externa." Camoens also identifies the ancient Kory or Kolis with Comorin.[3] But in Ptolemy Kori and Comorin are distinct. Ptolemy, like the author of the Periplus and other writers, regarded Cape Comorin as the most important projection of India towards the south, and as a well established point from which the distances of other places might conveniently be calculated.[4] In the geographical poem of Dionysius, it is described as towering to a stupendous height above the waves.

The early Portuguese speak of a small kingdom of Comori, the prince of which had succeeded to the kingdom of Kaulam (Quilon). This, Dr. Caldwell points out, must have been the state which is now called Travancore. It is well known that the families of Travancore and Quilon were collaterally related to one another.

Fra Bartolomeo, while mentioning the Church of St. Xavier as standing on a hill near the Cape, mentions that, "On another hill, a few miles farther up the country, is a monastery inhabited by pagan philo-

1. Gildemeister, 185.
2. Caldwell, Dravidian Grammar, p. 67; Gildemeister, 185, Ramusio, 1, 133.
3. Comoens, X, 107; Miekle's Translation.
4. Mc' Crindle, pp. 61-62.

CAPE COMORIN.

To face page 12.]

sophers, known under the name of gymnosophists or Yōgin (Yōgi)." In a note to this his editor adds, "They are real stoics and often impose upon themselves the severest penances. They are mentioned by Cicero, Plutarch, Clemens of Alexandria and Arrian. The last author says, besides other things respecting them, that they were accustomed to walk down into the sea at Cape Comorin, in order to purify themselves, a custom which they have retained to this day."[1] Between two to three miles to the north of the Cape runs a series of hills one of which is known as Maruṭwā Mala, on which even now live a number of Yōgies spending their lives in contemplation, but few are known to walk down into the sea now, though they do often bathe in the sea. There are on these hills a few temples perched on hillocks one over the other, besides the sheltering places improvised by *gosais* (gōsāīs) and other pilgrims, who take up their temporary abode there. Local tradition loves to relate how Hanūmān, the monkey messenger of Rāma, dropped on this spot the 'medicine-hill' he was carrying on his shoulders across the sea to Lanka, to revive Lakshmaṇa, by means of the efficacy of the medicinal herbs growing on it, from the stupor caused by the Rāvaṇa's *Brahmastram* (Brahmāsṭram). The hill is still reputed to produce medicinal herbs of untold efficacy; but, unfortunately for the denizens of this mundane hemisphere, these are visible only to the charmed eyes of the initiated few.

3. **Mount Delli.** Locally the mount is known as Ēli Mala[2]—N. Lat. 12° 2′, E. Long. 75° 16′. It forms the northernmost point of Malabar proper, though

1. p. 112.

2. Can it be a variant of Āli-mala, meaning the mount near the sea? Compare Ēlikara, the name of a kara or desom, part of a village. It means a kara near āli or sea.

tradition extends the country further north up to Gōkarṇam. It is a conspicuous isolated hill, or rather cluster of hills forming a promontory some sixteen miles north of Cannanore. From the earliest times it has been known as a conspicuous land-mark to mariners. Gasper Correa says that Vasco-da-Gama's pilots had foretold that the first land to be sighted would be a great mountain on the Coast of India in the Kingdom of Cannanore which the people of the country in their language called the mountain Delielly, "And they call it 'of the rat,' and they call it Mt. Dely, because in this mountain there were so many rats that they could never make a village there."[1] Upon this Mr. Logan observes, "*Eli* certainly means a rat, but the name of the hill is written with the cerebro-palatal l̄. The legend which Correa obtained was like that which conferred on it likewise the sounding title of *Sapta-Salia* (Sapta-Śaila) or seven hills, because *elu* (ēlu) means in Malayalam seven, and *elu* (ēlu) *mala* means seven hills, of which *Sapta-Saila* is the Sanskrit equivalent. Now, as a matter of fact, there are not seven peaks to this hill, just as probably the rats were no worse there than they were anywhere else on the coast. But Eli is clearly identical with Marco Polo's 'Kingdom of Eli' and Ibn Batuta's 'Hildi', and as the Ēli Kōvilagam, the second oldest of the palaces of the ancient line of Kōlattiri Princes, lies at a very short distance from the northern slopes of the hill, it is clear that the name of the hill was given to the palace or that of the palace to the hill. Its height is 855 ft."[2]

The earliest mention on record of the hill is perhaps in the Indian Segment of the Roman maps called the Pentingerian Tables. The Eli Maide [*Eli* (Ēli) + *Maidu* or Mēdu=hill in Tamil—Malaya-

1. Stanley's Translation, p. 145.
2. Malabar, Vol. I, p. 7.

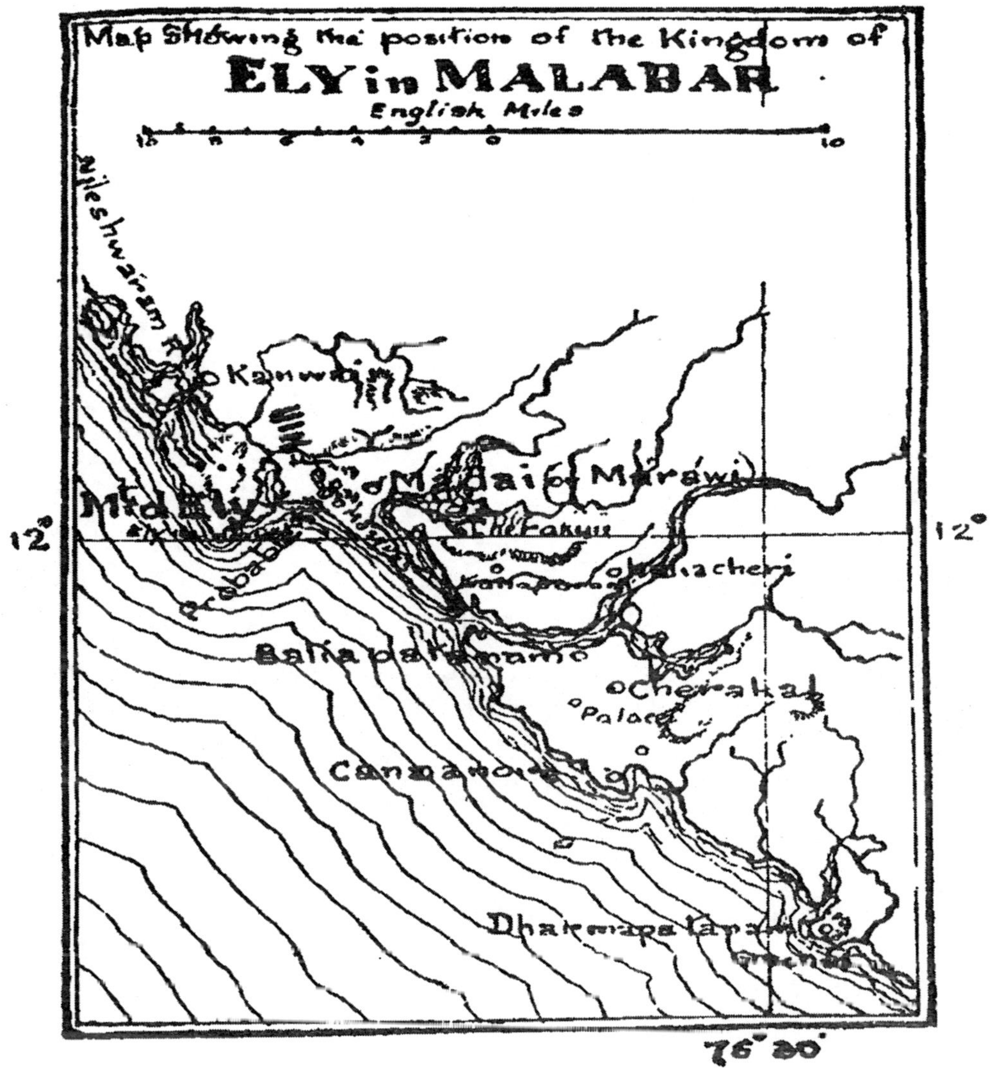

MAP OF THE KINGDOM OF ELY IN MALABAR.

To face page 15.]

lam; cf. Peermedu] of the tables is not unlikely an indication of Ēly or Ēli.[1] The Kēralotpaṭṭi, or Malayalam history of Kērala, makes mention of a fort called Mātayēliankōtta, so named after its constructors, Māda Perumāl and Ēli Perumāl. It is significant that the Tohfut-ul-Mujahideen, or Arab History of the Muhammadan settlement in Malabar, mentions a State called Hili-Marawi[2]. The name of Marabia or Marawi is preserved in Madavi or Mādāi situated 13½ miles north-west of Cannanore, upon the river which enters the bay about 7 or 8 miles south-east of Mt. D' Ely, and which is called by De Barros the Rio Marabia. There is an old temple here, and close by, and within the Mādāi township, is the hamlet of Payangadi or Palayangādi (old town or market), with an old tank known by the name of "The Jewish tank," near which stand the ruins of the old fort or palace of the Ēli or Kōlaṭṭiri Rajas. Mr. Sewell conjectures that the tank was probably constructed by a colony of Jews or Yavanās.[3] Dr. Gundhert, in the Madras Journal of Literature and Science, also alludes to a palace at Mādāi, while an old Malayalam poem mentions a Buddhist vihāra (chapel) as having existed in the place.[4]

Marco Polo (A. D. 1298) describes the vicinity of the hill as a "Kingdom towards the west about 300 miles from Comari" (Cape Comorin).[5] Rashi'duddin (A. D. 1247) refers to it as "the country of the Hili", lying between Manjarur (Mangalore) and Fandarina (or Kollam about 1½ miles north of Kovilkandy or Quilandy). Abulfeda (A. D. 1273) describes it as a "great mountain projecting into the sea, and

1. Hobson Jobson.
2. Pp. 54, 58, 59.
3. Archaeological Survey of S. India, Vol. I, p. 242.
4. Yule's Marco Polo, Vol. II, p. 387.
5. Book III, Ch. 24.

described from the promontory called Ras Haili.[1] Ibn Batuta (A. D. 1342) speaks of Hili as a "large and well-built town on a great bay (or estuary) which big ships enter."[2] Nicolo Conti (A. D. 1491) is perhaps the last of the medaeval voyagers who makes any distinct mention of D'Ely. "Proceeding onwards, he (Conti) arrived at two cities on the seashore, named Ras Comaria (Bakur, Malayalam, Vakkanūr) and Helly."[3] Barbosa (A. D. 1516) observes, "After passing this place along the coast is the mountain Dely on the edge of the sea. It is a round mountain, very lofty, in the midst of low land; all the ships of the Moors and the Gentiles............... sight this mountain........ ....and make their reckoning by it."[4] In A. D. 1527, the Portuguese Governor Lope Vaz sent his nephew Simon de Mello to burn the Moorish ships in the river of Marabia and at Mt. D'Ely. "He burned 12 of the Paraos that guarded the port and, landing, fired the town. The same he did at Mount Delli."[5]

Though Mount D'Ely is prominently mentioned in old books, it is rather strange that it finds no place in modern maps. The town of Monte d'Ely, however, appears as Monte Dib in Coronelli's Atlas (A. D. 1690) from some old source. It also appears as Ely in the Carta Catalana, and is marked as a Christian city.[6] Three leagues south from Mont D'Ely is a broad and deep river called Baliapatam (Mal: Valarpattaṇam), where, according to Alexander Hamilton, there was a factory belonging to the English East India Company.[7]

1. Gildemeister, 185.
2. Ch. IV. 81.
3. India in the 15th century, p. 6.
4. East Africa and Malabar, p. 149.
5. Faria, Vol. 1. p. 318.
6. Marco Polo, Vol. 11, p. 386.
7. A new Account of the East Indies; Vol. 1, p. 291.

4. **The Legend about the Origin of Malabar.** The legend has its variants. Our author gives one version of it, while another account of it is given by his Editor in the note. The Kottayam College Quarterly Magazine for July 1864 gives another and a more interesting and descriptive account of it, based on the Brahmāṇda Purāṇa.

"The Brahmāṇda Purāṇa contains a legend scarcely inferior in imagery to some of Homer's noblest pictures, but which, when stripped of its poetical garb, seems to point to an occurrence similar to those that have been related above (referring to changes in the physical configuration of the earth brought on by volcanic agency). It describes how the sons of Sagara dug a hole, and descended into the infernal regions, in quest of a certain horse that had been stolen by Indra and deposited there; and how, when they had been consumed by the fire of Kapilā's anger, one of their descendants implored Gunga to descend into *Patalom* (Pāṭālom) (the nether regions) and sanctify their ashes; and how at last Gunga yielded to his entreaties, and having flooded the abodes of Kapila, welled up through the hole dug by the sons of Sagara, and covered Gōkarṇam with destruction; we are then told that the 'inhabitants removed hither and thither; and when they saw that the holy Temple at Gōkarṇam was so speedily immersed in the ocean, they were deeply grieved, and consulted what they should do.' The result of this consulation was that they went up to the summit of the Sahya mountains in search of Paraśu-Rāma to whom their complaint was as follows:—' Hear the cause of our now coming, O thou who possessest mercy; we who once lived at Gōkarṇam are now afflicted by the sons of Sagara, who dug a hole and descended to the Infernal regions, and were burned with the fire of Kapilā's anger. And now all the country where the sons of Sagara dug has become ocean; and, because Gōkarṇam, the Great Temple, has sunk beneath the waves with its sacred waters, we are greatly distressed.' In this strain they supplicate Rāma, who at last vouchsafes to accompany them to the sea-shore. The description that follows is so striking that we shall be pardoned for attempting to keep up in some measure the poetical element:—

> With wonder great the mighty Bhargavan,[1]
> What time he stood upon Gokarnam's[2] shore,
> Beheld the scene: and when the wide domain
> Of ocean he espied, he southward turned,
> And with a voice in thunder, rolling, spake
> Like words as these: 'O sea-king, hither I,
> With these wise men, have come thyself to see;
> Delay not to assume thy form divine
> And grant thy presence, sire, to my demand.'
> Such words of Rama's[3] then heard Varunen,[4]
> But from his seat he moved not at the call.
> His boldness seeing, Bhargavan again,
> And yet again, called for the ocean-king:
> But not an answer yet gave Varunen,
> Nor to the light came forth; which seeing spake
> Bhargava-Rama,[5] if such mad contempt
> Be shown by worthless beings, what will men
> Of valour in their minds revolve and judge!
> 'Soon with my arrow will I dry this sea,
> Till not a drop of ocean shall remain.'
> He spoke and washed his feet; when straight from heaven,
> As swift as thought, a bow and arrow fell.
> Then worshipping the feet of Siva,[6] in
> His hand Bhargavan took the bow, and strung
> With wildest rage, and clutching in his grasp
> The arrow forged by Bhrgu,[7] both his eyes
> Starting their veins blood-red, he clanged the string.
> Then trembled the three worlds and all the Earth,
> With ocean, islands, mountains, deserts, quailed.
> And then upon the string that arrow dread,
> That, winged with flame, burns awful, like the fire

1. Bhārgavan. 2. Gōkarṇam. 3. Rāma. 4. Varuṇan. 5. Bhārgava-Rāma. 6. Śiva. 7. Bhṛgu.

Of the great day of doom, Bhargavan fixed,
And muttering *munthrums*[1] stood. Then hid the sun
His disk behind the cloud of dust that rose
From off the trembling earth, a comet streamed
Across the sky, the lightning flashed, and blood
Rained thick. Then terror seized the tribes of heaven,
Sidhen[2] and *muni*, *charanen*[3] and all
The singers of the Gods, the cause unknown,
Ran here and there, and mad with fear, lay, hid.
And the inhabitants of ocean all,
Huge aligators, fishes, serpents, whales,
And crocodiles and tortoises were scorched.
The waves rolled up and deluged all the shore,
And all the waters of the ocean boiled.

And so it goes on, till, at the entreaties of the various denizens of the deep, which are rendered peculiarily uncomfortable, Varuṇan is glad to humble himself before Paraśu Rāma and offers to obey him in anything he commands. Upon this, Paraśu Rāma, laughing, removes the dread arrow from the bow, while he commands Varuṇan to bring up the holy temple and remove his waters to a respectful distance. Varuṇan complies and promises to remove his seat as far from the shore as Rāma bids; whereupon Rāma sends away his bow and arrow; and having taken a golden spoon, such as is used for sacrificial purposes, he flung it over the waters. It fell at Cape Comorin, whereupon the waters removed from the shore (for 200 yōjanās) and Gōkarṇam, the great temple, became level with the earth; the city, the village, the holy waters, the temple, the desert, came in sight little by little; and all the sages blessed Paraśu Rāma.

Can there be a doubt that this legend chronicles, in the style of the poets, the effects of volcanic agency on this coast centuries ago; first, that there was once a subsidence, probably sudden, at Gōkarṇam; and secondly, that there was afterwards a perceptible up-

1. Manṭrams. 2. Siḍhan. 3. Chāraṇan.

rising, most probably in this case gradual, of at least some portion, if not of nearly all the coast between Gōkarṇam and the Cape."[1]

This latter view receives confirmation from later investigations. For, in discussing the recent geological history of South Malabar, between the Bēypore and Ponnāny rivers, Mr. Philip Lake, B. A., F. G. S., of the Geological Survey of India, points out that, before the laterite period, Malabar stood 500 ft. lower than at present, and the sea washed the foot of the Ghauts. South Malabar was then a bay bounded on the north by the Camel's Hump and its outlying ranges, and on the south by the Cochin hills. In the middle of the bay rose islands which are now the Wallaūr or Wolaṭṭūr Hill, Kundōṭṭi Hill, Urotmala, Pandalūr, Prāṇakōd, and the Anangamala. Pandalūr and Prāṇakōd hills were probably united. The land generally rose and at first a ledge of low-lying ground appeared round the central islands—Urotmala, Pandalūr and Prāṇakōd. This is now the highest parts of the plateau. The land rose higher and higher, and the ledge became broader, till at last it joined the Ghauts near the peak of Kanyankombu, thus dividing the bay into two. This line of division is now the watershed between the Pandkod and Ponnāni rivers. At length the present level was reached.[2] This process of formation must have extended to the South also.

5. **Descent of Namburi** (Nambūri) **Brahmins.** Our author must have derived his information as to the conversion of the fishermen into Brahmans from Maharatta sources.[3] Sir William Hunter repeats the

1. pp. 3 to 5.
2. Memoirs of the Geological Survey of India, Vol. XXIV, part 3, p. 35.
3. Malabar, Vol. I, p. 274.

NAMBUTIRI BRAHMINS.

To face page 21.]

story in his Orissa. But it need hardly be said that it has no foundation in history, and carries with it its own refutation.[1] Of the story the Travancore Census Commissioner observes, "Sir William Hunter would, most outrageously, it is felt, call them (the Nambūries) Brahmanical fishermen, and would refer to their polygamy, their post-nuptial marriage, the prohibition of holy matrimony among all but the eldest son in a household, and to the ceremonial fishing as part of the marriage ritual among the Yajur-Vēdic branch of the caste, as the relic and record of a pre-Brahmanic stage. But infant marriage has not been the prescribed institution of the vēdic Brahmans. Nor has the aim of marital union been anything other than the uninterrupted maintenance of a righteous lineage. Old maidens did not always mean unsuccessful would-be-Benedicts, and polygamy was as much the result, though indirect, of the gradual decadence of the spirit of self dedication to religious life among females, as carnal or noncanonical alliances of junior sons represented the lowering of religious ideals among males. And if anthropometry, as far as it has gone, may be trusted to enlighten us on the subject, the researches of Mr. Fawcet go to show that 'they (the Nambūries) are the truest Aryans in Southern India.'[2] The banks of the Nerbuda, the Kṛshṇa and the Kāvēri are believed to have given Brahmans to Malabar. The writer has come across Nambūries who have referred to traditions in their families regarding villages on the East Coast whence their ancestors originally came, and the sub-divisions of the Smārṭa caste, Vaṭama, Bṛhaṭcharaṇam, Ashṭasahasram, Sankēṭi &c., to which they belonged. Even to this day an east

1. Prāchīna Kēralam and the recent report to the Travancore Government on the Tenancy question may, however, be looked into.

2. Bulletin on the people of Malabar.

coast Brahman of the Vadadēśaṭṭu Vadama caste has to pour water into the hands of a Nambūri Sanyāsi as part of the latter's breakfast ritual. Broach in Kathiawar, one of the greatest emporiums of trade in the middle ages, is also mentioned as one of the ancient recruiting districts of the Nambūri Brahmans. Broach was the ancient Bhṛgucachchha where Paraśu Rāma made his Avabhṛtasnānam, final bathing, after his great triumph over the Kshestryās, and where to this day a set of people called Bhārgava Brahmans live." [1]

6. **Origin of Malabar.** The legend adverted to in Note 4 is not to be rejected altogether as puerile. It has, indeed, a core of truth in it. It in fact chronicles in the imaginative style of the poets the effects of volcanic action on the coast centuries ago. The low lands of the Malabar Coast have evidently been raised from beneath the sea-level by subterranean forces. Instances are not wanting of the formation by natural forces of large tracts of land on the coast even in modern times. The island of Vypin, 13 miles long by one broad, on the north side of Cochin, was thrown up by the sea not long ago. It is known in the locality as *Putu-Vaipu* (Puṭu-Vaipu), i. e., new formation, and the people there commence an era from the date of its formation in A. D. 1341. It would appear that, prior to this, a small river flowed by the town of Cochin, with only a narrow outlet for the discharge of the freshes that came in torrents during the rainy season down the Ghauts, at the well-known opening at Crānganūr about 20 miles to the north of this Vaipu. In the year 1341, an extraordinary flood occurred which forced itself into the sea at Cochin, and opened a capacious estuary, converting the land-locked harbour of Cochin into one of the

1. Travancore Census Report, Part I, p. 295.

finest and safest ports in India. The soil of the low-lying lands on the sea-coast, consisting of sea-sand and calcareous matter combined with various kinds of earth and clay, attests the nature of the formation. The nature of the sub-soil brought up at the sinking of an artesian well recently in British Cochin makes it clear that the strip of land on which the town is now situated lay not long ago submerged in the sea.

Fra Bartolomeo says that in his day the natives believed that the sea formerly extended even to the foot of the Ghauts, evidently referring to the tradition we are now discussing. He, however, was of opinion that the tradition had no foundation, though he is willing to concede "that some of the plains found in this country have been produced by conflicts between the waves of the sea and the torrents of rain." "The devastation occasioned by such inundations," says he, "can hardly be described. Grand-children sometimes can scarcely point out with any certainty the spot where their grand-father resided, because it has assumed a form totally different." There is, indeed, strong reason to suppose that in the early years of the Christian Era the sea-coast ran along the eastern shore of the backwater, which extends at present to over 40 miles from Changanāsēri to Pallippuṟam; and it is extremely doubtful if the long strip of land which forms its western bank, and on which now stand the flourishing sea-ports of Alleppey and Cochin, had any existence then. The towns mentioned by Ptolemy as lying on the sea coast between Muziris (Crānganūr) and Barkari (Varkalay near Quilon) can nowhere be identified as the coast now exists, whereas some of them, Podoperoura, Semne and Korthora, may be identified with Uḏayampērūr (the Diamper of the Portuguese), Chembu and Kothur, all of which are situated on the eastern shore of the backwater.[1]

1. The Tamils Eighteen Hundred years ago by Mr. Kanakasabhai, p. 19.

In a report on the mud bank at Alleppey in Travancore, Mr. Rhode, a former Commercial Agent of the State, observed, "I cannot give dates, as I have no records, but it is certain that the coast from about north of Calicut to south of Quilon was once well above the level of the sea, and was after a long period totally submerged, and then again was thrown up by volcanic action, and has again been partially covered by the sea. I state this because, in cutting the Varkalay Tunnel, trees were found, and also shells have been found on the coast which are known to belong to a class of shell-fish that only lives in deep water. Remnants of a fort at Poracaud were visible 30 years ago, and at Calicut and Vypin massive buildings are now in the sea."[1] "It is curious," says Dr. Day, "that this law of encroachments of the sea is now the rule on the western coast, because tradition and an examination of the geology of the country both lead to the conclusion that the sea formerly washed up to the Western Ghauts; thus Malabar has been literally raised from the sea." Dr. Day refers to a manuscript account of Malabar by Hernan Lopez de Castunheda in 1525, where, it is said, that, little more than 2300 years ago, the sea came up to the Western Ghauts.[2]

The theory, that the sea coast originally ran along the line of the eastern shore of the backwater, receives support from the names by which certain places situated on that line are still known. About 8 miles to the north of Cochin, on the eastern side of the backwater, lies the village of Kadakkara, or more correctly

1. Report on the Administration of Travancore, 1881-82.

2. Vol. 22. Mad. Jour. of Lt. and Sc. N. S. 6 pp. 260 and 264—1861. See also articles, "Ñārakkal or Cochin Mud Banks" by Dr. Francis Day, Civil Surgeon, Cochin and "The Mud Bank at Ñārakkal near Cochin—Its composition as exhibited by the microscope" by Lieut. Mitchel.

(*kadal*=sea + *kara*=shore=) Kadalkkara, signifying 'sea-shore'. To the south of it, almost in close proximity, is another village called Ēlikkara, which, there can be no doubt, should originally have been (*Ali*=sea+ *kara*=shore=)Ālikkara, also meaning 'sea-shore'. Next to Ēlikkara, to its south, lies Kaṭamakkuṭi, meaning 'the abode of the sea fishermen'. Close to it lies the island of Vypin or the land newly formed. Again 18 miles to the south of Cochin, on the eastern coast of the great backwater, lies the town of Vycome, or 'that which was newly formed'.[1] The coast line, as known at the time of Megasthenes, fourth century B. C., certainly ran along the eastern shore of the backwater. For he mentions Tropina, identified by eminent scholars with Ṭrippūniṭṭura, a few miles inland from Cochin and on the backwater side, as lying on the sea coast.[2]

According to Tamil Historical Texts, the people in the south, 1800 years ago, remembered that, in former days, the land extended further south of Cape Comorin, and that a mountain called Kumārikkōdu and a large tract of country watered by the Pahruli existed south of Kumāri. It is said that, during a violent irruption of the sea, the mountain Kumārikkōdu and the whole of the country through which the Pahruli flowed disappeared.

There are other local instances of the irruption of the sea and the subsidence of the land. The Buddhist

1. To the south of Vycome and not far from there is a small village called Vechūr. The meaning of this word is alluvion. To the east of Vycome is the village called Kadaṭṭuruṭṭi, (=kadal + ṭuruṭṭu=) island in the sea. It is also significant that in the Śuka Sandēśam there is no reference to these coast-lying places.

2. R. C. Dutt. Ancient India, Vol. II, p. 30; Indian Antiquary, quoted by Professor Mc'Crindle in note on page 142 of his Ancient India as described by Megasthenes and Arrian.

annals of Ceylon record one such on the south-western coast of that island in the second century B. C.[1] The island of Rāmēśwaram, which is 11 miles long, is only two miles away from the main-land, and, till but three or four centuries ago, there was a rocky causeway connecting Rāmēśwaram with the mainland. It is said that, about the 15th century, this connection was severed by the sea bursting through the chain of rocks that formed the causeway. The abrupt manner in which Point Rāman on the coast terminates, and its geological formation, which can be traced across the ridge of rocks to the island, almost confirm the supposition, and the opinion is strengthened by the records of the temple at Rāmēśwaram which state that, until the early part of the 15th century, the island was connected with the continent of India by a narrow neck of land, and that the *Swamy*(Swāmi)(idol) of Rāmēśwaram was on particular festivals carried to a temple on the mainland. The sandy ridge known as Adam's Bridge connects Rāmēśwaram with Ceylon, thus accounting for the so-called bridge built by the monkey soldiers of the Rāmāyaṇa.[2]

Extricating ourselves from the halo of legend that surrounds and obscures the Brahman sage Paraśu Rāma, we see in him the leader, perhaps, of the earliest Aryan colony into South India. The miraculous powers by which he is supposed to have reclaimed the land are part and parcel of his asserted semi-divine character. The very existence of such a personage as Paraśu Rāma has been questioned by some authorities; while others assert that he is an incarnation of Vishṇu, although it is difficult to fix his date with any approach to accuracy. His encounter with his great name-sake, the hero of the Rāmāyaṇa, and

1. The Tamils, 1800 years ago, p. 21.

2. The Gazetteer of S. India, p. 385.

his slaughter of the Kṣheṭrya race have been pronounced by Mr. Talboys Wheeler to be pure myths.[1]

But Mr. Romesh Chunder Dutt thinks that the story of Paraśu Rāma probably conceals a great historical truth. " He is said to have fought against the Kṣheṭryas and exterminated that caste 21 times when he was conquered by the Kṣheṭrya Rāma, the hero of the epic. It would seem that this story indicates the real rivalry and hostilities between the priestly and warrior castes—indications of which we have found in a literary form in the Upaniṣhads."[2] Paraśu Rāma, however, is a post-vēdic god and it is doubtful if he can be accorded a very high antiquity. Mr. Dutt points out that, in the Anuśāsana Parva of the Mahābhāraṭa, section 52, Yuḍhiṣhtira enquires how Paraśu Rāma, the son of the Brahman Jamaḍagni, was possessed of the qualities of a Kṣheṭrya. " It is indeed remarkable," says Mr. Dutt, "that Jamaḍagni's name occurs in the Rig Vēda, but not that of his renowned son Paraśu Rāma. That character therefore is a later invention, and the story of his wars with the Kṣheṭryas is probably based on actual hostilities, which may have taken place early in the epic age (B. C. 1400 to 1000) between stalwart priests and proud kings just when the caste system was taking shape."[3]

According to Rev. William Taylor, the nearest conjecture we can form regarding the date of Paraśu Rāma is that he lived sometime within the thousandth year after the flood according to the orthodox Christian chronology. He thinks that assuming the astro-

1. History of India, Vol. II, p. 67.

2. Ancient India, Vol. 1, p. 212. Hunter's Indian Empire, p. 104.

3. Ancient India, Vol. I, p. 153.

nomical principles detailed by him elsewhere[1] to be correct, there must have been a great retiring of the mass of the waters from the northern hemisphere during the period within 500 years to 1000 years after the flood; and, unless the level of the Malabar Coast be gradually beneath that of the Coromandal Coast, from this also a similar retiring of the waters must have taken place at the same time.[2]

7. **Kerala** (Kēraḷa). Our author does not himself call the country by the name Kēraḷa. However, his editor does so in his note. In Sanskrit literature, from the earliest times, the country is designated Kēraḷa, and that is the name by which the Malayālīs love to call their native land. Kēraḷa is a Sanskrit word. The land was certainly known to the Aryans at a very early period. Kāṭyāyana (first half of the fourth century B.C.) and Paṭanjali (B. C. 150) make mention of it, though Pāṇini (beginning of the seventh century B.C., if not earlier still) does not. The Mahābhāraṭa,[3] the Rāmāyaṇa,[4] the Vāyu Purāṇa,[5] the Maṭsya Purāṇa,[6] and the Mārkaṇḍēya Purāṇa[7] make mention of Kēraḷa and Gōkarṇam. The latter name appears also in the Bhāgavaṭa, Paḍma and Skānḍa Purāṇās. The Mahābhāraṭa, the Rāmāyaṇa and the Harivamśa refer to the Kēraḷās as a class of despicable people in the south, such as the Hūṇās, Pulinḍās, Chandālās, Svapachās, etc. They attribute the degeneration of the times to the existence of such

1. Trans: of Orient: Hist. MSS., Vol. I, p. 153.
2. Ibid, Vol. II, p. 65.
3. IV—41 1668; III—1991; Sabhā Parva, Ch. p. 31.
4. 1—41.
5. Chap. 45 and 124, Ed. Bib: Indica.
6. Chap. 112, V. 46, Poona Lithograph Edition.
7. Chap. 59, V. 45, Ed. Bib: Ind.

nations of the lowest origin.[1] To them were also ascribed the atrocities of warfare.[2] As to the dates of these epics and Purāṇās: the Rāmāyaṇa is later than the Mahābhārața; while Pāṇini refers to the latter, he is altogether silent about the former. Professor Bhandarkar classes the Vāyu, the Maţsya and the Bhāgavaţa as among the later Purāṇas. Of these, the oldest appears to be the Vāyu, and next to it the Maţsya, and the Bhāgavaţa the latest.[3]

The second and the 13th Edicts of the great Budhist Emperor Aśōka, (B.C. 257) refer to the ruler of Kērala as Kēralapuţra, and class his country as one of the Prāţyanţās or border-lands of the Empire. He is named along with Chōla and Pāndya in the south and Antiochus in the north.

In the first century A. D., Pliny refers to the ruler of Kērala as Calobōţrās and mentions Muziris, the first emporium of trade in India, as his capital. Muziris has been satisfactorily identified by Dr. Burnell with the modern Crānganūr or Kodungallūr, a sea-coast town 20 miles to the north of Cochin. From Pliny we may gather that the country ruled by Calobōţrās extended southwards to Neacyndon, Nilkanda or Kallada, near Quilon, where the sway of the Pāndyan king began.

The Periplus, written probably in the first century A. D., also refers to Keprobōţras and the land he ruled, which it calls Limurike. It extended from Nouro and Tyndis in the north to Nelcynda in the south.

Ptolemy, second century A. D., mentions Karoura as the capital of Limurike where Kērobōţrās lived.

1. Dr. Oppert on the Weapons, Army Organisation and Political Maxims of the Ancient Hindus, p. 33.

2. Nīţiprakaśika: Mad. Jour. of Lit. and Sc. for 1881.

3. Early History of the Dekhan, p. 26.

The description given by Pliny, Arrian, and Ptolemy of Limurike, or as the Pentingerian Tables call it Damurike, enables us to fix approximately the extent of the sway of Calobōṭrās, Keprobōṭrās or Kērobōṭrās. Limurike or Damurike has been shown by the learned Bishop Caldwell to represent the Drāvida or the Tamil-Malayālam country.[1] From Pliny it is somewhat difficult to gather its northern limit; but, after making mention of the important port of Muziris, he goes southward, and names Neacyndon, which, according to him, belonged to the Pāndyans. In this the Periplus agrees with him. Ptolemy calls the place Melkynda and locates it in the country of the Aioi, identified by Caldwell with South Travancore. Ptolemy and the author of the Periplus are at one in making Tyndis the most northern port in Limurike. The Periplus gives its distance at 7000 stadia or nearly 12° of latitude, if we reckon 600 stadia to the degree. Notwithstanding this authoritative statement, which makes Limurike begin somewhere near Calicut (11° —15′ N. Lat.), its frontier has generally been placed nearly 3° further north, Tyndis having been located at Barcelore. This error has been rectified by Sir Henry Yule, whose adherence to the data of the Periplus has been completely justified by the satisfactory identification of Muziris with Crānganūr instead of with Mangalore, as previously accepted. It is, perhaps, necessary to point out here that Tyndis, too, has been satisfactorily identified by Dr. Burnell with Kaṭalundi near Beypore, the former south-western terminus of the Madras Railway near Calicut.

The Kērobōṭrās of Ptolemy, Keprobōṭrās of the Periplus and Calobōṭrās of Pliny have been identified by Bishop Caldwell with the Tamil Kēralapuṭra. It is the same as the Kēralapuṭra of the Aśōka Edicts.

1. Comparative Grammer of the Dravidian Languages.

The insertion of the letter "p" in one of the above names is pointed out to be an error, perhaps of the transcriber. "The name in Sanskrit, and, in full," says the learned Bishop, "is *Keralaputra*, (Kēraḷapuṭra) but the Kēra and Kēla are Dravidian abbreviations of Kēraḷa. They are Malayāḷam, however, not Tamil abbreviations, and the district over which the Tamil Kēraḷapuṭra ruled is that in which the Malayāḷam language is now spoken."[1]

The Rev. Mr. Foulkes contends that Chēra and Kēraḷa denote the same country, the term Kēraḷa being but the Canarese dialectical form of the word Chēra. He points to a general concurrence of the authorities that Chēra and Kēraḷa are synonymous names, notwithstanding the difficulty caused by the supposed identity of Kongu and Chēra.[2] Dr. Rottler's Tamil Dictionary has under the word "Kēraḷan" "The king Chēran who reigned on the Malabar Coast." "I have no doubt," says Dr. Caldwell, "that the name Chēra and Kēraḷa were originally one and the same, and it is certain that they are always regarded as synonymous in native Tamil and Malayāḷam lists." Dr. Gundhert has, in his Malayāḷam Dictionary, under the word *Keram* (Kēram) "Canarese pronunciation of Chēram," "Chēra=Malabar," and under the word Kēraḷam "Chēram=the country between Gōkarṇam and Kumāri."

The Chēra or Kēraḷa kingdom at one time loomed large on the map of Southern India. According to Dr. Burnett, the period from the third to the seventh century appears to have been the most flourishing one in the modern history of the kingdom. It then extended over the present Mysore, Coimbatore, Tondinad, South Malabar and Cochin. It formed one of

1. Intro. to the Comp. Gram. of the Drav. Lang., p. 95.
2. Salem Dist. Manual, Vol. I.

the great triarchy of ancient Hindu kingdoms in the extreme south of India, and had already acquired a name before the third century B. C. Professor Dowson describes it at a later period as extending to the Mysore frontier in the north, the district of Salem in the east, and the Travancore coast up to Calicut in the north-west. Its capital was Ḳarūr. Dr. Caldwell is disposed to identify Karūr with the Karoura of Ptolemy, which, he says, occupies the same site as the present important town of the same name in the Coimbatore district, situated on the left bank of the Amarāvaṭi, a tributary of the Kāvēri. The authority of the learned Bishop is high indeed. But there are some noteworthy considerations which induce us to shift the locality of Ptolemy's Karoura, the capital of Chēra or Kērala, to an altogether different place. Early Tamil records point to Vanji as the capital of the Chēra kingdom, and, according to the Tamil metrical Dictionary, Tivākaram, the modern name of Vanji is Karūr. Ancient Tamil works describe Vanji as being situated west of the Western Ghauts. In the Periya Purāṇa, Vanji is mentioned as the capital of the Chēra king, and it is indeed significant that it was also known as Mākōṭai. In the Syrian copper plate grant of Bhāskara Ravi Varma, the ruler or Perumāl of Chēra or Kērala about the eighth century A. D., Kodungallūr or Crānganūr is called Mākōṭaipaṭṭaṇam, *i. e.*, the town of Mākōṭai, and this is generally accepted as being the capital of the Chēramān Perumāls. The Rev. Willam Taylor, in his preface to his Translation of Tamil Historical Manuscripts, assures us that the Śēra (Chēra) metropolis was no other than Ṭiru Vanji, the capital of the Chēra dēśam. Thus early records, known traditions, and old inscriptions, all point to Ṭiruvanchi or Ṭiruvanchikkuḷam (rendered into Śrī Vanji Kōviḷakam or palace of the prosperous Vanji king), lying adjacent to Crānganūr, as the capital of the early rulers of Chēra or Kēraḷa.

It has been already remarked that Crānganūr has been satisfactorily identified with the Muziris of Pliny and Ptolemy. Pliny, who died in A. D. 77, and who seems to have written his work two years before his death, says that "Calobōṭrās reigned there (Muziris) when I committed this to writing." But by the middle of the second century A. D., when Ptolemy wrote, Chēra must have either changed its capital, or constituted one more seat of Government; for, Ptolemy, as we have observed, names Karoura as the capital of Limurike. It may indeed be that there were two capitals, the northern and the southern; the capital for the interior and the capital for the coast; or Calobōṭrās or Kērobōṭrās must have removed his capital from Muziris on the coast to Karoura in the interior. For it will be found that Ptolemy names the latter as one of the interior cities of Limurike. Still it need not be that Kērobōṭrās removed his capital so far into the interior as Karūr in the Coimbatore district. If Ṭiruvanchikkuḷam is not itself Karūr, the capital of Chēra, a more likely site than the Karūr of the Coimbatore district is Ṭirukkārūr in North Travancore, now a deserted village, situated at the foot of the Ghauts, three miles from Kōṭamangalam and 28 miles east by north of Cochin. The remains of an old temple, and the walls of some old buildings are still to be found there. The people there still point to a plot of ground as the place from which Paraśu Rāma is said to have taken his final farewell of the Nambūries. It is further significant that, in the Kēralōṭpaṭṭi, Karūr or Ṭirukkārūr (the prefix Ṭiru simply means 'prosperous') is mentioned as the capital of one of the Chēramān Perumāls, and the tradition is still remembered by the people of the place.

For about two centuries after Ptolemy, we have no authentic references to Kēraḷa. But, towards the latter end of the fourth century, we see it referred to in the famous Gupṭa inscription on the Allahabad Lat of Aśōka. It is there recorded that Samuḍra Gupṭa captured and then liberated, among other Rajas, Manṭaraja of Kērala in the region of the south. Whether this is the product of the imagination of an oriental court panegyrist, or whether Samuḍra Gupṭa found it feasible to advance so far south as Malabar or not, it is noteworthy that one of the Chēramān Perumāls, who ruled over Malabar subsequently, went by the name of Sṭhāṇu Ravi Gupṭa. The late Mr. Venkiah of the Indian Archaeological Department, however, questions the correctness of the reading of the word Gupṭa occurring in the second of the Syrian copper plates.

A little later on, we have Varāhamihira, the great Hindu astronomer (about A. D. 550), noticing in his Bṛhaṭsamhiṭa both the country and its people by the names Kērala and Kairalakās respectively.[1] The word Kairalaka appears in that form in the Allahabad Inscription of Samuḍra Gupṭa.[2] Varāhamihira locates the country in the Southern Division, and names Bālaḍēvapaṭṭaṇam and Marīchipaṭṭaṇam as important towns therein. Profr. Kern, Varāhamihirā's translator, identifies these places with the Baliapaṭṭaṇa (Mal: Valarpaṭṭaṇam) and the Muziris of Ptolemy and other Greek geographers.

Inscriptions and copper plate documents of the Western Chālūkya dynasty show that, almost for 500 years after this, the Chālūkyan kings had made temporary conquests of Kērala. In an inscription of the Western Chālūkya king, Pulakēsi I (fifth century A. D), Kērala is mentioned as possessing a chief who was conquered by that sovereign.[3] In the Mahākūṭa

1. Chap. 14, V. 12; also Chap. 16, V. 11.
2. Gupṭa Inscriptions, p. 8, line 13.
3. Sewell's Archae. Survey, Vol. II.

inscription of Mangalēśa (567 to 610 A.D.), we are told that the victories of his brother and predecessor, Kriṭṭivarma I (489 to 567 A.D.), included the kings of Kērala, Mūṣhaka, Pāndya, Chōlya and Aluka.[1] Professor Monier Williams identifies Mūṣhaka with that part of the Malabar Coast lying between Quilon and Cape Comorin, and that is exactly the locality called Mūṣhaka or Mūṣhika in the Kēralōṭpaṭṭi. It may be remembered that Dr. Burnell stops a long way north of Quilon in giving the southern boundary of the Chēra or Kērala kingdom. Of Pulakēśi II (610 to 634 A. D.) it is said that, after the conquest of Kānchīpura, he fcrossed the Kāvēri and invaded the country of the Chōlas, the Pāndyās and the Kēralas.[2] But these preferred to submit rather than fight a formidable foe. However, they soon revolted and Pulakēśi's son, Vikramādiṭṭya I (652-3 to 680 A.D.),[3] a man of ability and daring adventure, had to march against them and break their combined power.[4] In the epithets applied to Vikramādiṭṭya I, father of Vinayādiṭṭya Saṭyāśraya, a clear allusion is made to a confederacy that was formed against him by the three kings of Chōla, Pāndya and Kērala. He is said "to have rent open with the thunderbolt, that was his prowess, the proud summits of the haughtiness of the three mountains which were the kings of Chōla, Pāndya and Kērala."[5] Vikramādiṭṭya's son, Vinayādiṭṭya, seems to have assisted his father in conquering the southern kingdoms between the 11th and 14th years of his reign (692 to 695 A.D.), and the king completely subjugated, among others,

1. Fleet's Sans. and old Can. Inscript. No. 185. Ind. Ant. Vol. XIX, p. 7.

2. Bhandarkar's History of the Dekhan, p. 39.

3. Burnell's South Indian Paleo. 2nd Ed. p. 18.

4. Ibid. p. 43; Fleet San. and old Can. Inscript. No. XXIX. Ind. Ant. Vol. VI, p. 87.

5. Ibid. p. 43; Fleet San. and Old Can. Inscript. No. XLVIII. Ind. Ant. Vol. VII, p.303.

the Kēraḷās in the south.[1] Vinayāḍiṭṭya made tributaries of the kings of Kēraḷa or Kāvēra, as it is read in some of the grants, and of the Pārasikās, who, as Professor Bhandarkar says, were probably the Syrians settled on the coast of Malabar.[2] Vinayāḍiṭṭya's grandson, Vikṛamāḍiṭṭya II, (began to reign in A. D. 733)[3], also claims to have fought with the Chōlās, the Pāndyās, the Kēraḷās and the Kalabhrās and to have reduced them. In a grant, dated A. D. 758, by Kṛiṭṭivarma II, son of Vikṛamāḍiṭṭya, we are introduced to him in a seaside residence at a place called Jayamambha, situated on the shore of the southern ocean, of which a graphic description is given, where he dwelt in peace after "withering up Pāndya, Chōḷa, Kēraḷa, Kalabhra and other kings."[4]

About this time, the Rāṣhṭṛakūṭas overthrew the Chāḷūkyās. The fourth prince of the Rhethōr family, Ḍanṭiḍurga, son of Inḍra I, was a great ruler. His own grant attributes to him an easy victory over the army of Karṇāṭa. He is said to have defeated the lords of Kānchi and Kēraḷa, the Chōḷa Srī Harṣha and Vijayanṭi.[5] Ḍanṭiḍurga's date has been fixed by means of grants as A. D. 725—55.[6] The Rāṣhṭṛakūṭa king, Govinḍa VI, claims to have conquered the Kēraḷās. He reigned about A. D. 803 to 814-15.[7] For 200 years and more after this, the Chāḷūkyas were completely thrown into the shade by the Rāṣhṭṛakūṭas, till, about A. D. 973, Ṭailapa, the Chāḷūkyan, rose and restored the decaying glory of the dynasty.

1. Fleet No. XLIV. Ind. Ant. Vol. VII, p. 209.
2. History of the Dekhan, p. 44.
3. Burnell's Paleography, p. 18.
4. The Chāḷūkyās and Pallavās by Lewis Rice. Ind. Ant. Vol. VII, pp. 26 and 27.
5. Ind. Ant. Vol. VI, p. 61.
6. Logan's Malabar, Vol. I, p. 265.
7. Ibid.

Ṭailapā's grandson, Vikramāḍiṭṭya Tribhuvanamalla, was a great conqueror. Bilhaṇa, in his Vikramakāvya, speaking of Vikrama's prowess, says, "The wives of the king of Kērala wept when they thought of Vikrama's former deeds." In the fourth *Sarga*, Bilhaṇa expressly says that Vikrama first marched against the Kēralās and conquered them. Vikrama reigned between A. D. 1008 and 1018.[1] At the beginning of the eleventh century, the Chōla king, Rājēnḍra II, is said to have conquered Māgōḍai or Ṭiruvanchikkulam and seized "the crown praised by many, and the garland of the sun; family treasures which the arrow-shooting king of Kērala rightfully wore; many ancient islands, whose old and great guard was the sea which resounds with conches; the crown of pure gold worthy of Lakṣhmi, which Paraśu Rāma, having considered the fortifications of Sānṭimattava impregnable, had deposited there, when in anger he bound the kings twenty-one times in battle."[2] The inflated language of poets and the fulsome panegyrics of inscription writers vaunting the victories and conquests of their patrons have, however, to be taken with the proverbial grain of salt. After this, it is not often that we see Kērala mentioned in any authentic records.

We have here made an attempt to summarise the earlier notices of Kērala or Malabar as it can be gathered from what may be taken as authentic records, refraining from making any reference to the Kēralōṭpaṭṭi, which professes to give in detail an account of its reclamation, colonisation and early system of government. But the book, as it is, can have but little claim to historical accuracy. In its present form, it is full of anachronisms, absurdities, and contradictions, or is an ill-digested and uncollated collection of different versions, huddled together in inextricable

1. History of the Dekhan, p. 62.
2. South Indian Inscriptions, Vol. III, p. 28.

confusion. After giving an account of the Paraśu Rāma legend, the work proceeds to say that Rāma organised a Brahman theocratical government. The Brahmans are said to have divided the country into *kalakams* (kaḷakams) or divisions, over each of which was placed a governor elected by the members of the 64 *gramams* (grāmās), or Brahman villages, constituted by Paraśu Rāma. The names of these kaḷakams were:—(1) Perinchellūr, (2) Payyannūr, (3) Paṛappūr and (4) Chengannūr. After some time, a Protector or *Rakshapurushan* (Rakṣhāpuruṣhan), elected by the members of the four kaḷakams, was placed at the head to supervise the administration of the country. For the decision of questions of importance, the representatives of the various kaḷakams together with the Protector formed a consultative council. The Protectors were allowed a sixth of the produce of the land for the maintenance of their dignity as well as to carry on the government. They were also known by the name of Avarōḍhi Nampies. This system did not last long. The kaḷakams being situated at long distances, and there being no means of easy communication, combined action became impossible, and the Nampies became tyrannical and avaricious. A meeting of the people of Kērala was convened at Ṭiruṅāvāye where it was unanimously resolved to invite a Perumāl, *i. e.*, ruler, from outside to rule over the country for a period of twelve years. Thus the Brahmans are said to have invited in all 25 Perumāls from the neighbouring provinces of Chēra, Chōla and Pāndya. Some of them did not rule for the full term of 12 years, as a few died prematurely, while others had to be replaced because of their tyrannical government. The first of these is said to have been brought from Coimbatore in the year 216 A. D. Subjoined is a comparative list of the names of the Perumāls as given in the Kēralōṭpaṭṭi and the Kēralaviśēṣha-māhāṭmyam and the Cochin Administration Report for the year 1875—6.

	Kēralōṭpaṭṭi	Kēralaviśēṣha-māhāṭmyam.	Cochin Report.
1.	Chēramān Kēralan	Chēramān Kēralan	Kēya Perumāl
2.	Chōla Perumāl	Chōla Perumāl	Chōla ,,
3.	Pāndy ,,	Pāndy ,,	Pāndy ,,
4.	Bhūṭarāya ,,	Bhūṭarāya ,,	Vaṇṇam ,,
5.	Kēralan ,,	Kulaśēkharan	Thulu ,,
6.	Chengal ,,	Chengal ,,	Inḍran ,,
7.	Chōlia ,,	Chōlian ,,	Āryan ,,
8.	Kulaśēkhara ,,	Bāṇan ,,	Cūna ,,
9.	Bāṇa ,,	Ṭulubhan ,,	Kuṭṭy ,,
10.	Thulubhan ,,	Inḍran ,,	Munda ,,
11.	Inḍran ,,	Āryan ,,	Ēli ,,
12.	Āryan ,,	Kandan ,,	Kompan ,,
13.	Kandan ,,	Kuṭṭy ,,	Vijayan ,,
14.	Kuṭṭy ,,	Māṭon ,,	Valluvan ,,
15.	Maṭan ,,	Ēli ,,	Hariśchanḍran
16.	Ēli ,,	Vijayan ,,	Mallan ,,
17.	Kompan ,,	Vallabhan ,,	Kulaśēkharan
18.	Vijayan ,,	Kulaśēkharan	Chēramān ,,
19.	Vallabhan ,,	Chēramān ,,	
20.	Hariśchanḍran		
21.	Mallan ,,		
22.	Kulaśēkharan		
23.	Āḍi Rājan ,,		
24.	Pāndy ,,		
25.	Chēramān ,,		

Approximate Dates.

Kēya	A. D. 216—225
Chōla	225—236
Pāndy	236—245
Bhūṭarāya	245—257
Kērala	257—269
Chōlia	281—293
Kulaśēkhara	293—305
Bāṇa	305—317
Thulubhan	317—329
Inḍran	329—341
Āryan	341—353
Kandan	353—365
Kuṭṭy	365—366
Mādan	366—378
Ēli	378—390
Kompan	390—402
Vijayan	402—414
Vallabhan	414—426
Hariśchanḍran	426—438
Mallan	438—450
Kulaśēkhara II	450—462
*	*
*	*
*	*
Ādi Rāja Perumāl	765—777
Pāndy II	777—789
Chēramān	789

It is, perhaps, necessary to add that these dates are only approximate, and are at the best but conjectural, having been calculated by taking the date of Kēya Perumāl's installation, as given by the Kēralōṭpaṭṭi, as the starting point, and by allowing the period assigned to each Perumāl by that work.

The last of the Perumāls, known by pre-eminence as Chēramān, is alleged to have become a convert to Muhammadanism and undertaken a pilgrimage to Mecca, having, previously to his departure, divided the country between his friends and dependants. On the disruption of the Kēraḷa empire, numerous petty principalities arose, over which the Zāmorin Raja of Calicut is said to have exercised a sort of a shadowy suzerainty till the arrival of the Portuguese in A. D. 1498.

In considering the extent of Kēraḷa, we have to note that the Kēraḷōṭpaṭṭi alludes to a division of the country on two occasions, once by the Brahmans during their direct sway, and at another time by one of the Perumāls, whom the Brahmans had elected as their ruler. Of the first division, the Kēraḷōṭpaṭṭi says that the Malanād or Malabar or hill country was divided into four parts, namely:—

(1) The Ṭuḷu kingdom, extending from Gōkarṇam to Perumpuḷa (the large river), *i. e.*, the Cānarās, (north and south), very nearly as at present constituted.

(2) The Kūpa kingdom, extending from Perumpuḷa to Puṭupaṭṭaṇam, the seat of the Thekkankūr (Southern Regent) of the North Kōlaṭṭiri dynasty, situated on the Kotta river, *i. e.*, North Malabar as at present defined, less the southern half of the Kurumbarnād Taluk.

(3) The Kēraḷa kingdom, extending from Puṭupaṭṭaṇam to Kaṇṇeṭṭi, *i. e.*, South Malabar including the southern half of Kurumbarnād Taluk, the Cochin State and North Travancore.

(4) The Mūṣhaka kingdom, extending from Kaṇṇeṭṭi to Cape Comorin, *i. e.*, South Travancore.

The other division was made by Ārya Perumāl. He, it is said, inspected the whole country and arranged it into four divisions or provinces:—

(1) The Ṭulu country from Gōkarṇam to Perumpuḷa.

(2) The Kērala country from Perumpula to Puṭupaṭṭaṇam.

(3) The Mūṣhika country from Puṭupaṭṭaṇam to Kaṇṇeṭṭi.

(4) The Kūvala or Kūva country from Kaṇṇeṭṭi to Cape Comorin.

Though these divisions were made for administrative purposes only, it is significant that, in naming them, the term Kērala is applied only to a fourth part of the whole country, notwithstanding that the Malayālīs still consider Gōkarṇam and Kanyākumāri (Cape Comorin) as the Dan and Beersheba of Kēralam.

8. **The Advent of Brahmans.** The question as to when the advent of the Brahmans into Malabar took place is a much debated one. A theory has been recently advanced to the effect that the Nambūries settled in Malabar at the end of the seventh or the beginning of the eighth century A. D. It will be well to deal with the arguments which have been adduced in support of this theory, and to discuss generally the date of the Brahman settlement in Malabar or Kērala.

It is supposed by many that the earliest home of the Aryan or Indo-Germanic stock, from which the Brahman, the Rajput, and the Englishman derive their common descent, is Central Asia. From this common camping-ground, different branches of the Aryan race radiated towards various centres, some towards the East and some towards the West. Speaking of this dispersion of the Aryans from their original home, Sir Monier Williams says, "Starting at a later period than the primitive Turanian races, but like them, from some part of the table-land of

Central Asia—probably the region surrounding the sources of the Oxus near Bokhara—they separated into distinct nationalities and peopled Europe, Persia, and India. The Hindu Aryans after detaching themselves from the general body of emigrants, settled down as agriculturists (probably at some period between 2000 and 1500 B. C.) in the districts surrounding the Indus, the five rivers of the Punjāb, and the sacred Saraswaṭi, these seven rivers being called *Sapta Sindhu* (Sapṭa Sinḍhu). Thence, after a time, they overran, by successive irruptions, the plains of the Ganges, and spread themselves over the region called Āryāvarṭa occupying the whole of Central India, and either coalescing with, and, so to speak, Āryanising the primitive inhabitants they found there, or driving all who resisted them to the south and to the hills."[1]

From Āryāvarṭa successive batches of colonists seem to have marched southwards and to have settled in the Dekhān as far south as the banks of the Gōdāvery and the Kṛṣhṇa. The first colony of Brahmans is said to have been led to the southern extremity of the Peninsula by Agasṭya, a *maharshi* (mahaṛṣhi), the father of Tamil literature, soon after the conquest of Ceylon by Śrī Rāma; and the event, assuming it to have been more or less contemporaneous with the foundation of the aboriginal dynasties of Pāndya and Chōla, may be taken to have occurred in about the fifth or sixth century B.C.[2] The great epic of the Rāmāyaṇa is itself supposed to be a narrative of the advance of the Aryans into Southern India, and we know the reference it contains to Paraśu Rāma, the reputed founder of Kērala, who really was the leader of a great Brahman colony to the south.

Mr. W. Logan in his Manual of the Malabar District discusses the question at some length, and

1. Hinduism, p. 3.
2. Manual of the Tanjore District, p. 164.

comes to the conclusion that the Vēḍic Brahmans must have arrived in Malabar in the early years of the eighth century A. D., and that they must have come by way of the coast from the Ṭuḷu country (South Cānaṙa).[1] He is almost certain that the Vēḍic Brahmans proper had not migrated to the south in 605 A. D.[2] The following facts are adduced by its adherents as conclusive proofs of this theory:—

(1) It is certain that when Hiuen Tsiang, the Chinese pilgrim, visited Southern India east of the Ghauts, in A. D. 629-45, either he found no Vēḍic Brahmans at all, or they were in such numbers and influence as not to deserve mention. The naked heretics whom he met in large numbers were, as Dr. Burnell points out, Digambara Jains, that is, adherents of the 24th Ṭirṭamkara.

(2) The settlement deed of the Jews at Crānganūr is not attested by the Brahman hierarchy, whereas they have attested the Syrian deed. It is therefore reasonable to conclude that the Brahman hierarchy had, between the dates of these two deeds, acquired the power and influence which has never since deserted them. If this reasoning is correct, the rise of Vēḍic Brahmanism on the Malabar Coast cannot be placed earlier than the latter half of the seventh or the beginning of the eighth century, and not later than 774 A. D.

(3) There are two traditional accounts, other than Malayāli, preserved in the Mackenzie MSS. "The Cānarēse account, taken from the Sṭalamāhāṭmya of Bāṇavāsi, relates how a certain Mayūra Varma, a Kaḍamba king of Bāṇavāsi, impressed with reverence for a Brahman who refused to eat in a country where

1. Malabar, Vol. I, p. 275.

2. Ibid, Vol. I, p. 261.

no Brahmans were settled, established this man in his capital. Mayūra Varmā's son, named Chanḍrāngaṭan, it is said, invited a large colony of Brahmans and located them in Kērala, Ṭuluva, Haigiri, Konkaṇa and Corada. The Kērala Brahmans are said to speak Malayālam. It was after this, so it is further said, " that Paraśu Rāma came to the country, bringing with him sixty-four families, among whom he established his own Vaiḍīka (ascetical) system."

" The Mahratta account states that Paraśu Rāma turned the Bōyijāṭi (fishermen caste) into Brahmans, in order to people Kēralam. They were to summon him from Gōkarṇam, whither he had retired, if they had any cause for sorrow or regret. They summoned him unnecessarily, and he cursed them and ' condemned them to lose the power of assembling together in council, and to become servile. They accordingly mingled with Śūḍra females and became a degraded race.' ' About this time one Mayūra Varma, considering these Bṛahmans to be contemptible, sent for others from Hai-Kṣhēṭram, and located them in different places in his dominions.' Mayūra Varma was a Kaḍamba king, and was ' selected,' so the tradition runs, to rule over 'Kērala and Caurāṣhṭaka Dēsam'."

It is asserted that the Chinese traveller Hiuen Tsiang did not notice the existence of Brahmans in Southern India to the east of the ghauts, and the argument is that it was improbable that, if they had settled on the west coast, he would have overlooked their existence. But if, as Mr. Logan himself asserts,[1] Hiuen Tsiang did not visit the Malabar coast, it is not at all surprising that he makes no mention of the Brahmans of the west coast. It is, however, scarcely correct to say that Hiuen Tsiang did not visit the Malabar coast, and that he has overlooked the

1. Malabar, Vol. 1, p. 262.

existence of Brahmans there. For it is certain that from Drāvida he proceeded to a country which he calls Mo-lo-kūch'a identified, as we have seen, by Dr. Hultzsch with Malai-nādu, the hill country—Malabar.

In noticing the travels of the Chinese pilgrim, Mr. Talboys Wheeler observes, "Hiuen Tsiang had proceeded to Conjeeveram along the eastern coast. In his return route he crossed the Peninsula to the western coast, known as the Malabar side; and then turned towards the north through Travancore and Malabar. Here he found the people illiterate, and devoted to nothing but gain. Most of the monasteries were in ruins, but there were hundreds of flourishing temples and the usual swarms of naked heretics"[1] According to Sir William Hunter, Hiuen Tsiang travelled from the Punjab to the mouth of the Ganges, and made journeys to Southern India. Everywhere he found the two religions, Brahmanism and Buddhism, mingled. "On the Madras coast Buddhism flourished, and, indeed, throughout Southern India the faith still seems to have been in the ascendant, although struggling against Brahman heretics and their gods."[2] It is true that the late Dr. Burnell was of opinion that the 'Nigganṭās' or 'Nigranṭās' mentioned by Hiuen Tsiang were not Brahmans but Digambara Jains. This view he based on the fact that Nigganṭās are "continually used to denote Jains" in the Attihapalmdaka Gāṭha. But he himself confesses that he has no information as to the age of this work.[3] On the other hand, these 'naked heretics,' or Nigranṭās, are generally supposed by eminent scholars to have been naked mendicant Brahmans.[4] "The Chinese

1. History of India, Vol. III.
2. The Indian Empire, p. 154.
3. Indian Antiquary, Vol. I, p. 309.
4. Bothlink and Roth, St. Petersburg dy. s. v. Lassen, Ind. Alterthumskunde, III. 692, IV. 233.

pilgrim to India in 640 A. D.," says Sir William Hunter, " relates how the Brahmans, or, as he calls them, heretics, were again establishing their power. The Buddhist monastries had, even at that time, difficulty to hold their own against Brahman temples." Again, " the Chinese pilgrim Hiuen Tsiang gives a full account of the court and people of Vallabhi (630-640 A. D.). Buddhism was the state religion, but heretics (i. e. Brahmans) abounded ".[1] The ruined state of the Buddhist monasteries and the flourishing condition of Brahman temples must have produced upon him a strong impression. There is indeed some significance in his calling the Malabar Brahmans ' naked heretics,' for the Namburies are notoriously a scantily clothed race. They were 'heretics' to the Buddhist pilgrim, for they were the irrepressible enemies of his own faith. It was one of their class, the renowned Vēḍānṭist, Sankarāchārya, who drove Buddhism finally out of India. It was, perhaps, to their influence that Hiuen Tsiang ascribed the ruined condition of the Buddhist monasteries. Surely he must have found Buddhism fast losing ground, and Brahmanism once more gaining its prestige and position.

We next come to the argument that, because the Jewish deed was not attested by the Brahman hierarchy, while they have attested the Syrian deed, it is reasonable to conclude that they had in the interval, between the dates of these two deeds, come to Malabar. This can scarcely be called a valid argument. For the Jewish deed does not profess to be attested by all the important communities then inhabiting Malabar. The Syrian Christian community, which had already settled at Crānganūr so early as A. D. 52, and attained an enviable pre-eminence, is conspicuous

1. History of the Indian People, pp. 83-85; The Indian Empire, pp. 154, 169, 171.

by its absence among the roll of witnesses. Again the Ṭīērs, Īluvās or Islanders, who had "certainly settled in the country at the time when the deeds of privileges were granted to the Jews and Christians, (A. D. 700 to 825)"[1] do not find a place among the witnesses in the Jewish deed, though they are referred to, and their privileges, the 'foot-rope right,' and the 'ladder right,' not to speak of the 'Varakōl-share-staff,' specifically mentioned in a deed of a later date, to wit, the second of the Syrian deeds (about A. D. 824). But Mr. Logan himself admits that "the Islanders (Ṭīērs) must have been settled in the country before the middle of the sixth century A. D." For he says, "It is not at all improbable that Ṭīērs had arrived in Malabar before the time of Kosmos Indikopleustus" (A. D. 522-547).[2] It may therefore be reasonably maintained that the non-attestation of the Jewish deed by the Brahman community does not prove its non-existence in Malabar at the date of that deed.

The Canarese and Maharatta traditions remain to be noticed. The former attributes the introduction of Brahmans into Malabar to Mayūra Varma, king of Bāṇavāsi, and to his son Chanḍragupṭa or Chandrāngaṭa. It then adds that it was after this that Paraśu Rāma came to Malabar with his 64 families of Brahmans. Admittedly both the Canarese and the Maharatta accounts are founded on tradition, and when we find them in glaring contradiction to the traditional accounts extant in Malabar, we have to decide between the relative value of the traditions. Now let us see which of these traditions is supported by historical facts. Who was this Mayūra Varma, and at what period did he flourish? Dr. Gundhert informs us that he was a king of North Malabar who introduced Brahmans into Ṭuḷuva.[3] He does not say

1. Malabar, Vol. I, p. 257.
2. Ibid, Vol. I, p. 143.
3. Malayalam Dictionary.

that Mayūra Varma introduced them into Kērala. Ṭuluva is the country extending from Gōkarṇam to the Perumpuḷa, a river five miles north by east of Mount D'Ely, comprising the Cānarās (north and south) very nearly as at present defined. It formed one of the four divisions into which Malanād or the 'hill country' was divided. Kērala was another division extending from Puṭupaṭṭaṇam to Kaṇṇeṭṭi, that is, South Malabar, including the Kurumbarnād Taluk, the Cochin State, and north Travancore. Though Ṭuluva was a part of Kērala, as it originally stood, it does not follow that, because Mayūra Varma introduced Brahmans into a part of the country over which he ruled, he must have been the first to introduce them into Malabar as a whole, or into every part of it. According to Mr. Sewell, Mayūra Varma was the Kaḍamba king of Bāṇavāsi who introduced Brahmans into his kingdom from the north[1]. Mr. Logan fixes the date of Mayūra Varma's accession in the last years of the seventh or the beginning of the eighth century A. D. This would certainly synchronise with the alleged date of the advent of Vēḍic Brahmans into Malabar. But this date is arrived at by calculating back from the date of Ṭailapa, who is said to have reigned from A. D. 1077 to 1108, through the sixteen generations that had elapsed between Mayūra Varma's time and Ṭailapa's, and allowing for each twenty-four years, which is considered to be a fair average reign for Indian kings. This, it must be admitted, is a somewhat arbitrary calculation. Now, in the genealogical list of Kaḍamba kings, contained in Mr. Sewell's Sketch of the Dynasties of Southern India, no particular date is assigned to Ṭailapa, and, what is more, the period assigned to Kṛiṭṭivarma II, with whom, as Mr. Fleet observes, we reach historical ground, is A. D. 1068—1076-7. Ṭaila I, or Ṭailapa,

1. A Sketch of the Dynasties of Southern India, p. 40.

preceded Kṛiṭṭivarma II. It is also noteworthy that Mr. Fleet points out that a number of Rāṣhṭrakūṭa inscriptions show that, at any rate up to 947 A.D., a family of Mahāmaṇḍalēśvarās of a different name preceded the Kaḍambās in the government of Bāṇavāsi. The Cānarīs tradition adds that it was after Mayūra Varma that Paraśu Rāma came to Malabar with his 64 families of Brahmans. This would make Paraśu Rāma live somewhere about the eighth century A. D. But there are references to him in the Rāmāyaṇa and the Mahābhāraṭa, and, accepting the criticisms of such eminent oriental scholars as Weber and Lassen, we may say that these two great epics were composed, at the latest, in the first century A. D., though references to the Mahābhāraṭa in Pāṇini (about B. C. 350) would indicate its existence at a much earlier date. It is impossible, therefore, that Paraśu Rāma, who must have lived at a period long anterior to the composing of the epics, should have come to Malabar after Mayūra Varma, who is said to have flourished in the latter part of the seventh or the early part of the eighth century A. D.

For aught we know, Mayūra Varma may have brought with him a colony of Brahmans for settlement in his country of Kunṭala. An inscription translated and commented upon by Mr. Fleet in the Indian Antiquary refers to this fact. It reads thus: "He (Mayūra Varma) performed the sacrifice called Aśwamēḍha, and, having himself brought eighteen Brahmans in succession from Ahikṣhēṭra and having established them in the radiant country of Kunṭala, and having acquired prowess, Mayūra Varma was resplendent in the government of the earth." From this it is evident that Mayūra Varma established his Brahman colony not in Malabar but in Kunṭala, which has been identified with Kolaṭṭūr in the extreme north-west of Mysore.[1] Eighteen Brahmans are

1. Indian Antiquary. Vol. X. pp. 250, 288.

said to have been brought from Ahichchaṭra. This may mean either that Mayūra Varma brought eighteen families, or that he brought eighteen successive colonies. There is, however, another account of his having brought colonies of Brahmans, recorded by Fleet in his comments on the inscription quoted above. He says, "But, at the same time, it is worthy of remark that there is another tradition that Mayūra Varma I not simply introduced but brought with him twelve thousand Brahmans of thirty-two families, purified by performing *Agnihothra* (Agnihōṭra) sacrifice, fromthe Agrahāra of Ahichchaṭra, and established them in the Agrahāra of Sṭhaṇuguḍhāpura or Ṭanaguṇḍūr, the modern Talgund or Talguṇḍi, in Mysore."[1] The assertion of the Bāṇavāsi Sṭhalamāhāṭmyam is not therefore without some truth, but it must have evidently gone astray in recording that Mayūra Varma located his colonies in Malabar.

The Mahrāṭṭa account is still more curious. It says that Paraśu Rāma turned fishermen into Brahmans in order to people his land of Kēraḷam. That the tradition was not altogether foreign to Malabar is clear from our author's reference to it.[2] Unlike the Cānarīs tradition, the Mahrāṭṭa account attributes the peopling of Kēraḷa with Brahmans to Paraśu Rāma. In this it agrees with the Malabar tradition. It, however, says that Paraśu Rāmā's Brahmans were a degraded class, and consequently Mayūra Varma, the Kaḍamba king, had to import a purer set from elsewhere. This no doubt gets over the anachronism regarding the period of Paraśu Rāma, but it, at the same time, acknowledges the existence of Brahmans in Malabar long before Mayūra Varma brought his colony.

Mr. Logan finds an argument in favour of his theory in the fact that the Malayāḷīs used in early days

1. Indian Antiquary, Vol. X, pp. 250, 288.
2. See also Hunter's Orissa, Vol. I, p. 254

to bury the bones of the dead in sepulchral urns such as are to be found in profusion in various parts of the district. On the authority of "one of the numerous Chinese pilgrims who flocked at this time (605 A. D.) to India," he says that "the bones of the dead are burned and their ashes placed in a So-tu (Sṭhūpa), a practice which Malayālīs certainly observed originally, if the evidence of the rude stone monuments of the district signifies anything."

The original faith, it seems, was that,

> " So long as the bones remain undisturbed and undefiled,
> So long does the soul enjoy heaven."

" But with the advent of the Vēḍic Brahmans came a change in this respect. These posed before the rude chieftains with whom they came in contact as 'god-compellers.' Their sonorous *Mantrams* (Manṭrams) and spells could compel the gods to take the wandering ghosts of even the worst of men direct to heaven. There was no necessity for costly death houses, and for furnishing such with all the deceased's weapons and implements in use by him during life. A few sonorous phrases, a ringing of bells and burning of incense, and the thing was done; and it only remained to scatter the ashes of the deceased upon the surface of some holy river to ensure him a welcome into the heaven of Inḍra."[1] A belief in the necessity of *Sradha* (Srāḍha) ceremonies and in the removal of the ashes worked its way southwards into Malabar in the wake of the 'god-compelling' Vēḍic Brahmans.

The whole argument appears to be that burial, a non Hindu custom, was in practice in Malabar till it was displaced by cremation and the observance of the Srāḍha ceremonies, both of which are essentially Brahmanical customs, and that there is no reason to think that this change in the faith of the Malayālīs

1 Malabar, Vol. I, p. 261.

had taken root before the beginning of the seventh century A. D. This, taken along with the other arguments adduced, would, it is supposed, prove that the great Brahman immigration into Malabar did not probably take place till a century later.

Mr. Logan has not adduced any reason to show that the inhabitants of Malabar were not Hindus before the seventh century A. D., and it will appear, further on, that Hinduism had been introduced into Malabar at a much earlier age. The practice of burial was not at all foreign to the Hindus in the earliest ages; and the eminent German scholar Dr. Roth was the first to point out from a passage in the Rig Vēḍa,[1] that in ancient ages burial was practised by the Hindus. Other passages from the Rig Vēḍa,[2] show that this custom was followed by the other one of burning the dead and burying the ashes. In the epic period (B. C. 1400 to 1000), the practice of burying the dead had ceased altogether; and the dead were burnt and only the ashes were buried. We find an account of this in the 35th chapter of the Yajur Vēḍa. The bones of the deceased were collected in a vessel and buried in the ground near a stream, and a mound was raised as high as the knee and covered with grass. The relatives then bathed and changed their clothes and left the cemetery. The same ceremony is more fully described in the Āraṇyaka of the Black Yajur Vēḍa.[3] According to the Rig Vēḍa, the last rite in the burial service consisted in tenderly committing the body to its 'house of clay',[4] with the words " Return to thy mother Earth; may she be kind

1. X, 18, 11.
2. X, 15, 14 and X, 16, 1.
3. Dutt's Ancient India, Vol. I, p. 279. See also Religious Thoughts and Life in India, by Sir Monier Williams, pp 281, *et seq.*
4. Rig Veda, VII, 89, 1.

to thee and lie lightly on thee," and with other similar words, which are thus freely translated :—

"Open thy arms, O Earth, receive the dead
With gentle pressure, and with loving welcome
Enshroud him tenderly, e'en as a mother
Folds her soft vestments round the child she loves."[1]

In the light of the above citations, it is impossible to hold that the burial of the dead is a non-Hindu custom, or that the native tradition (if such a tradition really exists) that "so long as the bones remain undestroyed and undefiled, so long does the soul enjoy heaven," is not in harmony with orthodox Sanskrit texts. If the Malayālīs originally observed the custom of burial, as pointed out by Mr. Logan, they only followed the general Hindu practice, and, if they did in time change that practice into one of cremation and the burial of ashes in urns, they simply followed the changes in the custom observed by the general body of Hindus. But there is nothing to show that the change took place at or within a fixed period. The argument that there is no reason to suppose that this change in the faith of the Malayālīs had taken root before the beginning of the seventh century A. D. does not appear to be sound, for no positive evidence of any kind is adduced to show, or even to indicate, that any such change had ever taken place—much less at or after the beginning of the seventh century A. D. It is certainly impossible to indicate in any definite manner the time when the Malayālīs ceased to bury their dead and commenced to cremate them.

Now, turning our attention to the Śrāḍha ceremony, it is noteworthy that no evidence of any sort is adduced to show that the Malayālīs were not in the habit of offering *pinda* (piṇḍa) to the manes of the

1. R. V. X, 18, 11—Religious Thoughts and Life in India, p. 280.

departed before the beginning of the seventh century A. D. If the argument is that, because it is an essentially Brahmanical ceremony, it must have been introduced by the Vēḍic Brahmans into Malabar when they emigrated into that country in the eighth century A. D., it cannot certainly be used to prove that the Brahman immigration itself took place only in the eighth century, for that would be begging the question.

The Śrāḍha, or 'feast of the dead,' is the outcome of one of the most primitive ideas of men. It had its origin in the belief, among the earliest races, that the spirit or ghost of man had a separate existence, and that it lingered behind after death. Such a belief has existed in all ages and amongst all communities, civilised or uncivilised, and is not altogether foreign even to our modern materialistic age. The aboriginal idea of propitiating the ghosts of the departed is still traceable in some of the acts of even Protestant Christians themselves, such as the decoration of graves with flowers. Mr. Talboys Wheeler points out that the idea of a 'surviving duplicate' finds exquisite expression in Collins' poem on the death of Thomson :—

> "Remembrance oft shall haunt the shore
> When Thames in Summer wreaths is dress'd ;
> And oft shall stay the dashing oar
> To bid his gentle spirit rest."

It is believed that the spirit of the departed delights to hover round places and persons that were dear to it in the days of its earthly career. Men thought that it was only right that the spirits of their dear departed should be provided with the food and other necessaries of life. This idea was so very powerful that along with the body were buried not simply grain and water, but also earthenware vessels, iron weapons, and implements of various sorts—perhaps to enable the spirit to find food and cook it on its onward progress to the other world.[1] With the advance of civilisation, the original idea was improved upon, and, in lieu of the grain and water buried along with the bones or the body, oblations of food and libations of water began to be offered to the manes of the deceased. "The Śrāḍha, or feast of the dead, was," in the words of Mr. Wheeler, "in its earliest form a pleasing expression of natural religion, which long preceded the advent of a priestly caste or the introduction of a systematic ritual."[2]

It is alleged that the Vēḍic Brahmans came in the wake of the conquering Western Chālūkyās and the Rāṣhṭrakūṭās and their allies. The former, it is said, were Vaiṣhṇavites, and their emblem was a boar, and the Paṅṅiyūr (pig-villages) faction of Nambūrīs was no doubt at first in a position of equality with the Śaivite faction, but the Rāṣhṭrakūṭās were chiefly Saivites, and the Chovvūr faction of the Nambūrīs managed in the end to get the ascendancy.[3]

The Aryan colonisation of Southern India was effected not by force of arms, but by the arts of peace. The Dravidian races of the south had to submit to the superior intelligence and administrative skill of the Brahmans from the North. "The introduction of the Dravidians within the pale of Hinduism appears to have originated," says the late Bishop Caldwell, "not in conquest, but in the peaceable process of colonisation and progressive civilisation. There is no tradition extant of a warlike irruption of the Aryans into Southern India, or of the forcible subjugation of the Dravidians; though, if such an event ever took place, some remembrance of it would probably have survived." Again, the same learned authority says: "The Aryan immigrants to the south appear

1. See illustrations VIII and X, Malabar, Vol. I.
2. History of India, Vol. II, p. 519.
3. Malabar, Vol. I, p. 275.

to have been generally Brahmanical priests and instructors, rather than Kṣhaṭrya soldiers, and the kings of the Pāṇḍyās, Chōlās, Kalingās, and other Dravidians appear to have been simply Dravidian chieftains, whom their Brahmanical preceptors and spiritual directors dignified with Aryan titles, and taught to imitate and emulate the grandeur and cultivated tastes of the Solar, Lunar, and Agni-kula races of kings.''[1]

The Pallavās of Kānchi, who were as much followers and staunch supporters of orthodox Hinduism as the Western Chālūkyās, preceded the latter in the suzerainty of Kērala, and it is hard to give credit to the theory that the Vēḍic Brahmans chose to follow in the wake of the Western Chālūkyan hordes rather than follow the Pallava conquerors of Kērala. The Chālūkyan inscriptions, referred to by Mr. Logan, record in the fulsome adulation of oriental court panegyrists that the Chālūkya heroes "withered up Pāṇḍya, Chōla, Kērala, Kalabhra and other kings," and "uprooted the clumps of thorns among the kings of the south." Beyond these adulatory expressions, there is nothing in the inscriptions themselves to show that they had any direct dealings with Kērala or that they held the country in subjection. Much less is there anything in these inscriptions to warrant the assertion that the Vēḍic Brahmans came in the wake of the Chālūkya conquerors. The first Western Chālūkya irruption is said to have taken place in the early part of the seventh century A. D., in the reign of Pulakēśi II.[2] He began to reign, according to Mr. Sewell, in 610 A. D. But long before this, in the latter end of the fourth century A. D., Samuḍraguptạ,

1. Comparative Grammer of the Dravidian Languages, Introduction, p. 114. See also quotation from Professor Max Muller to the same effect, in a note on p. 115.

2. Malabar, Vol. I, p. 250

a distinguished Hindu king of the Gupṭa dynasty from the north, had subjugated Kēralam. The famous Gupṭa inscription on the Allahabad Lāt of Aśōka throws much light on the extent of this great king's power and influence. Referring to the conquests made by the king, the inscription says:—"Whose great good fortune was mixed with, so as to be increased by his glory produced by the favour shown in capturing and then liberating Mahēnḍra of Kōsala, Vyāghrarāja of Mahākānṭāra, Manṭarāja of Kērala, Mahēnḍra of Pişhṭapura, Swāmiḍaṭṭa of Koṭṭūra on the hill, Ḍamana of Eranḍapalla, Vişhṇugōpa of Kānchi, Nilarāya of Avamukṭa, Hasṭivarman of Vengi, Ugrasēna of Palakka, Kuvēra of Ḍēvarāşhṭra, Ḍhananjaya of Kusṭhalapura, and all other kings of the region of the south."[1]

The Gupṭas were generally orthodox Hindus,[2] so that the Brahman emigrants from the north had a fair opportunity of migrating southwards in the wake of the conquering hordes of Samuḍragupṭa. He is one of the earlier kings of the Gupṭa dynasty which, according to many scholars, reigned from the second to the fourth century A. D.

The Rāşhṭrakūṭas came from the north and, under their king Ḍanṭiḍurga, subverted the older dynasty of the Chālūkyās in the Karṇāṭaka country. They did not come much into contact with the kings of the south.[3] Mr. Logan, however, conjectures that, with the conquest of the Western Chālūkyās, the tributary lien on Kērala must have passed to the Rāşhṭrakūṭās. Though one grant of the Rāşhṭrakūṭa king Govinḍa III records that he conquered Kērala, Mr. Logan doubts whether the victory was very complete. "At any rate," says he, "there is apparently nothing yet

1. Dutt's Ancient India, Vol. III, p. 64.
2. Ibid, Vol. I, p. 23.
3. Sewell's Sketch of the Dynasties of Southern India, p. 93.

on record to prove that the Rāṣhṭṛakūṭās conquered Malabar."[1]

From the formal division of the Nambūrīs into Paññiyūr and Chovvaram Grāmās, it is argued that because these two divisions represent the Vaiṣhṇavite and Ṡaivite factions, and because the Western Chālūkyās and Rāṣhṭṛakūṭās were respectively representatives of the Vaiṣhṇavites and Saivites, it may be concluded that each faction followed its leader as he conquered the country. But we find it difficult to reconcile this with what Mr. Logan himself says in another part of his book, " that a more or less successful resistance, probably with Brahman aid, was made by the Malayālīs against the aggressions of the Western Chālūkya dynasty."[2]

A further coincidence pointed out is that Paññiyūr literally means 'pig village', and the emblem of the Western Chālūkyās was a boar. That the Chālūkyās and the Rāṣhṭṛakūṭās were representatives of the two factions remains to be proved. Moreover, it is not shown that they were followers of the Vaiṣhṇavite and Saivite schisms respectively. Their complete conquest of the country is not beyond doubt. At any rate, the Rāṣhṭṛakūṭās had admittedly no complete control over Malabar. Yet we are asked to believe that the Saivite faction of the Nambūri Brahmans, who had placed themselves under the protecting aegis of the Rāṣhṭṛakūṭās, had come off best in their quarrel with the Vaiṣhṇavites. The Malabar Brahmans have never been known to be *Dvaities* (Ḍvaiṭīs), that is, those who differentiate between Ṡiva and Viṣhṇu as a point of religious dogma. They worship both deities alike as different manifestations of the same godhead. Properly speaking, they accord no precedence to any

1. Malabar, Vol. I, pp. 265-6.

2. Ibid, Vol. I, p. 120.

single head of the Trinity. In their view, all the three are of equal position, their functions being sometimes interchangeable.

The fact that the emblem of the Western Chālūkyās was the boar does not signify much. Dr. Burnell says that he has not been able to find an example of the seal of the Kalyāṇa or Western branch of the Chālūkyās. He gives four examples of the Kalinga or Eastern branch, two of the seventh, one of the tenth, and one, of the Chōla successors of the Chālūkyās, of the twelfth century. These, he says, are remarkable in having a device like those of the Vallabhi dynasty of Gujarat. The characteristic mark of the Chālūkyās, the boar, is found from the tenth century—a mark which seems to have been used by both dynasties and is clearly referred to by the author of the Smṛṭichanḍrika.[1] It is therefore doubtful whether the Western Chālūkyās used the mark of the boar as their emblem before the tenth century A. D., and we are unable to draw the inference that the Paṅṅiyūr faction of Nambūrīs adopted, in the latter part of the seventh or the beginning of the eighth century the name of 'pig-villagers', because the boar was the distinguishing emblem of their patron. The boar appears to have been a favourite mark with the mediaeval kings of the south. The Chōlās of the twelfth century, who displaced the Chālūkyās, had the mark of the boar as their emblem. So also the kings of the Vijayanagara dynasty of the sixteenth century. The *Mitakshara* (Miṭākṣhara) alludes to '*Garudavarahadirupayo*', (Garuḍavarāhāḍirūpayō),[2] but Dr. Burnell is at a loss to know what king or kings used the Garuḍa seal. The tradition in Malabar with regard

1. Burnell's Elements of South Indian Paleography, 1st Ed. p. 75.
2. Ibid p. 64, line 16.

to the two great Nambūri factions is that Paraśu Rāma divided the sixty-four Grāmās, introduced by him, into the Paññiyūr Grāmakkār (boar-villagers), and the Chovvūr Grāmakkār (bird-villagers), the former being the worshippers of *Varaham* (Varāham), the incarnation of the boar, while the latter were the worshippers of *Sarabham* (Śarabham) (Garuḍa), a kind of huge bird reputed to be the *Vahana* (Vāhana) or vehicle of Vişhņu.[1] Some attribute this division to the great Chēramān Perumāl, whose object in effecting it was to preserve the balance of power between the Zamorin and the Rajas of Cochin; for this, the Pērumāl is said to have appointed the Zamorin, or the Raja of Calicut, the head of the Paññiyūr Grāmakkār, while under the Rajas of Cochin were placed the Chovvūr Grāmakkār. Another reason for establishing these factions, according to our author, was " to create a martial spirit, lest by living in perpetual peace the Malabar people should sink into effeminacy, and thus become a prey to the surrounding nations. The Miţakşhara was written, as has been shown by Dr. Buhler, in the reign of the Chālukya king Vikramādiţya V, that is, at the end of the eleventh and the beginning of the twelfth century.[2] It is therefore not difficult to understand where the author of the Miţakşhara observed the use of the mark of the boar and the bird as emblems.

It will be observed that Mr. Logan invariably uses the term Vēḍic Brahmans to denote the Brahman immigrants, who are said to have followed the Chālukyās and the Rāşhţrakūţās into Malabar, and whose descendants, the modern Nambūri Brahmans, are

1. Madras Journal of Literature and Science, No. 9, N. S. p. 32.
2. Bombay Journal, IX., pp. 134-8. Burnell's Paleography, 1st Ed. p. 64.

supposed to be. By Vēḍic Brahmans we understand Brahmans who are followers of the Vēḍās. The earliest form of the religion of the Indo-Aryans was Vēḍism out of which grew Brahmanism. "It taught," Sir Monier Williams says, "the merging of all the forces of Nature in one universal spiritual being—the only real Entity—which, when unmanifested and impersonal, was called Brahma (neuter), when manifested as a personal creator was called Brahmā (masculine), and when manifested in the higher order of men was called Brahman ('the Brāhmans'). Brahmanism was rather a philosophy than a religion, and in its fundamental doctrine was spiritual Pantheism." Brahmanism *minus* the Vēḍas would be something very much akin to Catholicism *minus* Christianity; so that by the term Brahmans we understand those of the class who acknowledge the Vēḍas; and, if there were Brahmans in Malabar before the seventh or eighth century A. D., they must necessarily have been Vēḍic Brahmans.

The existence of a class of Brahmans in Malabar at the present day who are denied the right of studying the Vēḍas does not at all detract from our argument. For various reasons Nambūrīs of the Payyannūr Grāmam, Mūssaṭūs, Śāsṭrangakār, Grāmaṇīs and such others, have been declared disqualified to study the Vēḍas—some as hereditary physicians whose calling necessitated the constant use of surgical instruments, and others as having deviated from the strict line of rigid religious life absolutely enjoined on the Brahmans as a class, as having taken to arms as 'protectors of the realm' (Rakṣhāpuruṣhans), and as consequently having shed blood in battle. The very reasons assigned for their disqualification show that originally they had the right of studying the Vēḍas, but that they had subsequently been deprived thereof on account of certain acts of theirs not calculated to uphold and glorify the sanctity of the priestly class in its pristine purity. These cannot be classed as non-Vēḍic in the sense that they do not acknowledge the divine authority of the Vēḍas, or follow their behests, for they do conform, and have always strictly conformed, to the Vēḍic system and ritual, and they do still proudly array themselves in their daily life under the banner of one of the three Vēḍas.

We may now endeavour to determine approximately the date at which the Brahmans colonised Malabar. But it is almost impossible to obtain any direct historical evidence on the point.

Local tradition, as has been already pointed out, attributes the peopling of Malabar with Brahmans to Paraśu Rāma, who is supposed to have reclaimed the land of Kērala from the sea. There can be no doubt that the Dravidians had pushed southwards long before the Aryans. They seem to have entered the Punjab by the north-western passes, met the Kolārians, another branch of the new Aryan race, coming from north-east, overcome them, and pushed forward in a mighty body to the south. They now inhabit Southern India as far down as Cape Comorin.[1] To the compiler of the Rāmāyaṇa the whole of India to the south of the Vinḍhya mountains was almost a *terra incognita*. To him it was a long stretch of forest land (the Ḍanḍakāraṇya), inhabited by monkeys, bears, Rākṣhasās (demons), and other aborigines, relieved here and there by the presence of holy Ṛṣhīs (ascetics), who had retired into the forests to spend the evening of their life in penance and meditation. Modern oriental scholars regard the story of the Rāmāyaṇa as an allegory illustrating a historical fact—the spread of Aryan civilisation to the south, more

1. The Indian Empire, p. 80.

specially to Ceylon.[1] In their progress southwards from their camping ground in the plateau of Central Asia, the Aryans had conquered, peopled, and Hinduised, by the end of the epic period, the whole valley of the Ganges and the Jumna from Delhi to North Behar. Towards 1000 B. C., Hindu settlers had come as far southwards as southern Behar, Malwa, Southern India, and Guzarat. Nor did they stay there. As they advanced, the aborigines submitted to the higher civilisation and the nobler religion of their conquerors. By the fourth century B. C., the whole of Southern India had been Hinduised, and the three great Hindu kingdoms of Chēra, (*the Canarese form of 'Kerala'*) Chōla, and Pāṇḍya had been established, stretching as far south as Cape Comorin.[2]

To whatever period we assign the events recorded in the Rāmāyaṇa, we may safely assert that, with the conquest of Ceylon by Vijaya of Bengal, Aryan civilisation was introduced into that country. Ceylon was conquered by Vijaya, son of Subāhu, king of Śāla in Magaḍha, in the fifth century B. C., and made into a Hindu kingdom. It is true that Vijaya is not represented as having marched through the Peninsula, like Rāma, the hero of the Rāmāyaṇa, on his way to the Island. He and his colony of adventurers are said to have been cast adrift on the ocean on account of their misconduct, and the sequel was that they discovered and colonised Ceylon. According to the Ḍīpavamśa, composed in the fourth century A. D., and the Mahāvamśa, composed somewhat later, this conquest of Ceylon took place in the year 543 B. C.[3] Vijaya had to cross over to the continent for a wife, and he married a Pāṇḍya princess,[4] on whose father he

1. Weber's History of Sanskrit Literature, p. 192.
2. Dutt's Ancient India, Vol. I, p. 25.
3. Ibid Vol. I, pp. 31—32 and Vol. II, p. 31.
4. Upham's Mahavamsa, p. 10.

is supposed to have bestowed an annual settlement. The Singhalese believe that the Pāṇḍyan kingdom was in existence long before Vijaya's conquest of Ceylon. "These circumstances seem," says Dr. Caldwell, "to carry up the era of the first introduction of Aryan civilisation into the Pāṇḍya country, probably at Korkai, to a very early period; shall we say about 700 B. C.?"[1]

Raghu, the ancestor of the hero of the Rāmāyaṇa is represented as having subdued the Pāṇḍyās and exacted tribute from them; for an interesting verse in the Raghuvamśa says that, "they (the Pāṇḍyās) having prostrated themselves before Raghu, presented to him their glory, the collected excellence of the pearls of the ocean into which the Ṭamravarṇi flows."[2] Kālidāsa, the well-known author of the Raghuvamśa, must have lived, according to Mr. Dutt, in the fifth or sixth century, "when Paurāṇic Hinduism flourished, when temples and images were revered, and when the Hindu Trinity was worshipped." "An earlier reference to the Ṭāmravarṇi in the Mahābhāraṭa induces us to conclude that Southern India was not unknown to the Aryans of the time. In the Āraṇya Parva we read: "Also I will remind thee, O son of Kunṭi, of the fame of the Ṭamravarṇi, in the hermitage connected with which the gods, desirous of heaven, performed austerities."

With the Greek invasion of India and the embassy of Megasthenes (317 to 312 B. C.) to the Court of Chandragupṭa, we light on historical ground. The reference by Megasthenes to the country of the Pāṇḍya, which he says is called after the name of the 'Indian Heracles', is significant. The Indian Heracles has

1. History of Tinnevelly, p. 14.
2. IV, 50.

been identified with Kṛshṇa,[1] admittedly a Brahman deity. Pliny reports from Megasthenes that the 'Pāṇḍae' alone among Indian nations were ruled by women. Though this statement is clearly inapplicable strictly to the Pāṇḍyās of Madura, it is undoubtedly applicable to the peculiar social usage of Malabar, where inheritance is always traced thṛough the female members of the family.

At a later period (258 B. C.), the great Buddhist Emperor Aśōka sent his missionaries to Southern India. The second of the well-known edicts of king Piyaḍāsi (Aśōka) classes Kērala as one of the Pṛāṭy-anṭas or neighbouring nations who were independent. The edict records that the great Emperor "has provided medicines of two sorts, medicines for men and medicines for animals. Wherever plants useful, either for men or for animals, were wanting, they have been imported and planted. And along public roads, wells have been dug for the use of animals and men." The charity of Aśōka was not limited to his own empire. It extended beyond his borders to the kingdoms of Chōla, Pāṇḍya, Saṭyapuṭṛa, and Kēralapuṭṛa, as far as Ṭambapāni (Ceylon). Aśōka is further said to have sent his own son Mahinḍa to Tissa, king of Ceylon, about 242 B. C., and it was through him that Ceylon was converted to Buddhism. It also appears that, after the death of king Tissa and Mahinḍa, Ceylon was overrun and conquered twice by Dravidian conquerors, who were finally expelled by Waṭṭa Gāmiṇi about 88 B. C. That there were several conquests of Ceylon by the nations inhabiting the mainland cannot be questioned. The Singhalese accounts say that Ceylon was often invaded by the Tamil Chōlās from the continent. Their tradition is that the Chōlās invaded Ceylon as early as the third century B. C., again in the second century B. C., and a third time in

1. Lassen, Ind. Atl. 1, 647 ff. Weber's History of Sanskrit Literature, p. 136.

the second century A.D. The Singhalese retaliated by invading the mainland in great force on more than one occasion.[1]

We have already shown that the island of Ceylon was once connected with the mainland and that there must have been communication between the two countries in very early times.

If the missionaries of Aṡōka were Buddhists, Vijāya and his followers from Bengal were Hindus, not reckoning Raghu and his descendant Rāma, the hero of the Rāmāyaṇa, who led the Aryan invasion to the south. Rāma and his host of monkeys and bears (evidently the aborigines who inhabited the Ḍaṇḍaka forest) are said to have marched through the Peninsula down to Cape Comorin, whence they crossed the sea by building a bridge that carried them across to Ceylon. It would be idle to speculate whether the early Aryan invaders made any impression on the religious beliefs of the people whom they conquered. The evidence afforded by the cromlechs and sepulchral urns discovered in profusion in various localities in Malabar show that the Malayālīs of the age to which those interesting remains belong had adopted the Hindu mode of burial as laid down by the Rig Vēḍa. It is also significant that the trident or 'Hindu Ṭṛṡūla'[2] is one of the chief implements found in the sepulchral remains in Malabar.[3]

In the introduction to his Descriptive Catalogue of the Mackenzie Collection, Professor Wilson observes: "The introduction of the Hindu religion into Malabar or the principal tracts on the Malabar Coast appears to have occurred about the same time as into Drāvira. The Brahmans were brought, it is said, by Paraṡu Rāma from Ahikṣhēṭṛa which in the Mahābhā-

1. Malabar, Vol. I, p. 257.
2. Malabar, vol. I, p. 186.
3. Ibid. Illustration No. X.

raṭa is a city in the north of India. They were called Arya--Brahmans from being natives of the holy land Āryabhūmi, Central or Brahmanical India according to Manu, and we have seen that one of the written characters of Malabar, that which is most allied to Nāgari, is still called Āryaka, as probably of Brahmanical introduction. Probably traces of these events may be indicated by the Arica Province and Purros Mons of Ptolemy, although the former is rather misplaced, whilst Āḍisaṭṛa is possibly connected with Ahikṣhēṭṛa of the legend, if there be not indeed some further reference to the local traditions in the Aii or Aiorum Regis of Ptolemy." After pointing out that Aii may stand for the Sanskrit *ahi*, a serpent, the reference embodying the local tradition of the serpents driving out the Brahmans, the learned Professor goes on to say:—"At any rate, these coincidences are sufficient to show that Hinduism was established on the Malabar Coast anterior to the Christian era."

We have further evidence of the existence of Brahmans in Southern India on the Western Coast in the early years of the Christian era. Ptolemy names Bramagara as the second town in the Province of Limyrike, and he places it half a degree to the east of Tyndis (Kaḍaluṇḍi near Beypore), that is, really to the south of it, since Ptolemy makes the Malabar Coast run east instead of south. Professor McCrindle conjectures that this name Bramagara may be transliteration of the Sanskrit Brahmāgāra, which means 'the abode of the Brahmans'. The Brahmans of the south of India, adds the Professor, appear in those days to have consisted of a number of isolated communities settled in separate parts of the country and independent of each other. This, as Lassen remarks,[1] is in harmony with the tradition according to which Arya Brahmans

1. Ind. Atl. Vol. III, p, 193.

were represented as having been settled by Paraśu Rāma in 61 (64?) villages, and as having at first lived under a republican constitution. It may also be noted that, in section 74, Ptolemy mentions a town called Brāhmē, belonging to the Brahmnoi Magoi, that is, sons of the Brahmans.[1]

"At the time of the Periplus" (about 100 A. D.), says Sir William Hunter, "the southern point of India (and therefore of Kērala or Malabar) was apparently a seat of their (Brahmans') worship. A temple to the wife of Siva stood on Cape Comorin."[2]

The existence of the worship of Śiva in the south in early days is a further proof that Brahmanism had gained a firm footing in the Ḍrāviḍa country. The tradition is that it was introduced into Southern India by the well-known ṛṣhi Agasṭya, who has the reputation of being the "father of Tamil literature". The Chinese pilgrim supplies evidence of Śiva's worship before the seventh century A. D. (that is, before Mayūra Varma), and the fact that his "dread wife" had a temple at Cape Comorin at the time of the Periplus strengthens the belief that the Hindu God Śiva had his votaries in the southern extremity of Malabar in the early days of the Christian era. In such circumstances it is, indeed, incredible that Hinduism, which, as we have shown, had spread through Ceylon and the Ḍrāviḍa country, did not make its way to Malabar, though the Pāṇḍyās of Madura has extended their borders across the Peninsula to Malabar and the countries beyond. The Aryans of the period were a venturesome race. Leaving their original home in Central Asia, they had penetrated far into the south, advancing with rapid strides till they found themselves checked by the roaring ocean. They had even crossed over to

1. Ancient India described by Ptolemy, p. 51.
2. The Indian Empire, pp. 91- 95, 196.

Ceylon and made settlements there. They had made permanent settlements in the Chōḷa and Pāṇḍya countries. Having driven the aborigines into the wilds of the Ghauts, and having advanced as far south as the southern extremity, it is difficult to imagine that they stopped short of entering Malabar, as if they had been peremptorily told, "Thus far shalt thou go and no farther." It is far more difficult to believe that the Brahmans waited till Mayūra Varma of Bāṇavāsi induced them, in the latter part of the seventh or the eighth century, to leave their hearths and homes in the north and seek "fresh fields and pastures new." In adopting Mr. Logan's theory, we have to leave out of account the southern Aryans altogether. But we may rest assured that the southern Brahmans were not the people to view with calm indifference the appropriation of the virgin soil of Kēraḷa by their brethren from the north. The fact is that they had obtained a firm foothold in Kēraḷa long before Mayūra Varma was even thought of. It may be observed here that Professor Wilson states, in the Introduction to his Descriptive Catalogue of the Mackenzie MSS., that tradition uniformly points to an extension of Hinduism and civilisation from the extreme south of the Peninsula. All known facts, therefore, tend to prove that the Brahmans had settled in Malabar long before the Chālūkyan or Rāṣhṭṛakūṭa conquest of the country.

Dealing with the period of the arrival of the Nambūrīs in Malabar, in the Malabar Quarterly Review, the late Mr. Justice Narayana Marar arrives at the conclusion that the ancestors of the present Nambūrīs must have come and settled in Malabar between the first and fourth centuries of the Christian era. He argues, "that there are certain customs and observances prevalent among the Nambūrīs, but not followed by the Brahmans of the other parts at the present day, which enable us to assert with some amount of certainty that the advent of the Aryans into Malabar must have been earlier than the fourth or fifth century of the Christian era. A form of marriage known as the *Sarvaswadanam* (Sarvasvaḍānam) marriage is still in force among the Nambūri Brahmans, who trace it to Ancient Hindu Law, the formula used during the marriage being the following text from Vasiṣhṭa:—'I give unto thee this virgin (who has no brother) decked with ornaments, and the son who may be born of her shall be my son.' This form of marriage is not recognised in the Miṭākṣhara, which, in such matters, governs almost the whole of India at the present day. Similarly, the adoption of a son in the *Dvayamushyayana* (Ḍvayamuṣhyāyana) form *i. e.*, as the son of two fathers (the natural and adoptive) is the ordinary form of adoption recognised in Malabar, while, in countries governed by the Miṭākṣhara law, it is considered as obsolete. Now, though the Miṭākṣhara is the work of Vijñānēśwara who lived under the Chālūkya king Vikramāḍiṭya of Kalyāṇa, (1026—1127 A. D.), it simply embodied the customs and usages that were in force among the Hindus for a long period prior to the date of it, for the author does not purport to do anything more than expound the law as laid down by Yājñavalkya, not however, as supposed by some, the priest of Janaka, king of Viḍēha who flourished in the Epic Age, (B. C. 1400—1000) but the author of the Ḍharma Śāsṭra known by that name, which has been fixed to belong to the fourth or fifth century after Christ. Yāgñavalkya himself being not a law-giver, but only a compiler of the customs and usages prevalent in his time, it would be only fair and reasonable to infer from these circumstances that the Nambūrīs separated from their kinsmen and migrated into Malabar at a time when the Ḍvayamuṣhāyana form of adoption had not become obsolete and the Sarvasvaḍānam marriage was still a recognised form of affiliation among them, *i. e.*, before the fourth or fifth century of the Christian era."

An inference is also drawn from the difference in the custom regarding the marriage of girls. "The rigid insistence of child-marriage under penalty of forfeiture of caste in other parts is absolutely unknown among the Nambūrīs of Malabar. The custom in vogue in Malabar is in accordance with ancient Hindu Law, while that prevalent outside is a later innovation forced upon the people by the necessities of the times." Mr. Dutt points out in his Ancient India that the frequent invasions of foreigners in the Buddhist age (B. C. 320 to 400 A. D.) and the general insecurity of the times fostered the baneful custom of child-marriage, and the custom became a religious duty after the Hindus had lost their independence. "The foreign invasions alluded to must have reference to the Indo-Scythian, Persian, Greeco-Bactrian and Tartar invasions, commencing from the sixth century B. C. and continuing, with varying fortunes, for nearly twelve centuries afterwards, in the course of which on several occasions the Hindus lost their independence to the foreigners even in the centuries before Christ. Child-marriage therefore must have grown up into a recognised and inviolable custom during this period, and, as it is the exception, and marriage after puberty the rule amongst the Nambūrīs, it may fairly be presumed that they separated from the other Brahmans before the practice developed into a custom, *i. e.*, at all events, before the fourth century of the Christian era."

Mr. Narayana Marar thus fixes, on the one hand, a limit of time later than which their settlement could not have taken place, and then tries to see whether there is anything which would enable us to fix a similar limit, on the other hand, earlier than which they could not have come. He thinks that it will not be far wrong to say that they could not have come to Malabar before the Christian era.

The argument is that the Nambūrīs are strict followers of the later development of the Hindu religion bearing the impress of Buddhistic influences, and if they had come to Malabar before the advent of Buddhism, we should naturally expect to find Vēḍic Hinduism in its pristine purity and simplicity to be still the religion of the Nambūrīs. "They are, however, followers of a later Hinduism which is the outcome of the action of Buddhistic teachings and influences on the earlier Hinduism of the ancient Aryans, and which is the religion of the Hindus throughout India at the present day. And this points to the conclusion that the Nambūrīs must have come to Malabar after the changes enumerated above had been completely effected in the religion and practices of the Hindus by the influence and example of Buddhism. Though Buddha lived and preached in the latter part of the sixth and the beginning of the fifth centuries before Christ, it was not till the time of Aśōka the Great, that is, in the beginning of the third century B.C., that the ascendency of Buddhism was established throughout India and the great blow dealt to ancient and Aryan Hinduism. Buddha's teachings became so popular, and exerted so potent an influence on the minds of the people, that the Aryans found their hands forced, if they desired to save their position and make a stand against the aggressions of Buddhism without being overwhelmed by them, to re-adjust their religion, manners and observances so as to bring them into conformity with popular sentiments and requirements. This was how the revolutionary changes above referred to came to be effected. Allowing a reasonable time for the complete working of this process, we shall not, I presume, be far wrong if we assert that the Nambūrīs could not have come to Malabar before the Christian era."

There is some force in the argument ; but it presumes that the change in the form of Hinduism indicated could not have reached the Nambūrīs in the far south, and that they must have brought their present religion intact from their original homes. There were indeed natural barriers between their new and old homes that prevented frequent intercourse between the settlers in Malabar and those whom they had left behind. But it would not be correct to conclude from this that, once the Nambūrīs separated from their brethren and took up their abode in Malabar, they remained everafter unaffected by the changes that occurred in the manners and customs of those who had remained in their original homes. It is admitted that one of the edicts of the Buddhist Emperor Aśōka mentions Malabar or Kērala as a neighbouring independent kingdom to which Aśōka had sent missionaries, and that it may therefore be plausibly argued that the Nambūrīs first settled in Malabar with the ancient Vēḍic Hindu religion, and then, just as Buddhism spread over all the other parts of India and succeeded in reforming the Vēḍic religion, it did its work in Malabar as well. But it is contended that, "remembering the fact that the peculiar position of Malabar kept it absolutely secluded from the rest of India, we are forced to the conclusion that the argument presupposes the fact that the change brought about by the contact with Buddhism were the direct results of the teachings of Buddhist missionaries. That, however, was not the case. Those changes were the result of the attempts made by the Hindus to accommodate their religion to the necessities created by the Buddhists, and there is no reason whatever why the form taken by the innovations introduced by the Brahmans in Malabar should resemble even in the minutest details the form of the innovations made by them elsewhere, from whom, according to the supposition, they had long ago separated, and with whom apparently they carried on no further intercourse."

We need not for the purpose of the present argument discuss the question whether the changes that Vēḍic Hinduism underwent in the light of the advancement of Buddhism were forced on the Hindus by the

Buddhists, or whether the Hindus voluntarily accommodated themselves to the necessities created by the new religion, if we consider Buddhism to be a new religion at all in its origin, for Buddhism has not inaptly been called the hand-maid of Hinduism. Either way it was possible for the Nambūrīs who had brought with them the Vēḍic religion to be affected by the changes that were going on amongst their brethren in the north, and it may fairly be doubted if the innovations introduced by the Brahmans in Malabar resembled even in the minutest details the form of innovations introduced elsewhere. It is assumed that the Brahman settlers of southern India had apparently no further intercourse with the north. But why should this be so? We shall later on be able to show that there were means of communication between the extreme south and the extreme north, that the route of the hero of the Rāmāyaṇa from Ayōḍhya to Lanka can very well be traced on the map of India, and that it is clear that the author of the Rāmāyaṇa had a clear knowledge of the route he describes. We have seen that in the fifth century B. C., Vijaya, a son of the king of Magaḍha, is said to have gone by sea to Ceylon, conquered the island, and established a Hindu kingdom there; and it is admitted that the conquerors of Ceylon under Vijaya had constant intercourse with southern India. This, at any rate, shows that means of intercourse between the north and the south even by sea was not altogether wanting. Buddhism may be said to have established its ascendency throughout India by the time of Aśōka, and we have one of the edicts of the Great Emperor making special mention of the fact that he had despatched missionaries to Kērala among other countries. Later on, we have the evidence of the Tamil poems, the Chilapaṭikāram and the Maṇimēkalai, composed in the first century A. D., to show that Cape Comorin had been for a long time past a sacred bathing place for the Hindus, and "that Brahman pilgrims came from Benares to bathe in Kumāri and wash away their sins. Similarly the Brahmans of southern India went round the Pothiya hill, which was famous as the residence of the Vēdic sage Agasṭya, then bathed in the sea at Kumāri, and travelled northward to the Ganges to bathe in the sacred waters there. Pilgrims from the banks of the Ganges to Kumāri and from Tamiḷakam (which included Kērala) to Benares appear to have kept up communication between the Northern and Southern Aryas."[1] While therefore we may agree with Mr. Narayana Marar that the Brahman colonisation of Malabar must have taken place before the fourth century of the Christian era, it is not possible to hold with him that it could not have taken place earlier than the first century A. D.

9. **Backwaters, Rivers and Canals.** The channels referred to here are evidently the lagoons or backwaters, which are a peculiar feature of Malabar, extending from the Railway Station at Ṭirūr to Trivandrum, the capital of Travancore, a distance of over 200 miles, affording easy and cheap communication. Originally, they lay detached in a manner obstructing continuous communication, but, in course of time, they have been connected one with the other by means of artificial canals. In Travancore this enterprise was first undertaken by Her Highness Pārvaṭi Rāṇi, in whose reign the canal between the capital and the Kaṭhinamkulam backwater, a distance of 11¾ miles exclusive of the lake at Vēli, through which it passes, was dug. The Varkalay barrier presented the most formidable obstacle to uninterrupted water communication, but this was overcome by digging a canal through the rocks, and cutting through them two tunnels, each of about 1,500 and 2,500 feet length respectively, which were opened for traffic in 1877. The

1. The Tamils 1800 years ago by Mr. V. Kanakasabhai, p. 21.

A CANAL VIEW.

To face page 77.]

remaining important canals are the Parūr, Quilon and Chovare, which connects the intervening lakes with the Cochin system of backwaters. These extend towards the north almost to Chēṭṭva from where commences the Ponnāni canal which carries on communication up to Ṭirūr, one of the stations of the South Indian Railway.

In days gone by, when wheeled and pack-bullock traffic was all but unknown, this system of waterways afforded the easiest, the cheapest and, perhaps, the only means of carrying on traffic, and it is not difficult to understand how the back-water system exercised considerable influence on the political, industrial and commercial development of the country. It will be found that all the foreign nations who started the enterprise of commerce and conquest on the western coast were eager to get hold of sites for factories and fortresses at advantageous positions on the line of these backwaters. Thus the Portuguese and, after them, the Dutch, established their factory at Cannanore together with its outpost at Mt. D'Ely point, commanding the river navigation of North Malabar. The English factory at Tellicherry, with its outwork on Ḍharmapaṭṭaṇam Island was selected with the express purpose of securing the pepper trade of the locality, which was extensive. For a similar purpose did the French establish themselves at Māhe. Similarly, the Portuguese, the English, the French, the Dutch and the Danes secured sites within the dominions of the Zamorin of Calicut and the Rajas of Cochin and Travancore. The Danish factory at Edava in Travancore, insignificant as it was, was well placed, as it stood, at the time, at the head of the water communication in the south. The Dutch, the Portuguese and the English fought for the possession of Chēṭṭva, because it stood at the mouth of a broad river and an extensive backwater system on the north. So with Cochin. But for its deep land-locked harbour, affording safe anchorage to ships of large draught, and its unsurpassed facilities for communication with the interior, Cochin would never have been heard of. The Dutch at Ṭangachēry had similarly the command of the river navigation leading to Quilon. The site chosen by the English at Anjengo was altogether inhospitable and unattractive, its only redeeming feature,—and that was the main reason which influenced the East India Company to select the site—was that its position was not only useful politically, being situated in the heart of an important and enterprising Native State, but was advantageous to commerce as standing promiently at the head of the river communication around.

The Europeans were not the only nation who saw the advantage of a settlement upon a river-bank. Every Mahomedan settlement in Malabar will be found to be placed either on the banks of a navigable river, or at its mouth, or at its confluence with the backwater. Near the head of the navigable portion of the Valarpaṭṭaṇam river was settled one of the earliest Mahomedan colonies. In the village of Ṭṛkūr (Erroocur of the Atlas), situated on the main branch of the river, will be found another early Mahomedan settlement.

A journey by backwater is one of the most pleasant experiences of those who travel in the south of India. But the rainy season should be avoided altogether, as the storms of the monsoon render the lakes rough and the passage difficult, if not dangerous. But as the rain wears off, and the silver streaks of the moon illuminate the horizon on a cloudless night, the panorama presented to the eye of the traveller, viewing the scene from the deck of his boat, as it glides smoothly along the calm surface of the backwater, is supremely beautiful. Myriads of fireflies, with their weird twinkle, light up the coast line, fringed with luxuriant vegetation, while the starry heavens reflected in the blue, limpid water below make the fairy scene complete. The solemn stillness of the night is only ruffled by the splash of the oars or the darting of fish hither and thither, giving occasion for the phosphoroscent water to make its glow appear, and lend an additional charm to the already enchanting scene.

Ibn Batuta, in the early years of the 14th century, travelling by backwater from Calicut to Quilon accomplished the journey in ten days. It seems he would have enjoyed it much, but for his companion and guide, whom he took from Calicut, and who was always the worse for liquor. In five days the traveller reached a place which he calls Kānjirakara, "which stands on the top of a hill, is inhabited by Jews, and governed by an Emir who pays tribute to the king of Kowlam (Quilon). All the trees (we saw) upon the banks of this river, as well as upon the sea shores, were those of the cinnamon and bakum, which constitute the fuel of the inhabitants: and with this we cooked our food. Upon the tenth day we arrived at Kowlam, which is the last city on the Malabar Coast. In this place is a large number of Mahomedan merchants, but the king is an infidel."[1] Varthema (A. D. 1500) calls the water communication from Calicut to Kāyamkulam a river. He says, "And so we departed (from Calicut), and took our road by a river which is the most beautiful I ever saw, and arrived at a city called Cacolum (Kāyamkulam) distant from Calicut 50 leagues."[2]

Fra Bartolomeo, writing in the 18th century, mentions the following as among the most remarkable of these rivers: "The Cariapatnam, the Coleci, the Valaveli, and the Modalapusha, which runs past Atinga Ceringa and Anjenga also the Paru which flows past Chidaculam, Paru and Mainada, and, uniting itself with several other rivers, forms, from Cochin to

1. Lee's Translation, p. 174.
2. P. 178.

Codungalore towards the north, a kind of stagnant lake, so that people can travel through the greater part of Malabar by water. The rivers of less note are: the Veypoor and Porotta, the Feira d'Alva, which in its course washes Malayatoor, Cognur, Ciovara, Varapole Angicaimal and Cochin; the Alangatta which after running past Alamgattu, Cennotta and Codungalore discharges itself into the sea at Aycotta; also the Cetwa, the Paniani, the Calicut, the Mahe, the Baliapatnam and several others which extend a great way into the country and form an innumerable multitude of islands."[1]

The Malabar rivers generally take their names from the places they flow past, and as localities not unfrequently change their names, many of the rivers have come to be known by names different from those mentioned by Paoli.

The following are the principal rivers in Travancore:—

1.	The Periyār		Length	142	miles.
2.	,,	Pampa	,,	90	,,
3.	,,	Kallaḍa	,,	70	,,
4.	,,	Kollakkaḍavu	,,	70	,,
5.	,,	Mūvāṟṟupuḻa	,,	62	,,
6.	,,	Karamana	,,	41	,,
7.	,,	Ṭamṟavaṟṇi	,,	37	,,
8.	,,	Neyyāra	,,	35	,,
9.	,,	Mīnachil	,,	35	,,
10.	,,	Vāmanapuram	,,	35	,,
11.	,,	Iṭṭikkara	,,	30	,,
12.	,,	Parayara	,,	23	,,
13.	,,	Kōṭa	,,	20	,,
14.	,,	Kiḻḻiyār	,,	15	,,

1. Pp. 103--4.

A RIVER VIEW : THE ALWAY RIVER

To face page 82]

The following extract from the Census Report of Cochin sufficiently details the river system in that State : —

"The country is well watered by innumerable torrents, which pour down the hills. The chief among them are the Bhāraṭappuḻa or Ponnāni river, which with its tributaries of Chemmanṭōḍu and Veṭṭikkappuḻa drains the Pōṭṭuṇḍi and portions of the Machāḍ forests, the Chiṟṟūr river, the Karuvannūr river, the Chālakkuḍi river and the Periār or Ālwaye river. The Ālwaye in its course to the sea from south-eastern Travancore has but a short section within the limits of the State. At Ālwaye it bifurcates, and flows into the Arabian sea by two mouths, one into the opening at Crānganūr, and the other into that at Cochin. The drainage of the major portion of the forests of the Mukunḍapuram Taluk is performed by the Chālakkuḍi river whose feeders, the Kappaṭṭōḍu and Kaṇankariṭṭōḍu, form deep ravines and narrow gorges in the mountains. The river after its descent from the forest flows through picturesque and fertile tracts, and empties itself into the right arm of the Ālwaye river at Elenṭikkara, about six miles to the east of Crānganūr. The Maṇali and the Kuṟumāli, of which the latter is fed by the Chemmaṇi, the Muppuḻi and the Varulendian tapping the Paṟavaṭṭāni and Kōḍaśśēri forests, unite into the Karuvannūr river. Portions of the Ālwaye and the Chālakkuḍi rivers are much frequented during the hot season as bathing places. Both these rivers have great commercial value, being navigable all the year round for small country boats and barges. On the low lands, some of these rivers, which form the chief outlets for the drainage of the State, unite into shallow and irregular shaped lakes, or backwaters, which are the most remarkable of the physical features of the country. They open out into the sea at Chēṟṟuwāye, Crānganūr and Cochin." [1]

1. Intro. p. XXXI of Report of 1901.

The rivers of British Malabar are:—

1.	The Nīlēśvaram	47	miles long.
2.	,, Ēli mala or Deli	30	,,
3.	,, Ṭalipaṟamba	41	,,
4.	,, Valaṟpaṭṭaṇam	74	,,
5.	,, Anjarakaṇḍi	40	,,
6.	,, Tellichērry	14	,,
7.	,, Māhe	34	,,
8.	,, Kotta	46	,,
9.	,, Agalapuḻa or broad river	16	,,
10.	,, Elaṭūr	32	,,
11.	,, Kallāi	14	,,
12.	,, Bēypore	96	,,
13.	,, Kaḍalunḍi	75	,,
14.	,, Ponnāni	156	,,
15.	,, Chēṟṟuwāye		

Lakes in Travancore :—

The largest lake in Travancore is the Vembanāḍ lake, being 32 miles long. Its extreme breadth is nine miles.

The Kāyamkuḷam is 19 miles long and its extreme breadth two miles.

The Aṣhṭamuḍi near Quilon 10 miles long, and nine miles broad.

The Parūr.

The Anjengo 12 miles long and two and a half broad.

The Vēli.

The Kaṭhinamkuḷam.

Lakes in Cochin State :—

1. Manakkōṭi
2. Ēnāmākkal
3. Chāṭṭanāḍ
4. Cochin.
5. Kaiṭappuḻa.

10. **The Quilon coast is steep and rocky.** The Periplus of the Erythrean Sea notices the Quilon coast as part of what it calls " Parali. " The country so called comprised the line of coast including South Travancore and South Tinnevelly, and formed Ptolemy's country of the Aioi or the Ahi Dēśam of the Sanskrit Purāṇās. It commenced at what the Greek mariner called the Pyrhos or "Red cliffs," south of Quilon, and included not only Comorin but also Kolkhoi on the Tinnevelly coast. The remarkable line of low and beautifully coloured cliffs of Varkalay are also noticed by Mr. King of the Indian Geological Survey. Paralia is the Greek word for coast, and, according to Professor McCrindle, designated generally any maritime district. But Burnell identifies Paralia with Puraḷi, an old name of Travancore. Yule agrees with Burnell, and adds that from this name the Raja takes the title of *Puralisan* (Puraḷīśan), the lord of Puraḷi.[1] That the title was used to denote the Rajas of Travancore is evident from well-known poetical works in Malayalam.

11. **Stone adapted for building purposes.** This stone is known as laterite, and it is the finest building material available in Malabar. It is hewn when fresh with a kind of axe, and exposure hardens it. Mr. Philip Lake remarks that it is the great water-bearing stratum, and that it is to the laterite that Malabar owes the perennial character of many of its streams. The rock being porous takes a large quantity of water in the rainy season, and serves as a reservior during the hot weather.[2]

12. **Limestone and Lignite.** Major Heber Drury, the Editor of these letters, was assistant to General W. Cullen, British Resident in Travancore,

1. See also Dr. Gundhert's Malayalam Dictionary under the word *Puralisan*.

2. Geology of South Malabar.p 37.

who devoted much attention to the geology of Travancore. In this note Major Drury adopts the General's view that limestone and lignite are to be found on the Quilon coast and at Varkalay. A note by the Travancore State Geologist of the Northern Division, Mr. T. C. Chakko, on the Quilon limestone, published recently in the Travancore Government Gazette, throws considerable doubt on its existence there. Dr. W. King of the Geological Survey of India also failed to discover any limestone there. Mr. Massilamani, State Geologist of the Southern Division, has reported that limestones "occur in small patches at the cape (Comorin) at Vaṭṭakōṭṭa Fort, near Kanakapur and at Layam. They are shelly and usually siliceous. Underneath the shelly limestone at Cape Comorin is a porous travertine like siliceous limestone, full of broken sea-shells, forming the cliffs there. Owing to the heavy sea prevailing there during rough weather, large blocks fall down and are strewn along the shore. They form a break-water, and protect the cliffs from further damage for a time." Again, "Besides the limestone in beds, there also occur the globular, compact, loose pieces ot limestone peculiar to the Tropics, and known in India as Kunker."

Mr. Massilamani refers to another class, "the charnockites, which are found in Maruṭva Hill, Erachipolum and other places," which "will, when polished, make a beautiful ornamental stone, and will compare favourably with any of the European granites and syenites. The art of polishing hard stones is in the primitive stage, and the stone masons are not inclined to welcome any new method."

Of laterite Mr. Massilamani says:—"This common rock, the product of gneisses and other crystalline rocks, is found in abundance in various places. It is used as a building stone. Though soft when quarried fresh, it hardens by exposure and stands well the destructive action of weather. Much interest has lately been aroused by the discovery that laterite was not a silicate of aluminium as was formerly supposed, but that it contains a large amount of hydrated aluminium oxide (beauxite), as much as 52 to 59 per cent, while silica is only 0·58 to 2·65 per cent, and hence can be easily utilised as a source of extracting the metal aluminium. It compares favourably with the material now being mined so largely in South France. It has been determined that laterite can be converted into aluminium oxide."[1]

13. **Rice.**—Rice is the staple of food in Malabar, and its cultivation gives occupation to a large portion of the population. A fair proportion of the cultivable area of the country is devoted exclusively to the raising of this cereal; not only in the deltaic littoral and the swampy regions of the backwater, but also on the terraced plateau to the east, rising tier after tier till they reach the watershed above, rice grows luxuriantly. To our author it is curious that so dry a plant as rice grows in water. But, as early as B. C. 20, Strabo has pointed out that "the rice (*oryza*) according to Aristobulus, stands in water, in an enclosure. It is sowed in beds. The plant is four cubits in height with many ears, and yields a large produce. The harvest is about the time of the setting of the Pleiades and the grain is beaten out like barley."[2] Rice was known to the Greeks from very early times. Atheneus quotes Megasthenes (B. C. 300) to show that *oryza heptha*, cooked rice, formed the food of the Indians, and mentions a wine made from rice as an Indian beverage. Rice was exported in large quantities into Greece, and the derivation of the Greek word *Oryza*, denoting rice, has been traced by scholars to the Tamil word *arisi* (ariši) (of which the Malayalam *ari* is but a contracted form). Bishop Caldwell observes that

1. Page, 9.
2. Strabo XV--i 18 in Bohn's Ed. T. III. 83.

the Greek word for rice, *Oryza*, dates from the time, whenever that was, when rice was first introduced into Europe, and it cannot be doubted that here we have the Tamil word "ariśi" rice deprived of the husk, this being the condition in which, then, as now, rice was exported.[1] So also Dr. Oppert, who adds that there is no Sanskrit or Aryan root for the Greek word *Oryza*, while it is clearly traceable to the Dravidian word "ariśi", thus affording one more proof of the non-Aryan element in the early trade between the East and the West.[2]

Varthema gives us a curious description of "the practice they (the people of Malabar) follow in sowing rice." He says, "The men of Calicut, when they wish to sow rice, observe this practice. First they plough the land with oxen, as we do, and, when they sow rice in the field, they have all the instruments of the city continually sounding and making merry. They also have ten or twelve men clothed like devils, and these unite in making great rejoicing with the players on the instruments, in order the devil may make the rice very productive."[3] It must certainly have exercised the imaginative faculty of the mediaeval traveller very much before he could discover why the people made such great rejoicings on the occasion. Varthema may very well be pardoned for likening the frolicsome fellows dressed in fantastic attire to devils, when we read the gruesome description given by Abdur-Razak (A. D. 1442), the Mahomedan ambassador from Sha Rokh to the Zamorin. Of the people of Calicut, he says, "as soon as I landed at Calicut, I saw beings such as my imagination had never depicted the like of," and, waxing poetical, the astonished ambassador exclaims:—

> "Extraordinary beings, who are neither men nor devils,
> At sight of whom the mind takes alarm;

1. History of Tinnevelly, p. 23.
2. Lecture on Ancient Commerce of India.
3. Travels of Varthema, pp. 167-8.

If I were to see such in my dreams
My heart would be in a tremble for many years" ![1]

It may be that Varthema is referring to the custom obtaining in many parts of Malabar, till but recently, where, on the occasion of the first sowing of the seed in the year on lands belonging to large religious establishments, the temple authorities turned out with music and all the paraphernalia attached to the shrine to superintend the process.

It did not surprise Grose to see rice growing in water, for, he remarks that, "the growth of this grain has a particularity not unworth mentioning which is, that as it loves a watery soil, so to whatever height the water rises, wherever it is planted, the growth of the rice keeps measure with it, even to that of 12 or 14 feet; the submit of the stalk always appearing above the surface."[2] In his day the cultivation of rice was reckoned as an honourable occupation in Malabar and those that followed it had precedence over mechanics. "It is," he says, "sown in the month of June, in the soil that is a mere puddle, occasioned by the overflowing of the rivers on their grounds. When it is a hand high, they take it up, and replant it in just such other soil. Their harvest is gathered in the beginning of winter. Their plough is a very simple machine, and a branchy bough serves for a harrow."[3] This is at best but an indifferent description of the method of cultivating rice in Malabar.

As remarked above, this grain is cultivated both on wet and on dry land. There are different sorts of paddy raised in Malabar. Of these some grow only on wet land, while others want a dry soil. While some soils yield three crops a year, others yield only one, and

1. Major's India in the 15th Century.
2. A voyage to the East Indies, Vol. 1, p. 48.
3. Ibid, p. 341.

the highest yield in each case goes up to 20, even to 70, fold of the seed sown.

The implements of husbandry are not far removed from their primitive condition. A rude plough, tipped with iron, is used for ploughing. It generally but scrapes the earth, leaving a shallow furrow. Deep ploughing is seldom practised. Bullocks and buffaloes of an inferior breed are the draught animals used for ploughing. Manure, such as cow-dung, ashes, and leaves of certain trees, is somtimes used. Before ploughing commences, these are left to rot in the fields and then ploughed into the earth. The sowing is done by the hand. Very often plants are raised on seed beds attached to the fields, and then transplanted into them. Where water is scarce, it is brought by means of channels and baled into the fields.

In the swampy or marshy parts, the soil is turned up by spades, and detached heaps are formed on which the seed is thrown. When they come up and attain a certain age, they are transplanted—rather re-planted in the same field. In such fields as are often supplied with alluvial deposits washed down by the numerous rivers that rush from the ghats during the rainy season, artificial manure is seldom, if ever, used. There is extant in Malabar an old Malayalam poem in manuscript, said to be a translation of a Sanskrit work on agriculture, called Kērala Kalpam, believed to have been compiled by Paraśu Rāma for the benefit of his people in Kērala. In the rural parts of Malabar, especially in the north, the poem is taught in village schools, and the methods of cultivation now practised by the agricultural classes are mostly in accordance with the precepts laid down in this poem. The following is a short account of it as given by Mr. L. K. Ananthakrishna Ayyar:—

"The following story is told to account for so much rain in Kērala. In days of yore, there was, at one time, no rain in the kingdoms of Chēra, Chōla and Pāṇḍya, and all living beings were dying of starvation. The kings of the three kingdoms could not find means to mitigate the sufferings of their subjects. They consulted with one another and resolved to do penance to the god of rain. Temporarily leaving the administration of affairs in the hands of the ministers, they went to the forest, and did penance to Indra, the god of rain, who, at the intercession of the great gods, took pity on them and blessed each of them with rain for four months in the year. Well pleased, they returned to their kingdoms. They, however, soon became discontended, because the first had not enough of rain, while the other two had too much of it. They went to the rain-god again, and conveyed to him their grievances. He thereupon directed the kings Chōlan and Pāṇḍiyan to give two months' rain to the king Chēran. All the three rulers now felt quite satisfied. The king Chēran got eight months' rain for his kingdom, while the other two were satisfied with two months' rain in their own kingdoms. Their days of birth, namely, Ṭiruvāṭira (the sixth asterism) in Miṭhunam (June-July) of Chēran, Svāṭi (the 15th lunar asterism, Arcturus) in Ṭulām (October-November) of Chōlan, Mūlam (the 19th constellation) in Kumbham (February-March) of Pāṇḍiyan are worthy of remembrance. For, on these auspicious days commence the monsoons, namely, the South-West monsoon in Malabar, the North-East monsoon or ṬulāV-aṛṣham in the kingdom of Chōla, and the rainy season in the kingdom of Pāṇḍya. What are called ambrosial showers of rain are said to fall on these kingdoms during the two weeks beginning from the aforesaid dates. It is the belief of all castes among the Hindus even now that seeds of plants sown on these days will produce a rich harvest. These days are alled *Nattu-Velas* (Ñāṭṭu-Vēlās) (the best time for planting) in the respective kingdoms and held sacred by the people of these countries.

The unit of measurement of the quantity of rain falling upon earth is called a *para*. It is the measurement of the Dēvās, which consists of the quantity of rain falling upon land, 60 yōjanās or 600 miles in length and 100 yōjanās or 1,000 miles in breadth[1].

Among the old set of agriculturists in Malābar, the belief is that, if Vişhu (first of Mēṭam) falls upon a Saturday, there will fall one para of rain in Kērala; poor harvest and poverty among people will be the consequence. If it comes on a Sunday or Tuesday, there will be two paras of rain; the crops will be somewhat good. If on a Monday, three paras of rain will fall, and the harvest will be rich and the crops abundant. If on a Thursday, four paras of rain will fall; the crops will be abundant and the harvest so rich that no sign of famine in the land nor poverty among the people will be seen.[2]

The lands which should not be taken up for sowing are :—

The lands overgrown with (1) phlomis, (2) chengaṇa (a kind of grass), (3) bamboos and thorny plants, (4) hard stony grounds and (5) tracts frequented by

1. അറുപതുയോജനവിസ്താരത്താൽ
ഏറീടുംശതയോജനനീളം
പറയുടെമാനമിതെന്നെല്ലാരും
പറയുന്നുണ്ടേ വാനോരമര്

There is a Sanskrit variant to this which runs thus :—

ഷഷ്ഠിയോജനവിസ്താരം
ശതയോജനമുന്നതം
ആഢകസ്യപ്രമാണന്തു
ദേവമാനേന ഗണ്യതേ.

2. ശനിവാരേ വിഷുസംക്രമമായാൽ
തനിയേ പറയകാലം പോൽ
ഭൂവിപറരണ്ടുകാലത്താകും
ശശിബുധവാരേ വിഷുവൽസുഷ്ഠേ.
മിരിമൂന്നത്രേ പറയകാലം
വെള്ളം പെറനാലങ്ങതിലേറുക
ഇല്ലെന്നത്രേ നിമിത്തമോക്കിൽ.

wild beasts.[1]

On the contrary, lands with a mixture of sand and earth, those drained by springs from the hill-sides and sewage impurities as well as those manured by river-silt can be well taken up for cultivation.

Men who are unfit to be cultivators:—

They are:—

(1) Men with no piety to God, with no respect for their *Guru* (preceptor) and Brahmans,

(2) Men addicted to drinking,

(3) Men with no frugal habits,

(4) Dull and sleepy men,

(5) Men who do not keep proper accounts of income and expenditure,

(6) Men who do not provide themselves with a sufficient storage of grain for the wages of workmen under them,

(7) Men without the necessary implements of industry, viz., (1) crowbar, (2) hatchet, (3) sword, (4) axe, (5) spade and (6) various kinds of wickerwork,

(8) Men who cannot maintain themselves in Kaṙkaṭakam (July and August),

(9) Men having no farm house, and with no straw for bullocks in Kanni (September-October),

(10) Men having no adequate wages to be given to workmen.

The lands that should be taken up for cultivation should be well fenced, and manured with leaves, dung of cattle and ashes. The bank between fields should be sufficiently strong and grass should not be allowed to grow on them, as it may draw the manure off the fields.

1. [illegible]
കാട്ടിലൊന്നും വിതച്ചാലുണ്ടായിടാ,
ചെങ്കണ്ണായെന്ന പുല്ലുമിതുപ്പുള്ള
അങ്ങു കാട്ടിലൊട്ടും വിതക്കൊല്ലാ
ഇല്ലിപ്പടലങ്ങൾ ഏറിയ കാട്ടിലും
കല്ലൻ കാട്ടിലുമെന്നും വിതക്കൊല്ല,
കാട്ടുജാതികളേറിയ കാട്ടിലും
വിതച്ചാലങ്ങു കിട്ടുവാനും പണി

Manner of ploughing and manuring:—

The plough must penetrate deep into the ground to turn the layers of earth. The bullocks must never be thrashed, but must be cheerfully led. They must be enticed by songs. The ground for sowing seeds and for transplanting must be ploughed not less than six times. A bullock and a buffalo must not be yoked together.

Bullocks used for ploughing and other agricultural purposes should have (1) the hind part round and fat, (2) the back-bone nearly straight and raised, (3) white, black or red spots (active), (4) thick nose, (5) raised head and bent horns, (6) no decaying teeth, (7) bent and small horns, (8) should be small and fair like ponies, (9) should have soft dung, (10) long tail, (11) and should eat their food quickly.

Bullocks to be rejected are those that have (1) long hoofs, (2) small tails, (3) bent back-bones, (4) thick and heavy horns, (5) marks of leprosy, (6) decaying teeth, (7) the hind legs touching each other while walking, (8) belly like a rattan box, (9) no horns, and (10) that pass loose dung. Buffaloes should be dark coloured and have their bodies round.

Cattle-shed must have its floor paved with wooden planks, well cleaned, and partitioned. The dung must be removed to a distance, as its smell is very offensive to them.

Inauspicious times for sowing:—

1. Night (Poor harvest).

2. *Gulikakalam* (Guḷikakālam Time of the son of Saturn; fatal time).

A day is, according to Hindu Astrology, divided into 60 *ghatikas* (ghaṭikās = nāḷikas) or 24 hours. The are the *gulikakalams* (Guḷikakālams) for the week days:—

Day		
Sunday	26th ghaṭika	(4 —24 P. M.)
Monday	22nd do	(2 —48 P. M.)
Tuesday	18th do	(1 —12 P. M.)
Wednesday	14th do	(11—36 A. M.)

Thursday	10th	ghaṭika	(9 —24 A. M.)
Friday	6th	do	(8 —24 A. M.)
Saturday	2nd	do	(6 —48 A. M.)
Night			
Sunday	10th	ghaṭika	(10 P. M.)
Monday	6th	do	(8 —24 P. M.)
Tuesday	2nd	do	(6 —48 P. M.)
Wednesday	26th	do	(4 —24 A. M.)
Thursday	22nd	do	(2 —48 A. M.)
Friday	18th	do	(1 —24 A. M.)
Saturday	14th	do	(11—36 A. M.)

Seeds sown during those inauspicious times yield no produce.

3. *Kanni*, *Vrischigam* and *Dhanu Rasis*(Rāśīs):—A day is divided into 12 rāśīs or the 12 signs of the zodiac; namely (1) Aries (2) Taurus (3) Gemini (4) Cancer (5) Leo (6) Virgo (7) Libra (8) Scorpio (9) Sagittarius (10) Capricornus (11) Aquarius (12) Pisces.

The time set apart for each rāśi is given below:—

Malabar months.		Rāśi.		Ghaṭikās.	
(1)	Meṭam	do	(Aries)	4¼	do
(2)	Eṭavam	do	(Taurus)	4¾	do
(3)	Miṭhunam	do	(Gemini)	5¼	do
(4)	Kaṙkaṭakam	do	(Cancer)	5½	do
(5)	Chingam	do	(Leo)	5¼	do
(6)	Kanni	do	(Virgo)	5	do
(7)	Ṭulām	do	(Libra)	5	do
(8)	Vṛśchikam	do	(Scorpio)	5¼	do
(9)	Ḍhanu	do	(Sagittarius)	5½	do
(10)	Makaram	do	(Capricornus)	5¼	do
(11)	Kumbham	do	(Aquarius)	5¾	do
(12)	Mīnam	do	(Pisces)	4¼	do
			Total	60	

The crops raised by seeds sown in Kanni rāśi will be stolen, while those obtained from the seeds sown on the Vṛśchika rāśi will be destroyed.

4. *Gandantam* (Gaṇḍānṭam=a perilous time). The first quarter of the three asterisms, Aśvaṭi (first

constellation, head of Aries), Makam (the 10th constellation) and Mūlam (19th constellation, extremity of scorpion's head); and also the last quarter of Āiliam (9th asterism, forefeet of Leo), Kēṭṭa (18th lunar asterism in scorpion) and Rēvaṭi (27th constellation, Pisces).

The seeds sown during this period will produce nothing to the farmer.[1]

5. *Vishanadika* (Viṣhanāḍika = Poisonous period). Four Indian hours in each *nakshatram* (Nakṣhaṭṟam = star) that presides over the day.

6. *Pantamnal* (Panṭamnāl). The second, seventh and twelfth after the waxing and waning of the moon. So also the first day.[2] A house thatched on these days will take fire.

7. The sixth day after the waxing and waning of the Moon (Ṣhaṣhṭi).

8. *Velierakkam*. (Vēlierakkam = Low tide).

9. *Pannikkaranam* (Paṅṅikkaraṇam),[3] *Pasukkaranam* (Paśukkaraṇam) and *Kazhuthakkaranam* (Kaḻuṭakkaraṇam). A *Karanam* (Karaṇam) is the 11th constellation of the lunar fortnight.

10. *Rasis* (Rāśis). Aspected by evil planets or malifics.

11. *Latam and Argalam* (Lāṭam and Aṟgaḻam).

12. *Vaidrithayogam* (Vaiḍhṛṭayōgam). Sun and Moon standing in the same Ayana and like declension.

13. Days of eclipse.

14. *Adhimasam* (Aḍhimāsam). Thirteenth lunar month occurring every fourth year.

15. When Jupiter aspects Venus and *vice versa*.

16. Saturdays and Sundays.

Auspicious days for sowing :—

(1) *Rohini* (Rōhiṇi)—4th nakṣhaṭṟa, with Aldebaran.

1. *Vishti* also is prohibited.
2. പ്രതിപദമവാസ്യം.
3. A half day of each fortnight.

Punartham (Puṇaṙṭam)—the 7th nakṣhaṭṙa, Gemini and Sirius.

Puyam (Pūyam)—the 8th lunar asterism.

Cancer—the head of Hydra.

Astham (Asṭam)—the 13th constellation, Coma Berenices.

Uthram (Uṭṭṙam)—12th asterism, tale of Leo.

Mulam (Mūlam)—the 19th asterism, the extremity of scorpion's head.

(2) *Simhakkaranam* (Simhakkaraṇam) } [1]
Pulikkaranam (Pulikkaraṇam)
Anakkaranam (Ānakkaraṇam)

(3) *Rasis* (Rāśīs)—Miṭhunam, Kaṙkaṭakam, Simham, Makaram and Mīnam.[2]

The following extract from the same source on paddy cultivation in the Cochin State will also be found interesting. It applies equally to other parts of Malabar.

"Paddy cultivation in the State is generally of three kinds:—(1) Dry seed cultivation, (2) Sprouted cultivation and (3) Transplanted paddy cultivation.

Dry seed cultivation.—For this kind of cultivation, the fields, after the preceding crop have been cut in Vṛśchikam (November—December) and Ḍhanu (December–January), are ploughed. The ploughings are continued several times till Mēṭam (April—May). Some ashes are sprinkled every now and then on the fields. After a few showers of rain in Mēṭam, the seeds are sown broadcast. Some farmers plough in the seed, while others cover it with a hoe. The ashes are again thrown on the fields. The weeds (Kaḷa or that which has to be removed or lost) are removed a month after the seeds have been sown. The banks are repaired, and the

1. For these and other terms, vide my Notes on Malabar Astrology.

2. Castes and Tribes of Cochin.

water is confined on the field. Weeds are again removed in July. The harvest falls in the latter part of Kanni or Ṭulām. This method of cultivation is applied to a single crop of Kaḻama, Āriyan, and Ariviri (varieties of paddy) and the harvest is in Vṛśchiḳam. Should a double crop be raised, the sowing takes place in Mēṭam, and the harvest in Kaṙkaṭakam (July—August) and Chingam (August—September). The second crop is begun in two weeks.

Sprouted cultivation.—The fields for this are ploughed a dozen times, and are always kept full of water, except when the plough is at work. The field is drained, until the water does not stand deeper than a hand's breadth. At each ploughing, some leaves of any bush or weed, that can be procured, are put into the mud, which is smoothed by dragging over it a plank yoked to two oxen. The water is drained off by two or three channels formed with a hoe. The prepared seed is sown. As the corn grows, more and more water is allowed to rest on the field. The kinds of rice thus cultivated are fifteen in number, and require from three to six months. This cultivation is resorted to in fields on which dry seeds cannot be sown.

Transplanted rice cultivation.—The manner of ploughing and manuring is the same as in the case of sprouted seed and performed in the same season. If the ground be clean, the seedlings are transplanted immediately from the fields in which they are raised into those in which they may be reared into maturity. When they are planted, the fields contain three inches depth of water, which gradually increases as the plant grows. Good farmers plough the ground more than twelve times before hand.

The auspicious time at which seeds are sown for dry seed cultivation is during the Bharaṇi and Kāṙṭṭika

Ñāťťu Vēla, *i. e.*, from the 14th of Mēṭam (latter part of April) to the 10th of Eṭavam (about the end of May). Time for the sprouted cultivation is during the Makīram Ñāťťu Vēla which begins from the 23rd of Eṭavam and lasts till the 7th of Miṭhunam. The transplanted cultivation begins during the Ṭiruvāṭira Ñāťťu Vēla (*i. e.*, 7th of Miṭhunam to the 21st).

Mōṭan cultivation.—The dry lands are well ploughed and the sowing takes place in Mēṭam (March—April) and the harvest in Chingam (August—September).

Punja cultivation.—Sowing is in Kumbham and the harvest about the end of Mēṭam and the beginning of Eṭavam.

Kōle cultivation.—This kind of cultivation is peculiar to Cochin, Travancore and Malabar. It means the cultivation of paddy in fresh water lakes after draining away the water. The whole of the Trichur lake is thus cultivated. The beds are partitioned and temporarily bunded into plots of varying extent, and the water is pumped out before sowing. It is a speculative undertaking, for, if the bunds put up give way owing to some mishap, or, if the monsoon sets in very early, there is danger of the whole crop being submerged and lost. In normal seasons the outturn is good, and a good kōle harvest saves the State from the effects of a bad harvest in other fields. There has been of late an improvement in the methods of draining the lakes, as steam engine is used instead of the primitive water wheels. The sowing begins in Makaram and the harvest in Mēṭam or Eṭavam.

All lands in the State may broadly be divided into wet lands and *parambas*. Of the former, those situated on the margin of the back-waters are generally embanked for rice cultivation, and they afford much scope for reclamations and improvements. As these lands are submerged under salt water, their cultivation is taken up only after the showers of rain diminish the brackishness of the water. The soil is clayey and brackish; and ploughing is out of the question. The cultivation is carried on in the simplest way possible. The fields are dug up into square or rectangular plots, each a square yard or two in area, and sprouted seeds are sown over these plots and covered over with the same soil; in a few days, they take root and grow into luxurious plants. In other fields, sowing begins in May, a few weeks before the monsoon. There are some fields which give two and three crops, but the salt water fields give only one crop. A good harvest depends upon the timely showers of rain, as the plants are otherwise scorched by the sun, and the water is rendered more brackish. Leaves, cattle-dung and ashes are the chief kinds of manure."

Major Walker in his *Report on the Land Tenures of Malabar* observes that, "There is grown in Malabar upwards of fifty kinds of *nellu* or paddy, which have different periods of reaping and sowing, and which are distinguished by the natives for their different qualities." He then gives a list of those grains, with the season of their sowing, reaping and time of vegetation.

There are certain ceremonial observances at the first sowing of paddy in the year observed by those who are agriculturists by profession. The agricultural year commences with Vişhu which falls on the first of Mēṭam (April-May). The village astrologer or kaṉiyān is consulted to fix an auspicious day for the turning of the first sod of the season, on which day the master of the house provides himself with a variety of seeds in small baskets made of the leaves of the Kānjiram (*nux vomica*). These are placed in the yard beside a lighted lamp and a heap of rice. A pair of bullocks as also a new plough-share fastened to a plough are brought, and these are adorned with rice flour mixed in water. These are then carried to the field in procession where

HARVESTING PADDY.

To face page 98.]

the headman of the Pulayas or agrestic slaves raises a small mound of earth whereon some manure and seeds are thrown. The cattle are then yoked to the plough and a square piece of ground is ploughed. A few furrows are made and care is taken that the plough is dropped towards the right side. As at every ceremony, the god Gaṇapaṭi is invoked and offerings made to him, after which the master sows the seed in the furrows already made, the head Pūlaya in the meanwhile praying for a good season, a plentiful harvest and health and prosperity to his master and his family. A cocoanut is then broken on the ploughshare and, according as it breaks into exact halves or otherwise, the nature of the forthcoming harvest is predicted. If the two halves are exactly equal, it forbodes a moderately good harvest. If the hind portion is larger than the front one, it means an excellent harvest. If the cut passes through the eye of the cocoanut or if all the water within is spilt in the process, it bodes misfortune. The two halves after breaking are taken with the water in them and a leaf of the ṭulasi plant (*ocimum sanctum*) is put into each. This is another means of ascertaining what is in store for the agriculturist. If the ṭulasi turns to the right, it means a prosperous harvest, if to the left, the contrary. The party disperses after distributing the unused seed amongst the workmen, and the ceremony closes.

Of the agricultural festivals observed in Malabar, Nira, Para and Puṭṭari are noticed elsewhere. There is one ceremony, Uchāral, which may appropriately be described here. It is that which proclaims the end of the agricultural season and comes on at the end of the month of Makaram (January-February). The second crop of the year will have been harvested by the time, and, as the hot season commences now, Bhūmi Ḍēvi, the goddess of earth, retires to take rest till the rains set in. "At the beginning of this period, the Malayāli observes a festival in honour of the goddess' menstruations which, like the Roman Februria, are supposed to take place at this time. On the last three days, during which all granaries are closed, paddy is not sold and no implement of agriculture is touched. Even the rice to be eaten during these days is pounded before hand. On the first day, before the evening, the granary is closed, some thorns and shrubs of broom being fixed to the door with cow-dung and some ashes spread in front of it. The next two days are holidays for all: the house must not be swept, nor the floors smeared with cow-dung, and even the garden may not be swept or watered. On the fourth day, the granary is opened and a basketful of leaves is taken to the field and burnt with a little manure, perhaps to indicate that the cultivator remains in possession. Uchāral is the date on which all agricultural leases should expire, and demands for surrender of property cannot be made at any other time; but, by a liberal interpretation, the courts have extended the term to the day of Vishu. Special Uchāral festivals are held at Chērpplaššēry in the Walluvanāḍ Taluk and near Shoranur at which straw models of cattle are taken in procession to the temples of Bhagavaṭi."[1]

14. **Prices at the period.** Forbes in 1770 makes the same remark as that of this writer. He says that, "in the rainy season, when no ships frequent the port, a turkey cost only half a rupee, fowls and ducks in proportion; the beef, though small, was well flavoured and very cheap; as were fruit, vegetables and other refreshments for the numerous vessels which touch there in the fair season."[2] But later on Anqutail Du Perron (1757- 1758) found living in the hotel at Cochin much too expensive, and had to remove himself to the private quarters of the Carmelite missionary, Father Anastase, who resided in Muttancherry, and share with

1. Malabar Gazetteer, pp. 149--60.
2. Oriental Memoirs, p. 207.

him his primitive domicile of two rooms and his simple fare of eggs and rice.

15. **Animal food.** Not only in Malabar, but in all India, the Brahmans have a mortal abhorrence to animal food of any kind, and make use of nothing that has had life. This aversion to animal food is affected by other castes also in Malabar, notably by those among the Nairs who, forgetting for the moment who and what they are, assume an air of caste-superiority over their fellow-men, and pretend to despise all animal food. Even among the Brahmans, the eschewing of animal food is the outcome of the later development of Brahmanism as distinguished from Hinduism. The Hindus of the Vēḍic age, irrespective of caste or class, whether they were of the priestly order or not, were originally no strangers to flesh eating. "Elaborate rules," says Mr. R. C. Dutt, "have been laid down in the Sūṭrās on the subject of food; and animals and birds which may be used as food have been carefully distinguished from those which should not be so used. Beef was still used as an article of food, but was gradually falling into disuse on account of the growing disinclination to kill animals except at sacrifices. On this point Dr. Bhuler has drawn attention to a remarkable passage from Manu's Ḍhaṙma Sūṭṙa, which has been quoted by Vasiṣhṭa. Manu's Ḍhaṙma Sūṭṙa exists no longer, having been replaced by the later metrical code of Manu, which is no doubt based on the older Ḍhaṙma Sūṭrās."[1]

The flesh of animals occupied a most prominent place at domestic ceremonies among the early Hindus, for instance with regard to Annaprāśana or the first feeding of the child with solid food. Aśvalāyana and Sānkhyāyana prescribe various sorts of food, viz., "Goats' flesh, if he is desirous of nourishment; flesh of partridge, if desirous of holy lustre; boiled rice

1. Ancient India, Vol. II, p. 104.

with ghee, if desirous of splendour." According to Parāśara, "Flesh of the bird called Bharawaji, if he wishes fluency of speech; fish if swiftness was desired etc." So also at the Aṣhṭaka ceremony.[1]

With the early Hindus, it was no sacrilege to eat beef. In a very learned paper on "Beef in Ancient India", Dr. Rajendra Lala Mitra has pointed out that the slaughter of animals formed an essential part in several religious rites. In the autumn or spring season, a ceremony was performed called Śūlagava or "spitted cow," i., e., roast beef. Another ceremony was known as a Gavāṃanayana, or the sacrifice of the cow, otherwise called ēkāṣhṭakā. So there are other rites such as the Atiratra, the Niruḍha Paśubanḍha which required the sacrifice of a cow or an ox. The Maḍhupaṙka or honey-meat, which was offered to a respectable guest,—a priest, king, bridegroom or Vēḍic student, a teacher, a father-in-law, an uncle or a man of rank,—had to be accompanied with the sacrifice of a cow in honour of the guest. Numerous passages in the Rig Vēḍa point to the fact that beef was a common article of food with men, and as such a favourite offering to the gods. Speaking of Inḍṙa, Muir in his Sanskrit Texts says:[2] "He is also spoken of as eating the flesh of bulls, or buffaloes, at the same time that he drinks the draughts of Sōma." From the fact of these animals being offered in sacrifice, it may perhaps be inferred that they also formed a portion of human food.[3]

Not only in the Vēḍic age, but even in the Epic Period, animal food was freely used. Mr. R. C. Dutt points out that in the Aiṭaṙēya Brāhmaṇa, 1, 15, we learn that an ox or a cow which miscarries is killed when a king or an honoured guest is received. The

1. Ancient India, Vol. II, pp. 112—123.
2. Vol. V, p. 90.
3. Ibid, p. 463.

Brāhmaṇa of the Black Yajur Vēḍa discusses the kind and character of the cattle which should be slaughtered in minor sacrifices, and details are laid down. Thus a dwarf one is to be sacrificed to Vişhṇu, a drooping horned bull to Inḍra, a thick legged cow to Vāyu, a barren cow to Vişhṇu and Varuṇa, a black cow to Pūşhan, a cow having two colours to Miṭra and Varuṇa, a red cow to Inḍra &c. [1]

But it has to be noted that from very early times an undercurrent of feeling made itself felt against eating beef—a feeling based evidently, not only on utilitarian but also on aesthetic grounds. Thus we read in the Śaṭapaṭha Brāhmaṇa :—

"Let him not eat (the flesh) of either the cow or the ox; for the cow and the ox doubtless support everything here on earth. The gods spoke : 'Verily, the cow and the ox support everything here: come, let us bestow on the cow and the ox whatever vigour belongs to other species (of animals).' Accordingly they bestowed on the cow and the ox whatever vigour belonged to other species (of animals); and therefore the cow and the ox eat most. Hence, were one to eat (the flesh) of an ox or a cow, there would be, as it were, an eating of everything, or, as it were, a going on to the end (or to destruction). Such a one indeed would be likely to be born (again) as a strange being (as one of whom there is) evil report, such as, 'he has expelled an embryo from a women,' 'he has committed a sin,' let him therefore not eat (the flesh) of the cow and the ox. Nevertheless, Yagnavalkya said, 'I for one, eat it, provided that it is tender.' "[2]

Though Āpasṭamba[3] was no supporter of bovine life and sanctioned the eating of the meat of milch-

1. Ancient India. Vol. I, pp. 253—4.
2. Sacred Books of the East. Vol. XXVI, p. 11.
3. Ibid. Vol. II, p. 64. Apastamba 1, 5, 17, 30.

cows and oxen, Gauṭama expressly prohibits it; and though Yagnavalkya relished it, provided that it was tender, he lays down directions for expiating the sin caused by the slaughter of a cow.

Dr. Rajendra Lala Mitra thinks that the use of the beef as food fell into disuse when sacrifices themselves went out, and that, with the extreme solicitude for animal life that formed the most marked characteristic of Buddhism, it was finally abandoned.[1] There are evident traces of the influence of Buddhism in Southeren India on the West Coast from very early times.

The cow soon came to be regarded as a sacred animal and with good reason, regard being had "to the utility of the animal to man and the claim to motherhood from the milk which sustained the breeder." As pointed out by Dr. Schroeder in his *Prehistoric Antiquities of the Aryan People*, "the cow, which, like the bull, is intimately connected with the Indo-European mythology, has during her life-time a double significance. On the one hand, she is the milk-giving creature (Skt. ḍhēnu), on the other, she is especially the beast of burden and draught of the primitive age. In Gauṭama's time, the cow's life was considered so sacred that in battles men cried quarter by calling themselves cows, and the cry was respected. No sin is committed by injuring or slaying foes in battle, excepting those who declare themselves to be cows or Brahmans"[2].

The doctrine of metempsychosis, which was imported into the Hindu religion at a later stage of its development, also acted as a strong deterrent to the use of animal food. Belief in the transmigration of souls engenders in the Hindu a tenderness for animal life in every animated creature, none being thought too minute or too low to contain the soul of

1. Jour: A. S. B. XLI—Part. 1, p. 174 *et seq.*
2. Gautama, Sacred Books of the East, Vol. II, p. 226, Note.

a dear departed parent or relative. Fra Bartolomeo relates that, in his time, "King Rama Vurmar of Travancore forbade fishing in the river at Anjengo for some days after the death of the king's mother, lest any fish into which the royal soul had transmigrated might be caught and killed."[1] Two centuries before Bartolomeo, Varthema speaks to the same observance at Calicut where, on the death of the king, "the fishermen were not allowed to catch any fish for eight days."[2] Purchas too in his quaint way attributes the worship of the cow to the "supposition that the souls of men departed do most of all enter these beasts."[3]

In the 17th century, a similar superstitious belief seems to have been prevalent in England. Count Cominges, French Ambassador in England, writes in his *Relation de l' Angleterre en l' annee (1666)*: "Fish, oysters, deer are plentiful; so are ravens which peasants forbear killing, some because they think them useful for the soil by their feeding on 'vermin'; others, more simpletons, because they fancy that the soul of King Arthur animates a raven, and that they might by mischance deprive of life of the greatest king who ever ruled over their country."[4]

Forbes, in his *Oriental Memoirs*, says that, "One of the principal reasons for the Hindus regarding the cow with such religious veneration, is, that they believe that the soul transmigrated into that animal immediately preceding its assumption of the human form."[5] Fra Bartolomeo observes "that, when near the point of death, they (the Pagans) take in their hands a cow's tail, and, according to their belief, if they die in this

1. P. 144.
2. P. 144.
3. P. 625.
4. Nineteenth Century and After for April 1914, p. 788.
5. Vol. I, p. 44.

N.

manner, they are immediately transported to paradise."[1] In letter XXVII our author also refers to this. "When a native is dying, he takes hold of the tail of a cow which is brought alive to his bed-side: and some imagine that by doing so they are conducted to heaven. Thus the cow's tail serves much the same purpose to them, as wax tapers to the members of the Romish Church." Evidently these writers are referring to the gift of a cow to a Brahman, made by the dying man at his last breath, and considered to be a meritorious conclusion of one's career in this world.

In Malabar, the sacredness of the cow is supreme. As Grose observes, "They (the Hindus) purify themselves with its urine; they burn its execrement into a greyish powder, with which they sprinkle their foreheads, breasts, and bellies; they also, when the dung is recent, make a compost of it with which they smear their houses, pavements and the sides of them in the style of a lustration. In short, so excessive is their veneration for this animal, that there could hardly be a Gentoo found, that, if under a forced option to kill father, mother, or children, or a cow, would not with scarce a hesitation prefer sacrificing any or all of the former."[2]

According to Manu XI, 60, the killing of a cow is only an Upapāṭaka, a minor sin, and verses 109 &c. lay down rules for expiating the sin. The penance prescribed by Gauṭama[3] for killing a cow is the same as that for the murder of a Vaiśya. Yagnavalkya considers it a minor sin, and lays down directions similar to those prescribed by Manu.[4] Even Āpasṭamba, who was no respector of the sacredness of the life of the bovine race, declares that the same

1. P. 23.
2. Voyage to the East Indies, 1766, vol. I, pp. 184-5.
3. Chap. XXII, 18.
4. Yagnavalkya III, pp. 263-264. Mandalik's Edn. p. 171.

penance as for the killing of a Śūḍṛa must be performed "if a milch-cow or a full grown ox (has been slain) without a reason. A reason for hurting a cow is, according to Hara Ḍaṭṭa, anger, or the desire to obtain meat. In a general note, appended to Sir William Jone's translation of Manu, reference is made to an extract from Maḍana Raṭna Pṛaḍīpa which quotes a text of a Smṛṭi declaring the slaughter of a ḅull at a sacrifice to be not permissible in the present Kali age.[1]

In Malabar, cow-killing has always been reckoned a criminal offence, and in some of the Hindu States of the coast, at least in Cochin, it is still penal, though no specific punishment is prescribed by law for it. Purchas, writing in the 16th century, says:—"The soldiers are Nairs, none of which can be imprisoned or put to death by ordinary justice; but if one of them kill another, or else kill a *cow* * * * * the king after information gives his warrant to another Nair who, with his associates, kill him wherever they find him, hewing him with their swords, and then hang on him his warrant to testify the cause of his death."[2] According to Barbosa, the culprit had to undergo the ordeal of the oil before the punishment of death was inflicted, so that he had a doubtful chance of escape if he came out of the ordeal unscathed.[3] "In those provinces wḥere these Pagans have superiority," says Bartolomeo, "he who kills a cow is punished as a murderer. I once saw five natives of Malabar suspended from a tree in a forest near Ambalapuḷa (Travancore) on account of this supposed crime."[4] Even the ill-treatment of the cow, much more the selling of the animal for slaughter, was penal. Mr. Forbes observes that a subject of Travancore who is detected in selling a bullock to a European for slaughter is impaled alive.[5]

1. Sir. W. Jones' works, Vol. I. Cal. Ed. 1874, p. 353.
2. P. 627.
3. P. 118.
4. P. 284.
5. P. 238.

Writing in the early years of the 19th century, Hamilton gives an instance of the ludicrous extent to which veneration for the cow is carried in Travancore. He says, among other cases which came before the Resident while acting as Diwan, was an appeal from the decision of the Kāriakār (Judge) who had directed certain property to be given up to a man on his oath. This suit being referred by the Resident to an assembly of Pandits for their opinion, they reported that the decision of the Kāriakār was correct and just; but, as the oath taken had been rendered void, owing to the death of a cow, in the house of the person who had sworn, before the term of 40 days had expired, the property must be relinquished to the opposite party."[1]

Though merely to kill a cow is a crime punished with death, our author points out later on, in his tenth letter, that "No Raja has power to sentence to execution a Brahman however serious his crime."

The Brahmans in all Hindu States, and more especially in Travancore and Cochin, where their influence is paramount, have from very early times taken care to get themselves exempted, as much as possible, from punishment; at least the sentences passed on them were far more lenient than those passed on the other castes for the same crime, and this was strictly in keeping with the ordinance of Manu. "Never shall the king slay a Brahman though convicted of all possible crimes; let him banish the offender from his realm, but with all his property secure and his body unhurt." Even now in these States they are exempt from capital punishment, however heinous or dastardly the crime they have committed be. "If it is proved," says Bartolomeo, "that a Brahman has killed a man or a *cow*, all the other Brahmans of the same Grāma or district unite against him; cut off his *cudumi* (tuft

1 Account of the East Indies, p. 311.

of hair); take from him his sash (sacred thread), deprive him of the sacerdotal dignity, and expel him from the caste. He is then put upon an ass with his face towards the tail, and in that manner conveyed beyond the boundaries of the place."[1] The very oaths that the Rajas of Malabar take at their coronation enjoined on them "to protect cows, Brahmans and women."[2] According to Purchas, the same commandment is handed down to the Nair noble when he is dubbed a knight by the king. "He is dubbed or created by the king who commandeth to gird him with a sword, and laying his right hand upon his head muttereth certain words softly, and afterward dubbeth him, saying 'Have a regard to keep these Brahmans and their kine.' These are the two great commandments of the Brahman law."[3]

It is only the twice-born, viz. the first three in the scale of Hindu castes, who are prohibited from using meat as an article of food; and, in Malabar, they alone abstain from it, though there are those among Śūḍrās who fancy it to be a praiseworthy act from a religious point of view to abstain from animal food, and do so voluntarily. There are others who, from sentimental considerations regarding the taking away of animal life, abstain from meat. A great majority of Malayalees, however, are meat-eaters. All castes below the twice-born, the Ampalavāsies alone excepted, are not prohibited from eating meat. Beef is eaten only by the Pariahs, who are outside the Hindu caste system. The Nairs partake of fish, and the flesh of all clean animals. Many of the lower classes are always not very particular about the nature of the flesh meat they use.

16. The Natural Divisions of Malabar.

With regard to Malabar, taken as a whole, two main

1. P. 229.
2. See letter 27.
3. P. 627.

natural divisions may be marked out: one, the littoral and deltaic, and the other, the mountainous and sub-montane. The deltaic region expands almost from the southern point a good way northwards, broken in upon, here and there, by hilly ranges branching from the Ghauts and coming down to the sea coast. The country lying to the west of the main watershed presents the unmistakable appearance of a plateau or of land of a terraced character, which is most prominent about Trivandrum and northwards past Cochin into the Malabar country. In British Malabar this terraced character may be best seen at Malappuram.

In North Malabar, it is most conspicuous in the Chiṙakkal Taluk, north and south of the Ṭali-paṙampa river. Mr. Logan points out that these terraces touch the sea and form low cliffs at Mount D'Eli, at Cannanore, at Ḍhaṙma Paṭṭaṇam, and Tel-licherry, and thence almost continuously on to Mahe, at Kollam near Quilāndy, and for a few miles north of it, and lastly at the Elaṭṭūr river mouths. The deltaic or littoral region is just on a level with the sea, and is marked by the extensive chain of backwaters, lagoons, marshes and canals, fed by innumerable streams and rivers that scour the country down the table-land and bring rich alluvial deposits to fertilise and enrich the low-lands. In whatever aspect we view it, whether in regard to rainfall, climatic conditions, the nature and fertility of the soil, the amount of water supply, and facilities for communication and transport, the belt of land stretching along the coast presents clear points of advantage over the regions in the interior. The scrubby growth of grass on the higher level stands in strong contrast with the luxuriant vegetation that characterises the coast-land, while there is very little on the higher level to set off against the wealth producing cocoanut tree of the coast.

17. **Mineral productions.** Malabar has but few mineral productions. Of South Travancore

A TYPICAL FOREST SCENERY.

To face page 110.]

A TYPICAL FOREST SCENERY.

To face page 111.

Mr. Bruce Foote of the Indian Geological survey observes that, "Valuable minerals and metals are conspicuous by their absence," and this remark may truly be applied to the whole of Malabar.

Gold.—It is surmised that the gold that decked Solomon's Temple in the halcyon days of Jewish sovereignity came from the Malabar Coast, whence also came the ivory, peacocks, apes and sandalwood that formed part of the cargo of Hiram's shipmen "that had knowledge of the sea."[1]

There can be no doubt that gold was at one time found in Malabar. If, as Mr. Wigram thinks, Megasthenes' Nareae can be identified with the Nairs of North Malabar[2] and Capitalia with the Camel's Hump which is 6,000 feet in height and a conspicuous landmark for mariners, then "the extensive mines of gold worked by the inhabitants living on the other side of the mountains" would be the gold mines of Wynad. Anyhow, in the name of the river Ponnāny, we have indubitable philological evidence of the existence of gold.[3] Mr. Philip Lake observes that washing for gold has been carried on in many of the rivers, principally at Nilampūr and Maṇṇārkad. The gold of Nilampūr has attracted a good deal of attention.[4] There is no doubt that the sands of many of the rivers of South Malabar are highly auriferous, but the source of the

1. See Dr. Caldwell's Comparative Grammar of the Dravidian Languages, Introduction to. Dr. Burnell's Elements of South Indian Paleography, 1st Edn., p. 5.

Dr. G. Oppert's Lecture on the Ancient Commerce of India, p. 25.

Rev. Richard Collins—Missionary Enterprise in the East, p. 39.

Ind: Ant., Vol. 1, p. 230.

2. See Introduction, Malabar Law and Custom.

3. Compare the words Ponmudi, Ponmana, Ponnoorkode in all of which place-names the prefix *Pon* denotes gold.

4. A short account of it will be found in the Manual of the Geology of India, Vol. III, p. 180, *et seq.*

gold must be looked for higher up, in the Wynad and in the ranges of the Aṭṭapāḍy Valleys.[1] It is worthy of note that *Ponnarippu*,—a tax on "washing for gold"—was one of the sources of revenue of the early Malabar Rajahs.

As desired by the Travancore Government, Mr. King of the Indian Geological Survey once conducted a searching examination of the regions supposed to present the most favourable indications of the existence of gold-bearing rocks, *viz.*, in the neighbourhood of Malappāra, Koññiūr and other localities in the hill plateau. Mr. King reported that the supposed reefs were to all appearance of nearly pure quartz rock, occurring with the other strata of gneiss series, and that, though they locally gave the very faintest traces of gold, there was no reason to expect that better results would be obtained if worked on a commercial basis. Practically there are no auriferous quartz reefs, as usually understood, in the area pointed out, neither did he expect that such would be found in those parts of Travancore he was able to visit.[2]

Iron.—There is a good deal of iron ore of excellent quality throughout Malabar. In the 18th century, Fra Bartolomeo was told by Mr. Hutchinson, the English agent at Anjengo, that the hills round Varkalay and Kaṭhinamkulam in Travancore contained abundance of iron. There are in the locality some pure beautiful springs of water supposed to possess excellent medicinal properties and frequently resorted to by the people. "The water seam supplying the springs on the seashore," says Dr. King, "was tapped by the tunnel operations, and there was a slight temporary decrease in their discharge. The leaking of the water in the tunnels and at the cuttings over the freshly opened alum clays, and the mixture of ferruiginous

1. Memoirs. Geo: Sur: of Ṣouth Malabar, p. 38.
2. Records of Geological Survey of India for 1882, p. 87.

waste from above, thus gave rise to considerable surmise as to the existence of natural chalybeate and other waters. Such are, however, only produced temporarily, though they will be collecting for a long time, and they might be found efficacious in some cases of the skin diseases so common on this coast."[1] It is, however, noteworthy that the springs in the vicinity of Varkalay were resorted to long before the tunnels were thought of. Of iron in South Travancore, the State Geologist reports:—"Of the ores of this metal, magnetite occurs in the Yeddamalay Hills. A search for a vein or a bed failed. The mineral is in small grains disseminated throughout the rocks forming the main mass of the hills. During rains, the decomposed portions of the rocks are carried down the hills, and by the time they reach the plains, the particles become separated, and by the natural sifting action of the running water, owing to its weight, the black magnetite is left behind, largely mixed with quartz grains, in ravines, gullies and brooks.

"More than sixty years ago, this was gathered by the people of the neighbouring village of Marungoor, adopting the method now in vogue at Cape Comorin for the separation of garnet, the magnetite was recovered and smelted for iron and steel. This must have been done on a large scale, judging from the great amount of slag found near Marungoor and Kamadesanbudoor. The mineral, as seen in the sand, is one of the best ores of iron. The supply however is inconstant, and there is no fuel to work it profitably. In these days of cheap imported steel, it is too much to hope for the revival of this industry in South Travancore.

"This mineral is also found in the slopes of the Murtwa Hills".[2]

1. Record of the Geological Survey of India for 1882, Vol. XV, p. 99. Note.

2. P. 8.

Early in the 19th century (1800 A. D.), the native iron works of Vellāṙṙūṙ, in South Malabar, were noticed by Dr. Buchanan, who gives a description of the crude method of their working. He says that in all the hills of the country the ore is found forming beds, veins, or detached masses, in the stratum of indurated clay found in great abundance in the hills of Malabar.[1] The ore is composed of clay, quartz in the form of sand, and of the common black iron sand.[2] Since the days of Dr. Buchanan, various attempts have been made to establish on this coast iron works on a large scale; but with little or no success, the failure being due chiefly to want of fuel. However, iron ore is at present found in the Porūr Amśam of the Ēṙnāḍ Taluk, and formerly at Chembrēri and Pāṇḍikāḍ. The iron is said to be of very good quality, but the workmen seem not to know how to make steel. Mr. Philip Lake observes, "In Walluvanāḍ Taluk, mines are now worked in Nemini and Ṭochampāra amśams: but, some time ago, there were mines in Mangaṭa, Aṙakkapaṙampa, Mēlāṙṙūr, and Veṭṭāṙṙūr. The ore used is sometimes magnetite and sometimes hoematite. In Mangaṭa the old mines are in laterite, and do not reach downward to the unlateretised part of the gneiss. In Aṙakkapaṙampa the ore is found in a quartz run, and the upper surface of the ore is lateretised. In Nemini the ore is magnetite, and occurs in crystals in the gneiss."[3]

Other minerals.—In Travancore besides iron graphite, lignite, alum and sulphur also exist. In many places in the Neḍuvangāḍ Taluk, plumbago mines are worked at present; and an interesting account of the working of the graphite will be found in the Manual of the Administration of the Madras

1. Mr. King also notices this kind of clay in Travancore.
2. Canara and Malabar, Vol. II, p. 113.
3. Geo. Sur. Mem., p. 37.

Presidency. Plumbago is found also in the Taluks of Iraṇiel and Ṭōvāla.

"Next in importance to plumbago," says the State Geologist, "new to the State and probably to the whole of India comes a remarkable occurrence of pyrrhotine in the Valley Hills in the Ṭōvāla Taluk. This mineral, as far as the present indications go, occurs in a large mass almost unmixed with any other veistones, rising out of the surrounding gniesses. Most probably it extends to a great depth." Again, "India being rather poor in sulphur, if it can be proved that this mineral pyrrhotine extends on a large scale in Travancore, the Government may be sure of a steady income in the near future, as sulphur from this compound is easily separated by simple roasting, and cheap sulphuric acid can be manufactured directly." The State Geologist has also reported the presence of nickel in the massive pyrrhotine in the Ṭōvāla Taluk.

Salt is manufactured at Rājakkaḷamangalam and Ṭāmarakkuḷam both in South Travancore. Mica has also been recently found. "North of the parallel of Trivandrum there are stronger occurrences of granite, in which," says the Geological Record, "mica is abundant and in largest masses."[1]

Precious stones.—Precious stones were known to exist in Malabar in early days—at any rate, in those countries which constituted the early Chēra or Kēraḷa kingdom. The Periplus of the Eurythrean Sea mentions gems (carbuncles?) as being exported in large quantities from Muziris (Cranganore or Koḍungallūr) and Nilkanda (Kallada near Quilon).[2]

Speaking of Kāñjirapilli, a town in North Travancore once celebrated for its trade with Madura, Fra Bartolomeo says, "In the mountains there are found

1. Volume XV., p. 90.
2. Mc Crindle, pp. 34 to 36.

diamonds, sapphires, opals, rock crystals. We are informed by Ptolemy that in his time also these were found near Pūnjāṟṟil (not far from Kānjirappiḷḷi), but they must now be exceedingly scarce, for I was acquainted at Barcale (Varkalay) with several Brahman families who had expended their whole fortunes in searching for precious stones and by these means had reduced themselves to poverty."[1]

Again, "Precious stones are found * * in the neighbourhood of the Ghauts, particularly in the districts of Pūnjāṟṟil, Śencōṭṭa, Āṟṟinga and Vēlidūr (all in Travancore) on the Coast of Malabar. The Brahmans and other opulent persons are accustomed to purchase from the king certain pieces of land where they expect to find these valuable stones, and to dig for them at their own expense. But this is a very hazardous undertaking which very frequently does not defray the expenses, and by which many families in India are reduced to beggary."[2]

The diamond spar, employed for polishing these stones is found in great abundance on the Coast of Malabar. The art of cutting precious stones was also well-known in the country, and we read that, in the days of Fra Bartolomeo, "the king of Travancore had a seal ring set with a valuable stone on which was cut the words 'Srī Paḍmanābhan', the name of the king's family deity. Vimila Dharma Surdadu, the king of Ceylon, who became a convert to Christianity, and was at baptism given the name of Don John of Austria by the Portuguese, had a similar ring with him, on which Buddha was represented in human form."[3]

In Travancore, garnets were plentiful and Mr. King says regarding them, "In fact one might say that Travancore is essentially a country of garnetiferous

1. Pp. 118--119.
2. P. 392.
3. Pp. 394--395.

gneisses. The garnets themselves are only locally obtainable, it being impossible to break them from the living rock, while they are generally decomposed or weathered. They are generally of small size, but are very rich in colour, the precious garnet being very common. Other minerals, such as red, blue, and yellow sapphire and jacinth, are found among the garnet sands so common on the seashore at certain places. The seasands are also full of titaniferous iron grains. While on this subject I may instance the beautiful and long known constitution of the shore sands at Cape Comorin, where on the beach, may be seen the strangest coloured streaks or ribbons of good width, of bright scarlet, black, purple, yellow and white sands of all these minerals and the ordinary silica."[1] These sands are now a source of income to the Government of Travancore, who levy a royalty for its removal, and great quantities are being shipped from Comorin. The finer sort of sand is used by goldsmiths in polishing gold, and there is an ever increasing demand for it. Of the sand on the seashore at Comorin the State Geologist says, " The shore at the Cape is almost unique in India in its abundance of the sands which, in their variety of colours—red, white and black—and in the shape the grains take, make the spot a place of attraction to many in Travancore; people from outside have not failed to admire the beauty of the sand on the shore.

" Of the three varieties—red, white and black, all of different composition—the red is the most useful consisting, as it does, chiefly of garnet, a valuable abrasive in the absence of corundum and emery which are higher than garnet in the scale of hardness. There is a fairly brisk trade at the Cape in this sand which is being exported for making grinding wheels, artificial whet stones, etc. It is sent to Alleppey chiefly, whence it is forwarded to Bombay; the final destination is not known.

1. P. 89.

"Garnet is found in abundant quantities in South Travancore, being a conspicuous constituent of the rocks. All the brooks and the rivers carry small particles of this mineral, and, where the current is not strong, they deposit it in their beds. Whereas, inland, in river beds and gullies, the garnet sand is mixed very much with quartz, felspar, ilmenite and magnetite grains, at the Cape, owing to the nature of the currents and the shifting action of the waves, they are separated and deposited at different spots. It is but natural that the red sand should shift its position almost hourly, and in different parts of the year. At certain times, it disappears altogether; this I say with reserve, my authorities being those who gather the sand.

"The garnet sand is mixed with varying proportions of quartz, felspar, ilmenite and broken shells of marine organisms. It is usually separated by letting down the sand in a stream against the wind; garnet, being heavy, falls almost vertically, whilst others are carried forward. Where there is a large amount of ilmenite, it is useless to attempt this method, as this mineral is as heavy as garnet. A woman is usually in charge of this operation and earns 7 chuckrams (4 as. 8 ps.) for a cart load of ten sacks, each sack being 1½ cwt. To carry the sand from the beach to the cart in the road, a woman is paid one chuckram (7 ps.) each sack, and she usually earns eight chuckrams a day. Young girls get generally about half of it. The man who gathers the sand gets on the average 7 chuckrams a day.

"For trading purposes the sand is placed in three different classes:—(1) almost pure red sand; (2) red sand with some quartz; (3) red sand mixed with quartz and other minerals which have not been separated. The prices paid at Koṭṭaṙ, which seems to be the centre of this trade, are 2 Rs., 16 chuckrams and 14 chuckrams a sack respectively. The working expenses, calculating for a cart load of 10 sacks, amount to Rs. 2 and 3 chuckrams. Under exceptional circumstances, expenses may amount to Rs. 2—7 chuckrams. The selling price for a cart load of the first class article is Rs. 20, and the trader thus makes a profit of Rs. 17¾. In case of class II, taking the working expenses as Rs. 2, as not much of shifting is done, the profit amounts to Rs. 3 chuckrams 20. In case of III, the working expenses are still less as no separation of the red sand seems to be attempted. The total may amount to Re. 1 and 21 chuckrams and the trader has a clear gain of Rs. 2 and 7 chuckrams. The export duty is three chuckrams a cwt., irrespective of the variety of sand, and, as each cart has generally 15 cwts., the Government is benefited to the extent of Re. 1 and 17 chuckrams for each cart-load of sand exported.

"The value of the garnet sand at Cape Comorin is probably enhanced by the presence of 'bright scarlet, black, purple, yellow and white sands,' of ilmenite, sapphire and jacinth.[1] At the time Dr. King made his report, more than twenty-six years ago, the more modern methods of separation and analysis by heavy liquids,—a procedure now in vogue, especially in the preparation for analysis of sands of composite character—was unknown, and accordingly his statement must be taken with some reserve. The presence of jacinth or zircon is easily accounted for as a particular class of rocks in South Travancore has this mineral as one of the constituents. If an analysis reveals the presence of sapphire, a thorough search must be made for this valuable gem. The result of the analysis now being made for me in London by Mr. Gurnnell is anxiously waited for."

The State Geologist classes the garnet of South Travancore among the "inaccessible or insufficient minerals." He says, "The mineral which forms the characteristic constituents of the rocks in South Travancore when it is transparent and of the right colour is freely

1. Dr. King's Report, Records of the Geological Survey of India, Vol. XV, Part 2.

used as a gem, especially the variety known as *almandine*; this is cut *en cabochon* with a hollow at the back to receive a bit of foil. The range of colour lies between a violet or purple to brownish red or reddish brown. The crimson or the fiery red variety is found in the rocks in South Travancore. But till a method is devised for separating it from the main mass without damage, it must remain where it is. Very often it is picked up amidst debris of decomposed rock masses and in slopes of hills and are then passed off for rubies by the local jewellers."[1]

Among the "inaccessible or insufficient minerals of economic value" are mentioned (1) garnet (2) pyrites (3) jasper and (4) iron. Among those "reported to be present" are (1) mica in large quantity at Eraniel (2) antimony in the Ashamboo Hills (3) ruby in the Ashamboo Hills and (4) coal. With regard to the last, the State Geologist says, "This is nothing but lignite * * * All reports of coal in South Travancore must be set aside as inventions."

18. **Seismic Influences.**—Seismic influences cannot be said to be altogether unheard of or unknown in Malabar. Not to mention the natural convulsion that raised the land of Malabar from beneath the sea-level, there have been more recent instances of changes brought on apparently by subterranean forces. The island of Vypīn, lying just to the north of the harbour at Cochin, is an instance in point, it having been thrown up by the sea about the year 1341 A. D., from which date people in the vicinity have commenced an era known as *Puthuvaippu* (Puṭuvaippu) or new formation. There are no volcanoes in Malabar, but earthquakes are not unfrequent. There are clear evidences of "unstable equilibrium" all along the coast-line. The sea at Alleppey is considerably further from the town than it was but a few years ago, which shows that the shore is rising: the same is the case at Cochin to an extent that, we think, can scarcely be accounted

1. P. 8.

for by accumulating sand, while to the north of Cochin the sea is evidently encroaching, and in some parts has for years caused great destruction of property. At Ṭṛkkuṅṅappuḻa in Travancore, the sea was more than a couple of miles away from the shore till a few years ago, and the ruins of a splendid temple that was washed away by the sea were visible distinctly within the memory of those now living. Captain Hamilton in the 17th century found the remains of a fort out in the sea at Poṟakāḍ near Alleppey. "We are not altogether strangers in Kēraḷa (Malabar) to the shocks of earthquakes," remarks a writer in the *Kottayam College Magazine.* "In 1856 specially, repeated shocks were felt: in 1823, 1841 and 1845, shocks have been recorded at Trivandrum. In several cases the shocks have seemed to have been promulgated from the north-west: and in September 1856, a ball of a pendulum in the Trivandrum Observatory, 17 feet long, is recorded to have been moved about four inches in the direction N. W. by N. and S. E. by S., which is about the direction of the coast line."[1] So recently as October 1899, a sharp shock was felt all through Malabar.[2]

Fra Bartolomeo remarks, "Though water has the superiority in Malayāḷa and the whole land is in a

1. P. 5.

2. Earthquakes noticed at Trivandrum:—Logan's Manual, Vol. I, pp. 34-35.

February 1823.
September 19, 1841.
November 20, 1845.
March 17, 1856.
August 11, 1856-5 h. 51 m. 25 s. A. M.
August 22, 1856--0 h. 15 m. 10 s. P. M. and
September 1, 1856--0 h. 15 m. 0 s. P. M.

At Calicut:

31st December 1881--7-10 A. M. (Madras time).
28th February 1882 about 6-16 A. M. (Madras time).
14th October 1882--2 P. M.

manner inundated, traces may be found amidst it of earthquakes, and also, though seldom, of the effects produced by electric fire. In the month of December 1784 (not very long after our author wrote his letters), a general agitation of the earth was perceived there in the night time, which continued about two seconds. Such a phenomenon is called in the Malabar language *Bhoomikulukkam* (Bhūmikulukkam), and in the Sanskrit *Bhoochalana* (Bhūchalana). The mountains of Barcale (Vařkalay) and Kidaculam (Kaṭhinamkuḷam) which contain a great deal of iron and other highly inflamable substances, are, in all probability, the principal reservoirs which give rise to such concussions in the earth.''[1] "I can with justice assert,' continues the Carmelite Father, "that the hypothesis respecting the effect of electric fire on water is very well known to the Brahmans, as to other Indian philosophers, and by its means they are able to account for many phenomena, the nature of which would otherwise be inexplicable. According to their doctrine, the *Oruma*, that is, the union or peaceful combination of the elements, particularly of water and fire, preserves the equilibrium and tranquillity of all created things. The *Arima*, on the other hand, that is, discord and enmity of the elements, particularly of water and fire, occasions contentions, convulsions, and explosions, by which the earth, the atmosphere, and the sea, are thrown into the most violent agitation. As long as the *Oruma* takes place between the elements, they remain peaceful and quiet; but when the fire obtains the superiority, the *Arima* instantly begins, and occasions earthquakes, volcanic eruptions, thunder and lightning; in a word everything that the Brahman comprehended under the words *Gvalana* and *Svalana* which signify inflamation, combustion, and the other effects of fire.''[2]

---

1. P. 454.
2. Pages. 45, 47, 48.

PERSONS SUFFERING FROM ELEPHANTIASIS.

To face page 123.]

LETTER II.

1. **Indigenous Disorders.** Our author gives a sufficiently fair description of elephantiasis as prevalent in Malabar. It is generally known as "Cochin-leg"; just as the goitre came to be known as the Derbyshire neck, because of its prevalence in that country, elephantiasis came to be called the "Cochin-leg", because of its being very common in Cochin. Not long after our author wrote his letters from Cochin, Ives referred to it, observing, " We could not but take notice at this place (Cochin) of a great number of the Cochin or Elephant legs."[1] Writing about Cochin, Mr. Forbes says, "I have seen many with a leg thicker than their body: on the naked limb of the natives it has a disagreeable appearance; to the leg of a European, with a silk stocking, a shoe and a buckle something ludicrous is added.[2] Dr. Day found as many as 5 per cent. of the entire native and European population of the town of Cochin to be affected by elephantiasis. Males and females are about equally affected and children as young as four years, though it is unusual before 15 or 16. It is regarded as a family disgrace, and is much dreaded.[3]

In Travancore, the Census Commisioner, Dr. Subrahmanya Iyer, reports:—' Elephantiasis have been returned from 22 (out of 31) Taluks, though the instructions issued related only to two. The total number enumerated is 5,924—3,522 males and 2,402 females. The Taluks of greatest prevalence are, of course, Shērṭṭalay (Chērṭṭale) and to a much smaller extent Ampalappuḻa, the relative ratio being 8:1. While one in every 27 persons, or a little less than 5 per cent.,

1. Voyages, 1757 A. D., p. 193.
2. Vol. 1, pp. 207—208.
3. Land of the Perumāls, p. 426.

as Dr. Day has estimated, is afflicted with elephantiasis in the Taluk of Shērṭṭalay, about 194 persons have to be examined on an average to detect one case of elephantiasis in the adjoining Taluk of Ampalappuḻa. Next to these Taluks comes the mountainous Taluk of Paṭṭanāpuram with 27 elephantoid cases. In all the other Taluks, except Trivandrum, where we have 7 cases, most of them probably forming part of the floating population of the capital, the number is 5 or below 5."[1]

Its geographical distribution indicates more or less its origin also. The littoral region, lying along the swampy lowlands of the coast where the ground is damp and the water-supply bad, is the home of the disease. As the ground ascends towards the terraced plateau in the east, it decreases in proportion, and, as you reach the higher level of the Ghauts, it disappears altogether. And yet the mountainous tracts cannot be said to be entirely free from it; for instance, Paṭṭanāpuram stands out as an exception to this theory.

"The Taluk of Shērṭṭalay," says the Travancore Census Commissioner, "where, according to Dr. Waring, (1855), 2,133 out of a population of 48,591 or 1 in 23 had elephantiasis, is an instance of this kind. 'It is an ideal mosquito district. The yearly rainfall is 100 inches, the land is lowlying, water-logged, swampy and full of creeks. There are hardly any wells, the people obtaining their water from shallow pools and tanks. Northern Orissa, where elephantiasis is also extremely common, seems to have similar physical features; and a like description applies to large districts in Bengal and elsewhere where elephantiasis is extremely endemic'.[2] The converse, however, is not true. There are many mountainous islands in the eastern Archipelago, in the South Pacific and in the Indian Ocean, such as Sumatra, the Fiji islands, Mauritius and

1. P. 245.
2. Hygiene and Diseases of Warm Climates, Davidson.

Madagascar, where a large number of the inhabitants suffer from elephantiasis. According to Saville, in the mountainous island of Huahine, at least seven-tenths of the male population who have reached the age of puberty are suffering more or less from *Bucnemia tropica* (elephantiasis)."

"Among the influences that determine the geographical distribution of elephantiasis, the sea breeze is sometimes mentioned. But elephantiasis is found in the centre of Africa, on the western side of Lake Nayasa, the centre of the Soudan, and hundreds of miles up the Congo ; and it is entirely absent as an endemic disease in many islands well within the endemic zone, Formoza for instance. The sea breeze theory is not free from objection."[1]

Coming to the *quasi* popular idea as to the nature and cause of the disease, Forbes thinks that it is the same as the *lepra arabum*, while Day has no doubt that it is closely allied to leprosy. Many commentators of the Bible are of opinion that the leprosy mentioned there may be taken to be elephantiasis, the only consideration urged against this construction being "that it would certainly lessen the value of the miracles!"[2]

Ives, in his Voyages, observes, "This is a disorder peculiar to the inhabitants of the Malabar coast, and specially those of Cochin. It seems to be merely an oedematous swelling, arising from an impoverished state of the blood ; and in many persons the leg is of so enormous a size as to occasion its being called elephant leg, having greatly the appearance both in shape and bigness of the leg of an elephant. I could not learn that any remedy for this disorder had been discovered by the natives, and, as they seldom or never apply to Europeans for assistance, I believe they are seldom, if ever, cured ; but were they to do so,

1. P. 244.
2. Lawson's British and Native Cochin, p. 73.

probably it would but little avail, since an alteration from the poorest to the most cordial and nutritious diet would certainly be recommended to them, and we well know, that every caste of Indians are so much wedded to their own particular customs, they would sooner choose to die than materially to alter their usual course of living, even if their circumstances permitted it. The generality of those who labour under this disorder, seldom are able indeed to call in any assistance, being composed of the very poorest of the people, who feed chiefly on sardines, and cannot purchase even the smallest quantity of rice to boil with the fish for their daily subsistence. I was informed that these poor wretches are supported for whole weeks together, perhaps months, with no other aliment than what this species of fish afforded, and their drink is water only, unless by way of regale, they now and then procure a draught of the simple unfermented juice of the cocoanut tree called toddy."[1]

Some reference may be made here to the native system of treatment for the disease as prescribed by the *Ashtangahridayam* (Aṣhṭāngahṛḍayam), a medical treatise in Sanskrit of very high authority in Malabar.

If the elephantiasis is caused by the influence of rheum, the patient should be bled by opening a vein at two fingers' length above the heel of the foot after the leg had been smoothened by the application of medicated oils and ghees for some time, and after a process of sweating it has been gone through. The patient should take, for the period of a month, castor oil in cow's urine. After the oil has digested, he should be fed on rice, husked out of old paddy and boiled along with milk and a few pieces of dried ginger. He should be given a preparation of sesame oil, ghee, and the marrow of bones and flesh, mixed together and boiled. If this system of treatment does

1. Pages 93-94.

not effect a cure, recourse should be had to cauterisation.

If the elephantiasis is due to the influence of bile, the patient should be bled by opening a vein below the heel, and should be placed under proper diet and medicine such as would retard the effects of bile.

If it is the result of the influence of phlegm, the patient has to be bled by opening the artery on the great toe of the leg affected. The diet should be barley and other astringent things, mixed with honey. He should chew the gall nut (*Terminalia Chebula*), in gradually increasing numbers. The leg should be smeared with a preparation of mustard, ground along with the root of either the *cheruvazhuthina* (Cheṙuvaḽuṭina) or the *Koduthuva* (Koḍūṭṭuva) plant.[1]

Mrs. Manning, speaking of the diffusion of the medical science of India, obseves, "Greek physicians have done much to preserve and diffuse the medical science of India. We find, for instance, the Greek physician Actuarius celebrates the Hindu medicine called *Triphala* (Ṭṛphala). He mentions the peculiar products of India, of which it is composed, by their Sanskrit name Myrobalans. Aetius, who was a native of Amida in Mesopotamia and studied at Alexandria in the fifth century, not only speaks of the myrobalans, but mentions them as the proper cure for the disease called elephantiasis."[2] The myrobalans mentioned by Aetius is the *Terminalia Chebula* of the Aṣhṭāngahṛḍaya.

There is a curious tradition in Malabar tracing elephantiasis to the curse of St. Thomas, the Apostle, on his murderers and their posterity.[3] The tradition is not of recent growth. Dr. Fryer, who visited India about 1680, says that "about this mount

1. Part II, Chapter 30, Vol. 8 to 12.
2. Ancient and Mediaeval India, Vol. I, p. 351.
3. Day's Land of the Perumals, p, 427.

(i. e., St. Thomas Mount in the vicinity of the town of Madras) live a caste of people, one of whose legs is as big as an elephant's, which gives occasion for the divulging it to be a judgment on them, as the generation of the assasins and murderers of the blessed Apostle St. Thomas, one of whom I saw at Fort St. George." "Such," exclaims Sir W. Kaye, "the miraculous origin of elephantiasis!"[1] The tradition is preserved in the name by which elephantiasis was called by the Portuguese[2].

Among the natives of the country, it is popularly believed that it is caused by the drinking of the water into which the roots of the screw-pine have entered, thereby poisoning it, and this belief is influenced more or less by the fact that a "Cochin leg" bears some sort of resemblance to the root stock of the screw-pine.

As to its real cause we cannot do better than quote *in extenso* a few passages from Dr. Subrahmanya Iyer's Report on the Census of Travancore.

"It is generally admitted that elephantiasis, as met with in tropical countries in an endemic form, is a disease caused by the presence in the blood of the embryos of a parasite, *Filaria Nocturna*, first discovered by Demarquay in 1863, and described for the first time by Bancroft in 1876, after whom it has been named *Filaria Bancrofti*. These embryos are sucked in from the blood of an affected person by a species of female mosquito which serves as an intermediary host to the parasite. 'On filling herself with blood she (the mosquito) returns to some shaded spot near water, on which, after from 3 to 5 days, she deposits a little boatshaped agglomeration of eggs. She then dies, either on water or, falls into it after death * * *. Any *filaria* she may have fostered have now an opportunity to escape into that element * * *. At

1. Christianity in India, p. 4 Note.

2. *Pejo de Sants Toma*.

this point there is a hiatus in our knowledge which, until some one has the hardihood to subject himself to a very obvious but somewhat risky experiment, has to be filled in by conjecture'. In all probability, 'the *filaria*, after swimming about for some time, is at last swallowed in drinking water by man. Having arrived in this way in the human stomach, it works its way through the tissues of its definitive host, and, guided by that strange instinct which pilots so many parasites to their final habitat, comes to rest at last in some lymphatic vessel. Here it continues to grow and mature. Finally, being joined by one of the opposite sex, impregnation ensues. Its young after a time are poured into the lymph stream; thence into the blood; so completing the life cycle and starting a new generation of *filariae*. The periodicity of *F. Nocturna* being nocturnal, is evidently an adaptation to the habits of the intermediate host, the mosquito."[1] The parasite generally lives for a number of years. Various diseases are caused by the action of the parasite. But of all the filarial diseases, elephantiasis is the most frequent and very common in the endemic areas. It generally affects the extremeties and the genital organs---the latter variety being almost *nil* in Travancore (not so, however, in Cochin)—and is due to the blocking of lymph vessels by the undeveloped young parasites and hypertrophic changes as a consequence thereof."[2]

"My belief is," says Davidson, "that extended investigation will show that the distribution of elephantiasis is determined by a variety of factors, the principal of these being the distribution of one or more species of mosquito capable of acting as the intermediary host of *F. Nocturna*; and that this in its turn depends on such circumstances as an adequate rainfall, a summer temperature of at least 80° F., a suitable soil and stagnant water. Only second to these in

1. Hygiene and Diseases of Warm Climate, Davidson.
2. Part I, pp, 243--4.

importance is the character of the drinking water supply; the habits of the people with regard to its use and management; and as determining the explosion of the lymphangitio which is the immediate first step in the development of the disease, the occupations and personal habits as affecting their liability to injuries and irritation of the legs and scrotum."

It is, perhaps, a little difficult for the lay mind to correctly grasp the exact process by which the *Nocturna filaria*, sucked in by the female mosquito from the blood of an affected person, passes into the lymph vessels of another, blocking the passage. But the noxious insect has not only been arraigned before the bar of scientific opinion, it has also been convicted of the heinous crime of propagating, not simply elephantiasis, but also other sorts and kinds of epidemics. One has, therefore, to accept the verdict till it is reviewed or reversed by a tribunal of equal or superior jurisdiction.

2. **Mal-de-terre.** After elephantiasis, our author mentions one more disease, which, he says, disturbed him almost every month, and which the natives termed *mal-de-terre*. The symptoms described are those of cholera of a mild type, and the native remedy mentioned is indeed a curious one. Grose and Forbes call the disease *mordechin* or *mort-de-chien*, while Bartolomeo terms it *mordexim*. It was known as *morexi* or *mordexy* to early travellers. Yule and Burnell derive the word *mort-de-chien* from the Portuguese *mordexim* which represents the Konkani and Maharatti *modachi*, *modashi*, or *modwashi*, 'Cholera', from a Maharatti verb *moawen* 'to break up', 'to sink' (as under infirmities, in fact 'to collapse').[1] Johnson, in his *Infirmities of Tropical Climates* says that, "*mort-de-chien* is nothing more than the highest degree of *Cholera morbus*."[2]

1. Hobson Jobson, p. 449.
2. P. 405.

The earliest description we have met with of this fell disease is that of Gaspar Correa (1543 A. D.). "This winter they had in Goa a mortal distemper which the natives call *morxy*, and attacking persons of every quality from the smallest infant at the breast to the old man of fourscore, and also domestic animals and fowls, so that it affected every living thing, male and female. And this malady attacked people without any cause that could be assigned, falling upon sick and sound alike, on the fat and the lean; and nothing in the world was a safeguard against it. And this malady attacked the stomach, caused as some experts affirmed by chill; though later it was maintained that no cause whatever could be discovered. The malady was so powerful and so evil that it immediately produced the symptoms of strong poison; *e. g.*, vomiting, constant desire for water, with drying of the stomach; and cramps that contracted the hams and the soles of the feet, with such pains that the patient seemed dead, with the eyes broken and the nails of fingers and toes black and crumpled. And for this malady our physicians never found any cure; and the patient was carried off in one day, or at the most in a day and night; insomuch that not ten in a hundred recovered, and those who did recover were such as were healed in haste with medicines of little importance known to the natives. So great was the mortality this season that the bells were tolling all day * * * * * * * * insomuch that the Governor forbade the tolling of the church bells, not to frighten the people * * * * and when a man died in the hospital of this malady of *mordexi* the Governor ordered all the experts to come together and open the body. But they found nothing wrong except that the paunch was shrunk up like a hen's gizzard, and wrinkled like a piece of scorched leather * * * *."[1]

1. Correa, IV, pp. 288—289.

Couto ascribes it to the use of bad and brackish water and certain green and dry leaves,[1] while Bartolomeo thinks that in "Malabar it is occasioned by the winds blowing from the mountains which carry with them a great many nitrous particles, and which commonly commence immediately after the rainy season, when the wet weather is succeeded by a great heat and continued draught. On the coast of Malabar, this is the case from the beginning of October till the 20th of December; and on the coast of Coromandel in April and May. People are then liable to catch colds: and the consequence is, that malignant and bilious slimy matter adheres to the bowels, and occasions violent pains, vomiting, fever, stupefaction; so that persons attacked with this disease die very often in a few hours. It sometimes happens that 30 or 40 persons die in this manner, in one place, n the course of a day unless speedy relief be administered.[2] This disease played great havoc occasionally in Malabar. Correa says that in 1503 the Zamorin lost 20,000 men of his army by a disease which was just like this. And in the year 1782, Bartolomeo mentions that it ranged with such fury that a great many persons died of it.[3] It is interesting to note that in Tranvancore the people still call it by the name *Nirkomban* (Nīrcomban), a term by which in Bartolomeo's time the people of Malabar used to denote *mort-de-chien* or *mordexi.* Winslow, in his Tamil Dictionary, explains *nir* as meaning water and *combar* as signifying a kind of cholera or bilious diarrhoea.

With regard to cures employed, Carletti (A. D. 1599) says that there is no remedy discovered, and yet he observes that " there is a herb proper for the cure, which bears the same name of mordexina". Dr.

1. Dec. IV, liv. IV, Chap. 10.
2. P. 409.
3. P. 410.
4. See also Dr. Gundhert's Malayalam Dictionary.

Fryer (A. D. 1675), Bluteau (1702 A. D.), La Roqua (1716) and Grose (1760), all say, with our author, that the native physicians applied the cautery as a remedy for the disease. Under the word mordexim, Bluteau explains that it is properly a failure of digestion, which is very perilous in those parts, unless the native remedy is used. This is to apply a thin iron, like a spit, and heated, under the heel, till the patient screams with pain, and then to slap the same part with the sole of a shoe. It may be due, as Grose remarks, to "the powerful revulsion of which it (the heel) rarely fails of a salutary efficacy", but it is difficult to understand what special virtue the sole of the shoe can have to work a remedy to so bad a distemper.

According to Bartolomeo, "the bitter essence of *Droya Amara* is the best remedy for this colic; as it opens the pores, counteracts the effects of the saltpetre, warms the body, brings on perspiration, and in that manner, inspires it with new life * * * . The above essence is pretty dear, and it was not possible to procure it in such quantity as to supply all the patients (afflicted with epidemic in 1782). In its stead, therefore, we employed *Tajara*[1], coconut brandy, distilled over horse's dung (having perhaps the same efficacious property as the sole of a shoe !). All those recovered to whom this beverage was given, but the rest died in 3 or 4 hours. This circumstance made so much noise among the pagans, that the fame of our medicine and the cures it performed, was spread as far as Cochin. (The Padre was then a resident of Verāpulay about 8 miles from Cochin). When the physicians of the Dutch East India Company at that place, Messrs. Martensard and Enric, were informed of this circumstance, they not only gave our medicine their approbation, but even employed it in their practice."[2]

5. Can it be chārāyam ?

6. P. 410.

3. **Other diseases**. After mentioning elephantiasis and mal-de-terre as two of the prominent distempers indigenous to Malabar, Visscher dismisses the subject as a painful topic. But, however unpleasant the subject may be for discussion, it would be interesting and, indeed, advantageous to know the nature of the diseases that were once prevalent in Malabar, and the native remedies applied to them.

Fra Bartolomeo, in his *Voyage to the East Indies* gives a detailed description of both the diseases and remedies, and his account is so full and interesting that I make no apology in quoting it at length:—

"The diseases which prevail among the inhabitants of the southern part of India, that is, of Malabar, Canara, Mysore, Madura, Tanjore, Marava and Parava are as follows:—

Shralanova (Shralanōva), the wind colic. This is (Śūla ṅōvu).

Sanivali, nervous cramps and convulsions.

Adisaram (Aṭisāram), flux or dysentery.

Calladappa, the graval and stone.

Grahani, the blood flux.

Mujali, a kind of gout.

Kazhalappani (Kaḻalappani), St. Antony's fire, with feverish symptoms.

Pani, violent fever.

Tridoshajvaram (Ṭṛḍōṣhajvarom), the fever which has three bad properties; that is, the violent fever.

Malampani, a fever that lasts only one day, and is cccasioned by a certain wind which blows from the ghats.

Vidathapani (Viṭāṭṭapani), the continued fever.

Denaradenapani, the tertian fever.

Nalampani (Nālāmpani), the quartan fever.

Kshaya (Kṣhaya), phthisis.

Rajakshaya (Rājakṣhaya), consumption of the lungs.

Nirvaszicia, involuntary emission of urine.

Premeham (Přemēham), gonorrhoea benigna.

Andram (Āntřam), the hemorrhoids.

Mahodaram (Mahōḍaram), the dropsy.

Kamala, the jaundice.

Sanni, phrensy combined with convulsions.

Velupa or *Kushtam* (Veḷuppu or Kuṣhṭham), leprosy.

Nirtiripa or *Nircomban* (Nīřṭiripa or Nīřcomban), an intestinal colic which proceeds from cold. This disease is in common called *mordexim*, of which Sonnerat, drolly enough, makes *mort-de-chien*, dog's death. In the months of October, November and December, it prevails much on the coast of Malabar; for about that period certain winds blow from the ghats, and carry with them a multitude of nitrous particles.

Astisrava (Asṭiśřāva), an inflamatory disease which affects the whole body and consumes the marrow of the bones.

Ciardhi (Chchařḍi), vomiting which proceeds from bile or other causes.

Ractapittam (Rakṭapiṭṭam), bilious fever, which is commonly followed by a flux of blood and putrid matter.

Tippolla (Ṭīppoḷḷal), burning ulcers on the exterior part of the body.

Masuri (Masūri), the small-pox: a disease which in India is exceedingly infectious, and sweeps off prodigious multitudes.

Ciori (Chori), the itch.

Arbuda, Cancer.

Ceraverpa (Chēravāṟppa), an ulcer, the fetid smell of which attracts the snake *Chera.* This snake, however, is not poisonous.

Araklesam (Araklēśam), buboes.

Sannivadam (Sannivāṭam), apoplexy.

Engal (Ēngal), asthma.

Cuima (Chuma), cough.

"Those who read this catalogue of diseases with attention, will find that the greater part of them proceed either from too great heat, or from catching cold. Some kinds of boils and ulcers, which break out on the legs during the rainy season, are difficult to be cured; while there are others, on the contrary, which cannot be healed during the summer. The women who lead an indolent life, and do not take sufficient exercise, are tormented with convulsions, spasms, and other hysteric symptoms * * *. Such persons should be made to beat unshelled rice; bark and the cold bath should be prescribed for them, and they should, above all, be cautioned to avoid everything that tends to disquiet and disturb the mind.

"People who complain of a weakness of the stomach and nerves are accustomed in the morning to chew a little opium, which they say strengthens the nerves and promotes digestion * * * .[1]"

"The venerial disease is very little known in the interior parts of India. As the Indians are remarkably attentive to cleanliness, and as both male and female live with the greatest temperance, use food easy of digestion, are in continual perspiration, wash the parts of sex three times a day, and adhere to other strict regulations rendered necessary by the nature of the climate, this detestable disease has not been able to make much progress in the inland provinces. In the towns, on the sea coast, however, where there is a very

1. pp. 403 to 406.

great influx of foreigners, who indulge in every kind of dissipation, and where the above salutary practices and regulations are almost entirely neglected, the venereal disease has greatly increased, but it prevails only among the low, contemptible castes, and the Europeans who are the original cause of this[1] as well as of all the other evils which the Indians have to complain of"—a too sweeping condemnation indeed![2]

"As the body, however, in the hot climate, is in continued perspiration, the above disease may be easily removed, provided the patient employs, immediately on its appearance, attenuating and detergent medicines. The most effectual is velladampa or sarsaparilla. From this wood the Indians prepare a decoction, which is sweetened with a little sugar; and if from 2 to 3 pints of it be given to a venereal patient, before the disease has acquired much strength, he will be soon cured. This disease would be much less destructive, in general, were suitable remedies used in proper time. Boerhaave, a man whose name I cannot mention but with the utmost respect, says expressly, 'that the venereal disease is far from being as dangerous in India as it is in Europe'. (See *Tractatio medico-practica de Lue Venera*, Hermain Boerhaave, Lugd, Bat. 1751.)"[3]

Bartolomeo then refers to the dreadful disease *mordexim*, which he calls also by the name of *Shani*. If by this term he means *sanni*, it denotes in Malayalam convulsions, paralysis, lock-jaw, apoplexy, delirium.[4] So also in Tamil. We have already quoted his description of it and the havoc it used to make in Malabar. He then goes on :—

"The tertian fever is easily removed by a decoction of vēppu, or Malabar china. Vēppu is the name of

1. This disease is known in Malayalam as *Paramki Punnu* or Feringhee sore. (See Gundhert.)
2. P. 408.
3. P. 409.
4. See Gundhert's Malayalam Dictionary.

a tree which has a very bitter bark, and green prickly leaves, which are also exceedingly bitter. It grows on dry, sandy soil, without any culture or care. The decoction is prepared from its leaves, which are called *veppela* (vēppela). The property of this tree is well known to the Brahmans; but the common people have very little knowledge of it.

"The *Kachil* (Kāchil), or inflamation connected with *gonorrhoea benigna*, is removed by means of rice-water mixed with a little sugar, and given to the patient to drink. Cold fomentation, and decoctions of bananas, milk, saltpetre and other softening, cooling and diuretic medicines are also prescribed. This malady is very prevalent on the coast of Malabar.

"All these diseases which proceed from a decomposition of the animal juices, enervate the Indians at an early period, and hasten their dissolution. They die, almost without any pain, in the same manner as consumptive persons; and become extinct like a lamp which has no longer oil. At the moment of their death no contraction is observed in the features, no convulsive throbs, and they never whimper or complain like so many of the Europeans, who quit the world in the most painful manner imaginable. Many of the women lose their lives the first time they bring forth.

"The small-pox, a disease which in India is highly infectious, commonly makes its appearance in Malabar after the rainy season; that is, in December and January and the months following. Thousands are swept off by it every year. At the periods when it prevails, parents abandon their children, and children their parents; for this disease, as already said, is so infectious and dangerous that people can never be too much on their guard against it. To this may be added, that the Indians are not capable of forming a proper judgment respecting the symptoms, and consequently treat their patients in a very improper manner. The doors and windows are shut, that the patients may not be exposed to the smallest breath of cool air, and heating things alone are given them. The most common medicines employed in this disease are sugar, boiled onions, the urine of a healthy child, coriander-seed, boiled rice, green pepper, carambola leaves, onion juice and other things of the like kind, partly useless and partly pernicious. The object of them, however, is to expel the poison from the body; but they never suffer it to ripen properly; and they prescribe for the patient neither emollient nor cooling things, which would tend to allay the internal heat, and to moderate the ferment of the animal juices. Rice-water and fresh air would be far more proper; but the Indians are obstinate in adhering to their deep-rooted prejudices, and, therefore, all attempts to persuade them are in vain."

Some of the early travellers, as also a few of the later writers on Malabar, represent the physicians of the country more in the character of the medicine-man among the savages than the followers of Aesculapius. According to them, they are astrologers, wizards, sorcerers, quacks, devil-dancers, and what not, combined. Speaking of the "physicians who visit the sick at Calicut," Varthema says:—"When a merchant, i. e., a pagan is sick and in great danger, the above-mentioned instruments, (drums, cymbals, etc.,) and the above-said men dressed like devils, go to visit the sick-man and they go at 2 or 3 o'clock in the morning; and the said men so dressed carry fire in their mouths; in each of their hands and on their feet they wear two crutches of wood, which are one pace high, and in this manner they go shouting and sounding the instruments, so that truly if the person were not ill, he would fall to the ground with terror at seeing these ugly beasts. And these are the physicians that go to see and visit the sick man. And although they should fill the stomach full up to the mouth, they pound three roots of ginger and make a cup of juice and this they drink, and in three days they have no longer any illness, so that they live exactly like beasts." We have frequently heard the wonderful tales related by the early travellers. The wonderful stories of the "lying Mandeville", that prince amongst travellers who trade on the marvellous, pale into magnificence before some of those of Varthema. It is, however, refreshing to read from Marco Polo, who, in his description of the kingdom of Coilum, (Quilon) says, "They have very good astrologers and physicians."[1] Dr. Francis Day, sometime Civil Surgeon of Cochin and Chief Medical Officer to H. H. the Raja of Cochin, describes the native practitioners of Cochin as being "very ignorant"[2] though, in the 18th century, Fra Bartolomeo found an altogether different class of medical practitioners there. "When a physician is sent for," says he, "you are sure to be visited by five or six. There are even boys who possess an extensive knowledge of botany; and this is not surprising, as from their earliest years they are made acquainted with the nature of plants, and their different properties. Did the religion of the Indians allow them to dissect animals and study anatomy, they would certainly attain to great proficiency in medicine; but as these are strictly forbidden, it may readily be conceded that the above sciences can make very little progress. I have, however, seen instances of Malabar physicians curing patients who had been totally given up by the Europeans."[3] Again he goes on to observe, "The Malabar physicians in general are superior to most Europeans in their knowledge of the simples." Sir Charles Lawson, who had lived in Cochin for some time, makes the same remark. Speaking of the herbalist's shops he found at Muttanchery in Cochin, he observes, "Next is a herbalist's. Here

1. Vol. II, p. 376.
2. Land of the Perumals, p. 421.
3. Pp. 422—23.

hanging from the roof around, before and behind the dealer, are bundles of dry roots and herbs. These are sold readily to the natives, who have a considerable, if not perfect, knowledge of the medicinal qualities of each, and often administer them with such results as have been vainly expected from European remedies."[1]

Fra Bartolomeo gives a description of the simples used in his time by the Malabar physicians, and it will not be profitless to refer to it here. He says:—"Among those which they employ in their cures, the following are most worthy of notice:—

"*Veppu*, (vēppu), the chinchina tree which has been mentioned already. In the Sanskrit language it is called *Nimba*, in the Tamulic *Aipu*, and in Portuguese *Amargozeira*. There are two kinds of it: one of them, which has black appearance, is called *Karinveppa*, the other, with green prickly leaves, which have an exceedingly bitter taste, is known under the name of *Aryakarinvepa*. The latter, properly, is that which produces the real Malabar china. The bark of this tree, however, is employed by the Indians only in cases of necessity; for a decoction of the leaves, if the coarser parts which subside to the bottom of the vessel be used, produces as powerful an effect. The Brahmans are accustomed to prepare, from the juice of these leaves, what they call *Karil*, that is, a sauce which they eat with their rice. The medicine is of excellent service in tertian fevers, in cases of worms, and in all disorders arising from indigestion and weakness of the stomach and nerves. If the green leaf be bruised, and applied to wounds or ulcers of a long standing, they cleanse them, and prevent them from spreading or becoming cancerous. In a word, they answer the same purpose as the china bark, and in much shorter time, because more power is contained in the juice of the leaves than in the woody parts of the stem and the branches. The properties

1. British and Native Cochin, p. 38.

of this tree being, therefore, so nearly allied to those of the real china, which grows in America, the Indians can very well dispense with the latter, especially since it loses much of its virtue by long voyages, as the saline volatile particles it contains evaporate by the way.

"The nettle *Codittuva* (Koḍiṭṭūva), as the Brahmans say, is an excellent remedy to purify and thin the blood; to expel the gout, leprosy, and malignant fevers; and to check coughs connected with spitting of blood.

"*Avanaka* (Āvaṇakku), the so called wonder and cross tree, in Portuguese *Figniro d' Inferns*, bears a fruit which by expression yields a salutary oil. It purifies and sweetens the blood, dissolves the corrupt juices, expels worms, and is of excellent service in the sciatica.

"*Ulatunwera* (Ūlaṭṭunvēra), the root of the tree *Ulam*, is an effectual remedy for the jaundice. It cleaness the urinary passage when obstructed by flimsy accumulations, and cures the *gonorrhoea benigna*. In the latter case the root is administered after it has been pulverised and mixed with sugar and milk. The *Ulam*, in Portuguese, *Pareira brava*, is that kind of large ivy which bears very small fruit enclosed in small husks like those of the coffee-berry. Its root only is officinal.[1] The *Ulam*, however, must not be confounded, as it has been by some, with the *Vallicagneram* (Vaḷḷikāññiram) which grows also in Malabar. Geofroy has given a particular description of this plant in his *Materia Medica*, where it occurs among the exotics.

"*Konna* (Koṅṅa), the *Cassiapurgans*, carries of bile, purifies the veins and is of a cooling nature; at least we are told so by the Brahmans. The arecanut, bananas, the cocoanut tree, the *Mava* or *mangueria*, the *Kaja*, *Ciamba*, *Plava*, and *Papamaram* have been described by Gemilli Careri, in the third part of his travels round the globe, where figures of them may be seen.

1. Perhaps the root of the *Cissampelos pareira*, L.

"The *Nellimaram*, is a large tree which bears the so called *Emblis*, a kind of plum used also in medicine, and in the Malabar language called *Nellika*. Its chief property, according to the natives, is that it carries off the bile and slime which give rise to most of the diseases in India. It is customary to pickle these plums, and to eat them with rice.

"*Karuva*,(Kaṫuva) or *Ilavanga*, is the name of that tree, the bark of which is the *Cassia lignea*, or wild cinnamon. It is of the size of a large European plum tree and has smooth green leaves, which are somewhat pulpy, and emit a strong smell. They are used in India as we use cinnamon. This Malabar cinnamon tree grows without any nursing or care, and were it cultivated, would approach to near that of Ceylon. The Dutch, however, do not wish it to thrive, and extirpate the trees in Malabar wherever they find them, in order that their cinnamon, which grows in the island of Ceylon, may not become of less value.

"*Muringa*, is the name of a tree which is highly valued by the inhabitants on the coast of Malabar. In the Arabic it is called *moriaben*, and in Persian *Tamen Guzarat Trerida*. Its leaves, as well as the fruit, both of which are very small, are eaten with rice. They are said to cure the colic, and expel poison. However this may be, it is certain that they afford a wholesome kind of nourishment. I several times caused soup to be made of the leaves as well as fruits of this tree, and always found it of benefit.

"The only Malabar plant which I can with certainty call an antidote of poison is a shrub, about three or four feet in height, named *Alpam*. The root is pounded and administered in warm water to those who have been poisoned. A Malabar proverb says, "*Alpam akathu, veszam porathu* (Alpam akaṭṭu, veṣham poṙaṭṭu); as soon as the alpam root enters the body, poison leaves it. I must, however, confess, that the Theriac of

Andromache (*Thericea andromaco*) is much more powerful.

"The Indian saffron, in Malabar language is called *mangel* (maññal), in the Portuguese *Acafrao Indico* and in the Sanskrit *Kunkuma*. The Europeans employ this plant, which has yellow leaves, merely for dyeing; but the Brahmans ascribe to it the property of curing the itch and the gout, extenuating the juices, and purifying the skin from all spots arising from scorbutic acridities.

"The Senna-tree, *Cassia Senna*, is called in the Malabar language *Nilavague* (Ṇilavāgu) and grows in the mountainous districts of Cape Comorin. Its leaves, it is well-known, are employed as a purgative.

"*Panikurka* (Panikkūṙka), the Malabar *Melissa*, in Portuguese *Cidreira Malabarica*, has broad, thick, round, prickly leaves, and is, therefore, very different from that of Europe. It, however, possesses the same power and properties; that is, it strengthens the head and stomach, and is to be recommended, in particular, to those subject to hysteric affections.

"*Ḳadelsalada*, dandelion, in Portuguese, *Almeyrao*, is, as is well known, a plant of a detergent nature, and purifies the blood.

"*Tottavadi* (Ṭoṭṭāvāḍi), is the name of the sensitive plant, as it is called, which, as soon as touched, contracts itself together.

"*Vayambu*, in Latin, *Acorus*, and in Portuguese, *Dringo*, the sweet-flag, grows on the coast of Malabar in ponds and stagnant water. It has long green leaves, and a very aromatic root.

"The *Scorzonera* root is called in the Malabar language *Ciadaveli* (Śaṭāvali) and in the Tamulic *Nirvalikizhanga*, (Nīṙvalikiḻanga). The Indians boil it; they preserve it also, and eat it with their rice.

In order that I may not be too prolix, I shall here give a list only of several plants and vegetable productions which I ought not to omit :—

Perumeirakam (Perumjīrakam), Lat. *Foeniculum*, Port. *Funcha*, fennel.

Velladamba (Vellaḍampa), Sarsaparilla, of which there are two kinds, one with white flowers and the other with red. The latter is the Malabar sarsaparilla.

Cherupula (Cheṙupūla), Lat. *Sax fraga*, sassafras.

Muszelcevi (Muyalchevi), Lat. *Sonchus*, Port. *Seralha*, lettuce.

Codaven (Kuṭavan), Lat. *Cochlearia*, Port. *Rabaca*, scurvy-grass.

Prami (Bṙahmi) or *Caipacira* (Kaippachīra), Lat. *Nasturtium fontanum*, Fr. *Cresson*,, water-cresses.

Cattutrithava (Kāṭṭuṭṛṭṭāvu), Lat. *Ocymum thyrsistorum*, the herb basil.

Pandila, Lat. *Trifolum pratanese*, purple trefoil.]

Gurgul (Guggul), Lat. *Scammonia*, scammony, bind-weed.

Panna, Lat. *Polipodium*, common polypody.

Irattimadhuram(Iraṭṭimaḍhuram), Lat. *Glycirrhizu*, liquorice.

Puliyarila (Puliāṙila), marsh trefoil.

Manday, Lat. *Eupatorium*, liver-wort.

Mandaram (Manḍāram), Lat. *Admirabilis malabarica*, Port. *Fula de merenda*.

Cattasha (Caṭṭāla), Lat. *Aloes*, Port. *Herva babosa*, Arab *Saber*, the aloe.

Madalam (Māṭalam), Lat. *Arbustum mali Punici*, Port. *Romoeira*, the pomegranate tree.

Pavaka (Pāvakka), Port. *Momordica*, the garden-balsam. Plants of it are called, in the Malabar language, Pāvel.

S.

Kiszanelli (Kīlānelli), Lat. *Millesolium*, common yarrow.

Makipuva (Mākipūva), Lat. *Absynthium*, wormwood.

Ceruciaca (Cheṙuchakka), the annanas.

Cannati panna (Kannāṭi panna) or *Madilpanna* (Maṭil panna), Lat. *Adiantum*, Port. *Avenca*, maiden hair.

Cirakam (Jīrakam), Port. *Erva dolce*, anise.

Velluram (Veḷḷūram). Port. *Malvaisco*, mallow; an emollient medicine, which is of great service.

Orumbulicica (Oṭumpuḷinchikka), Port. *Salbas canaru*, is a tree, the fruit of which answers the purpose of our soap. The natives of Malabar employ it for washing, not only their bodies, but also their clothes.

Curanthotti (Kuṙumṭōṭṭi), a plant about a palm in height, from the root of which is prepared a decoction said to be useful in the gout, cough, gonorrhoea, flatulency and feverish affections. This decoction must be mixed with sugar and milk.

Ellacalli (Elakaḷḷi), Lat. *Euphoribum spurge*, a very sharp and powerful medicine, which properly ought to be prohibited.

Ciangupusham (Chinganpaḷam), the root and leaves of this plant are used as a decoction for the gout, cholic and poison.

Calumba, a yellow root, known as a certain remedy for the tertian fever, pain of the stomach, and poison. It promotes also the menses and parturition. It has an exceedingly bitter taste, and is given in wine. I suspect it to be the same root as that called *Vallicanjiram* (Vaḷḷikāññiram).

Cumbla (Vaḷḷikānjiram Kumbla), a large tree, the root of which expels the gout, and carries off bile.

Ciaca (Chakka), the largest of all the fruits produced on the earth, for one of them is almost more than a man can carry. It grows on the plāvu tree, the wood of which is in the inside yellow. It has been described by Gemelli Careri and other authors. The raw seeds of this fruit have a strong aromatic smell and are called *Ciacacura* (Chakkakkuru), a decoction of them excites venery.

Trikolpakonna (Ṭṛkōlpakoṅṅa), is the Malabar name of a detergent kind of turpeth.

Cagnaravera (Cagnaravēra), is the root of the tree *Solor*.

Parutti (Paruṭṭi), is the name given to that tree which produces cotton.

Caruppa (Kaṙuppu), is the name of opium.

Umana (Ummam), Lat. *Datura*, Port. *Dutro*, is a plant with a dark blue flower, containing a seed, which, if given to any person to drink in wine or water, excites involuntary laughter, clouds the understanding, occasions dimness of sight, and at last brings on sleep * * *. This plant has been described by Father Schott, in the Appendix to the second part of his *Physica Curiosa*, which is entitled *De Mirabilibus Miscellneis*. I was acquainted with a Frenchman in Cochin who having been imprisoned and condemned to the gallows, swallowed some of these seeds with a view to avoid the shame of his punishment. The consequence was that he lost his senses, and fell into a deep sleep, which in three days carried him into eternity. This event may serve as a proof that too strong a dose of these seeds proves mortal.

Tettamparel (Ṭeṙṙāmparel), is a fruit of the size and figure of hare's dung. When put into a vessel which contains muddy water, it purifies it in such a manner that all the unclean slimy particles instantly deposit themselves at the bottom, and the water becomes clear and bright. The same effect is produced when a branch of the tree is put into a pool or muddy well. I should have doubted the truth of this circumstance had I not several times seen it with my own eyes. I have still in my possession one of these fruits, and can perform the experiment when I please.

Bhudianarti (Bhūṭiyuṇaṟṟi), in Portuguese *Pan de merda* or *Pan fujo*, is a kind of wood, of a dark red colour, which smells like human dung * * * *. It has a great similarity to *Assafoetida* called in Malabar *Cayam* or *Hingu*, with which the natives are accustomed to season their boiled rice.

Of the banana fig, one of the most valuable of Indian fruits, there are four different kinds, viz., *Cannpala* (Kaṇṇanpaḷa), the hollow fig; *Cadalipala* (Kaḍalippaḷa), or *Puvanca* (Pūvanka), the garden fig; *Eraden* (Erāden), the sugar fig, so called on account of its sweet taste; and *Nendraca* (Nēnṭṟaka), the roasting fig, which cannot be eaten raw.

The *Pala*[1] (Pāla) or proper Indian fig tree has been very incorrectly described by Pliny in his *Natural History*. He evidently confounds the Pāla with another tree called by the Portuguese *Arvore de raiz* (the banyan). This tree rises to the height of the common chestnut tree, but throws out from its branches a number of fibres, which become so long that they at last hang down to the ground, where they take root and produce other trees of the same kind perfectly similar to the parent tree. In this manner they continue till from one tree there at length arises a whole forest. Certain travellers are, therefore, not in the wrong when they assert that, in India, there are trees under which a thousand men might find shelter. The Indians are accustomed to plant such trees in the neighbourhood of their temples or pagodas, that they may defend the people, when assembled, from the rain and the sun. I saw several of these trees at *Tiruvandaram* (Trivandrum) and *Ciranga* (Chiṟayankīl) and could not help being wonderfully struck with this

1. The correct Malayalam name of the tree is Pēral.

singular *lusus naturoe*. The Europeans settled on the coast of Malabar call this *Arvore de raiz*, the pagoda-tree. It has been described by Nierenberg in his *Natural History*."[1]

Botany has been studied in Malabar with great effect for some time past, and has gone down only recently. The medical properties of herbs and roots are thoroughly understood, and they are applied with peculiar efficacy. The attention of those who wish to be convinced of the numerous articles that occur in the medicine and botany of Malabar may be invited to the monumental treatise published at Amsterdam under the title of *Hortus Malabaricus*, an enduring monument of Dutch learning, industry and research. The work appeared between the years 1686 and 1703 in 12 vols. with 794 excellent copper plate engravings. It is indeed surprising that Visscher makes no reference to it in his letters which were written not long after the last volume of the work was issued from the press. The first volume was issued at Amsterdam only 23 years after Cochin was conquered by Holland, so that the work of research and compilation must have commenced as soon as the Company obtained a firm foot-hold in Malabar.

"In compiling the *Hortus Malabaricus*"; says the Rev. T. Whitehouse, " several persons, both natives and Europeans, were employed. Three Brahmans (probably Konkans) by the respective names of Ranga Botto, Vinaique Pandito, and Appu Botto, together with another scholar of the Chogan caste, called Itti Achuden, gave information about the medicinal properties of the plants. All the country around was diligently searched by natives best acquainted with the habitats of plants ; and fresh specimens were brought to Cochin where the Carmelite Mathoens sketched them with such striking accuracy, that there can be no difficulty in identifying each particular species, when you

1. Pp. 412—13.

see his drawings. A description of each plant was written in Malayalam, and thence translated into Portuguese by a resident at Cochin, named Emmanuel Carneiro. The Secretary to the Government, Herman Van Douep, further translated it into Latin, that the learned in all the countries of Europe might have access to it. The whole seems then to have passed under the supervision of another learned individual named Casearius, who was probably a Dutch Chaplain, and a personal friend of Van Rheede (the Governor).[1] A book of its size on which such care was expended must have consumed a fortune before its publication; and confers honor, both on those who compiled it and the place where it was compiled."[2]

The *Hortus Malabaricus* bears, indeed, eloquent testimony to the knowledge of botany and medicine possessed by the Malabar physicians of the period. In

1. Van Rheede lies buried at Surat where he has a mausoleum amongst the Dutch tombs which are, as Freyer says, "many and handsome, most of them pargetted." "They stand," observes Mr. Forrest, "in a neglected patch of ground studded with fruit-trees, and some wild parasite is bursting asunder their walls.' Grand, noble, for the expanse it covers, its height, its peculiar style of culture, is the mausoleum erected over the last resting place of Mr. Van Rheede, to whom oriental history pays the tribute of eulogy in denominating him the Maecenas of Malabar. At a period when European residents in India wholly directed their attention to mercantile adventure, or attempted political aggrandisement, he could spare leisure to devote to scientific research; and his labours have provided Holland with many valuable manuscripts and other equally important curiosities, while some of his statements still challenge enquiry. His *Hortus Indicus Malabaricus*, a work in twelve volumes folio, is an evidence of his literary exertions.' The tomb approaches in shape a decagon with a double cupola of great dimensions and a gallery above and below supported on handsome columns. 'In the centre of the chamber, a single tombstone marks a vault with more occupants than the Dutch officials.' A wooden tablet recounts the particulars of 'Hendrik Adriaan Baron Van Reede', who died, aged 56, on the 15th of December 1691." (Cities of India pp. 60—61).

2. Some Historical Notices of Cochin, p. 22.

collecting his catalogue of simples, says Fra Bartolomeo, he had the invaluable aid of a manuscript containing observations by many regular physicians and botanists, natives of the coast of Malabar.[1] He also points out "that India alone contains more medical writings, perhaps, than are to be found in all the rest of the world. As printing has never been introduced here, all hands are employed in copying manuscripts, and particularly such as relate to the prolongation of human life, viz., medicinal and botanical. The greater part of the Indian manuscripts preserved in the Library of the late king of France, those of the Propaganda and Mr. Samuel Guise, and in the Borgian Museum, consists of works of this kind. The often before mentioned Dictionary, *Amarasimha*, under the head *Aushadhivarga*, that is, class of the simples, and medicines, gives the names of above 300 herbs and plants used in medicine."[2]

Here, it is hoped, it would be appropriate to put in a word about one of the indigenous systems of medicine of which Aṣhṭāngahṛḍaya is an exponent.

"In both branches of the Aryan stock, surgical practice, as well as medical, reached a high degree of perfection at an early period."[3] "Probably it will come as a surprise to many, as it did to myself, to discover the amount of anatomical knowledge which is disclosed in the works of the earliest medical writers of India. Its extent and accuracy are surprising, when we allow for their early age, probably the sixth century before Christ, and their peculiar methods of definition. In these circumstances, the interesting question of the relation of the medicine of the Indians to that of the Greeks naturally suggests itself. The possibility at least of a dependence of either on the other cannot well

1. P. 421.
2. P. 412.
3. Encyclopaedia Brittanica, Vol, XXIII, p. 672 of the 9th Edn.

be denied when we know as a historical fact that two Greek physicians, Ktesis about 400 B. C., and Megasthenes about 300 B. C., visited or resided in northern India."[1] "That Greek medicine adopted Indian medicaments and methods is evident from the literature. The contact between the two civilisations became intimate through the march of Alexander, and continued unbroken through the reign of the Diadochi and the Roman and Byzantine eras * * . During the rule of the Abbasidies, the Indian physicians attained still greater repute in Persia, whereby Indian medicine became engrafted upon the Arabic, an effect which was hardly increased by the Arabian Dominion over India."[2] "I wish to impress upon you most strongly that you should not run away with the idea that everything that is good in the way of medicine is contained within the ringed fence of allopathy or western medicine. The longer I remain in India and the more I see of the country and the people, the more convinced I am that many of the empirical methods of treatment adopted by the Vaidyans and Hakims are of the greatest value, and there is no doubt whatever that their ancestors knew ages ago many things which are now-a-days being brought forward as new discoveries."[3] About its past glory Europeans were made to sing the praises ; about its present condition, let an Indian speak out. "Whatever may have been the past glory of Āyuṟvēḏa, it would be self-deception on our part to think that we still sit on a high pedestal. The fact is unfortunately just the other way. The number of Āyūṟvēḏic physicians in India is legion, but soundly educated exponents of the ancient system are not numerous. Besides, there is yet a good deal of conservatism, which is contrary

1. Dr. Hoerule, Preface to his 'Studies in the Medicine of Ancient India'.

2. Dr. Neuberger, History of Medicine .

3. Sir Pardey Lukes, late Surgeon-General, for some time Principal of the Medical College, Calcutta, and late Director-General of the Indian Medical Service.

to the liberal spirit of Āyurvēḍa, and which must be overcome. Much of the old literature has been lost and what exists is not often studied in a scientific spirit. If the sound principles and methods of treating diseases with the time-honoured recipes of reliable efficacy were not there, the Āyurvēḍic system of medicine would have been dead by this time in the struggle for existence. So, let us not be slow in recognising the crying need for reform. We may have once made great progress in surgery, but we must confess that we now lag sadly behind * * and even in the great departments of medicine and pharmacy which are our great pride and mainstay, we must work hard to demonstrate and utilise the principles of medicine that we have in our books."[1]

In the socio-political organisation said to have been introduced into Malabar by the Nambūries, there was a special place assigned to the practitioners of the healing art. To eight Nambūri houses was assigned the hereditary profession of physicians of Kērala, and they are still known as the *Ashta Vaidyanmar* (Aṣhṭa Vaiḍyanmār) or the eight physicians. The names of the eight houses are :—(1) Chūnḍal, (2) Chīraṭṭamana, (3) Pulāmānṭōle, (4) Kuṭṭanchērry, (5) Ṭykāḍ, (6) Ālaṭṭūr Nampy, (7) Elayaṭaṭ Ṭykāḍ, (8) Vellōṭ.

The religious pride of the Brahmans coupled with their instinctive exclusiveness induced them, however, to lower the dignity of the medical profession by ordaining that these physicians be classed among the lesser Brahmans, who were not entitled to study the Vēḍās, as they may have to shed blood in the use of surgical instruments. The Aṣhṭa Vaiḍyans keenly felt the indignity and seldom, if ever, practised surgery.

The native system of medicine and surgery in Malabar is based on the idea that the human body is

1. Dr. Mahamahopadhyaya Kaviraj Gnananatha Sen, M. A., L. M. S.

composed of five elements—earth, water, fire, air and ether. Physical health is said to be preserved by the maintenance, in exact proportion, of the three general elements, rheum, bile and phlegm, or air, fire and water respectively.[1] The following extract from Mr. O. Caṇṇan's Introduction to his Malayalam Translation of the Sanskrit medical work Aṣhṭāngahṛḍaya with commentaries gives a fair idea of the native system of physic and the point of view from which the native physicians approach the subject. Referring to the three elements above enumerated Mr. Caṇṇan says, "Their harmonious admixture tends to constitutional nourishment, whilst anything that destroys or disturbs this harmony causes impaired health. Though, in a sense, pervading all the body, each of them is not without its allotted province; that is, air, or rheum, spreads itself below the navel; fire, or bile, between it and the heart; and water, or phlegm, above the heart and upwards. By the predominance of one of these humours over the others, the human health is deranged, whilst their proportionate evenness secures good health.

"Tastes are six in number; viz., sweet, sour, saltish, bitter, pungent and astringent, which are the attributes of substances, each preceding taste being superior to that immediately succeeding it. The first three—sweet, sour and saltish—appease rheum; and the remaining three—bitter, pungent and astringent—appease phlegm; while bile is appeased by astringent, bitter and sweet. According to another opinion, the three humours are said to be promoted by these tastes; viz., the rheum by bitter, pungent and astringent; the phlegm by sweet, sour and saltish; and the bile by pungent, sour and saltish. Substances have three forms of digestions; viz., the sweet and saltish will digest

1. Paras 14 and 23 of Appendix I of the Report of the Committee on the Indigenous Systems of Medicine, Madras, elaborate this subject.

sweetly, the sour in its original taste, and the pungent and astringent mostly turn acrid.

"Medicines are of two classes known as clearing and subsidiary. The first effects the cure by purging out the irritated humours; and the second by establishing the humours which have been disturbed in their respective positions.

"To secure health, we should try to purge out the bile and other humours according to season.

"Purgatives are essential as otherwise the humours, augmented by their stagnacy, will endanger even life. The humours allayed by fasting or by the use of medicines having digestive properties, will sometimes be irritated.

"If properly purged out, these humours are not liable to irritation."

"Oil bath, athletic exercises, simple bath and oil-syringing are also necessary, as these will restore health and establish the digestive powers, and likewise create intellectual brightness, personal beauty, acuteness of the senses, and prolongation of life. Refrain from doing anything disagreeable to the mind, feelings and thoughts, lest a deceitful conscience irritate all the humours; govern the passions and senses in order that they may not be led astray; remember the past and conduct yourself with due regard to the peculiarities of the time and place as well as your own constitution, and pursue the well-trodden path of the righteous.

"He who wishes for happiness in this as well as the next world should, in controlling the passions, successfully resist the blind rush of the thirteen mental vices known as (1) avarice, (2) envy, (3) malice, (4) enmity, (5) lust, (6) covetousness, (7) love or passion, (8) anger, (9) pride, (10) jealousy, (11) arrogance, (12) haughtiness and (13) self-conceit, inasmuch as a man, imbued with any one of them, is apt to vicious acts of divers sorts, resulting in iniquities, which gaining ground in successive births, will force themselves out in the shape of diseases, causing immense misery. Moreover when these evils take hold of the mind, their influence agitates it and destroys the mental ease and vitiates the vital air, which is wholly dependant on such mental ease; and as the very life, vigour, memory, etc., are all sustained by the vital air, its loss entails hazard to them, and injuring respiration gives rise to various diseases. By treading the paths of virtue and possessing a truthful nature, a charitable disposition, compassion, sympathy and continence, and by using such fare as is congenial to the mind, free motion to the vital air will be secured. For mental vices spiritual knowledge, combined with prudence and courage, is the best remedy, by seeking which, the mind will be liberated from evil passions and left to pursue a virtuous course." * * * * .

"Speak but little, and that significantly and opportunely, so as to be agreeable to your hearers, and let your speech be characterised by sweetness, veracity, and cheerfulness, and an open countenance graced with kindness and affabilility.

"Eat or enjoy nothing alone. Do not be over-credulous or suspicious. Be sagacious in guessing other minds; treat them with kind and greeting expressions, and do not over-vex or over-indulge the organs of taste with distasteful or delicious fare.

"Let your mental, vocal or bodily exertion cease before actual fatigue commences.

"Do not deal in, or drink, spirituous liquors, nor expose yourself to the east-wind, directly to the rays of the sun, or to the dust, snow and storm.

"Do not in a crooked position yawn, cough, sleep, or eat, nor shelter under the shadow of trees on the margins of rivers.

"As the wise have the world for their preceptor in all doings, you ought to study the movements of the righteous, keeping yourself steadily to their virtuous path.

"A tender feeling and unaffected charity towards all creatures, and a self-restraint, physical as well as vocal and mental, combined with a due regard to the interests of others, are moral virtues which complete the test of true uprightness.

"He that daily contemplates his own acts, as to whether and how he has actually realised the grand end of his existence on the day, the lapse of which has brought him nearer to the grave than on the previous day, cannot be overtaken by grief, in as much as his deliberations, secure in divine grace, will ultimately conduct him to the attainment of true wisdom, regarding the mutability of this world and the eternity of God; and, he will, thus, be freed from all sins and sorrows, and in the end gain everlasting happiness. Moreover, as each day passes, life becomes shorter, and patent is the fact that the exercise of morality can be prosecuted only while it exists, and as the extrication from sorrow is the result of a strict pursuit of virtue and abstinence from vice, a daily reckoning of the nature and amount of our virtuous deeds is a salutary remedy for all mental diseases.

"A strict adherence to the daily observances herein briefly summarised will lead to longevity, health, prosperity, reputation and eternity."

Having approached the subject in this way, the text and commentaries follow, the book being divided into six parts, containing 120 chapters giving "extremely explicit directions, first for the preventive and afterwards for the curative measures to be adopted in the multitudinous circumstances of life."[1]

4. **The Seasons.**—The seasons do not vary in the different parts of Malabar. The year may be divided into three well defined seasons—the dewy, the

1. Malabar Manual, Vol I, p. 218--20.

summer and the rainy. The first lasts from December to February. During this season, the mornings are at times foggy and the days pretty hot, but the nights are cold and chill with heavy dew-fall. The summer season commences from February, and lasts till June, when both days and nights are very hot. The intensity of the heat is mitigated by the land-wind, which, however, is not healthy, by the occasional showers of rain, and by the sea-breeze in tracts along the coast. Strong land-winds blow in the northern parts of Cochin and the southern parts of Travancore between the months of November and March. About the first week of June, the rains set in and lasts till the end of November with a short interruption in August-September. The South-West monsoon brings in the most rainfall, June and July being generally the months of heavy rainfall. The North-East monsoon bursts in October and the rains continue till November. While the annual rainfall is irregular in its distribution, and seldom varies much in quantity from year to year, the average differs in various tracts. The number of rainy days varies roughly from 100 to 140 per annum. For about nine months of the year, the sun is bright and hot "in this land of perpetual summer." During two months of the rainy season, the sun is at times invisible for three or four days together. During the greater part of the year, the air is moist and humid, and the rank vegetation that suddenly crops up with the outbreak of the monsoon conduces to make the climate enervating and somewhat unhealthy.

Average rainfall in Cochin—109.4 inches.
do Travancore—84·82 inches.
do Br. Malabar—116·4 inches.

There is a fine description of the bursting of the South-West monsoon at Anjengo given by Forbes in his *Oriental Memoirs*. "It generally sets in very early at Anjengo; it commences with great severity, and presents an awful spectacle : the inclement weather continues, with more or less violence, from May to October; during that period, the tempestuous ocean rolls from a black horizon, literally of 'darkness visible', a series of floating mountains heaving under hoary summits, until they approach the shore, where their stupendous accumulations flow in successive surges, and break upon the beach: every ninth wave is observed to be generally more tremendous than the rest, and threatens to overwhelm the settlement. The noise of these billows equals that of the loudest cannon and with the thunder and lightning, so frequent in the rainy season, is truly awful. I often stood upon the trembling sand-bank, to contemplate the solemn scene and derive a comfort from that sublime and omnipotent decree, 'Hitherto shalt thou come, but no further; and here shall thy proud waves be stayed!'[1]"[2]

There is also another passage regarding the "curious contest, not only between the deities of the sea and the river, but also between the finny race in their respective dominions. In those months when the South-West monsoon blows with the greatest violence, the floods pour down from the mountains, swell the rivers, inundate the plains, and, with astonishing rapidity, carry trees, houses, men, and beasts to the ocean: the finny tribes, disturbed in their calm retreats, are impelled to the embouchure of the river: where, led by instinct, or accidentally driven by the monsoon winds, they meet the monsters of the deep ready to devour them. The floods from the mountains impetuously rush to this outlet, and there meet a sandy bar, accumulated by the western surges, which presents a formidable barrier between the contending waters. Neptune's terrific billows dash furiously against the river stream, precipitating over the bar, and present a scene easier to conceive than describe. The floods contain

1. Job, XXXVIII-Vol. II.
2. Vol. I, p. 215.

immense shoals of fish, which, unused to such violent convulsions, attempt to escape the noise and fury by leaping over the bar into the distended jaws of the tyrants waiting to devour their timid prey. An alligator is sometimes involuntarily impelled to act a part in this extraordinary gymnasium; and of course perishes in the ocean."[1]

1. Forbe's *Oriental Memoirs*, p. 219.

LETTER III.

1. **Cochin.** The town of Cochin is situated on the southern side of a natural harbour. It was formerly the capital of the Native State which took its name after it. Previous to the year 1341 A. D., a small river flowed by Cochin having a narrow opening into the sea, the main outlet for the discharge of the waters that came in torrents down the Ghauts being at the well-known opening at Crānganūr, some twenty miles to the north of it. In the year 1341, an extraordinary flood occurred which brought down from the Ghauts such a large volume of water that it converted the land-locked harbour of Cochin into one of the finest and safest ports in India. As observed by Mr. Chisholm Anstey, "If it were not for the bar of shifting sand, it would be one of the finest in the known world: even as it is, it will be hard to match it in India. The deepest water is inside, just where the wonderful chain of inland navigation, called the back-water, finds one of its outlets to the sea. By means of that chain Cochin has not only smooth and safe access of the Ghauts eastward and to the Carnatic, but northward to the Goa territories and southward through Travancore to Cape Comorin." It was about this time that the island of Vypin, thirteen miles long by three miles broad on the north side of the harbour, was thrown up by the sea as a result of natural convulsions. The island is known as *Puthu Vaippu* (Puṭu Vaippu), i. e., new formation, and the people there commence an era from the date of its formation, A. D. 1341.[1]

1. "I was assured," says Fra Bartolomeo, "by Mr. John Truyns, the sworn interpreter of the Dutch East India Company at Cochin, that the origin of this new period, and the epoch when it began, are registered in the Chancery of the Company."—*Voyage to the East Indies*, p. 127.

The earlier notices of Malabar do not mention Cochin or its fine harbour at all. Neither the Periplus nor Ptolemy mentions it, though both give us accounts of places situated to the north and south of Cochin, such as Crānganūr (Muziris), Kallaḍa (Nilkynda), Comorin (Comar) and Kaḍalunḍi (Tyndis). Among mediaeval travellers, so far as known at present, Ma Huan (A. D. 409), a Chinese Muhammadan, attached to the suite of Cheng-Ho, an envoy of the Emperor Yong-Lo (A. D. 1403—1425) to foreign countries, is the first to give an account of Cochin. The Italian Nicolo Conti (A. D. 1440) follows him. It may be noticed that this is almost exactly a century after the formation of the harbour. Cochin attained its importance only about the time of the arrival of the Portuguese in India (A. D. 1498). Since then it has been the chief port of Malabar, passing from the hands of the Portuguese to those of the Dutch and from them to the English. Four centuries have rolled by since the white sails of the Portuguese glided slowly into the inner harbour, steering safely through the deep channel of the Vypin river, and anchored quietly in one of the finest natural harbours their wondering eyes had ever beheld. The march of time has indeed left its mark on the devoted town and its harbour. Both have gone through various vicissitudes of fortune. From a fishing village, the Portuguese raised it to a place of great commercial importance, building forts, churches, commercial houses, &c. After some time, the Dutch wrested the town from the Portuguese and improved it considerably, laying out streets and gardens. The English, in turn, took it out of the hands of the Dutch, but pulled down everything their predecessors had taken so much labour and expense to rear up, and all but succeeded in putting it back some what to its old position of comparative obscurity.

We have a *precis* of the most important details contained in Ma Huan's description of the seaport of

Cochin given us by Mr. Geo. Philips in *The Journal of the Royal Asiatic Society* for April 1896:—

"Cochin, the first port of which we shall treat, is described as a day and night's sail from Coilum, the present Quilon, most probably the Kaulam Malai of the Arabs[1] known to Chinese navigators of the Tang Dynasty (A. D. 618—915), as Muhlai. The king or ruler is of the solar race, and is a sincere believer in Buddhism,[2] and has the greatest reverence for elephants and oxen, and every morning at daylight prostrates himself before an image of Buddha. The king wears no clothing on the upper part of his person; he has simply a square piece of silk wound round his loins, kept in place by a coloured waist-band of the same material, and on his head a turban of yellow or white cotton cloth. The dress of the officers and the rich differs but little from that of the king. The houses are built of the wood of the cocoanut tree, and thatched with its leaves, which render them perfectly water-tight.

"There are five classes of men in this kingdom. The Nayars rank with the king. In the first class are those who shave their heads, and have a thread or string hanging over their shoulder; these are looked upon as belonging to the noblest families.[3] In the second are the Mahomedans; in the third the Chittis, who are the capitalists; in the fourth the Kolings,[4]

1. Vide Yule's Glossary under Malabar.

2. " Our traveller, " says Mr. Phillips in a note, " makes no distinction between Buddhism and Hinduism. The Chinese text * * * is clear as to Buddhism being meant". Bhud dism was, however, at one time prevelant in Malabar.

3. Perhaps the Nambūri Brahmans are here referred to.

4. Perhaps the same with the Quilins who are mentioned along with the Chetṭies by the early Portuguese writers. They are also known as the Kling or Cheling, a term used to denote the people of continental India who trade in the Malay countries and Strait Settlements or are settled in those regions, and the descendants of such settlers. See Yule's Glossary, pp. 144—372.

who act as commission agents; in the fifth the Mukwas, who are the lowest and poorest of all. The Mukwas live in houses which are forbidden by the Government to be more than three feet high, and they are not allowed to wear long garments; when abroad, if they happen to meet a Nayar or a Chitti, they at once prostrate themselves on the ground and dare not rise until they have passed by; these Mukwas get their living by fishing and carrying burdens.

"The merchants of this country carry on their business as pedlars do in China. Here also is another class of men, called Chokis (Yōgi), who lead austere lives like the Taoists of China, but who, however, are married. These men from the time they are born do not have their heads shaved or combed, but plait their hair into several tails, which hang over their shoulders; they wear no clothes, but round their waists they fasten a strip of rattan, over which they hang a piece of white calico; they carry a conch-shell, which they blow as they go along the road; they are accompanied by their wives, who simply wear a small bit of cotton cloth round their loins. Alms of rice and money are given to them by the people whose houses they visit.

"In this country there are two seasons, the wet and the dry. In the first two months of the rainy season there are only passing showers, during which time the people lay in a stock of provisions; in the next two months there is a continual downpour, day and night, so that the streets and market places are like rivers, and no one is able to go out of doors; during the last two months the rain gradually ceases, and then not a drop falls for another six months. The soil is unproductive, pepper, however, grows on the hills and is extensively cultivated; this article is sold at five tales the P'o-ho, which is four hundred Cattis of Chinese weight.

"All trading transactions are carried on by the Chittis, who buy the pepper from the farmers when it is ripe, and sell it to foreign ships when they pass by. They also buy and collect precious stones and other costly wears. A pearl weighing three and a half candareens can be bought for a hundred ounces of silver. Coral is sold by the Catti; inferior pieces of coral are cut into beads and polished by skilled workmen; these are also sold by weight. The coinage of the country is a gold piece, called fanam, weighing one candareen; there is also a little silver coin called Ta-urh, which is used for making small purchases in the market. Fifteen Ta-urhs make a Fa-nam. There are no asses or geese in this country, and there is neither wheat nor barley; rice, maize, hemp, and millet abound. Articles of tribute are sent to China by our ships on their return voyage."

Nicolo Conti calls the town Cocym. Barbosa, the anonymous *sommaris dei Regni* in Ramusio, and D' Barros mention it as Cochin, while Lisbon Editions of Barbosa and Conti have Cochin, Cocym, or Cochym. So also Gutchin of Spinger. G. Balbi has Cochi. It is remarkable that Nicolo Conti, in the fifteenth century, and Fra Paolino, in the seventeenth, both say that the town was called Kochi, after the small river that flowed by that place. It is locally known as Kochi, and *kochu* in the Malayalam language means small. It is also significant that the Sanskrit Kērala Māhāṭmyam calls it Bālapuri, a small town.[1]

In the early part of the fifteenth century, Nicolo Conti travelling in the east reached Quilon or, as he calls it, Coloen. Having quitted Coloen, he arrived, after a journey of three days, at the city of Cocym. "This city is five miles in circumference, and stands at the mouth of a river, from which it derives its name. Sailing for some time in this river, he saw many fires lighted along the banks, and thought that they were made by fishermen. But those who were with him in

1. Bālā means a young girl, and puri, a town.

the ship exclaimed, smiling, '*Icepe*! *Icepe*!.' These have the human form, but may be called either fishes or monsters which issuing from the water at night collect wood and, procuring fire by striking one stone against another, ignite it and burn it near the water; the fishes attracted by the light, swim towards it in great numbers, when the monsters who lie hid in the water, seize them and devour them. They said that some which they had taken, both male and female, differed in no respect as to their form from human beings." A marvellous traveller's tale indeed!—of the Mandeville type, however. Surely a sober traveller like Conti would not be gulled into believing such trash. Hence perhaps the express assertion that the story rests on the testimony of his travelling companions. So far as his personal observation is concerned, he stops a good way short of the marvellous and attributes the many fires he saw lighted along the banks to fishermen carrying torches in order to attract the shoals of fish that swim in great numbers towards the light. Four centuries have passed by since Conti visited Cochin. Yet the attention of the latest arrival in these parts will even to-day be attracted by the numerous fires lighted, all along the coast-line after it is dark by the descendants of Conti's 'Icepe' for no other purpose than for replenishing their fish baskets. Of course, the specimens male and female, which Conti's companions had the good fortune to secure did not look like fishes or monsters and "differed in no respect as to their form from human beings," for the simple reason that they belonged to that class of beings whom God created in his own image.

In this district, adds Conti, the same fruits are found as in Coloen, and these are jack fruit, the mango, and the pepper.

1. Major's India in the Fifteenth Century.

VIEWS OF PORTUGUESE COCHIN.

To face page 67.]

For about a century and a half after the formation of the harbour, the Cochin Rajas enjoyed the advantages of this outlet to the ocean. The country was enriched by the trade it carried on with China, Arabia, Persia, and with the coast towns of Western India and the neighbouring countries. But, latterly, its trade had begun to decline owing to the exertions of the more energetic Zamorin between whom and the Cochin Rajas a deadly enmity had existed from time out of mind. Backed up by his enterprising Arab and Moorish allies, the Zamorin had enticed away most of the merchants to Calicut, and the Christian traders were driven from the coast by the Mussalmans. Under these circumstances, the Cochin Raja viewed with extreme satisfaction the advent of the Portuguese.

Cochin was then "the capital of a kingdom of the same name, nineteen leagues south of Calicut. It stood upon a river, was very strong, and had a safe and capacious port. The land about it was low, and divided into many islands. It was built after the manner of Calicut and inhabited with Gentiles and Moors who came from sundry parts to trade. There were two, each of whom had fifty ships. Provisions were not plenty. But here was pepper enough, most of that which was at Calicut being brought from hence. Yet the greater resort of merchants was at this latter place which was therefore the richer of the two."[1] Such is the testimony of the early Portuguese.

Under the Portugese, Cochin rapidly grew into a large and flourishing town and soon became a centre of commerical importance. Before Goa was built, it was looked upon as the official residence of the Viceroy of India. It extended to a mile and a half in length and a mile in breadth and was well built, having many public structures which beautified the town and gave it an imposing appearance. Baldeus has preserved a

1. Astley's Collection of Voyages, p. 33.

plan of the Portuguese town of Cochin as it stood at the time of the Dutch conquest. It appears to have covered all the sandy waste to the west of the present town, and to have run along the sea-shore; in this part was situated the monastery of St. Paul; whilst in the opposite direction, it narrowed off along the banks of the back-water, till the walls met in two or three formidable bastians somewhere in the vicinity of the Muttancherry bridge; and hereabouts stood the monastery of the Augustine monks. The Franciscan monastry stood on the eastern side of the present Government church; whilst the foundations of the Dominican convent are still traceable around the plot of ground occupied some time ago by the Protestant Free Schools. The Jesuits too had their establishment within the walls of the town. The place is said to have had an imposing appearance from the sea, for the Government buildings were well constructed, whilst the Cathedral, and the churches of the Dominicans and Augustinians are said to have been truly splendid; and all were enclosed in strong fortifications, which, when well manned, could stand a long siege.[1]

Between the years 1563 and 1581, Caesar Frederick, merchant of Venice,. voyaged to the East Indies and visited Malabar.[2] He described Cochin as the "chiefest place that the Portugals have in the Indies next unto Goa"; "and there is great trade of spices, drugges and all other sorts of merchandise for the kingdoms of Portugale." He speaks of the great privileges enjoyed by "those Portugales which are married, and are citizens in the Citie, Cochin, of the Portugales." He adds that "by this name of Portugales, throughout all the Indies, they call all the Christians that came out of the West, whether they be Italians, Frenchmen, or Almaignes." With regard

1. Whitehouse.—*Historical Notices of Cochin*, p. 14.

2. *Hakluyt's Voyages*, Vol. V, pp. 392-395.

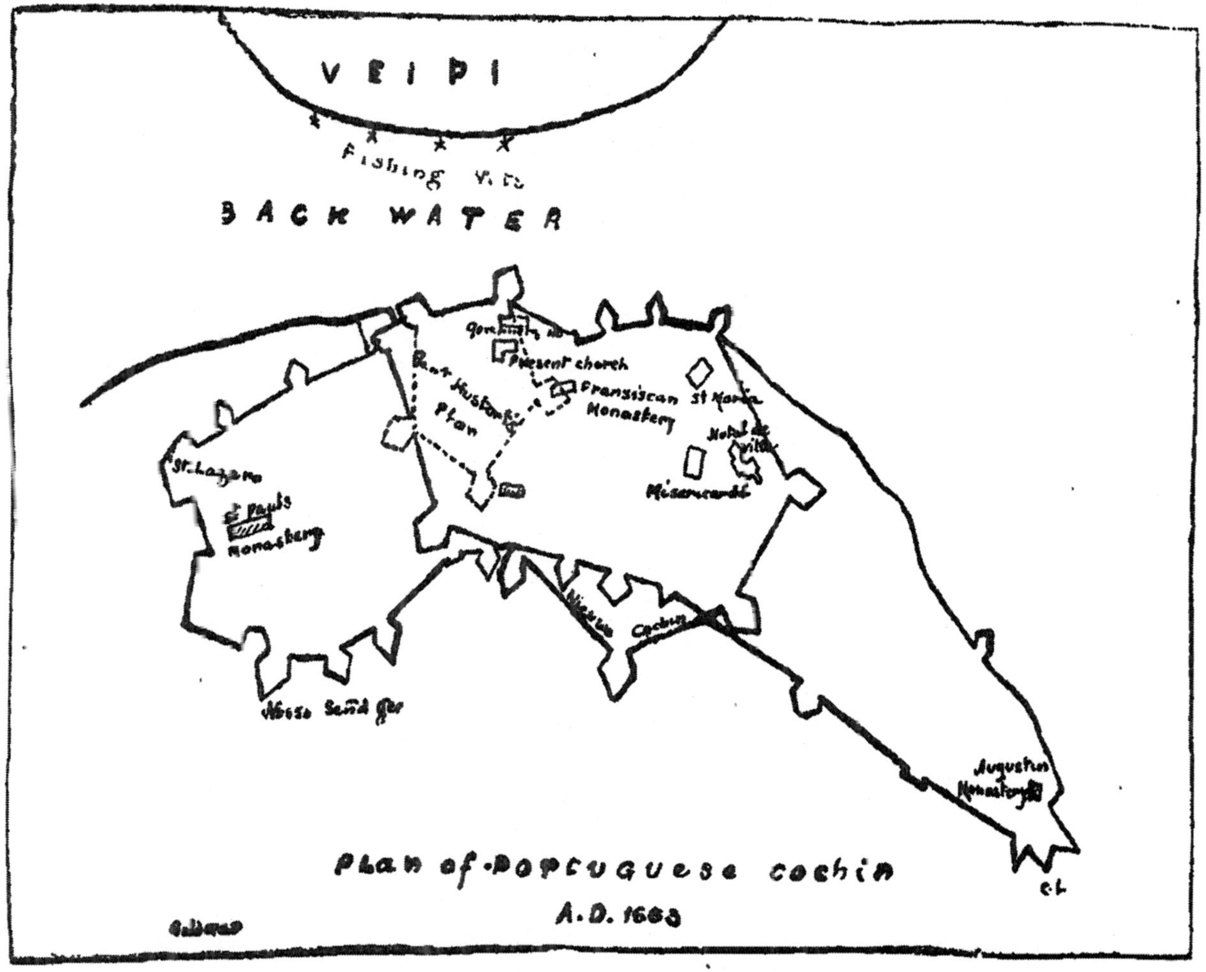

PLAN OF PORTUGUESE COCHIN 1663.

To face page 168.]

to the special privileges possessed by them, he observes: "All that marry in Cochin do get an office according to the trade he is of: this they have by the great privileges which the citizens have of the city because there are two principal commodities that they deal withal in that place, which are these; the great store of silke that commeth from China, and the great store of sugar which commeth from Bengala: the married citizens pay not any custome for these two commodities: for all other commodities they pay four per cents custome to the king of Cochin, rating their goods at their own pleasure. Those which are not married and strangers pay in Cochin to the king of Portugale eight per cents of all manner of merchandize."[1] "I was in Cochin," adds the traveller, "when the Viceroy of the king of Portugale wrought what he coulde to breake the privilege of the citizens, and to make them to pay customes as other did: at which time the citizens were glad to weigh their pepper in the night that they laded the ships with all that went to Portugale and stole the custome in the night. The king of Cochin having understanding of this, would not suffer any more pepper to be weighed. Then presently after this, the merchants were licensed to doe as they did before and there was no more speech of this matter, nor any wrong done."

There was considerable trade in export carried on between Cochin and Portugal. The ships bound for Portugal with cargo leave Cochin every year on the 5th of December or the 5th of January. "They lade ships in Cochin for Portugal and for Ormus," says Caesar Frederick, speaking of the articles of trade, "but they that goe for Ormus carrie no pepper but

1. William Barret (1584) makes mention of this privilege. With regard to the coins current in Cochin in his time he observes:—"The money of Cochin are all the same sorts which are current in Goa, but the ducket of gold in value is ten *tangas* of good money". *Hakluyt's Voyages*, Vol. VI, p. 21.

only contrabanda, as for sinamome they easilie get leave to carrie that away, for all other spices and drugs they may liberally carrie them to Ormus or Cambaia, and so all other merchandise which come from other places, but out of the kingdome of Cochin properly they carry away with them into Portugale great abundance of pepper, great quantities of ginger, dried and conserved, wild sinamome, good quality of arecca, great store of cordage of caire made of the bark of the tree of the great nut, and better than that hempe, of which they carry great store into Portugale."

From "A declaration of the places from whence the goods subscribed doe come" made about this time, we see the following articles mentioned against the name "Cochin": "Pepper, gawrie, sandals, wilde chopra, lignum aloes, galangoe, spodio-di-cana, folium indicum."[1]

The first Englishman to visit Cochin was Master Ralph Fitch to whom belongs the honour of being the "Pioneer Englishman", who had journeyed to India even before the first voyage of James Lancaster who sailed from Plymouth in 1591. The beginning of the English trade with the East is generally dated from this voyage. But Ralph Fitch had, in the company of other merchants, completed his voyage to India by the time Lancaster sailed from Plymouth. "In the yeere of our Lord 1583", says Fitch, "I, Ralph Fitch of London, merchant, being desirous to see the countreys of the East India, in the company of M. John Newberie, merchant (which had been at Ormus once before), of William Leedes, jeweller, and James Story, painter, being chiefly set forsooth by the right worshipfull Sir Edward Osborne, Knight, and M. Richard Staper, citizens and merchants of London, did ship myself in a ship of London called Tyger." He carried with him royal missives to Indian and China kings, was taken

1. *Hakluyt's Voyages*, Vol, VI, p. 24.

prisoner on his way by the Portuguese, escaped from their custody, completed the journey and returned visiting many important places on the way.

Among the places visited was Cochin where he lived several months. " Thus passing the coast," says Fitch, "we arrived in Cochin the 22 of March, where we found the weather warm, but scarcity of victuals; for here groweth neither corne nor rice, and the greatest part commeth from Bengala. They have here very bad water, for the river is farre off. This bad water causeth many of the people to be like lepers, and many of them have their legs swollen as bigge as a man in the waste, and many of them are scant able to go. These people here be Malabars, and of the race of the Naires of Calicut: and they differ much from the other Malabars. These have their heads very foel of haire, and bound up with a string, and good archers with a long bow and a long arrow, which is their best weapon: yet there be some calivers among them, but they handle them badly.

" Here groweth the pepper; and it springeth up by a tree or pole, and is like our ivy berry, but something longer like the wheat eare; and at the first the bunches are green, and as they waxe ripe they cut them off and dry them. The leafe is much lesser then the ivy leafe and thinner. All the inhabitants here have very little houses covered with the leaves of the coco-trees. The men be of reasonable stature; the women little blacke, with a cloth bound about their middle hanging down to their hammes, all the rest of their bodies be naked: they have horrible great ears with many rings set with pearles and stones in them. The king goeth incached; as they do all: he doth not remain in a place above five or six days: he hath many houses, but they be but little; his guard is but small: he remooveth from one house to another according to their order. All the pepper of Calicut and course cinamom groweth here in this countrey. The best cinamom doth come from Ceylon, and it is pilled from fine yoong trees. Here are very many palmere or coco-trees, which is their chief food: for it is their meat and drinke: and yeeldeth many other neces sary things, as I have declared before ."[1]

Just before the Dutch capture of Cochin, Sir Thomas Herbert, the Englishman (1653), describes Cochin "as the chief place the Portuguese have in the Indies, where is the greatest trade of spices, drugs, and all other merchandise ."

The Dutch captured the town in 1663 and considerably altered it, removing everything they deemed "obstructive to their rule, their religion or their convenience." Most of the houses and streets were allowed to stand, though the latter were re-named. The chief were as follows:—de Linde (Lime tree) Straat, de Lily Straat, Heere (Gentleman) Straat, de Peeter enlie (Parsby) Straat, de Bue (Broad) Straat, de Sime (Smith) Straat, de Osse (ox) Straat, de Kalven (calf) Straat, etc. They formed a botanical garden on the ground belonging to the Roman Catholic Church and named the street leading to it from the Government House, Bloomendaal (Flowerdale) Straat. The only building of consequence which the Dutch erected was the Commander's house which stood at the N. W. angle of the Fort, its walls being washed by the river where it debouches into the sea. They also raised a pile of buildings on the old parade ground, the chief of which were *het ammesnite Huys* (ammunition depot) and de Lyfwagt.[2]

Baldeus speaking of Cochin says, "The Jesuit Church and College facing the sea-shore, had a lofty steeple, and a most excellent set of bells. The college which was then three stories high, and contained about

1. Ralph Fitch, England's Pioneer to India, by J. Horton Ryley, 1899, pp. 185--6.

2. Whitehouse.

20 or 30 apartments, was surrounded with a strong wall."

In John Nieuhoff's *Remarkable Voyages and Travels into the Best Provinces of the West and East Indies*, we find the following description of Cochin, under date 1662:—"Some authors make mention of two different Cochins, viz., the old Cochin lying about a league and a half from the sea-shore. The Portuguese call it Cochin Dacima, or Higher Cochin, because it lies higher up the river; by the Dutch it is called Cochin Malabar, where the king keeps his residence, being situated upon the banks of a river, and pretty well-peopled and adorned with several goodly structures and pagodas. The other, called new Cochin, is scarcely a league from the sea, and was in the possession of the Portuguese." Caesar Frederick also gives similar descriptions of the two Cochins.[1] "Among other steeples," writes Nieuhoff, "that of St. Pauls (the Jesuit Church) being magnificently built of square stones exceeded all the rest in height as beauty. The Austin Friyer's, Franciscan's and Jesuit's had likewise their several convents magnificently built with very pleasent gardens and walks." Another traveller (Sieur de Rennefort) of the same period speaks of twenty-three churches built by the Portuguese in Cochin and its suburbs; and, as if these had not been sufficient, the Dutch discovered the foundations of one designed to be much bigger than any of the others. The Jesuit, Pierre Martin, in the Letters Edefiante's &c., contrasting with the Dutch period, tells us (in a tone of lamentation) that when under the dominion of Portugal, "One saw in Cochin, on every hand a great number of apostolic men, who went to carry the light of faith amongst the idolatrous nations." Once in possession of Cochin Van Goens, the Dutch Commandant, played the vandal. "You must know," writes Tavernier, "that at the taking of

1 See *Hakluyt's Voyages*, Vol. V., p. 393.

Cochin, the Jesuits had in that city one of the fairest libraries in all Asia as well as for the great quantity of books sent them out of Europe as for several rare manuscripts in the Hebrew, Chaldiac, Arabic, Persian, Indian, Chinese and other oriental languages. For in all the conquests of the Portugals, their first care was to summon all the learned people of several nations, and to get all their books into their hands. During the little time the Jesuits were in Ethiopia, they had copied out all the books that came into their knowledge and sent all these books to Cochin. But to tell ye what became of this library : General Van Geons made no conscience to expose it to the ignorance of his soilders, so that I have seen the soldiers and sea-men tear several of those beautiful volumes to light their tobacco. "[1]

Dr. John Fryer visited Cochin in the course of his voyage to India (1672—1681) and describes it as "once a famous mart of the Portugals wrested from them and made impregnable by the Dutch."

We get glimpses of Cochin, when in the possession of the Dutch, from accounts left us by Mr. Forbes and the French author, Anqutail Du Perron, as well as from Bartolomeo who was in the country for a long time. Anqutail Du Perron visited Cochin towards the latter part of the year 1757 and stayed till the beginning of 1758. He lets us have a peep into the inner life of the governing class, the personnel and the system of Government, &c. Forbes (1772), on the other hand, gives us an idea of its commercial position. The latter describes it as "a place of great trade presenting a striking contrast to Goa : a harbour filled with ships, streets crowded with merchants and warehouses stored with goods from every part of Asia and Europe marked the industry, the commerce and the wealth of the inhabitants."[2] Ives in 1757 found Cochin

1. Whitehouse,—*Lingernigs of Light in a Dark Land.* See quotation at p. 168.

2. Vol. 1, p. 208.

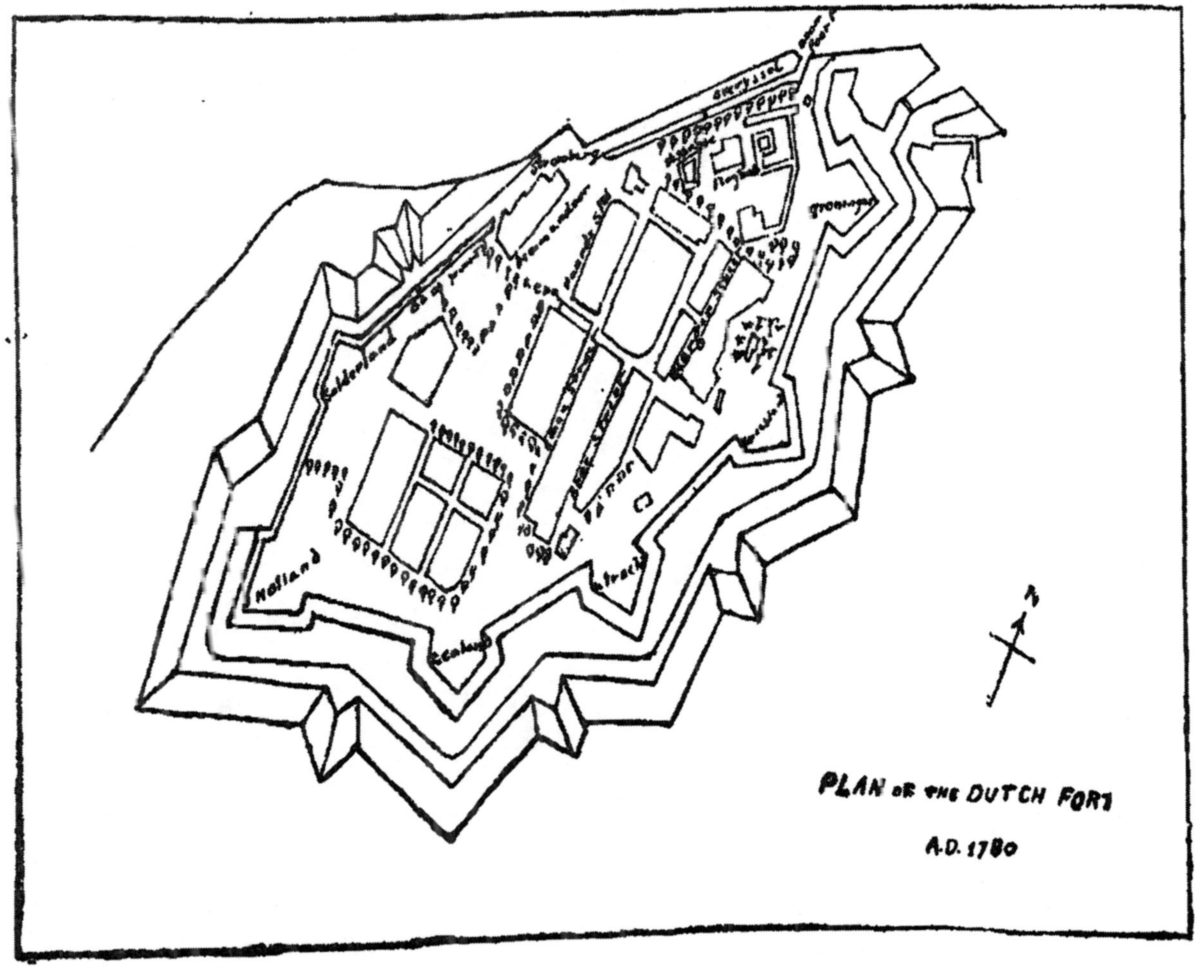

PLAN OF THE DUTCH FORT IN COCHIN 1780.

To face page 174.]

"not unpleasant, but in point of grandeur, regularity and indeed, in every other respect, it fell greatly short of Colombo."[1] Bartolomeo tells us that after the Dutch had become masters of Cochin, they carried off from it a great deal of riches. After that period, he adds, the beautiful cathedral was converted into a warehouse for the Dutch East India Company. "This edifice is now employed for preserving the sugar which the Company obtains from Batavia, and the cinnamon they receive from Ceylon together with nutmegs, cloves, iron, copper, cordage, rice, pepper, and various other articles of merchandise, which they bring hither from foreign countries, and sell partly to the Indian princes, and partly to Arabian as well as other native and foreign merchants. Cochin is intersected by beautiful streets: the arsenal is well provided with all kinds of military stores, and the citadel is strongly fortified. The latter, in the year 1778, was supplied with new ditches, bridges, batteries and bastions, under the direction of the the Governor Adrian Moens. It lies on the southern bank of the Coci, and commands the harbour, which is open to merchant vessels, but into which no ship of war is suffered to enter."[2]

Cochin remained with the Dutch till the year 1795 when, taking advantage of the rupture with Holland, the English under Major Petrie appeared before the town which was surrendered to him on the 20th of October. It was formally ceded to the British only in 1814.

On the occupation of Cochin by the British, they continued the Dutch form of Government. They had always to keep a watchful eye on the Raja of Cochin who appears not to have been very much pleased at the change of the European Governors of Cochin. There were constant outbreaks in Cochin and the

1. P. 194.
2. P. 130.

adjoining districts and at times these extended to the town itself; so much so that the Government thought it necessary to reimpose in Cochin the Regulation of July 22nd 1793 restraining the bringing of arms and ammunitions into the town. The Raja expected external aid from other European nations and the Dutch prisoners of war fomented his unpleasant relations with the English by presenting him with a portrait of Napoleon promising to procure support from that quarter. Thereupon the Raja's people assumed an insolent attitude, and the Cochin garrison had to be directed to "strictly exclude all the servants of the Cochin Raja from British territory, lying around the town." This state of unpleasantness continued for some time, the Cochin Dewan making attempts to encroach on British power till at last, inspired by the Travancore Dewan Velu Thampy, the Cochin minister, Paliath Achan, joined the former in violently attacking Cochin and attempting to murder the British Resident, Col. Macaulay, who was then living in what is now the Court house and Cutchery. Six hundred of the Travancoreans made a mad rush on the Resident's house at half-past two A. M., on the 29th December 1808, obtained possession of it and destroyed everything. They failed in finding Col. Macaulay, as he had already effected his escape along with his escort and got on board a *Pattimar*. This revolt continued and, on the 21st January 1809, the late Dutch Governor's house was broken open and plundered and the garden destroyed. On the 25th the Travancoreans once more attacked Cochin advancing from the south, setting fire to and burning the custom house at Mattancherry and breaking down the Mattancherry bridge on their way. But they were soon driven back. The rioters continued to hover about Cochin for some time more till efficient measures were adopted to put down the insurrection. A British army marched into Travancore and brought the erring Dewan and his associates to book, whereupon the Cochin Raja accepted

VIEWS OF COCHIN (from the sea — 1772 ; from the land side — 1780.

To face page 176.]

an offer of friendship, expressed his sorrow for the conduct of his minister, Paliath Achan, who was sent into exile, and his family title of hereditary prime minister to the Cochin Raja was taken away. There were a few troops left in Cochin till the year 1860, when the last vestige of the military occupation ceased.

"The early history of Cochin under the British rule," observes the Rev. Mr. Whitehouse, "is not calculated to reflect credit upon the Hon. East India Company. Utterly neglected for a long period with a declining trade, and an impoverished population, generally deprived of all religious and educational advantages, one cannot wonder that it gradually sunk, lower and lower, commercially, socially and morally."[1]

Bishop Middleton, writing in 1816, describes Cochin thus:—"It proved to be in a condition, in all respects sufficiently miserable: some of the principal edifices neglected, and falling into decay: the Dutch church shut up for want of a minister, the school in the fort destroyed, the children left unbaptized, the sick unassisted, and without the last consolatory offices: and a total apathy amongst the inhabitants respecting education and religion."[2] Such had been the state of the place for nearly fifteen years when Bishop Middleton visited Cochin. At the time of the British conquest, there were in the town several buildings of importance, not to say of great magnificence. Of those reared for religious purposes by the pious hands of the Catholic Portuguese, not a few were pulled down or desecrated by the Calvinist Hollander. The magnificent Portuguese Cathedral of Santa Cruz had been converted by the Dutch into a storehouse for their merchandise, and the English in their turn had its nave blown up, on the plea that it occupied too much

1. Historical Notices, p. 31.

2. Life of Middleton, Vol. 1, p. 233.

space. Its tower was, however, retained for use as a flag-staff and lighthouse. Its height will give us some idea of the Cathedral itself. It stood sixty-seven feet, eight inches high above the level of the grass. The light was shown at an elevation of sixty-seven feet above the tower except during the South-West monsoon, when it was placed at thirty-two. It was struck down by a flash of lightning on the 11th of May 1809, when all traces of the once magnificent Cathedral were finally blotted out.

The Church of the Franciscans had been appropriated by the Dutch for their form of worship. In the palmy days of the Portuguese Empire in the East, its spacious nave had seen the gorgeous performance of the Catholic form of worship in all its pomp and glitter. Its chancel had afforded a temporary home to the mortal remains of the great Portuguese navigator Vasco-da-Gama. The date of its erection is not known, but inscriptions on the pavement show that it had existed in 1546; and the fact of the internment of Vasco-da-Gama in its chancel makes it certain that it was erected before 1525, so that we may conclude that the church was built within 25 years after the Portuguese had obtained a footing in Cochin, and was, therefore, perhaps the first European Church in India. It is now known as the Protestant church and is used for the established form of worship. In the hands of the British, it was not to have escaped the vandalism of the East India Company. Mr. Lawson tells us that "some barrels of gunpowder had been already placed inside and everything was ready for its demolition, when, at the eleventh hour, the officer in command relented, and so happily this interesting pile has no trace of our sad levelling principles." Mr. Lawson gives us an interesting description of its condition in his days (A. D. 1860):—

"The church cannot lay claim to any great architectural merit. It has a tall gable towards the west, with arched windows and porch, columns and pinnacles of a very obsolete fashion—the exterior is more or less blackened by wind and storm, and butresses, six feet square at the base, support the walls which are four feet thick. The nave, a hundred and fourty-two feet long, fifty-one broad and to the angle in the strong braced roof above fifty feet high, is airy, bright and simple; long benches are arranged right and left to the reading desk and pulpit, and the stone pavement is occasionally irregular from the deep carvings on the monumental slabs. A broad spanned arch separates the nave from the chancel, extending across which behind the communion table is a handsomely carved screen with tablets gold on blue let into alternate panels. Though the interior is well nigh as innocent of ornament as that of a Methodist chapel, its historic interest has made the inhabitants of Cochin highly proud of their old church.

"Many of the inscriptions on the tombs are interesting for their quaint yet characteristic style.

"This is a translation of one of the oldest:—

'Here lies Maria Memdes, who begs for the love of God, one Pater Noster for her soul, died on the 14th October of the era 1562 Anno.'

"This is inscribed over a sailor:—

'Here rests the old trading Captain Baren Hermans being son of Uchtman Haftencer. Deserves for praise a crown—Vixit 63 years, obit 29th April Anno 1673.'

"The two following are singularly precise:—

'Here rests mistress Lea Vander Koute, wife of the Honorable Herr, commander Isaac Van Dielen died the 29th December, Anno 1688, being aged 32 years, minus a few hours. And Lea Gertruda Van Dielen, little daughter of both, died 11th November previous, aged three years, five months and seventeen days.'

'Here under rests the Honorable Herr Isaac Van Dielen, Commander and chief officer on the coast of Malabar, Canara and Vingorla. Died 25th December in the evening between 10 and 11 o'clock, being aged forty-one years, seven months and twenty days Anno 1693.'

"And this appears to be the most recent:—

'Hereunder rests, for holy Resurrection the body of the deceased, well born, Herr Reinen Van Harm, in life Senior Merchant, second,[1] and head administrator of this Government. Born at Campen on the 12th December 1734. Died the 16th March 1789 aged fifty-four years, three months and four days.'

"Since 1794 no burials have taken place in the church, the vaults were filled up, and the doors seldom unlocked until in 1817 the Bishop of Calcutta appointed a clergyman to this coast, and after a long period of but monthly services, the present Chaplain was established to this town individually by the Additional Clergy Society. His comfortable Parsonage is close by surrounded by a large garden containing a rare collection of tropical fruits and flowers."[2]

A few years before this, on the 9th of November 1857, Mr. Chisholm Anstey visited Cochin and he gives us a graphic, but doleful, account of the town as it then stood. He makes the following entry in his private journal:—

"I was agreeably surprised with the appearance of the town. It is not that the destruction was less complete than the vandals of Leadenhall Street designed. On the contrary, it is hard to imagine a more faithful and exact performance of the will of a superior than was rendered here in 1806 by the Company's

1. i. e., Second in rank to the Governor-General of Batavia.

2. Lawson's British and Native Cochin, pp. 23—26.

Proconsuls to their intelligent and honorable masters. The stupendous quays, shattered into enormous masses by the company's mines of gunpowder, still encumber the anchorage, and make embarkation and disembarkation difficult. Not a vestige remains of most of the public buildings. The magnificent ware-houses of the Dutch East India Company, which won admiration from the rest of the world, and envy from our own Company, were the first to be sprung into the air. There is a solitary Tower left—the 'Flagstaff' they call it now—to tell where stood the Cathedral of Cochin, and where the body of Vasco-da-Gama was buried. His grave has been defiled by us, and its very place is now forgot. 'You are within fifty yards of it, but on which side I cannot say'—was the only indication which a well-read and careful investigator of local antiquities—himself a resident here for some years past—could give me of the whereabouts of him, who opened the Indian ocean to *our* commerce—to *all* commerce. One church—diverted from the Portuguese to the Dutch worship, and from the latter to the Protestant Establishment—is the only one which the Company's Guy Fauxes were pleased to spare. That too is the only building left us whereby to justify our faith in the chronicles which record the ancient wealth and splendour of Cochin."

The journal then goes on to state that Cochin came into British hands in 1796, the British being the allies of the Stadtholder; and in 1806 it was feared that the ministry of Charles James Fox might restore Cochin and other Dutch Colonies to Holland, and so the only port south of Bombay where large ships could be built would be withdrawn from the East India Company. "So in that year the British authorities gave the word to blow up with gunpowder the fortifications, public buildings, etc., and great was the company of Guy Faux: great also the success. The Company's Gazetteers are still able to record that not only war and trade and Government were made impossible, but animal life itself. 'Scarcely a private house', we are told, 'of any size or value remained standing': all who could do so 'left the place'; 'all who could not', it is coolly added, 'sunk into abject beggary, though some formerly possessed titles, and held high rank and station' * * Really it cheers one to think that there is a complaisance which can chronicle such things, and not be ashamed! Still, in its ruins it is inviting enough: were it not for the misery of the indigent, which its now renaissant trade will in time extinguish. One can trace out the ruins for a mile square from the sea, even beneath the forest growth and herbage. * * * Now that free trade and liberty of the press have wrested, (1851) tardily enough, from Leadenhall street, the bare permission to those who will, to go out and live at Cochin and trade there, if they can, there are signs of life even amongst these ruins. In this wretched fishing village, for in 1815 it was no better, there are already now in 1857 seventeen thriving mercantile establishments: amongst them all they exported last year from Cochin not less than 600,000 sterling worth of Cochin and Travancore produce. The Company has suffered the backwater navigation to fall into ruin. But all is of a-piece with the policy which sprung the mines of 1806 upon the wharves and magazines of the same commerce. I could not help reflecting thus, as to-day I saw the *Persian*, a ship more than 700 tons, lying off one of the ruined quays to which she was moored, and which, albeit in ruins, was still so useful that the cargo could be carried on board along a foot plank without the need of a boat."[1]

The learned translator of Correa adds: "Thoronton, McCulloch, and the French Geographical Dictionary of Guibert agree in stating that this destruction took place in 1806, but no trace of it is to be found in the 'India Office or Admiralty Indexes'."[2]

1. Quoted by Stanely in his Correa, pp. 428-30.

2. See Thoronton's *Gazetteer* and Edge's Description of the Sea-ports of Malabar.

A decade after Anstey's visit, Col. James Welsh passed by Cochin and has left us an interesting description of the place. He observes that "the hand of time, the not less destructive hand of John Bull, and the extreme poverty of the remaining inhabitants, have alike combined to reduce this once flourishing city, to a small insignificant town." He then refers to the great facilities which Cochin possessed for ship-building. "A ready access to the finest timber for maritime purposes, with the facility of launching vessels of any size, have still secured to the port the almost exclusive privilege of ship-building, and the ship-wrights and carpenters are, therefore, expert and numerous. Here, of late years, some of the largest and best ships in the Eastern and Chinese trade, have been built: and several frigates were also constructed for the Royal Navy; but heavy duties, with the causes already mentioned have now reduced it to insignificance as a trading port."[1] The ship-building trade has altogether deserted Cochin and the expert ship-wrights and carpenters now live only in the memories of old residents; steam, steel and iron have taken the bread out of their mouths. The trade of Cochin is, however, looking up. There are several European firms engaged in exporting pepper, ginger, nux-vomica, cocoanut oil, coprah, cardamoms and other articles of great value. The coir manufacturing industry is also not neglected. The advent of the railway to Ernakulam on the opposite coast will no doubt give an impetus to Cochin's prosperity in the future. But till the harbour is improved, and steamers of large draught are enabled to enter the inner harbour by maintaining a uniform depth, Cochin can never hope to attain its once undoubted prominence.

2. **Decline of Portuguese Power.** By the end of the sixteenth century, the Portuguese Empire had begun to wane after having attained its zenith

1. Col. James Welsh,—Military Reminiscences, Vol. II.

some time before. Another power from the west had begun to try conclusions with Portugal for empire in the East. Casting off the shackles forged for them by the tyranny of Philip II of Spain, and conscious of the independence secured in the face of great odds, the undaunted Hollander had set his persevering energy on the acquisition of commercial supremacy in the East, and if possible, of an Oriental Empire. The Portuguese policy of conquest, conversion, and commerce had its halcyon days. Elements of deterioration and decay had begun to eat into the vitals of the Portuguese empire in the East. The sudden acquisition of ill-gotten wealth and the easy subjugation of vast tracts had turned the heads of the proud Portuguese officials. The race of heroes such as the Abuquerques and Pachecos had given place to a base set of captains and administrators whose only thought was money. Avarice and debased luxury had enervated a nation that had hitherto produced heroes and statesmen. Goa, their capital in India, came to be known as Goa Dourado or Golden Goa, a place of fabulous wealth. The interior life of Goa represented, as Dr. W. W. Hunter observes, on a more magnificent scale, the social types and standards of the Portuguese settlements in India. The description of that life shows to what low state the Portuguese had fallen by the commencement of the sixteenth century.

"The intensely military spirit, and its contempt for peaceful industry, ended in a reaction of profligacy and sloth. Portuguese society in Goa divided itself into two idle populations—an idle population of men in the streets and gaming saloons, and an idle population of women in the seclusion of their own homes. The gambling houses, sumptuously furnished and paying a heavy licence tax to the Government, were the resort of dancing girls, jugglers, native actors and buffoons—haunts of iniquity, in which the more determined players stayed sometimes for days together and were provided with board and lodging. The ladies of Goa soon obtained an equally unenviable name. Shut up as much as possible from male society, they lounged half-dressed through the tropical day, singing, playing, quarrelling, gossiping with their flattering slaves, and especially devising means to elude the vigilance of their husbands. A European *zenana* life grew up and produced ugly consequences. A lady valued herself in her female coterie upon the number and daring of her intrigues. The travellers who visited Goa during its palmy days tell strange tales of the hardihood with which the Portuguese matrons pursued their amour—not scrupling to stupefy the husband with drugs, and then admitting the paramour to his chamber. The perils of such interviews gave zest to jaded appetite, and the Goanese became a by-word as the type of an orientalised community, idle, haughty and corrupt.

" But the Portuguese of Goa, although clad much like natives in their own houses save for the large rosaries round their necks and with their children running 'up and down the house naked till they begin to be old enough to be ashamed,' made a splendid appearance when they stirred abroad. The ladies in gorgeous apparel were carried in not less gorgeous litters, guarded by domestics, to the great functions of the church—their 'dress mostly of gold and silver brocade' adorned with pearls, precious stones, and with jewels on the head, arms, hands and round the waist; and they put on a veil of the finest crape in the world which extends from head to foot. They wore no stockings, but slippers studded with gems and raised on cork soles 'nearly half a foot in height.' 'They do not wear any mask but paint their cheeks to a shameful degree.' These ladies, when they enter the church, are taken by the hand by one or two men, since they cannot walk by themselves on account of the height of the slippers'. Each is thus helped 'to her seat some forty or fifty paces off, taking at least a good quarter of an hour to walk that distance, so slowly and majestically does she move'—after the fashion of the high born Venetian ladies of that time.

"When a gentleman rode forth, he was attended by a throng of slaves in gay and fanciful liveries, some holding painted umbrellas, others displaying richly inlaid arms; while his horse glittered with gold and silver trappings, jingling silver bells, reins studded with precious stones, and gilt stirrups wrought into artistic patterns. The poor aped the rich and resorted to amusing makeshifts to exhibit an air of grandeur. Gentlemen who lived together had a few silk suits between them in common. These they used by turns when they went out, and hired the services of a man to hold an umbrella over them as they strutted through the street ."[1]

The system of private trade often encouraged at home gradually proved a source of political weakness. As early as 1524, complaints arose that the captains "do not want war, as it is too expensive and bad to endure, and of small gain and little advantage." In 1524, a new Governor found the royal service in great straits, owing to the number of officers who had left it to turn merchants—a business which offered greater chances of profit and less danger to life and limb. After three years' experience, he was anxious to resign "as he saw around him only corruption and dishonesty." In 1549, a confidential report thus summed up the position: "each one considers only himself!"[2]

The Government at home found itself unable to keep their lieutenants abroad in check and, after the union of Portugal with the Spanish Crown in 1580, the revolt of the Netherlands had crippled the resources available for the Indian commerce and Government. The pay of the officers in India had to be curtailed, and

1. Hunter's History of British India, Vol. I, pp. 156 *et seq.*
2. Ibid, p. 178.

even this reduced pay came to fall into arrears. They, therefore, justified their rapacity on the ground of insufficient salaries and began openly to conduct expeditions on their own behalf.

"If the system produced bitter fruits in Asia, it had its roots in Portugal herself. Not only could the Lisbon Court never screw up its courage to give fair commercial salaries for fair commercial work, but it used India as a refuge for depraved or destitute hangers-on upon its bounty. As the slave tillage of Portugal concentrated large tracts among a small body of great proprietors, the lesser nobility and gentry sank into indigence. Their blood disdained the degradation of trade at home, and the antechambers of the grandees were besieged by poor relations clamouring for employment or bread. India seemed to offer, if not a fortune, at any rate a grave. In either case, the suitor was got rid of. It became the asylum for those who had claims that could not be satisfied, or who had rendered services that could not be acknowledged, or had received promises that could not be fulfilled. Young women were shipped off from Lisbon with the dowry of an appointment in India for the man who would marry them. One favoured damsel carried in her trunk the Governorship of Crānganūr. The multiplication of offices was pushed to an extent which would have been ludicrous, if it had not proved fatal, in Portuguese India. But even nominal posts could not be invented to keep pace with the demand. Each of the four outward ships of a single year brought sixty persons more or less without pay."[1]

So early as 1549, i. e., barely half a century since the Portuguese occupation of Cochin, a letter of Cosma Annes to the king of Portugal, dated the 30th of December, observed that things were going "from bad to worse" at Cochin. Again, in a letter addressed to the king by the Judge and Alderman of Goa, dated the

1. Hunter's History of British India, Vol. I, p. 183.

25th of November 1552, they bewail, "In India there is no justice, either in your Viceroy, or in those who are to mete it out". Their one object is "the gathering together of money by every means. There is no Moor who will trust a Portuguese. Senhor, we beg for mercy, mercy. Help us senhor, help us senhor, for we are sinking."[1]

We have in the following words a true picture of the Portuguese in Cochin. "Persons having purchased their ill-paid Government appointments, became grasping and mercenary, not probably so much for the love of money as for the necessity of obtaining it for their expenses; for, in those days, Cochin was a gay city, and the saying was, 'China was a good place to make money in, and Cochin to spend it at.' The style of living and the pay were consequently incompatible, and helping themselves was a necessity. The whole nation was groaning under priestly dominion, a dominion which set the bishop's mitre before the king's crown and the Church before the State, and woe to that Governor, who should dare to disobey the mandate of a priest. These people who aimed at an empire in India both spiritual and temporal, at wholesale conversions effected by conviction, bribery, fraud or violence, who considered no expenditure too large to effect their object, whose self-love had alienated all friends, and injustice created many enemies, were now on the eve of resigning their authority to others. Another power was now to become predominant in the East, another race was to try their hand at supremacy and another religion to be introduced. The Portuguese had become objects of aversion to their old allies, the Princes of Cochin, as they had deposed the Raja, and created his aunt, the Ranee."[2]

Some time before, disputes had arisen regarding the succession to the Cochin throne. There had been

1. Hunter's History of British India, Vol. I, p. 185.
2. The Land of the Perumals, pp. 114--115.

some conflicting adoptions into the family from collateral branches. At first the adoptions were made from the Mūṭṭa Ṭāvaḷi branch and the Paḷḷiviruṭṭi branch. The adoptees quarrelled among themselves, and two factions arose in the country headed by the rival adoptees. The Portuguese espoused the cause of the Paḷḷiviruṭṭi branch and expelled the Mūṭṭa Ṭāvaḷi Princes from the kingdom. Soon after, all the Paḷḷiviruṭṭi Princes died and a further adoption was made from Chāḷiyūr and Airūr. As if this was not sufficient to distract the country, a further adoption was effected from the Beṭṭāṭ or Ṭāṇūr family, on the ground that Beṭṭāṭṭnād had, on a former occasion, rendered material help to the Cochin Royal family, and that the Princes of that house were at the time very powerful on the Coast. The reigning Raja died, and the Portuguese at once set up the Beṭṭaṭ Prince on the throne with the support of a Travancore Prince, called by the Portuguese Rāmaṇa Kōil. The exiled Prince of the Mūṭṭa Ṭāvaḷi sought the aid of the Dutch, the rival European Power that had recently established itself at Colombo. Raja Vīra Kēraḷa Varma of the Mūṭṭa Ṭāvaḷi proceeded in 1662 to Colombo, interviewed the Dutch Governor-General and invited him to befriend the exiled Princes of Cochin. Previous to this, on the 12th March 1661, the Pāliaṭ Achan, the hereditary Prime Minister of the Cochin Raja, had, on his own behalf, met the Dutch admiral Van Goens on board the ship *Muscatboom* "in a friendly manner and entered into an agreement, the purport of which was that, as the Portuguese and other enemies had deprived him of his lands, he would place himself entirely under the protection of the Dutch who were to restore him by force to his territories, whilst he was to obey them in all things."[1] The Governor-General was glad to find an opportunity of securing a desirable location on the Malabar Coast. He acceded

1. Moen's Memorial, Dutch Government Records.

to the proposal of Vīra Kērala Varma and promised to restore him to his inheritance.

The Dutch were about this time planning the conquest of the Malabar Coast. Not liking the interference of the Moghul Emperor with their trade establishments at Surat and other places, they were on the look-out for a settlement on the Malabar Coast, where they could lord it over the feeble native powers and carry on unhampered a lucrative trade in spices and other articles. Cochin appeared to be vulnerable, and it offered a suitable site satisfactory in all respects and affording immunity from the rapacious exactions of the Muhammadan Government as from any opposition on the part of their European rivals in trade, the English, who had already begun to compete for the eastern trade.

The plan of operations proposed by the fugitive Prince of Cochin was for the Dutch Admiral Ryklof Van Goens to attack Cochin from the sea and effect a landing on the western side, while the Rajas of Vaṭakkumkūr and Ṭekkumkūr were to advance on the town from the north and the south from the land side. Accordingly the Dutch fleet under Van Goens appeared before Palliport and captured the Portuguese fort there. The native allies from the land side failed however to put in their appearance, and the Dutch fleet sailed back to Colombo. But they soon returned to the attack. Sailing from Colombo, Admiral Van Goens appeared with a fleet before Quilon, in the beginning of December 1661, and recovered that place from the hands of the Portuguese who had re-captured it from the Dutch in the absence of the Admiral. Thence the Dutch troops proceeded to Cranganūr towards the end of December 1661, and landed a large army at Aycotta (Aīikkōṭṭa=Ālikkōṭṭa). Having effected a landing, they proceeded to lay siege to the strong Portuguese fort at Cranganūr. It was bravely defended by the Portuguese Commander, Urbano Fialho Fereira, a man of great courage and valour. The Princes of Chālyūr and other adherents and nobles of Raja Gōḍavarma of the Veṭṭaṭ faction supplied vessels for the defence of the fort on the seaside where the Pāliaṭ Achan, minister of Cochin, and his following stood guard at a quarter which was reckoned weak. The Dutch effected a landing here. The Governor of Cochin had great confidence in the courage and capacity of the Commander of Crānganūr and continued supplying him with ammunition and other materials for standing an assault. The attack lasted for many days continuously, and the Dutch, finding it a difficult task, raised the white flag and despatched an emissary to arrange for peace. But Fialho Fereira replied with contempt that he would supply the Dutch with ladders to scale the walls if they dared. The Dutch emissary returned and the attack was resumed. Pāliam, who had more than once before proved faithless to the Portuguese, again played his old trick. He slipped out of the fort unobserved and joined the Dutch whose Commander was taken to his place at Chēnnamangalam, where it was agreed that the Dutch should restore the Mūṭṭa Ṭāvaḷi Prince to the throne of Cochin. He then disclosed to the Dutch the weak quarter of the fort. On the 15th January 1662, the final engagement took place. It was very fierce, and the Commander Urbano Fialho Fereira was cut down after exhibiting prodigies of valour. The fortress was then surrendered to the Dutch who at once took possession of it and sent all the Portuguese soldiers to Europe.

Seven days after, the Dutch fleet approached Cochin by way of Vypin and crept along the coast till they came opposite to the fort. On the Island of Vypin towards its southern end, they found a church and a large house belonging to the Roman Catholic Bishop of Cochin which were at once seized and made the head-quarters of the Dutch Admiral. He then constructed a strong post close by and called it "Fort Orange." Leaving a garrison of 800 men to guard this post, Van Goens re-embarked with the rest of his men to attack Cochin from the south.

At this juncture, the Pāliaṭ Achan invited the Bishop of Cochin to proceed to his place at Chēnna-mangalam, guaranteeing the Bishop's safety there. The Bishop found it difficult to comply with this request; wherenpon the Achan sought for a personal interview, intimating that he had very important communications to make. The Bishop requested the Governor of Cochin, Ignatio Sarmento, to depute some one to be present at the interview. It was thought that, if measures were adopted at once to bring about an understanding between the Malabar Princes and the Portuguese to instal the Mūṭṭa Ṭavaḷi Raja on the Cochin throne on the demise of the then reigning Ṭaṇūr (Beṭṭaṭ) Raja, the hands of the Portuguese would be strengthened and the imminent fall of the Cochin Fort could be averted. Unfortunately for the Portuguese, there was no time to bring about this arrangement. The Mūṭṭa Ṭavaḷi Raja had already met the Dutch General on board his vessel and offered his services. He spoke Portuguese remarkably well, showed considerable acquaintance with military affairs, and made arrangements to supply the Dutch with fresh provisions from the neighbouring villages.

The Dutch now began to press forward. On landing, the Dutch Commander informed the Nairs that he had not come to fight with them or their legitimate sovereign, but that his only desire was to fight with the Portuguese. The Nair adherents of the Beṭṭaṭ Princes, however, disputed the advance of the Dutch and a dash on the Palace at Mattancherry was at once made. A battle was fought in front of the Palace. The Nairs fought with desperation and made a furious

PALACE IN COCHIN (DUTCH BUILDING).

To face page 192.

onset hacking the Dutch right and left with their long swords which they held with both hands; many of the Dutch were beaten down. But there was no method in their fighting and they were no match for the disciplined array of European soldiers that confronted them. Three of the Beṭṭaṭ Princes were cut down, gallantly fighting. The brave Dutch, in spite of the furious Nair onset, soon rallied and found no difficulty in driving back their enemies within the palace-walls where a fearful struggle took place, resulting in the death of four hundred Nairs. Tavernier says that 1600 Nairs were killed in this battle.[1] A Dutch ensign named Henry Adrian Van Rheede, (afterwards Governor of Cochin from 1673 to 1677), boldly entered the Palace and secured the person of the Ranee, Gangādhara Mahā Lakṣhmi, who is described as "an old woman, very plain in appearance, but covered with gold ornaments and jewels." For this act of bravery, the General at once promoted Van Rheede to a Captaincy. Her nephew, the Raja, who had accompanied the Dutch as their ally, interceded in her behalf, on which account she was treated with great kindness and consideration by the Dutch Commander. Tavernier observes that, after six days, the Queen was given into the custody of the Zamorin who was the most powerful of the petty kings of the Coast to whom the Dutch had promised that, if they took the town of Cochin, they would give him that of Crānganūr, provided that he was faithful to them. This engagement took place in February 1662. Of the Ranee's *Kariakars* or officers, Rāghavan Kōvil escaped with his wounds. Two Nambūries of Muriaṭiṭṭa Illam were carried to the Dutch fleet in chains.

Of the Beṭṭaṭ faction, Gōḍa Varma escaped to Ernakulam on the other side of the backwater, and the Dutch proposed to pursue and attack him there. The Raja of Poṛakāḍ, a staunch ally of the Portuguese and an ardent adherent of the Beṭṭaṭ Princes, now appeared

1. *Travels*, Ball's Edition, Chap. XVI, p. 241.

on the scene with large reinforcements. Supplies were thrown into Ernakulam and the place strongly entrenched. On this, the Dutch gave up the idea of pursuing the Beṭṭaṭ Princes across the water.

The Dutch force was then divided into three companies which were placed thus : one on the sea side of the town, the other on the land side, while the third was ordered to occupy a position near the river. Regular approaches were formed and batteries placed in position.

On the day following the engagement at the Mattancherry Palace, the Dutch attacked the Fort of Cochin led by a brave officer named Was who was killed almost at the point of carrying the fort by storm, whereupon the storming party retreated in confusion. The original plan of delivering the assault before sunrise was delayed, and by the time the storming party advanced, the Portuguese had discovered the scheme and were prepared to renew the attack. The old Portuguese spirit of Pacheco and Almeyda showed itself and the defenders fought bravely for weeks together, so that the besiegers were forced to give up their attempt discomfited, although the Dutch Commanders strained every nerve to take the fort by storm.

The Bishop of Cochin, Fr. Joseph Sebastioni, felt that Cochin was about to fall into the hands of the Dutch who were no friends of the Catholic faith, and concerted measures to secure his own safety. He applied for an interview with the Dutch General Van Goens who told the Bishop that, if he would send his secretary, matters could be arranged. The Bishop at once despatched his secretary Fr. Gothi Pedro to meet the General. Fr. Gothi was informed that the General would supply the Bishop with passports to proceed to Persia if he was willing to leave Cochin without delay, but that all final arrangements must wait till the war was over. This was no pleasant prospect for the Bishop, and he made up his mind to leave Cochin for Maṫṫam, near Shertalay, 20 miles south of Cochin, to join his flock there, an attempt in which after some hardships he fortunately succeeded. Winter was now fast approaching, and, at the end of a month, the besieging force had become reduced to 1400 men, while the ally of the Portuguese, the Raja of Poṙakāḍ, reinforced them with 6,000 Nairs. About this time, five ships arrived from Goa with reinforcements, but the harbour was so closely guarded by the Dutch that the Portuguese found considerable difficulty in entering it. The Governor Ignatio Sarmento with the assistance of the Bishop's secretary, Fr. Gothi, however, succeeded at last in eluding the vigilence of the Dutch and brought the ships into the harbour. The men were safely landed and were received with great joy and acclamation. The Dutch stood very much in need of war materials, especially fuses. The monsoon now suddenly burst forth with unusual fury, and, just as those within the walls of Cochin were fearing that the fort would soon fall into the hands of the besiegers, the latter made up their minds to raise the siege and retire to Batavia.

This they effected so quietly and in so clever a manner that the Portuguese within the fort did not know that the Dutch had given them the slip till noon on the following day. All night a Dutch constable named Boerdrop had been running about bawling out, at the top of his voice, words of command, such as 'stand,'' "halt," "who is there?"; a friendly Jew in the meanwhile sounded the gong till early vespers; and these stratagems put the besieged off their guard.

The Portuguese were elated at their unexpected success. In the excess of their joy they thought that the Dutch had finally given up their attempt to capture Cochin. Instead of strengthening the fortifications and securing the aid of the natives, they sought to wreak vengeance on the Jews who, they thought, had enabled the Dutch to slip unobserved; Jews' town was plundered and an attempt was made to destroy the Synagogue, but they succeeded only in carrying off the Pentateuch which was subsequently recovered in 1668. The Canarians (Konkanies) who had found an asylum in the Cochin State from the religious persecution of the community at Goa had rendered some assistance to the Dutch. The wrath of the Portuguese now fell on them. Their houses were plundered, their temple pillaged, and their market looted.

The sudden flight of the besiegers gave Gōḍa Vaṙma Raja who was roaming about the vicinity of Paḷḷiviruṭṭi a thrill of joy and he at once proceeded to Cochin surrounded by a large following. The chiefs and the nobility lost no time in flocking to his standard. He now entered the fort walls with all the pomp and glitter of an oriental magnate and the townspeople accepted him as their sovereign with great acclamation.

On the other hand, the Mūṭṭa Ṭāvaḷi Raja and the Pāliaṭ Achen found their cause lost. The Dutch who had come with the avowed purpose of assisting them had sailed away leaving them to shift for themselves. In this sorry plight they had to fly for their very lives. But the Dutch had left only with the intention of returning in greater force at the earliest opportunity. On leaving, they had promised the Mūṭṭa Ṭāvaḷi Prince that they would return when the dreaded monsoon had passed off, and the Raja was anxiously waiting for them. Fearing that the Dutch had given up their attempts to capture the town and oust the Portuguese, the Raja, Veera Kēraḷa Vaṙma, proceeded once more to Colombo accompanied by one of the Chāḷiūṙ Princes and Pāliaṭ Kōmi Achen. He succeeded in hastening the Dutch to return to the siege without delay, but died on board the ship on his return journey and was cremated at Anjēri Maṭhom at Mattancherri.

On their leaving Cochin, the Dutch did not withdraw or abandon the strong position they had secured on the island of Vypīn, whence they continued to harass the Cochin Fort. From Vypīn they poured shot and shell into the town, committing great destruction to life and property. Bishop Sebastioni gives us a harrowing description of the scene he witnessed in the town. He says that he had to go within the fort walls to transact some business with the Commander and thus became a participator in the suffering of its denizens. The roof of the house in which he was living was torn away from over his head by cannon balls. The lives of the inmates were in great jeopardy. The balls weighed something like 24 lbs; two of them linked together struck the portico of his house and shattered its beams and roof. Another shot broke the front door into splinters. As the penitent prelate was one day at his prostrations in the front yard of his house, absorbed in contemplation and prayer, he was rudely awakened to the realities of life on this mundane sphere by a cannon ball falling close at his feet. But Providence had willed that the Bishop should not be hurt and he escaped.

The Portuguese were thus reminded of the probability of the Dutch returning to the attack as soon as the monsoon was over, and an earnest requisition was sent to Goa for reinforcements. These reinforcements were, however, not destined to reach Cochin, for the ships that brought them were caught in a tempest near Honore and the whole fleet was lost.

The fort was not capable of sustaining a long defence. So early as 1623, Don Francisco da Gama Carde La Vidigveria who had come as Viceroy had reported that "Cochin which used to be the most prosperous settlement had then hardly any trade and was almost in a state of ruin and without any means of defence, whilst the enemy (the Dutch, English, etc.), were in great force in the Indies." No attempt seems, however, to have been made to improve the defence, though strict orders were issued to injure the trade of the English in Cochin.

The Dutch once more appeared before Cochin on the 25th of October 1662 under a new General named Hustaart. Fra Bartolomeo mentions Peter Van Bitter and C. Valkenberg as the admirals in command of the Dutch Fleet. The army sent from Batavia to resume the siege landed at Palliport (Pallippuram) where the Dutch had in the previous year erected a fort with palms. From this place it marched to Vypīn within the range of the guns of Cochin. Here also, as we have found, the Dutch had in the previous year occupied a position capable of forming a base of operations against the fort on the opposite side of the river that separated Vypīn from Cochin. They entrenched themselves on the southern end of the island, so far as the nature of the ground permitted, and placed some batteries in position; but their distance from the town made them practically of little or no use. Before long, three ships arrived with reinforcements and siege materials which were soon followed by the Governor of Amboyna bringing two more ships with a further contingent. A number of Sinhalese were also brought from Ceylon. Four hundred men of the Amboyna contingent were left at Vypīn, while the bulk of the army re-embarked and landed near Cochin in the vicinity of the church of St. Andrew where the Portuguese, assisted by the Raja of Cochin, were waiting to receive the attack of the Dutch. The Dutch General offered terms to the Portuguese Governor of Cochin. He intimated that the Directors of the East India Company had authorized the Government of India to permit all Portuguese who might subject themselves to the Company to trade freely and to have absolute freedom of religion in as many churches as they liked to maintain. The Dutch Commander added that, if the fort was surrendered, he would undertake that the Dutch should have only one church and that their soldiers should occupy the fort. The Portuguese Commander Ignatio Sarmento refused the profered terms. The Dutch successfully effected a landing, though the Portuguese bravely resisted the attempt, their loss being but slight, as the Portuguese had only aimed at the boats. The Dutch, observing a detachment of the Portuguese marching along the sea coast in the directior of the church of St. John, ordered their cavalry to reconnoitre them; whereupon, the Portuguese, retreating to the east, in their desperation set fire to the convent of St. John to prevent the Dutch occupying it.[1] The flames were, however, soon extinguished and the Dutch fixed it as their headquarters. The same day ten men from each Company were ordered to proceed to capture the Mattancherri palace which had been the year before the scene of a bloody conflict between the Dutch and the Nairs of the Raja of Cochin. They found the palace deserted and had therefore to return disappointed.

The Dutch then began to entrench themselves and raised small forts made of palms, one laid upon another, behind cover of which they erected batteries and placed their guns in position. A battery with four pieces of

1. The unrelenting spirit in which the Dutch conducted themselves is evidenced by an incident recorded by Tavernier. "A French soldier named Christofel who was in their (the Dutch) pay seeing a basket attached to a rope which was hanging from a bastion, went boldly to see what it had inside without fearing musket shots. But he was much surprised when he found that it was a poor famished infant which the mother had placed there in order to escape the sorrow of seeing it die of hunger;--for already some time had elapsed since the Dutch had commenced the siege of Cochin, and since any food had entered the town. The soldier smitten with compassion, took the infant and gave it of whatever he had to eat, at which the General of the army was so indignant, saying that the soldier should have left the infant to die, that he assembled the council of war and proposed that he should be shot. This was very cruel, and the council, moderating the sentence, only condemned him to the lash."—p. 237.

cannon was erected near the church of St. John near the sea. Another was erected near the church of St. Thomas where was the hospital for the sick and the wounded. A third was raised at Calvaṭṭi with seven pieces of cannon and two mortars whence bombs and stones were thrown into the town, and which caused great destruction to the buildings within the fort. At this spot there was a river which the Dutch attempted to bridge by means of sacks filled with earth, so that they might cross under cover of the point of a bastion which impinged directly on the river and assault the "Pepper house", a large store surrounded by the sea. Perceiving this, the Portuguese hastened to garrison it and supplied two guns for its defence. The scheme to bridge the stream was therefore given up. Thus weeks passed without anything important taking place. Several assaults were made which were all vigorously repulsed with great loss to the Dutch. In the last of these assaults the Dutch Governor of Crāngānūr who commanded the party was taken prisoner, and the General lost no time in withdrawing the survivors from a weak position. In November, Admiral Van Goens joined the besiegers with large reinforcements and military appliances and the brave Portuguese made up their minds to stand a siege. In December, the Raja of Poṙakāḍ brought a strong Nair contingent and entrenched himself at Ernakulam on the opposite coast and threw supplies into the fort. Thereupon the Dutch crossed over in boats, determined to attack him. The Nairs under Portuguese officers met the attack most valiantly and a bloody encounter took place at the landing place. The Poṙakāḍ troops met the Dutch while they were still in their boats, pulled them out by the hair of their heads and stabbed them most dexterously. For a time the advance of the Dutch was arrested. Fresh troops were soon brought up under the command of Captain Ree and the Poṙakāḍ contingent was routed.

Towards the close of December, the Dutch resolved to make another assault. Bishop Sebastioni says that, some days before the final assault, the Dutch Commander sent two Captains with a white flag to the Portuguese Governor, seeking an interview. General Ignatio Sarmento sent two *Palkees* to bring them inside the fort, their eyes being blindfolded. These captains were accompanied by a boy, who, by some mistake, was not blindfolded. The boy was intelligent enough to observe the condition of the fort, its defences, its weak points, the position and location of the defending forces within, etc. He also carefully studied a map of the fort he found in the Governor's house. The information thus gathered enabled the Dutch General to successfully accomplish his object.

The Dutch General in conjunction with the troops of the Muṭṭa Ṭāvaḷi Raja and the Pāliaṭ Achan at last determined on storming the fort. It was resolved to make the assault at the same point where the last attack had been made, that is, towards the Calvaṭṭi side. With this object, a large frigate was sent to Vypīn to bring the men who had been stationed there. On its return journey, the whole frigate was lost, as it accidentally struck on a sand-bank and foundered, all the soldiers and sailors on board, excepting ten men, being drowned. The escaped men swam ashore and landed near Cochin only to fall prisoners into the hands of the Portuguese. This misfortune did not, however, make the General desist from the resolution he had already formed. The assualt was kept up continuously for eight days and nights, troops being relieved every three hours. There was great consternation within the walls of the fort. Gōḍa Vaṛma Raja and his Nayars had already deserted the Portuguese to find shelter in a place of security. So also the Raja of Poṛkāḍ. The battering rams of the enemy were hard at work demolishing the walls all round. There was a close blockade of the harbour, the entrance being securely guarded by the Dutch ships. The Dutch fleet commanded the sea. Towards the east, Ernakulam was in the hands of the Dutch, and the only source of food supply was cut off. All hopes of succour from Goa were given up. Within the walls, most of the buildings were destroyed, and men, women and children were wandering helpless in great alarm. The clergy were trying their level best to console the distressed people in their great extremity. A penitential procession was formed to avert divine wrath, but all to no purpose. The town was doomed to fall into the hands of the Dutch. For, on the Calvaṭṭi side, a wide breach was already made and the Dutch entered the fort. The Dutch General had made a last and determined attempt to carry the fort. His scheme was to deliver the assault by night, but a French Lieutenant under him, named St. Martin, advised him to defer it to the morning, as there was great danger of the besiegers falling in the darkness of night into pits made by the enemy in the ramparts. At sunrise, next morning, every thing was ready and by 10 o'clock the assault was made by four companies, each containing about 150 men. Simultaneously on three points, the Portuguese fought most bravely, and both parties lost heavily. The Portuguese had the advantage of being aided by two hundred men of the Dutch army, who had deserted and joined them in revenge for having been kept out of six and a half month's pay in consequence of the loss of Tonan, a town in Java. This made them unwilling to serve the Dutch any longer. Tavernier observes that, without these soldiers who constituted an important aid to the Portuguese, Cochin would not have held out for two months. Among them was a Dutch engineer of great ability who, on account of the bad treatment he received from his own side, went over to the side of the enemy.

At one point, Captain Perre Du Pon succeeded in gaining a position on the wall and entered the town on the Calvaṭṭi side. The Dutch made themselves masters of a rampart, and remained all night under arms. The Portuguese General brought up a strong detachment to displace them; but they had to face a heavy fire from their own guns captured by the enemy and turned against them from the ramparts already taken. In spite of this, they fought fiercely. Perre Du Pon, however, managed to hold out till reinforcements came up to his assistance. The attacks on the other parts were not so successful and resulted in considerable loss to the assailants. Simon Gomez de Silva and other Portuguese Captains had advised the digging of trenches and the barricading of the streets to check the rushing advance of the enemy during the day. But this served only to accelerate the fall of the town, as the attempts on the part of the Portuguese to stop their advance induced the Dutch to press on with greater determination. As night drew on, the situation became most perilous. Bishop Sebastioni says that the air was rent with the yells of the victorious Dutch and the wailing of the suffering women and children within the walls. It was pitch dark, the gloom being relieved only by the flashes of firing guns. The sufferings of the inmates of the fort were intense. All hopes had ended, and, to avert the impending carnage, a white flag was shown and two commissaries were sent early in the morning who were graciously received by General Van Goens. The capitulation of the town was agreed on and certain concessions prayed for. The Dutch General answered that it was too late to ask for concessions, but that he would try to check all excesses. Thereupon the Portuguese General Ignatio Sarmento, arrayed in mourning and followed by his captains, delivered the keys of the Fort into the hands of the Dutch General Rykloff Van Goens. The whole day was spent in burying the dead. The Portuguese carried off for burial the bodies of some clerics, while the Dutch had the other dead bodies dragged to the river by the Chinese who were in their service. The wounded were removed to the hospital. All respectable women and children were given shelter inside the houses and all were supplied with passports. The Portuguese were allowed to take with them all gold, silver, and other valuables from the churches, or as the Dutch chaplain of Cochin says "with their false Gods and images," but were strictly forbidden from removing stores and spices. A bonfire had, however, been already made in another quarter of the town of the ornamentations of some of the churches at the very church doors. The Portuguese were ordered to confine themselves within their houses where they were promised protection from injury. After this, according to Bishop Sebastioni, the town was given up to loot for three days. The Bishop adds that the cruelties and atrocities perpetrated by the victorious troops passes description. The whole town was wailing. Those who were a moment before living luxuriously in palatial mansions were suddenly turned out into the streets and had to content themselves with roaming about as beggars without having even a roof to shelter their devoted heads. Some high-placed ladies died of fright. But the Bishop being an avowed partisan, we have to accept his account of the loot with some reservation. For, Tavernier, a disinterested and independent French traveller, gives a different account. His statement as to what took place on the capitulation does not support the Bishop. "The Portuguese, according to the terms of the capitulation, left Cochin with arms and baggages, but as soon as they were outside the gate of the town where the Dutch troops were in order of battle, they were obliged to give up their arms and place them at the foot of the General, with the exception of officers, who kept their swords. The general had promised the soldiers the loot of the town, but not being able to keep up his promise for reasons he explained to them, he led them to hope that he would pay them six months' wages; this a few days afterwards was reduced to eight rupees each."[1]

1. Pp. 241-2.

Besides the regular troops who defended the fort, there were four hundred Topasses in the place, who had greatly assisted the Portuguese, but were not included in the hasty terms which were made when the place was taken. Fearing the Dutch soldiery in the hour of their triumph, these men drew up on parade, just within the Fort at which the Portuguese were to go out, and the Dutch to enter, and swore that they would take terrible vengeance, and set the whole town on fire if they were not forthwith treated on the same terms as the Portuguese. Van Goens attended to their request, and offered to take such of them, as were willing, into the service of the Dutch, a proposal to which many of them at once acceded.

The following were the terms of the Capitulation under which the town was surrendered to the Dutch, the treaty being signed on the 7th January 1663 at the headquarters of the Dutch army in Cochin and ratified by both sides on the following day:—

"That the town of Cochin be surrendered with all its jurisdictions, income, and lands with all documents and papers referring to the same and whatever else that may be there held in the name of the king of Portugal, rights and titles to the same being made over to the Commander or his representatives.

"That all artillery, merchandise, victuals, moveable and immoveable goods, slaves and whatever else may be there be similarly handed over to the said Commander.

"That all free persons who may have borne arms should swear not to serve against the Dutch State for the next two years.

"That the soldiers and all others belonging to the army should leave the town with flags flying, drums beating, fuses alight, musket balls in their mouths, and two field pieces, to some place outside the town where their arms were to be piled before the standard of the Commander. All unmarried trueborn Portuguese to be sent back to Europe.*

"That the married Portuguese and Mestizoes should start for Goa and be permitted to take with them their beds and such other articles as the Commander and his council might allow.

"That all free 'Toepassen' and 'Canarins' should remain at the disposal of the Commander.

"That the clergy should be allowed to take with them their images and Church ornaments, excepting such as might be of gold or silver.[1]

"That all free persons, and those belonging to the Church, if subjects of the king of Portugal, and who might be wandering through the country should be included in this treaty".[2]

When everything was settled and the Dutch had assumed the Government of Cochin, the Zamorin asked for the town of Crānganūr in accordance with the promise made to him, and it was given to him. Before the town was given him, the fortifications were demolished. Naturally the Zamorin was much annoyed at this, but he had for the time being to put up with the chagrin. Soon after, treaties were concluded with the Mūṭṭa Ṭāvaḷi Raja of Cochin and the Raja of Poṛakāḍ. In accordance with the original agreement with the Mūṭṭa Ṭāvaḷi Raja, that Prince was at once installed on the throne of Cochin. "A few days after," says Tavernier, "the General had a crown made to place on the head of a new king of Cochin, the other having been driven away, and on the day which he selected for this grand performance, he seated himself on a kind of throne, at the foot of which a Malbari called Montani (Mūṭṭa Ṭāvaḷi), conducted by two or three captains, placed himself on his knees to receive the crown from his

1. These clauses are not in the copy of the capitul: tion in the the Cochin State Archives.

2. Danvers, Vol. II, pp. 327-8.

hands and to take possession of a kingdom of very limited extent, that is to say, some small territories in the neighbourhood of Cochin. This General when coming from Holland had been a ship's cook, and this crowning of a miserable Malabari by the hands of a man who had more frequently brandished a pot-ladle than a sword, was without doubt a brilliant spectacle."

Some writers[1] charge the Dutch General with keeping to himself the information he had received, on the day before the final assault, of peace having been concluded in Europe between Portugal and Holland, so that it might not interfere with the capture of the town. It is also said that, on his being taunted with this by the Portuguese later on when the trick was found out, Van Goens coolly replied that he was only playing the same game which the Portuguese themselves had played on the Dutch at the capture of Pernambuco in Brazil not many years ago. The Portuguese did indeed repeatedly claim for the restoration of both Cochin and Cannanore on the ground that these places were captured after the peace. The treaty in question had been signed on the 6th August, 1661, and was ratified by the king of Portugal on the 24th May and by the States-General on the 4th December 1662 respectively. Its publication did not however take place till the 12th March 1663. By clause VI of the treaty it was only stipulated that those places that might have been captured *after its publication* were to be restored, so that the claim of the Portuguese was clearly untenable.

3. **Founders of Cochin.**[2] For the better understanding of what is to follow it may be necessary here to refer to an incident that took place before the Portuguese came to Cochin. Vaṅṅēri was wrested from the Raja of Cochin by the Zamorin some time before the

1. Whitehouse—Historical Notices, p.242. The Abbe Raynal—History of Settlements and Trade in the East Indies, Vol. 1, p. 218; Day—The Land of the Perumals, p. 117.

2. The author here refers to Alphanso Albuquerque and the King of Portugal.

advent of the Portuguese on the coast. The loss of the villages comprising Vaṅṅērināḍ had always been a sore point to Cochin, as from time immemorial the kings of Cochin went through their coronation ceremony in a place called Chiṭṭṙakūṭam in the Perimpaḍappu village. The Zamorin held to them tenaciously for the same reason. Raja Rāma Vaṙma (1698—1722) is said to have taken a solemn oath on his accession to the *Musnad* that he would not be crowned anywhere except at Chiṭṭṙakūṭam and that he would never wear a crown till he went through the ceremony of coronation there. Unfortunately, Cochin never succeeded in regaining possession of Perimpaḍappu and Rāma Vaṙma's successors, respecting his oath, never afterwards performed the ceremony, nor did they ever wear a crown.[1]

Not that the Rajas of Cochin made no attempts to get back possession of Vaṅṅērināḍ, but their attempts have always been unsuccessful. Travancore was to have assisted Cochin in wresting this tract from the Zamorin and we see a note added to the copy of the treaty between the two Rajas in the archives of Ṭṙippūṇiṭṭuṙa that it was so specially agreed. Both the Rajas applied to Batavia for assistance from the Dutch. But the lukewarmness of the latter put off the proposed expedition till it was too late, as complications, consequent on Tippu's invasion of Malabar, rendered any such attempt impossible. Hyder had, while the Cochin Raja was tributary to Mysore, once promised to restore the place to Cochin and had in fact passed orders to that effect. But, unfortunately for Cochin, the Nawab died before the transfer was effected, and his son Tippu Sultan failed to conform to the wishes of his father in this particular, though in other respects the grants made by Hyder to Cochin were scrupulously respected. On the cession of Malabar to the English by Tippu, the Raja presented his claim to the villages before the joint commissioners appointed by the Bengal and Bombay Governments to adjust the claims of the Malabar

1. Cochin State Manual, Note, p. 103.

Princes to the tracts from which the Sultan had ejected them. But the commissioners did not see their way to admit the Raja's claim as Vaṅṅēri was in the possession of the Zamorin at the time Hyder conquered Malabar. The Cochin Rajas have thus lost for ever their dream of perfecting their coronation by crowning themselves at their ancestral home, unless the benign British Government, in the plentitude of their good feelings, makes a gift of the village as a matter of grace to the Raja.

After Vasco-da-Gama's departure for Europe, the Zamorin, with whom the Cochin Raja had a family feud, threatened to invade the Cochin Raja's territories with an army of 50,000 Nairs which he had assembled at Ponnāni. He, however, promised to withdraw, if the Raja of Cochin would surrender to him the Portuguese factors whom Gama had left behind him. The Portuguese themselves requested the Raja to give them up, so that Cochin might be saved from the threatened invasion. But the Raja refused the request and nobly replied that "loss of kingdom would be a smaller evil than breach of trust." The Zamorin's army poured into Cochin; a battle was fought before the walls of Cochin, in which the Raja was wounded and narrowly escaped with his life. The town was taken and given up to fire and sword. While Cochin was in this extremity, six Portuguese vessels were sighted, and next day they entered the river, and the Zamorin scuttled without a blow. These ships were commanded by Alphanso de Albuquerque and his brother Francisco.

In gratitude for this happy deliverance, the Cochin Raja permitted Alphanso de Albuquerque to build a fort at the mouth of the river. The foundations were laid on the 26th of September, 1503. It was constructed in the form of a square, each face being 180 yards long, with bastions at each corner, on which ordnance was mounted. The walls were composed of trunks of cocoanut trees, firmly fixed into the ground, and bound together with iron hoops and large nails. Earth was rammed in between the two rows of timber and the whole was surrounded by a wet ditch. The Raja sent workmen to construct the fort, and often went to see the progress of the work. It was soon finished and was called Fort Manuel after the reigning king Emmanuel of Portugal. Faria Y. Souza, however, calls it Fort St. James, and Joan de Barros observes that Francisco de Albuquerque, who superintended its construction, having a singular devotion to the Apostle James, and the vessel in which he sailed being called by the name of this saint, desired that the fort should be designated *Santiago*. Whitehouse conjectures that perhaps Manuel *Cotta* (Fort Manuel) was its civil and Santiago its ecclesiastical name.

4. **Episcopal See**. In 1557, at the request of Sebastian, one of the churches in Cochin, called St. Cruz or Santa Cruz (Holy Cross), was raised by the king of Portugal to the diginity of a Cathedral, and a Dominican elevated to the post of Bishop.[1] The first Bishop of Cochin was Don Father Jorge Thenmuda, O. P. or George Themuda of the order of St. Domingo. He was nominated by Donna Catherina, Regent of Portugal, and was confirmed by Pope Paul IV. He was consecrated at Lisbon in 1588, and arrived in India the same year. He governed the Diocese of Cochin from 1559 to 1567.[2]

5. **Restrictions on Commerce**. The following extracts from Day give us a fair idea of the rapacity of the Dutch East India Company and the way in which trade on the Coast was heavily handicapped:—

"The pay of the various officials was no criterion as to their emoluments, which were augmented by

1. Day, p. 109.
2. Augar, Church History of Travancore, p. 219.

numerous perquisites. Then the Dutch Commandant or Governor of Malabar received the following:—All foreign ships and sloops entering the river, with the Governor's permission, either for the purpose of trade, or otherwise, paid for anchorage; viz., from 1½ to 2 masts, Rs. 160 to the Governor; if from 2½ to 3 masts, Rs. 200. The Shawbunder likewise received Rs. 10. Persons on receiving leave to build a Bombara, or Dow, paid Rs. 100 to the Governor, Rs. 50 to the Second-in-Council, and Rs. 25 to the Shawbunder.

"On the sale of all private merchandise, 1 per cent. went to the Governor, who also received 5 per cent. on the value of timber exported, 1 per cent. on that of all coprah, Re. 1 for every 1000 cocoanuts, the same on every bale (consisting of 80 pieces) of Colechi cloth, one fanam on every Chōṭana (16 quarts) of cocoanut oil, Rs. 4 on every last of *nelly* (paddy) and Rs. 8 on each last of rice.

"A Bombara or Dow, leaving Cochin, paid Rs. 44 to the Governor for its passport; a shibar, bottilla or pattimar, of 1 mast, Rs. 11; and a maldive, Rs. 10. On issuing passports to country craft, ships and sloops, the following fees were paid: for vessels of 15 candies, Rs. 10 to the Governor; of 40 candies, Rs. 12; of 60 candies, Rs. 14; of 80 candies, Rs. 16; of 100 candies, Rs. 18; and on every additional candy, the Secretary received Rs. 2. A munchew and other small vessels paid from Rs. 3 to 3½; the endorsement of a passport cost Rs. 3. Pattimars and dhonies bringing letters or passengers, required no passports * * * *

"Every one had a certain percentage of whatever passed through his hands, from the Cashier to the Auctioneer, always paid by the person who received anything from the Company, or paid anything to it. Persons bringing slaves paid so much a head for their certificates to the Secretary. Fishermen gave 8 pounds of fish daily. The owners of the country vessels with gram or provisions a bunch of 100 betel-leaves, and 2 rolls of jaggery and so on."

Again, "All vessels passing along the backwater paid taxes at Cochin, Palliport, Cranganur, Paponatty and Quilon: whilst tolls were exacted on all liquors, metals, food or slaves imported or exported: 12½ per cent. on the produce of trees; and 30 per cent. on that of some of the land; even the fishermen were charged for the right of using nets."[2]

The Abbe Rayanal mentions the following as the articles of trade. "Their (Dutch) articles of sale consist of a small quantity of alum, benizon, camphire, tutenague, sugar, iron, calin, lead, copper and quicksilver. The vessel that carries this slender cargo returns to Batavia laden with caire or cocoa tree bark, for the use of the port."[3]

"The articles which are of the most current vent of those sent hither by the Company," says Stavorinus, "are cloves, nutmugs and mace."[4]

6. **Residences and Gardens.** This idea seems to have been realised later on. For the Governor and many of the upper classes seem to have built garden houses on the coast to the south of Cochin, and also on some of the picturesque islands with which the backwater was studded. Du Perron was taken by his landlord to his country residence on the island called Kanatcha on the way to Verapolay, the seat of Carmelite missionaries. Du Perron also mentions such houses being picturesquely situated on Rāmanṭuruṭṭu or Candle Island. The site now occupied by the British Residency at Bolghotty was the seat of a charming villa with a large airy room projecting into

1. Pp. 172—3.
2. P. 174.
3. History, Vol. I, p. 219.
4. P. 275.

the backwater, and the gardens around were a favourite resort for the picnic parties of the Dutch gentry.[1]

7. **Fortifications.** The Dutch regarded the Portuguese Fort as being too large and made considerable alterations. It was resolved to reduce it to one-third its size, though General Hutstart was for reducing its dimensions still further, his idea being to build a strong and small Pentagon Fort, one-third the size, which was finally decided on. It had seven bastions, called after the names of the seven United Provinces, viz., Holland, Zealand, Utrecht, Friesland, etc.

Dr. Fryer (1672—81) deemed the Dutch fortifications impregnable. Ives (1757) describes them as irregular but strong enough to resist any country power, with 40 or 50 guns facing the sea.

The Dutch Admiral Stavorinus (1775—1778) gives the following description of the city and its fortifications:—

"This city stands at the north-west point of an island, which is about eighteen Dutch miles in length, and two in breadth; to the south, the island is formed by the mouth of the river of Cali Coylang; and to the north, by that which runs from Cranganur, and separates it from the island of Bypin. The form of the city is nearly semi-circular, and it is about a mile and a half in circumference: on the landside it is fortified by six large bastions and cavalier, and to the eastward it has an irregular out-work; on the waterside, it is provided with a substantial wall, in which there are loop holes for small arms, and which terminates at the east end in a ravelin before the cavalier; a wet ditch runs round these works, and before it is a covered way and glacis tolerably well executed. The fortifications have been repaired and restored by Governor Moens out of the very ruinous condition into which they had been suffered to fall by former Governors.

1. Whitehouse—Historical Notices, p. 27.

" Although it cannot be said that the greatest part of these fortifications are constructed according to the exact rules of art, yet the place is sufficiently fortified to withstand a *Coup de main* and it would require a regular seige to take it. Approaches cannot even be made from any other quarter than from the south, where there is a dry and level plain; for, to the eastward as far as the river, there are several morasses which would render an attack on that side extremely difficult; besides, the place is fortified the strongest on that side and is the weakest by the seaside. In order to remedy this defect in some measure, a kind of ravelin has been constructed between the bastion Gilderland and the beach, but it is not, in my judgment, of sufficient strength, or importance, to deter an enemy from making an attempt on that side.

" The city cannot be attacked by the vessels from the river, until the fire of the bastions Gilderland and of the revelin Overysel be silenced, which could only be done by batteries to be erected at the southern extremity of the opposite island of Bypin. The security of the place would, however, be much augmented by the destruction of the wood which lies about a mile and a half south-east from the city, whereby the enemy would be deprived of a very important advantage for the carrying on of their operations, namely, the timber, etc. necessary for constructing of batteries, and for filling up the morasses, stagnant pools, and ditches in their way. The woods which cover the southern part of Bypin, and which extend down to the beach opposite to the city, ought equally to share the same fate.

" Cochin has three gates; one to the westward, called the Bay-gate; one to the eastward, called the New-gate; and one to the northward leading to the river, called the Water-gate.

" The principal buildings are the Church and the Government-house. The former is a pretty large, oblong edifice in which there is a very indifferent organ; the structure is a roomy, commodious and airy mansion, fronting a large plain, and appropriated for the residence of the Governor; opposite to it stands the mainguard, and on the left side are the barracks for the bodyguards of the Governor."[1]

8. **Heathens dwell not in Towns.** Orthodox Hindus do not, as a rule, even now live in the town.

9. **Mud Banks at Narakal** (Ñārakkal). The muddy bay or the mud banks of Alleppey and Ñārakkal form a peculiar feature of the Malabar coast, quite unique of its kind, perhaps not known elsewhere. There are four such banks as yet discovered, the more important ones being those already mentioned. There are minor ones off Quilandy and Calicut.

The earliest notice we have of the 'Alleppey-Porkad bank' is that of Captain Alexander Hamilton and dates so far back as A. D. 1678 to 1723, and is contained in an extract from his account of the East Indies in Pinkerton's *Collection of Voyages and Travels.* He says, "Mud bay is a place that, I believe, few can parallel in the world: it lies on the shore of St. Andrea, about half a league out in the sea, and is open to the wide ocean, and has neither island nor bank to break off the force of the billows which come rolling with great violence on all parts of the coast in the south-west monsoon, but, on the bank of mud, lose themselves in a moment, and ships lie on it, as secure as in the best harbour without motion or disturbance. It reaches about a mile along shore, and has shifted from the northward in 30 years about 3 miles."

"A MS. note has the following remark: This singular accumulation of mud still exists, and still affords the same convenience for anchorage in the worst weather. The present account was published in 1723, and now in 1825 the mud bank has shifted from St. Andrea in N. Lat 90° 41′ to Poonganot in N. Lat. 90° 25′, being 15 miles in 102 years." Mr. Maltby,

1. Voyages of Stavorinus, pp. 228—32. Ed. of 1798.

British Resident in Travancore, 1860, observes that the mud bank now (1860) is in Lat. 9° 28′ 30″.[1]

Captain Heber Drury, in 1858, in his *Notes on an Excursion along the Travancore Backwater*, referring to the advantages Alleppey possesses as a commercial depot, observes: "yet undoubtedly its greatest advantage as an emporium arises from the singular natural backwater formed in the open roadstead, and which consists of a long and wide bank of mud, the effect of which is so completely to break the force of the waves, that large vessels in the stormiest weather can securely anchor in the open roads, where the water is as calm as a mill pond. It is this extraordinary deposit which has earned for Alleppey the name of 'Mud Bay.'"[2]

Of the Ñāṟakkal Bank, the earliest account we have is that of the Dutch Admiral Stavorinus, who wrote about it in 1777, in these terms:—

" The Coast is safe and clear everywhere along the Company's establishment, except at the mouth of the river of Crānganūr, where there is a reef at the north side which stretches out to the sea, about three quarters of a league ; it is called the reef of Aycotia by our navigators ; before Coylang (Quilon), there is a similar one, but which does not extend half so far out. South of the above mentioned mouth of the river of Crānganūr, there is a bay, formed by mud banks; likewise one not far from Porca, and another south of Cochin : the banks forming which extend full a league out to sea, and into which vessels may run with safety during the bad monsoons, and may be in twenty and less feet of water, almost without anchors or cables, in perfect security against heavy seas, when these roll in upon the leeshore, as they break their force upon the soft mud banks, and within them nothing but a slight motion is percieved."

Amongst those who have in more recent years investigated scientifically the origin of these mud banks

1. Geological Survey Records, Vol. XVI, p. 17.
2. Madras Journal of Lit. and Sc. Vol, XX, N. S. 3, p. 217.

and their effect on a rough sea during the monsoon in producing safe and smooth anchorages both at Alleppey and at Ñārakkal, we may mention Major Heber Drury, Messrs. Crawford and Rhode, former Commercial Agents of the Travancore Sirkar at Alleppey, Lieutenants Taylor and Mitchel of the Royal Navy, Dr. Francis Day, some time Civil Surgeon of Cochin, and Messrs. King and Foote of the Geological Survey.

Speaking of the Alleppey mud bank, Major Drury thus wrote in 1858:—"The origin of the deposition of so large a quantity of mud in the open sea about two or three miles from the shore, and so many miles from any bar or outlet from the backwater has never been satisfactorily accounted for. From the circumstance of there being no natural outlet for the vast accumulation of waters which are poured down from the various mountain streams into the basin of the backwater, nearer than 36 miles on either side, it is not improbable that there exists a subterraneous channel communicating with the sea from the backwater through which the large quantity of mud is carried off and thrown up again by the sea in the form of a bank. Being subject to tidal action, the bank is more or less shifting at certain seasons, but not to a material extent. It imparts a dirty brown colour to the water for a considerable distance, and, close to the shore, the water is usually of a thickish consistency, being deeply impregnated with mud and slime."[1]

Mr. Crawford in a report submitted to the British Resident and dated 20th June 1860 has the following observations on this subject:—

"Lieutenant Taylor attributes the smoothness of the water to the soft mud at the bottom which, when stirred up by a heavy swell from seaward, so deadens the activity of the wave as to render the shore line free from surf.

1. Mad. Journal of Literature and Science, Vol. XIX, N. S. p. 217.

"A number of years ago, I brought to the notice of General Cullen (a former British Resident of Travancore) that the perfect smoothness of the water in the roads and at the beach at Alleppey was attributable not so much to the softness of the mud at the bottom as to the fact of the existence of a subterraneous passage or stream or a succession of them, which, communicating with some of the rivers inland and the backwater, become more active after heavy rains, particularly at the commencement of the monsoon, than in the dry season, in carrying off the accumulating water, and with it quantities of soft mud. General Cullen, the Resident, sent a quantity of piping and boring apparatus in order to test the existence or otherwise of what I had urged. Accordingly I sank pipes about 700 yards east from the beach and at between 50 and 60 feet depth: and, after going through a crust of chocolate-coloured sand stone, or a conglomerate mixture of that and lignite, the shafting ran suddenly down to 80 feet; fortunately, it had been attached to a piece of chain, or it would have been lost altogether. Several buckets from this depth were brought up, the contents of which corresponded in every respect with the matter thrown up by the bubbles as they burst at the beach, which I shall try here to describe as accurately as I can. Due west of the Flagstaff and for several miles to the south, but not north of that, the beach will after or during these rains suddenly subside, leaving a large tract of fissure varying from 40 to 100 or 120 yards in length; the subsidence is not so quick at first but when the cone of mud once gets above the water the fall is as much as five feet in some instances, when the cone bursts, throwing up immense quantities of soft soapy mud, and blue mud of considerable consistence in the form of boulders, with fresh water debris of vegetable matter, decayed and in some instances green and fresh. These bubbles are not confined to the seaboard, but are, I am inclined to think, both more active and numerous in the bed of the roads with the flagstaff bearing from E. N. E. to the south, until it bears N. E. by N. or over south of that. About five years ago, for about four miles down the coast and from the beach out to sea for a mile and a half, the sea was nothing but liquid mud, the fish died and as these cones reared their heads above the surrounding mud they would occasionally turn over a dead Porpoise and numerous other fish: the boatmen had considerable difficulty in urging their canoes through this to get outside of it; the beach and roads presented then a singular appearance; nothing to be seen but these miniature volcanoes, some silent, others active, perfect stillness all around the ships on the roads as if in some dock, with a heavy sea breaking at seven fathoms outside.

"There are numerous deep holes; some of them I measured in 1852; one in particular just at the end of the Conal Kad as much as 60 feet in depth. These holes may or may not communicate directly with the roads, but I think it will be found that the principal sources of active communication are more inland and the back-water perhaps only an auxilliary. About three miles above Chengaṅṅūṙ (16 miles east of Poṙcāḍ) in the river of that name, there is one or two 'Linus', which I only had an opportunity of visiting twice; the first time I had not the means of ascertaining the depth; the next I lost both lead and line.

"The depth of this passage (the supposed underground passage) is not so great as you approch the beach as noticed above; for while extending the canal from the Timber depot in March last about 200 yards from the beach at 12 feet, we suddenly and unexpectedly broke through the substratum, when a column of fresh water, mud and vegetable debris, and about nine inches in diameter, spouted up, which, when left alone, gradually subsided as the upper stratum of sand filled in round the column of the spring * * *.

"I have omitted to state one important particular, that is, should no rain fall, as has been the case this year, the sea in the roads and at the beach is not *nearly* so smooth ; up to this time we have had none of the mud cones bursting at the beach, neither on the roads, as the waves tumble in perfectly clear: there was a heavy surf from the 26th ultimo to the 9th instant, but never in any instance for these last 11 years has the rain held off so long as in this, and the roads and beach have always by the end of May been perfectly smooth."

Mr. Rhode, who succeeded Mr. Crawford in the Alleppy Commercial Agency, and who seems to have interested himself in the subject, agreed with his predecessor in thinking that the mud bank was due to hydraulic pressure caused by the level of the vast backwater being, in the S. W. monsoon, some four feet higher than the sea. The mud volcanoes that Mr. Rhode saw bursting up in the sea during the rainy season looked as if a barrel of oil has suddenly been started below the surface. Mr. Rhode observes that "the theory that the mud bank is immediately connected with, and due to, the height of the backwater being above the sea was, I think, conclusively proved this monsoon, as, at the height of the floods, when the canals were six feet above ordinary level, the area of the smooth water off Alleppey was so great that it was only by means of a good telescope and standing 20 feet above sea-level that I could see the breakers and heavy rollers beyond the half circle of smooth water. This flood was on the 13th June, and was followed by a rapid fall, and the half circle of smooth water of the sea beach contracted as the water fell. The floods again rose inland, and the smooth water circle expanded in proportion." Mr. Rhode also points to the existence of deep pot holes in the Vembanāḍ or Alleppey lake, 20 to 70 feet in depth, while the average depth of the lake itself is only a few feet, and remarks that this strengthens the theory of subterranean rivers connecting the backwater with the sea.

With regard to the Ñāṙakkkal mud bank Dr. Day observes, "The mud flat is now said to extend for half a mile south of Ñāṙakkal and to the north about four miles. The smoothest portions of the sea are between the villages of Ñāṙakkal and Nāyarambalam, one and a half miles to the north. W.N.W. from Ñāṙakkal the sea at soundings less than three fathoms, invariably retains its stillness, between three and five fathoms there is a slight swell. To the south of Ñāṙakkal the mud bank is narrower, and the deep water and stillness nearer the shore. To the north, the soundings are shallower and the water smooth further out to sea." [1] Dr. Day thinks that the Ñāṙakkal mud bank is due to the alluvial deposits washed into the sea by the S. W. monsoon by the rains on the coast. He says that "should any obstruction be at their outlets deposits some times take place, as at the Cṙānganūr and Quilon rivers, where mud banks have been so formed. Whether the impediment to the alluvial deposit being carried out to sea is merely owing to the action of the S. W. monsoon causing a great impetus to the waves as they meet the river at its exit, or whether other causes also obtain, must be questioned. In forming the Ñāṙakkal mud bank, a reet of rocks, the Aycotta reef, at the mouth of the Cṙānganūr river appears to have prevented the S. W. monsoon from causing a divergence of the river's mouth to the northward (as invariably takes place on the western coast unless that bank is protected); this reef (Aycotta) has probably assisted in theformati on of the Ñāṙakkal, or, more properly speaking the Cṙānganūr mud banks."[2]

The theory of hydraulic pressure, and subterranean communications between the backwater and the sea forcing the mud and debris of the lake into the sea, which, it is supposed, has formed the Alleppey mud bank, can scarcely account for the Ñāṙakkal bank; for, on either side of the bank, there are wide outlets into

1. Land of the Perumals, p. 35.

2. Records of the Geological Survey, Vol. XVII, p. 21.

the sea, viz., those of Cochin and Cranganur. Further no deep pits or pot-holes have been as yet found to exist in the Cochin-Cranganur backwater.

"The consensus of observation," says Dr. King of the Indian Geological Survey, "and opinion certainly leads to the conclusion that there is an underground discharge of water at any rate into the sea from the lagoon and the river system behind the Alleppey-Porcad Coast during flood time, the inland waters being at a higher level than the sea. The accounts of such a condition of affairs at Ñarakkal bank, are, however, not so clear, besides there is the free opening at the Cochin river mouth. Still underground discharges of lesser intensity may take place; while the lesser pressure likely to be brought to bear on this part of the sea-board may also account for the absence of violent exhibitions like those of Alleppey."[1]

As to the nature of the mud, Mr. Rhode found it to be of a peculiar character and so soft that a light lead (4lbs.), put over the end of a pier, apparently showed two fathoms of water, but on drawing up the line, six feet was found to be water and six feet soft oily mud.

Dr. Day observes that the Ñarakkal mud feels unctuous and sticky, but is not gritty, unless mixed with the sand. It is of a very dark greenish colour. Under the microscope it shows "very minute angular fragments of quartz, the largest hardly visible without a lens: this is the sand. Secondly, Foraminiferous shells of the genus Rotalia, and a few fragments of larger shells. Thirdly, Diatomaceae, of which were discovered species from upward of 20 genera. Fourthly, a few spicales of sponges and corals, very minute: and some amorphous matter, which was not destroyed after long boiling in strong acids." On a more elaborate enquiry, the mud was found to be very tenacious

1. P. 26.

and resistant of pressure, like a stiff piece of jelly. "An examination into its composition resulted in the discovery of 62 species, belonging to 30 genera of the class Cryptogamia, and sub group Diatomaceoe."[1]

Dr. King says that "the mud is full of organic matter, and that it contains a sensible amount of oil, some of which may have been derived from the decomposition of organism."

With regard to the action of the mud on the water above, it is supposed by Dr. Day that, acting like an immense spring, it yields to the pressure of the waves, and the water thus loses its force and becomes quiescent: whilst the mud expanding is prepared for a fresh encounter.

"Regarding the water over the mud," says Dr. King, "it is only known to calm down during the South-West monsoon. There is no observation showing how it may be affected in stormy weather or at other seasons. Still I was led to understand, when in personal communication with Mr. Crawford in 1881, that the calming of the anchorages does not take place until after the monsoon has commenced, and there has been a stirring up of the sea and the mud. The quieting of the waters is intensified according to the amount of the rainfall during the monsoon, but even if no rain fall, there is a certain amount of quiescence. The calmness continues throughout the monsoon, apparently, without any fresh stirring up of mud. In one locality at least, the water is subject at times to violent agitation through the bursting up of gigantic bubbles of water, mud or gas,—it is not quite clear which—and these features also appear to be intensified during heavy rainy weather in the monsoon periods. The water over the banks becomes considerably freshened, even to the extent—as I was told by Mr. Crawford—of being drinkable; also according as the monsoon rains are light or heavy. At such times, also,

1. Madras Journal of Literature and Science, Vol. XII, N. S. p. 264

the water gives off fetid odours, and the fish inhabiting it are killed off in large numbers; but whether owing to the freshening of the sea water, or to the exhibition of poisonous matter and vapour in the water, is not clear: perhaps the destruction of life may be due to both causes.

"The old idea of the mud bank acting as an elastic barrier against which the wild seas sank into such marvellous quietude must be given up in part at least, now that we have got the more reasonable soother of troubled waters in the oily constitution of the mud. There is of course the difficulty of citing, or indeed, the absolute want of authoritative observation of the action of oil on troubled waters; but tradition and anecdote are undoubtedly in favour of it, while there are the newspaper accounts of the experiment which was tried a year ago in the harbour of Peterhead, when a stream of oil was cast upon the heavy seas at the harbour's mouth with such success, that vessels were enabled to run in with comparative ease.

"In the case of the mud banks, it can easily be conceived how the stirring up the mud in the beginning of the monsoon should produce temporary calmness, but there is considerable difficulty in accounting for the long continuance of quiescence without any fresh stirring up. There is certainly the fact that the upper stratum of mud continues in an extreme state of liquidity or attenuation in the water, and that thus a sort of restlessness and freeing oil particles may be going on for a long period; but I think we must look to further supply from hidden sources, which are indicated by the more violent burstings forth of water or mud or oil in the form of 'cones'. * * * The amount of oil derivable from the decomposition of the animal and vegetable matter of the organisms in the mud would be, I am inclined to think, hardly sufficient to account for the features exhibited; hence it is necessary to look to other sources for the oil, and even to a source for the continued supply of the mud itself, which is evidently carried away by littoral currents.[1] Summing up his observations, from which we have already quoted largely, Dr. King concludes, "Thus, the conclusion seems inevitable that the banks, their smoothing influence and their position within certain ranges of the coast may be entirely due to the following causes: first, the discharge of mud from under the lands of Alleppey, Poŕacāḍ and Ñāŕakkal, this being effected by the percolation or underground passages of lagoon water into the sea; second, the presence in this mud of oily matter, derived perhaps in part from the decomposition of organisms, but principally from the distillation of oil in sub-adjacent lignitiferous deposits, belonging, presumably, to Vaŕkalay Strata; third, the action of littoral currents, which, slowly and through long periods of years, carry the mud down the coast to certain points whence it is dissipated seawards,—by the Quilon river at Ñāŕakkal, and at Poŕacāḍ, because it is there beyond the range of replacement."

Mr. Philip Lake of the Geo. Survey, who is perhaps the latest scientist who has investigated the question, observes, "The chief point, then, in which I differ from the previous observers, is in considering that the Alleppey bank is formed, not from the backwater mud, but from an older river deposit found only at particular points along the coast. This would explain its non-appearance at other points where the conditions seem equally favourable. With regard to the existence of subterranean channels, it may well be doubted whether any could exist in such unstable deposits as are found here."

"The Ñāŕakkal mud bank is very probably, to a large extent, formed of the silt carried down by the Crānganūŕ river. It does not appear to be very much affected by the rise of the backwaters. It is, in fact, very much what the Alleppey mud bank must have

1. Pp. 25--26.

been before the greater part of it was covered up by more recent deposits."[1] Mr. Lake points out that there is not the least resemblance between the mud of the bank and the backwater mud. The mud of the bank is greenish in colour, oily, very tenacious, and owing to its fineness, very mixible with water. It is very fine clay, and, of ordinary clays, is more like the under-clay of a coal-seam than any other. The mud of the backwater, on the other hand, is full of vegetable debris, black, lumpy and contains a high percentage of carbon. It will not mix well with the water, and is hardly a true mud[2]. He is inclined to think that the stratum of oily mud will be found at some depth below the water deposits, and that, in fact, it was the silt carried by the rivers into the sea when the coast line was further east than it is at present, before the sand bars cutting off the back waters from the sea began to be formed.

It will be clear from a review of the above observations that scientists are not yet agreed as to the exact source of the mud of the mud banks, or as to how the mud acts on the water above so as to produce a perfectly smooth-water anchorage.

The term "mud bay" or "muddy bay", as applied to these banks, is a perfect misnomer, though used by the earliest pioneers of navigation. In fact there is no indication of any bay either at Alleppey or Ñāṟakkal. The shore line, as it is from the Cṟānganūṟ spit to the Ṭangachēry reefs at Quilon is perfectly straight. Dr. Day, however, argues that at Ñāṟakkal a bay did exist at one time. He says that "though the northern projection of the coast at the mouth of the Cṟānganūṟ river, forming the northern extremity of the 'mud bay' is still present, the southern projection, or that between Nāṟakkal and the mouth of the Cochin river, is gone, having in fact been covered by the sea (at this place a church stood which is now submerged): had it not

1. Geological Records, Vol. XVIII, p. 47.
2. P. 46.

been so, a mud bay would still be present''. But Dr. King, while accepting the fact of a portion of the land near the Cochin end of Ñārakkal having been submerged, points out that there is no knowledge of this land having had the form of a projection like the southern arm of a bay.

A peculiarity with regard to the Alleppey bank has also to be noticed. It is known to shift its position. Captain Hamilton observes that it has shifted from the northward in 30 years about three miles. The MSS. note to the passage from Hamilton, extracted in Pinkerton, adds that in 1825 it had shifted from St. Andrea in N. Lat. 90° 40′ to Poonaganot in N. Lat. 90° 25′, being 15 miles in 102 years—an average of nearly one mile in eight years. More recently, in the year 1902, it shifted further south towards Poṙacāḍ. It is note-worthy that the progress is steadily southwards. Dr. King attributes this southerly movement to littoral currents acting over long periods on tenacious muds, which may really only be evolved in large quantities at intermittent periods.

10. **Calicut.** The ancient town of Calicut, once famous as the seat of the great Zamorin, has passed through various vicissitudes of fortune. It lies on the sea-coast in the Lat. 11° 15′ north.

Mr. Logan thinks that the tradition preserved in the Kēralōṭpaṭṭi regarding the founding of Calicut and its rapid rise as a trading centre are probably founded on fact. The Zamorin in his attempts to obtain supremacy in Malabar had warred with the Poṙlāṭiri or chief of Polnāḍ for almost 48 years, and at last secured admission into the Poṙlāṭiri's stronghold by bribing that chief's treacherous minister and faithless mistress; and, in order to have a firm hold on Polnāḍ, the Zamorin had built a fort at Vēlapuram in Calicut. About this time "a merchant (Chetti) from the east coast, who had been on a trading voyage to Mecca, reached Calicut, with a ship overloaded (it is said) with gold. The ship was about to sink in consequence, and the merchant brought it close on shore at Calicut, took out a box of treasure, laid it before the Zamorin and told his story. The Zamorin directed him to bring his treasure ashore, and store it in his palace. The merchant accordingly built (it is said) a granite cellar in the king's house, and deposited therein as much of the treasure as could not be conveniently taken away in his ship. He then sailed for his own country, and after a time returned to Calicut, opened the cellar in the presence of the Zamorin, counted out the treasure, and finding it correct, divided it into two portions and offered the Zamorin one-half of it. But the Zamorin replied, "I do not want your treasure, you may take away the whole". The Chetti, being convinced that this was the most truthful of all kings and Swarūpams (dynasties), then asked and obtained permission to trade at Caliçut. In this way the bazaar was founded. The Chetti's name is Ambarēśan, and, so the Kēraḷōṭpaṭṭi runs, "the cellar erected by him in the Kōvilagam (king's house) bears even to this day the name of Ambarēśan Keṭṭ (Ambaresan built)."

There is another version of the same story preserved in the Kēraḷōṭpaṭṭi almost to the same effect. It says "that in the town of Muscat two sons were born to a Mahomedan; after they had grown up, the father addressed the elder of the two sons saying:—'after my death, you two will fight with each other. The other will kill you. Both of you should not be in the same place. You had better go to some land and pass your days. I shall give you enough gold for that.' Thus the father sent away the elder son in a ship. He visited various countries and laid presents before their respective sovereigns. The presents consisted of pickle boxes full of gold, and he used to represent to each king whose honesty he wished to test, that the box contained only pickles. All the kings he visited, on discovering what the boxes really contained, concealed the fact, and appropriated the gold, but at last the experiment was tried on the Zamorin, and the Zamorin at once called him up and said :—'You mistook one thing for another. This is not pickles, but gold.' The traveller thereupon concluded that here at last was a trustworthy king, and so he settled down at Calicut and became the Kōya (Mahomedan priest) of Calicut."[1]

It is not possible to ascertain with any approach to accuracy, even approximately, the time when the event happened. If it ever did happen, it must certainly have been some time after A. D. 825. For the Zamorin himself claims to have come into possession of Calicut only on the alleged distribution of the Kērala Empire, which event is generally ascribed to that date. Soon after, the Zamorin, with the assistance of the Moors, subdued the greater part of Kērala, and assumed a doubtful supremacy over all Malabar. Hence perhaps the reason for styling Calicut the capital of Malabar.

Ibn Batuta in 1324 describes Calicut as "one of the great ports of the Districts of Malabar and in which merchants from all parts are found. The king of this place is an infidel, who shaves his chin just as the Haidari Fakeers of Room do. When we approached the place, the people came out to meet us, and with a large concourse brought us into the port. The greatest part of the Mahomedan merchants of this place are so wealthy, that one of them can purchase the whole freightage of such vessels as put in here; and fit out others like them."[2]

The Chinese Mahomedan Ma Huan (A. D. 1403) also gives a description of Calicut:—

1. Malabar, pp. 276—8.
2. Lee's Translation, p. 172.

This seaport, of which Ma Huan gives us a most lengthy account, is described as a great emporium of trade frequented by merchants from all quarters. "It is three days' sail from Cochin, by which it is bordered on the south; on the north it adjoins Cannanore (K'ān-nu-urh); it has the sea on the west; and on the east, through the mountains, at a distance of 500 li (167 miles), is the kingdom or city of K'an-pa-mei, (Koyampadi, a former name of Coimbatore?), a great seat of cotton manufacture, where is made, as also in the surrounding districts, a cloth called Chih-li (Chih-li-pu) cloth. It is made up into pieces, four feet five inches wide and twenty-five feet long; it is sold there for eight or ten gold pieces of their money. They also prepare raw silk for the loom, which they dye various shades of colour and then weave into flowered pattern goods, made up into pieces four to five feet wide and twelve to thirteen long. Each length is sold for one hundred gold pieces of their money."

"To return to Calicut, much pepper is grown on the hills. Cocoanuts are extensively cultivated, many farmers owning a thousand trees; those having a plantation of three thousand are looked upon as wealthy proprietors. The king belongs to the Nayar class, and like his brother of Cochin is a sincere follower of Buddha, and as such does not eat beef; his overseer, being a Mahomedan, does not eat pork. This led, it is said in times past, to a compact being made between the king and his overseer to the effect that, if the king would give up eating pork, the overseer would give up eating beef. This compact has been most scrupulously observed by the successors of both parties up to the present day. The king at his devotions prostrates himself before an image of Buddha every morning; which being over, his attendants collect all the cow-dung about the place, and smear it over the image of the god. Some of the dung the king orders to be burnt to ashes and put into a small cotton bag which he continually wears upon his person; and when his morning ablutions are over, he mixes some of the powdered dung with water and smears it over his forehead and limbs; by so doing he considers he is showing Buddha the greatest reverence.

"Many of the king's subjects are Mahomedans, and there are twenty or thirty mosques in the kingdom, to which the people resort every seventh day for worship. On this day, during the morning, the people being at the mosques, no business whatever is transacted; and the after part of the day, the services being over, business is resumed.

"When a ship arrives from China, the king's overseer with a Chetti go on board and make an invoice of the goods, and a day is settled for valuing the cargo. On the day appointed, the silk goods, more especially the khinkis* (kincobs), are first inspected and valued, which when decided on, all present join hands, whereupon the broker says, 'The price of your goods is now fixed, and cannot in any way be altered.'

"The price to be paid for pearls and precious stones is arranged by the Weinaki broker, (Chitti Weinaki) and the value of the Chinese goods taken in exchange for them is that previously fixed by the broker in the way above stated.

"They have no abacus on which to make their calculations, but in its place they use their toes and fingers, and, what is very wonderful, they are never wrong in their reckonings.

"The succession to the throne is settled in a somewhat curious manner. The king is not succeeded by his son, but by his sister's son, because his nephew, being born of his sister's body, is considered nearer to him by blood. If the king has no sister, the succession goes to his brother; if he has no brother, it goes to a man of ability and worth. Such has been the rule for many generations.

"As in Cochin, the money in circulation is the Fanan and the Ta-wih. Their weights are the P'o-ho and the Fan-la-shih, and there is a measure called a Tang-ko-li (Fan-sek-la?)

"The king's present to the Emperor is usually a gold plaited girdle set with all kinds of precious stones and pearls."

"It may not be out of place to note that Ma Huan states that the commander of the Chinese Fleet which left China in 1408, did on his arrival at Calicut erect a stone with a Chinese inscription on it to commemorate his visit. Are there any traces of it still remaining?"[1]

The next account we have of Calicut is from the pen of Abdurazak, the ambassador whom Sha-Rohk, the Persian Emperor, sent to the Zamorin in 1442—and that is a very pleasing account indeed. "Calicut is a perfectly secured harbour, which, like that of Ormuz, brings together merchants from every city and from every country. In it are to be found abundance of precious articles brought hither from maritime countries, and especially from Abyssinia, Zirbad, and Zanzibar. From time to time ships arrive there from the shore of the House of God and other parts of the Hedjaz, and abide at will, for a greater or longer space, in this harbour. The town is inhabited by infidels, and situated in a hostile shore. It contains a considerable number of Mussalmans, who are constant residents here, and have built two mosques, in which they meet every Friday to offer up prayer. They have one Kady, a priest, and for the most part they belong to the sect Schafie. Security and justice are so firmly established in the city, that the most wealthy merchants bring thither from maritime countries considerable cargoes, which they unload and unhesitatingly send into the markets and bazaars, without thinking in the meantime of any necessity of checking the account or of keeping watch over the goods. The officers of the Custom-House take upon themselves the charge of

1. Mr. Geo. Phillips' translation, Journal of the Royal Asiatic Society, April 1906.

looking after the merchandise, over which they keep watch day and night. When a sale is effected, they levy a duty on the goods of one-fortieth part; if they are not sold, they make no charges on them.

"In other ports, a strange practice is adopted. When a vessel sets sail for a certain point, and suddenly is driven by a decree of Divine Providence into another roadstead, the inhabitants, under the pretext that the wind has driven it there, plunder the ship. But at Calicut, every ship, whatever place it may come from, or wherever it may be bound, when it puts into this port, is treated like other vessels, and has no trouble of any kind to put up with."[1] His description of the people is rather uncanny:—"The blacks of this country have the body nearly naked; they bear only bandages round the middle, called *lankoutah*, which descend from the navel to above the knee. In one hand they hold an Indian poignard, which has the brilliance of a drop of water, and in the other a buckler of ox-hide, which might be taken for a piece of mist. This costume is common to the king and to the beggar."[2]

Two years after Abdur-Razak, we have a description of the town given by Nicolo Conti, the Italian, perhaps the first Christian traveller who has noticed Calicut. After leaving Cochin, he visited a number of places in the interior, and proceeded to Calicut which is described as a maritime city, eight miles in circumference, a noble emporium for all India, abounding in pepper, lac, ginger, a larger kind of cinnamon, myrobalans, and Zedary."[3]

The next notice we have is from Athanaseus Nikiten, a Russian traveller (1468—1474), who says "Calecut (Calicut) is a port for the whole Indian sea, which God forbid, any craft to cross, and whoever saw it, will not go over it healthy. The country produces

1. Major's India in the 15th Century, pp. 14—15.
2. P. 17.
3. Ibid. p. 26.

AD.

pepper, ginger, colour-plants, muscat, cloves, cinnamon, aromatic roots, *adrach* and every description of spices, and everything is cheap, and servants and maids are very good." Further on, he describes Calicut as having "a big bazaar."[1]

Towards the close of the 15th century, a Genovese, named Hieroinimo Di Santa Stefano, visited Calicut which he calls a "great city." He gives an account of the peculiar customs and manners of the people, but writes very little about the city itself, its government or its trade.

Ludovico Di Varthema (1503—1508) gives us a fuller account of Calicut in every respect than any other traveller. Varthema not simply travelled through the country, but stayed at Calicut for some time, and had occasion to judge of the place, its government, its people, and their peculiar customs; and, in spite of the supremely ludicrous descriptions and observations with which the account of his travels abound, he may be taken, with a great deal of reserve, to give us a tolerably fair idea of the country and its people.

In his book of travels, he treats about "Calicut," "Concerning the King", "Religion of the people," "The manner of the eating of the King of Calicut," "The Brahmans—Priests of Calicut," "The Pagans of Calicut," "What classes they are," "Dress, Food of King, Queen and people of Calicut," "Ceremonies after the death of King," "The manners of living and administration of justice," "Mode of worship of the Pagans," "The fighting of the people," "The palace of the King of Calicut," "The practice they follow in sowing rice," "The Physicians who visit the sick at Calicut," "Animals and birds," "Serpents, etc. found at Calicut," "The light of the King of Calicut," and "How a great number of people came to Calicut to receive pardon."

1. Major's India in the 15th Century, p. 20 and Intr. xxvii.

In 1588, Ralph Fitch visited Calicut as a trader, and was perhaps the first Englishman to set his foot on the shores of Calicut. He notices it as a large kingdom, extending from the Cochin Raja's territories to Goa in the north; but does not give us any description of the city itself.

After the arrival of the Portuguese, we have frequent references to Calicut and its king, the Zamorin, with whom the filibustering Portuguese could never pull on well. Barbosa, Castanheda, Faria Y Souza, Linxhoten, and others give us accounts of Calicut more or less exaggerated.

Pyrard de Lavel was there in 1607. He was much struck with the high degree of civilization to which Calicut had attained, in spite of a century of desolating war. "There is no place in all India," says he, "where contentment is more universal than at Calicut, both on account of its fertility and beauty of the country and of the intercourse with the men of all religions who live there in full exercise of their own religion."[1] "It is the busiest and the most full of all traffic and commerce in the whole of India. It has merchants from all parts of the world, and of all nations and religions, by reason of the liberty and security accorded to them there, for the king permits the exercise of every kind of religion, and yet it is strictly forbidden to talk, dispute, or quarrel on that subject."[2] "As for justice, it proceeds from the king alone, and throughout all his kingdom there is no other judge but he. For all that, justice is well administered, and awarded to all gratuitously".[3]

Sig. Pietro Della Vella, a noble Roman, in the course of his travels, reached Calicut in December 1623 in a Portuguese ship which carried an embassy from the Viceroy of Goa to the Zamorin of Calicut,

1. Vol. I, p. 336.
2. P. 404.
3. P. 470.

bringing the Viceroy's answer to the Zamorin's overtures for peace. Della Vella says, "The city of Calicut lies 11° 22′ distant from the Equioctial towards the North. After dinner, I landed also with the captain of my ship, and some other soldiers; we went to see the bazaar, which is near the sea-shore. The houses or rather cottages are built of earth and palm leaves, being very low; the streets also are very narrow but indifferently long; the market was full of all sorts of provision, and other things necessary to the livelihood of the people, conformable to their custom; for, as for clothing, they need little, both men and women going quite naked, saving that they have a piece either of cotton or silk hanging, down from girdle to the knees and covering their shame; the better sort are wont to wear either all blue, or white striped with azure, or azure and some other colour, a dark blue being most esteemed amongst them. Moreover, both men and women wear their hair long, and tied about the head, the women with a lock hanging on one side under the ear becomingly enough, as almost all Indian women do; the dressing of whose head, is in my opinion, the gallantest that I have seen in any other nation. The men have a lock hanging down from the crown to the head, sometimes a little inclined on one side; some of them use a small coloured head band, but the women use none at all. Both sexes have their arms full of bracelets, their ears pendants, and their necks of jewels; the men commonly go with their naked sword and bucklers or other arms in their hands, as I said, as those of Balgate." He then refers to the Mahomedan pirates from whom the coast came to be called the pirate coast, and observes that "it is famous in India for the continual robberies committed at sea by the Malabar thieves; whence in the bazaar of Calicut, besides the things above mentioned, we saw sold good store of the Portugal's commodities, as swords, arms, books, cloths of Goa and the like merchandises taken from Portugal vessels at sea: which things because stolen, and in regard of the excommunication which lies upon us in that case, are not bought by Christians. Having seen the bazaar, and stayed there till it was late, we were minded to see the more inward and noble part of the city, and the outside of the king's palace. * * * . Accordingly we walked a good way towards the Palace, for the city is great, and we found it to consist of plots beset with abundance of high trees, amongst the boughs whereof, a great many of wild monkies; and within these close groves stand the houses, for the most part at a distance from the common ways or streets; they appear but little, few of their outsides being seen, besides the low walls made of a blackstone surrounding these plots, and dividing from the streets, which are much better than those of the bazaar, but without any ornament of windows; so that he that walks through the city, may think that he is rather in the midst of uninhabited gardens, than of an inhabited city. Nevertheless it is well peopled, and hath many inhabitants, whose being contented with narrow buildings is the cause that it appears but small"[1]

Dr. Fryer, travelling between 1672 and 1681, has the following notice of Calicut:—

"Having taken in what bales of pepper this place (Ṭāṉūr) afforded; we weighed by two in the morning and by four in the afternoon. Anchored against that Anciently Traded Port of Calicut in the Latitude of 11 deg. 30 min. North.

"Ashore the first House facing us was the English: near it were placed six small pieces, resounding our Salutes at our Entry.

"On the backside lay two great Guns, dismounted, of Brass, all that is extant of the Portugal Town and Castle (which ran out as far into the sea as our Ships now ride, near four miles) overflowed by water; nothing

1. Pp. 181—2.

remaining of it but only what is taken upon chronicle.

"What is also left of Calicut, is not equivalent to what must be expected from the gleaning of so many Ages of Traffick; unless as Antiquaries esteem most of those things are Moth-eaten by Time, which Vermin has been plaguy pernicious here. For the city that stood upon Stilts, is tripped up, for down it is gone, and the Temple, whose Marble Pillars durst compare with those of Agrippa's in the Roman Pantheon, is Topsyturvy. And if any one that comes after me make you believe it to be not above Four Miles in length, and in that not an House befitting a Christian; here and there a Mosque and Burying Places with Tanks: A good long Buzzar with Trash and Ripe Fruit; another with Opium, and Spices of the coast, changers and Jewellers, infenced and rude in Building, he tells you but the truth. Indeed it is pleasantly situated under Trees, and it is the Holy See of Zamerhine or Pope. The citizens are urbane, being trained up to commerce; but the Trade gone to Goa, along with the Portugals: who at their first arival into the bay, found more ships by 500 than we did, without either chart or Compass, who most of them transported their commmodities to the Red Sea, along the Coasts; or to the Gulf of Persia. and thence they were carried overland to Scandaroon, Alleppo or Constantinople, unto the hands of the Venetians, from whom we were served with them, and by that means they gained for themselves the power and Greatness of the State."

Between the visits of the Roman noble and the English Doctor, Calicut must have had a rather serious fall. In the meanwhile, the Dutch had arrived, and the Portuguese, who contributed in no small degree towards the commercial prosperity of the city, had quitted the scenes of their glories. The Zamorin, proud of his position as assumed sovereign lord of

Malabar and conscious of the help of the Moors, had always quarrelled with the Portuguese, mainly because the Portuguese were befriending his longstanding enemy, the Cochin Raja. The Zamorin must have by this time fallen considerably in estate, for we find him described about 1664 as ruling "From Ticori (Ṭṛkkoḍi) to Chēṭṭwa," a distance of about 22 leagues, and keeping up "some faint resemblance of grandeur." [1]

Speaking of Calicut, Mr. Forbes (A. D. 1772) says :—"Calicut road where the ships anchor is deemed unsafe for those not well acquainted with the navigation, several vessels have been wrecked upon the ruins of the old city, now under water; as the mean town, just described, formed no part of the emporium where de Gama landed. Calicut is said to have been then a large city, where the Zamorin, the sovereign of the country, held a splendid court, and merchants resorted from Persia, Arabia, Africa, and different parts of India to purchase pearls, diamonds, spices, ivory and other costly articles."[2]

11. **The English in Malabar.** We have already seen that Ralph Fitch was the first Englishman to set his foot on the shores of Malabar. He arrived in Cochin as a merchant on the 22nd of March 1588 and remained there till the 2nd of November. In 1591, Captain Raymonds made an unsuccessful attempt to reach India in three English ships. Again, in 1596, Captain Wood made a similar attempt and failed. On the 31st December 1600, the English East India Company of London was formed, and, in August 1607 or 1608, the first English ship reached Surat under Captain Hawkins, and, in 1612, the English factory there was established. So early as 1606-7, we find a petition to the king from the Company of merchants trading into the East Indies for letters from His Majesty to certain Eastern Princes, and among these "To the

1. Malabar, p. 341.
2. Oriental Memoirs, Vol. 1, p. 206.

king of Calicut, praying that we, His Majesty's merchants, coming thither as good friends to traffic and trade, may be friendly entertained and permitted to trade in all liberty and freedom with peace and safety of our persons, ships and goods. And that His Majesty hath sent him a present by his servant the bearer hereof."[1] We do not know if such a letter was ever given.

In 1615, Captain Keeling with three English ships, the same that had brought Sir. Thomas Roe on his well-known embassy to the Great Mogul, arrived off Calicut, and as he was passing down the coast on his way from Surat to Bantam, there came, according to Purchas, "on the 4th of March, a Ṭōṇi (canoe) aboard us, with messengers from the Zamorin to the General. The next day the Governor sent a present, and entreated the General to go to Crānganūr which the day after we did* * *. On the 8th the General went ashore with master Barkeley, Cape merchant and others, when they received kind usage, and concluded to settle a factory"[2]. Three factors, a gunner, and a boy were accordingly left there, George Woolman being appointed chief. In April they moved to Calicut, where Woolman died a few months later. On the 21st March 1617, Captain Pepwell arrived with his fleet, and finding matters in a very unsatisfactory position, determined to withdraw the factory. Most of the goods left there had been sold, but it was impossible to obtain payment. The Zamorin's principal object in entertaining the English was to obtain their active assistance against the Portuguese; and when this was not forthcoming, he ceased to interest himself in their proceedings. "The country itself," said the factor in charge, "neither gave vent to ours, nor produced commodities in any quantity or at reasonable rates to return for England"[3].

The following letter from George Woolman, who

1. Letter Book of the East India Company, Vol. IV, p. 805.
2. Purchas, Vol. I, p. 603.
3. Ibid.

had been left at Calicut by Captain Keeling, addressed apparently to Captain Pepwell, gives us a fair idea of the circumstances under which Keeling landed at Crānganūr, and of what happened after Keeling's departure.

"Calicut, 15th of July 1616.

"George Woolman to (Captain Pepwell).

"Right Worshipful,

"Our duties remembered, &c. may it please you to understand that whereas it hath unhappily fallen out since the departure of Right Worshipful General Keeling, Esq., whose letters directed to your Worship, as touching the business done and agreements made between the Great Zamorin and he for the settling here in this country of Malabar, as also our advices, which we according to commission despatched away for the Mogal's Dominions to our English factories, were by the way intercepted, our post robbed, who returned unto us with unfavourable news this present month. This news seemed very distasteful unto us, being moved with jealousy that the Portuguese laid for them; but as yet we are not certain of anything, otherwise than our post affirmeth.

"The loss of our advice was not so much to be regarded as the loss of our General's letter, directed unto your Worship, the contents whereof are unknown unto us, and for that respect it fell out very crossly, in missing of his advice; but your Worship must have patience, and with the information from us to your Worship what we have seen hitherto so that we shall see now and between your Worship's arrival, God permitting, I hope will resolve you suddenly what is to be done as touching merchandising affairs.

"Now under correction, if it please your Worship to give leave, we will in a word (for not being tedious) relate unto you in what manner it fell out with us to fall upon this coast.

"This place of Callicutt is in latitude betwixt 11d—10 [m] and 11d—20 [m] and directly again [st] this place we stood in with the shore, giving chase to a sail, and approached as near the shore as we could after him, which we found to be a Malabar belonging to Callicut, as we understood which fell out contrary to our expectation. And being near the shore there came many boats aboard our ship, amongst which one came with news from the Zamorin to our General certifying him that his king the Zamorin was very desirous to have some conference with the English nation, not to prejudice them any kind of way, but that his propositions he meant to declare unto them should be as beneficial to our nation as profitable to himself. Upon which our General with his council considered of it, and determined to speak with the Zamorin, who was at Crănganūr, laying siege to the fort the Portugal hath near adjoining. This place of Crănganūr is in latitude 10 [d]-15 [m (Sup: 64. It is really 10°-13′-50″). There we arrived the 5th of March in the evening. The 7th of March our General was going toward shore and there was some twelve sail of frigates making towards them to intercept him, which caused him to return aboard again. But that day it was so ordered amongst the ships for riding near the shore within shot that our General went ashore at pleasure. There he spent a whole day in conferring, so that before his coming aboard the business was concluded in manner and form as you shall understand by the copy of agreements which we have sent your Worship herein closed. March the 19th we were put ashore, being five in number, three as factors, two as attendants. Our fleet departed the 2nd of March. Our cargazon left with us was but small to see to, but too great for the place we find it. April the 22nd we arrived at Callicutt by sea, with our cloth and some benjamin with a quantity of tin at the Zamorin's house to be sent after us, wanting as then conveyance for it. This tin and benjamin we took in a

Portugall ship upon this coast. The ship our general took along with him. We have here some sword blades and looking glasses ; they are very good presents but bad merchandise. So that we dare not advise your Worship to bring any commodity whatsoever while (probably 'until' is meant) we see further of it.

"The Governor did enforce the merchants to deal for part of our cloth, the price being made at 35 fannons (Fanams) per coviods, Portugall measure (the fannon at 6d. Sterling) ; five months' time, and at the end of it I pray God send us our money ; but our chiefest hope relies on the Governor. The cloth (though it be little they here desire) they would willingly have no other colour but stammels and red. But as I said before, we dare not write for any ; and while the Portugall be feared away from Achin (a mistake for Cochin) I think there will be little to be done in this place or parts, for they have been the ruining of this place, that the merchants dare not adventure by sea for them.

"The Portugalls are very much afraid of our being here in this country, fearing it will be very prejudicial unto them for future times.

"It would be very Royal for our King and country if it please His Majesty to accept the Zamorin's proffers, and will be without (without doubt ?) very commodious a thing very easy to be done with a few expert men. There was one Stamfort, a gunner's mate of one of our ships, that was left here with us in nature of an attendant unto us as also upon occasion to assist the Zamorin; within eight or ten days after his coming ashore ran away like a rogue to the Portugalls ; and by the way he fell into company with the king of Achin's (Cochin as before) soldiers, and they conducted him to their king, who are all one with the Portugalls. This fellow hath done much villainy since his going and doth practise himself against the

Zamorin ; the which hath been a great disgrace unto us. The Zamorin doth make light of it before us, but it grieveth him full sore we know.

"Here was a boat put ashore on this coast since our coming with certain Portugalls in her, who were presently apprehended and sent to the Zamorin, one of the which is a man's son of good account in Cochin who with the rest the Zamorin detains whilst they send our man again. There hath been great suit made by the Portugalls to the king of Cochin for him, but he will not release him till the ships come, and then he will present him to your Worship, as it is given out it is his intent. This news we have ; other news none worth writing.

"We desire your Worship, if so it please you, to let us hear from your Worship. There will be boats of Malabar daily at Surat trading this way, being that time of year serves them. Thus ceasing to trouble you, we rest with our prayers to the Almighty to bless your proceedings."

"*Post Scriptum*:—Pepper they hold here at a very high rate, too high for us I think to do any good upon, at 28 ryolls of eight per bahar (the bahar contains 20 maunds, the maund agreeing measurement with 26 lbs. English weight). But howsoever, I think it be my best course to provide the proceed against your coming, if I can be permitted. If there were any money worth the carrying away I would very hardly deal in anything this year ; neither am I certain what course I shall take as yet. Thus craving pardon, I rest."

The copy of the agreement referred to in the above letter is also of great interest, as perhaps the first communication addressed by a Malabar king to a Sovereign of England. It also foreshadows the nature of the agreements subsequently entered into with native Princes generally.

"The Zamorin of Calicut to King James[1] Underecoon Cheete,[2] the Great Zamorin or King of Calicut &c. to James, by the grace of God, King of Great Britain, France and Ireland, &c., Greeting.

"Whereas your subject and servant William Keelinge Esquire, arrived in my kingdom in the month of March 1615 (1616) with three ships to my port of Crānganūr, in latitute 10 degrees 15 minutes, and at my earnest solicitation came on shore to see me, where was concluded by me for my part, and by himself for the English nation, as followeth, viz.,

"As heretofore I have ever been an enemy to the Portugales, so I purpose to continue for ever.

"I do hereby faithfully promise to be and continue a friend to the English, and my successors after me, to endeavour the taking in of the fort of Crānganūr, and to possess the English thereof as their own, together with the island thereof, containing in length in sea-coast nine miles, and in breadth three miles, provided I purpose to build therein a house for some of my own people to the number of hundred persons.

(1) This carelessly drawn document embodies the agreement made by Captain Keelinge with the Zamorin of Calicut, in March 1616. There is another contemporary copy among the Pepwell papers in *Marine Rec. Misc.* Vol. II, but it presents no difference of any importance. A third copy (modern) will be found in Vol. VIII (p. 307) of the Factory Series. Purchas has printed the agreement at p. 603 of his 1st Volume. *Letter Book, p.* 64.

(2) 'Underecoon Cheete' which is given as the name of the Zamorin stands probably for "Punturakkon (king of Puntara)" which is, according to Logan's *Malabar* (Vol. 1, p. 273. N), "still one of the titles of the Zamorin Maharaja Bahadur of Calicut." Peyton (in Purchas, Vol. 1, p. 531) says, "the king's name is *Pendre Quone Samorine.*" "Cheetti" is the Malayalam "Cheet" or "Theet", Royal writing; the Malabar chiefs always begin their written communications thus:—The Royal writing of so and so to. *** &c. Yule and Burnell in Hobson Jobson observes that "'Cheete' appears to be the Malayalam Chetti generally applied to a member of a trading caste". But this rendering of the word here is not correct. It does not stand for Chetti but for Chīt or Thīt.

Can it be "Kundalaken cheet?"

" I will also endeavour, with the aid of the English, hereafter to take in the fort and town of Cochin, belonging formerly to my crown and kingdom, and then deliver it into the possession of the English as their own proper land and possession, provided that the charges of the surprise thereof be equally borne, the one half by myself, the other half by the English nation, and the benefits of the spoil thereof, in whatsoever quality, the one half to belong to me and the other half to the English nation; the Zamorin to have thenceforward no right, title or interest in the town, fortress, precincts or appurtenances of Cochin at all.

" And the Zamorin doth likewise covenant for himself, his heirs and successors, that the whole trade of the English in whatsoever commodity, either in or exported, shall pay, yield, or allow no manner of custom, imposition, tax or toll, or any other duty of whatsoever quality.

" And to this covenant, which the shortness of time did not permit to amplify, I, the Zamorin, have sworn religiously by the great God I serve to perform accordingly; and that not for myself only, but for my successors after me. In witness thereof I have laid my hand upon this writing as within.

" And the said Keelinge doth promise to acquaint the King His Majesty with the premisses, and to endeavour His Majesty's undertaking thereof accordingly.

" In the post of Cran-gnor, dated aboard the Dragon, the 10th of March, Anno 1615 (1616). Endorsed: Translation of the Zamorin's letter for England and privileges to our nation, March 1615 (1616)."[1]

Thus the factories at Calicut and Crānganūr were established in the year 1616. These were subordinate to Bantom. In 1618 the Company failed in its trade at Calicut owing, it is said, to a want of sincerity on the part of the Zamorin.[2]

1. Letter Book, Vol. IV, pp. 65 et seq.
2. See Sir George Birdwood's Report p. 227.

BOLGHATTY RESIDENCY.

To face page 246.]

Some years after, in June 1664, two of the English Company's servants proceeded to Calicut, and appear to have been permitted to settle down there on agreeing to pay duty to the Zamorin on the trade carried on by them.[1]

It is noteworthy that it was with the Zamorin of Calicut that the English Company's earliest extant engagement was concluded in September 1664 shortly after the taking of Cochin by the Dutch. It ran thus:—

"Royal writing from the King Zamorin to Mr. Riviri and Mr. Vetti in the year 840 (September 1664).

"On (account of) the contract made by you from the year 840 (in the month of) September about fanams, a deduction may be made yearly of one thousand fanams as usual. I will recover only the amazia. Our account shows fanams 400 for bracelets and fanams 50 (paid) to the Tupay, making in all fanams 450. This sum (please) recover from our writer at the Custom House and make entries in the old accounts. The Thousand fanams (you may) take yearly from the result of your trade."

The trade of the English Company seems to have prospered after this in spite of the opposition of the Moors who had great influence with the Zamorin, and the Dutch who took advantage of every opportunity to injure the English trade. For, our author remarks that in his time the English had the largest business at Calicut and were the most favoured of the foreign nations by the Zamorin.

Between the years 1611—15, the United French East India Company was formed. In 1642 Richelieu founded "La Compagine des Indes" with exclusive privileges for 20 years. In 1664, Colbert formed the French "Compagine des Indes." Their factory at

1. Malabar, p. 341.

Surat is described by Dr. Fryer as "better stored with monsieurs than with cash; they live well, borrow money, and make a show."

From Hamilton we learn that the French had formed a temporary settlement at Tellicherry prior to the English, and that they had a factory at Calicut in 1698. Their business, however, must have been very little, for he says that they had neither money nor credit, and were "not in a condition to carry on trade."[1]

12. **Moors in Malabar.** We have already seen that, according to tradition, a Moor had built the market at Calicut, and the flourishing condition of its trade was almost entirely due to the Moors. Naturally, they had great influence with the Zamorin. It was with their assistance that that prince had attained the overlordship of Malabar, and was enabled to preside at the national festival of Mahā-Makham or Māmānkam at Ṭirunāvāye.[2] The Portuguese encountered considerable opposition on their first arrival in Malabar from the Moors, who succeeded in thwarting the endeavours of the new arrivals to gain over the Zamorin to their side. There was always a fierce struggle between the Portuguese and the Moors for ascendancy in the Malabar trade.

In the 14th century Ibn Batuta found the Moors of Calicut so wealthy that "one of them could have purchased the whole freightage of such vessels as put in there and fit out others like them."

In the 15th century, Abdur Razak describes Calicut as containing "a considerable number of Mussalmans, who are constant residents here, and have built two mosques in which they meet every Friday to offer up prayer. They have one Kadi, a priest &c.; for the most part, they belong to the sect of schafei." He further observes that, in a despatch sent by the

1. Malabar, p. 354.
2. Malabar, p. 279.

Sovereign of Calicut to the Shah of Persia, occurs the following passage, which points in no unmistakable terms to the great influence the Mussalmans wielded at the court of the Zamorin:—"In this port (Calicut), on every Friday and every solemn feast day, the Khotba is celebrated, according to the prescribed rule of Islamism. With your Majesty's permission, these prayers shall be adorned and honoured by the addition of your name and of your illustrious titles."

With the advent of European nations, their influence as well as their trade declined, and, finally, in their death struggle with the Portuguese, they succumbed.

13. **The Jealousy between the Dutch and the English.** These allegations are more or less borne out by facts and are corroborated by contemporary accounts. Referring to the proceedings of the Dutch at Chēṭṭwa, Mr. Logan observes: "The English Company, on the other hand, and, if Hamilton's account is correct, the chief of the English factory, Mr. Robert Adams, had, in particular, interests of their own to protect. Ever since the place had been in the Zamorin's hands, the English chiefs had made, as Hamilton expresses it, 'a good milch cow' of it, by vending, presumably on their own private account, 'between 500 and 1000 chests of Bengal ophium (opium) yearly up in the inland countries where it is very much used. The water carriage of the river being cheap and secure, the price of ophium high and the price of pepper low, so that their profits were great both ways'." Hamilton also observes that the Zamorin acted on the advice of Mr. Adams in resorting to stratagem to recover possession of the fort at Chēṭṭwa from the Dutch. When the stratagem succeeded, and the Dutch sailed for Cochin, Mr. Adams hoisted the English flag over the unfinished works on the plea that, in February 1715, he had obtained permission from the

Zamorin to build a warehouse at Chēṯṯwa and keep a person there for trade purposes.

The fact of the loan advanced by Mr. Adams is also borne out by Hamilton, and Mr. Logan says that "Hamilton's belief that part of the money spent by the Zamorin in this war was borrowed was fully justified, for the Tellicherry records show that the company took great exception to the loans, which Mr. Adams had made of their money to the Zamorin, the Punnaṯṯūr Raja, the Prince Regent of the Kōlaṯṯiri dominion and others. Notwithstanding the most persistent dunning, the Zamorin's debt amounted to the large sum of fanams 6, 68, 122·04, when Mr. John Braddyl eventually took charge of the factory. Mr. Adams did not regularly deliver over charge of it. He proceeded with Mr. Braddyl to Ṭānūr to recover some of the money lent. Mrs. Adams, after some restraint (subsequently withdrawn) had been used to prevent her leaving Tellicherry, came down the coast 'on board the Decker for Fort St. George', picked up her husband at Calicut, and the records do not say what further became of them."

Of "the late war", our author has to say something more in his next letter.

That there existed great jealousy between the Dutch and the English appears clear, and we shall have to say something of it later on.

14. **The National Assembly of the Malabars.** These national assemblies form a peculiar feature in the early political organisation of Malabar. They had existed even in the pre-historic days of Brahman government, and had even then acted as a curb on the despotic tendencies of the administrators. Tradition as well as early records, so far as they are now extant, point unmistakably to the fact that the early Brahman oligarchy of Malabar was subject to the curb applied now and again by these national assemblies. The Kēralōṯpaṯṯi refers to these assemblies

1. Malabar, p. 350—1.

WHERE KOOTTAMS MEET.

To face page 251.]

or Kūṭṭams. There were three of this sort, and these were composed of representatives of the various divisions into which the country was divided. The Nairs who formed the majority of the population, and who belonged to the "protecting class", corresponding to the Kshetryas of other parts of India, were essentially a martial race. For military purposes they had divided the land into Dēśoms, presided over by Dēśavālīs, and Nāḍs, presided over by Nāḍuvālīs. Each Nāḍu was again sub-divided into Ṭaṝās. Thus while a Ṭaṝā formed the unit of civil administration, a Dēśom represented the unit of military organisation. The Ṭaṝās, or villages, were presided over by Kāraṇaveṝs or elders, who were also known by the names of Mukhyasṭhans or Pṝamāṇīs or principal men. The Nairs were originally organised into guilds or bands of "Six hundred", "Five hundred,', and "Five thousand", and each guild seems to have had assigned to it the protection of all the people in a Nāḍu or country. Now the three kinds of Kūṭṭams or assemblies mentioned above are (1) the Kūṭṭam of the Ṭaṝa or village, (2) the Kūṭṭam of the Nāḍu or district, and (3) the Kūṭṭam of all Kērala or Malabar. The last, under ordinary circumstances, assembled only once in 12 years, and when the whole Kēralam assembled, it did so at Ṭiruṅāvāye, on the banks of the Ponnāni river, on the occasion of the Mahā-Mākham festival. The first, or Kūṭṭam of the Ṭaṝa, the meeting of the villagers, as represented by the Kāraṇaveṝs of families or Ṭaṝavāḍ met to discuss matters of local interest; the second, or the Kūṭṭam of the Nāḍu, the meeting of the representatives of a number of villages which form a district, for the discussion of matters of wider importance; and the third, the Kūṭṭam of all Kērala, for the discussion of affairs of national concern. Of the three, the assembly of the Nāḍ was the most potent. "The Nāḍ or country", as Mr. Logan observes, "was a congeries of Ṭaṝas or village republics, and the Kūṭṭam or assembly of the Nāḍ was a representative body of immense power, which, when necessity existed, set at naught the authority of the Raja and punished his ministers when they did 'unwarrantable acts.' "[1] The existence of these Kūṭṭams is evidenced by (1) old tradition, embodied in the Kēralōṭpaṭṭi, (2) ancient documents, (3) accounts furnished by mediaeval writers of repute, and (4) the existence of later similar organisations specially amongst those who have not been much affected by the great changes that have taken place in recent times.

The Kēralōṭpaṭṭi says that, after the introduction or rather the election of Perumāls to rule over Kērala, the Brahmans, fearing that the power of the rulers would grow despotic, if left to themselves, organised the country into 18 divisions, and supplied the Rajas with assemblies which were always to be consulted in all matters of government, the Rajas themselves being strictly enjoined not to do anything without consulting the assemblies. Three such assemblies are named in the Kēralōṭpaṭṭi. viz., Paravūr Kūṭṭam, Ayrāṇikkulam Kūṭṭam, and Irinjany Kūṭṭam.

Organisations such as those of the "Five hundred", "Six hundred" and "Five thousand", which must have been originally designed to act as checks on the despotic power of the ruling authority, and as means of preserving the rights and privileges of the people in tact, were in force all over the land from Gōkarṇam to Cape Comorin from very remote times. We see the " Six hundred " mentioned in the early Syrian Copper Plate No. III of Logan's collection, where the assent of that body is obtained by the Perumal in granting certain privileges to the Christian colonists. It says, " With the sanction of the Palace, Major Vyāraka Ḍēvar, who has given to these (the Palliyar) the 72 jenmi rights (viduperu), such as for marriages (or processions) the elephant's back, the earth, the water &c. (or

1. P. 89.

'earth and water on the elephant' at all events, marks of nobility), and with the concurrence of His Excellency the Ayyan Adigal, His Excellency Rama, the ministers and officers, the 'Six hundred' and the Lords of Punnaṭṭala and Pulācuḍi, let Anjuvaṇṇam and Maṇigrāmam, carry out this unrestricted possession right in the manner described by this copper deed for the time that earth, moon and sun exist." Again in the Ṭiruṅelli copper plate we read, "this is placed under (the control) of the 'Five hundred' and 'Five thousand' of Puraigilaṅāḍu."[1] These grants are said to belong to the 8th and 9th centuries A.D. respectively. The latter was by Bhāskara Ravi Varma (A.D. 700), while the former was by Sṭhāṇu Ravi Gupṭa (A. D. 824).[2] The Ṭiruṅelli plate evidences the existence of the organisation of the Nair community into the "Five hundred" and "Five thousand" in North Malabar, and the Syrian Copper Plate shows that in the next century a similar organisation had existed in the south. Deed No. 4 of Mr. Logan's collection, the date of which it is impossible to ascertain from the data contained in it, makes a distinct reference to the organisation of the "Six hundred."[3] Three centuries later, we see the "Six hundred" mentioned in a stone inscription from Travancore in the extreme south. Inscription No. 9/60 of Professor Sundram Pillay's collection speaks of the "Six hundred" of Vēṇāḍ (Travancore) and of the 18 districts or Nāḍs into which Vēṇāḍ was divided. It says, in making reference to a gift to the Ṭirukkunagarai Temple:—"From this time forward, the manager of the temple of Ṭirukkunagarai shall, under the supervision of the 'Six hundred' of Vēṇāḍ and of the District officers and agents, take sole possession of all things whatsoever in this Śērikkal, with the exception of the paddy land or &c." It proceeds to stipulate that a certain quantity of paddy, ghee, &c., shall be supplied

1. Ind. Anti. Vol. XX, pp. 285 *et seq.*
2. Malabar, p. 267.
3. Malabar, Vol. II, p. 122.

to the temple every day, and provides punishment for neglect. "If the supply fails once, double the default shall be paid. If twice, twice the default and fine. If thrice, the 'Six hundred,' the officers and the Valanjiars of the 18 districts shall institute enquiries &c. &c."

There can be no doubt of the existence of village associations and assemblies that had considerable share in the management of the local affairs of the country in that quarter. In an inscription dated Kollam year 384 (A.D. 1209) we read, "In the presence of the Ṭiruvananṭapuram Association and its Sabhanjita (chairman) assembled in the Southern (Hall) of Miṭrānanḍapuram (under the solemn presidency) of (the Bhattāraka) &c." Commenting on the above, Professor Sundram Pillay remarks that " it is impossible to doubt that, in 384, Trivandrum, like so many other villages, had a Sabha or association, with a Sabhanjita, chairman, or secretary of its own, and that it used to meet on occasions of importance in the old temple at Miṭrānanḍapuram, about a couple of furlongs to the west of the shrine of Srī Paḍmanābha. The south-western corner of the court yard of this temple is still pointed out as the sacred spot where the Sabha used to meet of old, and the word "Tek" or south, in our inscription, gives no dubious guide to that spot. The raised floor of this hall still remains, but the roof, which must have resounded with the voice of many a wise council, is now no more. Fragments of apparently very old inscriptions in the Miṭrānanḍupuram Temple speak also of memorable meetings of the Sabha in the same " Southern Hall."[2] We next come to what Professor Sundram Pillay styles " one of the great charters of Travancore," a Proclamation in the year 410 M. E. by Srī Vīra Iravi Kērala Varma Tiruvaṭi, fixing and regulating the land tax payable to the Government. It reads thus :—" Hail! Prosperity! In the year opposite Kollam year 410, with Jupiter in Scorpio, and the

1. Some Early Sovereigns of Travancore, p. 42.

2. P. 44.

Sun 27 days old in Aries (i. e., the 28th Mēḍam), is issued the following Proclamation, *after a consultation having been held* among the loyal chieftains of Srī Vīra Iravi Kērala Varma Tiruvaṭi, graciously ruling Vēṇāḍ, the members of the Sabha (or Association) Kodainallūr and the people of that village," &c. &c. * * * * "In seasons of drought and consequent failure of crops, the members of the Sabha and the people of the village shall inspect the lands and ascertain which have failed and which not * * *. If all the taxable lands appear to have equally failed, the Sabha and the villagers shall report the matter to Swami" * * *. "If the members of the Sabha and the inhabitants agree among themselves, and pray in common for a postponement of the payment &c." Upon this Mr. Sundram Pillay remarks, "Here is proof, if need be, of the independent nature and constitution of our old village associations. The Sabhas being mentioned side by side with the people, it is impossible to take them as mere occasional assemblies of the inhabitants, summoned together, for the time being, by those in charge of the administration. Here they appear as permanent well-constituted public bodies that acted as a buffer between the people and the Government." Here we may remember what, according to the Kēralōṭpaṭṭi, the duty of the Kūṭṭams and the peculiar Nair organisation was. It was, as that work expressly puts it, "to prevent the rights from being curtailed or suffered to fall into disuse." As Mr. Logan remarks, "They were, in short, the custodians of ancient rights and customs; they chastised the chieftains' ministers when they committed 'unwarrantable' acts, and were the 'Parliament' of the land."

For want of reliable and authentic records, we are unfortunately not in a position to pursue the enquiry further, and show that there was a never ceasing continuity in the system above discussed. But, though the hiatus cannot be filled up at present, there can be no doubt that it will be filled up as historical records come to light as the result of the researches of competent scholars.

Early in the history of Travancore, we see the Yōgakkārs (corporation) of the Paḍmanābha Swāmi's Temple and the Eṭṭuvīṭṭil Piḷḷamār or chieftains of the eight houses keeping the authority of the Raja in check. These Eṭṭuvīṭṭil Piḷḷamārs were originally the heads of the local Nair Ṭaṙa organisation of the "Six hundred" who were charged with the maintenance of the rights of all classes and with preventing any such from falling into disuse. The Rajas tried for a long time to gain ascendency and to keep in subordination these Nairs, but with little success. The contest continued for a long time and ended only in the early part of the 18th century, when the great Māṙṭṭāṇḍa Vaṙma, with the assistance of the Naika rulers of Madura and the English settlers at Anjengo, succeeded in completely annihilating the authority of the Piḷḷamāṙs.

We have ample evidence to show that the people were never slow to assert their rights and safeguard their interests, whenever occasion arose. We have a very significant instance of this in the case of Nānjanāḍ in South Travancore. The great Tiruṃala Naik of Madura made repeated incursions into Nānjanāḍ. Between the years 849 and 869 M. E., (1674 and 1694 A. D.), these incursions and their attendant privations became more and more unbearable. Yet the people stuck to their allegiance. The attacks from Madura became more and more frequent, and the attempts on the part of the successive Rajas became less and less successful. New taxes had to be imposed, which pressed heavily on the people already groaning under the oppression of the Naika hordes. The greedy officers of revenue and the minions of the Yōgakkāṙ and Piḷḷamāṙ began to coerce the people into making payments of illegal cesses. At length, in 878 M. E., the Nāṭṭāṙ or citizens assembled at

Vaḍaśśēri, on the first Alpaśi, and resolved to protest unitedly against such acts of Government which, in their opinion, subjected them to serious troubles and loss. Assembling once more at Āśṭamom near Nagercoil, on the 14th Māṟkaḻi, they asserted their loyalty to the reigning sovereign, but resolved to continue to pay Anjali Mēlvāram alone, but not Koṭṭappaṇam, unusual taxes. The resolution continued, "We should honourably keep up all the privileges or rights which our ancestors enjoyed in old days." "In thus asserting our rights," the relosution goes on to say, "if any Piḍakai or village, or any single individual is subjected to loss by acts of Government, we should support them by re-imbursing such loss from our common funds. If at such times any one should get into the secrets of the Government and impair the privileges or rights of the country, he should be subjected to a public inquiry by the Nāṭṭāṟs."

The assembly again met on the 15th Vykāśi, 891 M. E., at Īśānṭimangalam, and recorded a resolution which, after enumerating their troubles, proceeded to say, "Though there had been thus numerous kinds of troubles in the country, the Kāryakkāṟs, and Svarūpakkāṟs (officers) have not, under royal command, redressed our grievances and enabled us to live in peace, we should leave uncultivated the whole country between Mankalam and Manārkuḍi from the Kar season of 92 M. E., and if, after that, the Kāryakkārs and Svarūpakkāṟs, under royal command, redress our grievances and enable us to live in peace, we may then cultivate our lands. We should keep up all privileges (or rights) in the country as in the days of our ancestors. If any in the country get into the secrets of the Government and undermine the established privileges of the country, we should inquire into the matter, and make such persons answer for the same, both as a house (family) and as individuals personally. While thus managing our affairs, if the country, or any Piḍakai or village, or any house, become subject to troubles, we should, as a body, make ourselves strong by making a united stand, and emigrating (if necessary)."

These resolutions, made binding by "taking oath at the feet of our Lord Ṭāṇumalayapperumāḷ and our Lord Bhūṭanāṭhaswāmi," make it clear that the Nānjanāḍ people were very tenacious of their rights and privileges, that they were prepared to make a bold and united stand to preserve them intact and unimpaired, and that they would even go the length of expatriating themselves rather than submit to unwarranted impositions.

The "Kūṭ" organisation of Canara, described by Mr. J. Sturrock, I. C. S., as "riotous assemblies"[1] was, according to the Honorable Mr. Huddleston, probably identical with the Kūṭṭam of Malabar.[2] If so, the assemblies of the Nāṭṭār of Nānjanāḍ afford a close parallel to the "Kūṭs" of Canara.

Dr. Fryer (1672—1681) describes the "Several Petit signiories of Malabar" as "having a government most like aristocracy of any in the East, each State having a representative, and he to act according to the votes of the Nairos gentry in full assembly".

The incident to which our author refers in the text happened in the year 1720. Twenty-six years later, certain civil commotions seem to have taken place at Calicut of which we have unfortunately no details. But, when, in connection with it, the agent of the Honorable English East India Company at Tellicherry called on his representative at Calicut for an explanation, the latter observed, "These Nairs, being the heads of the Calicut people, resemble the Parliament, and do not obey the king's dictates in all things, but chastise his ministers when they do unwarrantable acts".[3]

1. Manual of the Canara District, Vol. I, p. 83.
2. Malabar, Vol. II, p. 206.
3. Tellicherry Diary, May 28th—1746; Malabar, p. 132.

A further reference by our author in his Eleventh Letter to these national assemblies and the manner in which they are held and the rules that guide them shows that they had existed in his day in the Cochin Raja's territories, and that their function was to check the arbitrary power of the Rajas.

The highly artificial constitution of the assemblies, the rules by which they were worked and the means of punishment resorted to to enforce the attendance of its constituent members[1] all point unmistakably to a long-standing institution which acted as a strong weapon in the hands of the people to defend their rights and privileges against the unwarranted aggressions of the royal authority.

The village republics, already mentioned, seem to have existed in early times on the Western Coast as in other parts of India. Socially and politically they exercised considerable influence on the community. They formed centres of local self-government. They managed all local affairs, possessed common funds, levied cesses to meet certain local expenses, and acted as arbitrators or judges in matters of dispute arising between persons living within the limits of their local jurisdiction. These small republics in which the Nair inhabitants were represented by their Kāraṇavaṟ or elders presented a striking resemblance to the "village republics" of the East Coast districts. They were self-contained and exercised their authority through the agency of their own officers. They had their own temple, their own pasture land, their own artisans, their own washermen, barbers, and men of other occupations, in short, all that was necessary to make life happy and comfortable. Every villager shared the joys and sorrows of his co-villagers. When there occurred a death in any family, the villagers would proceed to that house, and attend to his cremation and help the

1. See Letter XI *infra*.

relatives of the deceased to perform his funeral ceremonies. On the 16th day after the date of the death, the villagers would be treated to a feast in the house of the dead individual. For marriages, the villagers had the right to be invited. For thatching the houses, a man from each house had to go. In short, socially, the villagers lived a life of arcadian simplicity, their rights safe-guarded by its Kūṭṭam, and their persons and their houses protected at night by the village watchmen who went about with religious scrupulousness in their nightly rounds.

The representatives met occasionally in assembly at appointed places, generally on a wooden platform raised on posts with a thatched roof overhead situated in front of the village temple under the cool shade of the village banyan tree, and not far removed from the pagoda tank. There, under the presidency of the Āśān or headman, who was also known by other names, such as Mukhyasṭan or Pṙamāṇi, as localities varied, the affairs of the local village were discussed and settled. All sorts of social disputes and such petty offences as did not require the intervention of the superior authorities were placed before the meeting and disposed of according to the votes of the majority. The requirements of the village temple were attended to, the annual festivals, such as the uṭsavam, etc., were settled, the funds necessary to meet the expenses were raised, and matters of dispute adjusted. No one dared disobey their orders on pain of incurring social penalties far more stringent and far more efficient than any punishment that judicial tribunals could award. In their hands the penalty of social ostracism was a potent weapon. Whoever set at naught their authority or disobeyed their orders was visited with expulsion from society. He lost all his privileges and became almost an outlaw. Like Ishmail of old, his hands were against all and the hands of all were against him. Every one shunned him. He could not attend the village temple or bathe in the temple-tank; no barber would shave him, no washerman would wash for him. He became a social leper and a political non-entity. The ban followed him wherever he went, and he was treated in the same manner everywhere. Life was rendered not worth living, and, finally, he had the choice of either putting an end to it or of submitting to the orders promulgated by the assemblies. In cases of continued obstinacy, the ban was sometimes extended to his family and friends. Of course this relentless system has been softened a good deal in its working under the authority of the British Government. Yet the system still lingers, at any rate in the interior, however shorn of its powers. The early British administrators would seem to have ignored altogether the Ṭar̤a organisation of the Nairs. They adopted the Mysorean system of sub-divisions for revenue purposes, which was subsequently changed into the hobali and Amśam system, without caring to know that the Nair Ṭar̤ās were originally not mere revenue or administrative divisions, but were organisations to which was entrusted the management of local concerns. The village assemblies and Panchayats as *quasi* political associations ceased to exist henceforward. These were however not dead for all purposes. In the interior parts of the country, where society has not been very much affected by recent changes, to a certain extent in the cities and towns also, they linger and continue to do much quiet useful work. It is still possible to make use of them as units for purposes of local self-government. Around them will gather the sweet traditions and pleasant memories of a glorious past, which would certainly act as an incentive for them to put forth endeavours to achieve something substantial in the future. Guided by sympathetic hands, and charged with the management of such local matters as might safely be entrusted to them, they could still be turned into efficient auxiliaries, able and willing to relieve the administration of much of its petty toilsome labours. The sense of responsibility which the people once felt in the management of their local affairs, and which at present is fast passing away, may then be revived with the result that, ere long, each citizen will begin to feel that he is an integer having rights and duties which require careful attention. "The self-contained villages of India," observed Sir George Birdwood at a meeting of the East India Association, "each of them a little republic, had been the salvation and the religion and traditional civilization of 'India of the Hindus' through all the political shocks and convulsions through which the country had passed during the 2,000 years, anterior to its pacification by the British, and with whatever good intentions, we had really done India a dubious service in intermeddling so radically as we had with the immemorial village system of the Hindus. Every separate village was regarded by its people as the 'hub of the Universe' and from the beginning of their history, they had looked on at the struggles of successive invaders, for the political possession of the country, as we do at military tournaments in the Agricultural Hall at Islington, or a battle scene on the stage of the Imperial Theatre at Earl's Court, as, in short, pageants in which they had no concern except for their amusement. The municipal and civic instinct was strong in India, and what I have always felt with regard to our efforts to create enlarged civic organisations in India was that we ought to do more to develop the civic institutions already existing in the country rather than attempt so strenuously to introduce the exotic forms of these institutions". He added that he was speaking from personal experience. He had lived in these villages (of Western India) the life of the villagers and, on two occasions, as the guest of village patels and had studied the reports of Sir George Wingate on the Revenue Survey of Western India, and other similar documents on the spot, and all this had fixed in him the conviction that there was much more civic spirit and civic life in India "at least in Western India", than was dreamt of in this country. The experience of those who are closely acquainted with village life in Malabar is the same.

The Malabar Rajas were originally simply heads of feudal chieftains. On the disruption of the Chēra Empire, the greater chiefs of Travancore in the south, and their kinsmen, the Kōlaṭṭiri, in the north, seem to have assumed independence, while the Cochin Rajas, who are alleged to be the heirs of the last Chēramān Perumāḷ, ruled within certain prescribed limits in the middle of Kērala. Very soon the Zamorin, backed by his Moorish allies, subdued all the minor chiefs, and set himself up as the Suzerain of all Malabar, but it is very doubtful if this position was ever acknowledged, though often asserted, but as often resisted by the greater chiefs of Kērala. Dr. Fryer calls these minor chiefs, "Arch-Rebels against the Zamorin of Calicut, paying him only some slight acknowledgments of his supremacy, as their chief Bishop, and joining with him against the Great Mogul, else striving to supplant each other." However that may be, all the Rajas of Malabar, the Zamorin, Cochin, Travancore, and Kōlaṭṭiri not excepted, depended for their position and power on the goodwill and allegiance of the minor chiefs and the people. These chiefs held their lands on feudal tenure, undertaking to follow their liege lords at the head of their men to defend them whenever necessary. The whole Nair community formed the militia of the land, liable to be called for active service by the feudal chiefs at any moment. There were no standing armies then. In not a few cases, the feudal chiefs were known as heads of so many men, as for instance "Ayyāyira Prabhu Kaṟṟāvu, the lord of the 5,000 men". Bows and arrows, spears and axes, swords and shields formed their sole weapons of offence or defence. The use of gunpowder was all but unknown. With the appearance of foreign nations on the coast, who came originally as merchants, but remained in the country as aspirants to political supremacy, the whole aspect of affairs changed. They introduced fire-arms and weapons of precision, lent officers trained in European tactics to organise and instruct the armies of native princes, mixed themselves up in internecine quarrels, setting one prince against another and finally acquiring from all parties concerned advantages that enabled them to satisfy their ambition of obtaining a permanent footing in the country. Thus, in the year 1723, the English at Anjengo under their local chief, Dr. Alexander Orme, father of the great historian, "resolved in spite of money expenses to put down the enemies and subject the country to the king" (of Travancore). A few months earlier, the king had entered into a covenant with the Governor of Anjengo, the self-same Alexander Orme, the Sixth article of which said, "The Government of Travancore will be in league and united in good friendship with the honorable Company". They were only too eager to come to the assistance of the king and make common cause with him against the local chieftains. The power of the feudal barons and of the popular and representative assemblies did not conduce to the advancement of their commercial enterprises. They preferred to have on the throne a despotic sovereign, unaided by council or clergy, who could, of his own accord, assign them monopolies of the produce they came in quest of, and enforce the same with a strong arm. Such a person they found in the great Mārṭāṇḍa Vaṙma, who is described by Fra Bartolomeo as "a man of great pride, courage and talents, capable of undertaking grand enterprises, and from his youth accustomed to warlike operations." The political ideal of that prince was the foundation of a military state, whose power should be centralised in the king, and the English Company readily fell in with his views. It will be observed that engagements entered into by Travancore with the foreign nations invariably provided for the supply of fire-arms and munitions of war, and it was not long before a powerful standing army was organised, officered by clever European adventurers and trained in the western system of warfare. The institution of this standing army tolled the death-knell of all popular rights. Before its advancing might chief after chief succumbed, till the Travancore flag flew as far north as Cochin. It was not long before that the Raja of Cochin sought the aid of his late enemy Raja Mārttāṇḍa Varma of Travancore "in putting down all dignities in his country," a step resolved upon apparently to deal a death-blow to popular rights. The last clause of the treaty of the 12th Ḍhanu 937 M. E., 22nd December 1761, contained the following stipulation:—"The Raja (of Travancore) will assist me (the Raja of Cochin) agreeably to my design in abolishing the dignities of all rank in my country as also in the concerns appertaining to them."[1] In pursuance of this stipulation, the Raja of Travancore actively interfered in the affairs of the Nāḍuvālīs and chiefs of Cochin and compelled them to surrender their properties and rights to the Raja of Cochin, leaving to them only means sufficient for their bare maintenance. This was in the year 1761, and ever after this we hear nothing of the meeting of the assemblies mentioned by Visscher.

We have already observed that the great Kūṭṭam or assembly of all Kērala was held once in 12 years at Ṭirunāvāye at the Mahāmākham festival. Originally it was presided over by the Valluvanāḍ or Vellāṭṭiri Raja, which arrangement continued till the 12th or 13th century, when the Zamorin, becoming supreme in Kērala, assumed the presidency of the assembly. The last celebration of the festival took place in the year 1743, and the political changes that convulsed Malabar soon after made it impossible to celebrate it any longer. Ordinarily the next celebration

1. Malabar, Vol. III, p. 110.

should have come on in 1755. But before this the aggressive policy of the Zamorin embroiled him with all neighbouring powers. He was fighting with the Raja of Cochin and the Dutch in the south, and with Valluvanāḍ and Palghat in the north. At first he carried everything before him in Cochin, but very soon he was driven out of Cochin territory by the Travancore Raja coming to the assistance of Cochin. In the north also his star was on the wane. The Palghat Raja had turned to Hyder in his extremity, and thus introduced into Malabar a power that before long set the country ablaze and paved the way to British supremacy. Hyder very soon conquered Malabar, and brought the Rajas under complete subjection. He accepted proposals from them to become tributaries, and constituted them petty despots over their various possessions. "By this new order of things," as Mr. Murdoch Brown of Anjarakandy observed to Dr. Claudius Buchanan, "the latter (the Rajas) were vested with despotic authority over the other inhabitants, instead of the very limited prerogatives that they had enjoyed by the feudal system, under which they would neither extract revenue from the lands of their vassals nor exercise any direct authority in their districts. Thus the ancient constitution of government (which, although defective in many points, was favourable to agriculture, from the lands being unburthened with revenue) was in a great measure destroyed, without any other being substituted in its room. The Raja was no longer what he had been, the head of a feudal aristocracy with limited authority, but the all-powerful deputy of a despotic prince, whose military force was always at his command to curb or chastise any of the chieftains who were inclined to dispute or disobey his mandates." Tippu's persecution of the people made matters worse. His fanatic endeavours to convert the people to Islamism were warmly supported by the Mopla inhabitants of Malabar, whom he used as his unscrupulous instruments. The whole country from one end to the other was devastated by fanatic Mussalman hordes. The sword or the Koran was the alternative offered. Everywhere the Hindus were persecuted, and robbed of their riches, their women and their children. Those who could elude the vigilance of the Mysoreans hid themselves in the forests and carried on a predatory warfare. Others fled to Travancore leaving their cherished hearths and homes behind, a prey to Moslem frenzy. The Rajas and chiefs deserted their people and fled for their very lives, and anarchy prevailed throughout the land. The ancient system of government and constitution of society was gone never to return. The Moplas increased in number and influence, while the Nairs diminished in proportion. At this juncture, the English stepped in to save Malabar from destruction, and invited the Nairs and the Rajas who had left the country to return and join the Company's forces. It was then found that the Nairs had dwindled into an inconsiderable number. Lord Cornwallis, the Governor-General, conducted the campaign against Tippu in person. When Seringapattam had fallen and Tippu's army had been expelled from Malabar, the East India Company reinstated the Rajas in their respective possessions. But they returned, not as the feudal chiefs of old, but as the deputies of an all-powerful suzerian, who had always a strong army to enforce and sustain their authority. The feudal system had broken. The Nair organisation, which had been hitherto the bulwark of the rights and privileges of the people, had vanished into the limbo of oblivion. "No other kind of administration," says Mr. Brown, "was known to the Rajas, who laid claim to their respective districts, than that which they had exercised or witnessed under Hyder, and which was a compound of corruption and extortion. To these men, however, the most unfit that could have been selected, was the whole authority of government over the natives entrusted. Two evils of great magnitude were the consequence of this measure. The extortions and corruptions of the preceding administrations were continued, while the ancient feudal institutions of military service were revived and all the Nairs hereby attached to the different chieftains and these again to the Rajas. Nothing could exceed the despotic rapaciousness of these men, to oppose which there was no barrier; for, it is well known, that none of the inhabitants dare complain against a Raja, whatever injuries they may have sustained, assassination being a certain follower of complaint."[1] As time passed on, the Company discovered the cloven foot introduced by them. Oppression and tyranny became the order of the day. The Moplas, who had been deprived of the great power they had exercised so recently, resented the loss, while the Nair followers of the Rajas under the protecting *aegis* of the Company set themselves up to seek revenge on their former despoilers. The result was awful, and the Company had soon to cancel their engagements with the respective Rajas and assume direct authority. But in doing so, the earlier British officers failed fully to understand and realise the ancient privileges of the people, constitution of society, and government in Malabar. The administrative machinery established by the Company was therefore altogether new, and based on a system of official hierarchy, in which the people as a body had no place or voice. The 'village republics,' in whose hands much of the local administration remained, and which had continued faithfully to do their work from the earliest times, were completely ignored and ceased to exist. Thus by strange vicissitudes of fortune, the Nairs who were once the 'protectors' of the land, the 'eyes,' the 'hands' and the 'givers of orders,' as the Kēraḷōṭpaṭṭi pithily expresses their state functions, the 'Parliament' of the country,

1. Canara and Malabar, Vol. II, p. 191.

the "chastisers of ministers," fell low in the political scale, and were reduced to mere dumb units of society without power or influence. Well may Mr. Logan, the author of the official account of Malabar, an officer who had enjoyed peculiar facilities for correctly studying the institutions of the country, bewail the turn events had taken in Malabar. "I would more specially call attention," says Mr. Logan, "to the central point of interest as I look at it, in any descriptive and historical account of the Malayāli race—the position, namely, which was occupied for centuries on centuries by the Nair caste in the civil and military organisation of the province,—a position so unique and so lasting that, but for *foreign* intervention, there seems no reason why it should not have continued to endure for centuries on centuries to come. Their functions in the body-politic have been tersely described in their own traditions as the 'eye', the 'hand' and the 'order,' and to the present day we find them spread throughout the length and breadth of the land, but no longer—I could almost say, alas,—'preventing the rights (of all classes) from being curtailed or sufferred to fall into disuse.' This bulwark against the tyranny and oppression of their own rulers secured for the country a high state of happiness and peace, and if *foreign* peoples and *foreign* influences had not intervened, it might, with almost literal truth, have been said of the Malayālis that 'happy is the people who have no history.' "

LETTER IV.

1. Quilon. The town of Quilon is older than the era to which it has given a name. It is now eleven centuries since the Kollam era began, and, ever after its commencement, it has been current throughout Kērala—the British districts of Malabar, and the Native States of Travancore and Cochin. At one time, it was current also, to a limited extent, towards the Tinnevelly side. Quilon had its vicissitudes of fortune. It was at one time a great political and commercial centre. The Nestorian Christians found here an asylum on their arrival on the coast. It was the seat of the first Roman Catholic Bishopric in India. It enjoyed a large trade with China and Arabia, and had also political relations with Kublai Khan, the great Mongol Emperor of China. Its port has been described by early travellers as one of the largest in the world, and its markets the finest in India. In appearance and political importance it rose to such an eminence as even to occasion a proverb in Malayālam that he who has seen Quilon cares not for his house.[1] With the arrival of the Arabs and the Portuguese in Malabar and the rise of the ports of Calicut and Cochin as commercial competitors, its importance began to decline, its manufactures became neglected, its harbour gradually lost its natural facilities for shipping, and it came finally to be reduced to a third rate port. But there are signs of revival. With the railway running across the ghauts from the east coast right into the centre of the town of Quilon, and a chance, distant though it be, of the harbour being improved, one may hope that Quilon will regain its former important position on the western sea-board.

The Kollam or Quilon era commenced with 825 A.D., and it is commonly believed that it commemorates

1. കൊല്ലംകണ്ടവനില്ലംവേണ്ട.

the foundation of the town. This, however, is a mistake, for we see a reference to the town in an episcopal letter written by Jesu Jabu of Adiabene, the Nestorian Patriarch of Babylon, who died in 660 A. D., to Simon, Metropolitan of Fars (the old name of Persia), in the 7th century. The passage in the letter says that, not only is India, "which extends from the coast of the kingdom of Fars to Colon, a distance of 1200 parasangs, deprived of a regular ministry, but Fars itself is lying in darkness."[1] It is, however, necessary to add that Yule and Burnell point out that "this is an arbitrary and erroneous rendering in Assemani's Latin. The Syriac has Kolah, and probably therefore refers to the port of the Malay regions noticed under Colay and Quedda".[2]

The names under which early writers have noticed the place seem to vary very much. Cosmas (6th century) calls it Male; Solyman (851), Koulam malay; Benjamin of Tudela (1166), Chulam ; the Chinese annals, quoted by Pauthier in his edition of Marco Polo, Kiulan; Abulfeda (1273), Coilon or Coilun; Marco Polo (1298), Rashiduddin (1300), and Wassaf (1310), Kulam; Friar Odoric (1322), Polumbum ; the Palatine MS. of Odoric (same date), Colonbio ; Jordanus (1328), Columbum; Letter of Pope John XXII to the Christians of Quilon (1330), Columbo ; Ibn Batuta (1343), Kaulam; John Marignolli (1348), Columbum ; Nicolo Conti (1430), Coloen ; Varthēma (1510), Colon ; Barbosa (1516), Coulam, and Sammario Ramusio, Colour; and G. D. Empoli (1530), Colam.

In Malayālam the town is known as Kollam, and an interesting note by Bishop Caldwell in Yule's Edition of Marco Polo[3] discusses the derivation of the term. Abulfeda and Odoric describe the position of the place as "at the extreme end of Balad-ul-Falfal, *i. e.*, the pepper

1. Assem. III, pt. II, p. 437, quoted in Marco Polo, Vol. II, p. 377.

2. Hobson—Jobson, 1 Ed. Note on p. 569.

3. Vol. II, p. 377.

country or Malabar," and as "at the extremity of the pepper forest towards the south." Colonel Yule ventures the query, "May not its real etymology be Sanskrit Kolam, 'black pepper'?" which called forth the following note by Dr. Caldwell :—"I fancy Kola, the name for pepper in Sanskrit, may be derived from the name of the country Kolam, North Malabar, which is much more celebrated for its pepper than the country about Quilon. This Kolam, though resembling Kollam, is really a separate word, and never confounded with the latter by the natives. The Prince of Kolam (North Malabar) is called Kōlasṭr̄i or Kōlaṭṭiri. Compare also Kolagiri, the name of a hill in the Sanskrit Dictionaries, called also Kollagiri. The only possible derivations for the Tamil and Malayal̄am name of Quilon that I am acquinted with are these:—(1) From Kolu, the 'royal presence', or presence-chamber, or hall of audience. Kollam might naturally be a derivative of this word; and in confirmation I find that other residences of Malabar kings were also called Kollam, *e. g.*, Koḍungallūr or Cr̄ānganūr. (2) From Kolu, the same word, but with the meaning 'a height' or 'high ground'—hence Kollei, a very common word in Tamil for a 'dry grain field, a back yard'. Kolli is also in the Tamil poets, said to be the name of a hill in the Chēra country, i. e., the Malabar Coast. (The Chēra king has the name Kolli Kavalam in Tamil annals). Kōlam in Tamil has not the meaning of pepper; it means 'beauty' and it is said also to mean the fruit of the jujuba. (3) It might possibly be derived from Kol, to slay; Kollam, slaughter, or a place where some slaughter happened. * * *
In the absence, however, of any tradition to this effect, this derivation of the name seems improbable."

The name by which the Malabar Era is known in Sanskrit is significant, viz., Kōlamba according to an inscription from Ṭr̄ikkaṇāmkuḍy in Tinnevelly, dated 1468—9 A. D. It reads, "In the year Bhavaṭi (644) of the Kōlamba Era, King Āḍiṭṭya Var̄ma, the ruler of

Vanchi who has attained the sovereignty of *Chera baya Mandalam*, hung up the bell * * ."[1] It may be remembered that Jordanus and Marignolli had long before this referred to the place as, 'Columbum.'

The disruption of the Chēra Empire and the Mecca pilgrimage of the last Chēramān Perumāl is attributed to the year 824-5 A. D. "In a Syriac extract (which is, however, modern) in Land's *Anecdota Syriaca*,[2] it is stated that three Syrian missionaries (two of them, perhaps, Nestorean Persians, Mar Sapor and Mar Peroz), came to Kaulam in A. D. 823, and got leave from the king, Shakirbirti, to build a church there."[3] Shakarbirti could not evidently have been the name of the king. It was rather the title of the king, it being known as Shakrbriti or more correctly Chakravartti, or the Emperor. It will be observed that one of the Syrian Christian copper-plates makes mention of Vīra Rāghava Chakravartti as ruling in Malabar about 774 A. D. The second charter of the Syrian Christians, granted by Sthānu Ravi Gupta about 824 A. D., gives permission to Mar Sapor to transfer to the Tarisa church and community at Quilon, a piece of land near the city with the hereditaments attached to it, with the overlordship of several families of 'low-caste soil-slaves.' Mr. Logan conjectures that this grant must have been impelled by the political exigencies of the time, occasioned by the invasion of Malabar by the Rāshtrakūtās.

According to the Mahomedan accounts, Chēramān Perumāl, while on his death-bed at Zaphar, despatched missionaries to Malabar for the spread of his new faith and one of them, Malik Ben Habub, after landing at Cranganūr, proceeded to Quilon, built a mosque, and settled there, making that place the centre of his proselytising operations. And this, according to the

1. Ind. Ant. Vol. II, p. 360.
2. Latin, 1—125; Syriac, p. 27.
3. Hobson-Jobson, p. 569.

Tohfut-ul-Mujahideen, is the origin of the Mahomedan colony at Quilon.[1]

The next notice we have of it is by the Arab traveller, Solyman (852 A. D.), who, in his book, *Chaine de Chroniques*, says that the Chinese ships used to touch Quilon on their homeward voyage from Siraf on the Persian Gulf. At Quilon, the Chinese ships paid a heavy post duty of 1,000 Dinars. These ships, though large, were flat-bottomed, and could therefore cross the bar at Quilon with ease, and enter the lagoon which formed so fine a harbour. Quilon was, according to Solyman, 'the most considerable port in South India at the time.'[2]

We have an interesting account of Quilon, the city and its people, two centuries after, by the Rabbi Benjamin of Tudela, who travelled in the east between 1159 and 1173 A. D. But all that he relates of India is suspected by Yule to be mere hearsay. His account is none the less interesting and may be extracted here. "Seven days from thence is Chulam (Collam) on the confines of the country of the Sun-worshippers. They are descendants of Kush, are addicted to astrology, and are all black. This nation is very trustworthy in the matters of trade, and whenever foreign merchants enter their port, three Secretaries of the king immediately repair on board their vessels, write down their names and report them to him. The king thereupon grants them security for their property, which they may even leave in the open fields without any guard. One of the king's officers sits in the market and receives goods that may have been found anywhere, and which he returns to those applicants who can minutely describe them. This custom is observed in the whole Empire of the king. From Easter to New year (April to October), during the whole of the summer, the heat is extreme. From the third hour of the day

1. See Rowlandson's translation.

2. Reinaud's *Voyages par les Arabes et les Persians.*

(9 in the morning), people shut themselves up in their houses until the evening, at which time every body goes out. The streets and markets are lighted up and the inhabitants employ all the night upon their business, which they are prevented from doing in the day-time in consequence of the excessive heat. The pepper grows in this country; the trees which bear this fruit are planted in the fields, which surround the town, and every one knows his plantation. The trees are small and pepper is originally white, but when they collect it, they put it into basins and pour hot water upon it; it is then exposed to heat of the sun and dried in order to make it hard and more substantial, in the course of which process it becomes black in colour. Cinnamon, ginger and many other kinds of spices also grow in this country. The inhabitants do not bury their dead, but embalm them with certain spices, put them upon stools, and cover them with cloths, every family keeping apart. The flesh dries upon the bones and as these corpses resemble living beings, every one of them recognises his parents and all the members of his family for many years to come. These people worship the sun; about half a mile from every town, they have large places of worship, and every morning they run towards the rising sun. Every place of worship contains a representation of that luminary, so constructed by machinery (our author calls it witchcraft) that upon the rising of the sun, it turns round with a great noise, at which moment both men and women take up their censers, and burn incense in honour of the diety. 'This their way of folly'[1] All the cities and countries inhabited by the people contain about 100 Jews, who are of black-colour as well as the other inhabitants. The Jews are good men, observers of the law and possess the Pentateuch, the Prophets, and some little knowledge of the Thalmud and its decisions."

A writer in the *Jewish Chronicle* of the 19th October 1906 doubts if Benjamin visited Quilon at

1. Psalm, XLX, 13.

all. He says, "In a copy of Benjamin's itinerary published in Amsterdam, 5485 A. M., the place said to have pepper and black coloured Jews is Hoolah or Hula in Arabia, about 100 miles inland and west of El Katiff. No mention of his visit to India is made in his work. He says[1] that he came up to Samarcand, and thence retraced his journey to Kohistan,[2] then to Krishu Island, and then to El Katiff, then to Hoolah, and then to Karak Island.[3] The Jews he found in Hoolah were certainly a section of Yemen Jews whose colour is like that of the natives there, and the pepper was either a genus of that country or one carried by merchants from India. The summer there, according to Benjamin, lasts from Passover to New Year and it is too hot to expose oneself to the sun, while, in Malabar, it is the time for winter, and the summer is not so hot as to require all public transactions to be carried out during the nights as it is in Hoolah. The natives there, Benjamin says, worship the sun and embalm their dead ; both of these practices are unknown in Malabar. Above all, it is absurd to think that Benjamin reached Quilon from El Kattif in seven days. There is not even a tradition that Jews ever colonised Quilon. About 180 years after Benjamin, a Moorish traveller, Ibn Batuta (his itinerary was edited and translated by M. Defremery and Dr. Sanguinetti, 1858—59), who travelled through Malabar, had seen only Mahomedans and natives of Quilon, and the Jews he met with were in a place midway between Calicut and Quilon governed by an Emir of their own."[4]

In 1263—75, Al Kazwini, the Mahomedan geographer, compiled his account of India from the works of others, and among other places he mentions "Kulam (Quilon), a large city in India. Mis'ar bin Muhalhil, who visited the place, says that he did not see either a

1. P. 40.
2. P. 42.
3. P. 44.
4. P. 31.

temple or an idol there. When their king dies, the people of the place choose another from China. There is no physician in India except in this city. The buildings are curious, for the pillars are (covered) with shells from the backs of fishes. The inhabitants do not eat fish, nor do they slaughter animals, but they eat carrion," and he goes on to describe the pottery made there and contrasts it with China-ware. "There are places here where the teak tree grows to a very great height, exceeding even 100 cubits."[1] The mention of the choice of a king from China to succeed the one deceased suggests the probability of there being a Chinese Factory or Settlement, at the time, in Quilon governed by one of their own chiefs who was succeeded on his death by another brought from China. Of such settlements we read frequent allusions in the writings of old travellers. In Gaspar Correa's account of the Voyages of Da Gama, there is a curious record of a tradition of the arrival in Malabar, more than four centuries before, of a vast merchant fleet 'from the parts of Malacca, and China, and the Lequeos' (Lewchew); many from the company on board had settled in the country and left descendants. In the space of a hundred years, none of these remained; but their sumptuous idol temples remained.[2] Mendoza, after mentioning a "towne called unto this day the soile of the Chinos, for that they did reedify and make the same * * . On the coast of Coromande, which is the cost against the kingdome of Norsinga towards the sea of Cengala," observes, "The like notice and memory is there in the kingdom of Calicut, whereas he, many trees and fruits, that the naturals of that countrie do say, were brought thither by the Chinos, when they were lords and gevernours of that countrie."[3] These passages are quoted by Yule in his Marco Polo.[4] He

1. Malabar, pp. 284-5.
2. Stanley's transl., Hak. Soc., p. 174.
3. Mendoza, Parke's transl., p. 71.
4. Vol. II, pp. 391-2.

says in a foot-note, "It appears from a paper in the Mackenzie MSS. that, down to Colonel Mackenzie's time, there was a tribe in Calicut whose ancestors were believed to have been Chinese.[1] And there is a notable passage in Abdur Razzak which says the seafaring population of Calicut were nicknamed *Chini bachagan*, 'China boys.' "[2] It is also significant that the Dutch Captain, Nieuhoff, in noticing Quilon, speaks of two Quilons, "the upper or Malabar Koulang, the other the lower Koulang; in the first the king and queen kept their ordinary residence; the last was formerly in the possession of the Portuguese, as lying near to the seaside." Speaking of lower Quilon, he says: 'Its suburbs which are very large and stately, are by the Portuguese called Coulang China,' probably because that was the portion occupied by the Chinese Settlement. Similarly, Marignolli says Cynkali, the name by which Crānganūr was known to some early travellers "signifieth Little India, *i. e.*, Little China, for Kali is 'little'."[3] Garcia de Orta (1563) mentions a Chinese stone with (apparently) an inscription as having been taken away by the Zamorin from Cochin.[4]

Marco Polo (1298) gives us fuller details of the country, its people, its products, &c. He says: "When you quit Malabar and go 500 miles towards the south-west, you come to the kingdom of Coilum. The people are idolators, but there are also some Christians and some Jews. The natives have a language of their own, and king of their own, and are tributary to no one.

"A great deal of brazil is got here which is called *brazil Coilumin* from the country which produces it;

1. See Taylor's Catal. Raisonne, III, 664.
2. India in the XVth Cent., p. 19.
3. Cathay, p. 873.
4. *Colloquios da India*, *Varuhagiu's reprint* f. 58b and 59 cited by Dr. Burnell in his *Elements of S. Indian Paleography*, 2nd End . p. 57—Note 2.

it is of very fine quality. Good ginger also grows here, and it is known by the same name of Coilumin after the country. Pepper too grows in great abundance throughout this country * * *. They have also abundance of very fine indigo * * *. And I assure you that the heat of the sun is so great here that it is scarcely to be endured ; in fact if you put an egg into one of the rivers, it will be boiled, before you have had time to go any distance, by the mere heat of the sun.

" The merchants from Manzi (China) and from Arabia, and from the Levant come thither with their ships and their merchandise, and make great profits both by what they import and by what they export.

" There are in this country many and divers beasts quite different from those of the other parts of the world. Thus there are lions black all over, with no mixture of any other colour ; and there are parrots of many sorts, for some are white as snow with red beak and feet, and some are red, and some are blue, forming the most charming sight in the world. There are green ones too. There are also some parrots of exceeding small size, beautiful creatures They have also very beautiful pea-cocks, larger than ours, and different from ours ; and what more shall I say ? In short, everything they have is different from ours, and finer and better. Neither is their fruit like ours, nor their beasts, nor their birds ; and this difference all comes from excessive heat.

" Corn they have not, but rice. So also their wine they make from (palm) sugar; capital drink it is, and very speedily it makes a man drunk. All other necessaries of man's life they have in great plenty and cheapness. They have very good astrologers and physicians. Man and woman, they are all black, and go naked save for a fine cloth worn about the middle. They look not on any sin of the flesh as a sin. They marry their cousins german, and a man takes his brother's wife after the brother's death ; and all the people of India have this custom." [1]

The Chinese trade with Quilon noticed by Solyman in the eighth century must have existed earlier still, for Ma Huan tells us that Quilon was known to the Chinese navigators of the Tang dynasty (618—913 A. D.) This trade had, in the face of the opposition of the Moors, who were gradually establishing themselves on the coast, languished a good deal, and was almost vanishing when it obtained a new impulse from the hands of the enterprising Mogul Emperor, Kublai Khan. We have already seen that, even before Marco Polo, the Chinese must have had a settlement at Quilon. Marco Polo himself was employed by the Khan in a diplomatic capacity, and visited Quilon while he was a Chinese Mandarin in the service of the Khan. According to Yule," Kublai had a good deal of diplomatic intercourse of his usual kind with Kaulam (Quilon). De Mailla mentions the arrival at I' Swanchan (or Zayton, the chief port of China at the time) in 1282 of envoys from Kiulam, an Indian State, bringing presents of various rarities including a black ape as large as a man. The Emperor had three times sent thither an officer called Yang-Ting-pi (ix—415).[2]" " Some rather curious details of these missions are extracted by Pauthier from the Chinese annals. The royal residence is in these called A-pu'hota, and the king is styled Pinati. Barbosa also calls the king of Kaulom Beneti—deri, and Dr. Caldwell explains that Penati or Benati represents Vēṇāḍan, 'the Lord of the Vēṇāḍu,' or Vēṇāṭṭu, that being the name of the district to which belonged the family of the old kings of Kollam; and Vēṇāḍan was their regular dynastic name. The Rajas of Travancore who superseded the kings of Kollam, and inherited their titles, are still poetically styled Vēṇāḍan."

1. Vol. II, p. 375 6.
2. Vol. II, p. 379.

We learn from Marco Polo that the king of Quilon had benefited largely from the Chinese trade, and that he was a powerful ruler governing a tract extending to the mouth of the Ṭāmraparṇi.

The chief articles of export from Quilon were brazil wood or sapang, indigo, ginger and pepper, which last was in great demand in China. Marco Polo estimates that Kuisay, the largest city in China at the time, alone consumed daily 43 loads of pepper, each load weighing about 200 lbs. Even after the merchants paid almost 40 per cent. of the cost price as freightage and duty, they are said to have realised large profits from the pepper trade.

Not long after the visit of Marco Polo, John of Monte Corvino, the first Roman Catholic Missionary to China and the first Archbishop of Peking, touched Quilon on his way to his See. From him we learn that the Mahomedans, who had already settled there in large numbers, were gradually ousting the Chinese, the Christians, and the Jews from their commercial position on the coast.

Abulfeda defines the position of Quilon as at the extreme end of the pepper country, towards the east, whence ships sailed direct to Aden; on a gulf of the Sea, in a sandy plain, adorned with many gardens. He adds that the brazil tree grew there, and that the Mahomedans had a fine mosque and square.

Friar Odoric (1322) also places it 'at the extremity of the pepper forest towards the south,' and calls it 'Polunbun,' 'in which is grown better ginger than anywhere else in the world, and the variety and abundance of wares for sale in that city is so great that it would seem past belief to many folk.'

In 1324, Friar Jordanus came out to Quilon as a Roman Catholic Missionary to recover the heretical Nestorians to the true Roman fold. He was subsequently appointed by Pope John XXII, Bishop of Quilon or Colunban, the first Catholic See in India. In his work entitled *Mirabilia Descripta*, he gives us an interesting account of the country. He tells us that 'the king of Colunbun is called *Ligna* but his kingdom Mohebar.' Yule, who has translated and edited the Friar's work for the *Hakluyit Society*, explains that "The king whose name was *Ligna* may probably have been connected with the sect of the Lingayets still existing in Southern India, whose members wear a representation of the *Lingam* or Śaivite emblem round their neck and have many peculiar practices. He was certainly a Nair, as appears from what Jordanus has said of the law of succession." This need not necessarily be; for Col. Yule was perhaps not aware that in Malabar the Kṣheṭṝyās also follow the Marumakkaṭṭāyam law of descent in the female line. "Among the Rājās of Coorg, who were both Nairs and Lingayets," continues Yule, 'we find the name *Ligna* borne by several during the last century.'

The system of inheritance referred to above is thus described by Jordanus:—'In this India never do the legitimate sons of great kings or princes or barons inherit the goods of their parents, but only the sons of their sisters,'—an absolutely correct statement of the Marumakkaṭṭāyam law as extant in Malabar even to-day. Of the character of the people, he gives the following pleasing account:—"The people of this India are very clean in their feedings; true in speech, and eminent in justice, maintaining carefully the privileges of every man according to his degree as they have come down from old times." And it may be remembered that the functions of the Nair community in the body-politic, according to the Kēralōṭpaṭṭi, were those of supervision (kaṇ=the eye), the executive power (kai=the hand, as the emblem of power), and the giving of orders (kalpana=order, command) so as to prevent the rights from being curtailed or suffered to fall into disuse.[1] It is also pleasing to read the tribute he pays to the spirit of religious toleration that has always been a distinguishing characteristic of the rulers of Malabar. He says, 'And let me tell you, among the idolators, a man may with safety expound the word of the Lord, nor is any one from the idolators hindered from being baptised.'

The trade of Quilon was, according to Jordanus, extensive and consisted chiefly of pepper, cinnamon, ginger and brazil wood.

Jordanus found a flourishing community of Nestorian Christians in Quilon and other towns on the Coast. Of these Nestorians, who were in his eyes schismatics, the Friar observes, 'In this India there is a scattered people, one here another there, who call themselves Christians, but are not so, nor have they baptism, nor do they know anything else about the faith! Nay, they believe St. Thomas the Great to be Christ.' Of these he succeeded in bringing a considerable number back into the Roman communion. He built for them a Church at Quilon, known as St. George's Church. No trace of this church now exists, but it is mentioned in subsequent years by the Friars and Missionaries who ministered to its congregation for a long time after, and it is indeed probable that this was the church that the Portuguese found at Quilon, when they first visited the place in 1502. Col. Yule has, in the preface to his edition of Jordanus, given us the opening lines of the Bull of Pope John XXII, dated 5th April 1330, addressed to the Christians of Colunbun and intended to be delivered to them by Jordanus, who was nominated Bishop of that place. The Bull commences as follows:—

"*Nobili viro domino Nascarinorum et universis sub co Chiristianis, Nascarinis de Columbo, Venerabilem fratrem nostrum Jordanum Catalani, episcopum*

1. Malabar, p. 135.

Columbensem, Proedicatorum Ordinis professorem, quem nuper ad episcopalis aignitatis apicem anctoritate apostolica duximus promovendum.'' and so on.

The Pope goes on to recommend the missionaries to their goodwill, and ends by inviting the Nascarini (Nazrāṇi, Christians in India) to abjure their schism, and enter the unity of the Catholic Church.[1] It is doubted whether Jordanus ever took possession of his See.

John De' Marignolli, a Minorite Friar of the Fransiscan Monastery of Santa Corce, Florence, was sent by Pope Benidict on a mission to Cathay in 1338, in response to a request from the Christian Alans, who formed part of the army of the great Khan, 'For a legate wise capable and virtuous to care for their souls.' On his way back from China, he touched at Quilon, lived there for over a year, and preached in St. George's Church, founded by Jordanus. He received for his offices, from the Christian congregation of Quilon, a tithe of 100 gold fanams per mensem and a bonus of 1,000 fanams on his leaving the place. He was an ambitious man and was particular that the good people of Quilon should not forget him. "To emulate the glory of Alexander the Great", he says, "I erected a stone as my land-mark and memorial, and anointed it with oil. In sooth it was a marble pillar with a stone cross upon it, intended to last till the world's end. And it had the Pope's arms and mine engraved upon it with inscriptions in both Indian and Latin characters. I consecrated it and blessed it in the presence of an infinite number of people, and was carried on the shoulders of the chiefs in a litter, or palanquin like Solomon."[2] But alas for the vanity of human wishes! The column which was to endure till the world's end soon crumbled under the corroding influence of the elements and very little of the inscription remained.

1. p. 7.
2. Cathay, II, pp. 342—5.

Even as it was, very soon a tradition gathered around it, attributing it to St. Thomas, the founder of Christianity in Malabar, and it continued to be pointed out as a conclusive and unerring testimony of the Apostle's visit to the coast. So much for the holy Friar's worldly vanity.

Though the trade of Quilon was gradually on the decline, it was still important. When Ibn Batuta came to Quilon, Chinese ships still used to frequent the port. Ibn Batuta's visit to Quilon was due to an accident. He had left Delhi as Ambassador from the Great Mogul to the Emperor of China in company with the Chinese Ambassador to the Sultan. Landing at Calicut, he spent a few months there as the guest of the 'Samorin', who made arrangements for his passage to China in Chinese junks. When about to start, a sudden storm compelled the junks to put to sea, and Ibn was left behind. He was told that the Kakam (vessel) which was to have carried him must touch Kaulam (Quilon), and thither he determined to go by back-water. It was a ten days' journey, whether by land or by water. So he set off by the lagoons. On the tenth day, he touched Quilon, which he describes as one of the fairest cities of Malabar, with splendid bazaars and wealthy merchants and a fine mosque and square. "There was also a Mahomedan Kazi and Shabandar (master attendant). Kaulam was the first port at which the Chinese ships touched on reaching India, and most of the Chinese merchants frequented it; but the Mahomedans had already succeeded in wresting a considerable portion of the trade from their hands. They lived in separate quarters under the rule of their own Kazi. The king was an infidel called *Tiruvari* (Ṭiruvaṭi), a man of awful justice, of which some striking instances are given by Ibn Batuta. One day when the king was riding with his son-in-law, the latter picked up a mango, which had fallen over a garden wall. The king's eye was upon him; he was immediately ordered to be ripped open and divided asunder, the parts being exposed on each side of the way, and a half of the fatal mango, beside each."[1] "During my stay at Quilon," says Batuta, "a Persian archer, who was wealthy and influential, killed one of his comrades and then took refuge in the house of one Alawedji. The Musalmans wanted to bury the dead body, but the officers of the king would not allow them to do so, until the murderer was seized and punished. The officers of the king took the body in a bier to the gate of Alawedji and left it there to rot. The smell soon compelled Alawedji to hand over the murderer to the officers of the king, who refused a large bribe offered by the Persian, and had him forthwith tried and executed. The body of the victim was buried."

The name of the king given by Ibn Batuta, *Tiruvari* (evidently Ṭiruvaṭi), affords us a clue to identify the then ruling dynasty of Quilon with that of Travancore. The Travancore king is still known, specially in Tamil poetic literature, as Vēṉāṭ Aṭikaḷ Ṭiruvaṭikaḷ,[2] i. e., 'the feet of Vēṉād, the adorable feet.' It is, however, only a title, and we see the mistake often made of the sounding titles assumed by the princes of Malabar being taken for the proper names of families or individuals. A notable instance of this is that of the title of 'Chēramān Perumāl or the lord of Chēra' being assumed to be the personal name of the last ruler of Kērala.

We learn from Ibn Batuta that even in his time Calicut had become a strong competitor with Quilon for commercial supremacy. The Zamorin had attracted towards his capital most of the wealthy and enterprising Arab merchants by the grant of favourable monopolies and privileges. The Chinese trade had passed the stage of languishing, and was being steadily

1. Cathay, pp. 420—1.

2. See Professor Sundaram Pillay's dedication of his *Some Early Sovereigns of Travancore.*

driven from the coast; and we learn from Joseph of Cranganūr, who visited Portugal and Rome, that, in the beginning of the 16th century, the Mahomedans with the powerful aid of the Zamorin massacred all the Chinese inhabiting the ports of Malabar.

In the 15th century, the Noble Venetian, Nicolo Conti (1441), describes 'Coeloen' as 'a noble city the circumference of which is 12 miles,' and notices its flourishing trade in 'ginger called by the natives *Colobi* (*i. e.*, Colombi, or of Kaulam or Quilon), pepper, brazilwood, and the cinnamon which is called (*i. e.*, by Western travellers) crassa (*i. e.*, *Cairella grossa*, coarse cinnamon or cassia), and describes the jack, amba (mango), and a tree he names *Cachi*.'

Quilon continued to be an important place till the beginning of the 16th century, when Varthema speaks of it as 'a fine port', and Barbosa as a 'very great city with a very good haven, with many great merchants, Moors and gentiles, whose ships traded to all the Eastern Ports as far as Bengal, Pegu, and the Archipelago.'

Half a century after Ibn Batuta, the Portuguese arrived on the Malabar coast, and the queen of Quilon invited Cabral, promising to supply him with pepper and spices at a cheaper rate than he could obtain them at Cochin. But this offer was politely declined. However, a second offer made to Vasco-da Gama was successful, and trade was established with the Portuguese in 1502. In 1519 Portuguese factor, Heytor Rodrigues, on pretence of repairing the factory, commenced to build a fort at Tungachery which was soon completed and armed. The already languishing trade of the port now received its death-blow from the hands of the friendly Portuguese. Under cover of the agreement giving the Portuguese the control of the pepper trade, Rodrigues seized 5,000 bullock-loads of that article, which certain traders from the East Coast had collected in barter for 5,000 bullock-loads of rice, which they were on the point of taking across the ghauts, *via* the Āriankāvu Pass. From that time forward, East Coast merchants were afraid to cross by that pass for trade at Quilon, and that trade-route gradually fell into disuse. The pepper trade was diverted to the rival port of Cochin, which was rapidly rising in importance under the auspices of the Portuguese Crown[1].

In 1588, the English traveller, Ralph Fitch, passed by Quilon, which he describes 'as a fort of the Portugals: from whence commeth great store of pepper which commeth from Portugall: for oft times there ladeth one of the carracks of the Portugall.'[2]

The fort continued to be held by the Portuguese, till, in the beginning of December 1661, the Dutch Admiral, Ryklof Van Goens, captured it from them.

Captain Nieuhoff was appointed Chief Director of the Dutch East India Company at Quilon. He arrived at Quilon, as such, on the 7th of January 1662, and gave immediate orders for repairing the castle. He gives us the following description of Quilon :

"The city is fortified with a stone wall of 18 to 20 feet high, and eight bastions ; its suburbs, which are very large and stately, are by the Portuguese called Colang China. For Koulang is separated into two bodies, one of which is called the upper or Malabar Koulang, the other the lower Koulang; in the first the king and queen kept their ordinary residences; the last was formerly in the possession of the Portuguese; here the friars of St. Paul and the Franciscans had each a monastery, adorned with stately chappels and steeples. Besides which there were four other Portuguese churches here, dedicated to as many Romish Saints ; they had no less than seven goodly churches, among which was the famous church built many years ago by the Christians of St. Thomas, which was left standing,

1. Danvers, Vol. I, p. 346.
2. P. 185.

after we reduced the place into a narrow compass; in this church is the tomb of a certain great Portuguese captain, who was Governor of Koulang 60 years. The houses of the inhabitants were very stately and lofty, built of free stone; among which the Stadthouse surpassed all the rest; it was two storeys high, and had very curious stone steps on each side. But the castle, the residence of the Portuguese Governor, surmounted all the rest in magnificence; it lies very near the sea-side, at one end of the city, being covered on the top with coco leaves, as likewise two of its turrets, the third being tiled with pantiles. Just upon the sea-shore is another four-square tower where I set up the Company's flag on the top of a mast. In the midst of it is a very lofty edifice, which the Portuguese used for a chapel, which I ordered to be made up into divers convenient chambers, and to be fitted for the use of the Company's officers. This castle is the strongest the Portuguese ever were masters of on the Coast of Malabar, being built some hundred years ago by the famous engineer Hector de la Casa (who died in A. D. 1560).

"This city as I told you before was drawn into a less compass by the Dutch, which they fortified on the land-side with two half and one whole bastion. Most of the churches and other public edifices were pulled down, except the castle, St. Thomas' Church and some monasteries, which remained standing within the said precinct. * * *

"The harbour is very convenient for small vessels, but not for great ones, because the south-wind blows directly upon the shore and forces the waves with great violence thither; they call it Coyclanal. About a league to the west of Koulong the great river Eqwick disembogues into the sea. * * *

"On the side of Koulong China, along the seashore, the Jesuits had built a great village for the Parvees, a poor sort of Malabars living upon fishing, where the Governor of the king of Travankor and Prince Baryette Poelo (Vaṭayāṯṯu Pilla) kept their residence, which are about a mile in circuit and surrounded with an earthen wall, with some points like bastions, on which are mounted good store of great cannon, which command the roads, without which there is scarce any access to them.

"The best houses are built along the river-side, with very good gardens, stocked with all sorts of trees, fruits, flowers, and herbs, but especially with citrons, which grow here not on trees, but shrubs; their houses are seldom above two storeys high, their stairs within of stone, their rooms above stairs are paved with green and yellow four square stones, the cieling of which is commonly of Indian oak, some being finely carved, others painted. They commonly have an arbour or summer-house belonging to each garden, which is commonly near the river-side, where they spend generally their evenings, and divert themselves with anything."

The Dutch remained in possession of the fort for a century and upwards, though harassed by Travancore now and again. From a memorial of Van Angelbeck, Dutch Governor of Cochin, we learn that "the inhabitants (Christians) of Quilon had been from 1663 the company's subjects, and were governed without the least interference of the Raja of Travancore, whose subjects they had never been, as after the Raja of Quilon died, they came under the rule of the Signatty, or Chief of Culli-Quilon (Kāyamkulam)."

At first, the Raja of Travancore claimed from the fishermen ten chakrams (a small coin, 28½ to a Rupee) and fish annually, not because they were subjects of the Signatty, but because they extended their fishing excursions to parts opposite his territory. While those who were married in the Roman Catholic Church at Nīnṭakara, situated in Travancore limits, were obliged to pay a fee of ten chakrams.

After Travancore annexed the Culli-Quilon territory, the fishermen paid 30 chakrams annually for every large net, and 15 for each small one, and this was the origin of the so-called poll-tax. Dutch officials collected it, while the Travancore officials had to apply to them for the amounts. By degrees, the Travancore Revenue Officers commenced interfering with the limits of Dutch Quilon, and the commandant there, Kosier, was of such a lazy temperment that he took no notice, and thus the inhabitants came to be partially governed by Travancore people.

Subsequently much trouble was occasioned in wresting Quilon from Travancore, but all disputes were set at rest in 1788. A conference was held in the October of that year at Māvēlikkaray, when the Raja observed that many of his subjects had taken up their abode in Quilon, and were he to give them up, he should be pecuniarily a loser; it was promised they should be turned out; and it was agreed

1st that the remaining inhabitants shall submit to no increase of the obligations to which they were formerly subject;

2nd that the taxes shall be collected by Dutch officials, who shall pay the amount into the Raja's treasury; and

3rd that the Raja's officials shall interfere no more in the affairs of Dutch Quilon.

Not long after, on the 20th October 1795, the Dutch fort of Cochin surrendered to the British under Major Petrie; and with it passed the dependencies under Cochin, the most prominent of which was Ṭangachērry or Dutch Quilon. These were finally ceded to the British Government by the Paris Convention of 1841.

Under the treaty concluded with the English East India Company and Travancore, a subsidiary force had to be stationed in Travancore, and Quilon was the place chosen for its location. Vēlu Ṭampi Dalawah, who succeeded the famous Raja Kēšava Dāss as Prime Minister of Travancore, and who subsequently rebelled against the English, took great interest in improving Quilon. He built new bazaars and invited merchants from Madura and Tinnevelly to settle there, and did all he could to make it a flourishing centre of trade. Large and spacious buildings were erected for the public offices, as also a Hindu pagoda, and a royal residence. Quilon continued to be the head quarters of the Travancore Sirkar till the Huzur Cutchery was removed to Trivandrum. Since then the town has been going down in importance. But there are signs of a prosperous future for it. It is now the terminus of the Travancore-Tinnevelly Railway and signs are not wanting of its rise in commercial importance.

2. **Signati**. Signati is Jeyaṭungaṅāḍ, Jayasimhaṅāḍ, Ḍēsingaṅāḍ or Chengaṅāḍ corrupted into Singnati by the Portuguese. It represents the old kingdom of Quilon, ruled by a collateral branch of the Travancore royal family. The kingdom of Quilon was annexed to Travancore by Maharaja Mārttāṇḍa Varma in 1742—3 A. D.

3. **Aiwike.** This part of the country was noticed so early as the first century A. D. by Ptolemy, who calls it the Aiorum Regio, or the country of the Aioi. The Aioi were a people who, according to Prof. McCrindle, occupied the southern parts of Travancore. "The name," says he, "is perhaps a transliteration of the Sanskrit *Ahi*, a snake, and if so, this would indicate the prevalence among them of serpent worship. He points out that Cunningham in his *Geography of Ancient India*[1] states that in the Indo-Chinese map of India, the alternative name of Malayakūṭa is Hai-an-men, which suggests a connection with Ptolemy's Aioi. The entrance to the backwater at Kalikoulan is called the Great Aybicca Bar, and an entrance further south, the little

1. P. 522.

Aybicca Bar. The first part of these names may also be similarly connected." The Dutch factories were very well situated for purposes of trade, for, according to Fra Bartolomeo, "On the east of Collam (Quilon) and towards the interior part of the country be Permanadu and Cirumuttu, two beautiful and uncommonly fertile districts, which belong to the kingdom of Koṭṭārakaray, and which produce great quantities of pepper, ginger, cardamom, gum, lac, cotton and various kinds of valuable wood. The river on which these articles are transported takes its rise in the ghauts, and proceeding past Collare (Kallaḍa), Tuyam and on the north side of Collare, discharges itself into the sea, towards the south, not far from the town of Aybicca. At the last mentioned place, the king of Travancore causes small ships to be built from time to time and in general gives employment to a great number of seamen."[1]

4. **Kulli Quilon.** Kalli Quilon or Kāyamkuḷam was a well-known port on the Malabar Coast in early times. During the middle ages, it was in a flourishing condition, and now forms an important town in Travancore. It is no longer a seaport, but only a broad, shallow sheet of back-water, known as the Kāyamkulam Lake, having been formed in front of the town, between the coast and the sea on the west. The country around is very productive, specially in pepper, and, after it ceased to be a port, it used to send all its produce to Poṟacāḍ for shipment. Passing Poṟacāḍ southwards, Barbosa mentions Kāyamkuḷam as the first town in the kingdom of Coulam (Quilon) "in which dwell many Gentiles, Moors and Indians, Christians of the below mentioned doctrine of St. Thomas. And many of these Christians lived amongst the Gentiles. There is much pepper in this place of which there is much exportation."[2] DeBarros, as well as

1. P. 117.
2. P. 157.

the *Sommario dei Rgni* in *Ramusio*, makes mention of the place. According to the Abbe Reynal, the quantity of pepper the Dutch exported from the coast of Malabar was 2,000,000 lbs. per annum, and it is noteworthy that a fifth of this was obtained from Kāyamkulam alone.

5. **Porcad**. Poṙcāḍ is a port situated about ten miles south of Alleppey. DeBarros calls it Porca, while the Lisbon edition of Barbosa has Porqua. We have already seen that the mud-bank of Alleppey extends to or has shifted to Poṙacād, thus affording safe anchorage for ships of all sizes even in bad weather. In former times, it was a place of much greater importance than at present. Barbosa gives the following description of the place: "Porca has a lord of its own. Here many Gentile fishermen reside, who do nothing and have no other occupation than that of fishing during the winter, and of plundering on the sea during summer such as fall in their way. They possess certain small boats, like brigantines, which they row skillfully, and collecting many of these together, they themselves being armed with bows and arrows, they surround any ship becalmed, and, after forcing it to surrender by means of their arrows, they proceed to plunder the crew and the ship, casting the men naked on the ground. The booty they divide with the lord of the country, who countenances them. This kind of boat is called Cation."[1] The Malabar pirates were a notorious race who infested the coast all along from Gujarat downwards, and were a source of much terror and anxiety to coasting voyagers from so early a date as that of the Greek mariners. Pliny, Arrian, Ptolemy and other ancient authors mention them as the *Molandis*.

"Piracy," says Mr. Mc Crindle, "which from very early times seems to have infested, like a pernicious parasite, the commerce of the Eastern Seas

1. Ramusio, Vol. I, p. 312.

flourished nowhere so vigorously as on the Konkan coast, along which richly freighted merchantmen were continually plying. Here bands of pirates, formed into regularly organised communities like those of the Thugs in the interior of the country, had established themselves in strongholds contiguous to the creeks and bays, which were numerous on the coast, and which afforded safe harbourage to their cruisers. The part of the coast, which was subject to their domination, and which was in consequence called the Pirate Coast, extended from the neighbourhood of Simylla to an emporium called Nitra, the Mangarath of Cosmos, and the Mangalore of the present day. Whether the native traders took any precautions to protect their ships from this high-way men of the ocean is not known; but we learn from Pliny that the merchantmen which left the Egyptian ports heading for India carried troops on board well armed for their defence."[1] But, according to the Periplus, the Pirate Coast extended still further south. For Muller quotes at length a passage from Pliny[2] which must have been excerpted from some Periplus. It runs thus: "To those bound for India it is most convenient to depart from Okelis. They sail thence with the wind Hippalos in 40 days to the first emporium of India, Muziris (identified with Crānganūr) which is not a desirable place to arrive at on account of pirates infesting the neighbourhood, who hold a place called Nitrias, while it is not well supplied with merchandise." "The Malabar Pirates," says Dr. Hunter, "held a chain of precipitous strongholds and difficult creeks, from near Bombay to Cape Comorin, and it was a confederacy of one of their chiefs (Timoja) with Albuquerque which had captured Goa for the Portuguese. Their fleets scoured the route in squadrons of 20 ships a-piece, at a distance of five miles apart, so that once a merchant craft come in sight, they could close

1. Ptolemy, p. 46.
2. Vol. I, XXVI 104.

in on her and render escape impossible—a strategy commented on by Marco Polo. More cruel still were their forays on shore, plundering and burning hamlets and killing the inhabitants or carrying them off as slaves."[1]

These piracies seem to have declined in Hamilton's time, for he says, "Porkat or Porkah is of small extent, reaching not above four leagues along the seacoast. The prince is poor, having but little trade in his country, though it was a free port of pirates when Evory and Kyd robbed along the coast of India, but since then the pirates infest the northern coasts, finding the richest prizes amongst the Mocha and Persian traders."[2] But Paolino points out, speaking of Cannanore, that the whole surrounding district, which towards the north extends as far as the Mountain Illi (D' Ely) is inhabited by these pirates. He adds that these unite themselves to other pirates who reside on the Angedib Islands near Goa, and capture all the small vessels which sail from Goa to Cochin. The huts in which their wives and children live stand on the eastern side of Mount Illi. Two centuries before Paolino, Ceaser Frederick speaks of the coast from Cannanore to Cranganūr being infested by pirates. The coast line, a hundred and twenty miles, he says, is " full of thieves, being under the king of Calicut, a king also of the Gentiles, and a great enemie to the Portugales, which when he is alwayes in warres, hee and his country is the nest and resting for stranger thieves, and those be called Moores of Carposa, because they weare on their heads long red hats, and these thieves part the spoyles that they take on the sea with the king of Calicut, for he giveth leave unto all that will goe a roving, liberally to goe, in such wise, that all along that coast there is such a number of thieves, that there is no sailing in those seas but with great ships and very well armed or else they

1. History of British India, Vol. II, p. 231.
2. Pinkerton, Vol. VIII, p. 383.

must go in company with the army of the Portugals."[1] The pirate hordes on the Western coast were finally destroyed by Admiral Watson and their stronghold captured by Clive in 1756. Later still, the fishermen pirates of Poṙacād continued to be active, harassing and robbing boats that ply on the back-waters to the coast of Poṙacād, a part of which is known as Kallaṙ-cōḍe (land of thieves). The country around is very fertile, forming what is known locally as Kuṭṭa-nāḍ, which is considered the granary of Travancore. There are vast expanses of low-lying land covered by water during the rainy season, forming lakes extending for miles and miles together. As the cultivating season approaches, the water is drained into a channel that flows through this land by means of water-wheels and the land, when dry and fit for cultivation, is sown with paddy. Poṙacād was formerly a place of much greater importance than at present. Baldeus calls it 'Percatti' and in Keith Johnson's Atlas it is written 'Parrakad.'

6. **Cranganore.** Of all places in Malabar, Cṙān-ganūr is, perhaps, the most important from a historic point of view. We catch glimpses of its early glory through a long vista of misty antiquity. Situated on the western sea-board at a point where the river system that afforded untold facilities for communication with the interior opened its mouth into the sea, Cṙān-ganūr formed a great emporium of trade from very early times. The Phoenicians, the Egyptians, the Greeks, and the Romans, each in turn, carried on commerce with the East. The fact of the Phoenician intercourse with South India is based on indubitable philological evidence. The Hebrew names by which the ivory, apes and peacocks, the gold and sandal-wood that Solomon's shipmen carried away, as mentioned in the Bible indicate the geographical limits of Phoenician trade, so far as the Indian coast is concerned. The first three are called

1. Hakluyt's Voyages, Vol. V, p. 392.

Habim, Kafim, and Tukim in Hebrew. The first is said to be *Ibha* (Sans. Elephant), the second is similar to *Kapi*, an ape, and the third, Dr. Caldwell says, is the Hebrew word for a pea-fowl, which is Thuki, and is a Dravidian word. "The oldest Tamil word found in any written record in the world," says the learned Bishop, "appears to be the word for pea-cock in the Hebrew text of the Books of Kings and Chronicles, in the list of articles of merchandise brought from Ophir (about B. C. 1000) in Solomon's ships, which formed a portion of the great mercantile fleet of the Phoenicians. The old Tamil word *Tokai* became in Hebrew Tuki." In the Almug tree or Algum tree, scholars have recognised the sandalwood. Prof. Max Muller says that "one of the numerous names of this tree in Sanskrit is *Valguka*. This *Valguka*, which points back to a more original form of *Valgu*, might easily have been corrupted by Phoenician and Jewish sailors into Algum, a form as we know, still further corrupted at least in one passage of the old Testament into Almug. Sandalwood is found indigenous in India only, and there chiefly on the "coast of Malabar."[1] Mr. Bosworth Smith tells us that the gates of the ancient city of Carthage were made of sandalwood imported from Malabar.[2] Earlier still, Moses specifies the appropriation to relegious uses, and in large quantities too, of cinnamon and cassia which were peculiarly the productions of Ceylon and Malabar. A well-known passage in the Bible[3] attests to the fact that these valuable aromatics figured prominently in the temple service of the Jews. The traditions of the Malabar Jews carry back the date of their settlement on the Malabar Coast to the time of their escape from servitude under Cyrus in the sixth century B. C. If there be any truth in this, it was not at all difficult for them to have maintained their connection with their motherland, for we

1. Lectures on the Science of Language, Vol. I, p. 322.
2. Carthage and the Carthagenians.
3. Exodus, xxxv. 23—24.

have it from Herodotus that the Red Sea trade in myrrh and franckincense, cinnamon and cassia was in the hands of the Egyptians and Phoenicians. Cinnamon and cassia were specially Malabar products, and Ktesias, the Knedian (B. C. 400) makes mention of cinnamon under the name of Karpion identified by Dr. Caldwell with the Tamil-Malayalam word *Karappu*.

"Thirty-five years ago," says M. Zēnaide A. Ragozin, "no one would have thought of connecting India (pre-Āryan India), with archaic Babylonia, and, if a solitary fact pointing that way was once in a while picked out by an exceptionally inquisitive and observant mind, it was suffered to remain unexplained, as a sort of natural curiosity, for the inferences it suggested were too startling to be more than hinted at." M. Ragozin refers, as an instance, to the use of the word *mana*, pointed out by the late Francois Lenormant, as early as the Rig Vēḍa, to denote a definite quantity of gold—a word which, he says, can be traced to ancient Chaldea, or Semetic Babylonia, with the same meaning, and which afterwards passed into the Greek monetary system (mnā, still later Latinized into mina). "Well, this little fact," continues M. Ragozin " simply points to a well established commercial intercourse between Dravidian India (for the Kolarians never came as far west as the land by the Indian Ocean) and Babylonia and Chaldea. And now, years after, chance brings two more discoveries, individully as trifling, yet linked together, the three form a chain of evidence as complete as it is strong. In the ruins of Mugheir, ancient Ur[1] of the Chaldies, built by Ur-Ea (or Ur-Bagash), the first king of united Babylonia, who ruled not less than 3000 years B. C., was found a piece of Indian teak.[2] This evidence is exceptionally conclusive,

1. Ur of the Chaldees. A Dravidian derivation may be suggested for the word Ur. It may be the Tamil word ūr denoting village. Thus Jerusalem would be the ūr or village of Salem.
2. Sayce. Hibbert Lectures for 1887, pp. 18, 136, 137.

because, as it happens, this particular tree is to be located with more than ordinary accuracy: it grows in Southern India (Dekhan), where it advances close to the Malabar Coast, and nowhere else; there is none north of the Vindhya. Then again, the precious vocabularies and lists of all kinds of things and names which those precise old Babylonians were so fond of making out and which have given us so many startling surprises, come to the fore with a bit of very choice information, namely that the old Babylonian name for muslin was Sinḍhu, *i. e.*, that stuff was simply called by the name of the country which exported it."[1]

From these facts, M. Ragozin argues that the Āryan settlers of Southern India had, at 'an amazingly early period,' excelled in the manufacture of muslin, that the Āryans of the Punjab being not acquainted with the sea, or the construction of sea-going ships, their Dravidian contemporaries who were enterprising traders carried the article to some commercial centre on the western coast where the largest vessels lay which carried on the regular export and import trade. "This internal evidence," observes M. Ragozin, "is still further strengthened by another item of information, which, though coming from a very different quarter, dovetails into it exactly. Professor Max Muller has long ago shown that the names of certain rare articles, which king Solomon's trading ships brought him, were originally not Hebrew. These articles are sandalwood (indigenous on the Malabar coast and nowhere else), ivory, apes, and peacocks, and their native names, which could easily be traced through the Hebrew corruptions, have all along been set down as Sanskrit, being common words of that language. But now, quite lately, an eminent Dravidian scholar and specialist (Dr. Caldwell) brings proof that they are really Dravidian words, introduced into Sanskrit. This is a dazzling ray of light, and proof so conclusive, when added

1. Cf. Calico and Calicut.

to an already strong and compact case, that further corroborative evidence would be welcome, but scarcely necessary."[1]

In return for the extensive commercial benefits derived from the East, the Phoenicians seem to have left to India the priceless legacy of a form of writing. Dr. Burnell observes that "all known facts tend to prove that the earliest date of the introduction of the Phoenician alphabet into India, which became the South Aśōka character, cannot have been earlier than 500 B. C., the date of the Aśōka inscriptions." He then proceeds to point out the difference between the South Aṣōka alphabet and the Vaṭṭeḷuṭṭu alphabet, "the most ancient Tamil and almost the present Malayalam character." His conclusion is that these two alphabets are derived from one and the same source, and that the Sematic, that is, the Aśōka alphabet was moulded for the expression of Sanskrit in the north, and the Vaṭṭeḷuṭṭu for the Dravidian in the south, and that the latter reached Southern India by way of the three ports of Muzuris, Tundis and Nilkanda. Of these, Muzuris has been satisfactorily identified with modern Craṅganūr.

The Greek intercourse with Malabar is also proved by philological evidence. Leaving the word *Karappu* or *Karuva*, used to denote cinnamon, we have in the Greek word Oryza (rice), the Tamil word 'ariśi', and the Malayalam 'ari'. As Dr. Oppert remarks, "the word 'Oryza' dates from the time, whenever that was, when rice was first introduced into Europe, and it cannot be doubted that here we have the Tamil word 'ariśi,' rice deprived of the husk, this being the condition in which, then as now, rice was exported."[2] Again the Greek word Zingeber (ginger) is considered by Dr. Burnell to have a distinctly Malayalam origin. He thinks that the word is derived from the Malayalam

1. Vedic India, pp. 305—7.

2. Ancient Commerce of India.

name of the plant and the Greeks probably took it direct from that source. In Mạlayalam, ginger is called *Inchi* and *Inchiver* is Iñchi-root. Ginger is chiefly exported even now from Malabar, and in earlier times the Greeks procured it almost exclusively from that province, so that there is every probability that the name is Dravidian and not Sanskrit.[1]

It was not long before the great Roman Republic overran the Macedonian Empire, and the flourishing Greecian commerce with the 'Glowing Orient' passed on to Rome. It received a marked impetus with the beginning of Roman rule in Egypt (B. C. 30). The well-known saying, "Conquered Greece conquered her conquerors" receives no better illustration than, perhaps, in the matter of commerce, letting alone literature and the arts. It was through the Egyptian Greeks that the Romans carried on their sea-borne trade with the East. Egyptian ships, manned by Egyptian crew, brought Indian treasures to Roman shores, and these were highly priced in the Roman mart. About A. D. 47, the voyage to India was made easy by the discovery of a new route across the ocean by a Greek mariner named Hippalos. The *Periplus* says that "Hippalos was the pilot who first, by observing the bearings of the ports and the configuration of the sea, discovered the course across the ocean; whence, as, at the season when our Etesians are blowing, a periodical wind from the ocean likewise blows in the Indian Sea, this wind which is the south-west, is, it seems, called in those seas Hippalos."[2] Though spoken of as a new discovery, Vincent is of opinion that "there was a direct passage by the monsoons both in going and coming from India in use among the Arabians before the Greeks adopted it, and that Hippalos, frequenting these seas as a pilot or merchant, had met with Indian or Arabian traders who

1. Ind. Anti., Vol. I, p. 352.

2. After the name of the pilot who first discovered the passage by means of it.

made their voyage in a more compendious manner than the Greeks, and that he collected information from them which he had both the prudence and courage to adopt, just as Columbus, while owing much to his nautical skill and fortitude, was still under obligations to the Portuguese, who had been resolving the greatest problem in the art of navigation for almost a century previous to his expedition." Dr. Oppert also thinks that Hippalos only rediscovered the South-West Monsoon, which, he says, was known to the Phoenicians, and the knowledge of which had fallen into oblivion since their time. The result of this discovery was that mariners were enabled to strike boldly from the mouth of the Arabian Gulf across the ocean, and the Western Monsoons carried them to Muzuris, a harbour on the Malabar coast. "To those bound for India," says Pliny, "it is most convenient to depart from Okelis (now Galla or Calla, a small bay within the Straits of Babelmandeb). They sail thence with the wind Hippalos in 40 days to the first emporium of India, Muziris, which is not a desirable port to arrive at on account of pirates infesting the neighbourhood, who hold a place called Nitrias, which is not well supplied with merchandise. Besides, the station for ships is at a great distance from the shore, and cargoes have both to be landed and shipped by means of little boats. There reigned there, when I wrote this, Calabothras." The Periplus of Arrian, written probably in the first century A. D., also says that Muziris was the seat of government. Muziris, as already observed, has been identified with the modern Koḍungallūr or Cranganūr by Drs. Gundert, Caldwell and Burnell. It is the Muyrikkōḍu of the early Syrian copper-plates, and the Muchiri of the early Tamil poets. It was also known as Makōṭai, a term which appears in the Syrian copper-plate of Bhāskara Ravi Varman, where it is said that the king gave the grant from his seat at Makōṭai-paṭṭaṇam (town of Makōṭai). It is, indeed, noteworthy that even to this day among the community who were the recipients of the bounty of the Perumāḷ, Koḍungallūṟ is known as Makōṭaipaṭṭaṇam. Sanskritised into Mahāḍēvarpaṭṭaṇam. Ptolemy mentions Muziris as an emporium in Limyrike, which, as already observed, has been identified by Dr. Caldwell with the Damurike of the Peutingerian Tables, i. e., Ṭamiḷakam of the Tamil poets.

"To the kingdom under the sway of Keprabothras," says the author of the *Periplus Maris Erythroei*, "Tindis is subject, a village of great note situated near the sea. Mouziris which pertains to the same realm is a city at the height of prosperity, frequented as it is by ships from Arriake and Greek ships from Egypt. It lies near a river at a distance from Tindis of 500 stadia, whether this is measured from river to river or by the length of the sea voyage, and it is 20 stadia distant from the mouth of its own river."[1] This description answers exactly to the situation of Crānganūṟ and its suburb Ṭiruvanchikkuḷam. These places are not much more than 500 stadia either from Tindis, identified by Dr. Burnell with Kaḍaluṇḍi near Beypore, or from Nelkanda or Kallaḍa near Quilon, identified by the same learned authority. Arrian says that it is two miles distant from the mouth of the river on which it is situated, and according to Pliny it was not a desirable place for shipping purposes, though the first emporium of trade on the coast. The station for ships was at a great distance from the shore, and cargoes had to be landed and shipped by means of boats hewn out of a single log of wood. At Crānganūr, the ships have still to stand off at sea and though its shipping trade has been shifted to the better harbour and port of Cochin, the Travancore Sirkar still unloads its cargo of salt consigned to the Sirkar depot at Paḷḷippuṟam here. The salt has to be brought to the depot in Ḍhoṇīs (boats;

1. Para 54.

the country boats are generally hewn out of a single log of wood), the ships themselves being unable to enter the harbour for want of water.

The following articles are mentioned as exported from, or imported into, Muziris, and this gives us some idea of the natural and artificial products of the country around this great emporium of trade:—

Imports :—Coral; Tortoise shells of the best kind in all the Erythroean—that of the Golden Khersonesos; Malabathram, an unguent or perfume; Spikenard (Sans. *nalada*, cuscus); Wine in small quantities; Sandarke, a red pigment—red salphuret of arsenic—also a resin from the *Thuja articulata* or *Callitris quadrivaivis*, a small coniferous tree of North Africa; it is of a faint aromatic smell and is used as incense; Corn; Arsenic; Tin; Lead; Stibium—a sulphuret of antimoney—a dark pigment used for dyeing the eye-lids; Copper; Glass of a coarse kind; Chrysolite (topaz); Cloth in small quantity, stuffs in which several threads were taken for the woof in order to weave flowers or other objects.

Exports :—Pearl in considerable quantity and of superior quality; Pepper in large quantities; Gems (carbuncles) exported in every variety; Diamonds; Hayacinth or Jaenith. According to Salmasius, this is the ruby. In Solinus XXX, it would seem to be the Amethyst (Sans. Puṣhkaraja).[1]

The Tamil Poems, *Chilappadhikaram* (the Epic of the Anklet) and the *Mani-Mekalai* (the jewel belt), mention Chenkudduvan as ruling over the Chēra or Kērala country in the second century A. D. That appears to have been the period of Chēra ascendency, as Chenkudduvan was, during his reign, the arbiter of the destinies of South India. He resided at his capital Vanji (Ṭiru+Vanchi + kuḷam= Ṭiruvanchikuḷam near Crānganūr) at the mouth of the Periyār (Alwaye river).

1. McCrindle's Commerce and Navigation of the Erythroean Sea.

The *Chilappadhikaram* was composed by the king's younger brother Iḷanko-Aṭikal or the 'royal monk,' who, after renouncing the world, resided at Kunavayil near Vanchi. It is also said that Chenkudduvan's son 'Yānaik-kaṇ' 'he of the elephant-look,' was ruling as Viceroy under him at Tondi on the coast (Quilāndy in North Malabar).[1]

The Roman intercourse with Malabar is also evidenced by the find of Roman coins in many parts of the country. These coins range from those of the times of Augustus to those of that of Nero (B. C. 27 to A. D. 68). The Pāṇḍian kings as well as the ruler of Malabar, seem to have sent more than one embassy to Rome. The one to Augustus is noticed by Strabo, and subsequently to him in the *Chronographia* of Syncellus (A. D. 800). Dr. Oppert speaks of Indian envoys with precious presents being sent to Augustus, Claudius Antonius Pius, and Julianus. "According to the Pĕutinger Tables (226 A.D.)," says Mr. Sewell, "there was at one time a temple of Augustus with a garrison of two Cohorts or 1200 men at Koḍungallūṙ (Crānganūṙ)." This, if true, no doubt indicates something more than mere commercial relations between Rome and Malabar. The company of Romans that lived in Madura possessed, according to Mr. Tracy, the right of minting coins, which indicates some sort of political power. But Sir William Hunter points out in his History that the statement regarding the stationing of the Roman cohorts and the setting up of the temple of Augustus "does not find support from the edition of the *Tabula Itineraria Peutingerianci* by Kanad Muller (1888) or in the earlier Leipsic facsimile of 1824, or in Ernest Des Jardin's fine work *La Table de Peutinger*, Paris, 1869, nor can I discover evidence in any previous edition."

"It is to Crānganūṙ," observes Col. Yule, "that all Malabar traditions point as their oldest seaport of

1. Tamils 1800 Years Ago.

renown; to the Christians it was the landing place of St. Thomas the Apostle. The tradition is that the Apostle landed on Malankara, a small island in the lagoon or backwater close to Cranganūr in A. D. 52., and planted Christianity for the first time in India; and it is significant that the Metropolitan of the Jacobite Syrians in Malabar still takes his title of Bishop of Malankara from that little island."

A Tamil poet describes Muchiri or Muziris or Koḍungallūr (Cranganūr) situated near the mouth of the Periyār as follows:—"The thriving town of Muchiri where the beautiful large ships of the Yavanas, bringing gold, come splashing the white foam on the waters of the Periyār, which belongs to the Chērala (Chēra or Kērala) and return laden with pepper."[1] "Fish is bartered for paddy, which is brought in baskets to the houses;" says another poet, "sacks of pepper are brought from the houses to the market; the gold received from ships, in exchange for articles sold, is brought on shore in barges at Muchiri, where the music of the surging sea never ceases, and where Kudduvan (the Chēra king) presents to visitors, the rare products of the seas and mountain."[2*] Mr. V. Kanakasabhai identifies the Muchiri of the above extract with the Muziris of the Greek geographers. Muchiri, according to the Tamil poets, was situated near the mouth of the Periyār and was frequented by Yavana (Greek) merchants. The Greek geographers style the river-mouths Pseudostomos, which signifies in Greek 'false mouth,' a correct translation, says Mr. Kanakasabhai, of the Tamil or Malayalam expression, Alimukham, by which the mouth of the Periyār below Koḍungallūr is known even now.[3]

If, as Prof. McCrindle observes, the author of the *Periplus Maris Erythroei* wrote his account between

1. Erakkaddur Thyankannanar Akam 148.
2. Paranar,—Puram, 343.
* The Tamils 1800 Years Ago, p. 16.
3. Ibid, p. 19.

the years A. D. 80 and 89, the Keprobotras or the Calobotras whom Pliny met at Mouzirs must have been the Chēra king Athan II. (A. D. 55—90), or at any rate, his successor, Chenkudduvan or Imaya Varman (A. D. 90—125), leaving a margin of a few years on either side for possible mistakes. It was the younger brother of the latter, Ilanko-Aṭikal, or the 'royal monk,' who composed the poem *Chilappadhikaram*, which throws considerable light on the social and the political conditions of the country at the time. It gives a fair description of Vanchi, the Chēra capital and of the Periyār, the river at the mouth of which it was situated.

We now come to the copper-plate grants of the period of the Chēra kings, Bhāskara Ravi Varman and Vīra Rāghava Chakravarṭṭi. By the first of these, the king conferred certain privileges on the Jewish colonies of the Malabar coast which they still possess to some extent. The deed says that the king was living at the time of the grant at Muyiri Kōḍu which has been, as already observed, identified with the Muchiri of the Tamil poets and the Mourins of the Greek geographers. In another deed executed in the reign of the Chēra king Vīra Rāghava Chakravarṭṭi, in favour of the Syrian Christians of Malabar, the grantee Iravi Cortan of Mahāḍēvapaṭṭaṇam is invested with the lordship of Maṇigrāmam. The Mahāḍēvapaṭṭaṇam mentioned here is same as the Makōṭaipaṭṭaṇam of the Tamil Dictionary, which again is modern Koḍungallūr or Cranganūr. There has been considerable controversy and difference of opinion with regard to the date of these documents. Of the first, Dr. Burnell thinks that it cannot be later than the eighth century A. D., nor older than the beginning of that century.[1] Probably not later than the ninth century, nor earlier than the seventh, says Bishop Caldwell;[2] about 750

1. Ind. Ant., Vol. III, p. 334.
2. Grani. Dr. Lang, Intro.

THIRUVAṆCHIKULAM TEMPLE (INNER SHRIM).

To face page 309.]

A. D., says Dr. Burnell.[1] Mr. Wish gives 139 B. C., while Sir Walter Elliot brings it down to 861 A. D.; Mr. P. Sangunny Menon assigns to it the year 230 A. D.[2] So also Mr. Kūkal Kēlu Nayar.[3] Mr. Kanakasabhai observes, with regard to this deed, that it is dated in a year equivalent to 192 A. D., and is therefore the oldest copper-plate inscription preserved in Southern India. Of the second deed, Dr. Burnell is positive that A. D. 774 can be its only date. Dr. Keilhorn has, however, pointed out that it need not necessarily be so, as the year A. D. 680 also suits as well the astronomical data furnished by the deed. The late Mr. Venkiah of the Indian Archaeological department drags it down to the 11th century A. D., mainly on philological grounds. Anyhow, there can be no doubt that these afford satisfactory evidence of the early existence and prosperity of the Chēra capital Cranganūr.

As the capital and seat of the Chēramān Perumāls, Crangānūr enjoyed considerable prosperity. The Palace of the Perumāls, known as Allal Perinkōvilakam, was situated in the vicinity of the great pagoda at Ṭiruvanchikkulam, which, as already observed, formed a suburb of Cranganūr. Around and close by the palace were situated the Ṭalies or the assembly halls of the representatives of the Brahman aristocracy, by whom the Perumāls were elected to rule over Malabar for a term of 12 years. These Ṭalies (there were four of them) represented the four divisions into which the country was divided for administrative purposes, and over each of which was placed an unmarried Brahman President for a term of three years, whose duty was to preside over the administration of his division. According to the Kēralōṭpaṭṭi, these Ṭalies were known as Mēl Ṭali, Kīl Ṭali, Chingapuraṭ Ṭali, and Neṭiya

1. S. I. Paleography.
2. History of Travancore, p. 45.
3. Jour. of Lit. and Sc., Vol. V, No. 9.

Ṭaḷi. There were also minor Ṭaḷies, whose location may still be traced to those places which continue to have the affix Ṭaḷi added to their proper names, such, for instance, as Calicut Ṭaḷi, Changanāṭ Ṭaḷi, Koṭṭay Kuññaṭ Ṭaḷi, Nīlēśwaram Ṭaḷi. The Syrian copper-plate makes mention of the four chief Ṭaḷies, whose representatives are called by the Perumāḷ to witness the execution of the deed. A division of Malabar into four Ṭaḷies, or Kaḷakams, as they were called then, had existed even before the advent of the Perumāḷs. The Brahmans, who were reputed to have held sway in Malabar previous to the Perumāḷs, had established four Kaḷakams, the head-quarters of each of which was located in a temple of fame. At these temples, the Brahman inhabitants of the locality met to deliberate on affairs of local importance, the representatives of all the Kaḷakams meeting in a general assembly at the capital to assist the Rakṣhāpuruṣhan or Protector appointed to rule over Kērala for a fixed period. These Kaḷakams were located at (1) Perinchellūṟ, (2) Payyannūṟ, (3) Paṟappūṟ and (4) Chengaṇyūṟ. When it was found necessary for the Brahmans to call in Perumāḷs from outside Kēraḷa, it was left to these four Kaḷakams to elect kings. The Ṭaḷies of the Perumāḷs were but the continuation of the Brahman Kaḷakams, and it is said that the Brahmans preserved and strengthened them as a bulwark against the possibility of the elected kings becoming too powerful.

The last Chēramān Perumāḷ, Bhāskara Ravi Vaṟma, lived at Cṟānganūṟ, and ruled over Kēraḷa for 36 years, or three times the term for which he was originally elected. In him the Brahmans possessed a ruler congenial to their wishes, who not simply protected and pampered them, but also added lustre to their native land by his broad-minded policy of religious toleration and free commerce. The Jews, Christians and Muhammadans found in him a kind patron, who afforded facilities for their firm establishment in the country. He granted them immunities and privileges still highly cherished. It is alleged that his foreign proclivities led him to succumb to the religious influences of Muhammadan preachers, and to become a convert to the faith of Islam, and set out on a pilgrimage to Mecca after distributing, what came to be regarded by him, his country, among his many dependants and relatives. Cṟānganūṟ is pointed out as the port from which the Perumāḷ set sail on his voyage to Mecca, and a locality close by has the reputation of being the exact spot where the so-called distribution of the country took place. The Muhammadan conversion, the Mecca pilgrimage and the partition of the country are all but mere tradition and have to be accepted with great reservation; though the incident of the alleged conversion is made the basis of the introduction of Muhammadanism into Malabar, and of the disruption of the early Chēra Empire into a number of petty states.

The foundation of the Jewish and Christian communities as guilds with rights and privileges like those possessed by the Nayar community, at Cṟānganūṟ, is attributed to the latter Perumāḷs, if not to the last of them. If the introduction of the Muhammadan community into Malabar is also traceable to the last Perumāḷ, it is remarkable that Cṟānganūṟ can claim the merit of having first given shelter to all the three communities which have in no small degree contributed towards the prosperity of Malabar. St. Thomas, the Apostle of the Syrian Christians, is said to have landed at Malankara, an island at the Cṟānganūṟ mouth of the Periyār river near Paḷḷipōrt or Paḷḷippuṟam in A. D. 52, and to have built seven churches on the coast, the chief of which was located at Cṟānganūṟ itself. The Christian community continued to live there prosperously for a long time. When the Portuguese arrived in India, the Christians at Cṟānganūṟ sent a deputation to Vasco da Gama in 1502 with a request that the king of Portugal would take them under his protection. The Portuguese king, who had made proselytizing a state policy, sent Roman priests with instructions to bring the Syrian Christians over to the Roman fold, and, till but recently, Cranganur was the seat of a Roman Archbishopric. A seminary had also existed there for the religious instruction of Native Christians for ordination. When the Dutch possessed themselves of Cranganur (where the Jesuit Archbishops resided), it was the seat of learning, science and religion in Malabar. Here was a noble Jesuit College, containing a splendid library, the structure itself, says Baldeus, being not inferior to many in Europe: whilst within the fortress walls, a magnificent cathedral reared its stately head, and around it were the gorgeous and costly tombs of the Archbishops and Bishops, who had formerly held sway over this famous citadel. Beyond the walls at Palliport was the college of the Christians of St. Thomas for the instruction of youths of that persuasion in the Syriac tongue. The last building was subsequently converted into a leper hospital, and the masters and pupils removed to Changanassery, which, from that period, they termed Vaipucottah. The Carmelites subsequently erected a seminary at Varapulay. Of the buildings within the fortress of Cranganur, no record now remains, as they were totally destroyed. [1]

The early intercourse betweeen the East and the West makes it probable, as Basnage supposes, that the first Jews who arrived on the Malabar coast came in Solomon's fleet of merchant-men.

From the days of the last Perumal till the time of Al Biruni (970—1039), for a century and more, we have little or no account of Cranganur available.

1. Day, p. 238.

Mediaeval travellers refer to the place under various forms of the same name.

Al Biruni	970 A. D....		Jangli.
Benjamin of Tudela	1167	....	Gingaleh.
Friar Odoric	1281	...	Cyngilin.
Chinese Annals	1286	....	Shinkali.
Rashiduddin	1300	....	Chinkali or Jinkali).
Shemseddin Dimishqui	1320	....	Shinkli.
Friar Jordanus	1328	....	Singuyli.
Abulfeda	1330	....	Shenkala.
Marignolli	1349	....	Cynkali.
Nicolo Conti	1444	....	Columguria.
Barbosa	1505	....	Cranganore.
Assemani	1510	....	Chrongalor.

Colonel Yule thinks that the name Shinkali or Shigala was probably formed from Ţiruvanchikuḷam. He points out that the data to identify Crānganūr with the Gingaleh of Rabbi Benjamin are too vague, though the position of that place seems to be in the vicinity of Malabar.[1]

Al Biruni mentions Jangli as a kingdom on the west coast. He mentions in order Sindabur (Goa), Faknur (Barkur in South Canara), Manjarur (Mangalore), Hili (D'Ely), Sadrasa (not satisfactorily identified yet), Jangli (Crānganūr or Ţiruvanchikuḷam), and Kulam (Quilon). The men of all these countries, he tells us, are Samanics, *i. e.*, Bhuddhists.

The Rabbi Benjamin informs us that, in his day, the place contained about 1,000 Israelites, and no wonder, because that was the location of the first Hebrew colony, and it remained there till its desolation in 1524, and the final dispersion and emigration to Cochin in 1565.

1. Hobson-Jobson, p. 627.

AN.

Friar Odoric mentions Cyngilin as one of two cities of great importance situated in the Pepper Forest, the other being Fandarina (identified with Pandarani, a port which stood about 20 miles from Calicut). He places Quilon at the southernmost extremity of the Forest. Buchanan, in his *Christian Researches*, observes that, up to the present century (19th), there was a tract on the Malabar Coast called the 'Pepper Jungle.' Anyhow it is significant that the island on which the British Residency in Cochin is situated still goes by the name Molaku-Kāḍ, which means 'Pepper Jungle' in Malayalam and this name has been twisted into Bolgotty in English.

The Great Mongol Emperor Kublai Khan appears to have established some sort of political relation with the kingdom of Crānganūr also. We read in Marco Polo of the endeavours made by the Khan to carry on intercourse with the western countries of Asia. But his officers made the initial mistake of claiming homage and political supremacy as the basis of all intercourse with people outside China. This led to unsatisfactory results in Japan and Java. The Khan was, however, more fortunate elsewhere. In 1286, he is said to have established the sort of intercourse that he wanted with the kingdoms, Mapacal, Sumantala * * * and Sengkili. The Chinese annals mentions Sengkili as one of the western kingdoms which sent tribute(*i. e.*, envoys and presents to Kublai), and, as it is coupled with other countries which may be identified with Malabar and Somnath, it is highly probable that Sengkili or Crānganūr is intended.[1] We have already seen that the Khan had diplomatic relations with the king of Quilon.

Rashiduddin says, " Of the cities on the shore (of Malibar) the first is Sindabur (Goa), then Faknur (Baccanore or Barkur), then the country of Majarur (Mangalore) * * * then Chinkali (or Jinkali), then Kulam (Quilon)"

1. Cathay, Vol. I, pp. 75—77.

Shemseddin Dimishqui has the following observation :—

" * * * *Le pays de manibar, appele pays du Povre comprend les villes sinvantes. La ville de Shinkli, dont la majeure partie de la population est composee de Juifs. Kaulam est la derniere ville de la cote de Poivre* "

Friar Jordanus, after mentioning 12 kings of Greater India, proceeds to say, " * * there is one very powerful king in the country where the pepper grows, and his kingdom is called Molebar. There is also the king of Singuyli. "

Abulfeda in Gildemeister has the following notice of the place. " *Etiam Shabiyat (Chalyat) et Shinkala urbes Malabar icac sunt, quaram alteram Judaici incolunt*". * * (185).

John Marignolli observes, " And in the second India, which is called Mynibar, there is Cynkali, which signifieth little India " (Little China) " for Kali is 'little'."[1]

Nicolo Conti, after leaving Cochin, visited a place called by him Colunguria, which, he says, is situated at the mouth of a river, Paluria, identified with the Periyār or the Alwaye river, at the northern mouth of which stands Crānganūr.

Barbosa, in the early part of the sixteenth century, notices it as Crangalor, and says that it is occupied by a varied population of " Gentles, Moors, Indians, Jews and Christians of St. Thomas ; they have there a church of St. Thomas, and another of Our Lady, and are very devout Christians, only they are deficient in doctrine." Ortelius and Hormanus name the place correctly as Crānganūr, and it was taken by the Portuguese in 1505. Here Lopo Suares inflicted a crushing defeat on the Zamorin, who had collected there materials for an extensive campaign against the

1. Cathay, Vol. I, p. 373.

Raja of Cochin in 1502. The town was completely destroyed by the Portuguese.

Assemani, not long after, incidentally tells us, "*Scigala* (*i. e., Shigla or Shikala or Shenkala of Abulfeda*) *alias et Chrongalor vocatur, ea quam Cranganorium dicims Malabariac urbem, ut testatur idem Jacobus Indiarum episcopus, ad calcem Testamenti Novi ab ipso exarati, anno Graecorum 1821, Christi 1510, et in fine Epistolarum Pauli, Cod. Syr. Vat. 9 et 12.*"[1]

The Portuguese built a fort at Crānganūr in 1523, and they contemplated at first making it the seat of their Government in Malabar. They, however, gave up that idea, as they found Cochin a more eligible place. Crānganūr continued to be in the possession of the Portuguese till the year 1662, when it was taken by the Dutch. That was really the beginning of the end of Portuguese power in Malabar, if not of their Eastern Empire itself.

We have an account of the capture of the Portuguese Fort of Crānganūr given us by Captain Nieuhoff who seems to have taken part in the attack. After the capture of Pallipōrt, the Dutch "design upon the city of Crānganūr," we are told, "was laid aside for that time, after we were thoroughly informed concerning its condition, and that we were not sufficiently provided for such an attempt. So we proceeded on our voyage again the next day," (the 5 of March 1661). The Dutch tried their fortune in the south and succeeded in taking Quilon. "By this time," (December 1661), continues Nieuhoff, "it being resolved to prosecute the career of our victories, the Commodore Roodhaes with eight ships sailed towards the city of Crānganūr, to block up the entrance of that river, the rest being to follow with all convenient speed. The 19th (December) I went on board the Commissary James Borchorst, but on a sudden, there arose such a

1. *Diss. de Syr. Nest*, p.440 and p. 732.

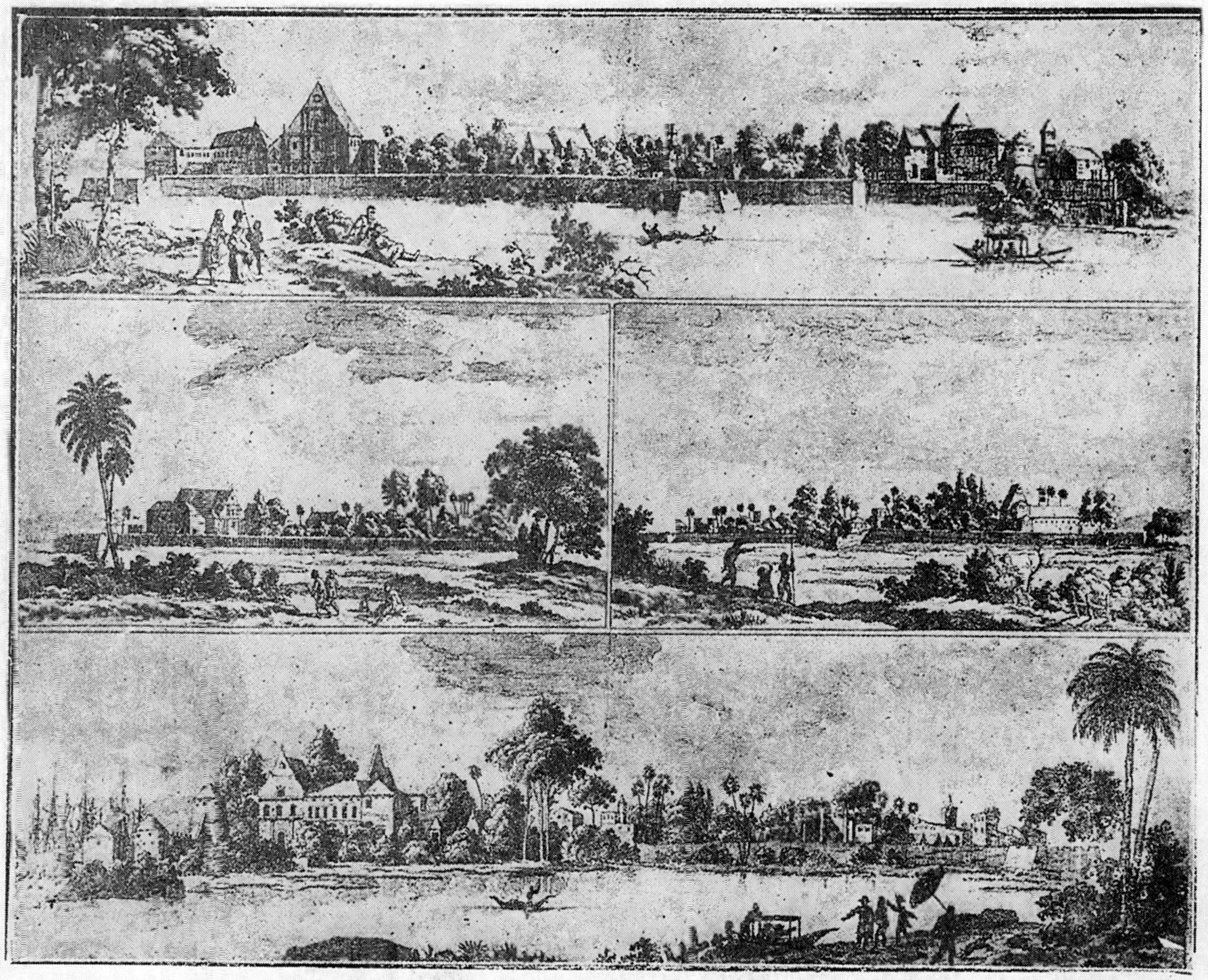

To face page 316.] VIEWS OF PORTUGUESE CRANGANORE.

RUINS OF CRANGANORE FORT.

To face page 317.

tempest that with much ado I could get ashore again. * * * * Through God's mercy, all our great ships escaped the danger of this storm without any considerable damage, except what was in their rigging which, however, most fell upon the smaller vessels." Leaving a garrison at Quilon, Mr. Van Goens "set sail the same day with the ships the 'Walnut-tree' and the 'Ulieland' towards Crānganūr, Commodore Gotske being to follow with the rest * * * . The 29th we set sail in the 'Exchange' to follow the fleet * * * . The 1st of January 1662 by break of day we found ourselves within a league of the city of Cochin, passed close to the shore without attracting attention of the garrison. The same day about noon we came into the road, at the entrance of the river Pallipōrt, and the next day having embarked our men in boats, and our ammunitions with two field pieces in another, we landed them without any opposition, except that the enemy discharged some of his great cannon against us from Crānganūr but without any loss on our side.

"We had posted our forces in three several places, the better to cut off all correspondency betwixt the enemy and the country. The next following day we brought two tons of rice, and two brass guns ashore, and soon after our whole train of artillery, with all other necessaries requisite for such an undertaking. For some time we had kept the place blocked up both on the land and river side, but now we began to open our trenches with such success, that in a short time we carried them on under the cannon of the city, the garrison being all this while not idle on their side, but endeavouring to hinder our approaching by their continual fire-arms, which they did with such dexterity, that they killed many in the trenches. * * * Fourteen days after we had carried our trenches to the body of the place, during which we had several smart skirmishes with the enemy, it was resolved to venture a general assault; pursuant to this resolution, I was sent with two servants to confer with Commodore Gotske and Mr. Roodhaes, concerning the most convenient place the assault was to be made in . * * * Mr. Gotske and Roodhaes had been before informed concerning the condition of the place by a certain Negroe (Nair) and where it might be most conveniently assaulted, of which they having given me a circumstantial account, I returned forthwith, and was with the Admiral by next morning, who thereupon resolved to assault the city, and, as he left me, said, 'To-morrow the city shall be ours.'" * * * * *

"In the meantime our forces mounted the breach and assaulted the town with great fury under the favour of the smoke of their cannon and fire-arms, which by the wind was forced towards the city. * * * The enemies defended themselves with a great deal of bravery for a considerable time, but our men pushing on the assault, with the utmost vigour, they were at the last, forced to give way, and to leave us masters of the city. Mr Polman and Shuilenburgh, two of our Captains, were dangerously wounded, 80 common soldiers were killed in the assault and a great many more wounded. The loss of the enemies' side was much greater, 200 Portuguese being slain during the action, besides a great number of Negroes (Nairs) who were all thrown into the river. We found the taking of this place to be another piece of work than that of Koulang (Quilon) and we were upon the point of sounding the retreat, had not the Commanders by their own example animated the soldiers to do their utmost, it being almost surprising how with so small a force we were able to attack and conquer so strong a place as this. After the city was plundered, it was laid level with the grounds, except one stone tower, which standing upon the river, was preserved entire, and a garrison put into it for the security of the river."

Of the city of Cr̄ānganūr, Nieuhoff gives the following description :—"This city of Cr̄ānganūr (for there is no other on the coast of Malabar nearer to the sea-shore) lies about four or five leagues to the north of Cochin; being the capital city of a kingdom of the same name, bordering to the north upon Cochin and to the south upon Koulang. It was very famous among the Indians by reason of its antiquity; being situated upon the bank of a river, about a league from the sea-shore defended by a wall of earth, and a stone breastwork; which had seven bastions and the wall of earth three more. At the point near the river is remaining to this day a strong stone tower for the defence of the river, which served instead of a bulwark on that side. On the other point was a small fort which commanded the river, and all ships going out or in. Several goodly stone houses were in this city, and among the rest a church excelling all the rest; on the opposite side the river, towards the side of Cochin, is the redoubt called Pallipōrt, built for the better defence of the river; upon a long island called Baypin extending to the river of Cochin. The Royal Palace is not far from hence, in a very pleasant country; the king then reigning being a prince of great bravery, and well-versed in military affairs, in the flower of age."

The Ducth, who looked to commerce before empire, discovered ere long that they had to maintain a military establishment the expenses of which, they thought, were not commensurate with the profit they derived from the Malabar trade. Mr. Swaarderkroon in his 'Memorial' on the Malabar Coast in 1698 said, "It is to be regretted that the company carried so much sail here in the beginning, that they are now desirous of striking them, in order to avoid being overset."

In 1680, the destruction of the forts in Cannanore, Crānganūr and Quilon was agitated on account of the enormous expense incurred in their up-keep, and the supreme Government at Batavia even offered Crānganūr and Quilon for sale to the Portuguese from whom they had conquered them. But nothing was finally settled. In October 1696 it was resolved not to keep up the fortifications at Crānganūr and other places; but the opertion of the resolution was postponed till the revision of the general affairs of the company on the coast by the supreme Government at Batavia. On the 19th of August 1697, the matter was finally settled. Only the ancient interior works of the Fort at Crānganūr were to be preserved with a reduced garrison of 20 Europeans, which was judged a sufficient number for the purposes of the company there.

The Dutch had come into possession not only of the Portuguese fort of Crānganūr, but also of the territory of the Raja of Crānganūr, lying around it. This they had acquired by a treaty with the Zamorin whose vassal the Raja was, dated 17th December 1717; but they had allowed the line of the Rajas to continue as their vassals. Subsequently the Zamorin made several attempts to retake Crānganūr, but these were always baulked by the Dutch with the assistance of the Cochin Raja. When complications arose between the Dutch and Hyder Ali, Crānganūr became a place of great moment. Hyder wished to possess the fort and the territory around, so that he might have an open way for his contemplated invasion of the kingdom of Travancore. Having subdued Malabar, he proceeded southwards, and opened negotiations with the Dutch to allow him to pass through their possessions to Travancore. The Dutch found their position on the coast very weak, and proposed to destroy their forts at Chēttwāye, Crānganūr and Quilon, rather than see them pass to Hyder. In 1767, the Governor of Cochin, C. Breekpot, received strict orders from Batavia to destroy these forts, but he refrained from doing so in the presence of the Mysoreans. Breekpot's predecessor, Wayerman, had directions to blow up the Crānganūr fort, but he had excused himself with the plea that, if he did so, all the houses within it must share the same fate, whilst the cost of breaking it down by manual labour would be excessive. The truth was that the powers in Batavia did not actually realise the importance of the fort. Those on the spot were decidedly of opinion that Crānganūr was the key to North Malabar, and that its destruction would be suicidal. The Governors of Cochin pleaded strongly for its retention and improvement. They had, however, to yield to orders from head-quarters, and both Wayerman and Breekpot had to reduce the garrison of Crānganūr considerably. The Dutch had not to wait long before they felt the consequences of their ill-advised policy. The negotiations opened with them by Hyder had become protracted in consequence of the necessity of making frequent references to Batavia, whence orders were long in coming. The Mysorean was impatient, and pressed for immediate replies, and the Governor of Cochin, not being in a position to satisfy him, Sirdar Khan was ordered to reduce the forts of Chēttwāye and Crānganūr. Sirdar Khan crossed the Chēttwāye river on the 8th October 1776, and marched southwards to Crānganūr. On the 11th, he made an attempt to surprise the fort, but failed. The Dutch tried to obtain the opinions of the Rajas of Cochin and Travancore, whose interests were identical with theirs in the face of a common enemy. But they were lukewarm. Urgent applications were, therefore, made to Ceylon for reinforcements. The safety of Cochin itself was threatened. Hyder was collecting a strong fleet at Calicut to bring down troops by sea to Vypīn past Crānganūr, so that the fort of Aycōṭṭa might be taken first, and the Crānganūr fort besieged afterwards from the south, whilst Sirdar Khan could invest it from the north. Two armed sloops were placed at the mouth of the Crānganūr river to guard the entrance to the harbour and two merchant-ships were also employed to cover the coast. The forts of Crānganūr and Aycōṭṭa were repaired and strengthened. The

Travancore lines, which commenced from the rear of the Aycōṭṭa fort, were improved, and carried along the southern bank of the river towards the ghauts. Fortunately for the Dutch, a detachment of troops arrived by sea, and the Mysoreans retreated without delivering the threatened blow. They, however, invested Chēṭṭwāye, drove the Dutch from there, and subdued the whole island including the territory of the Raja of Crānganūr except the Dutch fort. Their further advance was impeded by the Travancore lines. The old negotiations were renewed and the reply recently received to Hyder's letter, despatched to Batavia, was sent to Hyder's camp with the customary presents. Hyder now disowned the acts of his general, Sirdar Khan, and professed his great desire for friendly relations with the Dutch East India Company. The Dutch desired very much to recover their lost possessions, and planned an expedition for that purpose in the early part of 1778. They stormed and took the Crānganūr Raja's Palace, and marched up to Chēṭṭwāye and attacked the fort, but, failing to carry it by storm, they retreated towards Crānganūr. The Mysoreans in their turn followed them and attacked the Crānganūr Raja's Palace, whence the Dutch had to retire with loss. In March 1778, the Diwan of Travancore met the Dutch Governor at Cochin, when the latter strongly impressed on the former the necessity of preventing Crānganūr from falling into the hands of the Mysoreans, as that would prove disastrous to the Rajas of Cochin and Travancore. He, therefore, requested the Diwan to co-operate with the Dutch in their attempt to keep out Hyder. Meanwhile, the crafty Governor was in correspondence with Hyder respecting an offensive and defensive alliance with him. But the Sultan spurned these overtures, and made the Dutch Governor clearly to understand that he was only waiting to have leisure to turn his arms against the Dutch East India Company. The Governor became alarmed, and, as a last resource, turned to the Raja of Travancore for assistance. He helped the Raja with competent engineers and military men to improve the lines. Hyder died in December 1782, and his son, Tippu, was a more unrelenting foe than his politic father. For a time, he had to fix his undivided attention nearer home. But in 1787, the Sultan set out on an expedition to "improve the morals and realise the revenue of the Malabar country," and marched to Calicut. The Dutch were alarmed at the approach of Tippu, and negotiations were at once set on foot to revive the Dutch Governor's desire of entering into an offensive and defensive alliance with Mysore. In an extant letter, dated September 1788, we find it stated that Tippu's sepoys would shortly be at Crānganūr to assist the Dutch against Travancore; and the writer who writes from Calicut ends by saying, "Time will show, if he (Tippu Sultan) really wishes to assist us, or is merely serving his own interests." Next year, Tippu requested his vassal, the Cochin Raja, to negotiate with the Dutch for the purchase of the forts of Cochin, Crānganūr, and Aycōṭṭa ; but the attempt to purchase them for Tippu failed. Meanwhile, the Raja of Travancore had sought the aid of the British, who deputed Major Bannerman to advise him on military affairs, especially with regard to the expected operations in the vicinity of Crānganūr and the Travancore lines. They also lent the Travancore king the aid of a detachment of British troops, encamped three corps in the rear of the " lines, " and declared that any attack on the Travancore lines would be taken as equivalent to a declaration of war against them. Governor Holland of Madras, who was suspected of being partial to Tippu, however, made the Raja clearly to understand that, if he proved to be aggressive, he could expect no assistance from the British. The detachment of the British troops was to assist the Raja only in Travancore territory ; and, as the fort of Aycōṭṭa and Crānganūr belonged to the Dutch, and stood on a portion of land claimed by the Raja of Cochin, who was an acknowledged tributary of the Sultan, it was open to Tippu to capture these forts, and force his way through the island of Vypīn into the territories of the Raja of Cochin, and pass on to Travancore, without embroiling himself with the English, and without in any way being impeded by the Travancore lines. In this predicament, the Raja of Travancore in consultation with, and under the advice of, Major Bannerman, the political envoy accredited by the Government of Madras to his court, and with the tacit consent of the Governor, negotiated with the Dutch for the purchase of the forts. Though Tippu himself had promised to pay double the price offered by the king of Travancore, the Dutch authorities thought that they would close the bargain with Travancore, as that would enable them to keep the Mysorean army at bay by involving the English in the storm that was slowly brewing. The purchase was effected in August 1789, and led to a good deal of controversy at the time, both the Governor of Madras and the Gover-ror-General disapproving of it at first. However, the transfer was made, and Travancore troops were admitted into the forts. This incensed Tippu, and he began his march to storm the Travancore lines. The attack was made on the 29th of December, and ended in complete failure. Mortified and enraged at this, the Sultan sent for siege-artillery to Seringapatam, and swore that he would not quit the place till he had demolished 'this contemptible wall.' In April, a breach was effected of about three quarters of a mile in extent, and resistance became impossible. The Mysoreans overran the country, and Tippu appeared before the Crānganūr fort, the garrision of which fled in utter dismay. Severe measures taken by the commander of the fort were, however, successful in bringing back the garrison. Tippu now tried to threaten the Dutch to surrender the fort into his hands. At this critical juncture, Colonel Hartley arrived from

Bombay with a regiment of Europeans and two regiments of sepoys, and landed at Crānganūr. A close examination of the fort showed that it was untenable; and, as the united corps were not deemed equal to undertake any offensive operations, Col. Hartley withdrew the Travancore garrison from the fort on the night of the 7th May, and early next morning, the Mysoreans occupied it. Previous to evacuating it, the garrison within had already begun the demolition of the fort, and Tippu's general, Lally, lost no time in completing it. Lord Cornwallis now declared war with Tippu who was soon brought to book. Both the States of Travancore and Cochin became tributaries of the English East India Company at the end of the Mysore war, and Crānganūr, which belonged to a petty chief under the suzerainty of the Cochin Raja, came under the British Government.

So early as 1616, the English East India Company had opened a factory at Crānganūr. The very first engagement made by the English with any Malabar power was entered into at Crānganūr with the Zamorin on the 10th of March 1615 [1616] by Captain Keeling. In this treaty, the Zamorin stipulated that he and his successors would continue to be friendly with the English, and promised "to endeavour the taking in of the fort of Crānganūr, and to possess the English thereof as their own, together with the island thereof." The object of the Zamorin in entering into this treaty was to curb the power of the Portuguese and their ally, the Raja of Cochin, with the assistance of the English. But Captain Keeling having sailed away without affording any assistance, nothing came out of the above engagement, and the English had to wait for 170 years and more to possess themselves of the place consecrated by the very first treaty entered into by them with any Malabar sovereign.

The present condition of Crānganūr is, indeed, deplorable. Having continued to be prosperous and important almost from pre-historic times till the middle of the 14th century, it has since fallen into complete ruin and decay. Crānganūr was already on the decline when the Portuguese arrived in India. "Years ago," says the Revd. Richard Collins, " by one of those strange vicissitudes which so often mark the progress of time, Crānganūr was shorn of her glory. It was no Nebuchadnezzar, no Alexander, no Titus, that blotted out her name from history, and 'laid her stones and her timbers and her dust in the midst of the waters;' and made her 'a place to spread nets upon' —a mere village, as she is now, of a few fishermen's huts. She fell a prey to the geological instability of the coast, before referred to. Like so many things of the earth, the very foundation on which she was built was insecure; the entrance to her harbour became chocked up; the remorseless monsoon washed away her bulwarks, and, losing her trade, she lost also her inhabitants." The opening of the Cochin outlet for the discharge of the monsoon flood of waters into the sea and the consequent chocking up of the Crānganūr outlet led to the forming of the present beautiful harbour of Cochin. That tolled the death-knell of the commercial prosperity of Crānganūr. Deprived of its natural harbour, it gradually dwindled into insignificance. Its trade fled northwards to Calicut and southwards to the new harbour of Cochin, and with its trade its prosperity also. The subsequent efforts of the Portuguese to revive Crānganūr were of no avail, and it now remains only a name in history.

Pliny described Crānganūr as *primum emporium Indiac*. Well did it deserve that proud distinction. Situated on the coast, eighteen miles to the north of Cochin, at a place where the great rivers that form the only means of communication with the interior debouched into the sea, it attained an unrivalled prosperity from very early times. It was through this port that the Hindus received from the Phoenicians

CRANGANORE TEMPLE.

To face page 326.]

their art of writing; it must have been from this port that the shipmen of Solomon of Israel, 'that knew the sea,' obtained their valuable cargoes of gold, ivory, sandalwood, etc.; it was to this port that the Greek merchant and mariner Hippalos, that Columbus of ancient times, in his voyage for the discovery of a sea-route to India, was carried by the western monsoons; it was here, according to common tradition, that the Apostle St. Thomas landed first, planted the Cross and preached Christianity in the opening years of the first century of the Christian Era (52 A. D.); it was here, not long after, that the Jews arrived after the destruction of the second temple and the final desolation of Jerusalem (A. D. 69) and founded a colony; it was at this port, that the Romans had, according to one version of the *Peutinger Tables*, set up a temple of Augustus and stationed a garrison to protect their trade; it was here that Thomas Cama landed from Syria, when he brought with him a fresh colony of Syrian Christians; it was here that the early Chēra kings had their seat, and the Chēra king Chenkudduvan held his prosperous court, and ruled over the Chēra Empire in the first century of the Christian era; it was here that the great Chēramān Perumāl, Bhāskara Ravi Varma, lived and ruled over Kērala prosperously for thrice the period of his allotted term. It was here that he was visited by certain Muhammadan pilgrims, who, according to tradition, succeeded in inducing the Perumāl to turn Muhammadan and undertake the Haj; it was here that the Perumāl, on the eve of his renunciation of religion and empire and embarkation for Mecca, is reputed to have distributed Malabar among the many princes who own it even now; it was here that his emissaries from Mecca founded a Muhammadan colony and built the first mosque in Malabar. The Portuguese, the first European nation to arrive and found an empire in India, had seriously thought of making Cranganūr their seat of Government, but preferred Cochin, as that place offered, since the formation of the harbour there in the year 1341, a better site. Nevertheless, the Portuguese fortified Cr̄ānganūr and made it the seat of the first Roman Catholic Archbishopric in India. The Dutch ousted the Portuguese, and were of opinion that Cr̄ānganūr was the key of Malabar. Verily it proved to be so when Hyder and Tippu led the Mysorean hordes to the west coast. The purchase by Travancore of the fort of Cr̄ānganūr and its destruction by Tippu led to the third Mysorean war, at the close of which Malabar passed into the possession of the English, who had, as early as 1616, established a factory there, and entered into a treaty with the Zamorin, perhaps the very first treaty between the English and an Indian sovereign. At present, the site of the fort is a wilderness which is being gradually cleared and brought under cultivation. Where once the noble Cathedral walls resounded to the sonorous prayers chanted by the Roman Cath olic priests, the jackals now keep up a chorus of monotonous howling. The old fort is no more. It is in utter ruins. Even its very site is soon changing its configuration. Its old moat is the haunt of crocodiles and paddy bird. The solitary tower that had for years withstood the corroding influence of the dashing waves has at last succumbed and fallen into the backwater. "The solitary stranger," says Day, "perhaps disturbs a snake in his path or an owl in the dense overhanging trees, but rarely a mortal will meet his eye." What strange tales would history unfold, if only the gift of speech were allowed to the stones and pebbles that lie embedded in the bosom of the river that flows by the once famous fort of Cr̄ānganūr!

There is a plan of Cr̄ānganūr, as it was, in Valentyers' great work on the Dutch Colonies. There is a view given in Baldeus also.

7. **Paravur**. Por̄acāḍ is evidently a misprint for Paravūr̄ or Par̄ūr̄. For the territories that lie on the opposite side of the Cr̄ānganūr river belong to the

Raja of Pařūř, whereas Pořacād is situated 45 miles to the south of Cochin.

7(a). **Palliport or Pallipuram.** Pallipōřț or Pallippuřam is situated on the island of Vypīn between Aycōțța on the one side and Cochin on the other. It is also known as Manappāḍ. The Portuguese had occupied the place and built a small fort to serve as an out-post to the larger and stronger one at Cřānganūr. They also built a Syrian College here in 1587 which was subsequently removed from there. The Dutch captured the fort from the Portuguese in February 1661. Captian Nieuhoff gives the following account of the capture: "Over against the isle of Baypin we met with 15 or 16 sail under the command of Mr. Adrian Vander Meyden, who was sent thither to attack the fortress of Palipatnam; we went immediately aboard the 'Ulieland,' where we paid our respects to the Admiral, who enjoined us to send all our land and sea men ashore, to assist at the taking of this fortress; which being done accordingly, and the Dutch forces marching in good order to the attack, they found to their great astonishment, that the enemy had deserted the place and left only one old woman and a boy behind them; thus we became masters of this stronghold, without striking a blow." [1]

The Dutch sold it along with the fort of Cřānganūr to Travancore. According to Day, "Here is a holy pagoda, where trials by crocodile-ordeals took place, after the prisoner had sworn before the idol. Just to the north of this is a ditch dividing the Cochin territory from that of the British and that of Travancore. This ditch is probably a remnant of the Travancore lines. In 1743, this territory was under the free lord Pāliaț Achan. To the north, and close to the ditch, is the Pallipōřț Lazarets, or Leper Asylum: it and the ground on which it stands, are British property. Originally a Portuguese building, erected as a Syrian

1. Voyages.

College, it was turned by the Dutch to its present use. Next to this is a fine church."

8. **The Zamorin's Capture of the Dutch Fort at Chettwaye.** We have other sources of information regarding this war with the Zamorin.

On the 10th of September 1691, the Dutch gave up Chēttwāye, situated at the northernmost extremity of the island, to the Zamorin in pursuance of their policy "of curtailing military expenditure in the East." The Zamorin took this opportunity to secure a strong position in the flank of his hereditary foe, the Raja of Cochin, and contemplated the erection of a fort there. The English were then in high favour with the Zamorin, and the agent at Tellicherry, Mr. Admas, who had his own interest also to serve, urged on that prince the necessity of having a strong position at his southern boundary. The Dutch, on being informed of this, in the year 1714, obtained from the Raja of Cochin with the consent of the Raja of Ayrūr, a plot of ground to which both Cochin and the Zamorin laid claim. The Dutch, with the assistance of the Rajas of Cochin and Ayrūr, forthwith commenced erecting a fort at the mouth of the Chēttwāye river, which was declared to be the boundary between the Zamorin's and the Cochin Raja's territories. The English, whose position in Malabar was being thus undermined, at once induced the Zamorin to thwart the Dutch; and, acting under the advice of Mr. Adams, the Zamorin had recourse to a stratagem. Captain Alexander Hamilton, who was then travelling on the coast, has left us an account of what took place at the time. He says, "The Dutch made small account who had the best title, but carried on their work with diligence. The Dutch were building the fort at Chēttwāye, and the Zamorin got some of his men in the disguise of labourers to be employed by them, and to take an opportunity of surprising the Dutch. The two lieutenants, who had the overseeing of the work, were one evening diverting themselves with a game at tables in a guard room about half a mile from the fort. They had left some of their soldiers go straggling about, and the disguised natives took the opportunity to kill the sentinels, signal to the ambuscade, and take the half-built fort. One of the lieutenants in attempting to retake it was killed, the other, thinking it impracticable to attack greater forces within than he had without, embarked for Cochin with his men. I was fortuned to be at Cochin where he and his men arrived, and by a court martial he was sentenced to be shot, which sentence I saw executed. The Zamorin caused the English flag to be hoisted, and the fort was destroyed."[1] Soon after this, the Zamorin, in February 1715, entered into an agreement with Mr. Adams, permitting the English to build a warehouse at Chēṯṯwāye and keep a person there for trade purposes. It will be remarked that Hamilton's account of the capture of the fort slightly differs from that of our author, who does not make mention of the stratagem by means of which the Zamorin and his adherents effected it.

The Dutch spared no time in retrieving this disaster. Councillor William Bakkar Jacobtz at once took the field at the head of 4000 troops and recovered all lost ground. The war ended, as Hamilton observes, in a "dishonourable and a disadvantageous peace" to the Zamorin and the English in the year 1717. On the 10th of April of that year, the Dutch formally resumed possession of Chēṯṯwāye fort and hoisted their flag. It was named Fort William, and Heer Wilhem Blasser, Captain-Lieutenant, and first Commandant thereof, died there on the 2nd of February 1729, as his tombstone lying at the Chēṯṯwāye public bungalow still attests.

9. **A Pagger.** A small fortified village or hamlet. It is a Malay word meaning a 'fence, enclosure.'

1. Hamilton's Account of the East Indies.

It occurs in the sense of 'Factory' in the Charters of the East India Company.[1]

10. **Mangatta Achen.** Mangāṭṭa Achen was the hereditary prime minister of the Zamorin and the Commander-in-chief of his forces.

11. **Mapranam.** Mapowvane stands for Māpṙa-ṇam, Towtamburi for Ṭaṭṭampuḷa, Avatorte for Akan-ṭuruṭ and Ourganoor for Urakam.

12. **Identification of some places and names.** Patracotti stands for Pāṭiri Kōṭṭa. "Poenctoar Namburi". This is a mistake for Punnaṭṭūr Nambidi.

13. **Terms of the Treaty with the Zamorin.** By the terms of the treaty, the Zamorin was obliged to rebuild the fort he had demolished at Cheṙṙwāye, to pay 10,625 rix dollars towards the expenses of the war; to pay the Dutch East India Company seven per cent on all the pepper exported out of his dominions for ever; and to give up his possessions south of Cheṙṙ-wāye, which were divided between the Dutch and their ally the Cochin Raja,—a bitter pill for the beaten Zamorin. The terms of this treaty were believed to be so advantageous that, when, later on, the Zamorin, under altered circumstances, wished to enter into a fresh treaty with the Dutch in 1758, the Dutch Governor preferred to leave the treaty unsigned, thinking that the treaty of 1717 should remain in full force, as this new one was rather detrimental to the Company's reputation.

14. **Kolattiri.** The Europeans use this term to denote the Kōlaṭṭiri or Chiṙakkal Rajas, who ruled over North Malabar. This country was known as Kōlaṭṭu-nāḍ.

15. **The Ali Raja of Cannanore.** With regard to this Chief, we derive the following information from Logan's *Manual of the Malabar District*. It is

1 P. 324.

said that Chēramān Perumāl invited a Muhammadan and his wife to come from his native land of Āryapuram, and installed them at Cannanore. The Muhammadan was called Āli Raja, that is, the Lord of the deep or the sea. "The Kēralōṭppaṭṭi," says Mr. Logan, "would trace the family history (of the Āli Raja) back to the Chēramān Perumāl, but tradition is tolerably unanimous that the first chieftain of the family was a Nayar, by name Arayankulangara Nayar, one of the ministers of the Kōlaṭṭiri, who is said to have lived about the eleventh or the beginning of the twelveth century A. D., and who embraced Islam and adopted the name of Muhammad or Muhammad Ali. Owing to his skill and ability, it is said, the Kōlaṭṭiri retained him as his minister even after his conversion, and his successors were known as the Mammali Kiṭāvūs, who were hereditary ministers of the Kōlaṭṭiris. Tradition says that Mahammad Ali and his successors were admitted to all the important counsels of the Kōlaṭṭiri and that they used to stand on such occasions with sword-point resting on a box, implying that, what ever was determined on, they would find the money to do it." Hamilton gives an interesting account of these chieftains after they had become independent of the Kōlaṭṭiri. He describes Cannanore as a pretty long town, "built in the bottom of the bay" and as independent of the Dutch, then stationed in fort Anjelo. It was, under "Adda Raja, a Muhammadan Malabar Prince, who upon occasion can bring near 20,000 men into the field." "His Government is not absolute, nor is it hereditary; and instead of giving him the trust of the treasury which comes by taxes and merchandise, they have chests made on purpose with holes made in their lids, and their coin being all gold, whatever is received from the treasurer is put into these chests by these holes and each chest has four locks, and their keys are put in the hands of the Raja, the Commissioner of Trade, the Chief Judge, and the Treasurer, and when there is occasion for money none can be taken out without all these four be present or their deputies."

16. **The Relations with the Portuguese and the Dutch.** The Portuguese were the bitter enemies of the Muhammadans, and naturally they came into conflict with the Āli Rajas. The relations between these chieftains and their suzerain, the Kōlaṭṭiris, also became strained, and, when the Dutch ejected the Portuguese from the coast, the Āli Rajas became their friends. The Dutch often made use of these chieftains to molest the English. On the appearance of the Mysoreans on the Malabar coast, the Āli Raja at once joined them. But the Mysoreans were eventually driven out of Malabar by the British, under whom Āli Raja is now a petty tributary within contracted limits and possessing little or no power.

17. **Anjengo. The English and the Ranee of Attingal.** "In the year 1684," says Mr. Logan, "the English East India Company obtained from the Rāṇi of Aṭṭingal a sandy spit of land at Anjengo[1] on the sea

1. According to some accounts, the first settlement made by the English in Travancore territory was a few years earlier than the one at Anjengo, but the dates of early travellers are very unreliable. Hamilton who sailed along the coast between A. D. 1683 and 1723 refers to the English factories of Ruttera (Vittur) and Brinjan (Villaniam), both to the south of Anjengo, as having been already founded. He says "when our factories were at Ruttera and Brinjan, they sent a yearly present to the Queen of Attingen whose court is about four leagues within land from Anjengo. In Anno 1685, when the present was sent, a young beautiful English gentleman had the honour to present it to her Black Majesty and, as soon as the Queen saw him, she fell in love with him, and next day made proposals of marriage to him, but he modestly refused so great an honour: however, to please her Majesty, he staid at court a month or two, and it is reported treated her with great civility." (Pinkerton, Vol. VIII, p. 383.)

Colonel John Biddulph, however, observes that, in 1688, Rani Ashure (Aswati, the first Star of the lunar month. The members of the royal house of Travancore are known generally as those born under such and such a Star. This is the Rani referred to as "the Princess' mother who had been born in the planet called

coast, about 20 miles north of Trevandrum, with a view to erect a factory [1] and fortify it." The place had been frequented by the Portuguese, who, after a time, were ousted by the Dutch. The choice of the site was in many respects unfortunate. There was no drinking water within three miles of the place. The open roadstead afforded very few facilities for shipping. There was no safe anchorage. Ships could not anchor under ten or eleven fathoms, and, to a considerable distance seaward, the coast was rocky. The surf, especially towards the south, was so bad that even ship's boats could scarcely land with safety. Hamiliton points out that the fort "might as well have (been) built near the red cliffs to the northward from whence they have their water for drinking and where there is good anchor ground and a tolerable good landing place for boats in the N. E. monsoon." But in other respects the selection was not bad. It commanded the line of water communication towards the north, and, when the place was fortified, some years later, the cannon of the fort commanded the river, the main artery of traffic, as well as the shipping in the roadstead. Pepper and calicoes of excellent quality were procurable in abundance. In 1690,

Ashwady " in the agreement, dated 5th April 1729, between the Princess of Atingah and Ezachiel King, to be quoted later on) invited the English to form a trading settlement in her dominions which lay extending along sixty miles of coast, and two were formed, at Vittoor (Returch) and Villanjuen (Brinjone); but for some reason, she became dissatisfied with the English, and the hostility of the Dutch, in spite of the alliance between the two countries in Europe, caused great trouble. The two settlements being, in the words of Hamilton, " naked places were subject to the insults of the courtiers whose avarice is seldom or never satisfied."

1. According to the Travancore State Manual, " the first political and commercial relations between Travancore and the East India Company began in 1673 when a factory was established at Anjengo." (Vol. III, p. 578)

permission was obtained from the Queen to erect a fort here, but there is no record to prove this.[1] But, according to Col. Biddulph, it was only in 1693 that the Rāṇi granted the site for a fort at Anjengo, together with the monopoly of the pepper trade of Āṯṯinga, and he attributes the grant to the successful diplomacy of John Brabourne who was sent to Āṯṯinga in the month of November of that year.[2] Soon, the Dutch protests and intrigues aroused the Rāṇi's suspicions. She ordered Brabourne to stop his building. Finding him deaf, she tried to starve out the English by cutting off supplies; but, as the sea was open, the land blockade proved ineffectual. She then sent an armed force against Brabourne, which was speedily put to flight, and terms of peace were arranged. The fort was completed in 1695, and a most flourishing trade in pepper and cotton-cloth speedily grew up. The fort was 86 yards square and was built in the Vaḍakkakam division. Anjengo became the first port of call for outward bound ships. The Anjengo fortification appeared so formidable to the Dutch that they closed their factories at Cochin, Quilon, and Cannanore; so says Bruce. Within two years of the erection of the fort, it had to withstand a violent attack from the Travancoreans. The piratical acts of the notorious Captain Kydd, who had been sent out on an expedition from England to put down European piracy in Indian waters, caused native powers to suspect the real character of the English Company which had made settlements on the coast. In November 1697, the Travancoreans attacked Anjengo on the plea that the factors were really pirates. Ever after this, the relations between the English factors and the Travancoreans remained strained. "About 1700, Rāṇi Ashure died, and the little principality", says Col. Biddulph, "fell into disorder. It was a tradition that only women

1. Logan. p. 345.

2. *The Pirates of Malabar and an English Woman in India Two Hundred Years Before*, p. 271.

THE RUINS OF PALLIPPURAM FORT.

To face page 329.]

The North East View of Angengo Fort on the Coast of Mallabar

ANJENGO FORT.

To face page 336.]

should reign, and Ashure's successor was unable to make her authority felt. The Poolas, (Piḷḷamār or nobles), who governed the four districts into which the principality was divided, intrigued for power against each other, and before long the Rāṇi became a puppet in the hands of Poola Venjamutta." We see from our author's seventh letter that the differences between the English factors at Anjengo and the natives came to a crisis in 1721, when the chief and his councillors were foully murdered and the English were not in a position to take immediate vengeance upon their enemies. These differences were, however, made up later. The enemies whom the English had to confront were really not the king of Travancore and the queen of Aṟṟingal, but the Eṭṭuvīṭṭil Piḷḷamār, who were a power in the State, holding vast estates and unbounded authority. The royal family had been for some time completely under their subjection, the kings being but mere puppets in their hands, while they acted as Mayors of the Palace, and governed the country, though in the name of the king. About this time, a prince of the Travancore house, more brave and daring than any before him, swore to exterminate the Piḷḷamār and to bring the country under his control and, for this, he sought the aid of the Anjengo factors. The incident of the massacre, which was perpetrated at the instance of the Piḷḷamārs, furnished a strong motive for the English to take the side of the prince. The English East India Company had made a settlement, at Anjengo mainly for trading in 'pepper and piece-goods' and the position of affairs in Travancore was then, and for some time to come, scarcely conducive to foster the Company's commercial enterprise. The country was divided into a number of small fiefs ruled by an oppressive and unscrupulous nobility under the direction of the Eṭṭuvīṭṭil Piḷḷamār, who were the heads of the Nayar Ṭaṟa organisation—an organisation which had been, as observed before, originally designed as a bulwark against royal power, but which had latterly

AQ.

deteriorated into an organised engine of oppression. The Yōgaṭṭil Pōṫṫimār, or the Brahman chiefs of the Paḍmanābha Swāmi temple of Trivandrum, also exercised authority to a large extent. These and the Eṭṭuvīṭṭil Piḷḷamār had quite thrown into the shade all royal authority, so that the English factors at Anjengo found the country not at all favourable for trade. The furtherance of their interests required the presence of a despotic monarch in a position to assign to them monopolies of the articles they wanted to trade in. The reigning Raja was weak and had called to his aid a prince of extraordinary ability, whose counsels prevailed in the court of Travancore. The prince at once set himself in opposition to the Brahmans and Piḷḷamārs whom he swore to exterminate. The unerring political sagacity of the prince pointed to the English as the rising power in India, on whom reliance could be placed; and, under his advice, the Raja entered into a treaty with Dr. Alexander Orme, the Chief of Anjengo, on the 25th April 1723, which ran as follows :—

"Covenant and conditions, which the Prince of Neyatingarai, by order of the king of Travancore, settled in the following agreement with the Governor, Mr. Alexander Orme, 25th April 1723.

"Article 1. The king of Travancore, by the end of June of the current year, is bound to order the erection of a fort in his country at Collache, and to give the die with people to coin fanams on account of the Honourable Company.

"2. If. within the time specified, a fort is not built at Collache, the Honourable Company may bring the die to Anjengo, and the Government will be obliged to send men to Anjengo to coin the fanams.

"3. The fortress which is to be built shall be at the cost of Government, as well as the pay of the people placed in it.

"4. The artillery and munitions of war for the fort, the Honourable Company is obliged to supply.

"5. After the erection of the fort at Collache, the die can be taken thither and the coinage of fanams carried on.

"6. The Government will be in league and united in good friendship with the Honourable Company.

"7. Thus, by order of the king of Travancore, was this treaty adjusted between myself, Prince of Neyatingara, and Commander Alexander Orme, on the part of the Honourable Company and I have affixed to this writing my signature and sent it by Ramen Ramen, who drew it up."[1]

Three months later, another engagement was entered into which has reference to the incident of 1721. The English had evidently to carry the war into 'the queen of Āṭṭinga's' country, owing to the massacre of the Chief of Anjengo and his men and the subsequent attack on the fort by the Piḷḷamārs. The terms of this engagement with Dr. Orme, of the 15th August 1723, make it clear that the enemies the factors had to fight in Travancore were the recalcitrant barons who were rebelling against their legitimate sovereign and not the king of Travancore or the queen of Āṭṭingal.

Dr. Orme had already entered into a treaty with the queen, copy of which was forwarded to the Council in September 1722. The treaty was guaranteed by the Rāṇi's brother, the king of Travancore, who is styled the Raja of Chiṇganathy (Signatti.)

" Copy of the ōla written by the king of Travancore to the Chief, Mr. Alexander Orme, 15th August 1723:—

" Received, through the Vicar, an ōla from the Commander, and understood its purports, as well as all the things the Vicar was requested to communicate to us. Herewith a list (of conditons), and I shall be bound to observe all that is declared in it."[1]

1. Malabar, Vol. III, p. 9.

" Owing to the loss sustained by the Honourable Company in the capture of Attinga, and the money and artillery which the enemies robbed in our country, the Honourable Company have resolved, in spite of money expenses, to put down the enemies and subject the country to the king, we are ready to do anything, which the Honourable Company may require, and shall personally come there and punish the enemies there in the best manner you may desire, regarding which we affirm to do without fail and wish to know when we must come there with our army. Besides this, Mr. Adams has much helped the king of Colastre, and, as the Commander is his brother-in-law, hope that the same favour will be done to this Government.

" All the other things, the Vicar will tell the Commander."

" Copy of the list (of conditions) made by the king of Travancore, who pledges to observe everything contained in it.

" Article. 1. Owing to the fault committed by Sendu Comodu against the Honourable Company, I will oblige him to give a writing, in public, begging pardon for the fault he has been guilty of against the Honourable Company.

" 2. The arms which he seized from the dead soldier, I will oblige him to return and pay a penalty for the fault.

" 3. For the parents of the dead soldier, I will oblige him to pay them 1,001 fanams by way of fine.

" 4. The vessels which pass by without paying the dues, excepting the ships of Europeans, the Honourable Company may send a watch-barge to seize all such vessels at Collache and direct them to pay the customs for the expenses of which I shall bind myself to pay 4000 fanams yearly to the Honourable Company.

"5. To all the ships on my borders and of my vassals, which should pay customs, I will give my writing.

"6. In future times, any of my vassals acting in such a manner against the Honourable Company, both jointly should punish them and for which I shall give my writing to the Honourable Company.

"7. In lieu of the dead soldier, I will be obliged to send another to the Honourable Company.

"8. As Collache has been made over to the Government of Landatu Curipa, at least on the half of the place which properly belongs to me, I shall soon direct a Banksaul to be made and a post for the banner to be planted.

"9. All the piece-goods and other things which the Honourable Company require, I shall order the merchants to supply.

"10. I shall soon confirm, by writing, that I shall not give to any other European nation any goods, which are necessary to the Honourable English Company.

"11. The customs on exports and imports of the goods, the Honourable Company may receive from merchants, but the rate of exchange should be adjusted.

"12. Every year in various kinds, which the Honourable Company require, I will order to supply up to 1,00,000 piece-goods.

"13. In order to adjust the dues leviable from merchants, the Honourable Company will be obliged to give in gold or other articles on account, to the extent of 6,000 fanams yearly.

"All these things referred to above, I did grant, since the Honourable Company asked me."[1]

1. Malabar, Vol. III, pp.11—12.

Eager as the English at Anjengo were to come to the assistance of the Raja, "in spite of money expenses, to put down his enemies and subject the country" to him, their strength in the south did not permit them to back up this resolution with armed forces. There is nothing to show that they did anything further to attain their avowed object than exchange arms and munitions of war for pepper, spices and piece-goods. To put down the rebellious chiefs, the king had to go over the border and seek the aid of his old enemies, the Nayakas of Madura.

However, amicable relations were restored and continued to subsist between the Princess of Āttingal and the Anjengo factors; and we see, on the 5th April 1729, the Princess entering into an agreement, "written on a silver ōla (cadjan-plate), with Ezachiel King Esqr., chief of Anjengo."

"Translation of an agreement written on a silver ōla entered into by the Princess of Āttingah and Ezachiel King Esqr., Chief of Anjengo, on the 5th April 1729.

"On the 25th Mēḍam 904 has been wrote this. This is the term agreed for the continuation of union of the English Company with the Princess of Āttingah: That all past accounts to the year 904 have adjusted and settled and have passed receipts. The duties, customs and all other things agreeable to a writing passed between the Princess' mother who had born in the planet called Ashwedy, and the Chief John Braban are to be continued, and from the year next ensuing of 905 (1730), the company will present yearly with 75 Venetians to the Princess, and soon after they can begin to receive pepper in the assistance of my Writers. To each candy they will give me the custom of 5 Rajees (50 chukroms) from which I allow 20 per cent to the comprny. The Chief must have goodwill and diligence to make the trade more augmented that, by which means, the Estate may have more profits. All pepper that may have in my country, I will cause to be transported to the fort of Anjengo free of any embarrassment whatever in these territories. And the Company must not give to any other person but to me the customs for pepper of my country. Should there be any embarrassment of whatever person, I will get it removed. All pepper of my country I will not give to any other person but to the English Company.

" In witness I, Tevan Changaren, Writer to the Princess, by her Royal Order, have wrote this ōla of agreement with my own hand in the govern of the Chief Ezachiel King.

" Shri Tulliom. "[1]

Later on, in 1731, the factors found themselves strong enough to exact reparation from the Princess of Āttingal for the wrong their former Chief and his Councillors had suffered ten years back at the hands of the Pillamārs who, it may be remembered, were the common enemies of the Princess and the English. Perhaps the factors who had the unanswerable argument of powder and shot behind them, justified themselves on the plea that the murder was committed and the subsequent attack on the fort was made by the Pillamārs in the name of the queen. On the 10th of January 1731, "Hezakial King, Chief of Anjengo" obtained " two ōlas by which the king of Travancore and the queen of Āttinga confirmed the grant of the gardens Palatady and Cottudals to the Honourable Company."

"Copies of two ōlas by which the king of Travancore and the queen of Āttinga confirmed the grant of the gardens of Palatady and Cottudals to the Honourable Company, in the time of Hezakiah King, on the 10th January 1731.

" Towards Cherreungue are the gardens of Palatady and Cottudali, which were formerly bought by

1. Malabar, Vol. III, pp. 17 and 18.

the Commander of Anjengo, but when, on the 15th April 1721, he and ten other persons went to Āṭṭinga to make presents to the queen, they were killed by the treachery of Pullayas and Karikars, who seized the money of the Honourable Company. Seeing the loss and the damage thus done to the Honourable Company, we have ceded the same gardens to them, giving up their revenues and the right of cutting trees and all other privileges, which the Company may take, and they and heirs may enjoy these gardens without any obstacle or having any obstruction; but we are obliged to ask for a free passage and protection on the part of the Honourable Company. Thus, in truth, we confirm (the grants) with our signatures to the Commander, on the 10th January 1731."[1]

By this time, the famous Mārṭṭāṇḍa Varma had succeeded to the throne of Travancore and set himself earnestly to retrieve the fortunes of his fallen house. In his attempts to subjugate the rebellious Pillamārs and other refractory noblemen, he always received timely help from the Anjengo factors in the shape of war materials.

" A contract made with the king of Travancore and the Honourable Company for 1500 candies of pepper on their part by John Spencer, Esqr., their Chief, and the king's by Quejavan Mattanden Poolah and Porico Mouza Marcar.

" The king of Travancore shall be obliged to deliver to the Honourable Company, from the 6th July 1758 to 30th July 1759, fifteen hundred (1500) candies of pepper at the rate of eighty-two (82) rupees per candy, exclusive of the customs to be paid as usual.

" Of this pepper, 1,200 candies shall be delivered into warehouse before the 31st January next, and the remaining 300 candies to complete the whole quantity by the 30th July 1759.

1. Malabar, Vol. III, p. 19.

"It is also conditioned that the Honourable Company for each 500 Candies shall deliver 200 arms and other things as usual, but not till each 500 candies is received first into warehouse.

"In confirmation we have passed this ōla of contract signed by us this 6th day of July 1758 and have received on account of this contract 10,000 rupees ready money, and an order on Tellicherry for the payment of 10,006 rupees there.

"Quejavan Mattandere
"Porico Mouza Marcar."[1]

"These are to certify that we, Mallen Chunbagaramen, Saruvadi Carriacar, and Matanda Pulla, Saruvadi Carriacar, Ministers from the king of Travancore, have contracted by His Majesty's order with Thomas Whitehill Esquire, Chief of Anjengo, for the Honourable English Company, to deliver (2000) two thousand candies of pepper at the rate of (82) eighty two rupees per candy of five hundred and sixty (560) pounds by the 31st December 1764, a thousand of which to be delivered by the 30th of April next. For every five hundred candies that is weighed off, the king shall be entitled to demand 200 muskets with bayonets and the other articles the same as the last contract which are as follows, viz :—

Scarlet, Superfine	500 yds. 7—2 per yd.
Coarse Red	1000 ,, 3—2 ,,
Red Perpets	5000 ,, 1 Rupee ,,
Lead	100 candies, 50 per candy.

1. From the Diary of Anjengo, dated 6th July 1758. Agreements similar to the above were annually made with Travancore. Vide Anjengo Diaries, dated 6th November 1759, 29th January 1770, 15th June 1773 and 2nd August 1779 (Malabar, Vol. III, p. 108).

AR.

Muskets with bayonets 800 12—2.

" Signed and delivered by us this 1st day of January 1764.

" Malem Pulla.

" Matanda Pulla. "[1]

The relations between the Anjengo factors and the Travancore kings continued to be very satisfactory after this, each assisting the other as far as each could. The Dutch had always watched the proceedings of the English factors with a jealous eye, and suspected that the amicable relations existing between the English and Travancore would, in the long run, lead to an estrangement between themselves and the king. The English at Anjengo had already once in 1696 burnt the Dutch factory there on the plea that it had given cover to one of their enemies. When, in the early part of the 18th century, the relations between the factors and the king were strained owing to the conduct of the Pillamārs, the Dutch at once took the opportunity of fomenting the ill-feeling and inducing the king to expel the English from Anjengo. About the year 1710, when the Dutch were assisting the king of Cochin against the Zamorin in the capture of the fort at Chēṭṭ-wāye, the local authorities reported on the hostile conduct of the Dutch, and the Bombay Government said that they "found it difficult to believe that, during the maintenance of a strict alliance between England and the Netherlands, the Dutch would venture to publicly aid the 'king of Āṭṭeng', in his designs on the English factory at Anjengo, although by underhand dealings they have created a difference which they strove to foment into an open rupture." With the gradual dwindling of their political supremacy on the coast, this

1. From the Diary of the Anjengo factory, dated 24th January 1764. Similar agreements were entered into by the Anjengo Residents. Vide their Diaries, dated 5th April 1782, 8th February 1784, 20th November 1787, 14th December 1788, 10th January 1790. and 20th November 1791, (Malabar, Vol. III, p.112.)

jealousy only increased, and, so late as in 1790, we find amongst the Dutch records of Cochin a formal resolution passed by the Council that the English factory at Anjengo should be destroyed.

When Anjengo was founded, it was given a prominent position in India, being second only to Bombay Castle, its Chief for the time being ranked second in Council. In 1776, it was reduced to the status of a Residency. In 1792, it was reported to be in hopeless decline. In 1809, during the 'Nair war,' when the English had to fight with the rebellious Diwans of Travancore and Cochin, the fort of Anjengo was blockaded. As soon as hostilities ceased and order was restored, the Commercial Residency was abolished, and, in 1810, Anjengo was handed over to the Political Agent in Travancore. In the year 1813, the factory was abolished, and not long after, the revenues of the villages were farmed to the Travancore State. During the Carnatic war, Anjengo was of great use to the English, as a depot for the military stores and as the place from which news of outward-bound ships reached Madras.

Ives visited Anjengo fort during the course of his voyages in 1757. "Anjengo fort," says he, "is small, but neat and strong ; it is a square with four bastions, having eight guns mounted on each, carrying a ball of eighteen pounds. Two of these bastions face the sea, the other two the country. Besides these, there is a line of eighteen or twenty guns, pointing towards the sea, of eighteen and twenty-four pounders. About a pistol-shot from the back of the fort runs a river, which, besides it being a security to the factory, adds much to the agreeable situation of the place. This river has its source in some distant mountains, and descending in a course from the north and east, it afterwards turns in several pleasing meanders so far to the west as to wash the bottom of our factory's garden; and at last winding to the south, it empties itself into the sea. Several beautiful small islands too, which are washed by its current, diversify the scenery, and greatly heighten the beauty of the prospect.

* * * *

" This settlement supplies our East India Company with pepper ; and its situation is also very convenient for giving proper intelligence to our ships touching here from Europe, or from any part of India. The present Chief, Mr. Spencer, is a man of an excellent character, both for probity and sagacity, the greatest harmony and satisfaction subsist among the inhabitants in his Government."

Ives also gives a description of the country around and of the pleasant days he spent at the settlement.[1]

Forbes, the learned author of the *Oriental Memoirs* was the Bombay Member of Council at Anjengo in the year 1772—3. He did not like the place. "I was not partial," he writes, " to Anjengo as a Residency, and the situation I held afforded no emolument equal to the sacrifice of my friends and a delightful society in Bombay." He has, however, left on record a description of the place :— " Anjengo, Lat. 8°-89′ North, 76°-40′ East Long., stands on a narrow bank of sand, its western side bounded by the sea, and the eastern by a river, where there are two rows of houses forming a street about 500 yards in length ; the north end terminated by the Portuguese Church, and the English burying ground ; the south by the fort and lower batteries. This fortress, which reached nearly from the sea to the river, contained store houses, accommodations for the garrison, and apartments for the Chief, who was a member of Council at Bombay. The civil servants and military officers resided in tolerable houses ; the natives generally in thatched huts. The Portuguese Church, white tombs, a respectable fortress, and other accompaniments

1. Voyages, pp. 192-3.

surrounded by cocoanut woods, gave Anjengo a pleasing appearance."[1]

Speaking of the industries of Anjengo, Forbes observes :—"Others made cordage and cables from the coir or husk of the cocoanut, a principal article of trade at Anjengo, where they also manufactured some common cotton-cloth ; but in the kingdom of Travancore were various and extensive manufactures of that article, which in every respect rivalled the long-cloth of the Carnatic. The English gentleman traded in cassia, but the Company had the exclusive purchase and exportation of pepper. Among the Anjengo manufactures may be reckoned the trunks, travelling cases, and camp baskets composed of cane work, covered with a composition of quicklime and butter-milk, mingled with a black powder, prepared from the burnt shells of cocoanut ; that is afterwards repeatedly varnished with the juice of a tree, common in Travancore, until it acquires a polished solidity capable of resisting the weather ; two or three families excelled in gold and silver filigree work, which they executed with the simplest implement; and imitated silver utensils of the best English fashion, with great facility and neatness."[2]

It is interesting to note that, besides that of Forbes, Anjengo is associated with other illustrious names of more moment in the literary world. It was the birth-place of Robert Orme, 'the British Thucydides.' He was born here in 1728, when his father, Dr. Alexander Orme, who had come out as an adventurer, was governor of the place, having secured the office through the influence of his brother-in-law, Mr. Robert Adams, Chief of Tellicherri. But the greatest of the shades that haunt the far off shores of Anjengo is that of Mrs. Daniel Draper, Sterne's 'Eliza' who was born here. The Abbe Raynal's apostrophe to Eliza Draper in his *History of the Settlement and Trade of the East and West*

1. Vol. I, p. 213.
2. Pp. 214-5.

Indies is well known. It begins with "Anjengo, thou art nothing, but thou hast given birth to Eliza!" and goes on in this way over five octavo pages in pica, every paragraph beginning with 'Anjengo' or 'Eliza.'

The present condition of Anjengo is thus described by Mr. J. J. Cotton of the Madras Civil Service. "The turtle who come to lay their eggs in the moon-light on the foreshore, and a handful of poverty-striken fishermen, who devote one-third of their Friday's haul to Mother Church, are now the sole inhabitants of Anjengo. All that is left of the town is a row of squalid houses, and the only street is a dead man's walk between the forsaken flagstaff and the crumbling cemetery, and the back-water on one side and the ocean on the other. The old fort is now quite deserted, and harboured the hyena and the jackal, till it was lately cleared of the thick brushwood under-growth. A portion of the lower mast of the old flagstaff still stands on the north-western angle of the fort."

The term Anjengo is the Anglicised form of the Malayalam name of the place Anchu+ţengu, which mean five cocoanut trees. Probably, when the place was first occupied, there stood only five cocoanut trees on the spot.

The earliest epitaph on a tomb stone to be found in the Anjengo Cemetery is that of "Deborah, the wife of John Braboorn Esquire, Commander of Anjengo. She was born the 4th of November 1676, Mar, the 25th September 1695, deceased September the 2, 1704." The latest of any note is—

"Sacred to the memory of
Mr. Philis Phillipez of Cochin
Superintendent of Police, Anjengo,
Who departed this life on the 3rd July 1827,
aged 55 years and 22 days.

This tomb is erected by his most afflicted Dons Peter John Philipez and Thomas Alexander Philipez."

Subjoined is a list of Chiefs and Residents of the English factory at Anjengo:—

Factory established in	....	1684
John Brabon, Chief about	....	1710[1]
Alexander Orme, do	....	1723
Hezikiah King, do	....	1729
William Wake, do	....	1735
The factory records extant commence from 1st August	....	1744

1. Col. Biddulph says that John Brabourne was sent in the month of November 1693 (p. 271).

Chiefs	Date of assuming charge	Date of retirement	Remarks
R. Bouchier ...		1st February 1750	Was chief on 1st August 1744
T. Byfeld ...	2nd February 1750	5th March 1751	
T. Hodges ...	5th March 1751	7th April 1752	
W. Hornby, acting ...	8th April 1752	14th May 1752	
G. Scott ...	15th May 1752	27th March 1757	
I. Spencer ...	28th March 1757	12th September 1758	
C. Crommelin ...	13th September 1758	20th April 1759	
T. Whitehill ...	21st April 1759	8th September 1769	Died at Anjengo
W. Taylor, acting ...	8th September 1769	9th December 1769	
P. E. Wrench ...	10th December 1769	16th February 1774	
S. Ewart, acting ...	17th February 1774	23rd March 1774	
N. Slackhouse ...	24th March 1774	12th February 1776	The Chiefship was now reduced to a Residency

Residents	Date of assuming charge	Date of retirement	Remarks
G. Bigger, acting ...	13th February 1776	31st December 1776	
J. Torlepe ...	177	8th December 1780	Diary missing
J. Morley ...	9th December 1780	10th December 1781	
J. Hutchinson, acting ...	11th December 1781	22nd March 1782	Mr. Hutchinson was appointed Cochin Commissioner, but, in five months, he returned to Anjengo and died there.
Do. confirmed ...	23rd March 1782	24th February 1796	
I. T. Dyne, acting ...	25th February 1796	17th July 1796	
J. Hutchinson ...	18th July 1796	11th October 1797	
I. T. Dyne, acting ...	12th October 1797	22nd February 1798	
G. Parry ...	23rd February 1798	3rd September 1803	
A. W. Handly ...	4th September 1803	1st July 1808	Died at Anjengo
I T. Dyne, acting ...	1st July 1808	27th October 1808	
I. Smee ...	28th October 1808	27th December 1809	
R. Coward ...	28th December 1809	10th December 1810	Factory abolished, and Anjengo transferred to the Political Resident, Travancore.

The British possessions in Travancore, such as Anjengo and Ṭaṃkachēri, have been recently detached from the Malabar Collectorate and constituted into a separate collectorate under the British Resident of Travancore and Cochin.

18. **The English at Tellicherry.** The English had established a factory at Tellicherry so early as A. D. 1683,[1] having obtained the grant of a site from the Vaḍakilamkūr (Northern Regent), who happened at the time to be the *de facto* ruler of Kōlaṭ-ṅāḍ. Hamilton, who was on the coast about the time, observes, "The place where the factory now stands belonged to the French, who left the mud walls of a fort built by them to serve the English when they first settled there, and for many years continued so, but of late (1727), no small pains and charge have been bestowed on its buildings; but for what reason I know not, for it has no river near it that can want its protection, nor can it defend the road from the insults of the enemies, unless it be for small vessels that can come within some rocks that lie half a mile off or to protect the Company's warehouse, and a Punch House that stands on the seashore, a short pistol shot from the garrison."

The date of the establishment of the factory cannot be exactly ascertained, but the first date of the *General Letter Book* of the factory of the date of the 6th May 1728, is the 24th October 1699. So that it may be safely presumed that it had existed before that, and the date given by Sir George Birdwood, viz., 1683, may possibly be correct. It is mentioned as one of the affiliated factories of Bombay, in 1702, along with Karwar, Calicut and Anjengo.

The necessity of fortifying the place soon became apparent. In 1704—5, one of the rival Kōlaṭṭiri princes of the Uḍaya Mangalam branch, in combination with the neighbouring Nair Chieftain of Iruvāḷiṅāḍ, the

1. Birdwood's *Report on the Old Records of the India Office.*

Kurangōṭ Nair, broke into the Company's warehouse and committed depradations. The Northern Regent was appealed to, and it was pointed out that, unless the place was fortified, the incident might recur. The Regent consented to the building of a fort, and it is said that he himself laid the foundation stone. A house-site of the Ponaṭṭil Poḍuvāl and a hill, Ṭiruvalappan Kuṅṅu, belonging to the Vallura Ṭangal were also taken up with the consent of the owners. The Company also bought up a street of weavers which had existed at the proposed site.

The town, according to Hamilton, lay at the back of the fort with a stone wall round it "to keep out enemies of the Chief's making; for, in 1703, he began a war that still continues, at least there were folks killed in 1723, when I was there." It is necessary to add here that Hamilton who was an interloper bore no goodwill to the factors of Tellicherry or their Chief. "The occasion of the war, as I was informed," says he, "began about a trifle. The Nair that was Lord of the Manor had a royalty, for every vessel that unloaded at Tellicherry, paid, two bales of rice duty, to him. There was another royalty of every tenth fish that came to the market there, and both together did not amount to £ 20 sterling per annum. The Chief either appropriated these royalties to his own, or the company's use, and the Nair complained of the injustice, but had no redress. These little duties were the best part of the poor Nair's subsistence which made it the harder to bear, so his friends advised him to repel force by force, and disturb the factory what he could, which he accordingly did (by the secret assistance of his friends) for above twenty years. The company are the best judges whether the war is likely to bring any profit to their affairs there or no."

On the 20th of August 1708, the Northern Regent formally gave and made over the Tellicherry fort to the Company under the following grant:

"Royal writing from Prince Badacalam curo of Pally Palace to the Honourable English Company in the year 883 (1708).

"The fort of Tellicherry has been built at the request and entreaties made by me as a friend. To acknowledge the love and friendship which the Company bears towards me and my palace, I give and make-over the said fort with its limits to the Honourable Company where no person shall demand, collect and plant. Our custom house will be obliged to give us what has been settled.

"This day, August 20th 883."[1]

This treaty was subsequently confirmed by the Kōlaṭṭiri himself and other members of his family.[2]

Mr. Robert Adams was for a long time Chief of Tellicherry, and directed the affairs of the Company on the Malabar coast. Born and brought up in the country, and knowing the language perfectly well, he wielded considerable influence with the various local chieftains, and it is believed that it was under his advice and with his assistance that the Zamorin fought with the Dutch for the possession of the Chēṭṭwāye fort. Hamilton observes that he advised Mr. Adams "not to embark his masters in that affair, because war was a different province from his," and he adds that it ended in "a dishonourable and disadvantageous Peace," in 1717. Mr. Adams continued to be the Chief of Tellicherry till the 10th March 1728, when he was relieved by John Braddyle. Tellicherry continued to be a place of great importance to the English, specially during the attempted Mysorean conquest of Malabar.

19. **The Danes.** Of the European nations who made settiements in Malabar, the Danes were the least successful. They owned but few warehouses or factories, and were such a poor and lazy lot that they

1. Malabar, Vol. III, p. 2.
2. Malabar, Voi. III, pp. 6—8, Treaty Nos. 8—10.

dropped out of existence in Malabar almost unnoticed. They owned two warehouses,one at Eḍava in Chirayankīl Taluk and the other at Colachel, both in Travancore. Captain Alexander Hamilton, writing early in the 18th century, says thus about Eḍava, " The Danes have a small factory here standing on the sea-side. It is a thatched house of a very mean aspect and their trade answers every way to the figure their factory makes."[1] Of the Colachel factory, the Abbe Raynal observes, in 1760, "The factory of the Danes at Kolhachy is nothing more than a small storehouse where they might nevertheless be supplied with two lakhs weight of pepper. But such is their indolence or their poverty that they made but one purchase and that of a very small quantity these ten years."[2]

On the 19th March 1726, the English also obtained the grant of a site at Eḍava for a factory from the queen of Āttingal. It runs in the name of Dr. Alexander Orme, Chief of Anjengo, and is as follows: —

"Copy of the ratification of the queen of Āttenga in regard to the Eḍava factory, in the time of Mr. Alexander Orme, dated 19th March 1726.

"All that which the Commander has spoken to Gristnavo, he has related to me; the place which is now granted in Eḍava for a factory, is not for any other interest of Government, but that of obtaining the favour and help of the Honourable Company during all the time, which this Government and the Honourable Company should last, as well as that of augmenting the custom duties of this Government. No Commanders, who came in these days here, have obtained such a place as this Commander, so that he may acquire greater fame in the service of the Honourable Company it is that I have granted this place. The presents sent by the Commander through Gristnavo to me and Pulamars have been received."[3]

1. Pinkerton, Vol. VIII, p. 383.
2. History of the Settlements of Trades, etc., Vol. I, p. 367.
3. Malabar, Vol. III, p. 13.

LETTER VI.

1. Malabar, an Expensive Settlement.

From the very beginning, the Dutch Settlement of Malabar was a matter of considerable anxiety to the East India Company, as the income derived from the Malabar trade was never commensurate with the expenses incurred in the government of the Settlement, and the military transactions rendered necessary by the interference with the internal concerns of the neighbouring native powers.

The desire to possess territorial sovereignty on the coast and to exercise political supremacy over the Rajas of Malabar, and the mistaken policy of carrying on trade at the point of the sword conduced chiefly to bring about unsatisfactory results.

The Dutch Admiral, Stavorinus, who visited Malabar (1775—78), gives us the following account of the position of the East India Company on the Malabar Coast:—

" The principal object of the Dutch in expelling the Portuguese from the coast was to possess a monopoly of the pepper trade. They, however, early met with much disappointment on this head, both by the bad faith of the Malabar princes, and by the constantly increasing competition of European rivals, who adopted a surer mode of obtaining as much pepper as they wanted by always following the market price, or even paying something above it, while our Company continually insisted upon the performance of the contracts, that no pepper should be furnished to any others, although a fixed price was never stated in them, and they only speak of the market price, as the rule to go by.[1]

1. Secret Considerations of the Commandant, De Jong, of the 25th of October 1757—5.

The selling of pepper to other nations was stigmatized as contraband trade, which ought to be put a stop to by compulsion, if other means were not sufficient; and force was resorted to at different times for that purpose. But these attempts were as little productive of the effects proposed as they were expensive, for the princes themselves were not able to restrain their subjects from carrying on this trade with other nations, by which they made double the advantage that they did in selling to us;[1] by all these vicissitudes and occurrences, the Malabar coast has been rendered, from the period that it was conquered, to a few years ago, one of the heaviest burthens of the Company in India; and this it was that made the Governor-General, Mossel, addressing himself to the Director-General, Golonesse, who maintained that the Malabar, where he had long been stationed as Commandant, was one of the most important possessions of the Company, use these words:—'I am so far from being of your opinion, that I rather wish that the ocean had swallowed up the coast of Malabar an hundred years ago.'[2]

" The observations of Mr. Mossel on the state of the Malabar Coast, need only be attentively perused to obtain a conviction of the great detriment which our establishments upon it have already been to the Company; they have been not so much intrinsically prejudicial as baneful, on account of the continual disputes and wars which we have been engaged in with the native princes and not a little by the infidelity and peculation of the servants who have been employed here..[3]

1. Secret Considerations of the Commandant, De Jong, of the 25th of October 1757—5.

2. Historie Philosophique et Politique d l' Abbi Raynal Tom I, p. 261. Edition de la Haye, 1774—5.

3. Mr. Mossel, however, was of opinion, that, by a better management, 'the Malabar' might be rendered a profitable possession to the Dutch; 'not so much by the pepper trade, as by the gains upon the spices, sugar, arrack and Jappan copper, which may be disposed of here.' He supposes that the profits upon this

"Since the accommodation of the last differences respecting the Zamorin, the Malabar has, however, again begun to make a tolerable figure in the Company's statements. We do not mean to take into consideration the sum written off in the year 1767, to make good the deficiency occasioned by the infidelity of the persons employed; the balance closed on the 31st of August 1774 shews that the expenses of the Malabar had amounted in the book-year, 1770—1771, to £ 205,570—17; and, on the other hand, the profits amounted to £ 325,687—17—8; leaving a handsome advance upon the whole of £ 120,117—0—8,[1] and their profits would, under the disinterested administration of Governor Moens, have been larger, had not the unhappy disputes, which I have before detailed, been the means of greatly augmenting the charges.

* * *

"Amongst the several conquests and settlements which the Dutch Company have made, or established, in the Indies, that of the Malabar is not one of the most advantageous or important to the Dutch. It costs the Company much money, on account of the destructive wars in which they have in consequence engaged, the rivalry in trade of numerous competitors, and, though

might 'annually be £ 250,000, and the charges on the whole £ 230,000 or £ 18,000 (about £ 6,636 sterling) less than the gains; to which is to be added, what might be gained upon the pepper; in 1778, lbs. 1,000,000 of pepper from the coast of Malabar, were sold in Holland at 17 Stivers (nearly 1 sh. 7 d.) per pound; the purchase cost on the coast is by the * * treaties, from four to five Stivers per pound. The pepper, however, must then be sent to Ceylon, and thence conveyed to Europe, whereby much expense is incurred, but not so much as not to leave a considerable profit.' Mr. Mossel's calculation of the charges, however, made upon the supposition that the Company's establishments on the Malabar Coast, amounts to no more than 300 or 400 persons; but we have seen on page 233 that, in 1776-1777, there were 867 Europeans, and 405 natives, in the Company's service here.

1. About £ 10,920 sterling.

last not least, the infidelity and peculation of their servants. It was but a short time after the first capture of these possessions from the Portuguese, that the direction, which had been established in them, was found to be too cumbersome and expensive, and a resolution was accordingly taken, in October of the year 1686, that the fortifications of Cochin, Crānganūr, Cannanore, and Coylang should not be kept up, the garrisons be withdrawn or reduced, and the number of the Company's qualified servants considerably diminished. But the execution of this resolution was, for various reasons, delayed, till after the opinion of Mr. John Van Hoom, the then Director-General, was delivered and till the general revision of the affairs of the Company was effected by the Supreme Government at Batavia on the 19th of August 1697. The result of this resolution was principally as follows :--

" I. That the fortifications of the city of Cochin, which by the large garrison it required, and the continual reparations to be made, in consequence of the great extent of the walls, were too expensive for the Company to maintain, should be reduced by one-half.

" II. That of the present fortifications of Cannanore, the Portuguese tower should only be preserved, with a garrison of twenty, or, at the most, twenty-five European soldiers, to which number the present garrison should be reduced.

"III. That, at Crānganūr,[1] the ancient interior works should only be preserved, with a garrison of twenty Europeans, which is judged a sufficient number for the purposes of the Company here.

"IV. That it is likewise judged advisable at Coylang no more should be retained than the old Portuguese

1. Cranganur was sold by the Dutch to the king of Travancore, taken from him by Hyder Ali, and retaken by the English in 1790. Cochin, Quilon, Quile-Quilon and the other settlements of the Dutch on the coast of Malabar, have shared the fate of the greater part of their Indian possessions and are actually in the hands of the English. AT.

tower, or as much of the present works as may be thought necessary for the interest of the Company, with fifteen or twenty men, to which number the establishment there should be reduced; and that the remainder of the fortifications of the three last mentioned places should be removed or demolished. It was further thereby determined that all military out-posts should be withdrawn, except that of Paponethy; Porca and Cali Coylong should be retained as Residencies or factories, in order to keep an eye over what might be going forward all along the coast, and to avail of such opportunities of trade as might occur ; that a book-keeper or assistant or else a trusty and intelligent serjeant, with two private soldiers or sea-men, should be stationed at each place, and also at Ṭengenapaṭṭaṉom, as soon as the disputes with the queen of Anjengo shall have been amicably adjusted.

"The vessels of all descriptions were to be reduced to one small yacht, two sloops, and three rowboats; for it was determined not to obstruct any more, by measures of constraint and harshness, the navigation of the Malabars, and their trade in the productions of their country, consisting chiefly in arecanuts, wild cinnamon and pepper, which the Company could not exclusively purchase from them.

" The number of pieces of artillery, which should thenceforward be employed upon the fortification should be fixed at ninety-five pieces of iron, and six pieces of brass, ordnance, with two mortars : and about five hundred and thirty Europeans, and thirty-seven natives, were judged sufficient for the service of the Company.

" Upon this the charges diminished considerably in the year 1698; and it is surprising that the resolutions just now detailed had not before been taken, and put in execution, since the experience of thirty years had already pointed out the injurious tendency of the former expensive establishment, with no adequate benefit. The ostentation of a great power, which cost the Company such large sums of money, had not the effect of producing in native princes that degree of awe and apprehension, which is indispensably necessary for carrying on an exclusive trade."[1]

The aim of the Dutch from the very beginning was to monopolise the whole trade of Malabar, driving the Portuguese, whom they had conquered, and the English, who were putting forth all their energies to share in the Malabar trade, from within the sphere of their influence. Thus, speaking of Karunāgappilli, Dr. John Fryer says of them, in 1657, "Being against Carnopoly, a Portugal Friar boarded us. It is some miles to the north of Caulam (Quilon) formerly inhabited by the Portugals, and from them taken by the Dutch, who have built a castle there, and Lord over the natives, so that at Carnopoly the Dutch exact customs for all the goods that they carry off to the sea, though there live but one boy and two Dutchmen. The Portugals have only five persons here. The English had also a factory for pepper, but they are gone both from hence and Purcate twenty miles more north; the cause we are unacquainted with, but believe the Dutch will leave nothing unattempted to engross the spice trade, for none has escaped them but this of pepper, cinnamon, cloves, mace, and nutmegs, being wholly theirs; and by the measures they follow, this also in time must fall into their hands. Nor indeed are pretensions wanting, they holding here rights by conquest (a fairer claim than undermining), they boasting they have in a manner subdued the natives; which is no hard matter, since the region of Malabar (in which general name I reckon as far south as the land's end Phalapaṭam (Baliapaṭṭam). North is divided into several petit signories, or arch-rebels against the Zamerhin of Calicut."

As an instance of the inordinate desire of the Dutch Company to monopolise the pepper trade, may

1. Voyages, pp. 234 *et seq.*

be mentioned the incident that, when Captain Nieuhoff was asked by the Raja of Karuṅāgappiḷḷi what quantity of pepper the company might require, he haughtily replied that "they wanted the whole and would have nothing unpacked."

To enforce the monopoly, the Dutch had, of course, to maintain large armed forces and build strong positions at necessary points, with the almost inevitable result of goading on the natives to engage themselves in daring smuggling expeditions. Thus smuggling was largely indulged in, while their own officers were not altogether immaculately impervious to the temptations of illicit trade. In 1756, Commandant Cunes, wrote that full ten cargoes of pepper, *i e.*, between eight and nine millions of pounds weight, might be annually exported from Malabar, but that half of this was taken over to the Coromandel Coast. This aspect of the matter had not escaped the notice of outside observers, for even so early as 1615, the English ambassador to the great Moghul, Sir Thomas Roe, wrote, "The Portuguese, notwithstanding their many rich residencies, are beggared by the keeping of soldiers, and yet their garrisons are but mean. They never made advantage of the Indies, since they defended them. Observe this well. It has also been the error of the Dutch, who seek plantations here by the sword. They turn a wonderful stock. They probe in all places; they possess some of the best, yet their deal pays consume all the gain."

The Abbe Raynal thus sums up the mercantile position of the East India Company in the year 1760:— " The events have not answered their expectations. The Company have not succeeded in their hope of excluding other European nations from this coast. They procure no kind of merchandise here but what they are furnished with from their other settlements, and being rivalled in their trade, they are obliged to give a higher price here than in the markets, where they enjoy an exclusive privilege."

As regards the articles of trade, we gather the following information from Dr. Fryer, who says that they monopolised the trade in pepper, cinnamon, cloves, mace, and nutmegs. Stavorinus in 1775--78 points to cloves, nutmegs and mace as being "the articles which are of the most current vent of those sent hither by the Company." The Abbe Raynal observes, "Their (Dutch) articles of sale consist of a small quantity of alum, benezon, camphire, tutunague, sugar, iron, calin, lead, copper, and quicksilver. The vessel that carries this slender cargo returns to Batavia laden with coir or cocoatree bark, for the use of the port. By these articles, the Company gains at most 360,000 Liveres (£ 15,750), which with 120,000 (£ 5,250) arising from the customs, make the sum of 480,000 Liveres (£ 21,000). In times of profound peace, the maintenance of these settlements costs 464,000 Liveres (£ 20,300), so that 16,000 (£ 700) only remains to defray the expenses of their shipping, for which that sum is certainly not sufficient. It is true that the Company gets two millions weight of pepper from Malabar, which is carried in sloops to Ceylon, where it is put on board the ships fitted out for Europe. It is likewise true, that, by virtue of these capitulations, they pay only 192 Liveres (£8-8 sh.) the candil, which weighs 500 lbs., for which other Companies give 240 (£ 10-10 sh.), and private merchants 288 (£ 12-12 sh.); but whatever advantage may be made of this article, it is reduced to nothing by the bloody wars it occasions." He further observes with regard to the losses annually sustained by the Company that "in 1779, it was found that the expenses of the Company amounted to 489,645 Francs, while the income came only up to 414,977."

2. **Retain Malabar for Pepper Trade.** The first reason given by our author why Malabar should be retained by the Dutch is that "we may remain

masters of the pepper trade in Malabar." This expectation was not fulfilled. The desire for political supremacy plunged the Company into the vortex of the quarrels rampant among the petty chiefs of the coast, and brought them into conflict with superior forces. The Dutch East India Company posed themselves as arbitrators ready and willing to settle all disputes arising in the families of the native princes. This soon led them into a long and disastrous war with the great Mārṭṭāṇḍa Varma, king of Travancore, which raged between the years 1741 and 1748. In 1734, a deputation from four Malabar princes waited on the Governor of Cochin, and sought his aid to stem the advancing tide of the Travancore aggression and to settle all disputes between local chiefs. The first of this was from the Raja of Kāyamkuḷam, complaining against the preparations made by Travancore for invading Kāyamkuḷam, and of the attempt made by the Travancore king to induce the Ṭekkankūr and Ampalappuḻay Rajas to join him. The Governor at first refused to give countenance to the Kāyamkuḷam Raja's representations, but subsequently informed the Travancore king that he should desist from violating Kāyamkuḷam territory. The deputation from Koṭṭārakkara or Eḷayaḍaṭṭunāḍ was more successful: for the Dutch took up the cause of the exiled Rāṇi of Eḷayaḍaṭṭunāḍ and the Dutch envoy, Mr. Van Imhoff, personally carried a message to the king, demanding the restoration of the princess, failing which, the Dutch Governor threatened to invade Travancore. The king refused the demand, and sneeringly rejoined that he himself had been thinking of invading Europe some day! The Rajas of Vaḍakkankūr and Mangāṭṭy or Ālangāḍ had also about this time invoked the aid of the Dutch Company. The result of all this was that a long and ruinous war ensued between Travancore and the Dutch, ending in the complete discomfiture of the Dutch. Peace was finally concluded on the 15th of

August, 1752, hostilities having been suspended since the 18th October 1748, when the draft treaty was sanctioned. As Stavorinus observes, "the 9th article of the treaty do not appear very honourable to the Company. It stipulates that the Company shall recede from all engagements which they may have entered into with the other Malabar princes, whom the king of Travancore might choose to attack, and on no account to interfere in their disputes, or afford them assistance or shelter; nor in any respect raise any opposition to the enterprise of the king." And this was for the paltry advantage of getting four annas for every 25 lbs. of pepper to be supplied to the Company from Travancore and *from the territories to be conquered by Travancore*. This betrayal of their allies by the Dutch tolled the death-knell of their status as a sovereign power on the coast, and hence-forward they had to content themselves to be a mere Company of merchants with little or no political significance. Of this humiliating position, they were painfully reminded by the Travancore king himself, who, on subduing all States lying to the south of Cochin, and advancing as far as the seat of the Dutch Government in Cochin, turned round and repudiated his obligation to supply the given quantity of pepper at the fixed rate, and informed them that they were no longer a sovereign power, but merely a Company of petty merchants, and that, if they required spices, they were at liberty to purchase them in open market. This treaty was a perennial source of annoyance, and Van Angelbeck, a subsequent Governor of Cochin, bitterly complained of it. "Anyhow," as Dr. Day observes, "the treaty does not appear to have brought either credit or money to the Dutch." Thus the desire "to remain masters of the pepper-trade in Malabar" finally wrought their ruin as a political power. It was this ambition that led the Dutch East India Company to introduce the system of monopoly into the pepper trade. De Jong, Commandant of Cochin, in 1757, in his *Memorial* points out that monopolies in pepper did not exist before the advent of the Dutch, and were " illegal combinations of rulers." as he remarks, " for defrauding the people." "The Portuguese," says he, "obtained it from the Rajas, who acted only as brokers between the owners and the Portuguese Government. When competition between the European nations arose in the pepper trade, monopolies were by degrees introduced, but such a power did not exist in the laws of Chēramān Perumāl, by which the rulers of Malabar are bound, and from which they cannot deviate without the consent of their subjects. This was the reason why the Rajas and Chiefs of Malabar feared to prevent smuggling, as they were well aware of the illegality of the system of monopolies. The Dutch had, therefore, to bring military force to check smuggling, which was very expensive, and consequently the Malabar command was almost invariably in debt. While the Dutch always insisted upon the performance of pepper contracts at a low rate, and attempted to enforce preference to all others in the matter of supply, their European rivals always paid the market price or a little above it. Thus, in the long run, their European rivals succeeded in driving them from the pepper trade."[1]

3. **The Portuguese keeping an eye on Malabar.** The Portuguese seem always to have kept an eye on Cochin. For Mr. Moens in his *Memorial* says that, in 1774, there were various ugly rumours current, regarding the Portuguese in connection with Cochin, that they were making preparations to reinstate themselves in India, and that they would first claim the town of Cochin on the pretext that it was taken after peace had been made in Europe between the two nations. These rumours were general and were

1. De Jong's Memorial.

considered probable, as the Portuguese were really making many improvements in Goa with regard to naval artillery and military efficiency, also with regard to the mode of government. But these rumours gradually disappeared.

"Volume XIII of *Vadulandsche D Historie*, page 378, says that, in the year 1669, it was agreed between Portugal and Holland that Cochin and Cannanore would remain Dutch as a pledge for arrears which were still due to the States by Portugal. Why so is a puzzle to which I can suggest no solution. The history does not say whether these arrears have ever been paid or whether any fresh settlement effected. But it is said that the Portuguese would have got the town, if they were willing to make compensation for the expenses incurred by the Dutch; but this amount was so large that they could not pay."

4. **Use of Figurative Language.** It was not always so. For, speaking of king Māṟṟāṇḍa Vaṟma of Travancore, the Abbe Raynal says :—" A neighbouring State had sent him two ambassadors, one of whom began a long harangue, which the other was preparing to continue—'Be not tedious,' said the prince, with an austere brow, 'life is short'."[1]

5. **Rules for managing the country.** Our author has, in this para, placed on record certain wholesome principles, the strict observance of which would have gone a long way to establish the position of the Dutch as a commercial and political power on this Coast. But successive Governors of Cochin seem to have cared little to keep before them clearly the sound advice given by Visscher.

The Dutch had assumed the protectorate of the kingdom of Cochin. We have seen that the reigning line had been restored to its ancestral possessions by

1. P. 367. AU.

them, and that they had undertaken that the integrity of the kingdom would in no way be disturbed. For some time, the Raja was assisted by them in withstanding the inroads of the Zamorin. The Dutch were drawn into a long desultory war with the Zamorin, lasting from 1701 to 1710, to protect the interests of the Cochin Raja. They soon found the war expensive; and, as the settlement at Cochin was not paying its way, the supreme Council in Batavia, in 1721, came to the very important resolution "that the Cochin Raja was no longer to be supported in his interminable fights with the Zamorin," and the Cochin Council was solemnly cautioned to live peaceably with all men. It was not long after this that Travancore became aggressive and began to extend its bounds northwards, absorbing, one after another, the tributaries of Cochin. Espousing the cause of the Chālūr Ṭampāns, who laid a claim to the Perumpaṭappil Mūppu Sṭhānam, the Travancore king crossed the border, carried war into Cochin territory, conquered Karappuṟam towards the west, subjugated the Ṭekkenkūr and Vaḍakkankūr countries towards the east, and marched up almost to the gates of the residence of the Cochin Raja at Ṭṛppūṇiṭṭuṟa, who again and again sought the help of the Dutch East India Company, his protectors; but to no purpose. The Company itself was at war with Travancore and was trying its best to terminate it by peace. In the negotiations that followed, the Dutch ambassador did, indeed, make an unsuccessful attempt to insert a clause in the proposed treaty that, should the Cochin Raja be attacked by Travancore, the Dutch would consider it as equivalent to a declaration of war. The most the Dutch were able to secure was a promise that the Raja of Travancore "would live in friendship with the Raja of Cochin, *provided he gave no cause to the contrary.*" The Raja of Cochin was thus left to make his own terms with his enemy, and the result was that before long, the two States went to war with each other without any interference from the Dutch, except a few useless protestations. The Dutch evidently thought that, under the circumstances, discretion was the better part of valour, and satisfied themselves with requesting the Travancore king to respect their limits, which lay two miles to the south of Cochin. While the Cochin Raja was placed in this difficult condition, his hereditary foe, the Zamorin, found his opportunity. The latter advanced from Ponnāni and overran the northern parts of the Cochin territory, the Raja's feudatories hastening to join the Zamorin's standard. Hemmed in between two fires and left in the lurch by his avowed protector, the Dutch East India Company, the unfortunate Raja deemed it expedient to come to terms with his new enemy, Travancore, and seek her help against his more ancient and more relentless foe, the Zamorin. The differences between Cochin and Travancore were soon made up, and a treaty concluded in 1761, by which Travancore undertook to expel the Zamorin from Cochin, which was effected soon after. After this, Cochin rightly thought that she was not bound by any ties of obligation or close friendship with the Dutch.

The resolution arrived at by the Supreme Council at Batavia; that the Cochin Raja was not to be supported in his interminable wars with the Zamorin, soon paved the way for the virtual separation of all bonds between the Company and the Raja.

The imprudent manner in which the Dutch Governor of Cochin assumed to himself the office of an arbitrator in disputes between the Malabar Chiefs, and the haughty way in which his proud envoy, M. Van Imhoff, attempted to enforce Dutch authority was the proximate cause of the war with Travancore, the close of which found the Dutch East India Company fallen very low in the political scale.

6. **No Hasty Wars.** Certain observations made by Stavorinus illustrate the consequence of a disregard of the fifth rule. He says, "Upon this, the people in the administration on the coast immediately set about attacking Travancore, without even asking orders from Batavia on the subject. It was, however, speedily requisite to send for assistance from Java in order to carry on the enterprise that had been begun." Again, "The consequence of this inconsiderate conduct was a great decline in the reputation and importance of the Company on the coast of Malabar; for they concluded a treaty of peace, by which their allies were wholly abandoned and left to themselves, without any conditions or interference on the part of the Company in their behalf, and, on the other hand, we entered into an exclusive alliance with the king of Travancore, as the most powerful prince in the country."[1]

7. **Selfish Wars.** The wisdom of the first stipulation said to have been extorted from the Raja of Cochin by Commandant Hertenberg cannot be doubted. But the attempt of the Dutch Commandant to pose as the arbitrator in disputes between the Malabar Chiefs led to serious consequences. When Commandant Maten took it upon himself to remonstrate against the Travancore king's attacking Kāyamkuḷam, and contended that the annexation of Koṭṭārakkara was unjust, and that that territory should be restored to the exiled Rāṇi, king Mārttāṇḍa Varma coolly rejoined that it was rather unfortunate that foreigners should be called upon to arbitrate between native princes, and that the Dutch East India Company would do well to confine itself to its commercial relations with Travancore, and not to burn its fingers in the political fire that was then smouldering.

8. **The Dutch Rule of Malabar.** We may gather the following information regarding the

1. Pp. 243—4.

administration of the Dutch Malabar Settlement from an account given by Stavorinus. The Chief bore the title of Governor and Director. He was generally a member of the Supreme Government at Batavia. If he was not so, he had only the title and rank of Commandant. He was assisted by a Council consisting of the second who was a senior merchant, the Fiscal, the chief of the military, the warehouse-keeper, the *Dispensier* or purveyor, and all the junior merchants in the Settlement either in or out of office. Latterly, the Comptroller of equipments was added to the Council, as the rank of Sea-Captain was given to him. The Council had a Secretary, who was a junior merchant, and also held the post of Malayalam Translator, besides being the Chief of Quilon. The out-posts or Forts of Cranganūr, Kāyamkuḷam, Poracāḍ, Pāppanimaṭṭam, and Cheṭṭwāye were in charge of Book-keepers or Residents. The Chief of the military possessed the rank and title of Major, and the Chief of the artillery that of Captain-Lieutenant.

With regard to the military establishment: at first, troops had to be maintained at Quilon, Culli-Quilon (Kāyamkuḷam), Cranganūr, Cannanore, and subsequently at Pappanotty (Pāppanimaṭṭam), Cheṭṭwāye and other places. In 1680, the destruction of the forts of Cannanore, Cranganūr and Quilon was agitated. An attempt was also made to sell Cranganūr and Quilon to the Portuguese. But nothing was done. In 1686, it was resolved that the fortifications of Cochin, Cranganūr, and Quilon should not be kept up and that reductions should be made. The total European force proposed to be maintained was 455, as well as 200 militia. The operation of this resolution was suspended till 1697, when the walls of Cochin had become so ruinous that directions were given that the forts should be reduced by one half. At Cannanore and Quilon, only one tower was to be left standing, and at Cranganūr, only the exterior works.

All military out-posts, excepting those at Pappanoty, Poracad, and Culli Quilon, were ordered to be withdrawn. As to the naval establishment, only one small yacht, two sloops, and three row-boats were to be maintained. The armament of the fort in Cochin consisted of 95 iron and six brass pieces of artillery, and two mortars. The garrison was composed of 530 Europeans, of whom barely above one-fourth or one-third was Dutch, the remainder were English and French deserters, renegade Germans, "and similar broken adventurers, who came for the purpose of mending or making their fortunes."

In 1776—1777, the whole establishment of the Dutch on the coast of Malabar consisted of 102 persons in civil and three in ecclesiastical establishments, 10 surgeons and assistants; 60 belonging to the artillery; 49 sea-men, and mariners; 613 soldiers and 30 mechanics—in all 867 Europeans, besides 405 natives.

9. **Native Christians.** The Syrian Christians of Malabar had, from almost the time of their settlement in the country, been allowed certain privileges by their generous rulers. They were loyal and faithful and their Hindu rulers honoured and trusted them. The Syrian deeds evidence this. They were allowed to have their own spiritual chief with certain temporal powers. Their own ruler was known as 'Beliartes'. His dynasty having become extinct some time before the arrival of the Portuguese, they presented his sceptre, which they had preserved, to Vasco da Gama on the Admiral's landing in Malabar. The Portuguese interested themselves on their behalf. We learn from Gouvea, the chronicler of the doings of Archbishop Meneses in Malabar, that "these Christians were at the time subject to Hindu sovereigns in all temporal matters; yet, by most ancient compact and custom, although they were scattered about in different principalities, it came to be universally regarded that, as in spiritual so in social

matters, they were ruled by their bishop alone; who, with his assistants, settled all their disputes, hearing most patiently the contending parties, and allowing them to speak as much as they liked; so much so that it is recorded how a certain woman, on one occasion, spoke morning and evening for the space of three whole days in support of her cause! Their privileges were most religiously regarded by the native Rajas; and, if they were trampled on at any time, they were not appeased, before the person who had insulted them presented the model of a silver arm, or some other valuable gift to their church, by way of satisfaction for the admitted offence."

The *Memorial* of Governor Moens says that, according to article IX of the treaty entered into with the Raja of Cochin, on the 22nd March 1663, "all Christians were placed under the protection of the Dutch Company, the article stating, that all are under the jurisdiction of the Company, and, should any be guilty of misbehaviour, he is amenable to the Company's laws." By a subsequent treaty, dated February 25th 1664, it was stipulated that "those Christians who reside in the Raja's territory should obey and perform their obligations to that Government, as the heathens do."

The relative position in which the Christian subjects of Cochin stood to the Dutch Company and the Raja is thus set forth by Moens:—"Most of the Christians rely too much on the protection of the Company and try with the help of this influence to escape from paying taxes to the king, which they are bound to pay. On the other hand, however, as the Christians are much despised by the heathens, they would have to suffer humiliations, and would be ill-treated, if they were not protected by the Company. They were, no doubt, under the protection of the Company, but are in reality subjects of the king, at least those who reside in his territory; because there are so many Christians, who live in the territory of the Company, and are, therefore, as a matter of fact, subjects of the Company. It is the same with the native Christians, who are now under the king of Travancore in so far as they inhabit the territory, which formerly belonged to the king of Cochin but has since been conquered by the king of Travancore. The Company retains its protection over them.

"But this protectorate is gradually pushed further, because, if they are obstructed in the exercise of their religion or ill-treated in other cases, and complain about this to the Company or ask for consolation, the Company speaks then on their behalf, and takes interest in their case and makes even the king or his ministers listen to reason.

"Besides the above protection, the Christian subjects have the privilege that they pay only half taxes to the king, whilst a heathen subject, having become a Christian, at once comes under the protection of the Company with this difference however, that he has still to pay the same taxes to the king as he did when he was a heathen, according to article IX of another contract, dated 25th February 1664."

Moen's successor, Von Adrian Angelbeck, in his *Memorial*, dated 1793, has given us a complete summary of the agreement between the Cochin Raja and the Dutch regarding the native Christians. After refering to the treaties of 1663 and 1664, he says that constant disputes arose with the Raja respecting the 'Inland Christians,' the Roman Catholic portion of which was claimed by the Dutch to be under their jurisdiction in accordance with article III of the treaty of 1663. Article IX of the first treaty ran thus: —"All Christians who had been formerly *subject to (the Government of) this fort* to be under the protection of the (Dutch) Company." As the text of the second treaty is not forthcoming, it is not possible to ascertain exactly the extent of the jurisdiction claimed. But it is significant that, when disputes arose between the Raja and the Dutch, in 1789, regarding the right of the Dutch to exercise jurisdiction over all Roman Catholic Christians, Mr. Powney, the English Commissioner, pointed to a difference in the wording between the Raja's Malayalam copy of the treaty and the Dutch one. In the Raja's copy, the Dutch were given authority over all Muṇḍukārs, (persons wearing muṇḍu or a piece of cloth round their loins stretching down to the knees or the ankles), located near the town of Cochin, as well as over those living along the coast. The Dutch copy, however, went further and added, after the word Muṇḍukārs, "viz., all Christians," words which were absent in the Malayalam copy with the Raja. The English Commissioner and the Raja insisted that, by the term Muṇḍukār, only fishermen were meant, while M. Van Angelbeck got the Carmelite priests of Varāppuḷa and other persons well acquainted with the language to declare that "it included all who followed the Latin ritual, and not only the fishermen, but also the Lascouns (peons), land cultivators, and handicraftsmen (if Christians), as well as Topasses." M. Van Angelbeck further contended that, by a subsequent convention, dated 1785, the term Muṇḍukārs was so defined as to include not only fishermen, but all the other classes before mentioned.

M. Van Angelbeck mentions two special rights as having been possessed by the Dutch from the earliest times of their connection with Cochin, viz., (1) that all Christians should be tried by them: (2) that the Raja could not impose new demands on the Christians, or increase their taxes above what was paid by their forefathers (without the knowledge, apparently of the Dutch). But, by the treaty of the 25th February 1664, "the subjects of the Raja who have been accustomed to contribute head-money and other demands shall not be freed from other obligations by becoming Christians." Any claim the Raja had on the Christians had to be made through the Dutch Commandant, who alone could attach their houses or gardens or imprison them. In 1785, the Raja found that his power was increasing, while that of the Dutch was on the wane. He, therefore, demanded a new agreement in curtailment of former privileges. Under this agreement, the Latin converts were henceforth to pay a tax to the Raja which was to be collected by their own headmen, but, should they fail to realise the same, the Dutch Government was obliged to collect it and pay it over to the Raja, who had the right to realise it, if that Government too failed to do so. The Dutch were still allowed to exercise a nominal jurisdiction over them. The convention further stipulated that, "Should Christians purchase, or rent lands from the heathen, they were liable to imposts, which the purely Christian lands were exempt from." With the surrender of Cochin by the Dutch to the English, the jurisdiction which the Dutch claimed over Christians in the Native State also passed to the British, who, in the revision of the Regulations of Cochin in the year 1814, handed over that jurisdiction to the Raja.

10. **Punishments for Crimes.** The different kinds of punishments awarded, mentioned by our author, are not exhaustive; neither is it likely that the Dutch confined themselves to European methods. The law, though nominally the same for both Europeans and natives, was in reality different in its application. Specially with regard to the natives professing different religions, Dr. Day observes, "If an European killed a slave, whether by an accidental blow or otherwise, he was severely punished, but rarely by death. The law laid down was that slaves might be corrected by their masters, in any way short of causing death. To obviate the chance of an exasperated master's giving a fatal

blow, there was an official, who, amongst his other duties, received complaints against slaves, and, on payment, caused them, if males, to be beaten before their master's door, if females within his house." * *

Impalement, and more rarely the nail torture, and that by fire and water, were employed, though our author does not mention them. The process of impalement practised and its effect on the victim are thus described by Day :—"An iron spike was thrust through the criminal's skin, in the lower part of the back, where a cross cut had been previously made for its insertion, then the point of the spike was guided by the executioner's finger so as to bring it out at the neck or shoulder, carefully avoiding injuring any large arteries, or vital organs, as such would afford the poor victim speedy relief. The lowest extremity of the spike was then made fast to a wooden post, which was raised perpendicularly, as fixed into the ground, and thus the culprit was supported, partly by the iron spike under his skin and partly by a small bench, placed underneath his feet, and raised about 10 inches from the ground. Tortured by thirst, but denied water, scorched by the sun, but denied shade, devoured by insects, but refused any means of keeping them away, his miserable existence terminated in a lingering death that, in some instances, was protracted for three days A shower of rain was hailed as the greatest blessing as it caused the wounds to mortify and death rapidly ensued." Surely such a cruel method of execution was never practised in Europe. Wolf says that, in Cochin, 'the Dutch substitute, for breaking criminals on the wheel, with breaking their thighs with an iron club.'

Europeans were rarely executed by hanging; but military executions by shooting occasionally took place. Close by the river and by the side of the Cathedral of Santa Cruz, used by the Dutch as a warehouse, stood a large gallows, while another stood on a low island about half a mile away (yet in sight of the former) known as 'Gallows Island,' where criminals were generally executed by hanging.

"There are no jails here," says our author. It would seem that this desideratum was supplied some time after, for we learn from Day that a jail as well as a house of correction for disorderly women had existed in Cochin. He refers to the following entries in the Diary of 1790. "February 13th—a Moor woman taken by the Patrols, this day sentenced to be whipped and imprisoned for two years. March 20th—the Christian prisoner Barki Chowry was this day tortured."

11. **Judicial Tribunals.** Later on, regular judicial tribunals were established. In 1796, fiscal (Dutch Superintendent of Police, Justice of Peace, and Attorney-General in criminal cases), Criminal and Civil Courts, and a Court of Appeal were constituted in Cochin, and continued to administer justice even after the British occupation, till the judicial system was finally assimilated to that of the British in 1814.

12. **Orphanage.** Originally there was an orphanage for the reception of illegitimate children and orphans of the poorer classes. They were taught various trades, and the boys, at a suitable age, were generally drafted into the army, and the girls respectably married. Apart from the orphan-house, was the College for the guardianship of orphans and minors (a Dutch institution answering to the court of wards), whose business was to take care of the property of the orphans.

13. **Acquisition of Lands and Fields.** Edourtien is Eḍaṭṭuriṭṭi in the Ponnāni Taluk, and Paponetti is Pāppanimaṯṯam close by. These were acquired in 1666.

"Bollogatti." This is the modern Bolghotty, the island on which the British Residency in Cochin now stands. It is a corrupted form of Mulakukāḍu, the name by which the whole island is known in Malayalam. The southern end of the island, on which the

Residency is situated, is known locally as Pōññikkara. It was acquired in 1665.

"Cruz de Milagre" is the modern Muriññali. It means the wonderful cross, and was so called because it was here that the Portuguese first planted the cross as a symbol that they claimed sovereignty over the country. Another account says that it was here that St. Thomas landed and set up the cross himself.

"Antge Caimal" is the modern Eṙṇākuḷam, so called because its possession was originally shared by Añchu Kaimals, or "five nobles", of whom the Cheṙia-orukāṭṭu Kaimal, otherwise known as Chērānellūr Kaṙṭṭāvu, still holds a large extent of property in Eṙṇākuḷam.

"Castella," two miles south of Cochin, formed the southern limit of the Dutch possession in Cochin.

"Binduverti." This is the island of Veṇḍuruṭṭi, two miles in length, and believed, according to tradition, to have been separated from the island of Bolghotty, which is now more than a mile distant, by only a small stream. The northern portion, it seems, was drawn off from the southern and was, therefore, called Pōññu Ikkara or 'the land that came away this side,' while the southern portion was called Veṇḍuriṭṭi or Viṭṭaṭuruṭṭi, i.e., the 'island left on that side.' The island of Veṇḍuruṭṭi formed a portion of the endowment of the Santa Cruz Chathedral in Portuguese times.

"Aroe" is the modern Arūr in Travancore, a few miles south of Cochin.

"Senhira Sande" is the present "Souṭi," while
"Mundenbeeli" is the modern Muṇḍenvēli and
"Main Code" is Mānākkōḍam.

In 1781, when Governor Moens handed over charge to his successor Van Angelbeck, he enumerated nine islands, including Veṇḍuriṭṭi, as well as 69 gardens and pieces of land, which were then the property of the Dutch. He observed that they had 42,089 fruit-bearing cocoanut and other trees, 4,507½ parrāhs of fields, and 19,716 salt-pans. The Dutch surrendered Cochin to the British in 1795, and, by the convention of Paris, ceded their Malabar possessions to them. The outlying *Pattams*, or leaseholds attached to the present Cochin Taluk, represent the landed properties possessed by the Dutch Company from which they received rents.

They are:—

No.	Pattam		Miles		
(1)	Ṭumbōle Pāṭṭam	....	33	miles to the south of Cochin	
(2)	Kāṭṭūr Pāṭṭam	....	31	do.	do.
(3)	Aṭṭāīakkād Pāṭṭam	....	27	do.	do.
(4)	Manakkōḍaṭ Pāṭṭam		27	do.	do.
(5)	Antony Fernandez Pāṭṭam	....	6	do.	south-east
(6)	Tekkēpurupunkara Pāṭṭam	....	6½	do.	do.
(7)	Muṇḍenvēli Pāṭṭam	...	6	miles to the south-east of Cochin	
(8)	Domings Fernandez Pālakkal Pāṭṭam	....	6	do.	do.
(9)	Santiago Pāṭṭam	....	5		south do.
(10)	Ṭaiveppu Pāṭṭam	...	4	do.	do.
(11)	Belicho Rodrigues Pāṭṭam	....	4½	do.	do.
(12)	Saint Louis Pāṭṭam	..	5½	do.	do.
(13)	Duart Lemos Pāṭṭam	....	5	do.	do.
(14)	Hendrick Silva Pāṭṭam	....	4½	do.	do.
(15)	Rāmanṭuruṭṭi Pāṭṭam	....	1½	do.	north-east

(16) Sondikalguvankare
Pelva Pāṭṭam .... 4½ miles to the south of Cochin

(17) Palliport Hospital
Paramba .... 16 do. north do.

Nos. 5 to 6 are together known as Kallenchēri. The proprietary right in the soil was vested in the Company, but the Dutch and Christian subjects were exempt from ground-rent taxation.

LETTER VII.

1. **Trade of the English in Malabar.** In this letter, our author gives us an account, from his point of view, of the trade of the English on the Malabar Coast and the disasters they have experienced. The rivalry between the various European nations to monopolise the Eastern trade is a matter of notoriety. To secure this, all means available, fair or foul, were resorted to without any qualms of conscience. While some were eager to secure profit by trade alone, others were more ambitious and sought trade only as a means to attain political supremacy and territorial sovereignty. This, of course, led to wars between the European nations themselves with the result that the English have, at last, outstripped all the others in the race for Empire in India. It was, in fact, the large profits made by the Dutch that excited the jealousy of the English and fired their ambition to try their hand at the Eastern trade, and then commenced that struggle for maritime and commercial supremacy in Southern and Eastern Asia that was continued for a considerable length of time. In this struggle, the Dutch were at first successful, owing chiefly to the support given to the Dutch East India Company by the Netherlands Government, the State regarding it as a national concern. In England, however, the English East India Company was looked upon in the light of a mere private speculation scarcely meriting recognition from the Government. As observed by Sir William Hunter, "the English Company was the weakling child of the old age of Elizabeth and of the shifty policy of king James ," while the Dutch Company "was the strong outgrowth of the life and death struggle of a new nation with its new Spanish oppressors." For a long time, the English were completely thrown into the shade, Holland

lording it over the seas. During the whole of the 17th century, she was in secure possession of the monopoly of the Malabar trade, besides that of the Eastern Archipelago. But, before long, the English succeeded in thwarting their enterprise in Malabar. Peace at home between the two nations was of little moment in the east, so long as the one could find an opportunity of worsting the other. The Dutch were always intriguing against the English, while the latter, in their turn, were never slow to conspire against the former. On the capture of Cochin, the Dutch had summarily ordered the English factors, who had established themselves there in 1634—5, to quit. The factors at Poṙacāḍ were similarly treated. The following extract taken from an article in the *Madras Mail* of the 18th February 1902 entitled "Dutch ascendency in India: Its enforcement in Malabar in 1709," gives us a fair idea of the position of the parties at the commencement of the 18th century on the West Coast:

" An illustration of the relative position of the two rivals at the beginning of the eighteenth century is afforded by a few unpublished manuscripts in the British Museum that possess some claim on the attention of your readers. It seems that, on the 26th April 1711, the Board of Trade (of which Lord Stamford was president) wrote to Lord Dartmouth, Secretary of State, to say, that, in pursuance of the directions signified to them by his Lordship a fortnight previously, they had considered a 'representation' of the East India Company, and the extracts of letters and other papers referred to therein, relating to the proceedings of the Dutch East India Company on the Coast of Malabar; and, having themselves prepared a 'representation thereupon', they transmitted the same to him. Their representation assumed the form of a memorial addressed to the Queen's Most Excellent Majesty, in which they took leave to lay before Her Majesty—Queen Anne—the state of the case as it appeared to them from

AW,

the information they had received from, and the documents submitted to them by the 'United Company of Merchants of England trading with the East Indies'. They reported that the Dutch, in order to monopolise the pepper trade on the Malabar Coast, 'had joined with the king of Cochin to make war with the Zamorin, who has been obliged to deliver up to them Chittoa (Chēťťwāye) and Ponnāni with the sole trade of those places, which are the two best on all the Malabar Coast for pepper.'

" It appeared that, on the 23rd November 1709, two Dutch ships, one of 30 guns, and the other of 20, and the Dutch brigantine arrived off Calicut, and anchored opposite the British factory there. On the 24th, they approached nearer the shore, dropped anchor, and promptly fired about 300 shots at the town, but did no damage beyond killing one 'Muckwa' boy, and one gold-smith's boy, and wounding a Moor woman. The Dutch Commodore now called upon the masters of three native vessels in the roads, and the Portuguese master of a British Ketch to proceed on board his ship. The master of the British Ketch obeyed the order, and was then directed to land, and warn the British factory 'to take care of themselves, for that the Dutch were resolved to burn, sink and destroy all they could, and that, if the factory wanted goods, they might go with the ships to Cochin, but the Dutch could suffer none to be shipped at Calicut. The factory sent an English representative to the Dutch Commodore to state that no notice could be taken of his verbal message, and to desire that, if he had anything to say, he would communicate it in writing and in English too, as they were unacquainted with Dutch. But the Commodore replied that he was unacquainted with English, so he again sent a verbal message, and warned the factory to be careful, for 'powder and balls had no eye.' It had already been observed by the people in the factory that in every broadside fired by the Dutch vessels, 'several of the guns were levelled at the factory, the shot flying all around them, one of which beat down a corner of the factory, whereof the Dutch had immediately notice sent them. The Dutch being satisfied with this display of force before the Zamorin's Capital, sailed away from Calicut to Chittoa, where they encountered no opposition, as the Zamorin had been unable to raise a force to protect the place. They landed, raised palisades, and laid the foundations of a fort on a spot of ground formerly granted to the English East India Company. They pulled down the house, wherein the Company had been wont to store its purchases of pepper, after rifling it of all that was in it; while they threatened the servants of the Company whom they found there, that, if they did not leave immediately, they would be put in irons, and shipped off as prisoners to Batavia. Then the Dutch returned to their ships, and set sail for Anjengo, where the English Company had another factory. Thus intimidated, the Zamorin made a grant of Chittoa to the Dutch, and relinquished to them some conquests that he had made from the Raja of Cochin.

"On the 4th January 1710, the Dutch Commodore, accompanied by the members of his Council, visited the Zamorin at Chāvacāt—Chowghaut?—a 'league' to the northward of Chittoa, 'where all the Dutch demands were by him granted, though with little or no sincerity on either side, the Dutch not knowing when they had enough,' and the Zamorin king, being not able to defend himself, disputed nothing, but complied with whatever they asked.' Thus it was that he made cession of the monopoly of the pepper trade in his dominions to the Dutch exclusively, and also gave them permission to raise a factory both at Ponnāni and Calicut, as well as a fort at Chittoa, the centre of the Malabar pepper country. The Board of Trade then stated :—

"'The Company does observe that the Zamorin—king (the most powerful of all the princes who inhabit the pepper country) being thus reduced, it may be easy for the Dutch to seize on, and secure all the other pepper trade that is produced in those parts, and, in that case, may set what price they please upon it in Europe, as they do on the other four sorts of spices, whose prime cost in the Indies is less than that of pepper, and not equally necessary. This will be a means greatly to increase their navigation to several parts of Europe, particularly to the Mediterranean and Turkey, where pepper is always demanded to make up the cargoes for those places. Besides this, should the pepper trade be wholly engrossed by the Dutch, it would very much enhance the freight paid by the English East India Company by reason that pepper filling up the spaces between the bales, chests, or other parcels, is a consideration for which the owners of shipping do take a less freight by at least £ 10 per ton than otherwise they could afford the same.'

"The Board's memorial was accompanied by the 'humble representation' also addressed to 'the Queen's Most Excellent Majesty' from the English East India Company and signed, on behalf of the Board of Directors, by Thomas Woolley, the Secretary. The Company complained of the hostile action of the Dutch in Malabar, especially of the firing on the factory at Calicut, notwithstanding that St. George's flag was hoisted upon it. As the Dutch was at war with the natives only, they had, according to the Company, committed an outrage on England, for which satisfaction should be demanded. They urged the importance of preventing the Dutch from obtaining a monopoly of the Malabar pepper trade. There was only one other source from which Europe could obtain pepper and that was Sumatra, 'and there the Company have, at the expense of several hundred thousand pounds, endeavoured to preserve a footing to their great loss, it would be to their interest to throw up the same, were it not that they are more concerned for the benefit of the nation than themselves'. But, as at Bantam so in Malabar, the Dutch had intimidated the native princes into granting them a monopoly, and had thus succeeded in obtaining supplies of pepper at the fourth of the price that the spice sold for in Europe. The loss to England of the pepper trade would result in the loss to her treasury of the import duty imposed on the article.

"The Company submitted for Her Majesty's consideration extracts from letters that they had received from their representatives in India. For example the Governor and Council of Bombay reported that

" 'The Dutch this year have been very troublesome, the king of Cochin being assisted with about 600 Europeans and 1000 Brigasses against the Samorine. They have already fought two battles, in which the latter was worsted, and, by our last advice, we are informed they were marching towards Chittoa, from whence all our southern pepper comes; and, if they take it, Calicut Factory will be of no use; therefore, we have desired your servants to withdraw to Tellicherry, and fortify that place, lest by bribery or other indirect means, the Raja should be prevailed on to oppose us. At Cochin, they have already built flat-bottomed boats to carry all materials for a strong fort, to be built in Chittoa, if they succeed in their design upon it, which it is much to be feared they will, having a strong power by land, and several ships, with which they range the coast, and destroy the sea-ports of the Samorine.

" 'The Bombay Government found it difficult to believe that, during the maintenance of a strict alliance between England and the Netherlands, the Dutch would venture to publicly aid the 'king of Atteng' in his designs on the English Factory at Anjengo, 'although, by underhand dealings, they have created a difference which they strove to foment into an open rupture.' The Government did not doubt that, all along the coast, the Dutch 'will use all base means to obtain their ends, yet we hope they may miss of their aim, which is certainly what they discourse, your servants at Calicut 'having received a message from the Samorine, acquainting them that the demands of the Dutch are to have us turned out of his dominions.'

"The manuscripts under notice do not throw light on the result of the joint representation to Queen Anne. But, if one cared to ' 'ave a dive', as an Aden boy might say, into the innumerable state papers at the Record Office, one might obtain full information on this point. It is, however, well known that, little by little, the English established their ascendency over the Dutch on the Malabar Coast, the Coromandel Coast, and elsewhere. The Dutch Colonial Empire fell in consequence of the short-sightedness of its directors. It was, according to Sir William Hunter, 'deliberately based upon a monopoly of the trade in spices, and it remained, from first to last, destitute of sound commercial principles.'

"Like the Phoenicians of old, the Dutch stopped short of no acts of cruelty towards their rivals in commerce; but, unlike the Phoenicians, they failed to introduce their civilisation among the natives with whom they came in contact. The knell of Dutch supremacy was sounded by Clive, when, in 1759, he attacked the Dutch in Chinsurah, both by land and water, and forced them to an ignominious capitulation. During the great French wars between 1795 and 1811, England wrested from Holland every one of her colonies, although Java was restored to her in 1816, and Sumatra exchanged for Malacca in 1854. At present, the Dutch flag flies nowhere on the mainland of India."

Mr. Grose, voyaging on the Coast about 1750, gives us an account of the rivalry between the two nations in South India and their respective position there:—

" As mere traders, the English would never have got the footing they had, if they had not added to that character the profession of arms, both at land and sea. This is so true, that the special privileges, fortified settlements, and favourable grants, obtained from the several Princes of India, well conformable to their original dates, appear to have been owing to the figure our nation formerly made there in war, when its victories over the Portuguese, who sunk as fast as we rose, gave it such a reputation, as that hardly anything was denied to it; and, to say the truth, it is principally on that old foundation, that the extraction of our commerce has since subsisted. I say principally only, because, no doubt, our frank, unaffected and generous national character, amidst all the faults of some of its subjects in power there, I can scarcely aver without any partiality, also once bore in the eyes of the Indians a very favourable comparison with the silly, senseless, sanguinary bigotry of the Portuguese; with the unsocial dryness, imperious conduct, and the keenness after gain of the Dutch; and the super-refined designing politeness of the French. And yet the advantages of these last over us in the affair of Madras, did not a little shake our estimation in those parts, no people being more apt to be dazzled and influenced by success than the orientalists, and those of India above all.

"The Dutch especially insult us in their insinuations to the country Governments, of our inferiority, in that we are not possessed of a head-place of arms, such as Batavia is to them, from whence our operations might be more timely, and more effectually applied to any exigence, than as there now exists a necessity for waiting for orders and aids from Europe. They do not consider, or at least do not add a candid confession, of the treacherous and cruel supplantment of us, in a time of full peace in the Spice islands, which are the mines, from whence they draw the means of supporting the extraordinary charges of that their boasted capital place in India; a competition with which our trade, circumstanced as it had been since that fatal epoch, could never well afford; though it is impossible but it might have gained a much more considerable extension, if either the settlements we actually have, had been better cultivated, useful new ones had been formed or other channels of commerce explored; or if, in short, more attention had not been given to the temptation of momentary profits and present dividends than to the founding of permanent establishments upon greater views, but of which the immediate requisite expense appeared to be as so much lost in the distant futurity of the returns. This narrow consideration it is, which, combined with a generally prevailing indolence, and the facility of humouring that indolence, since the opening of those fatal gulfs, the public funds, which, swallowing up the very element and support of trade, have set up a class of men called the moneyed interest to the destruction of the commercial one, upon the produce of whose stock, which itself has depauperated, it projects lazily to live; all these, I say, have more contributed to extinguish the ancient English spirit of discovery and extension than any certainty that could with reason be pleaded, of there being nothing further to be found or hoped for from it.

"One of the reasons that the Dutch East India Company flourishes, and is become more rich and powerful than all the others is, its being absolute and invested with a kind of sovereignty and dominion, more especially over the many ports, provinces and colonies, it possesses in those parts. For, it appoints magistrates, admirals, generals and governors; sends and receives embassies from kings and sovereign princes; makes peace and war at pleasure ; and, by its own authority, administers justice to all, &c., &c. The power of the Dutch by sea and land is very great in the East Indies; where by force, address and alliances, they raised themselves, and still support a great superiority, in spite of the English, Portuguese and other Europeans, that have some trade there; but so inconsiderable are these that all of them together do not enjoy what the Hollanders enjoy. The Hollanders gave law to the very English, in 1662, obliging them to a peace very advantageous to Holland and their East India Company in particular, after a bloody and expensive war that arose from jealousy and rivalship in commerce * * . For, in those parts, Holland commands and directs everything at pleasure, bringing sovereigns under subjection, conquering or reducing large and plentiful provinces, after it laid the foundation of its Empire upon the spoils of Portugal, and enlarged it by prescribing narrow limits to the jurisdiction and commerce of the English and disappointing or reducing that of the French and other Europeans".[1]

2. **Incidents at Attingal and at Anjengo.**— The incidents described in the early part of this letter led up to the serious results mentioned later. Apparently, the disputes were between the people of Āṭṭingal and the English at Anjengo. At this period, the authority of the Eṭṭuvīṭṭil Piḷḷamārs was in the ascendant and the Rāṇi was merely an ornamental figurehead.

We have an account of the incident mentioned in this letter given us by Hamilton, which puts a slightly different colour on the whole transaction; there is besides other evidence to show that our author's account is not wholly unprejudiced. The disputes mentioned in the early paragraphs of this letter culminated in open rupture between the English at Anjengo and the Kāryakār (Governor) of Āṭṭingal, and when hostilities commenced, Mr. Walter Brown of the Bombay

[1] Vol. II. p. 256 *et seq.*

Council was deputed to bring about an amicable arrangement. On his arrival at Anjengo, it was agreed that, as soon as the customary annual tribute to the Rāṇi was paid, all disputes should be laid at rest. Hamilton observes that, in April 1721, a demand for the annual tribute was made. "Those who demanded it assured him (the chief of the factory) that they came to demand it by the queen's order, and offered their receipt of it in her name." The chief had his own doubts about its reaching its proper destination, if paid into their hands, and offered to take it in person to the Rāṇi. On this, the chief was invited by the queen to Āṭṭingal and, in the words of Hamilton, "he (Mr. Gyfford), to appear great there, carried two of his Council, and some others of the factory (viz., Messrs. Burton, Fleming, Cowes and others) with most part of the military belonging to the garrison ; by stratagem, they were all cut off, except a few black servants whose heels and language saved them from the massacre, and they brought to Anjengo the sad news of the tragedy." This happened on the 15th of April 1721. Only a few invalids had been left behind in the fort. But these had time to prepare themselves for its defence, as the murderers did not at once besiege the fort. When they appeared, all attacks were resolutely repulsed by gunner Ince, who made a most valiant defence, and frustrated every attempt to scale the walls. The defenders were able to keep the enemy at bay, till reinforcements were sent up by Mr. Adams, chief of Tellicherry, and the seige was raised. Sir George Birdwood describes gunner Ince's heroic defence of Anjengo as worthy of a place beside Clive's defence of Arcot about 50 years later.

Col. Biddulph gives us a detailed account of the state of affairs at Anjengo about this time and of the conduct of the factors which led up to the tragic incident in which these terminated. The lady whose career in India forms the subject to the second part of the Colonel's work was the wife of the chief of the Anjengo settlement, Mr. Gyfford, who perished in the massacre.

"In 1704, a new Governor, Sir Nicholas Waite, was appointed to Bombay. For some reason, he left Brabourne without instructions or money for investment.[1] Their salaries and their private trading seem to have made the Company's servants very independent. We constantly find them throwing up the service and going away, without waiting for permission. Brabourne went off to Madras, after delivering over the fort to Mr. Simon Cowse, who had long resided there, apparently as a private merchant, and who proved, as times went, a good servant to the Company. The Company's service in those days was full of intrigue and personal quarrels. The merchant second in rank at Anjengo, John Kyffin, intrigued against Cowse so successfully, that Cowse was deposed, and Kyffin was made chief of the settlement. He appears to have been a thoroughly unscrupulous man. To enrich himself in his private pepper trade 'he stuck at nothing'. He took part in the local intrigues of Āṫṫingal, from which his predecessors had held aloof, played into the hands of Pūla Venjamuṭṭa, quarrelled with the other local officials, and behaved with great violence, whenever there was the slightest hitch in his trade. Kyffin's want of loyalty to the Company was still more clearly shown by his friendly dealings with their rivals, a procedure that was strictly forbidden.

" In June 1717, Kyffin made known to the Council at Bombay his wish to retire, and William Gyfford was appointed to succeed him, as soon as the monsoon would permit. So, in due course of time, Gyfford and his wife went to Anjengo; but, in spite of his resignation, Kyffin stuck to his office, and evidently viewed

1. This is the reason given by Bruce for Brabourne leaving Anjengo; but the death of Brabourne's wife, in 1704, probably had a good deal to do with his leaving the place. Her tomb still exists.

Gyfford with unfriendly eyes. In the following April, intelligence reached the Council at Bombay that Kyffin had had dealings with the Ostenders, and had been 'very assisting' to them; so, a peremptory order went down from Bombay, dismissing him from the Company's service, if the report of his assisting the Ostenders was true. If the report was not true, no change was to be made. A commission to Gyfford to assume the chiefship was sent at the same time. Interlopers and Ostenders, he was told, were not to receive even provisions or water. So Kyffin was departed, and Gyfford reigned at Anjengo in his stead.

"But the follies of Kyffin had roused a feeling against the English that was not likely to be allayed by Gyfford, who exceeded Kyffin in dishonesty and imprudence. He threw himself into the pepper trade, using the Company's money for his own purposes, and joined hands with the Portuguese interpreter, Ignatio Malheiros, who appears to have been a consummate rogue. Before long, religious animosity was aroused by the interpreter obtaining possession of some pagoda lands in a money lending transaction. Gyfford also aroused resentment, by trying to cheat the native traders over the price of pepper, by showing fictitious entries in the factory books, and by the use of false weights. The only thing wanting for an explosion was the alienation of the Mahomedan section, which, before long, was produced by chance and by Gyfford's folly. It happened that some Mahomedan traders came to the fort to transact business with Cowse, who had resumed business as a private merchant, but he was not at leisure, so they went to the interpreter's house, to sit down and wait. While there, the interpreter's 'strumpet' threw some *hooli* powder on one of the merchants. Stung by the insult, the man drew his sword, wounded the woman, and would have killed her, if he and his companions had not been disarmed. Gyfford, when they were brought before him, allowed himself to be influenced by the interpreter, and ordered them to be turned out of the fort, after their swords had been insultingly broken over their heads. The people of Āṭṭinga flew to arms, and threatened the fort. For some months, there were constant skirmishes. The English had no difficulty in defeating all attacks; but, none the less, trade was brought to a standstill; so, Mr. Walter Brown was sent down from Bombay to put matters straight. Pūla Venjamuṭṭa, who had all the time kept himself in the background, was quite ready to help an accommodation, as open force had proved useless. Things having quieted down, Gyfford, 'flushed with the hopes of having peace and pepper,' devoted himself to trade. He had, at this time, a brigantine called the *Thomas*, commanded by his wife's brother, Thomas Cooke, doing his private trade along the coast. The year 1720 passed quietly. Force having proved unavailing, the Āṭṭinga people dissembled their anger, and waited for an oppotunity to revenge themselves. So well was the popular feeling against the English concealed, that Cowse, with his long experience and knowledge of the language, had no suspicions.

"There had been an old custom, since the establishment of the factory, of giving presents yearly to the Rāṇi, in the name of the Company; but, for some years, the practice had fallen into abeyance. Gyfford, wishing to ingratiate himself with the authorities, resolved on reviving the custom, and, to do so in the most ceremonious way, by going himself with the presents for seven years. Accordingly, on the 11th April 1721, accompanied by all the merchants and factors, and taking all his best men, aboutone hundred and twenty in number, and the same number of coolies, Gyfford started for Āṭṭinga, four miles up the river. Here they were received by an enormous crowd of people, who gave them a friendly reception. The details of what followed are imperfectly recorded, and much is left to conjecture ; but Gyfford's foolish overconfidence is sufficiently apparent. In spite of their brave display, his men carried no ammunition. Pūla Venjamuṭṭa was not to be seen. They were told he was drunk, and they must wait, till he was fit to receive them. He was apparently playing a double part, but the blame for what followed was afterwards laid on his rival, Pūla Caḍamon Pillay. Cowse's suspicions were aroused, and he advised an immediate return to Anjengo, but Gyfford refused to take the advice. He is said to have struck Cowse, and to have threatened him with imprisonment. The Rāṇi also sent a message, advising a return to Anjengo. It was getting late, and, to extricate himself from the crowd, Gyfford allowed the whole party to be inveigled into a small enclosure. To show his good-will to the crowd, he ordered his men to fire a salvo, and then he found that the ammunition carried by the coolies had been secured, and they were defenceless. In this hopeless poition, he managed to entrust a letter addressed to the storekeeper at Anjengo, to the hands of a friendly native. It reached Anjengo at one o'clock next day, and ran as follows :—

'Captain Sewell, we are treacherously dealt with here; therefore keep a very good look-out of any designs on you. Have a look to your two trankers.[1] We hope to be with you to-night. Take care and don't frighten the women; we are in no great danger. Give the bearer a chequeen'[2].

" But none of the English were to see Anjengo again. That night or the next morning, a sudden attack was made, the crowd surged in on the soldiers, overwhelmed them, and cut them to pieces. The principal English were seized and reserved for a more cruel death. In the confusion,

1. Tranqueira (Port.), a palisade.

2. Meaning sequin, the origin of the modern Anglo-Indianism, 'chick'.

Cowse, who was a favourite among the natives, managed to disguise himself, got through the crowd, and sought to reach Anjengo by a little-frequented path. By bad luck, he was overtaken by a Mahomedan merchant who owed him money. Cowse offered to acquit him of the debt, but to no purpose. He was mercilessly killed, and thus the debt was settled. 'Stone dead hath no fellow,' as the chronicler of his death says. The rest of the English wre tortured to death, Gyfford and the interpreter being reserved for the worst barbarities. Ignatio Malheiros was gradually dismembered, while Gyfford had his tongue torn out, was nailed to a log of wood, and sent floating down the river.

"It is easy to picture to one's self the consternation in Anjengo on that 12th of April, when, soon after midday, Gyfford's hasty note was received, and the same evening, when a score of wounded men (topasses) straggled in to confirm the worst fears; 'all miserably wounded, some with 12 or 13 cutts and arrows in their bodyes to a lower number, but none without any.' Gyfford had taken away all the able men with him, leaving in the fort only 'the dregs,' old men, boys, and pensioners, less than forty in number. At their head were Robert Sewell, who describes himself as storekeeper, captain and adjutant by order of Governor Boone; Lieutenant Peter Lapthrone, Ensign Thomas Davis, and Gunner Samuel Ince. The first three of them were absolutely useless, and Gunner Ince, whose name deserves to be remembered, was the only one of the four who rose to the situation. His first care was for the three English women, whose husbands had just been killed. By good fortune, there happened to be in the road a small country ship that had brought a consignment of cowries from the Maldives. Mrs. Gyfford, for the third time a widow, Mrs. Cowse with four children, and Mrs. Burton with two, were hastily put on board, and sailed at once for Madras. No mention appears of Mrs. Gyfford having any children with her, but she carried off the factory records and papers, and what money she could lay her hands on. She was no longer the confiding girl, who had given herself to Governor Harvey eleven years before. She had learned something of the world she lived in, and intended to take care of herself as well as she could. She even tried to carry off Peter Lapthrone with her, but Sewell intervened and prevented it. So giving him hasty directions to act as her agent, she passed through the dangerous Anjengo surf and got on board. A letter to her from Lapthrone, written a few weeks later, relates that the only property he could find belonging to her were 'two wiggs and a bolster of some ophium' in the warehouse.

"Having got rid of the white women, Sewell and his companions set to work to hold the fort against the attack that was inevitable. From the old records, we get an idea of what the fort was like. As designed by Brabourne, it covered a square of about sixty yards each way, but this did not include the two trankers, palisaded out-works, alluded to in Gyfford's note. Ten years before, the attention of the Council at Bombay had been drawn to the bad condition of the 'Fort house, being no more than timber covered with palm leaves (cajanns) so very dangerous taking fire,' and the chief of the factory was ordered to build 'a small compact house of brick with a hall, and conveniencys for half a dozen Company's servants. And being advised that, for want of a necessary house in the fort, they keep the fort-gate open all night for the guard going out and in, which irregularity may prove of so pernicious consequence as the loss of that garrison, especially in a country where they are surrounded with such treacherous people as the natives and the Dutch,' it was ordered that a 'necessary house over the fort walls' should be built, and the gates kept locked after 8 o'clock at night.

"How far these orders have been carried out does not appear; but the Company's goods were still kept in a warehouse outside the walls: some of the Company's servants also had houses outside, and the palm-leaf roofs were still there. For garrison, they only had about thirty-five boys and pensioners, 'whereof not twenty fit to hold a firelock,' and, for want of a sufficient garrison, it was necessary to withdraw from the Trankers, which were thought to be so important for the safety of the place. Desperate as was the outlook, gunner Ince, exerted himself like a man, animating everybody by his example. By his exertions, seven hundred bags of rice, with salt fish for a month, and the Company's treasure were got in from the warehouse, and an urgent appeal was sent to Calicut. The surgeon had been killed with Gyfford; they had no smith or carpenter or tools, except a few hatchets, and the Attinga people, swarming into Anjengo, burned and plundered the settlement, forcing a crowd of women and children to take refuge in the small fort. Though no concerted attack was made at first, the assailants tried with fire-arrows to set fire to the palm-leaf roofs, which had to be dismantled; and all through the siege, which lasted six months, the sufferings of the garrison were increased by the burning rays of a tropical sun or the torrential rains of the monsoon.

"On the 25th April, they were cheered by the arrival of two small English ships from Cochin, where the intelligence of the disaster had reached; and received a small reinforcement of seven men with a consignment of provisions. A message of condolence also had come from the Raja of Quilon, who offered to receive the women and children; so one hundred and fifty native women and children, widows and orphans of the slain, were sent off. On the 1st May, an ensign and fifty-one men, collected by Mr. Adams from Calicut and Tellicherry, joined the garrison and gave some relief from the constant sentry duty that was necessary. The enemy, meanwhile, had contented themselves with harrassing the garrison by firing long shots at them; but it was rumoured that the Raja of Travancore was sending troops, and then they would have to sustain a serious attack. Gunner Ince, on whom the whole weight of the defence rested, let it be known that in the last extremity he would blow up the magazine. It is cheering to find that there was at least one man who was prepared to do his duty. Sewell and Lapthrone got drunk, and joined with the warehouseman, a Portuguese named Rodriguez, in plundering the Company's warehouse and sending goods away to Quilon; the soldiers followed the example, and plundered the rooms inside the fort, while the late interpreter's family were allowed to send away, to Quilon, effects to the value of one hundred thousand fanams, though it was known that the Company had a claim on him for over two-thirds of the amount, on account of money advanced to him. Davis was dying of a lingering illness, to which he succumbed in the beginning of July.

"On the 24th June, a vigorous attack was made on the fort from three sides at once. On one side, the enemy had thrown up an entrenchment, and, on the river side, they had effected a lodgment in Cowse's house, a substantial building close to the wall of the fort. This would have soon made the fort untenable; so a small party was sent to dislodge the occupants. At first, they were repulsed, but a second attempt was successful. Marching up to the windows, 'where they were as thick as bees', they threw hand-grenades into the house, which was hurriedly evacuated; numbers of the enemy leaping into the river, where some of them were drowned. Ince, then, bombarded them out of the entrenchment, and the attack came to an end. Several of the garrison were wounded but none killed; but what chiefly mortified them was that the arms of the men slain with Gyfford were used against them. After this, the land blockade lingered on; but no very serious attack seems to have been made. A second reinforcement of thirty men was sent down by Adams from Calicut, and the Rāṇi and Pūla Venjamuṭṭa sent 'refreshments', and promised that the attacks of their rebellious subjects should cease. The Rāṇi also wrote to the Madras Council, and sent a deputation of one hundred Brahmins to Tellicherry to express her horror of the barbarities committed by her people, and her willingness to join the Company's forces in punishing the guilty.

"Intelligence of the disaster at Anjengo did not reach Bombay till the beginning of July. The monsoon was in full force, and no assistance could be sent till it was over. Men and supplies were gathered in from Carwar and Surat; and, on the 17th October, Mr. Midford, with three hundred men, reached Anjengo. His report on the state of affairs he found there makes it a matter of surprise that the place had not fallen. The safety of the fort had been entirely due to gunner Ince. Sewell's behaviour was that of a fool or a madman. Together with Lapthrone, he had set the example of plundering the Company, and their men had done as much damage as the enemy. Sewell, as storekeeper, had no books, and said he never had kept any. Lapthrone had retained two months' pay, due to the men killed with Gyfford, and asserted his right to it. Much of the Company's treasure was unaccounted for, and Mrs. Gyfford had carried off the books. Midford sent Sewell and Lapthrone under arrest to Bombay, where they were let off with a scolding, and proceeded to restore order. The Rāṇi and Venjamuṭṭa were friendly but told him he must take his own vengeance on the raiders for their inhuman action. So he commenced a series of raids into the surrounding country, which reduced it to some sort of subjection. Soon there came an order for most of his men to be sent back to Bombay, where warlike measures against Angria were on foot.

A cessation of arms was patched up, and Midford installed himself as chief.

"He proved to be no honester than his predecessors. He monopolized the pepper-trade on his own private account, making himself advances out of the Company's treasury. In less than a year, he was dead; but, before his death, Alexander Orme, then a private merchant on the coast, was sent to Anjengo as chief of the factory, at the special request of the Rāṇi. Before long, Orme had to report to the Council that there were due to the Company, from Gyfford's estate, 559,421 fanams, and that 140,260 gold fanams had disappeared during Midford's chiefship, which could not be accounted for. Midford had also drawn pay for twenty European soldiers who did not exist. The Council ascribed Midford's misdeeds to his 'unaccountable stupidity', and the Directors answered that 'the charges against Mr. Midford are very grievous ones.'

"In September 1722, the Council received from Orme a copy of the treaty he had made with the Rāṇi. The following were the chief provisions: the ringleaders in the attack on Gyfford were to be punished and their estates confiscated; the Rāṇi was to reinburse the Company for all expenses caused by the attack on Anjengo; the Company was to have exclusive right to pepper-trade, and to be empowered to build factories in the Rāṇi's dominions wherever they pleased; the Rāṇi was to return all arms taken in the late outbreak, and to furnish timber to rebuild the church that had been burnt. The treaty was guaranteed by the Rāṇi's brother, the Raja of Chinganatta.[1] By the Directors, it was received with mixed feelings.

"'Last year's letters took some notice about the Affair at Anjengo, We had not then the Account of the Treaty Mr. Orme made with the Queen of Attinga and the King of Chinganetty, We are sorry to find it included in the Treaty, That We must supply Soldiers to carry on

1. Chinganatta or Dēsinganāḍ or Quilon.

the War against her rebellious Subjects for which she is to pay the Charge, and in the Interim to pawn Lands for answering principal and Interest, because it will certainly involve us in a trouble if We succeed, and more if We don't; add to this, the variable temper and poverty of those people may incline them to refuse to refund, and in time they may redemand and force back their Lands, If the articles are fully comply'd with they seem to be for the Company's benefit, But We fear we shall nave the least Share of it, To what purpose is her Grant to Us of all the Pepper in her Countrey, If our unfaithful people there get all for themselves and none for Us, as you Charge Mr. Midford with doing, We don't want an Extend of Lands, if We could but (obtain) pepper cheap and sufficient, And what benefit will it be to Us, to have the liberty of building Factorys, which in Event is only a Liberty to lavish away Our Money, and turning Quick Stock into dead, unless you could be morally certain it would be worth while to get a small residence in the King of Chengenatty's Countrey where it is said the Dutch make great Investments of Piece Goods cheaper and better, than they used to do at Negapattam, and therefore have deserted it, We consider further, if such Goods as are proper for Our Europe Market were procurable, how comes it We have had none hitherto, It is true We have had Cloth from Anjengo good of the Sorts, but Invoiced so dear that We forbad sending more unless to be purchas'd at the prices We limited, since then we have heard no more about it, But we are told it is Traded in to Bombay to some profit, what Security can you have that the King of Chenganatty's Guarranteeship will answer and give full satisfaction, These are what appear to Us worthy your serious and deliberate consideration to be well thought of before you come to a determination What Orders to give, We find by your Consultations in January 1722/23 You had sent down Treasure to Anjengo, to enable the Chief to levy Souldiers to revenge the Murder of the English, since you could not spare Forces which as there exprest is absolutely necessary, for else the Natives will have but contemptible thoughts of the English, who will then loose their Esteem, had We ever found a benefit by their Esteem, something might be said for it, But in the present Case We fear We shall by Our Esteem at too dear a Rate, We should be extreamly glad to be mistaken and to find in effect what your 120th Paragraph says in words, that you hope to make it a Valuable Settlement.'[1] "

3. **Reprisal on Attingal.** Perhaps there was no immediate reprisal attempted; but that, before long, A̅ṯṯingal was assailed by the Anjengo factors is evident from the letter addressed by the king of Travancore, the suzerain of the queen of A̅ṯṯingal, to Mr. Alexander Orme, Chief of Anjengo, dated the 15th of August, in reply to one from the Chief. That letter discloses the arrangement made by the English East India Company and the king, whereby the former agreed to assist the latter in purging the country of its eternal and inveterate enemies, the Eṭṭuvīṭṭil Pillamārs.

Some of the conditions of the agreement attached to the letter explain the more or less veiled resentment lurking behind the observations of our author regarding the English. The 9th clause of the agreement stipulated that "all the piece-goods and other things which the Honorable Company require I shall order the merchants to supply," while, by the next clause, it was added, " I shall soon confirm, by writing, that I shall not give to any other European nation any goods which are necessary to the Honorable English East India Company." The 12th clause said, "Every year in various kinds, which the Honorable Company require, I shall order to supply up 100,000 piece-goods." These and other stipulations of the agreement were, by

1. Letter from the Court of Directors to Bombay, 25th March 1724.
2. Pp. 272—90.

no means, palatable to the Dutch, who possessed a factory at Anjengo, and who were all along striving to monopolise the Malabar trade.

4. **Madagascar Pirates.** For the suppression of the Madagascar pirates, the English Government despatched Commodore Thomas Mathews to the East Indies with a strong squadron, consisting of the *Lyon*, 50 guns, *Salisbury*, 40 guns, *Exeter*, 50 guns, and *Shoreham*, 20 guns. The Company's ship *Grantham* was also placed under his orders, to act as a store-ship. In Byng's successful action with the Spanish, off Cape Passaro (August 1718), Mathews had commanded the *Kent* with credit, but, with the exception of courage, he apparently failed to possess a single quality for independent command. Irascible, domineering to his subordinates, and insolent to all others he was brought in contact with, he was entirely devoid of judgment or discretion. Twenty years later, when he became better known, Walpole wrote of his 'brutal manners', and Horace Mann nicknamed him 'Il Furibonds'. There could not have been a worse selection for the work in hand.

In February 1721, the squadron sailed from Spithead, with orders to rendezvous at St. Augustine's Bay. Soon after leaving the Channel, the *Salisbury* and *Exeter* were dismasted in a storm, and were obliged to put into Lishar to repair damages. Mathews continued his voyage with the *Lyon* and the *Shoreham* to St. Augustine's Bay. He found no pirate-ships there at the time, and good policy demanded that he should await the *Salisbury* and the *Exeter*. Instead of doing so, he continued his voyage to Bombay, where he arrived on the 27th of September. Before leaving, he entrusted to the natives of St. Augustine's Bay a letter for Captain Cockburn of the *Salisbury*, in which a number of particulars were given of the squadron. The proceeding was so ill-advised and so well calculated to defeat the object of the squadron's coming into Indian waters, that it was believed in the squadron that Mathews had done it purposely to put the pirates on their guard. Whether this was his intention or not, it serves to show the opinion held of him by those under his command. Soon after Mathews' departure, Taylor and La Buze reached St. Augustine's Bay, read the letter, and sailed at once for Fort Dauphin, in the south-eastern end of Madagascar. The *Salisbury* and *Exeter* arrived soon afterwards, and, getting no news either of Mathews or the pirates, sailed for Bombay[1].

5. **Marauders of Angria.** Of this expedition against the pirates of Angria, we have accounts which seem not to agree with one another in important particulars. Mr. Danvers, in a note, observes that the report on this transaction, which must have been sent home, is not now in existence amongst the India Office records, and proceeds to quote from a history of the wars with Angria, written by Clement Downing, an officer of the ship, *Salisbury*, which was engaged in the attack on the pirate. Downing agrees with our author in attributing treachery to the Portuguese. He says, " The day of attack having arrived, the Viceroy of Goa went on board his ship on the plea that he was taken very ill. The Commodore sent his own doctor to him to offer his service and supply him with such medicines as might be necessary, but he returned and reported to the Commodore that he did not perceive anything to be the matter with the Viceroy. On the appointed day, the whole army advanced to the attack with scaling ladders, whereupon the Angrians came down in a great body, with several elephants, which the general of the North perceiving, he broke the order of his wing; and the seamen being employed in storming the castle (which for certain they would have taken, had they been properly supported), the whole army fell into confusion. So soon as the enemy saw

1. The Pirates of Malabar, pp. 170—71.

that the Portuguese were on the retreat, and the whole army was confused, they came down upon them and made a terrible slaughter amongst the English soldiers and seamen; great part of our army was taken, with most of the ammunition thereto belonging. The whole army was now on the rout, and the Commodore came on shore in a violent rage, flew at the General of the North and thrust his cane in his mouth, and treated the Viceroy not much better. Thus the Angrians defeated us this time entirely by the treachery of the Portuguese who seemed to design only to lead our people on and then to leave them in the lurch; this seemed the more probable, for they never once offered to pursue them, but let them march off without any molestation. We got off most of our scattered forces, and what part of the baggage and artillery we had saved, and re-embarked, though we had great numbers killed and wounded.''

Col. Biddulph, whose account of the expedition will be quoted presently, also refers to the Viceroy's 'feigning illness' and observes that 'the English were left to shift for themselves,' in the subsequent arrangements made between the Portuguese Viceroy and the Angria. But Mr. Danvers does not refer either to the 'feigning of illness' by the Portuguese Viceroy or to the 'leaving of the English to shift for themselves.' In his account of the transaction, Mr. Danvers observes, "On the 28th December, the Portuguese camp was strengthened by means of a palisade, and, on the 29th, some skirmishing took place. The Viceroy was now taken ill, and, on the advice of his doctors, went on board his ship, leaving the command to Dom Antonio de Castra e Mello and Robert Cowan. On the 30th, the Angria was reinforced by 6,000 horse, which were sent to him by Baji Rao.

"On the 1st January 1722, the general, Baji Rao, sent word that San Raja, his lord, was a friend of the Portuguese, and that he really had no intention of assisting the Angria against him, although it was his duty to help his vassals: all he wished for now was that the Viceroy and the Angria should come to terms and conclude a peace. The Viceroy, perceiving he could do nothing against the enemy, who had such a superior force in point of numbers, listened to this proposal, and agreed to a cessation of hostilities pending negotiations, each party handing over to the other five officers as hostages.

"After a conference lasting several days, an agreement was concluded to the effect that all the territories under the Portuguese Crown should be exempted from tribute, either to the Angria or to the Maharattas; that the merchandise of the Sirkar which might be sent to Portuguese ports should be exempt from dues, as well as all Portuguese merchandise sent to the ports of the Maharaja; that the Portuguese Captains should, in future, abstain from giving convoy to the ships of the enemies of the Maharatta; that assistance should be mutually rendered by the one to the other whenever required; and that all vessels seized by either party should be returned. This document was dated from the camp of Alibaga, the 9th January 1722.

"This agreement, it was stipulated, was to be also binding on the English nation, as an ally of the Portuguese, and was to be ratified by them within eight days. The ships set sail on the 17th January. The Portuguese fleet carried the Viceroy to Goa, where he arrived on the following day. The Governor of Bombay sailed soon after for England. * * "[1]

We have a full account of the expedition given us by Col. Biddulph, which may be given hereunder:—

"Meanwhile, great preparations were being made for a fresh campaign againt Angria, and, while these bickerings went on among the subordinates, the Governor and Mathews were engaged in planning the

1. Vol. II, pp. 392—3.

attack. Long before Mathew's arrival, negotiations had been opened between the Portuguese Viceroy, Francisco Jose de Sampaio e Castro, and the Bombay Council for a joint attack on Colaba. Through the management of Mr. Robert Cowan, who had been deputed, in March, to Goa, for the purpose, a treaty of mutual co-operation had been drawn up, by which the Bombay Council undertook to furnish an equal force. The negotiation was not completed till the beginning of September, and Cowan, in recognition of the ability he had displayed, was given a seat in the Council. The combined forces were to assemble at Chaul, then a Portuguese possession, and march overland to attack Colaba. Forgetting the old adage about setting the skin of the bear while the animal was still alive, it was further agreed that Colaba, after capture, was to be the property of Portugal, while Gheriah was to be handed over to the English. The arrival of Mathews' squadron, therefore, brought a welcome addition to the Bombay armaments.

" A camp was formed for the expeditionary force; drilling was the order of the day; Cowan was named General, and various commissions as Colonels, Majors, and Captains were granted to officers of the navy who volunteered for land service. On the 30th October, a seven days' fast was ordered, to secure the divine blessing on the undertaking, and the chaplain was directed to preach an appropriate sermon.

" On the 29th November, the expedition left Bombay, and anchored off Chaul, where the Portuguese force had already assembled. The English force consisted of 655 Europeans and topasses, a troop of 40 horsemen and 1,514 sepoys. Mathews also contributed 200 seamen, of whom 50 were to serve the guns. The artillery consisted of two 24-pounders, two 18-pounders, four 9-pounders, six small field guns, two mortars, and eight cochorns. Thé Portuguese force consisted of

1,000 Europeans, 160 horsemen, 350 volunteers and 2,400 sepoys with six 24-pounders, six 18-pounders, ten field pieces and eight mortars, commanded by the General of the North. The Viceroy was also present. Such a force combined with the men of war, was sufficient, under proper direction, to have destroyed all Angria's strongholds along the coast.

"Some delay was caused by the necessity of building a bridge over the Ragocim river, and then the army advanced, to be quickly brought to a stand-still again, till sufficient transport could be brought from Bombay. On the 12th December, after marching round the head of the Alibagh river, the army encamped close to the Alibagh fort; while the men-of-war anchored in the roads. During the march, a few of Angria's horsemen had been seen from time to time. On one occasion, while the Viceroy, accompanied by Mathews, Cowan, and other Commanders, was riding to view the country, a horseman approached them under cover of a cactus hedge, and threw his lance, wounding Mathews in the thigh. Matthews vainly pursued him, beside himself with rage at his wound and at his pistols missing fire.

"On the 13th, an assault was made on the fort, though the heavy guns had not been landed. Outside the fort, there were fifteen hundred horse and a thousand foot sent by Sahoojee to Angria's assistance. The Portuguese were to face them, while five hundred English soldiers and marines, led by Naval forces, were to force the gateway and scale the rampart. Common sense demanded that Sahoojee's force outside the fort should be disposed of, and the heavy guns that had been brought with so much labour from Chaul should be mounted and used, before any attempt at an assault was projected ; but there was a woeful absence of ordinary capacity among the commanders. At four in the afternoon, the little force under Brathwaite, first lieutenant of the *Lyon*, who held the rank of colonel for the occasion, advanced to the assault. The gateway was blocked, and could not be forced; many of the scaling ladders were too short, and the affair resolved itself into a struggle by a small number who had gained the rampart to maintain themselves, while the rest remained exposed to the fire from the walls. In the midst of it, Sahoojee's force advanced on the Portuguese, who broke and fled in wild confusion leaving the English force to their fate. The assaulting party, seeing their danger, drew off, leaving many of their wounded behind them, the whole force gave ground, and soon there was wild rush for the camp, luckily not followed by the Maharatta horsemen. Thirty-three had been killed, and twenty-seven wounded; among the latter, Lieutenant Bellamy of the Navy who had behaved with great dash and bravery. Matthews' marines suffered heavily. Though wanting in discipline, they displayed much courage. All the field guns and a great deal of ammunition fell into the hands of the Maharattas. The whole blame was laid on the Portuguese, to whom treachery was imputed. Mathews, always violent, flew at the General of the North, assaulted him, and treated the Viceroy not much better. A little more enterprise on the part of the Maharattas would have destroyed the whole force. The following day some heavy guns were landed, and a four-gun battery was constructed. But the Portuguese had had enough of it and were determined to withdraw.

" From the beginning, there had been little cordiality between the ill-matched allies. In the English camp, Cowan was devoid of military experience or instinct, and commanded little confidence among men habituated to defeat in their attacks on Angrian strongholds ; while Matthews, violent and overbearing, claimed a right to direct operations that he knew nothing about. The Portuguese, on their side, proud in the recollection of the great position they had once held on the Malabar coast, and which, though now fast falling into decay, was still immeasurably superior to that of the English merchants, were disgusted at the constant drunkenness, quarrelling, and want of discipline among the English, and incensed at the charge of treachery, for which there was no justification. Feigning illness, the Viceroy betook himself to his ship. Angria saw his opportunity of breaking up the alliance, and opened negotiations with him. On the 17th, the Viceroy wrote to the English proposing a suspension of arms. With a bad grace, they were obliged to consent, seeing, in the negotiation, which was against the compact that neither should treat separately, further confirmation of their suspicion of treachery. Angria granted the Portuguese full reparation for injuries, and formed an offensive and defensive alliance with them. The English were left to shift for themselves. Full of wrath, they embarked at once and sailed for Bombay on the 28th."[1]

LETTER VIII.

1. Multiplicity of Kings and Party Hatred. Ibn Batuta (A. D. 1324) says :—"In the country of Malabar are twelve kings, the greatest of whom has fifty thousand troops at his command : the least five thousand or thereabouts. That which separates the district of one king from that of another is a wooden gate upon which is written, 'The gate of safety of such an one.' For, when any criminal escapes from the district of one king, and gets safely into that of another, he is quite safe ; so that no one has the least desire to take him, so long as he remains there."[1]

Friar Jordanus says, "In this greater India are 12 idolatrous kings and more. For there is one very powerful king in the country where pepper grows, and his kingdom is called Molebar. There is also the king of Singuyli and the king of Columbum, the king of which is called Lingna, but his kingdom Mohebar."[2]

On the arrival of the Portuguese in Malabar, they found the country cut up into the following little kingdoms mentioned by Faria-Y-Souza. "Cannanore, Tanore, Moringue, Cranganore, Parur, Mangate, Replim, Cochin, Diamper Pimenta, Tarangule, Cale Coulam, Coulam, Chengernate, Gundra, Travancore, Maturte and Pitemen."[3]

"Below this (Mount Delli) to Cape Comorin are 93 degrees, and is called Malabar, divided into three kingdoms, which own no superior. The kingdom of Cranganore (evidently a mistake for Cannanore or Kōlattunāḍ) has 20 leagues of the coast, in which are these towns,—Cota, Coulam, Nilichalam, Marabia,

1. P. 167.
2. Ch. V, para 1.
3. Vol. II, p. 244.

Boleapatam, Cannanore, the metrapolis, in the latitude of 20 degrees, Tremapatam, Chebu, Maim and Puriapatam. Here begins the kingdom of Calicut, and runs 27 leagues, and has these towns—Calicut, the metrapolis in about 11 degrees and 70 minutes of latitude, Coulete, Chale, Parangale, and Tanoor, the head of the kingdom, subject to the Zamorin or Emperor of Calicut, and Chetwaye, the last bound of this Empire. Next is the little kingdom of Cranganore, which borders on that of Cochin, then that of Coulam, and lastly Travancore, subject to Narasinga.''[1]

Writing in the middle of the 18th century, Fra Bartolomeo gives us the names of the following kings and chiefs as the representatives of those, among whom Perumāl divided his empire:—"Kings of the first rank were, the Zamorin and Perumpadipil, or the king of Cochin. To the second rank belonged the kings of Tanore, Codungalore, Parpurangari, Airur, Cannanur Edapilli or Rapolim, Cayamcollam, Temali, Parur, Punettur Alangatta, Angamali and Aynicara. Those of the third rank were called Karttava, that is, princes or lords. Such were the Karttava of Panamucatta, Nandielette, Ciangara Cotta, Puḍucōṭṭa, Māpraṅam, Mūriāḍ, Cunnṭṭēri, Cōḍaśśēri, Ceṫṫaṭūr, Puṭṭenpīdika, Curumbilāga, Ceṭṭia. Several of these petty princes and lords still existed at the time I arrived in Malabar.''[2]

The political condition of Malabar in the beginning of the 18th century was anything but satisfactory. Like Italy before it was united under the house of Savoy, Malabar was cut up into a great number of small independent principalities, with rival interest and mutual jealousies. These little principalities were so numerous that a Malayalam saying pithily put it that "though two steps might be made in one territory, a

1. Portuguese Asia, Vol. I, pp. 95—6.
2. P. 168.

third must pass the boundary." These princes did indeed acknowledge, in some vague, shadowy manner, the suzerainty of the greater chiefs. The Zamorin of Calicut claimed to have been invested with the over-lordship of Malabar by the last Chēramān Perumāl, while the Raja of Cochin claimed the Perumāl's throne as his direct descendant in the female line and lawful successor. The claims of these chiefs were thus antagonistic, and the Cochin and Calicut rulers ever kept alive their perennial quarrels. The Zamorin, backed up by his Arab and Moorish allies, often waged war against the Cochin Raja, who was strongly supported first by the Portuguese and after them by the Dutch. The whole country marshalled itself into two factions, the northern princes and their vassals, known as the Paññiyūr faction, supporting the Zamorin, the southern faction, known as the Chovvarakūr, espousing the cause of the Cochin Raja. This distracted state of the country continued till about the middle of the 18th century, when it reached its height. Fra Bartolomeo, a contemporary writer, gives us a vivid description of the state of Malabar at the time. He says, "These princes who were not unanimous among themselves, attacked each other's territories; carried away their subjects as captives; excited the chief men against one another; deprived several families of their property, and, as they were too weak to subdue an opulent and high-spirited people, gave to some private individuals full freedom to revenge the injuries which they had suffered. Scarcely a week now passed in which some murder was not committed. Children massacred their parents; and even the sovereign was no longer safe in his palace." "Such crimes," adds the pious *padre*, "could not remain unpunished; and the inhabitants soon experienced that chastisement which their cruelty deserved."[1]

Nemesis appeared in the person of the great Mārttāṇḍa Varma, king of Travancore. That sovereign

1. P. 171.

and his celebrated minister, Ramien Ḍelava, after annexing the territories of Quilon and Koṭṭārakkara, which were ruled by princes of collateral branches of the Travancore family, extended their conquests northwards, and incorporated with the king's dominions the principalities of Kāyamkuḷam, Ṭekkankūr, Vaḍakkankūr and Ampalappuḷa. The whole tract lying between Quilon and Arūkkuṯṯi was thus brought under the direct sway of Travancore. "Thus ended," says Fra Bartolomeo, "the dominion of the petty Malabar sovereigns and princes; thus was humanity avenged, and thus were the crimes punished and the licentiousness suppressed, by which this country had been distracted ever since the 10th century. * * Of a greater portion of the above events, I was myself an eye-witness."[1] After this, events marched with rapid strides. The Dutch were worsted by Travancore in an inglorious war, terminated by an ignominous treaty, which wrecked their political supremacy on the coast; the Raja of Cochin was shorn of a considerable portion of his dominions and confined within certain narrow limits, the Zamorin was driven back beyond the northern limits of Cochin, and the Mysorean invasion of Malabar soon paved the way for British supremacy, which was achieved in the opening years of the 19th century.

2. **Pandelakoers and Chodderakoers.** These stand respectively for Paṅṅiyūrkūr, i e., the Paṅṅiyūr faction, and Chōvarakūr, i. e., the Chōvvaram or Śukapuram faction. Tradition in Malabar attributes the division of the Malabar Brahmans into these two factions to the warrior sage, Paraśu Rāma, himself, the hero-saint of Kēraḷa. It is said that he divided the colony of Brahmans, he had introduced, into the Paṅṅiyūr Grāmakkār or boar-villagers, and the Chōvūr Grāmakkār or bird villagers, the former being the

1. Pp. 172-3.

worshippers of Varāham, the incarnation of the boar, while the latter were the worshippers of Śarabham (Garuḍa), a kind of huge bird, reputed to be the *Vahana* or vehicle of Viṣhṇu. There can be no doubt that, in the early history of the Brahman community in Malabar, there was a split into two factions, the Paṅṅiyūr Grāmam adopting the Vaiṣhṇavite faith, and the Chōvūr Grāmam, the Saivite faith. Mr. Logan observes that a more or less successful resistance, probably with Brahman aid, was made by the Malayalees against the aggression of the Western Chalūkyans, and, as the boar was the emblem of the Chalūkya dynasty, it is probable that the decline of the Paṅṅiyūr Grāmam and the ascendency of the Chōvūr Grāmam were brought about at this time.

3. **Origin of the above two Factions.** The real origin of these factions is lost in obscurity. It is very improbable that the factious spirit which marshalled the country into these opposing divisions, and which continued to exercise its evil influence for a long time, could have arisen at the bidding of any single individual, however powerful he might have been. It would be more reasonable to suppose that it was the outcome of the development of internecine quarrels social and political, which, in the long run, engendered a spirit of animosity between emigrants who had colonised Malabar from different places without any common ties of race, blood or language. It is possible that the Zamorin of Calicut and the Raja of Cochin took advantage of this and made use of it for their own ambitious projects of self-aggrandisement. The *Tohfut ul Mujahideen* says, "The Rajas of Malabar are of two parties; the first, those who support the Zamorin; the second, those who are in alliance with the Rajah of Cochin. Now this division is only occasioned by the circumstance of the rivalry of those two great chieftains,

1. Pp. 243—4.

and which, when it shall be at an end, this distinction of party shall cease."[1]

4. **Partition by last Perumal.** The general impression in Malabar, based, no doubt, on long-standing tradition, is that the last Chēramān Perumāl, in his old age, turned Mahomedan, and went on a pilgrimage to Mecca, after partitioning his empire amongst his friends, dependants, and relatives. There is, however, little historical evidence, so far as we know, to support this tradition. The question of the last Perumāl's conversion to Islamisim and the alleged pilgrimage to Mecca will be discussed presently, but here we shall make a few remarks on its sequel, the alleged partition of the Kērala Empire. The Kēralōṭpaṭṭi, a work of comparatively recent date and of more than doubtful authority, contains a detailed record of the tradition. Of the extent of the last Perumāl's empire, one version of the work says, "Between Gōkarṇam and Cape Comorin, within Kannetti and Puṭupaṭṭaṇam, there lie, on the south, Changalapuraṭṭa Aḷi (port), and, on the north, Puṭupaṭṭaṇam Aḷi (port), on the east, 18 mountain passes, on the west, the 18 entrances to the deep. Between these and the four corners, northwest, northeast, southeast and southwest lies the country of Chēramān (Paraśurāma's land), 160 kāṭam in extent." It is significant that this description does not take in the dominions of of the two Kōlaṭṭiris, i. e. Travancore in the south and Kōlaṭṭnād or North Malabar in the north. But the Mangalore edition of the Kēralōṭpaṭṭi records that Chērmānnād or Chēramān's territory was divided into three grand divisions and placed under three great sovereigns independent of one another. These again were subdivided into minor principalities, ruled over by chiefs who were held responsible to their immediate superiors, the three great independent sovereigns. Uḍaya Varman Kōlaṭṭiri was made Perumāl (sovereign) of the North (crowned king and lord of Kērala)

1. P. 62.

To him was given 350,000 Nairs together with Perumāl's dagger. These were assigned to him to stand guard on the right side of Valarbhaṭṭaṭṭhu Kōṭṭa (fort). The Śiva-temple of Ṭalipparampa was also given to him with injunctions to do what lay in his power to increase its sanctity. The Perumāl had the king anointed and enthroned by Nāyaka Nambūripād, the high priest. Under the king was placed subordinate chiefs, Chulali Kaimal and Nērpaṭ Kaimal with twelve kāṭams (leagues) of land, and 12,000 Nayars each. The Perumāl then blessed Uḍaya Varman and said to him, 'If I return, you shall be Ilamkūr (heir-apparent); if I don't return, you shall have Chēramān's Crown (chief authority.)'

The southern portion, comprising Vēṇāṭu and Ōṭanād, was given to Vēṇāṭṭaṭikal (the present Travancore dynasty), a descendant of Kulaśēkhara. To him was assigned 350,000 Nairs, armed to serve him in the new palace, known as Ōmanappuṭṭan Kōvilakam, on the right-hand side of the fort at Kalkulam. The Perumāl said to him, 'You must assist Kōlaṭṭiri, and expend money, and he was thus appointed ruler of Kuvalanād (one of the old divisions of Kerala).'

To the Sūrya Kṣheṭriya was given 52 kāṭams of land, and under him were placed 18 barons and 42 (or 72) ministers, of whom Pāliaṭ Mēnon was the foremost. Many fighting men were also given him. The Perumāl conferred on him the title of Perimpaṭappu (the greatly extended). This dynasty is now represented by the ruling family of Cochin.

Then follows an account of the distribution among minor chiefs. The Perumāl's younger brother, Kavisimharēru, (by no means a Malayalam name) was appointed to rule over Ṭulunād to the north of Perinapula. Under him were placed four minor chiefs, Parampar, Ajilar, Savittar, and Samanṭereru. Polnad, extending over six kāṭams with a population of

10,000 Nayars, was assigned to Poṙlāṭiri. He was ordered to live in the palace at Mallūr, and enforce the 16 ācharams (customs, observances) introduced by the Perumāl. What these were is not known. 36 kāṭams of land, with a population of 300,000 Nairs, were given the Kuṙumpṙaṭiri. To the Rajas of Quilon and Panṭalam, three and five kāṭams of land each were given. The unstinted bounty of the Perumāl was shared in a lesser degree by the minor chiefs of Parappūswarūpam, Veṭṭaṭṭuswarūpam, Kāyamkulaṭṭu Chervay Swarūpam, etc., etc. Ṭiruṅāvāye was given to the chief of Ārangōṭṭu Swarūpam (the Vaḷḷuvanāṭ Raja), who was entrusted with the due celebration of the Mahāmākham festival.

Under this arrangement, it will be observed that the Zamorin was excluded, and so, the Kēraḷōṭpaṭṭi proceeds to say that, as Chēramān Perumāl was about to set sail to Mecca, the survivor of the two Ēṙāṭi brothers, who had fought for the Perumāl in his life and death struggle with Kṛṣhṇa Raya of Ānagunṭi, went to the Perumāl at Ṭṛkkāryūr Chiṭṙakūṭam, but found that he had already partitioned his kingdom. The Perumāl had, however, left with him one ḍēśom (village), so small that a cock-crowing could be heard all over it, also one bit of thorny jungle. He gave the Ēṙāṭi these, and expressed his extreme regret that the recipient did not turn up earlier. Insignificant as the gift was, the Ēṙāṭi accepted it, as it was accompanied with the Perumāl's sword and with the Perumāḷ's blessing, 'die and kill and seize,' and 'make yourself master of all Malanād (Malabar).' The modern representative of the Ēṙāṭi is the family of the Zamorin of Calicut. The Zamorin, it is said, was forbidden to go to war with either the North or South Kōlaṭṭiri Rajas, (the Travancore and Chiṙakkal Rajas), but he might wage war with the other chiefs.

Besides the Kēraḷōṭpaṭṭi, the only other source of information we have is the Kērala Māhāṭmyam, a

Sanskrit work on 'the Greatness of Kērala' of some local reputation. But it gives no corroboration to this story. The Māhāṭmyam gives a different account of the origin of the four principal ruling dynasties of Malabar. Travancore and Kōlaṭṭiri are said to have derived their title from the brothers, Bhānu Vikṛama and Raṇa Vikṛama, whom Paraśu Rāma had appointed to rule in the south and in the north. These two royal houses, viz., those of Travancore and Kōlaṭnād, still continue to have community of pollution, and, whenever the Travancore line stood a chance of extinction, adoptions used to be made from the Kōlaṭ family or its collateral branches. The Cochin Raja is said to be descended from Lavapuṭṛa, a descendant of Ayōḍhya Kṣheṭṛyas, who was placed by Paraśu Rāma at Bālapuri (Cochin). As regards the Zamorin, the Māhāṭmyam observes that "from thence Paraśu Rāma proceeded to Gōpakūṭapuri (Ēṛnāṭu), and founded the Zamorin dynasty (Malayalam Ṭāmūṭiri) by depositing a Sāmanṭa virgin with the Brahman chiefs. Her son ruled in Curupuri, endowed with Paraśu Rāma's sword."[1]

Comparing the Māhāṭmyam with the Kēraloṭpaṭṭi, Mr. Logan says that the former is full of the usual inflated Brahmanical legends, and is not worthy of serious analysis as is its more popular form, the Kēraloṭpaṭṭi. He is, therefore, inclined to accept the version of the Kēraloṭpaṭṭi with slight modifications. He believes that the Perumāl, who turned Mahomedan and undertook the pilgrimage to Mecca, was not the last one, but a predecessor of his, named Palli Bāṇa Perumāl, that the Perumāls described as having reigned after the apostate were either the north or south Kōlaṭṭiris or the Ṭulu or Cochin chiefs, and that the principal actors on the Malayāli stage, after the flight or pilgrimage of the Mahomedan Palli Bāṇa Perumāl, ought to be the north and south branches of the Kōlaṭṭiris, and the other chiefs who *attained*

1. Madras Journal of Literature and Science, Vol. XIII.

independence in consequence of the Perumāl's flight. He fixes the 25th of August 825 A. D., the day of Ōṇam festival, as the identical day on which the southern Kōlaṭṭiri and perhaps also the northern branch broke away, possibly under pressure of foreign influences, or possibly out of disgust at Chēraman Perumāl's conversion to Islam, from their allegiance to the last of the Kērala Perumāls. Mr. Logan is also of opinion that it is not at all improbable that the northern Kōlaṭṭiris are descended from a matrimonial alliance between the last of the Kērala Perumāls and a lady of the stock of the southern Feudatory (the Travancore, south Kōlaṭṭiri Rajas). All this is but mere conjecture; and, so far as we have any data to work upon, it will be found that these conjectures are more or less imaginary. The partition of Malabar is made to hang upon the alleged conversion to Mahomedanism of Chēramān Perumāl and his pilgrimage to Mecca. A detailed inquiry into the question makes it clear that there is little or no historical basis, so far as known at present, for those allegations.

There is almost contemporary evidence of an altogether unimpeachable character to show that the various dynasties ruling over Malabar had actually existed and were in possession of their respective principalities long before the alleged division of the country by the last Perumāl; so that the theory of their having derived their authority from him cannot bear scrutiny for a moment. This consists of three ancient Malayāli deeds, which have excited considerable interest among historians and orientalists, not simply for their value on philological and ethnographic grounds, but also for the flood of light they throw on the early social and political condition of Southern India. By these deeds, the ancient kings of Kērala had conferred on the Jewish and Syrian Christian communities of Malabar certain peculiar privileges, which those communities still partially enjoy.

The first of these is " A grant of Anjuvaṇṇam to Joseph Rabban, given by the Perumāl, Bhāskara Ravi Vaṙma, attested by the chief Rajas of Kērala."

The witnesses to this are :—

(1) " Thus do I know Gōvaṙḍhana Māṙṭṭāṇḍan, owner (uṭayavaṙ) of Vēṇāṭu (Travancore).

(2) " Thus do I know Kōṭei Śrī Kaṇṭhan, owner (uṭayavaṙ) of Vēṇavali Province, perhaps an older name for Ōṭanaṭu. South vassals.

(3) " Thus do I know Manavepala Manaviyan, owner of Erala Province, the Province of the Ṭāmūṭiri.

(4) "Thus do I know Rairen Chāṭṭen, owner of the Valluva Province. Northern vassals.

(5) " Thus do I know Coṭṭi Ravi, owner of Neḍumpaṙayūr (Palghat Rajas)."

The second is a grant from Vīra Rāghava Perumāl to Iravi Cortan of Koḍungallūr, making over to him the Principality of Maṇigrāmam, and elevating him to the position of sovereign-merchant of Kērala.

The witnesses to the document are :—

" With the knowledge of Vēṇāṭu and Ōṭanāṭu (rulers) have we given it.

" With the knowledge of Ēṙṇāṭu and Valluvanāṭu (rulers) have we given it."

Dr. Gundhert, the eminent Malayalam scholar, whose translation of the deeds has been here accepted, explains that Ōṭanāṭu is Kāyamkulam, now in Travancore. Eṙnāṭu is the original province of Ṭāmūṭiri or Zamorin, and his neighbours were the Āraṅgōṭṭu Valluvanāṭu dynasty. Vēṇāṭu is well-known as Travancore.

The third is "an act" by which one *Marvan Sapir* transferred a piece of ground near the sea-shore with several families of heathen castes to a country church, the grant being made with the Palace Major's sanction

BB.

(probably the commissioner of Sţhaṇu Ravi Gupţa). The grant is made also with the sanction of the Ayyan Aţikal governing the Vēṇāţu (Travancore). His next heir, the second Raja Rāma, brother of the former, his officers, ministers, etc., are also cited as witnesses. The Travancore Maha Raja is still poetically styled the " Vēṇāţţaţikal Ţiruvaţikal."

We have had occasion to refer to the dates of these documents already, and, for the present purpose, we may accept provisionally the dates assigned to them by Mr. Logan (viz., A. D. 700, 744 and 824).

These three deeds, read together, evidence broadly the following facts :—

Kērala was, between the end of the seventh century and the first quarter of the ninth century, a kingdom extending probably from Quilon in the south to Calicut in the north, ruled over by the following kings at the period shown against their names :—

No. 1. (A. D. 700) Bhāskara Ravi Vaṙma.
No. 2. (A. D. 744) Vīra Rāghava Chakṙavaṙţţi.
No. 3. (A. D. 824) Sţhāṇu Ravi Gupţa.

We may also gather that *during* the time of these Perumāls, and *previous* to the periods of the *last* of them, the following dynasties were in possession of various portions of Malabar, as owners (uţayavar) and ruling over them :—

(1) Travancore or Vēṇāţu.
(2) The Zamorin or Ēṙṇāţu.
(3) Kāyamkulam or Ōţanāţu.
(4) Ārangōţţu or Valluvanād.
(5) Neḍumpaṙayūr or Pālakkāţu.

Of the four chief dynasties of Malabar, we have here the names of two, those missing being the houses of Cochin and Kōlaţţunād. It is said that the Hebrew version of the Jewish deed contains a statement that the name of the Cochin chief is not there, because he was the heir of the Perumāl. But, according to Dr. Day,[1] the Cochin Raja had the title of 'Ravilōka Ṣharajay' conferred on him by the Perumāl about 325 A.D. This assumes the existence of Cochin as a separate principality even before the alleged partition. Mr. Logan observes that "the absence of the Kōlaṭṭiri from among the array of witnesses in the above deeds leads to the surmise that the northern Kōlaṭṭiris had not up to this time attained to the dignity of a separate dynasty, whereas their cousins, the southern Kōlaṭṭiris, had;" while Dr. Gundhert observes that "it does not seem that, in the time of these three documents, the northern Malabar or Kōlaṭṭiri did belong to the Perumāls; for, if it did, its Rajas would certainly have obtained as high and conspicuous a place in the line of witnesses as their relations of Vēṇaṭu to whom in olden times they appear certainly superior." In controverting the latter position, Mr. Logan remarks that, so far as evidence is yet forthcoming, there is nothing to show that the north Kōlaṭṭiri dynasty had a separate existence in the eighth century A. D. But one would have expected Mr. Logan to refer, under the circumstances, to positive evidence to show that the north Kōlaṭṭiri was, at the time, very insignificant, or that it had not attained the dignity of a separate dynasty, rather than be content with the remark that there is no evidence forthcoming tending the other way. There is, on the other hand, the testimony of the Kērala Māhāṭmyam which describes "Kērala as being first under the rule of the united Travancore and Kōlaṭṭiri dynasties, the sway of which, being contracted by foreign aggressions in the north, paved the way for the independent rule of the Kōlaṭṭiri branch."[2] If we follow the boundaries of the Chēra or Kērala country, as given

1. P. 43.

2. Madras Jour. of Lit. & Sc., Vol. XIII, p. 1.

by Dr. Burnell and Professor Dawson, we see that they do not take in North Malabar, and this circumstance tallies with the statement of the Kērala Māhātmyam that the Kōlaṭṭiri was in absolute possession of his country of Kōlaṭṭūnaḍ. Bishop Caldwell is disposed to identify the ruler of Kōlaṭṭūnaḍ as the descendant of Kōla, one of the four sons of Akrīḍa or Ḍushyanṭa mentioned in the Harivamśa and other Purāṇās.[1]

Mr. Logan argues from a supposed declaration, alleged to be still made by the Maharajas of Travancore on receiving the state sword at their coronations, viz., "I will keep this sword, until the uncle who has gone to Mecca returns." From this, it is argued that the Southern Kōlaṭṭiris assumed independence only after the Perumāl had left the country, and then only on the understanding that it was to be laid aside directly he returned. If it were true that the Maharajas of Travancore have, at any time, made such a declaration, there might be some foundation for the argument. But *it is not* true that they have to make, or they do make, or they ever made, any such declaration. The statement rests on what the Rev. Samuel Mateer says in his *Native Life in Travancore*, and it is not possible for us to know the source of his information or the authority on which he records it. On the other hand, we have the highest possible authority for denying that such a statement has ever been made or has to be made. The Maharaja of Travancore having been approached on the question, His Highness observed, "I do not know where Mr. Logan got this information; but no such declaration as mentioned in the Malabar Manual was made by me when I received the State sword at Śrī Paḍmanābha Swāmy's Pagoda. I have not heard of any such declaration having been made by former Maharajas."[2]

1. History of Tinnevelly, p. 12.
2. State Manual, Vol. I, p. 225.

After a careful analysis of the Kēralōṭpaṭṭi, the Kērala Māhāṭmyam, and the Christian and Jewish deeds, Dr. Gundhert has come to the conclusion that "that part of the Kēralotpaṭṭi, in which the present dynasties of Malayalam are represented as dating their origin from the last Perumāl's distribution of the country, is fully disproved by this and the Jewish documents, and the relation of the Kērala Māhāṭmyam, according to which the several families were placed here and there by Paraśu Rāma for the purpose of protecting certain temples and Brahman villages, comes much nearer the truth, if we understand by Paraśu Rāma the old time of Brahmanical rule."

The popular tradition is, no doubt, an old one, and was current, when the Portuguese arrived on the Coast, for Camoens in his *Lusiad* dealing with the last Perumāl's alleged Mecca pilgrimage and distribution of his country writes:

> " Having no Heir, left the royal house;
> Before he parted, he did cantonize
> His realm. Those servants he love'd best, he brings
> From want to wealth, from subjects to be kings."
>
> *Fanshaw's Translation.*

Besides the authority of the Kērala Māhāṭmyam and the Syrian and Jewish deeds, we have the views of those who were in a position to form an opinion on the question to support our contention that the various dynasties that ruled over Malabar had their origin independent of the last Perumāl.

Dr. Maclean in his *Standing Information regarding the Official Administration of the Madras Presidency* says, " that Travancore and Cochin were, from the first, under the Rajas belonging to the land-owning class. Malabar was similarly ruled, but broke up in the ninth century into a number of petty principalities, among the chief of which was that of the Zamorin at Calicut, found still in authority by Vasco de Gama at the end of the 15th century." Fra Bartolomeo tells us that the kings of Travancore had their origin in Madura, and Major Heber Drury agrees with him. Mr. Talboys Wheeler observes that "there were originally 20 kings of Malabar; but so many differences arose between these petty sovereigns that they determined to elect an arbitrator. The office was not hereditary but elective, and it was to be held by a prince who was not likely to become too powerful. Accordingly, they appointed Chēramān Perumāl, literally a Governor from Chēra, and fixed his residence at Calicut." Mr. Wheeler, in a foot-note, mentions the names of these petty kings as those given by Faria Y Souza[1]. From this, it would appear that, rather than these chiefs deriving their title from the bounty of the last Perumāl, the Perumāl viceroyalty was instituted by them. We have already shown that the three ancient deeds referred to place it beyond doubt that some at least of the ruling dynasties of Malabar were in power before the last Perumāl. But it may be asked, if these princes already held sway over Malabar before and during the time of the Perumāls, what then was the authority of the Perumāls themselves? Mr. Ellis, in his analysis of the Jewish deed, says "that the Raja (the Perumāl) appears to have been a prince paramount. In this inscription at the end are cited as witnesses the names of numerous chiefs of minor principilities." [2]

The state of the country is thus described by Dr. Gundhert: "The most correct representation of the country ruled by the Perumāls is that of a feudal state with a powerful heirarchy close to the person of the king, and deeply rooted in each province through richly endowed colonies. Then four or more eminent vassals, say two in the south, two in the north, and lastly a

1. History of India, Vol. III.

2. Madras Jour. of Lit. and Sc., No. 30, Second Series.

number of other princes and hereditary dignitaries with sounding names and minutely defined privileges, all having Crown offices, such as those of the writer and of the subject of the document."[1]

5. Cheraman Perumal: His Alleged Conversion to Islamism and the Mecca Pilgrimage.

In the seventh volume of the *Asiatic Researches*, Professor Bruns of Helmstadt suggested, among others, the following desiderata :—" Is the story of Sheramaloo Permaloo, or Cheruma Perumal's conversion to the Musalman Faith, of his journey to Arabia, and of the Division previously made by him of his Territory, well founded or otherwise ; and what was the exact Period of those Events ?" " Who were the Chiefs among whom he divided his country ; and do any genealogical Records exist whereby the Descent of the present Rajas in Malabar, from those chiefs, may be traced ? "

Well nigh a century has rolled by, since these desiderata were suggested, and yet the subject therein referred to still lies hidden behind the clouds of a misty past. No doubt, the paucity of such authentic records as would elucidate the early history of Malabar has contributed most to this unsatisfactory result. But it cannot, at the same time, be denied that not a little of this dearth of information is due to the want of curiosity and enterprise among the educated community in Malabar.

All historical accounts, so far as they can be ascertained, agree in holding that the earliest form of government extant in Malabar was the republican dominated over, however, by the Brahman theocracy, then powerful in the country. The Brahmans of that period were not simply 'god-compellers' who, with their sonorous *mantrams*, mystic incantations, and slow

1. Madras Jour. of Lit. and Sc., Vol. XIII, pp. 124—5.

monotonous bell-ringings, professed to transport to heaven the manes of the deceased Malayalees, securing for them ethereal bliss for evermore ; they were, at the same time warriors and statesmen strenuous in protecting the dearly-cherished hearths and homes of those whom the departed manes had left behind on this sublunary stage. When the Brahmans found that their sacerdotal profession necessarily clashed with their secular and worldly aspirations, and that, for one reason or other, they could not carry on the government of the country satisfactorily, they, in conjunction with the people of Kērala, resolved at a *Koottam* (Kūṭṭam) or national assembly to elect a king, whose rule was to be limited to a term of twelve years. Thus the people of Malabar resolved to have an elected monarchy in preference to a Brahman republic. The choice, however, was not to be made from among themselves. Four of the villages, representing the four *Kalakams* (Kaḷakams) or divisions into which the country was once divided, were empowered to make a choice, and they, after mature deliberation, invited one Kēya Perumāḷ, a Kṣhaṭriya Prince of Coimbatore, to assume the reins of government in Malabar. This, according to the Kēraḷōṭpaṭṭy, is the orign of the Perumāḷ rule in Malabar.[1] Among the names of the Perumāḷs given in that work, we come across a Chōla Perumāḷ, a Pāṇḍy Perumāḷ and a Chēramān Perumāḷ referring, perhaps, to Perumāḷs or rulers invited from the adjoining countries of Chōla, Pāṇḍya, and Chēra. Twenty-five elected Perumāḷs seem so have ruled over Malabar between the years 216 and 825 A. D. The last of these was known, by pre-eminence, as Chēramān Perumāḷ.

Facts and circumstances, into which it would be foreign for our present purpose to go in detail, lead us to conclude that the alleged invitation of the Perumāḷs to rule over Kēraḷa by the Brahmans is but a euphemistic form of recording the undoubted historic fact of

1. Keralolpathy,—Mangalore Edition, page 17.

the conquest and subjugation of Malabar by the Chēra, Chōla and Pāṇḍya kings. The Perumāls were, if not the rulers themselves, the Viceroys of these kings, so that the Perumāl viceroyalty was based on a much higher authority than the alleged election, or invitation by the people of Kērala. The Perumāls seem to have governed the country subject to the popular rights it had enjoyed under the constitutional system of its former rulers. The native account goes on to say that the last Viceroy, known as Chēramān Perumāl, revolted against his suzerain and set up an independent government in Kērala supported by the people,ruled prosperously for a long time, turned Mahomedan in his latter days, distributed his empire among his friends, dependants and vassals, went to Mecca on a pilgrimage and died there a Mussalman saint.

The Moplah, or Mahomedan account embodied in the Kēralōṭpaṭṭi gives further particulars. It says that, having made a division of his kingdom, the Perumāl secretly embarked on board a Moorish vessel from Crānganūr.[1] He was hotly pursued by ships from that port; but carefully eluding their vigilance, he landed at the port of Sahar Mukhal on the Arabian coast. The Prophet was then in the 57th year of his age and was, at the time, sojourning at Jeddah. The Perumāl proceeded thither and had an interview with Mahomed who canonised him under the name of Thiauj-uddien *i. e.* 'the Crown of the faith.' He married Regiat, the sister of Hubib-ud-dien, king of Arabia and lived there comfortably for five years. Accompanied by Habib-ud-dien and his sons, the Perumāl, afterwards, undertook a journey to Malabar for the spread of Islam in that country. He did not, however,

1. According to Barbosa, "he embarked at the same place where the city of Calicut was founded; and the Moors held this time and place in much veneration, and would not after that go and load pepper any more in any other part, since the said king embarked there after becoming a Moor and going to die at Mecca." The East African and Malabar Coasts, p. 103, (Hakluyt Society).

BC.

live to see the object of his mission accomplished, as he died of an ague at Sahar Mukhal, where his remains were interred in a mosque he had erected.

The Tohfut-ul-Mujahideen (a history in Arabic of the first settlement of the Mahomedans in Malabar) observes that, " amongst the Mahomedans of Malabar, the conversion to Islamism of the king is believed to have taken place in the time of the Prophet, it having been occasioned by that monarch's perceiving in a vision, during night, the partition of the moon, which miraculous circumstance induced him to set out upon a journey to visit the Prophet; and having been blessed with an interview with him, he returned to the coast of Arabia, designing to return to Malabar, with the individuals above named, when he died there."[2] The author of the Tohfut is not inclined to believe the above account in its entirety and gives a version of what he declares to be " the common and earliest *tradition* regarding the propagation of the Mahomedan religion in Malabar." According to this, a company of poor Moslems, men who had devoted their lives to the exercise of religious austerities under the spiritual guidance of a Sheik and " who were on a pilgrimage to the footsteps of our forefather Adam at Ceylon " arrived at Cranganūr and had an audience with the king. He related to him the history of the Prophet, explaining also the tenets of Islamism, and, in confirmation of their truth, he narrated to the king the miracle of the division of the moon. Conviction of the Prophet's divine mission, under the blessing of Almighty God, having followed this relation, the heart of the king became warmed with a holy affection towards Mahomed, and, in consequence of this conversion, he, with much earnestness, enjoined the Sheik to return to Cranganūr after his pilgrimage, which the good Sheik did. The king secretly requested the Sheik to

1. Keralolpathy, pp. 74—75.
2. Lieutenant Rowlandson's Translation, pp. 55—56.

arrange for a vessel, in which he embarked after leaving instructions for the proper administration of his country in his absence. [1]

The legend, above narrated, rests wholly on oral tradition, uncorroborated, so far as known at present, by any contemporary record. It, therefore, requires careful consideration, and, notwithstanding the impress of popular sanction, which it undoubtedly carries with it, one may be pardoned for questioning its authenticity in the absence of any reliable independent evidence to establish its truth. It is, indeed, extremely doubtful, if any Chēramān Perumāl did ever become a convert to Mahomedanism. In fact, there never was such an individual of that name. The term Chēramān Perumāl denoted the ruler of Chēra, and, according to some, was the official designation of the Viceroys sent by the kings of Chēra to govern Malabar.[2] As the late Dr. Gundhert, the eminent Malayalam scholar, correctly observes, "Surely there has never been an individual Chēramān Perumāl, though his name is in every mouth on the coast. Chēramān is the name of the dynasty of Chēra or Kērala rulers, for these two names are the same." [3]

But taking the alleged convert to be the last of the dynasty of the Chēra rulers of Malabar, as accepted generally, it need hardly be pointed out that it was not possible for him in the ninth century A. D. (the period assigned to him by European scholars on what seems to be excellent authority.), *i. e.* three centuries *after* the death of Mahomed, to have seen the Prophet at Jeddah, as alleged by the Mahomedan account. One version of the Kēralōṭpaṭṭi would have it that the Perumāl proceeded to Mecca in A. D. 355. [4] This

1. Lieutenant Rowlandson's Translation, pp. 50—53.
2. Day's Land of the Perumals, p. 42.
3. Madras Journal of Literature and Science, Vol. XIII pp. 116 *et seq.*
4. Mangalore Edition, p. 74.

again would be about two centuries *before* the birth of the Prophet, an evident anachronism. The meeting, therefore, of the apostate king and the apostle of Islam must necessarily be a figment of the imagination—" a pious invention of the Mahomedans." [1] "There is but little truth in this account," remarks Sheik Zinuddien, the author of the Tohfut-ul-Mujahideen. [2] The Mahomedan Arabs hold with the Sheik that Mahomedanism was not introduced into Malabar till 200 years after the Hejira, and they are not prepared to accept the story of the last Perumāl's conversion. They contend that, if the statements of the Kēralōṭpaṭṭi and the Mahomedan legend were true, the name of such an influential convert as that of an Emperor of Kērala should have found a place in the works of the old commentators and been handed down to posterity. They further point out that no such name as the one said to have been taken by the convert king—*Th[illegible]-ul-uddien* or Crown of the Faith—denoting attachment to Islamism, was given in the Prophet's life time. The Arab merchant, Suliman, [A. H. 237 (A. D. 851)] " who wrote with knowledge, as he evidently visited the countries he wrote about" says expressly "that in Malabar he did not know of any one of either nation (Chinese or Indian) that had embraced Mahomedanism or spoken Arabic." [3] This almost gives the lie direct to the alleged conversion of the Perumāl. For, it is difficult to believe that the Arab merchant, visiting the coast so soon after the alleged conversion of the Perumāl—it is said to have taken place in 825 A. D.—would have failed to hear of the glorious acquisition to his faith of the Hindu Emperor of Malabar and the consequent support Mahomedanism had apparently derived from such a notable event. It cannot be said that the event was

1. Wheeler's History of India, Vol. III, p. 423, Note.
2. Lieut. Rowlandson's Translation, p. 56.
3. Logan's Manual of the Malabar District, Vol. I, p. 191.

not then generally known in the country; for the Mahomedan account of the pilgrimage assures us that, though the Perumāl and his new friends attempted to effect their exit from Malabar secretly "under the concealment of night,"[1] they were found out and hotly pursued by ships from Crānganūr.[2] The expedition of Malik Ibn Dinar, who had been commissioned, according to the Moplah manuscripts, by the convert Perumāl, before his death at Sahar Mukhal, to proceed to Malabar for the spread of Islam and who had been provided with letters of recommendation to the Malabar princes, is said to have reached the coast about A. H. 224 *i. e.* A. D. 856 or 13 years before Suliman wrote his account. The expedition is said to have been successful, for it is alleged that "they were received hospitably, and, in accordance with the Perumāl's instructions, land to build a mosque and a suitable endowment were given. Malik Ibn Dinar himself became the first Kazi of Crānganūr."[3] This was followed by the erection soon after of several mosques throughout Malabar. And yet Suliman makes no mention of these remarkable events.

None of the early travellers or geographers, whether Mahomedan, Christian, or Jew, has left us any record of the legend. So far as our present knowledge goes, it is with the arrival of the Portuguese on the Malabar Coast that we begin to obtain glimpses of the story *recorded*; and then it is not difficult to trace it to a Mahomedan source.

Suliman (850 A. D.), Al Biruni (970-1039 A. D.), Al Idrisi (1153-4), Benjamin of Tudela (1159-60), Rashidu' ddin (1247-81), Al Kazwini (1263-75), Marco Polo (1271-94), Abulfeda (1273-1331), Friar Odoric (1286-94), Friar Jordanus (1320), Ibn Batuta (1324-54), Abdur-Razak (1441), Nicolo Conti (1444),—no one of

1. Tohfut-ul-Mujahideen, p. 51.
2. Keralolpathy,—Mangalore Edition, p. 74.
3. Logan's Malabar, Vol. I, pp. 191—6.

these refer to the story of the Mahomedan conversion. It is, indeed, true that, in many cases, we have only second-hand information of the accounts left by the early travellers and, then, we have only translations of extracts. But, as already pointed out, the earliest of them, Suliman, who wrote soon after the occurrence, has not simply failed to refer to it, but positively avers that he did not find in Malabar any one whether native or Chinese who had become Mahomedan or spoken Arabic. Ibn Batuta [1] and Abdur-Razak, both of whom were Mahomedans, had spent some time in Malabar and have not failed to note the prosperous existence of those of their persuasion on the coast. "In most of their Malayalam districts," says Ibn Batuta, "the Musalman merchants have houses and are greatly respected." [2] Again, noticing Kawalam or Quilon, Ibn observes, "In this place is a large number of Mahomedan merchants." [3] Of those at Calicut, he remarks that "the greatest part are so wealthy that one of them can purchase the whole freightage of such vessels as put in here and fit out others like them." Coming to Fandarina (North Kollam), he found "the Mahomedans in possession of three districts in each of which was a mosque with a judge and preacher." Ibn has also not failed to record stories of conversions alleged to be brought about by miracles related to him. Speaking of Dadkannan (identified with Valarpaṭṭaṇam or Baliapaṭṭam) he says, "The king is an infidel. His grandfather, who had become Mahomedan, built its mosque and made the pond. The cause of the grandfather receiving Islamism was a tree over which he had built the mosque. This tree is a very great wonder; its leaves are green, and like those of the fig, except only

1. His real name was Abu Abdullah Mahomed. But he is better known by his surname "Ibn Batuta" which meant "The traveller".
2. Lee's translation of the Travels of Ibn Batuta, p. 172.
3. Ibid, p. 174.

that they are soft. The tree is called *Darakhti Shahadet* (the tree of testimony), *darakht* meaning tree. I was told in these parts that this tree does not generally drop its leaves; but at the season of autumn in every year one of them changes its colour, first to yellow, then to red, and that upon this is written with the pen of power 'There is no God but God; Mahomed is the Prophet of God;' and that this leaf alone falls—very many Mahomedans, who were worthy of belief, told me this; and said that they had witnessed its fall, and had read the writing; and further, that every year, at the time of the fall, credible persons among the Mahomedans, as well as others of the infidels, sat beneath the tree waiting the fall of the leaf; and when this took place, that the one half was taken by the Mahomedans as a blessing, and for the purpose of curing their diseases; and the other by the king of the infidel city, and laid up in his treasury as a blessing; and that this is constantly preserved among them. Now the grandfather of the present king could read the Arabic; he witnessed, therefore, the fall of the leaf, read the inscription and, understanding its import, became a Mahomedan accordingly." Ibn also refers to another miracle at Fattan (or Ḍharmapaṭṭaṇam) greatly to the glory of Mahomedanism. "Without the city was a mosque built by certain merchants which was destroyed by one of the Brahmans who had removed its roof to his own house. On the following night, however, this house was entirely burnt, and in it the Brahman, his followers, and his children. They then restored the mosque, and in future abstained from injuring it; whence it became the resort of the Mahomedan strangers." A miracle forsooth! It is surprising that Ibn Batuta, "the greatest traveller of all the Arabian Nation,"[1] "a cultured man of the world,"[2]

1. Dr. Birdwood's Introduction to his Report on the Old Records of the India Office, 2nd Edition.
2. The Madras Review, Vol. V., p. 69.

and "one endowed with boundless curiosity"[1] did not suspect the hand of the pious incendiary in the working of this truly marvellous miracle! After this, it is difficult to believe that an account, however imperfect, of the miracle of the vision of the split-moon and the conversion of the Emperor of Malabar to which it led would not have reached the ears of this enthusiastic traveller, if the story was current at the time. It is still more difficult to believe that Ibn Batuta would have failed to record the marvellous *tale*, if it had been told him. We may therefore, safely conclude that the story was not extant in Malabar, when Ibn Batuta visited the coast.

A hundred years after Ibn Batuta, Abdur-Razak[2] visited Calicut (A. D. 1442) on an embassy from "His Majesty the happy Khakan"—Shah Rokh—the professed object of the mission being the conversion of the Samorin to Islam. The Samorin Raja of Calicut had previously sent an ambassador to the great Shah of Persia, and Abdur-Razak's mission was in response to it. In his own words, "As soon as the sovereign of Calicut was informed of these occurrences, he prepared some presents, consisting of objects of value of different kinds, and sent an ambassador charged with a despatch, in which he said: 'In this port on every Friday and every solemn feast day, the Khotbah is celebrated according to the prescribed rule of Islamism. With Your Majesty's permission, these prayers shall be adorned and honoured by the addition of your name.' These deputies setting out in company with the ambassador from Bengal, reached the noble court of the Emperor, and the Emirs laid before that

1. The Calcutta Review for April 1901.

2. See Elliot's Historians of India, IV, pp. 98 to 103, also Major's India in the 15th Century, pp. 15 *et seq*—Hakluyt Society's publication. Abdur-Razak landed at Calicut on an embassy from Samarkand in June (?) 1442. Sewell, p. 106, Note 1.

monarch the letter and the presents by which it was accompanied. The messenger was a Mussalman distinguished for his eloquence; in the course of his address, he said to the Prince: 'If your majesty will be pleased to favour my master, by despatching an ambassador sent specially to him, and who, in literal pursuance of the precept expressed in that verse '*By thy wisdom and by thy good counsels engage men to enter on the ways of thy Lord*,' shall invite that prince to embrace the religion of Islamism, and draw from his beclouded heart the bolt of darkness and error, and cause the flame of the light of faith, and the brightness of the sun of knowledge to shine into the window of his heart, it will be, beyond all doubt, a perfectly righteous and meritorious deed.' The Emperor acceded to this request and gave instructions to the Emirs that the ambassador should make his preparations for setting out on his journey. The choice fell upon the humble author of this work."

Abdur-Razak's mission was, however, far from being successful. He had, indeed, an audience with the king; but the ambassador remarks, "the Samorin showed me but little consideration." Though he had the pleasure of meeting some distinguished friends at Calicut, it seemed to him to be a "disagreeable place, where everything became a source of trouble and weariness." Soon after, the king of Bidjnagara requested the Zamorin to send the Shah's ambassador over to him, and Abdur-Razak says, "the humble author of this narrative, having received his audience of dismissal, departed from Calicut by sea." The narrative left by Abdur-Razak shows clearly that he resented very much the treatment he received at Calicut and was much chagrined at the failure of his mission. Otherwise, it is difficult to account for the gruesome description he gives of the people of Calicut. "As soon as I landed at Calicut, I saw beings such as my imagination had never depicted the like of." Here he waxes poetic and pours forth :—

> " Extraordinary beings, who are neither men nor devils,
> At sight of whom the mind takes alarm ;
> If I were to see such in my dreams,
> My heart would be in a tremble for many years."

After thus easing his mind of his chagrin, he proceeds to give an account, accurate enough, of the dress, the customs, and manners, etc., of "the blacks of this country." It is remarkable that he makes no reference to the conversion of Chēramān Perumāl or of the story of his Mecca pilgrimage. Having come to Calicut on a mission with the avowed object of gaining over the Zamorin to Islamism, it is extremely unlikely that the ambassador would not have been informed by the Mahomedans of Calicut that one far greater than the Zamorin—one from whom the Zamorin himself derived his authority as sovereign of Malabar—had found consolation within the bosom of Mahomedanism and had piously undertaken the Haj.

Half a century later, the Portuguese heard the story on their arrival at Calicut,[1] and Camoens [2] sings of it in his great epic of the *Lusiad*:

1. " And there begins the country of Malabar, which was governed by a king who was called Sermaperimal, who was a very great lord. And after that, the Moors of Mekkah discovered India, and began to navigate near it, which was six hundred and ten years ago ; they used to touch at this country of Malabar on account of the pepper which is found there. And they began to load their ships with it in a city and seaport, Coulom (Quilon), where the king used frequently to be. And so for some years, these Moors continued their voyages to this country of Malabar, and began to spread themselves through it, and became so intimate and friendly with the said king, that they made him turn Moor, and he went away with them to die at the house of Mekkah, and he died on the road." Barbosa (1516).—*A Description of the Coasts of East Africa and Malabar*. Hakluyt Society's publication, p. 102.

2. The greater part of the *Lusiad* was written in India between A. D. 1553 and 1559. See Dr. Birdwood's *Report on the Old Records of the India Office*. 2nd Edition, p. 180.

"But certain strangers coming to the realm
From Mecha in the Gulf of Arabie,
Who brought the Law of Mahomet with them,
(in which my parents educated me,)
It so befell, with their great skill, and stream
Of eloquence, these to that degree
This Perimal unto their Faith did win,
That he proposed to dye a saint therein.
Ships he provides, and therein (curious)
For off'rings lades his richest merchandise;
To turn Monastic, and religious,
There, where our Legislative Prophet lies.
Having no Heir, left of the royal house;
Before he parted, he did cantonize
His realm. Those servants he lov'd best, he brings
From want to wealth, from subjects to be kings."

Canto 7, Stanzas 33 and 34.
Fanshaw's Translation.

It is significant that the Portuguese admittedly got this account of the tradition from a Mahomedan Moor, Monsayde by name, a native of Tunis, whose acquaintance they made on their first landing at Calicut and who subsequently accompanied Vasco de Gama on the return voyage to Europe, turned a Christian and died there[1].

"Among the swarming rout that thronged to view,
Cometh a Moslem, who was born and bred
In distant Barb'ry 'mid her barbarous crew.

* * * *
* * * *

The Moor Monsayde, thus his name was known."

Canto 7, Stanzas 24-26.
Burton's Translation.

1. In his transactions at Calicut, Gama was assisted "chiefly by a Tunis Mahomedan, who could speak Spanish and whom the Portuguese called Moncaide. Moncaide so openly took their side that he found it convenient to leave for Europe in De Gama's ships," Whiteway's *Rise of the Portuguese Power in India*, p. 81.

Others give his name as Bontaybo. Day's *Land of the Perumals*, p. 73. Castenheda quoted in *A new Collection of Voyages and Travels*, Astley, p. 43, Note b.

It was Monsayde, that first gave the new comers an idea of Malabar, its history, its people, their manners and customs &c.

If the imaginative mind of the Portuguese bard had deemed it right to enshrine the tradition in verse, the sober judgment of the Spanish historian refused to chronicle it as embodying an historical fact. Faria-y-Souza [1] declares the story of the Perumāl's voyage to Mecca " a false invention of the Moors."

Zeiruddeen Mukkadom, an Egyptian traveller of the fifteenth century, denounces the story of the pilgrimage as unfounded.[2] In the sixteenth century, *i e.*, a century after the arrival of the Portuguese in India, Sheik Zeenuddien, the author of the *Tohfut-ul-Mujahideen*, himself a Malabar Mahomedan descended from the original Arabian immigrants, [3] in recording the event, takes particular care to remark that he was giving only " the common and earliest *tradition* that exists." We have already pointed out that the good Sheik is not disposed to believe it. It is significant that he refers to it as a "tale." [4] In the seventeenth century, Faria-y-Souza declares it to be "a false invention of the Moors."[5] Jacob Canter Visscher, the Dutch Chaplain of Cochin, who wrote early in the eighteenth century, after giving in detail the story as related to him on Mahomedan authority, remarks that " the narration I have followed is, however, filled with trifles and does not hang well together." [6] Mr. Talboys Wheeler thinks that " the Mecca pilgrimage is, doubtless, a pious invention of the Mussalmans." [7] " The story rests probably upon

1. Faria-y-Souza wrote his *Asia Poriuguesa* in Spanish.
2. Madras Journal of Literature and Science. O. S. No. 20 p. 35.
3. The Madras Review, Vol. V, p. 65—Note.
4. Rowlandson, page 56.
5. See Faria quoted in *A New Collection of Voyages and Travels*, Vol. I, p. 29—Note
6. Visscher's *Letters from Malabar*, p. 121.
7. History of India, Vol. III, p. 423-Note.

no good foundation," says Major Heber Drury.[1] Professor Sundaram Pillai observes that there is no written record of respectable antiquity to lend support to the story of the Perumāl's conversion or the voyage to Mecca.[2]

Speaking with reference to the rise and progress of Mahomedanism in Malabar, the Rev. Mr: Whitehouse observes, "The traditions of the vulgar—who seem to attribute to *one* man what was really done by a succession of rulers bearing the title of Perumāl—will tell you that their favourite hero, Chēramān Perumāl, became a convert to Mahomedansim ; but, if one looks into the old Malayalam history of Kērala (as before observed), we find a distinct statement that it was Bāṇa Perumāl who turned Mussalman, and went to Mecca, and not the last of these princes, Chēramān Perumāl.[3] Here there is evidently a confusion with regard to the religion embraced by Bāṇa Perumāl. The native history says that he became a " Boudha, " which literally means a follower of Buddha, though in common parlance it is used, in Malabar, to denote all religionists other than Hindus. There is a consensus of opinion that Bāṇa became a Buddhist.[4] The reference to Bāṇa Perumāl's journey is thus accounted for by Dr. Day. " It appears likely that one of these kings (the Perumāls) did turn Buddhist and was dethroned. By degrees, both Jains and Mahomedans were included in the above term, as they both came from Arabia, and it

1. Drury's *Account of Travancore, Letters from Malabar*, p. 168.

2. Professor Sundaram Pillai on the Kollam Era.

3. Lingerings of Light in a Dark Land, p. 54.

4. Keralolpathi, pp. 29-30, Keralavisesha Mahatmayam, p. 95: Mack: MSS.; Day's *Land of Perumals*, p. 365 ; Indian Antiquary, Vol. IX, pp. 77-79, Note 4; Madras Journal of Literature and Science, Vol. II, p. 71.

became a common saying that Chēramān Perumāl became a Buddhist (Boudha) and went away to Mecca."[1]

The Mahomedan tradition is sought to be supported by the alleged existence of a tomb at Zafhar on the Arabian coast reputed to be that of the convert Perumāl.[2] Mr. Logan in the 11th Vol. of the *Indian Antiquary*, [3] and more recently, in his *Manual of the Malabar District*, has attempted to show that the tomb of the Perumāl is still, or was but till recently, to be found at Zafhar. In the *Antiquary*, he says:—"At Zafhar (on the Arabian coast) lies buried Abdul Rahiman Samiri, a king of Malabar. The inscription on his tomb-stone says that he arrived at the place A. H. 212, and died there A. H. 216. The tomb is regarded with much veneration as that of a Hindu (Samuri---Samaritan=worshipper of the Calf-Koran S. 20) king of Malabar who became a convert to Islam. If the dates are correct, then this is almost certainly the tomb of the Kodingaloor king mentioned in the *Tohfut-ul-Mujahideen*."

In the absence of some written record of respectable antiquity to corroborate the tradition of the conversion and the pilgrimage, one is disposed not to attach any evidentiary value to the tomb on the shores

1. "At the present time, no Jains trade to India, and their only remaining representatives are the Mahomedans, still called Buddhists (Boudhas), consequently it is commonly reported and believed, that Cheraman Perumal became a Mahomedan." Day's *Land of Perumals*, p. 365.

2. Even Mr. Logan is prepared only to *assume*, until evidence to the contrary is forthcoming, that the Mahomedan tradition is correct, and that the Hindu king of Malabar who lies buried at Zafhar in Arabia was indeed Cheraman Perumal. See Malabar, Vol. I, p. 244. But this is scarcely the proper frame of mind with which one ought to approach a doubtful point of historical importance.

3. P, 116.

of the Persian Gulf. Let us, however, proceed to inquire into the nature of the evidence as to the existence of the tomb, the alleged inscription thereon and the conclusions derivable therefrom.

The existence of the tomb at Zafhar, at present, rests solely on the information received by Mr. Logan from an Arab living in the outskirts of Zafhar. In the words of Mr. Logan himself, " the facts have still to be authoritatively verified."[1] Mr. Logan had tried his best to obtain exact information on the subject from the British Resident at Aden as well as from other sources, but without success.[2] In the latter part of the sixteenth century, the *Tohfut-ul-Mujahideen* mentions "as a fact well-known to all, that the king was buried at Zafhar, instead of on the Arabian coast of the Red Sea, at which place his tomb can be seen by everyone, and is, indeed, now flocked to an account of its virtues."[3] The author does not vouchsafe to us the authority on which he makes the statement, but contents himself with the observation that " it is well known to all." Later on, we hope to show that, in the sixteenth century, the tomb of a Malabar king might have existed at Zafhar and yet that it might not have been that of Chēramān Perumāl. The *Tohfut*, however, does not make mention of any inscription on the tomb, though, according to Mr. Logan's informant, it bears an inscription to the effect that the king, lying buried there, arrived at the place A. H. 212 and died there A. H. 216.[4] If there was such an inscription on the tomb specifying dates of arrival and demise, Śheik Zeenuddien would certainly have noted it, as that too must have been then " well-known

1. Logan's *Malabar*, Vol. I, p. 195.

2. Logan in the 11th Vol. of the *Indian Antiquary*, pp. 116 *et seq.*

3. Rowlandson, p. 56.

4. Here again Mr. Logan is careful to observe "that the dates on the tombstone still require verification." Malabar, Vol. I, p. 244.

to all." On the other hand, after giving the account current at the time in Malabar of the conversion and pilgrimage of the Perumāl and of the propagation of the Mahomedan religion on the coast, he observes :—" Touching the exact time when this event occurred, *there is no certain information;* but there appears good grounds for the *supposition*[1] that it happened about 300 years after the flight of the Prophet."[2] Here again, it is rather unfortunate that the good Sheik has not confided to us his "good grounds for the supposition." Lieut. Rowlandson, the translator of the *Tohfut*, points out that the company of Moslems referred to by the author, in his preface, as having emigrated to certain ports of Malabar and proselytised the natives were emigrants from Arabia in the reign of Hjaj-Ben-Yoosuff A. D. 710.[3] Though Mr. Logan is not inclined to agree with Lieut. Rowlandson in thinking that the Arab emigrants established themselves in Malabar in the time of the *Ummayidi* Caliph Valid I (705—15),[4] he admits that Arabs engaged in trade had, no doubt, settled in these places long previously[5] (*i. e.*, previous to the ninth century) and, indeed, an inscription on a Mahomedan granite tomb-stone still standing at Pantalayini Kollam recites, after the usual prayer, that "Ali-ibn-Udthorman was obliged to leave this world for ever to the one which is everlasting, and which receives the spirits of all, in the year 166 of Hejira

1. The italics are not in the original.
2. Malabar, Vol. I, p. 56.
3. Ibid, p. 5,—Note.
4. Ibid, p. 191.
5. Dr. Burnell says that the *Muhamadan* Arabs appear to have settled first in Malabar about the beginning of the ninth century; there were heathen Arabs there long before that in consequence of the immense trade conducted by the Sabeans with India (according to Agtharchides i., p. 64 of Hudson's Edition, cfr. also the Periplus of the Red Sea). S. I. Paleography, p. 57, Note 2.

(A. D. 788),[1] so called after Mahomed the Prophet left Mecca for Medina."[2] M. Adrian Van Moens, the Dutch Governor of Cochin, observes that, in the seventh century, a Mahomedan merchant named Malekmedina, accompanied by some priests, had settled in or near Mangalore.[3] These facts certainly render the account of the Mahomedan settlement on the West Coast under the Caliph Valid more than probable. It may be that the Mahomedans obtained a firm footing on the coast only later on; but it would scarcely be correct to hold with Sheik Zenuddien that there are "good grounds to suppose that the incidents detailed by him took place 200 years after the Hejira."

In these days of forged inscriptions, spurious genealogies and sham relics,[4] it is not possible, in the interests of truth, to accept the unverified statement of an irresponsible Arab, living in the outskirts of Zafhar, for the existenee of the Perumāl's tomb and the alleged inscription on it.

1. Mr. Logan in a note observes that "the date is a good deal weather-worn, but these figures are still fairly distinct."

2. Malabar, Vol. I, p. 194,

3, Day's *Land of the Perumals*, p. 365.

4. An instance of a forged Chera inscription of A. D. 247 is mentioned by Dr. Burnell in his *Elements of South Indian Paleography*, p. 34. No less a person than a late Archaeological Surveyor of the N. W. Provinces and Oude is said to have given in a "Monograph on Buddha Sakya Muni's Birth place" elaborate details of a wonderful *Stupa* of Kongamana, "every word of which is false" according to Mr. Vincent Smith who writes a Preface to Mr. P. C. Mukerji's explorations. Similarly minute details regarding the base of the broken Asoka Pillar, discovered in the Nepal Terai, had been given. However, when Mr. Mukerji and Colonel Lawrence Wascell, I. M. S., visited the ruins, they discovered, that the pillar, which was not *in situ*, had no foundation at all! Mr. Vincent Smith observes: "These fictions about the Kongamana *Stupa* do not stand alone. The inscriptions of the Sakyas alleged to have been found in the small *Stupas* at Sagariva are impudent forgeries, and when Dr. Fruhrer supplied the Burmese Priest UMA, with sham relics of Buddha, he endeavoured

BE.

But presuming the existence of the tomb and the inscription thereon, they, at most, show only that a Zamorin lay buried there. The name alleged to be inscribed on the tombstone, according to Mr. Logan's Arab informant, is *Abdul Rahiman Samiri*,[1] while the *Tohfut* says that "the king, of whom this *tale* is told, is styled by the people of that part of the world, as Samuri."[2] He could not have been surely one of the earlier kings of Koḍungallūr, who were officially designated Chēramān Perumāls. The native official designation of the king of Calicut is Sāmūri[3] or Sāmūṭiri=Ṭāmūṭiri, and the word appears in its original form in the name of the convert king on his tomb at Zafhar. Ibn Batuta calls him Al-Samari, while Abdur-Razak and the author of the *Tohfut* call him Samuri. Buchanan has both Samudiri and Zamorin. It is not unusual for converts of position to retain their original designation, in addition to the new names they receive from their new faith, so that their original *status* may not be forgotten. Accordingly, the Hindu king of Calicut, who became a Mahomedan and who undertook the pilgrimage to Mecca, might have tacked on his original

to support the imposition by a forged inscription of Upagapta, the *guru* of Asoka. In the course of my official duty, the whole case was investigated by me, and no doubt as to the facts is possible. I find that the reserved language in previous official documents has been sometimes misrepresented, and it is now necessary in the interests of truth to speak out plainly." After this, it is refreshing to read that the officer in question has been "permitted to resign" the service. See the *Pioneer* extracted in the *Madras Mail*, 20th November 1901, p. 5, Col. 3. "Dr. Fruhrer Exposed again."

1. Indian Antiquary, Vol. xi, p, 116. Malabar Voi. i. p. 196.—Note.

2. Rowlandson, p. 56.

3. "He seems to have adopted the high sounding title of *Kunnalakhon* or king of the hill (*kunnu*) and waves (*ala*). The Sanskrit form of this title *Samudri*, or as it is pronounced by Malayalis *Samutiri* or *Tamutiri* (or vulgarly Samuri or Tamuri) is that by which the Chief Raja of this house became known to Europeans as the Zamorin of Calicut." Logan, Vol. i, pp. 276—7.

title to his Mahomedan name, so that his former subjects might still recognise in him their old sovereign. This theory receives support from the circumstance noticed by Mr. Logan that "from the fact that the king is called Samiri (on the tombstone), some Moplas (Malabar Mahomedans) assert the king buried at Zahfar was really a Zamorin."[1] It is further significant that, while the name on the Zafhar tombstone is said to be "Abdul Rahiman Samiri," the name assumed by or conferred on the convert Perumāl, according to the Mopla legend, is "Thiaj-ud-dien" (crown of the faith).[2] It certainly looks rather unnatural to twist the word Samuri into Samiri and then give it a strange signification on the authority of the Koran, in order that the inscription on the tombstone may afford evidence of the truth of the story of the Chēramān Perumāl's conversion.

The Mahomedan historian, Ferishta, has no doubt as to the Malabar king who embraced Islamism. He says that a Zamorin turned Mahomedan, undertook a pilgrimage to Mecca, and that, from that period, "Mahomedans extended their religion and influence in Malabar, and many of the princes and inhabitants, becoming converts to the new faith, gave over the management of some seaports to the strangers whom they called (Nowjatis) Nowayits (literally the new race.)"[3]

We have to keep in mind that, till overthrown and almost annihilated by the Portuguese, the Mahomedans (Moors) were all powerful at the court of the Zamorin. The whole trade of Malabar was monopolised by them. Their machinations compelled Vasco de Gama, at first, to quit the coast of Calicut without achieving the object of his long and hazardous voyage to India. We have a lively poetic account of this in

1. Logan's *Malabar*, Vol. I. p, 196,—Note 2.
2. Ibid, p. 191.
3. Brigg's Ferishta, iv, pp. 531-3. (N̊ava-jāti=the new caste).

the *Lusiad*. Gasper Correa, the chronicler of Gama's voyages, says that "the Moors were very powerful and had so established and ingratiated themselves in the countries of the seaports, that they were more influential and respected than the natives themselves."[1] His account of the means by which they succeeded in thwarting the endeavours of Gama makes it clear that they were, all in all, at the court of the Zamorin at Calicut.

The Zamorins have not unfrequently been confounded with the Perumāls. Thus Faria-y-Souza, speaking of the Perumāls, says, "This dignity of Emperor signified by the word Samorin continued till the year of grace 347 according to the records of Calicut, but till 588 according to the records of Cochin."[2] Dr. Gustave Oppert, referring to the early Arab settlement in Malabar, observes that, when the Arabian pilgrimship bound for Ceylon was driven to the Malabar Coast, the reigning Zamorin was Chēramān Perumāl. He adds that "the then reigning Samorin of Calicut, Chēramān Perumāl, received them kindly, and becoming acquainted, through intercourse with the shipwrecked people, with the tenets of Islam, turned Mahomedan himself and went on a pilgrimage to Mecca."[3]

The confusion and the consequent mistake may be traced in the Kēralōṭpaṭṭi itself, a work in Malayalam purporting to deal with the early history of Malabar, but which, in its present garb, is either full of anachronisms, absurdities and contradictions or is an ill-digested and uncollated collection of different versions

1. Stanley's Translation, pp. 155 to 157. Hakluyt Society's publication. See also Whiteway's *Rise of the Portuguese Power in India*.

2. Faria quoted by Talboys Wheeler, History of India, Vol. III, p. 424.

3. A Lecture on *The Ancient Commerce of India* p. 31—by Dr. Gustave Oppert.

huddled together in inextricable confusion.[1] The Kēralōtpaṭṭi says that Chēramān Perumāl was sent, on the invitation of the Brahmans, to rule over Malabar for a term of twelve years by Kṛshṇa Rāyar of Ānagunḍy, and, on his not giving up his government at the expiry of the term, the Rāyar led an invasion into Malabar to subdue his overgrown vassal.[2] The Kṛshṇa Rāyar referred to here is evidently the well-known Kṛshṇa Rāya, successor of Vīra Narasimha of Vijayanagara; for we know of no other Rāyar dynasty in the history of Southern India to which he could have belonged.[3] According to Bishop Caldwell[4], Vijayanagara is also commonly known as Ānagunḍi, a Canarese name—elephant pit—which is properly a village on the other side of the Pampa or Ṭungabhaḍra on whose banks stood Vijayanagara. This account anticipates the coming into power of the Vijayanagara dynasty by almost seven centuries.[5] The mistake, no doubt, arose by attributing a subsequent and much later invasion of Malabar, or at least, of that part of the country under the sway of the Zamorin of Calicut, by Maharaja Kṛshṇa Rāya of Vijayanagara or Ānagunḍi to the Perumāl period. It will be seen from the Kēralapalama, a treatise in Malayalam on the doings of the Portuguese in Malabar, that the Portuguese Governor-General, Albuquerque, had about A. D. 1510,

1. The Keralolpathy is supposed to have been written in the 17th century by Thunchath Ramanujan Eluthachan, the Father of Malayalam Literature. See p. 111 of the Mangalore Edition. Also Sewell, p. 55. But there is not the least warrant for this assertion in spite of what the Mangalore edition asserts in its last paragraph.

2. Keralolpathy, Mangalore Edition, pp. 44 to 55.

3. There is no Krishna Raya among the Chola Rayas whose genealogy is given by Mr. Foulkes. Salem District Manual, Vol. I, p 39.

4. History of Tinnevelly, p. 45.

"Anagundi Krishna Rayer" or Krishnadeva Raya of Vijayanagar,—Sewell p. 57, Note 2.

5. "Of course, this is an absurd anachronism," says Mr. Sewell. See *Sketches of the Dynasties of South India*, p. 57. Note 1.

i. e. two years after the accession of Kṛṣhṇa Rāyar to the Ānagunḍi throne,[1] made a compact with that prince with a view to overthrow the influence of the Mahomedan Arabs and Moors of Calicut. The Portuguese envoys to the Court of Vijayanagara proposed that the Rāyar should cross the Ghauts at the head of a large army, while the Portuguese engaged to guard the seas against all Arab and Moorish vessels.[2] The embassy is referred to by Mr. Danvers, who says that Friar Luiz was despatched with a letter to the king of Narasinga (Vijayanagar) with the view of securing his assistance by land, whilst the Portuguese operated by sea for the destruction of the Zamorin.[3] Whether the Vijayanagara king responded to the embassy or not, it is certain that the Zamorins lived in wholesome dread of the Vijayanagara king. Even so early as A. D. 1442, Abdur-Razak remarks "that, although the Samorin is not under his authority, nevertheless he is in great alarm and apprehension from him, for it is said that the king of Beejungur has 300 seaports, every one of which is equal to Calicut and that, inland, his cities and provinces extend over a journey of three months."[4]

The Mahomedans were, from an early period, very powerful on the coast of Malabar, and the greatness of Calicut and its ruler was more or less due to the Arab and Moorish trade.[5] A

1. See Burnell's *South Indian Paleography*, 2nd Edition, p. 55; Sewell, pp. 108—109.
2. The Keralapalama, p. 113.
3. Danvers—*The Portuguese in India*, Vol. I, p. 183.
4. Major's *India in the Fifteenth Century*, p. 19.
5. " There can be no doubt, however, that, even in Malabar, which was free from such expeditions, Mahomedan influence was on the increase, and it is not at all improbable that it was about this time [end of the fourteenth century A. D.] that the influence of the Zamorins began to preponderate in Malabar; and this, there can be no doubt, was brought about [as indeed the Keralolpathi indicates] by a close alliance with the Mahomedan traders attracted to Calicut by the freedom of trade enjoyed by them." Malabar, Vol. I, pp. 290-4.

trace of their influence at the Court of the Zamorin may be found in the ceremony, which successive Zamorins have still to observe on the occasion of their coronation, when they have to receive *Pan* and *Supari* (betel and nut) from the hands of a man dressed as a Mopla woman or a woman herself, as some accounts say. After this ceremony, the Zamorins are supposed to be kept at arm's length by the members of his family and are said, by some, to be actually put out of caste by the ceremony, "and have to live separately thereafter to their manifold discomfort."[1] It may not be too far-fetched to suggest that the ceremony and the supposed degradation are a relic of the apostacy of one of the Zamorins and of his pilgrimage to Mecca, the change of religion being, perhaps, the result of a *liaison* which the then Zamorin had with a Mopla woman. However that be, it is significant that every new Zamorin has, it is said, to declare that he assumes the title and rules only until his uncle returns. It is probable that the apostate Zamorin died at Zafhar and was buried on

1. Logan's *Malabar*, Vol. I, p. 245. The ceremony is referred to by Mr. Fawcett in these terms:—"The new Zamorin comes to the bank of the Kallai river adjoining Calicut. There he is asked some questions, and he crosses the river in a *boat*—not over the bridge. Arrived on the Calicut side, he must partake of some betel-leaf from a Mopla man dressed as a [Mopla] woman, or, as some say, from a Mopla woman, and *he says that he assumes the title of the Zamorin and rules until his uncle returns.* The betel-leaf, received from a [Mahomedan] Mopla, which he chews, defiles him. He has lost his status in the caste, and he is supposed to be henceforth celibate." Madras Government Museum Bulletin, Vol. III, No. 3, pp. 295-6. The italics are not in the original.

Mr. Logan thinks that the ceremony is the relic of the time when the *Perumal* turned Mahomedan and left the country to its own devices. Malabar, Vol. I, p. 245. Would it not be more natural to attribute it to the incident of a real *Zamorin's* conversion and pilgrimage to Mecca? But the conversion to Mahomedanism, whether of Cheraman Perumal or of one of the Zamorins, rests, at present, only on tradition and conjecture unsupported by contemporary records.

the Arabian coast; and the tombstone referred to by the author of the *Tohfut-ul-Mujahideen* may, for aught we know, be that of a real Zamorin. But the conversion and pilgrimage should have taken place between the dates of Abdur-Razak's visit to Calicut (1442 A. D.) and of the arrival of the Portuguese in India (1498 A. D.). History and chronology have never been the forte of the Hindus. We have, indeed, several instances of native annalists referring persons and events of a comparatively modern date to a remote past and endeavouring to enshroud them in the mists of hoary antiquity.[1] As Mr. Sewell declares "the dates of the Kērаḷōṭpaṭṭi are probably entirely fictitious, and could not be for a moment depended upon."[2]

The Mahomedan, the Christian, the Buddhist, the Jain—each of these religions, claims the Perumāḷ to have embraced its tenets, and yet the Hindus tenaciously hold that he lived and died a devout follower of Śiva.

"Wherever it was," says Faria-y-Souza, the Portuguese historian, "that Chēra Perumāḷ then reigned, who, tired with the cares of a Crown and having some knowledge of the evangelical doctrine, as being a great favourer of the Christians of St. Thomas inhabiting at Crānganūr, resolved to end his days at Meliapore (modern Mylapore, St. Thome—a suburb of the town of Madras) serving in the church. By consent of all princes, he resigned the crown to Manichan

1. Speaking of the Vikramaditya Era, Dr. Burnell refers to another motive for the alteration of dates. "The passion for systematizing and thus falsifying even history in accordance with the popular astrological and religious notions of the day, has, it is evident from the above, led to repeated alterations in the dates assigned to real or fictitious events in Indian history." *Elements of South Indian Paleography*, p. 73. See also the remarks of Mr. Talboys Wheeler at pp. 410—412 of the 4th Vol. of his *History of India*, part 2. The conduct of the annalists is in striking contrast to that of certain Orientalists who want to modernise everything Indian, and who so dream their desires and try to realise their dreams.

2. Sewell's *Sketches of the Dynasties of Southern India*, p. 56, Note 7.

Herari, a page esteemed worthy and able to govern that empire. Perumāl died at Meliapore and it is thought that one of the bodies found with that of the Apostle was his."[1] Faria also refers to another relation, evidently Portuguese, according to which this Perumāl was one of the three kings who went to adore Christ at Bethlem![2] "Is not this a false invention of the Portuguese priests to rob the Mahomedans of a convert?" indignantly exclaims the Editor of *A New Collection of Voyages and Travels*. "This is false invention of the Portuguese," he adds, "since he (the Perumāl) began his voyage at least 347 years after Christ according to De Faria's own account. Forgers are never satisfied, and, by a certain fatality, invent stories to confute one another."[3]

Mr. Talboys Wheeler is disposed to think that, in all probability, the Perumāl turned a Buddhist monk in his old age.[4]

The story of the Buddhist king Nāsanga, as related in the Kērala Māhāṭmyam[5] (a Sanskrit work on the greatness of Kērala) fits in closely with that of Chēramān Perumāl as related in the Kēralōṭpaṭṭi. In the Kērala Māhāṭmyam, we read that a clever Buddhist woman, by name Māli, fascinated a *Rishi* and had by him a son for whom she procured the right to the crown by exchanging her infant against that born to the 11th Kōlaṭṭiri king. In due time, the boy became king of Malabar and governed the country through Buddhist officers, though he was also kind to the Brahmans. It further adds that the first Buddhist *Vihara* (chapel) was made by him at Nasamīpapura (Madaya or Palayangāḍi). Nāsanga was so powerful that even Parasu Rāma,

1. Asia Portugueza, Vol. I, p. 100.
2. Ibid, Vol. II, p. 224.
3. Vol. I, p. 29, Note, Astley's Collection.
4. History of India, Vol. III, p. 424.
5. Chapters 61 to 73.

BF.

incarnation of Vishṇu as he was, found it difficult to overcome him. Rāma is said to have extirpated the Buddhists and lopped off the hands and feet of the king, which as soon sprouted afresh. After describing the changes that Nāsanga introduced into the administration of Malabar and the difficulties that Rāma encountered in endeavouring to get rid of him, the Māhāṭmya proceeds, "The king was detained in the chase by Śiva in disguise, whilst the queen fell in love with *Krodha*, the minister, and made offers to him, the flat refusal of which prompted her desire a speedy revenge. She acts all the part of Potiphar's wife. But the faithful servant, when on the point of being executed, is discovered mounted on the heavenly chariot and, parting, advises the king to go to Mecca and worship there Vishṇu incarnate in all shapes (Viśwarūpāvaṭāra) in order to go to Vishṇu's heaven. The king did so." [1]

The latter part of the above story has its analogue in the Kēralōṭpaṭṭi with the variation that the Chēramān became a convert to Mahomedanism and undertook the Haj. There we read that the Perumāl's wife fell in love with Paṭamala Nāyar, chief of his body-guard, and made offers to him. The sturdy chief indignantly refusing, the haughty queen swore to take dire vengeance. She instigated the Perumāl to punish the chief for some supposed crime, and, while the faithful servant was on the point of being executed, the Ḍēvās (gods) alighted in a heavenly chariot and carried the Nāyar bodily to the upper regions. The Perumāl, seing the chariot ascending heavenwards, begged of his late servant to advise him as to how he could attain *Moksha*. The Nayar exhorted his quondam sovereign to give up his religion and to conform to the tenets of Mahomed. Adopting the advice, Chēramān gave up Hinduism, became a follower of the Prophet, and left for Mecca.[2]

1. Madras Journal of Literature and Science, Vol. XIII, p. 103.
2. Keralolpathy, Mangalore Edition, pp. 65-66.

Buddhism had penetrated into Southern India at a very early date. The great king Aśōka (280 B. C.) mentions, in one of his famous edicts, Kērala as one of the *Pratyantas* or countries neighbouring his dominions.[1] According to one version of the Kēralōṭpaṭṭi Bāṇa, a predecessor of Chēramān, is said to have been converted to Buddhsim by certain monks who had come from China,[2] and the Brahmans found considerable difficulty in getting rid of him. At length after a great struggle, the Perumāl was dethroned and the Buddhists had their tongues cut out and then expelled from the country. His successors had to take an oath by which they bound themselves never to allow any persons, not of the orthodox Brahman faith, to obtain public sanction to reside in the country. In Northern India, Brahmanism was once more getting rampant, and Buddhism, steadily dislodged from one stronghold after another, was fast losing ground. According to General Cunningham, from the fifth to the seventh century A. D., the decline was gradual and gentle, but, from the eighth century, the fall was rapid and violent.[3] In the seventh century, when Hiuen Tsiang, the Chinese pilgrim, visited Benares, the city was already more Brahmanical than Buddhist. Buddhism was in a state of decay. Passing through Malabar, he found most of the monasteries in ruins, while there were hundreds of flourishing temples with the usual swarms of "naked heretics."[4] Evidently, Brahmanism was putting

1. See Professor Wilson's translation of the Edict given in App. I, Vol. III.—History of India.

Dr. Burnell reads the words "Pratyanteshu" as "Samantesu." see note 4, *Elements of South Indian Paleography*, 2nd Edition, p. 11. See note post. Dr. Bhuler in the *Epigraphia Indica* reads the word as 'Pratyantcshu' and translates it to mean neighbouring. Vol. II, p. 466.

2. See Kerala Visesha Mahatmyam, pp. 89-90; Sewell, p. 57, Note 3.

3. The Bhilsa Topes, Chapter 12 and Archaeological Reports.

4. Wheeler's History of India, Vol III, p. 280.

forth all its might in ousting Buddhism from South India. Not long after, about the middle of the eighth century, occurred the confutation of the *Boudhas* of Malabar by Kumārila Bhaṭṭa and consequent persecution noticed briefly in the Kēralōṭpaṭṭi.[1] Kumārila, the holy apostle from Bengal, not simply preached against the Buddhists, but persuaded a king of Southern India to persecute them. The prince commanded his servants to put to death the old men and the young children of the Buddhists from the southermost point of India to the snowy mountains. "Let him who slays not, be slain," so ran the terrible behest of the fanatic Hindu king. That great opponent of the Buddhists, the renowned Vēḍānṭist Śankara, himself a native of Malabar and a Nambūṭiri Brahman, lived about the time of the last Perumāl [2], and began his successful controversies with the Buddhist priests in Malabar. Through his instrumentality, the Brahmans were able, not long after, to worst the Buddhists and finally to expel their religion from India. That certainly was neither the time nor the occasion for the Buddhists to get into their fold the last Perumāl, and the common report of the Buddhist conversion of the Perumāl related evidently to the apostacy of Bāṇa Perumāl, one of the predecessors of Chēramān.

Mr. Kūkkal Kēlu Nāyar, in his memorandum on the Syrian and Jewish Copper Plates, suggests that the

1. Wilson's *Descriptive Catalogue of the Mackenzie Collection*, p. 39.

2. Sankaracharya—

[*a*] Lived about the eighth or ninth century A. D. Professor Wilson's *Hindu Sects*.

[*b*] Born A. D. 788. Died A. D. 820-21. Indian Antiquary. Vol. IX, pp. 175, 263.

[*c*] Sankaracharya is generally placed in the eighth century; perhaps we must accept the ninth century. The best accredited tradition represents him as born on the 10th of the month of Madhava [April-May], in 788 A. D. Ind. Studies, Vol. XIV, 355, Note 1, p. 89. Barth's *Religions of India*.

Perumāl became a convert to Jainism, and that his departure to Mecca, called in Sanskrit Magaḍha (!), was due chiefly to the religious inducements of Majains called Jains or Boudhas, who, as a people, were then settled in Arabia, and many of whom visited Malabar. The original name of Mahajains, it is said, became in time corrupted into Magains or Magans.[1]

Jainism is closely allied to Buddhism and may properly be styled a sister of the latter.[2] By the fifth century A. D., it had penetrated to the extremity of the Peninsula, where we find fixed settlements of the Jainas. The Buddhists had preceded them, and to these we owe the first literary culture of the Tamil and Canarese languages.[3] Malayalam was still only a dialect of Tamil and had not yet developed into an independent language. In the seventh century, the Jains were the dominant sect in the Dekhan. Hiuen Tsiang mentions, as existing in the Dekhan, a class of people known as "Nirgranthas," naked heretics, or "those who have cast aside every tie." Dr. Burnell, on the authority of the *Atthapahudaka* (*i. e.* *Ashtaprabhritaka*) *Gatha*, takes them to be Jainas,[4] while Lassen,[5] Bothlingk and Roth[6] identify them with naked mendicant Brahmans.

1. Madras Journal of Literature and Science, Vol. XXI, p. 35 *et seq.* 30, *ff.*
2. Dr. Buhler has ascertained that the Jains are the heretical Buddhists, ex-communicated at the first Council. Burnell's *Elements of South Indian Paleography*, 2nd Edition, p. 12, Note 2.
3. Barth's *Religions of India*, p. 151.
4. Indian Antiquary, Vol. I, p. 309. See *Elements of South Indian Paleography*, 2nd Edition, p. 47, Note 6.
5. Ind. Alterthumskunde, III, 692, IV. 233.
6. St. Petersburg Dictionary, S. V.

See also Hunter's *History of the Indian People*, pp. 83-85. Also the Indian Empire, pp. 154, 169, 171. It may be remarked that the Niganthas (*i. e.* Nirgranthas) are frequently mentioned in the Pali "Dathavamso" [of the 12th century] as heretical enemies of the Buddhists *who worshipped Vishnu* [see III, 23]. Burnell's *South Indian Paleography*, p. 48.

The name occurs in the inscriptions of Aśōka, and it is said that, in all probability, it referred to the ancestors of the existing Jainism, if not to the Jainas themselves.[1] On the theory so strongly urged by Mr. Edward Thomas[2] that the early faith of Aśōka was Jainism, Mr. Logan has observed that Jain missionaries had come as far south as Malabar.[3] But after the confession of faith recorded in the Babhra Edict of Aśōka,[4] it is impossible to say that his missionaries were Jaina and not Buddhist. "It was by Buddhist missions," observes Mr. Barth that "the powerful Emperor came into relation with the kings of the Dekhan, over whom he appears to have exercised a kind of protectorate."[5] Mr. Logan refers to another circumstance as evidencing the prevalence of Jainism in Malabar, i. e. the peculiar style of temple architecture said to be left behind by the Jainas. Mr. Ferguson in his *History of Eastern Architecture*

1. Barth, p. 151, See 8th Edict of Delhi. 5 in the Corpus Inscrip. Indie plate XX.
2. *Jainism, the Early Faith of Asoka* by Edward Thomas, F. R. S., London, 1877, p. 42.
3. Malabar, Vol. I, p. 184.
4. See Cunningham Corpus Indic. pl. XV. Barth, pp. 117-130; also Mr. Edward Thomas' *Jainism, the Early Faith of Asoka*; and Appendix 1 to the 3rd Vol. of Wheeler's *History of India*.
5. Mr. Edward Thomas and Dr. Burnell read the word rendered into *Pratyanteshu* by Wilson as *Chamantesu* and *Samantesu*. Dr. Burnell observes: "The third word is read *pacantesu* by H. H. Wilson, and taken to be for *Pratyanteshu*, a word which is not supported by authorities. As *p* and *s*, and *c* and *m* only differ in a very trifling degree, I venture to read *Samantesu* which is far preferable." Dr. Burnell's reading of the inscriptions is :—

Tablet II "Evam api Samantesu yatha Coda Pa (*n*) da Satiyputo Ketalaputa." *Elements of South India Paleography*, p. 11, Note 4. For Mr. Thomas' reading on his *Jainism, the Early Faith of Asoka*, "Evamepi pa chanitesu yatha chosa" &c. The word "Samantesu" imports subordination, at any rate, protectorate.

notes the similarity which, he says, is most marked in the District of Canara.[1] More curious still; Dr. Buchanan Hamilton[2] points to the similarity between the architecture of the West Coast and of Nepal, and both he and Col. Kirkpatrick[3] remark that this, coupled with the strange notions as to conjugal relations and other peculiarities prevailing among the Nayars of the West Coast and the Newars of Nepal (the similarity in names may also be noted), point to a similarity of race which is both curious and interesting, but how and when the connexion took place it is difficult to determine. Mr. Ferguson also confesses his inability to offer even a plausible conjecture as to how or at what time a connexion existed between Nepal, Thibet, and Canara. No doubt, the Hindu temples and even the Mahomedan mosques in Malabar exhibit a style of architecture not far removed from that of the Jainas. In Travancore, it is found even in lay buildings. But it has to be remembered that there are, at present, in Malabar, few, if any, buildings as old as the eighth or ninth century A. D. Again Mr. Logan himself observes that the Jains seem to have made very little impression on the religious belief of the people; for even a regard for animal life, the great characteristic of the Jains, had, until recent years, very little hold on the people.[4] The Perumāl's converson to the Jaina faith rests wholly on the conjecture hazarded by Mr. Kēlu Nayar with almost nothing to support it and may, therefore, be taken for what it is worth.[5]

1. Logan's Malabar, Vol. I, pp. 270-1.

2. Account of the Kingdom of Nepal, pp. 29, 42, 51.

3. Nepal, p. 187,—Kirkpatrick Mr. Brian Hodgson refers to this similiarity and remarks that the Nayars of Malabar and the Newars of Nepal may perhaps belong to the same race.

4. Malabar, Vol. I, p. 184.

5. Dr. Hultzch characterises Mr. Kelu Nayar's observations as "wild speculations." See Vol. XX of the Indian Antiquary, pp. 285—292, Note 12.

The Hindus reject the story of the conversion itself and maintain that the Perumāḷ lived and died a Śiva devotee.

Pāchu Mūṭṭaṭu records that the Perumāḷ died a staunch Hindu at Ṭiruvanchikkuḷam, the ancient capital of the Chēra or Kēraḷa kingdom, in the 73rd year of his reign and the 100th year of his age,[1] and adds that the Mecca pilgrimage is not supported by records. The Kēraḷavakāśakṙamam asserts that he died in Malabar a Hindu.[2] Mr. Śanguṇṇi Menon, in his *History of Travancore*, holds that the Perumāḷ closed his earthly career at Ṭiruvanchikkuḷam,[3] dying a devout Hindu.[4] Both the Sanskrit Hālāsya Māhāṭmyam[5] and the Tamil Tiruviḷayāṭal Purāṇam[6] refer to Chēra Perumāḷ as a Śiva devotee. The Tamil accounts of the eleventh and twelfth centuries say that he ascended to heaven with Sunḍaramūṙṭṭi Swāmi.[7]

There is a picturesque description of this mysterious disappearance embodied in the Periya Purāṇam, a work composed not later than the twelfth century. Its version is that "while the Śiva Saint Sunḍara was at Ṭiruvanchikkuḷam, the Chēra capital, celebrating it in certain hymns which still exist, the time came for

1. The Keralavisesha Mahatmyam, p. 97. See p. 90 also.

2. P. 21.

3. A well-known Siva shrine close by Cranganur, the seat of the early Kerala Empire.

4. Pp. 85--86.

5. Chapter 48. Story the 42nd.

6. Tirumugan-godutta padalam, p. 227 of the Madras Edition of 1888. See also Nelson's *Madura Manual*, Part III, p. 26.

Tufor's Translation of *Oriental Historical MSS.* Vol. I, page 88.

See also the 37th Chapter of the *Periapuranam*, Madras Edition of 1884.

7. Sundara-Murthi Nayanar must have flourished prior to the eleventh century A. D. It is not possible to ascertain the exact date. See *South Indian Inscriptions*, Vol. II, Nos. 38 and 41.

him to depart the earth. Accordingly, one morning, the angels of Mount Kailāsa waited upon him with a white elephant and a commission to translate him athwart the sky to that rocky abode of Gods. Elated beyond measure, the Saint tarried not even to utter a parting word to his royal friend, but, ascending the celestial elephant, started forthwith on his travel through the azure blue. The Perumāḷ, coming to know what had taken place and unable to sustain the separation, mounted his steed and uttered a *mantram* in its ears which enabled it to ascend into air and overtake the paradisaical pachyderm. The ministers and generals of the king, beholding the miraculous scene, shook off their mortal coils with the help of their swords and followed their beloved king. So the aerial procession reached Mount Kailās, but the Perumāḷ found admission into the divine presence, only after he had composed the poem called Adi-ula, which one Machattan is said, in the Purāṇa, to have communicated to the world here below by reciting it in the town of Ṭiruppiḍavūr." "Such then", observes Professor Sunḍaram Pillai, "is the legend as embodied in the Periya Purāṇam, and all that it enables us to conclude is that a small Chēra prince mysteriously disappeared from his capital. There is nothing whatever in this or any other written record of respectable antiquity to lend support to the story of the conversion (to Mahomedanism) or the voyage to Mecca."[1]

Jacob Canter Visscher is not sure whether Chēramān turned a Mahomedan and went to Mecca or that he simply proceeded to the river Ganges in fulfilment of a vow.[2] Even this pilgrimage is denied by Major Heber Drury, who says that "like Charles V, the aged monarch, weary of the cares of state, retired to console his declining years with religion and solitude, and, taking up his abode within the precincts of a sacred

1. Professor Sundaram Pillai on the Kollam Era.

2. Letters from Malabar, pp. 49—50.

pagoda in the Cochin territory, died full of years, A. D. 352."[1] This view is supported by the Dutch Government records of Cochin, which state that the Perumāl retired for life to the pagoda at Ṭiruvanchikkuḷam. "The celebrated pagoda of Ṭiruvanchikkuḷam is still associated with the history of this Perumāl." says the Rev. M. Whitehouse. "Within its sacred precincts are still to be seen two stone statues of great antiquity venerated as memorials of the great Perumāl and his wife, Cherōṭṭi Amma, now regarded as demi-gods. It is also said that, at an annual feast called Paṭṭaṭṭānam, the Cochin Raja, as the most direct lineal descendant of the last Perumāl is required to make certain offerings to his departed spirit."[3] The Tohfut-ul-Mujahideen remarks that the "Pagans would believe that he (the Perumāl) has been taken up into heaven, and still continue to expect his descent, on which account they assemble at Crānganūr and keep ready there wooden shoes and water, and, on a certain night of the year, burn lamps as a kind of festival in honour of his memory.'

A careful survey of the evidence available on the question may fairly be said to lead to the conclusion that there is very little to show that the last Chēramān Perumāl became a convert to Islamism and undertook

1. Malabar, Vol. 1, p. 167,—Drury's *Account of Travancore.*

2. Day's *Land of the Perumals*, p. 45.

There is a tradition that the Perumal one day suddenly disappeared from the pagoda at Tiruvanchikkulam, that the deity of that temple went in search of him as far as a tank close to a mosque, but that the Perumal was not found. In token of this, the idol of the pagoda is taken in procession on one of the annual festival days to that locality and, after going round the mosque, is carried to a place called Cheraman Tara and Paramba, which are in the vicinity where the Perumal is said to have resided. See an article entitled *Origin and Early History of Keralam or Malayalam.* The Madras Times, December 18—1900. p. 5.

3. *Lingerings of Light in a Dark Land*, p. 3.

4. Rowlandson's Translation, p. 56.

the Mecca pilgrimage, while the probabilities are in favour of his having lived and died a devout Hindu. The Mahomedan legend is evidently the result of the mixing up of the early Buddhist conversion of Bāṇa,[1] one of the Chēramān Perumāls and of the much later Mahomedan conversion of one of the Zamorin Rajas of Calicut who claim to have derived their authority from the last Chēramān Perumāl.[2]

6. **Zamorin's Title to the Land.** Even if the Zamorin did derive his title to the kingdom of Calicut from the last Perumāl, it is extremely doubtful if he was a relative at all of the Perumāl. Much less is it certain what the degree or nature of the relationship between the two was, though the Cochin *Grandhavari* (chronicles) says that the first Zamorin was the son of the Perumāl before his conversion to Mahomedanism. The Kēralōṭpaṭṭi simply says that the ancestors of the Zamorin, two Ēṟāṭi youths, had rendered material help to the Perumāl in expelling a foreign invasion and that, on the eve of the Perumāl's sailing for Mecca, he made a gift of a narrow strip of land to them, with an injunction to conquer and rule. The Ēṟāṭī brothers came from Pūṇṭura near Coimbatore, and there is no reference to any relationship between them and the Perumāl. The Kēralamāhāṭmyam does not, as already shown, connect the Zamorin in any way with the last Perumāl. The last Perumāl is described by some of the early Portuguese writers as a Kṣheṭṟiya and by others as a Vaiśya or Śūḍṟa in caste. Both Barbosa and Faria-y-Sousa assert that the Zamorin was a nephew, i.e., sister's son, of the last

1. Mr. Logan is inclined to identify Bana Perumal, the Buddhist convert, with the Cheraman Perumal of the Mahomedan tradition. Malabar Vol. I, pp. 241—2.

2. The family of the Ali Raja of Cannanore may be mentioned as a prominent instance of a Malabar Mahomedan chieftain deriving his descent from a Hindu convert to Mahomedanism.

Perumāl and, curiously enough, the latter adds that he was a Brahman; and Castenheda agrees with him. In Cowell's edition of Elphinstone's *History of India*, we read that, "in the 17th century, there were two traditions extant as regards the origin of the Zamorins. According to one story, the kings of this line were all Brahmans and esteemed for piety and learning." Dr. Fryer styles the Zamorin "the chief Bishop" of Malabar. The Dutch *Road Book* of 1742 mentions that the Zamorin was the son of the last Perumāl, while the Cochin Raja was his nephew, being sister's son, and, as such, the rightful heir to the throne of the Perumāl according to the Marumakkaṭṭāyam law, the law of succession prevalent in the country. This, it is added, accounts for the former being a Śūḍṛa, while the latter is a Kśheṭṛiya. But Zeiruddeen Mukkadom, an Egyptian traveller of the 15th century, tells us "that the last Perumāl belonged to the Vaiśia or Śūḍṛa caste, and was called Shukkerwutty or Chakerwutty".[1]

7. **Perumal's Sword.** To the first volume of Mr. Logan's *Manual of Malabar* is attached a *Frontispiece*, being "an engraving from an original sketch" of "Chēramān Perumāl's sword given to the Zamorin with advice to die and kill and annex." Probably this is the sword referred to by our author. As the sketch appears in the illustration, there is an inscription in modern Malayalam characters. It must have been engraved on the sword, if it is the identical one given by the the Perumāl as asserted, at the latest, in the beginning of the ninth century A. D. But the Syrian and Jewish deeds of almost even date make it clear that the modern Malayalam characters had not yet come into use, the alphabet then in use in Malabar was the Vaṭṭeḷuṭṭu. The modern Malayalam, or Āryaneḷuṭṭu, is the product of the development of ages and attained its present shape only in the 17th century, having been introduced, it is said, by Ṭunchaṭṭ Eḷuṭṭachhan, "the father of Malayalam literature." Mr. Logan

1. Day, p. 43. Probably, the word is Chakṛavaṛṭṭi.

is inclined to think that Eḻuttachhan not simply introduced the modern Malayalam alphabet, but rather invented it. For, he says, "It was no less than a revolution when, in the 17th century, one Ṭunchaṭṭ Eḻuṭṭachhan, a man of the Śūḍra (Nayar) caste, boldly *made* an alphabet—the existing Malayalam one—derived chiefly from the Granḍha—the Sanskrit of the Tamils, which permitted of the free use of Sanskrit in writing and boldly set to work to render the chief Sanskrit poems into Malayalam."[1] Of the Vaṭṭeḻuṭṭu, the alphabet employed in the most ancient written documents extant, —the Jewish and Syrian copper-plates—Dr. Burnell says that it was "the original Tamil alphabet which was once used in all that part of the Peninsula south of Tanjore, and also in South Malabar and Travancore." He adds that the Vaṭṭeḻuṭṭu alphabet "remained in use in (Malabar) up to the end of the 17th century among the Hindus, and since then, in the form of the Kōleḻuṭṭu (sceptre writing), it is the character in which the Hindu Sovereigns have their grants drawn up.[2] It is, therefore, impossible to accept the sword, of which an illustration is given by Mr. Logan, bearing an inscription in modern Malayalam characters, as the identical one alleged to have been presented by the Perumāl.

We read in the Kēraḷachariṭṭram that this sword was burnt, when the Dutch sacked the Zamorin's temporary residence at Ṭiruvanchikkuḷam in the year 1671.[3]

8. **Perumal's Shield.** It appears that there is a shield preserved still in the Maṭṭāncherī palace in Cochin, which is pointed out as the identical one presented by the Perumāl. It, however, bears no inscription. That it should have survived eleven centuries amongst various vicissitudes throws considerable suspicion on its asserted identity.

9. **The Martial Spirit of the Nayars.** This was kept up by means of various institutions which were

1. P. 92.
2. Elements of S. I. Paleography.
3. P. 147.

designed for that purpose. Every year during the Ōṇam festival, sham fights were arranged throughout the country, when the adult members of the community ranged themselves into two parties under their respective leaders, and tried their strength in the open field. Large crowds used to gather to witness the combat, and even Nayar ladies, attired in gay apparel and decked with jewels, graced the occasion, bestowing smiles on the winning party. There is a fine description of an Ōṇam tournament given by Forbes in his *Oriental Memoirs*. The Christians also joined these sham fights held during Ōṇam, and one of the Decrees of the Synod of Diamper expressly prohibited them "from joining their heathen neighbours, during the Hindu feast of Ōnam." Duels were also much in vogue and were even encouraged, as these were a source of revenue to the State.

Mr. Logan gives the following account of duels in Malabar. "When mortal offence was given by one man to another, a solemn contract used to be entered into before the chieftain of the locality to fight a duel, the chief himself being umpire. Large sums (up to 1000 fanams or 250 rupees) used to be deposited as battle-wager, and these sums formed one source, (aṃkam) of the chieftain's revenue, and the right to levy them was sometimes transferred along with other privileges appertaining to the tenure of the soil. A preparation and training (it is said) for twelve years preceded the battle, in order to qualify the combatants in the use of their weapons. The men who fought were not necessarily the principals in the quarrel—they were merely champions. It was essential that one should fall, and so both men settled all their worldly affairs before the day of combat."

The custom of Kuṭippaka (literally, family feud) was another institution, which tended to brace up the martial spirit of the Nayars. According to this, when a man is slain, it is incumbent on his family to compass the death of a member of the slayer's family. The chieftain of the district intervened, when a man was slain and the body of the deceased was by him taken to his enemy's house, and the corpse and the house were burnt together. It is understood that an out-house is usually selected for the purpose, but it was a common saying that "the slain rests in the yard of the slayer."[1]

Sham fights, like the one witnessed by our author at Kalli Quilon, were not of unfrequent occurrence in Malabar. In the year 1519, Sequeira, the Portuguese Viceroy, with a band of more than 500 Portuguese, witnessed a duel on a very big scale between a chieftain of the Zamorin and a chieftain of Cochin. Four thousand men were engaged on each side, and, while the fighting was in progress, one of the Portuguese struck in with the Zamorin's men, whereupon the Cochin men sent a flight of arrows into the Portuguese spectators and killed five of them, putting the rest to flight.[2] These sham fights continued to take place periodically almost up to the period of the Mysorean conquest of Malabar, which immediately preceded the British occupation of the country. Sir Thomas Munro, reporting to the Madras Government, on the 4th of July 1817, regarding the land tenures and political oraganisation of Malabar, observes as follows :—" The Naruwai (Nāḍuvāli) was the military chief of the district, and was bound to attend the Raja on the field, or march wherever he was directed, with all the fighting men of his district, under the Desaways (Ḍēśavālis) or heads of their respective villages. It was also his duty, in times of peace, to assemble the Nayars of his district every two or three years, in order to exhibit, in the presence of the Raja, a mock or rather real fight, with the Nayars of another district ; for these combats never terminated without the loss of a few

1. Logan, p. 169.
2. Logan, p. 323; Keralapazhama, p. 155.

lives. The Naruwai paid, for the funeral of each Nayar slain, eight to sixteen rupees, and to each Nayar wounded sixteen to three hundred rupees, according to his rank and the nature of the wound. These combats, it is said, were instituted with the view of keeping up the martial spirit of the Nayars."

The institutions, known as Kaḷaries, were intended to foster the martial spirit of the Nayars, and to keep them fit for work in wars. These were fencing schools, and were generally attached to the Bhagavaṭi (goddess) temple of each village. Each Kaḷari is presided over by its Āśān (fencing-master), who supervised the massage and the physical culture of the pupils placed under his charge. This training enabled the young men not only to become excellent warriors but also to endure any amount of fatigue, and to show wonderful feats with their body. I shall here extract a short description of a Kaḷari or Malabar gymnasium, as described by a correspondent in the *Madras Mail*, to which paper I render my thanks for this quotation.

"There are several Nayar institutions in Malabar which, surviving unto the present day, bear ample proof that the people to whom they belong fitted themselves in every way for the martial profession they followed in the ancient political constitution of Malabar, before the European came and changed the aspect of affairs. I remember reading a year or two ago, a reference in your columns to a friendly tournament known as *Onathallu* (Ōṇaṭṭallu), which the Nayars get up at the great Ōṇam festival time, the combatants being picked youths from two factions. The following description of a Kaḷari or Malabar gymnasium, and of the usages connected with it may be interesting as showing that the Nayars bestowed as much attention, as the Greeks or Romans of old did, on the physical development of their youths. A village in olden days used to have its own Kaḷari, but it was also, and is still, common for private persons to have their own Kaḷaries, where their lads can be taught the national methods of self-defence. A gymnasium of this description consists of a pit, about 20 feet long by 15 feet broad, and 6 feet deep. It is topped by a thatched roof strongly constructed. The floor of the pit is covered close with little *cowries*, so well set down, each with its round side up, that a very smooth flooring is the result. Sometimes further smoothness is obtained by rubbing oil or lard over the *cowries*. In the gymnasium thus prepared, the Nayar youth takes his course of lessons in the now decaying art of fencing. The course begins,—that is, admitting old customs are abided by—on the first day of the *Karkatam* month (July) and ends, as far as the tutor is concerned, on the last day of the same month; for, according to the Malabar physicians of old, the most fit time for physical exercise and muscular development is when the monsoon is at its height. Special teachers impart instruction in fencing. They are known as Paṇikers in South Malabar, and Paravens in the north of the district, and socially they occupy an intermediate position between the Ṭīyar and Nayar, the latter having to bathe, if polluted by the touch of a Paṇiker.

"On the day the course opens, the tutor is given a present by each pupil in either coin or cloths. Both pupils and teacher rub themselves well over with oil, and, wearing only a narrow waist cloth, lightly bound, begin work. The pupil first practises lifting his leg to the height of his own uplifted arm. He is next taught to bend back, till his head touches the floor. After proficiency has been attained in these two trying movements, the pupil has to prostrate himself on the floor, in the first instance face upwards, and then face to the ground, while the preceptor, suspending himself from a strong rope attached to the roof of the gymnasium, proceeds most dexterously and elaborately with his feet, or rather, with his big toe, to "shampoo" his pupil, going all round the region of the heart, lungs, joints, etc. After this massage process, (which, by the way, is looked upon as very important), the student practises, with each leg and arm forming a right angle and with chest off the ground, raising himself up and down without bending his arms and knees. This stage of the course over, the tutor rubs the pupil down vigorously, using both hands for the purpose. When these preliminary tactics have been completed, the pupil may stand and proceed to take lessons in fencing. He provides himself with a stick (*moochan*) made of teak or some other strong wood. A similar stick is handed over to an opponent, and, the two being placed *vis-a-vis*, the fencer is taught to stand on his guard in correct positions with his balance properly arranged. The earlier movements consist of what may be described, in fencing technique, as simple head parries in a given number of motions, straight and oblique. The pupil next learns to lower his stick and parry its aim at his sides, chest, knees, ankles and the various other joints and vital parts of his body. After having gone through a regular course with a single stick, he proceeds to defend himself with two sticks, the lessons being so arranged as to instruct the pupil how to parry strokes by adroitly crossing both sticks and receiving his adversary's weapon on the outside of the cross so formed. A part of this lesson also consists in the teacher deftly getting behind the other and then attacking him. This move is frustrated without turning round, simply by bringing both sticks cleverly behind under the arms. Much stress is laid on a counter motion, in which the guard makes an attack on his opponent, when the latter is resuming his front position after his effort at the rear.

"The foregoing is only a general description of the very elaborate system of fencing practised by the Nayars of Malabar. It may be added that, after the pupil has gone through this course, he is instructed in somersaulting feats, as also in wrestling, principally with the right arm disengaged. He is taught several feint attacks, both in the "high" and "low" lines, so to speak, and is initiated into the secret of delivering certain aggressive movements, whereby the adversary is paralysed in a trice. In fact, this phase of Malabar fencing and wrestling reveals a very close aquaintance with the human anatomy. The entire course of instruction is so arranged that it extends over the whole month of *Karkatam*. During the following month, the pupil keeps in practice, and then leaves off till *Karkatam* comes round again. After four or five years of this programme, a promising pupil becomes a perfect fencer and wrestler. Pupils undergoing instruction have to abide by certain strict regulations. During the month of study, they must remain strictly continent, indulge in no long walks and avoid damp places. Before beginning the day's lessons, they take a hearty meal, and, after the lessons, they swallow a drink of hot water in which ghee and ground pepper are put. They have to rise before dawn, and are not allowed to sleep during the day time. They have also to avoid fire. After the day's exercise is done, the pupil must abstain from further exertion until the next day. The Paṇikers who teach the youth of Malabar these feats of strength and skill have such a reputation and are supposed to understand so perfectly the system of massage that a proverb says that a Paṇiker can make a man lissome even on a *pattayam* (a box), which interpreted means that he can rub a man down and make his muscles flexible, in the smallest possible space. A kaḷari is an institution common to all parts of Malabar, but the people of the northern part will tell you with pardonable pride that it prevails mostly in their midst and is most popular in the Kaḍaṭṭanāḍ locality, the scene of several deeds of daring of a great hero named Ṭacchōli Oṭēnan, who is said to have once jumped across a well, 66 feet in circumference. This well, which stands near the town of

Badagara, is still pointed out by the people as a relic of past greatness."

10. **Zamorin's Supremacy**. Beyond the statement of the early Portuguese travellers, there is nothing to support the theory of the Zamorin's supremacy over all Malabar. Neither the Kōlaṭṭiri Raja nor the Raja of Travancore was ever under the Zamorin. Besides styling the Zamorin Emperor of Malabar, the Portuguese accounts do not say how he exercised any authority over the other States. Indeed, Mr. Logan says that, from the 12th or 13th century, the Zamorins were present at the Mahāmākham festival as suzerains of all Kēraḷam, including Travancore, which, as a Malayali State, only attained to the first rank shortly after the date of the last Mahāmākham festival in 1743. It is added that those who acknowledged the Zamorin's suzerainty sent flags in token of fealty, and places where these flags used to be hoisted at festival time are still pointed out. But neither Hamilton's account of the festival held in 1695, nor even Mr. Logan's account of the previous one of 1683, obtained from the records of the family of the Zamorin Maha Raja Bahadur, contains any mention of the Travancore, Kōlaṭṭiri or Cochin Rajas or their representatives being present or their flags of fealty being hoisted. At any rate, in the 13th century, Marco Polo names the king of Quilon, i. e., Travancore as a powerful and independent sovereign. In 1347, the Arab traveller, Ibn Batuta, calls this king of Quilon, Ṭiruvaṭi, a well-known designation of the Travancore king. The early Portuguese found the king of Travancore the legitimate sovereign of not simply of the southern part of the West Coast, but also of the whole of the south of Tinnavelly. Duarte Barbosa, after noticing Quilon, proceeds southwards and points to Cape Comorin as the southernmost extremity of Malabar, and observes

P. 173.

that the kingdom of Quilon still goes on and comes to an end at the city of Kayal, where the king of Quilon made his continual residence. This king, Barbosa styles, Benat-diry, i. e., Vēṇāṭṭaḍiry or king of Vēṇāṭ (Travancore). "He is very rich and powerful," adds Barbosa, "on account of his many men-at-arms who are very good bowmen. He always has in his guard four or five hundred women, trained from girls to be archers; they are very active. He sometimes is at war with the king of Narasinga (Vijayanagar), who wishes to take his country, but he defends himself very well."[1] De Barros mentions that the Portuguese, on their arrival on the coast found Travancore a powerful kingdom "the king of which," says he, "our people called 'Rey Grandi,' because he is greater in his dominions and the state he keeps than those of the princes of Malabar." The celebrated missionary, Francis Xavier, describes the king as "the great king of Travancore," and speaks of him as having had authority all over South India.[2] Purchas also points out that "the Portugals called Travancore, the great king, as being greater in state than the former." According to Mr. Logan himself, who speaks on the authority of early Portuguese writers, "the Travancore king is said to have, at one time, levied tribute from Ceylon and ventured even to challenge to battle the powerful king of Vijayanagara". In Astly's *Collection of Voyages*, we read that, on the arrival of the Portuguese in Malabar, there were seven kingdoms on the coast. "South of that of D'Ely, of which the rulers of three only were properly kings and independent, viz., Kananor, Calicut and Coulam (Travancore), the rest being only nominal or dependent kings." Again, the account which Astly has gathered from the Portuguese travellers of the tradition regarding the partition of Malabar by the last Perumāl goes to say with regard

1. I, p. 173.
2. Life of Xavier-Coleridge.

to the Zamorin, "He, the Perumāl, also gave him (the Zamorin) his sword and a cap as ensign of state and commanded all the other princes, among whom he had divided his territories, to acknowledge him as their Zamorin or Emperor, *except* the kings of Koulam and Kananor." Purchas also gives a similar account. Whiteway in his *Rise of the Portuguese Power in India* says that "the suzerainty of the Zamorin over Kananor (Kōlaṭṭnāḍ) and the northern States was little more than nominal". Thus, over Travancore and Kōlaṭṭnāḍ, it will scarcely be correct to say that the Zamorin did ever exercise any supremacy; at any rate, so far as known, there is no evidence to show this.

With regard to Cochin, it is different. There were frequent wars between the Zamorin and the Cochin Rajas, in all of which Cochin seems to have been more or less worsted. As observed by Mr. Whiteway, "The position of the Raja of Cochin had become quite subordinate; he was periodically displaced and reinstated by the Zamorin, and he could neither coin money nor even roof his house with tiles."[1] The periodical invasion of Cochin by the Zamorin continued, but latterly at intervals, till, at last, the Cochin Raja succeeded in finally expelling the Zamorin from Cochin territory with the aid of Travancore in 1762.

11. **Two Pagodas.** The two pagodas mentioned in this paragraph are situated in the Ponnāni Taluk of the Malabar Collectorate. We have the following account of them in the second volume of the *Manual of the Malabar District*. "In the neighbouring Vaṭṭakkuḷam Amśom, there is an important Hindu temple called the Sukapuram temple. It is believed to be of great antiquity, and also to have been founded by the hero and demi-god Paraśu Rāma. It is dedicated to Ḍekṣhiṇāmūrṭṭi or Śiva, and is said originally to have been attached specially to the Nambūtiri Brahmans of Śukapuram, which was one of the 64 grāmams or

1. Barbosa, p. 156.

settlements founded by Paraśu Rāma. Even to this day, offerings are invariably made by the Nambūṭirīs belonging to the gramam on occasions of marriage or other ceremonies among them, and none who have performed yāgams or sacrifices are recognised as such until they are registered at this Pagoda. This registration takes place once in 12 years. The Śrīkōvil, or Garbhagṛham (shrine) of the temple, is a massive laterite structure, 50 feet in length, 45 in breadth and 40 in height, the roof being covered with copper sheeting.

"About six miles to the south-east of Eḍappāl village (which is five miles from Ponnāni) and about the same distance in the same direction from Śukapuram temple is another famous ancient Hindu temple. It is situated in Chēkōd Amśom (village). This also is believed to have been founded by the same hero and demi-god, Paraśu Rāma, being specially attached to the Nambūṭiri Brahman colony of Paṅṅiyūr (the Pandel of our author), another of the 64 settlements referred to. This temple is a small tiled building, the presiding deity being Varāhamūrṭṭi (according to the Hindu Purāṇās the third incarnation of Vishṇu). This is the chief temple of the Nambūṭirīs, designated the Paṅṅiyūr Grāmakkār of the present day".

In the *Mackenzie Collection*, there is a somewhat incoherent story given regarding the theft of an idol belonging to Paṅṅiyūr villagers by certain members of the Chovūr clan, with the result that the Paṅṅiyūr men declared that they would no longer associate with the Chovūr villagers, and hence the cause of the feud between the two clans. Perhaps our author alludes to some tradition of the sort extant in his time.

12. **Porcad and Paroe.** These were the Ampalappuḻa or Chempakaśśēri, and the Paṟūr Rajas, both of whom were Nambūṭiri Brahmans and, therefore, of the spiritual order.

Berkenkoor and Mangatti. These were the Vaṭakkenkūr and the Ālengād Rajas, who belonged to the Sāmanṭa caste. These four Principalities, Ampalappuḷa, Parūr, Vaṭakkenkūr and Ālengād, used to be called the four pillars of the kingdom of Cochin, for they formed the main support of the kings of Cochin in their wars with other chiefs, especially with the Zamorin, who, as we have already observed, never gave rest to Cochin.

13. **Succession to Cochin Throne.** As is well known, under the system of Marumakkaṭṭāyam law existing in Malabar, succession is in the female line, one's heirs being not the issue of one's own loins but the issue of one's sister. The eldest male member is the head of the family, and he is succeeded by his next junior in age, irrespective of his being the sister's son of the last. Thus, the deceased Raja is always succeeded on the throne by his next junior in age. While this is the rule of law, history tells us that, with regard to succession to the Cochin throne, custom had modified the law a good deal. At any rate, it does not appear that the next in age always succeeded his predecessor on the throne. The Cochin royal family was originally composed of five branches, claiming to be descended from five sisters of Chēramān Perumāḷ. These branches were known as (1) Mūṭṭa Ṭāvaḷi (2) Eḷaya Ṭāvaḷi (3) Muriññūr Ṭāvaḷi (4) Chāḷiyūr Ṭāvaḷi and (5) Paḷḷiviruṭṭi Ṭāvaḷi. It is said that the ancestress of the Eḷaya Ṭāvaḷi alone had issue, when the alleged partition of Malabar was made by the Perumāḷ, so that the succession to the Perumāḷ's throne came to that branch. But, in course of time, the ancestresses of the other branches had also issue, and the succession was regulated by seniority in age among the male members of all the branches. Naturally, disputes arose ; but the Eḷaya Ṭāvaḷi sems to have secured for a long time prominence by effecting adoptions into the influential houses of Māṭaṭṭenkūr, which

possessed territory and temple (Ḍēvaswom) estates up to Kannet near Quilon, of Villārvaṭṭam, and of Kurūswarūpam, both of which houses possessed extensive estates. As the Eḷaya Ṭāvaḷi rose in power, it managed to gather round it the nobility and the people, and all the estates of the realm together resolved that the succession to the Cochin throne should be reserved to the Eḷaya Ṭāvaḷi, while the senior in age of all the five branches was allowed the diginity of Perumpaṭappu Mūppusṭānam, to which were attached certain valuable temple jurisdictions. The other branches came to be treated as mere collaterals, from which adoptions were to be made to the Eḷaya Ṭāvaḷi whenever necessary. After some time, disputes appear to have arisen again, the members of the various branches insisting that seniority in age alone should regulate succession to the throne. The allied Swarūpams (dignities), probably including the "four pillars of the State," the chief of the Brahman community, and others assembled, and resolved that the succession to the Crown should be regulated by election, from among the five branches, of the most able and the most wise, and of the one whose horoscope was the best, and that the prince so elected should be crowned as king and govern the country. The reason given for this resolution is that, if senority alone was to be the criterion of succession, it might happen that the senior in age was an incapable man, and the cause of monarchy would suffer at his hands, and the country be exposed to danger. The senior in age was, however, not to be left out in the cold. For, the diginity of Mūppusṭānam together with the emoluments and privileges attached to it was to continue as before. When the Portuguese under Cabral arrived in Cochin (December 1500), the state of circumstances then found existing is thus described: "The Raja of Cochin should, in his old age, retire to a temple and live and die there as an ascetic.

It was necessary to have the sanction of the Zamorin for the crowning of the successor." The reigning Raja seized the opportunity of the presence of the Portuguese who had come there from Calicut, disgusted with the Zamorin, and made up his mind to break through the toils of the Zamorin.[1] In 1505, when Almeyda arrived on the coast, he found a strong controversy going on in Cochin regarding the succession to the throne. Uṇṇi Gōḍa Vaṙma, the Raja who was ruling when Cabral came to Cochin, had, in pursuance of the custom above described, retired to a temple on account of old age. His next two juniors had sided with the Zamorin in the war between the latter and the Cochin Raja, assisted by the Portuguese in 1502, and were, therefore, expelled from the country, and excluded from their rights. The Raja desired that the third prince should be installed in his place. The expelled princes were backed up by the Brahmans and some of the chiefs of Cochin, and, on the Raja applying to Almeyda, he installed with great pomp the third prince under the style of Uṇṇi Rāman Kōil, and endeavoured to make the succession contingent on the approval of the king of Portugal instead of the Zamorin. The elder princes naturally revolted, and hostilities ensued. Five years after this, Uṇṇi Gōḍa Vaṙma died and Uṇṇi Rāma Vaṙma, the ruling prince, resolved to relinquish the throne according to custom and retire to a pagoda. The exiled princes, on receiving information of this, came up to Vypīn at the head of an army provided by the Zamorin, and demanded to be restored to their rights. The old Raja felt irresolute, left his place of residence and retired into the country. Nuno, who was left in command in Cochin, hastened to him and advised him not to do anything precipitate, till Albuquerque should come up from Cannanore. A few days after Albuquerque arrived, and advised the old Raja to break through the old custom, as it was not to the interest of the Portuguese

1. Keralapazhama, p. 23.

that the next senior in age then should succeed him, as he was a declared ally of the Zamorin. It was with much reluctance and with a heavy heart that the Raja yielded, and it was only after the chiefs of Mulanturuttu, Paṟūr, and Pallippuṟam presented themselves, tendered fealty, and advised that the Brahmans should not be listened to in the matter, that the Raja consented to give up the long observed custom of retiring from active life: Albuquerque encouraged him with assurances of Portuguese support, and said, "Brahmans' word has ceased to rule this kingdom. The mighty arm of the foreigner must be respected in future. Seek asylum, therefore, in the royal favour of the king of Portugal, and you will never be forsaken." The Raja continued to rule and the custom was given up henceforward. He, perhaps, outlived his exciled juniors. For, it is said that, after this, the throne descended in regular succession to the next junior in age to the deceased Raja.[1] Evidently, our author refers to the voice that the feudatories mentioned by him had in the choice of the king from among the most capable members of the five branches.

14. **Continual Warfare between Cochin and Calicut Rulers.** Though it is not altogether correct to attribute the continual warfare, which existed between the Zamorin and the Raja of Cochin, to the division of the Malayāli community into the Paṅṅiyūrkūr and the Chovarakūr, there can be no doubt that the factious spirit generated by these, contributed a good deal to keep up the quarrel between the two houses. In fact, the cardinal point in Malabar politics for a long time had been the rivalry between the Calicut and Cochin Rajas, and both the Portuguese and the Dutch cleverly availed themselves of this to advance their own interest on the coast. The Portuguese, rebuffed by the Zamorin, sought the aid of Cochin, the Raja of which State received them with open arms, his main view being to

1. Keralapazhama, Chap. 44.

subdue Calicut, or, at any rate, withstand successfully the incursions of the Zamorin with the help of the Portuguese. Of course, the Portuguese were also benefited greatly by the aid rendered by the Raja. The Dutch, on the other hand, were not as successful as the Portuguese in pursuing this policy. Their commercial instincts did not allow them to maintain a sufficient military establishment on the coast, such as would enable them to back up the Raja of Cochin against the Zamorin. Soon after their assumption of the protectorate of Cochin, the Dutch East India Company was drawn into the interminable wars between the Cochin and the Calicut chiefs, which continued in a desultory fashion for a long time, causing considerable loss to the Company, so much so that, before long, the Supreme Government of Batavia had to come to the resolution, "that the Raja of Cochin was no longer to be supported in his interminable fights with the Zamorin," and the Cochin Council was solemnly cautioned to live in peace with all men around.

15. **No lasting Peace between the above Rajas.** We learn from Portuguese authors that the position of the Raja of Cochin had become quite subordinate to the Zamorin, he being periodically displaced and reinvested by that chief. The wars between Cochin and Calicut were never formally brought to a close, except perhaps once at the instance of the Dutch When the contending parties felt exhausted, they retired from the field for a time, only with a view to renew the struggle with greater determination and when better equipped. The system of warfare persued in Malabar, to which we shall have occasion to refer later on, permitted this sort of temporary cessation of hostilities, either side agreeing to postpone the fight for the time.

As far as we have been able to ascertain, this mode of warfare between the rival kings of Calicut and Cochin continued for over 250 years after the arrival of the Portuguese in Malabar. Let us here summarise the history of some of the wars between the Zamorin and the king of Cochin.

First War. The Zamorin had been incensed at the conduct of the Cochin Raja in receiving the Portuguese with open arms, and, on seeing that De Gama had sailed with his fleet to Portugal, he collected an army of 50,000 Nayars at Ponnāni, and demanded that the few Portuguese left behind in Cochin should be surrendered at once. The nobility and the chiefs of Cochin, fearing the might of the Zamorin, advised the Raja to give up the foreigners, and not to allow the country to be desolated for persons of whom he knew nothing. Public feeling ran higher than ever against the Portuguese, and they themselves advised the disconsolate Raja to allow them to proceed to Cannanore, saying, "Your Highness should suffer no indignity on our account. Send us over to Cannanore." The Raja answered, "It is better to be driven out of one's country than not stand by one's plighted word. My only desire is that your lives should be safe." To his own men he said, that he was determined to protect the friendless foreigners, and that, while there was life left in him, he would not tarnish his reputation by any act of treachery,—"a notable example," says Faria-y-Souza, "of fidelity in a heathen, scarce to be paralleled among Christians." The Portuguese requested their countryman, Sodre, to remain with his ships in Cochin to assist them. Turning a deaf ear to their repeated entreaties, Sodre sailed away to capture the Mecca merchant ships. After sailing round the Red Sea and plundering many ships, he was reaching the Arabian coast, when he and his ships with all his men were destroyed in a storm. The handful of Portuguese in Cochin were thus left to the unaided protection of the Raja. The Zamorin, who had been joined by a number of Cochin feudatories, now invaded the State, claiming the island of Cochin as belonging to the Raja of Eṭapiḷḷi. Before starting on the enterprise, the Zamorin called a council of his nobles and pointed out to them that Calicut had owed its prosperity and affluence to the mercantile enterprise of the Moplas, that, since the arrival of the Portuguese and their setting themselves as enemies of the Zamorin, the Cochin Raja has denied the suzerainty of Calicut and associated himself with them and that he should, therefore, be adequately punished. The whole council agreed to this, except the Zamorin's nephew called by the Portuguese "Nambiaṭirin," who said, "We should not confide in these Mopḷas. They are incessantly clamouring for war, but they would run away as soon as the fighting begins. It is not only the Raja of Cochin who has received the Portuguese with open hands; Vēṇāṭṭaṭikaḷ (i. e. Travancore) and Kōlaṭṭiri (i. e. Chiṙakkal) have also done the same. If we now proceed against Cochin, it will surely be said that we do so, because we are powerless to proceed against Kōlaṭṭiri. The Cochin Raja is punctually paying his tribute. Then, why trouble him now? Even if we succeed in killing the ten Portuguese who are there, shall we be able to kill the Portuguese over the sea? So my opinion is that we should not proceed on this war." To this the others replied, "It is a shame to give up the enterprise and retire without doing anything, after having collected an army of 50,000 men." Their views prevailed, and the Zamorin marched to Eṭapiḷḷi, and the chiefs (Kaimaḷs) of Eṭapiḷḷi, Cheru Vaippu, Kumbaḷam and others flocked to the Zamorin's standard. On March 31st and April 1st (1502), the Zamorin attempted to cross the frontier by forcing the passage of the Chēṫṫuvāye river near the Cṙānganūr island, which was defended by the heir-apparent of Cochin, known as Marumahan Raja, at the head of 5,500 Nairs, who succeeded in repelling the attack. However, in a subsequent engagement, said to have taken place at the Eṭappiḷḷi ford, Marumahan Raja was defeated and slain along with two other Cochin princes. It is said that the Zamorin stopped the supply of provisions to the Cochin forces by bribing the Raja's commissariat officer, and thus withdrew a large section of the Cochin army from the scene of action. The Nayars became importunate. A universal panic prevailed, and many quitted the town. The Zamorin once more promised that he would retire, if only the Cochin Raja would give up the foreigners. But arguments, threats, and entreaties were of no avail against his firm determination to keep to his engagement. The Zamorin's hordes now spread over the state, devastating the country with fire and sword. Taking advantage of the confusion prevailing in the town, of which the Zamorin obtained information from two Italian deserters from the Portuguese, he marched against the town. The Raja defended the place as long as he could, but, being wounded, withdrew with the remnant of his army to the island of Vypīn, whither he took the Portuguese with him. The Cochin territory was overrun, the town reduced to ashes, and it is said that the sacred stone at which the Zamorin was made Lord of the southern Malabar States was removed from Cochin to Eṭappiḷḷi. As the monsoon now commenced, the Zamorin retired to Calicut, leaving a strong force to hold Cochin. On the 20th September 1503, Francisco de Albuquerque arrived with six sails, when the enemy precipitately retreated to Crānganūr. Eṭappiḷḷy was attacked and captured, and subsequently given up to plunder, and hostilities ceased for the time. Of this war, we derive the following further information from Faria-y-Souza.

" While the people of Cochin were beseiged in the island, there sailed from Lisbon nine ships under three distinct commanders (1) Alphonso de Albuquerque (2) Francisco de Albuquerque and (3) Antony de Saldhana. * * * Their chief commander sent the king a present into the island, part whereof was 10,000

Ducats in money. Then on going ashore, the king ran and embraced him, crying Portugal! Portugal! Portugal! and the Portuguese, to return the civility, cried Cochin! Cochin! The Commander comforted the king, giving assured hopes in the assistance of his ships and the others he expected. Not to lose time, he fell upon those who held the island of Cochin for the king of Calicut, and, killing many, expelled the remainder, then passed to Vypīn, restoring that country to its lawful prince. The Lord of Replim (Eṭappiḷḷi) had his lands wasted with fire and sword, and only four Portuguese were lost in this action. The joy Tirunupara conceived in being restored to his allies moved him to grant us leave to build a fort in Cochin. The work was begun, when Alphonso de Albuquerque arrived, and it was called the Fort St. James, and a Church there built dedicated to St. Bartholomew. 500 men were put aboard some vessels taken from the enemy, who burnt Replim after a short defence made by 200 Nayars"

After laying waste the island of Replim, the Portuguese sailed for the island of Kumbaḷam, where they killed over 700 men; thence they advanced into the territories of the Zamorin, where they laid waste the lands, and killed a number of the inhabitants. A force of 6,000 men gathered to attack the Portuguese and drive them out of the country; but these were ultimately repulsed, though not without great difficulty. Albuquerque then patched up certain terms of peace with the Zamorin and sailed for Europe.

No sooner had Albuquerque sailed from India than the Zamorin formed a combination with other kings and lords of Malabar to attack Cochin, and collected a large fleet, well armed with cannon, which were made for the Zamorin by the Italian deserters. A numerous land force was also collected, which was placed under the command of the nephew and heir of the Zamorin, called by the Portuguese Nambia Darim,

1. P. 71.

assisted by Elan Kōil, the lord of Replim (Eṭappilli). The Raja of Cochin was alarmed at this, and sought counsel from the Portuguese Commandant, Durate Pacheco, whom Albuquerque had left behind him. Pacheco gave the Raja every encouragement and advised him to make preparations to withstand the forthcoming attack.

The army collected by the Zamorin is said to have amounted to 50,000 men, in which number were included 4,000 who were to attack Cochin by sea, whilst the rest of the forces were to assault it by land. The command of the defence was given to Pacheco, who had with him for the purpose 100 Portuguese and 300 Malabarese troops. With this handful of men, Pacheco boldly went forth to dispute the passage of the ford against the hordes of the Zamorin, leaving the king with his forces to guard the city of Cochin. The Moors in Cochin attempted to aid the attack by fomenting revolt within the city; but this was frustrated by the vigilance of Pacheco. After placing sentries at all available passes, to prevent any one from leaving the island, and having disposed of his available forces to the best of his ability for the protection of the island, Pacheco determined to assume the offensive and sent small parties across the river, which made marauding expeditions into the frontiers of Eṭappilli and adjoining country, where several villages were burnt and many of the peaceful inhabitants killed. As soon as the Zamorin learned this, he marched forward with his army towards Eṭappilli. On the 16th March 1504, the Zamorin reached Eṭappilli and advanced with his army on Kumbaḷam, near which place there was a practicable ford to the island of Cochin. This ford Pacheco prepared to defend, for which purpose he brought up what vessels he had available. In the largest ship, which was amply provided with cannon, fire-arms and all sorts of warlike stores, he placed five men under the command of Diogo Pereira, with orders to defend the city and fort from all attacks of the enemy. He placed thirty-five men in the fort under the command of Ferdinao Correa; twenty-six men in one of the caravals under Pero Raphael, and, as the other caraval was being repaired, he fitted out two small vessels, one of which he placed in command of Diogo Petrez with twenty-three troops and the other he reserved for himself with twenty-two men. To support this handful of men, the king of Cochin had only remaining with him a force of some 5,000 soldiers, as the remainder of his army had deserted him and gone over to the side of the Zamorin; of these, he gave 500 chosen men to Pacheco under the command of Kaṇṭan Kōru and Perum Kōru, described as Kōviladhikārikaḷ and the Kaimaḷ of Paḷḷuruṭṭi and Aṭavi (Āṭṭuḷḷi?) Paṇikkeṛ.

As the Zamorin's forces had not reached the ford by the time Pacheco had posted his vessels to defend it, he sailed with a body of men to Eṭappiḷḷi and engaged a body of archers, who attempted to prevent them from landing. These, however, after a fight of some hours, were driven back, and Pacheco burnt the town and carried off with him a large herd of oxen for slaughter. The Nayars were very much disgusted at this. Just then, a Brahman messenger arrived from the camp of the Zamorin and intimated that the next day has been decided upon to give battle and that his sovereign would not stop till Pacheco was killed. The Portuguese commander remarked that the Zamorin's astrologers were mistaken in choosing the day for battle, as it happened to be the first Sunday of a great Christian festival.

On the following day, the Zamorin marched out with his whole army. The Kēraḷapaḷama gives the following description of the approach of the Zamorin's army:—First came the five brass cannon constructed for the Zamorin by the Italian deserters. Next came the Raja of Ṭāṇūr known as Veṭṭaṭṭu-Mannan with 4,000 Nayars; then Kakkāṭ Kaṇḍan Nambiṭi at the head of 12,000 Nayars. The Koṭṭiaṭṭ or Porṇaṭṭukara Raja followed them at the head of 18,000 Nayars, and lastly, Curuva Kōil, the Raja governing the country between Cranganūr and Ponnāni, with 4,000 Nayars—in all four Rajas with 37,000 Nayars. These were followed by ten chiefs or barons, the names of eight of whom are given as follows :—

1. Paṭiññāreṭaṭṭu Kōvil—Raja of Cranganūr.
2. Elankōil Nampiāṭiri—Ruler of Eṭappilli.
3. Pāppu Kōvil—Ruler of Chāliaṭ.
4. Vēnganāṭ Nampiāṭiri—Raja of Kollankōḍe.
5. Vaññalachēri Nampiṭi.
6. Parappu Kōvil—Ruler of Beypūr.
7. Pāppu Kōvil of Parappanangāṭi.
8. Kaimal of Mangāṭ Nāḍ—Ruler of Ālengāḍ.

These brought up 20,000 and odd Nayars besides Arabs and Moplas. The whole army was placed under the chief command of Kōlikōṭe Nambiāṭiri. To support the land forces, the Zamorin had also fitted out a fleet of 160 ships including 26 paraos, which, at the suggestion of the two Italian deserters, had been covered with sacks filled with cotton, as a defence against cannon balls. At their instance, also twenty paraos linked together with chains were sent in advance of the fleet. The commanders of these paraos had orders to attack the caraval, and to endeavour to seize her with their grappling hooks as quickly as possible. Pacheco too adopted a somewhat similar plan, and by connecting three of his vessels together by chains and stationing across the stream, he effectually barred the passage of the river.

At the first attack of the enemy, the Cochin Nayars deserted, leaving Pacheco with only his 111 Portuguese to resist the attack. Their leaders, Kanṭankōru and Perunkōru, however, remained with the Portuguese. A fierce engagement ensued, and, after a short resistance by the Portuguese for some hours, a shot from a heavy gun broke the chain that connected the leading paraos, and caused four of them to retreat; the others, however, advanced, but ultimately eight were sunk, and thirteen others were forced to retire, whereupon the attack from that quarter began to flag. At this juncture, however, the prince of Eṭappilli, who had held his forces in reserve, advanced to the attack, and at the same time, the Zamorin attempted to force the passage of the ford with the main body of his army. The engagement was stubborn and long, but in the end, the Zamorin's troops failed in their attempt and retired, having lost no less than 1,030 men, whilst amongst the Portuguese, several had been wounded, but none killed.

"After this victory, the Portuguese at once set to work to repair their ships with all expedition, and they also refitted the other caraval. The Zamorin, acting on the advice of the sooth-sayers, did not at once renew the engagement; but Pacheco, being determined to give him no rest, crossed over to Cambalam, where he ravaged the country, burnt the villages, killed many of the inhabitants, and carried away a considerable amount of booty.

"In the meantime, the Zamorin, having received reinforcements from Calicut of 200 ships of war, eighty smaller vessels, and 15,000 men, sent one of his officers with seventy paraos to attack the ships that had been left to defend the city of Cochin, with the view of drawing away some of the Portuguese from the ford, and so dividing their forces. Immediately on hearing of this, Pacheco sailed to Cochin with one of the caravals and one of the smaller vessels; immediately he came within sight of Cochin, the enemy's vessels sailed away for Replim as quickly as possible, whereupon Pacheco, instead of following them, returned with all haste to his former position.

"On arrival at Cambalam, Pacheco found the Portuguese position in extreme danger. The caraval left there had been vigorously attacked and was riddled with holes, her rigging was demolished, and the protective sacks of cotton had been torn from her sides, whilst the smaller vessels were in an almost equally precarious state."

This was on Sunday the 25th of March, the auspicious day chosen by the Zamorin's astrologers to make a successful attack. The Portuguese, on their part, were also glad of the choice, as that was the day of the feast of Passover. Pacheco found the enemy pressing the attack by both land and water, when he unexpectedly arrived with his two vessels, and attacked them in the rear. The battle raged furiously for sometime; but, at length, the forces of the Zamorin began to give way, and ultimately took to flight after having lost 79 of their paraos and 290 men.

" The Zamorin was greatly enraged at this second defeat, and at once made preparations to renew the attack, which was made on Tuesday the 27th March. Pacheco ordered the men under him to keep themselves as much as possible out of sight, and to observe a strict silence, until he should give orders to the contrary. The enemy, supposing that the Portuguese were now mostly exhausted or wounded, and unable to offer further resistance, advanced again to the attack, shouting, and in great hurry and disorder; whereupon, at a given signal, Pacheco s men rushed on deck and with great noise attacked their assailants briskly with their cannon and other weapons. They speedily sank several of their paraos, scattered others, and committed great execution amongst the enemy, wh speedily broke and retired. The prince of Replim rallied the men and led them again to the attack, but they were afraid to approach the Portuguese closely; whereupon the Zamorin sent Nambia Darim with orders to at once force the passage of the ford and fall upon the Portuguese. He made the attempt, but his men met with such a warm reception that they were speedily

1. Danvers, Vol. I, pp. 107—9.

routed, and put to flight with a loss of sixty paraos and over 600 men.

"Being again frustrated in his attempts against Cochin, the Zamorin now withdrew. Pacheco followed and attacked his fleet for some distance as they retired, and afterwards crossed over and burnt several villages, killing many of their inhabitants."[1]

The feudatories of Cochin who had joined the Zamorin began now to return to their allegiance, seeing that that prince cannot make head against the Portuguese. The chief among them, Mangāt Mūṭṭa Kaimaḷ, who had hitherto tarried in Vypīn, now came forward with supplies for the Cochin forces.

The Zamorin's nephew and heir, called by the Portuguese Nambia Darim, advised his uncle to make peace and retire at least during the monsoon.

The Zamorin would probably have refrained from again renewing the attack but for the advice of the prince of Eṭappiḷḷi, of the Moors who were in council and of the two Italian deserters. These pointed out the loss of reputation he would sustain by acknowledging a defeat, and suggested that another attempt to cross to the island of Cochin should be made by the fords of Palignard and Palurt.[2]

"Being informed of the Zamorin's intention, Pacheco set out for Palignard with 200 of the king of Cochin's soldiers and a few Portuguese. Here he was met by a body of the enemy, which he defeated, taking fifty prisoners, and killing most of the rest. He then sailed for Palurt, about two miles distant, where he learned that the Zamorin intended to endeavour to force the pass at Palignard the following day; Pacheco, thereupon, left some of his officers and the largest ships at Palurt, and returned in haste with his smaller vessels to Palignard, having first taken the precaution to have

1. Danvers, Vol. I, p. 108.

2. Paḷangāḍ and Paḷḷuruṭṭi.

the trees opposite the ford at Palurt cut down, to prevent them from serving as a protection to the enemy.

"Pacheco observed that the fords at Palurt and Palignard could not be passed at the same time; for, whereas at high-water the latter could not be passed on foot, it was not deep enough for the smallest vessels, whilst that at Palurt could only be passed by ships at high-water, so that when the former could be crossed on foot, the latter had not sufficient depth for ships, nor was it sufficiently shallow to be forded.

"This discovery greatly facilitated the defence of those places; a few men were stationed at each, and arrangements made that, at a given signal, those from the one ford should hurry to the assistance of those at the other. Early the following morning, the prince of Cochin went to the assistance of Pacheco with 600 men. The first attack of the enemy was made at Palurt, where, at break of day, they began to attack the Portuguese ships with their cannon. A fleet of about 250 vessels was also seen approaching, but, before these could arrive, Pacheco crossed over with a small party, attacked the enemy's position, and succeeded in driving them off, when, having spiked their guns, he again retired to his ships.

"The enemy's vessels soon after arrived and began to attack the Portuguese ships, but, after a long artillery duel, their paraos were driven off and many of them sunk. The prince of Replim then made two unsuccessful attempts to cross the ford, being on each occasion forced to retire with the loss of many men.

"Being repulsed at Palurt, the Zamorin and Nambia Darim went with a large force to Palignard. The attempt to cross this ford was led by Nambia Darim, but he was twice forced to retreat with considerable loss, and, soon after his second failure, a plague broke out in the enemy's camp, which put a stop for a time to further hostile operations on the part of the Zamorin."[1]

The rainy season had now advanced, and the terrible havoc made by the plague in the Zamorin's camp induced him to retire for a while to Calicut. Believing that his defeat was due to his not properly propitiating his gods, the Zamorin withdrew to a temple to do penance for some time, forsaking his regal position during that period of his religious austerities. But the prince's mother, a lady of great courage, rallied him with ridicule, saying that the determination to do penance was the result more of cowardice than a sense of piety and induced him to leave the temple.

But, in the meantime, Pacheco took advantage of this respite to repair his vessels, to furnish himself with fresh supplies of arms and amunition, and to make all necessary preparations. Amongst other means of defence, he had a number of stakes cut, the ends of which were sharpened and hardened in the fire. These were driven deep into the mud at low water, so that they could not easily be drawn out, with the view of rendering the ford impassable on foot.

In due course, the Zamorin again advanced his army to the attack. His artillery consisted of thirty brass cannon, which was sent in advance of the main body of the army, guarded by 4,000 picked men. The first line of the main army consisted of 12,000 men, under the command of Nambia Darim; next came the prince of Replim with a similar number, and the Zamorin brought up the rear with 15,000 troops. To oppose this overwhelming force, Pacheco had only two vessels with forty Portuguese, and the 200 men sent by the king of Cochin, who were stationed in a place of great natural strength on shore, defended by a rampart. These latter, however, deserted, as soon as the attack was first commenced.

1. Danvers, Vol. I, pp. 109—10.

"The enemy, having placed their cannon opposite to the Portuguese ships, endeavoured to oblige them to leave their station at the ford. Pacheco made, at first, no reply to their attack; but, after a while, he drew his vessels nearer to the shore and commenced a vigorous attack upon the enemy with all his guns, which were directed with so much judgment that he soon obliged them to seek shelter in some neighbouring woods. Nambia Darim now advanced with his troops, and made an attempt to force the passage of the ford, but was held in check by the fire of the Portuguese guns. The Zamorin came up to his support with the rest of his army, and a most persistent effort was made to cross, the Zamorin personally encouraging his men, until a shot from one of the Portuguese vessels killed two officers by his side. He then retired a little, but the men were urged forward by their officers with the points of their swords. Upon entering the ford, however, they came upon the pointed stakes, which wounded them in their feet and caused many to fall down.

"When the advanced party of the enemy were thus thrown into confusion, the men in front being unable to advance on account of the stakes, or to retire by reason of those in the rear pressing upon them, the Portuguese poured in ceaseless broadsides from their vessels, and so held them in check, until the tide began again to flow, and the ford became impassable by reason of the depth of water. The Zamorin again had a narrow escape for his life, and at last withdrew his forces. This engagement lasted from break of day until nine o'clock, and it is alleged that the Zamorin lost here more men and ships than in any previous encounter with the Portuguese; whilst of the latter, although many were wounded, not one of them was killed.

"As soon as the enemy had retired, the king of Cochin came to congratulate Pacheco upon his success. The latter at once gave orders for suitable refreshments to be provided for his men after their recent exertions, and then looked to the repair and re-equipment of his vessels, so as to be prepared in case of a future emergency.

"The Zamorin was exceedingly indignant at the failure of his numerous forces to defeat the few Portuguese that were opposed to them. The prince of Replim, however, in order to appease him, endeavoured to accomplish by treachery what had in vain been attempted by force, and, to this end, he bribed certain men in Cochin to poison the water and food supplied to the Portuguese. Pacheco, having been informed of this, ordered fresh wells to be dug every day, and also that none of his soldiers were to buy any food without first making the vendor eat some of it.

"Failing in these attempts, the prince of Replim next determined to convey a detachment of men by water at night to Cochin, to set fire to the city, and then to fall upon the inhabitants. This project was, however, also frustrated by the vigilance of Pacheco, who, not content with maintaining his own position, made frequent inroads into the enemy's country, where he did a considerable amount of damage.

"In retaliation for these constant attacks, the Zamorin equipped a fleet to ravage the coast of Cochin; but, in several engagements with the Portuguese vessels, these suffered many defeats, whilst some of the enemy's paraos were captured. At length, the Zamorin determined to make another attack upon the Portuguese, to which end he brought an army of 30,000 men, in addition to a large number commanded by the prince of Replim, and a fleet consisting of 100 large ships, 110 paraos and eighty pinnaces, in addition to eight turrets constructed upon paraos, and a large float of timber, pitched and bound with tow, which it was intended to set on fire and send down upon the Portuguese vessels.

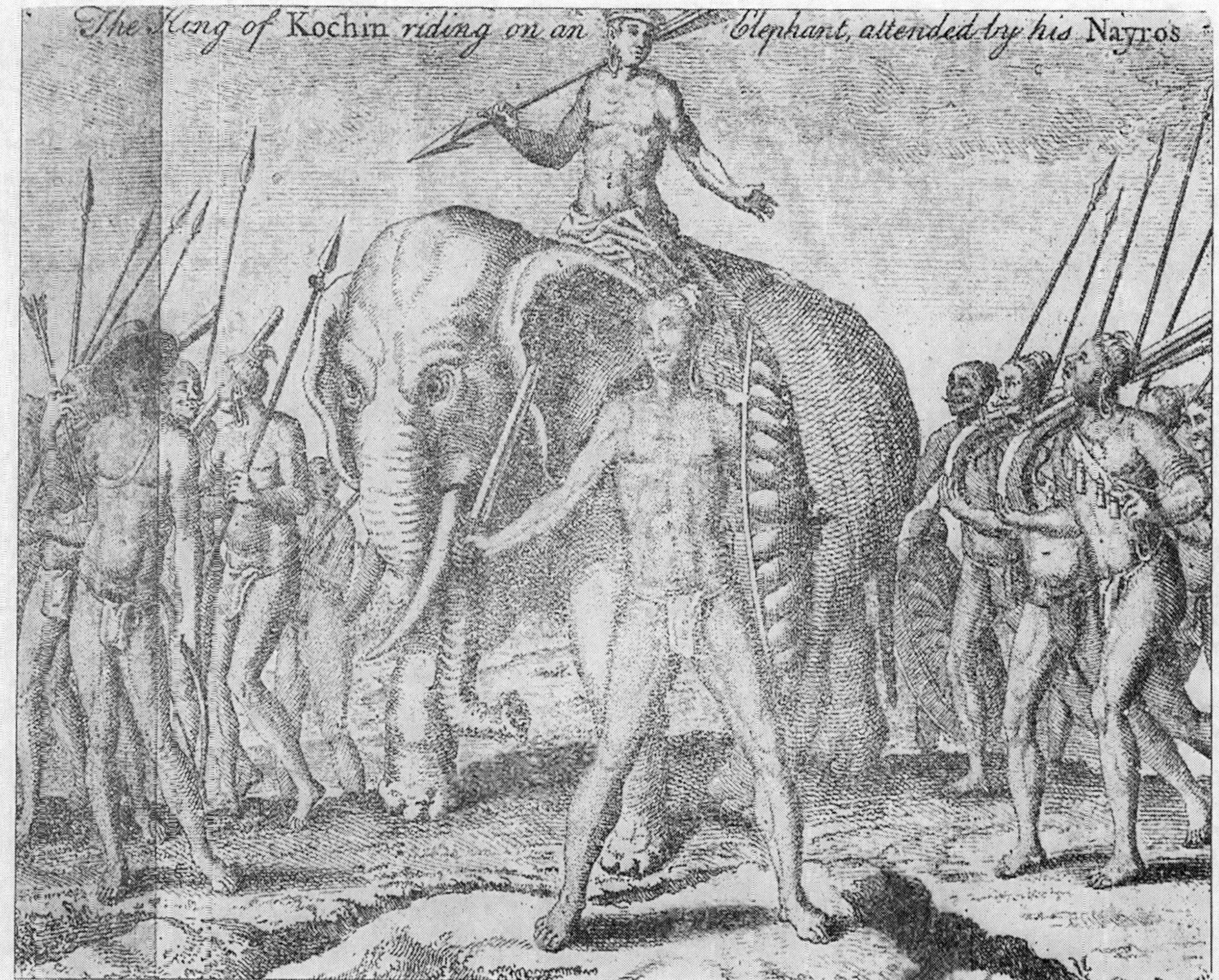

THE KING OF COCHIN WITH A FEW OF HIS NAYAR MILITARY ATTENDANTS.

To face page 499

"Pacheco, having been informed of these preparations by the enemy, protected his vessels by means of a number of masts, eighty feet in length, with which he made large floats, and anchord them at a distance from his ships' prows so as to prevent the too near aproach of the enemy's castles. As the land forces of the enemy approached, Pacheco set out for the island of Arraul, where he attacked and killed some of their advance parties, and then retired to his ships.

"At day-break, the enemy's fleet appeared in sight; the timber float was set on fire and sent down the river towards the Portuguese vessels, but the masts anchored in the stream effectually kept it off from doing any damage. The engagement then became general, and the Portuguese were on the point of being overpowered by the enemy, when a shot from one of their big guns brought down the enemy's largest turret; soon afterwards, a second turret was similarly destroyed, and many of the enemy's paraos were sunk.

"An attempt was, at the same time, made by the land forces of the Zamorin to cross the ford, which was opposed by Christopher Jusart and Simão Andrade in two small ships, aided by some paraos, and a native force of 1,000 men, commanded by the prince of Cochin. The engagement was most fierce, and lasted from break of day till the evening, during the whole of which time the Zamorin's large army was not only effectually kept in check, but large numbers of them were killed, and many of their ships destroyed.

"In the evening, the tide setting in very strong, brought that day's engagement to a close.

"The Zamorin, now despairing of success, would have retired his forces altogether, but was persuaded by some of his people to make one more effort to attain his object. He accordingly again attacked the Portuguese; but his army and navy, being now disheartened by repeated defeats, made but a feeble attempt, and were easily routed. The Zamorin, thereupon, withdrew, and returned to Calicut, thus bringing to an end this war; which had lasted for five months, during which it is alleged that the army of Calicut lost about 19,000 men, together with a considerable number of his ships. A peace was subsequently concluded between the king of Cochin and the Zamorin."[1]

On Pacheco's departure to Europe, the Cochin Raja, who styles himself as 'Kēraḷa Uṇṇi Rāma Kōil Ṭirumulpād', presented him with a shield, on which was emblazoned in gold five crowns to represent those of the five Rajas whom Pacheco had slain in the war, together with the names of the seven battles in which he had defeated the Zamorin, the whole being illuminated with the armorial bearings of the Raja. The shield was accompanied by a testimonial to the effect that it was presented as a token of gratitude, to be preserved by Pacheco and his heirs, for the protection afforded to the Raja on the occasion of the invasion of his State by the Zamorin at the instance of the chiefs of Vypīn, Cheṟuvypīn, and Aṭavil in the month of Mīnam 671 M. E., 1504 A. D.[2]

Second War. 1521. During the Viceroyalty of Sequiera, another war broke out, the cause of which cannot now be ascertained. According to Day, the Zamorin attacked the Cochin Raja in the absence of the Portuguese Viceroy, believing that he had then better chances of success, but was easily routed. But the Kēraḷapaḻama[3] tells us that the Cochin Raja wanted to take revenge against the Zamorin for the death of the Cochin princes at the ford, and determined that a similar number of the Zamorin's family should be slain so that they may be quit. As the Zamorin had destroyed the town of Cochin, Calicut should also be destroyed. The Raja

1. Danvers—*The Portuguese in Asia*, Vol. I, pp. 93—114; Faria-y-Sousa, Vol. I, pp. 73—79; *Keralapazhama*, pp. 36—60.

2. Keralapazhama, p. 66.

3. P. 164.

vowed that he would bathe in the tank of the Zamorin at Calicut. With this end in view, the Cochin Raja made an unprovoked attack on the Zamorin at the head of 50,000 Nayars. To oppose this invasion, the Zamorin brought an army of 200,000 Nayars into the field, and drove the Cochin Raja back. Cochin now asked the aid of the Portuguese, who, being then at peace with the Zamorin, only lent the Raja the services of 36 gunners, with whose assistance some success was secured; but the Brahmins soon prevailed upon the Raja, by cursing the land which gave protection to the Portuguese, to dismiss them, with the result that the Zamorin drove back the Raja's army with little or no difficulty.[1]

Third War. 1536. The Zamorin intimated to the Raja of Crānganūr, who was subordinate to him, his intention of attending the annual assembly held there in honour of Chēramān Perumāl. The Raja, who was always ready to seek any means of rendering himself independent, took counsel of the Cochin Raja, who sustained him in his idea, but refused to give any active support, suspecting that it might lead finally to the Portuguese erecting a factory at Crānganūr, and thereby diminishing appreciably the profits from Cochin trade. Thus deserted, the Crānganūr chief had to yield to his suzerain, who presided over the assembly. Having succeeded in this, he determined to do yet another thing, which brought him in conflict with Cochin itself. He determined to perform those ceremonies at the sacred stone, which his predecessor had removed in 1503 to Eṭappilli, and this, he thought, would enable him to claim lordship over the southern Malabar States. As the Raja of Cochin was particularly desirous that this should be prevented, the Portuguese, though their hands were full elsewhere, sent a force to his assistance. The stone was brought back from Eṭappilli to its former resting place in Cochin; but, unfortunately for the future peace of the country, the

1. Day, p. 102; Danvers, Vol. I, p. 351.

stopping by the Portuguese of the usual payments to certain Malabar chiefs not only alienated them from the Portuguese but also from the Cochin Raja, and was the cause of much trouble from that quarter.[1]

The exploit, by means of which the "sacred stone" was brought back, is thus described by Faria-y-Sousa:—

"September 1536. Martin Alfonso de Sousa now sent his force against the king of Replim, who had offended him of Cochin. Antony de Brito who had led the van met a vigorous opposition at this island, till Martin coming up they fled, who maintained the outworks. The king retired to this city, in which were 6,000 men. Next day Sousa attacked it; after some resistance, the king and all the defendants fled. As Sousa entered a mosque, he had like to be killed by a Moor, but receiving the stroke on his buckler, he ran through the Moor with a javeline. This victory cost us 14 men; the city was plundered and reduced to ashes. The principal part of the booty that fell to the king of Cochin, on whose account this action was undertaken, was a piece of marble, by him highly valued, because on it were carved the names of the kings of Malabar for 3000 years past, which was taken from him by the king of Replim; some brass plates with serpents engraved on them, esteemed a great relic by the conquered king; and his hat (some crown perhaps) lost in the flight, which among them is the greatest disgrace to the conquered and highest glory to the victor."

Fourth War. In 1550, the Zamorin and the Raja of Pimienta (by which the Portuguese meant the Vaṭakkenkūr Raja) entered into a league against the king of Cochin, a league which threatened the latter State with dangerous consequences. In pursuance of this league, "the king of Pimienta, with a force of 10,000 Nayars took the field at Bardela (an island and

1. Whiteway, pp. 250—1.

capital of the kingdom of Pimienta), the king of Cochin doing the same with his men, assisted by a force of 600 Portuguese. The two contending armies, coming to close quarters, fought desperately, and after several courageous charges, the king of Pimienta was carried off the field mortally wounded, and died before the battle was decided. On his death becoming known, his troops fled in great disorder, and were pursued into the city with great slaughter. The palace was burned, and this being considered the worst offence that could be offered, the enemy rallied their forces once more, and fell on their adversaries with such fury and determination that they forced them to retire in great disorder, with a loss of over fifty killed to the Portuguese.

" Five thousand Nayars, all sworn to avenge the death of their king, now entered the territory of Cochin, killing a large number and compelling others to seek refuge in the fortress, then commanded by Anrique de Sousa, who marched out and defeated the Nayars with a heavy loss. The joy at this success was soon dispelled by the arrival of the Zamorin and the princes of Malabar, with a force of 140,000 men. The Zamorin, with 100,000 men, encamped at Chembe, ordering the other princes (eighteen in number, including the king of Ṭāṉūr, lately a friend of the Portuguese, but now an enemy), with the remaining 40,000 men, to occupy the island of Bardela. The Governor, Jorge Cabral, on being informed of this state of affairs, made all necessary preparations for the impending storm by sending Manoel de Sousa e Sepulveda with four ships to Cochin, and having joined the vessels there, to blockade the island, until he should arrive. Sepulveda having sailed, the Governor soon followed with a fleet of 100 ships, and nearly 4,000 fighting men besides seamen. The first place they called at was Tiracole[1], a seaport between Calicut and Cannanore,

1. Ṭṛkkoṭi.

which was reduced to ashes. Coulete (in the kingdom of Calicut) and Ponnāni suffered the same fate, after a vigorous resistance.

"The Governor, who landed at Cochin with a force of 6,000 men(he having been joined by 2,000 men whilst there), found the king of Cochin had collected an army of 40,000 men. These forces having joined, a signal for an attack on the enemy was made, when those on the island showed a flag of truce. The Governor came to the conclusion that those eighteen princes were prepared to surrender upon their lives being spared. Finding, however, that they delayed in giving themselves up, he determined to attack them the next day. The next day came, and with it a flood which prevented him from executing his plans. As the enemy found themselves completely surrounded by such a large force, the king of Ṭaṇūr sent a message to the Governor to the effect that he wished to be on peaceful terms with the Portuguese. Many days were wasted in negotiations, and, as the king's object evidently was to gain time by delay, the Governor determined to attack the island the following day, namely, 29th November 1550; but just as all was in readiness, a vessel arrived with orders from the new Viceroy, Dom Affonoso de Noronha, to stay all proceedings. The result of this was that those eighteen princes and their whole army were suffered to escape."[1]

Fifth War. In the year 1565, the Zamorin and his Moorish allies, assisted by one of the petty Rajas, again invaded the Cochin State with success. The Cochin Raja and two princes were slain in battle on the 27th of January 1565, whilst his successor met with the same fate fourteen days later on the battle field at Puṭiakāvu on the 10th February.[2]

Sixth War. The Portuguese had espoused the cause of the Betetunad (Veṭṭaṭṭunāḍ) or Ṭaṇūr adoptees

1. Danvers, Vol. I, pp. 489-90.
2. Day, p. 352.

into the Cochin family, and had driven out of the country the Chāliyūr princes, who were the legitimate claimants to the Cochin Musnad. The exiled princes sought the aid of the Dutch, who captured Cochin from the Portuguese and restored their proteges to their inheritance. These had called in the aid of the Zamorin also, who now refused to go back to his own country. The Zamorin was, therefore, driven from Vypīn to Kōṭaparampa, and forced to cross the canal that formed the then boundary between the two kingdoms. The island of Chēṟṟuvāye remained in the Zamorin's possession, while the districts lying to the east of the river were returned to Cochin.

Seventh War. The Dutch had, in pursuance of their policy of curtailing military expenses, placed the Chēṟṟuvāye island in the hands of the Zamorin in the year 1691. That chief was not slow to perceive the advantageous position he had secured in the flank of his hereditary enemy of Cochin, and he lost no time in fortifying Kōṭaparampa, where he formed a strong encampment in 1701 to the menace of the Raja of Cochin. War at once broke out, and the Dutch were drawn into it in a desultory fashion. It lasted from 1701 to 1710. The Dutch and the Raja dislodged the Zamorin from Kōṭaparampa, and occupied the island of Chēṟṟuvāye. In 1714, the Dutch commenced the erection of a fort at the northernmost point of the island, where the back-water has its outlet into the sea. The Zamorin at once attacked the half-finished fort, took it and drove the Dutch back to Cochin. He then advanced southwards, and fortified Pāppanimaṟṟam, Kaṭṭūr, Māpraṇam, Ūrakam, Iruṭṭaññi, Kūṭṭumkal and other places. In the year 1716, Councillor William Bakker Jacobtz took the field at the head of a strong army, recovered Chēṟṟuvāye and captured Pāppanimaṟṟam and other forts, and brought the war to a close. We have a description of this conflict given us by our author in his fourth letter. The war was terminated in the year 1716—17 by a treaty concluded between the Zamorin on the one part and the Dutch and the Raja of Cochin on the other part, whereby it was agreed that the two Rajas would henceforward live in peace for ever. Six copies of the treaty were made, three in the Dutch language and three in the Malayalam language, and the three parties retained a Dutch and a Malayalam copy each.

Eighth War. In the year 1742, the Zamorin appears, in spite of the stipulation in the treaty of 1717, to have made an unprovoked attack on the Raja of Cochin. The English, who were fast gaining supremacy on the coast, intervened and compelled the Zamorin to retreat.

Ninth War. We now come to the ninth and last war. Dissensions in the royal family of Cochin had distracted the country for some time. Some Ṭampāns of the Chāliyūr branch openly rebelled and claimed the dignity of Perimpaṭappu Mūppu Sṭhānam. Their cause was warmly taken up by a few chiefs, and these appealed to Mārṭṭāṇḍa Varma, king of Travancore, who was eagerly on the look-out to find some pretext to make aggressions on his northern boundary. The Ṭampāns were formally taken under the protection of Travancore, and the king marched at the head of an army to the north. Town after town and district after district fell before him, and his redoubtable minister, Rāma Iyen Ḍalawa (chief minister). Ampalappulay, Ṭekkankūr, Vaṭakkankūr, and a number of other petty States were annexed. Karappuram, Kurunād, Kunnaṭṭunāḍ, Vaḍavucōde, Kurumala and a host of other places were occupied. While matters stood thus in the south, the Zamorin reckoned this a favourable opportunity to overthrow Cochin and then make an attempt on Travancore. Some of the chiefs subordinate to Cochin, such as the heir-apparent of Paravūr, the Muṭṭērippāḍ of Ālengāḍ, the Kaimal of Kōṭassēri, Murianāḍ Nampiār, and others threw up their fealty to their sovereign and swore allegiance to the Zamorin. The Zamorin approached by way of Chowghat, and the Nampūṭiri Brahmans of the Trichur grāmam invited him to Trichur.[1] With their assistance, Trichur was occupied in 1757, and the Zamorin held his court there. Proceeding southwards, Chennamangalam was captured, and Pāliyam, the seat of the Cochin Raja's hereditary Prime Minister and Commander-in-chief, rased to the ground. The Dutch, by way of a counter-move, proposed to attack Chettuvāye The Raja approved of this, and the combined forces of the East India Company and the Raja marched to Crānganūr. A severe battle was fought at Veluṭṭavāṭa, in which the allies were worsted, and the Dutch retired to Cochin. They, however, soon returned better-equipped, and an encampment was formed at Ṭiruvanchikkulam. While matters were in this position, the ministers of the Zamorin opened negotiations with the Dutch, and agreed to give up the island of Chettuvāye to the Dutch, to dismantle the fortifications at Veluṭṭavāṭa and Pāppanimattam, and to pay the expenses of the war. The Dutch accepted the terms without consulting the Raja, and retired to Cochin. Thus left in the lurch, the Raja felt that, standing by himself, he could not make head against the Zamorin. The Zamorin thought this the best opportunity to broach his idea of conquering Travancore and proposed an alliance with Cochin for this purpose. The Cochin Raja thought that he would come to terms with Travancore rather than join his ancient enemy in an enterprise which he felt would land

1. The Tirunavaya yogam was on the side of the Zamorin. But I doubt whether the Trichur yogam, as a body, sided with him. He tried to win it over to his side; but this is the reply he got:

[illegible];
[illegible]
[illegible]
[illegible];

and the poet was rewarded by the Cochin Raja with the grant of an extensive estate.

him in greater difficulties. He, therefore, proposed to negotiate with king Mārttāṇḍa Varma. Meanwhile, the heir-apparent of Cochin marched with a considerable army to Kumarapuram, and, with the assistance of Kakkāṭ Kāraṇavappāṭ, recovered the fortified positions at Iraṭṭachira and Vadakkēkara at Trichur. The Zamorin, however, lost no time in attacking the heir-apparent within the Sankēṭam of Trichur, and the Cochin forces retreated to Kumarapuram. The Zamorin, who held his court at Trichur, died there in 1760. Not long after, the Cochin Raja also died. His successor made up his mind to come to terms with Travancore, and seek the assistance of that State in expelling the Zamorin. With this view, he proceeded to Trivandrum, and concluded a treaty with the king of Travancore, whereby it was agreed that Travancore would drive the Zamorin out of Cochin territory, and restore the Raja to his ancient possessions, in consideration of which Cochin agreed to cede certain districts and pay the expenses of the war. The Travancore minister, Ayyappan Mārṭṭāṇḍa Pillay, and General D'Lenoy were despatched with an army to effect this purpose. By this time, the Zamorin had occupied the southern portions of the Trichur Taluk, besides Ālangād, Parūr, Māprāṇam and other places. The Travancoreans succeeded in dislodging the Zamorin from all these places. The Zamorin retreated towards the north and quitted the Cochin State. Messengers were then despatched to Paḍmanābhapuram, where the king of Travancore was then residing, and a treaty concluded between Travancore and Calicut, in which the Zamorin bound himself not to molest Cochin any more. Thus was the Zamorin finally expelled from Cochin, which he had terrorised over for the last 250 years and more.

16. **Death of Three Cochin Princes.** Perhaps the reference here is to the death of three Cochin

princes at the Crānganūr or Chēṫṫuvāye ford. The chronicles of Cochin mention a similar event as having oocurred at Paḷḷuruṭṭi, a couple of miles to the south of Maṭṭāncheri, in one of the wars with the Zamorin. The date of the occurrence is expressed in the cryptogram, Kşhaṭṙaṭṙayēhaṭāḍya, equivalent to 681 M. E., 1506 A. D. It is said that the three princes having been slain, the Zamorin walked hand in hand with the Beṭṭaṭ chief to view the dead bodies, and, on seeing them lying face downwards, and hands grasping the ground, turned one of the bodies with his foot, remarking with a sneer that the Kşheṭṙiya (meaning the Cochin prince,) still hankered after the soil though dead. This cowardly act of the Zamorin was at once resented by his chivalrous companion who, drawing his sword, cut off the leg that had turned the corpse. This, of course, led to a general scuffle, in which the Zamorin was worsted. It is said that there has been an irreconcilable feud between the royal houses of Cochin and Calicut ever after.[1]

17. **Custom of Retaliation.** We have already alluded to the custom of Kuṭippaka or family-feud, which demanded life for life. Reference may here be made to another prevalent custom noticed by early travellers as existing in Malabar.

Sheik Zeen-ud-deen observes that, if a chieftain was slain, his followers attacked and obstinately persevered in ravaging the slayer's country and killing his people, till their vengeance was satisfied. This custom was doubtless that which was described so long ago as in the ninth century A. D. by two Mahomedans, whose work was translated by Renaudot. " There are kings who, upon their accession, observe the following ceremony. A quantity of cooked rice

1. H. H. Vidvan Manavikraman Ettan Thamburan, the late Zamorin, was the first to visit Cochin after those troubulous times. He was given a right royal reception by H. H. the Ex-Raja of Cochin, who was then ruling the country.

was spread before the king, and some three or four hundred persons came of their own accord and received each a small quantity of rice from the king's own hands, after he himself had eaten some. By eating of this rice, they all engage to burn themselves on the day the king dies or is slain, and they punctually fulfil their promise." Men who devoted themselves to certain death on great occasions were termed "Amucos" by the Portuguese. Barbosa alludes to the practice as a custom prevalent among the Nayars. Purchas says, "They (the Nayars) are prodigal of their lives in the honour of their king. Osorius telleth of some, which like the renowned Deii, had vowed themselves to death, and not to return from the enemy without victory." Again, "The king of Cochin hath a great number of gentlemen which he calleth Amocchi and some are called Nairii. These two sorts of men esteem not their lives anything, so that it may be for the honour of the king."[1] The manner in which these served the king is well illustrated by what took place some time after the death of Marumahan Raja, the heir-apparent of Cochin, and two other princes at the Crānganūr ford. Only 200 of the immediate followers of the heir-apparent escaped from the disastrous battle in which he was killed. As they had survived their master, they shaved off all their hair, even of their eyebrows and devoted themselves to death. They made their way to Calicut territory, where they slaughtered all they met; 20 survived to reach the neighbourhood of the town killing as the chance offered. In turn, they were killed off one by one, until, in five years, the last was destroyed.[2] The proper Malayalam term for such men is Chāvēr,[3] i. e., those who took up or devoted themselves to death. Castenheda uses the proper term Chāvēr to denote them.

1. Purchas, II. 1708.
2. Whiteway.
3. Chāvēr. In Malayalam, Chāvuka=to die. Those who vowed to defend the person of the Raja and to die for him were given lands freed of all taxes. Those estates were termed

18. **Dignities.** In the Cochin royal family, there are at present three Sṭhānams or dignities viz., those of (1) the Mahā Raja i. e., the ruler (2) the Eḷaya Raja or the heir-apparent, and (3) Veroli (Vīra Eḷaya) Raja or the First Prince.. Thus it will be seen that they are reckoned in a different order from that mentioned by our author. Veeroli or Vīraḷam stands for Vīrakērala.

Kaimal means Lord or Chief.

Ragiadorr, Kāriakkār, Governor, or one who manages or governs. It appears to be a Portuguese word.

19. **Olas.** Ōlās or palmyra leaves are the materials on which the letters are written or rather inscribed with an iron style ; the letters themselves are sometimes called Ōlās.

20. **Keeping the full Number.** This seems to be a misconception. There is no law or custom by which there should always be a specified number of princes in the royal family, so that, on the demise of the reigning prince, the last place has to be filled up by incorporating into the family a new prince chosen from "the legitimate royal family," whatever is meant by this. But if there is any fear of the family becoming extinct, there is the custom of adopting both male and female members from collateral branches of the royal house.

21. **Exclusion from Administration.** It is the general practice of the Cochin and Travancore

chāvīṭṭu-viruṭṭi lands. Such holdings were recognised even at the recent Settlement in Cochin. De Gubernatis (154) has the following: "Their forces (at Cochin) consist in a kind of (Nayar) soldiers whom they call *amocchi*, who are to die at the king's pleasure, or when they lose him in war." He suggested that the word *amocchi* was derived from the Sanskrit, *amokshya*,' that cannot be losed' as the idea of being 'bound by a vow' underlay the conduct of the persons to whom the word was applied.

States not to associate the younger members of the family, not even the heir-apparent, in the government of the country. The wisdom of the practice is not apparent. Perhaps it is thought that their association in public affairs would bring about complications. Our author bases the practice on State reasons, but what these are is not clear ; more or less it is the result of a want of confidence, amity and good feeling between the various members of the family, which has been for long the bane of royal houses, it may be said, all over the world, the more especially in countries where the ruler is a despot, who holds his arbitrary sway unaided by any council and not tempered by the force of public opinion. Instances have not been wanting, though happily not in the States of Travancore and Cochin, of the next in succession being on the look-out to assassinate the reigning chief. Even in these States, the heir-apparent is, more generally than not, taken to be in opposition to the Raja, and instances have not been wanting, when their quarrels and misunderstandings have ended in open rupture. The consequence of this studied exclusion of the junior members from public affairs is that there is always a want of continuity of policy in the administration, the subject population having to submit themselves to the whims and caprices of successive rulers. Public opinion does not exist, and the people, as a body, is a negligible element. Things have, of course, changed with the march of time, but not to such an extent as could be desired. The benevolent despotism of the British Indian Government serves as a model to the Native States.

22. **Paliyath Atchen**. Even now, the Pāliyaṭṭ Atchen is the premier nobleman of the Cochin State. Till recently, he was the hereditary Prime Minister and Commander-in-Chief of the kingdom. He was the ruling chief of his own territories and possessed an excellent army. He held political relations directly with

the foreign nations who held power on the coast. He was entitled to and was levying transit duties. As sovereign of the territories over which he held sway, the properties of extinct families within his jurisdiction escheated to him. Our author says that the dignity of General-in-Chief of the kingdom had hitherto belonged to another family. This dignity was at first hereditary in the family of Nāykar Vīṭṭil Atchen, another chief of some fame. When and how the Nāykar Vīṭṭil family became dispossessed of the dignity does not appear. After them, it devolved on the Pāliyam family. The Kēralōṭpaṭṭi, however, says that Chēramān Perumāḷ, in constituting the Perimpaṭappu or Cochin dynasty, gave the Cochin Raja 42 (or 72) ministers, of whom Pāliyaṭṭ Atchen was the chief. Of these dignities of hereditary Prime Minister and Commander-in-Chief of the Cochin kingdom, the Pāliyam family was deprived by the British Government for rebellion in 1809. We have little or no record of the Pāliyam's doings during the Portuguese period. The Pāliyam, however, seems to have taken a prominent part in the sieges of Crānganūr and Cochin by the Dutch. Bishop Sebastioni more than hints that the Pāliyam had always proved faithless to the Portuguese and attributes the fall of Crānganūr to the betrayal of a weak quarter, where the Pāliyam and its followers had stood guard. The chief is said to have played a double game. While pretending to be friendly to the Portuguese, he was secretly treating with the Dutch.

So early as the 12th of March 1661, i. e., two years previous to the capture of Cochin, the Pāliyaṭṭ Atchen met Van Goens, the Dutch Admiral, and entered into an agreement with him, by which he placed himself under the protection of the Dutch East India Company, who were to restore him by force to the territories of which he had been deprived by the Portuguese and his other enemies, whilst, on his part, he undertook to obey the Dutch in all things. This agreement was entered into on board the ship *De Muscaatboom*. The following is the full text of the engagement:

" I, Paljetter Come Menone, chief of the island of Baypin, being in difficulties on account of the Portuguese and other enemies named, about having done great harm to my land and my subjects and having acted as my enemies and caused trouble to me, for which reasons, finding myself powerless to resist the said enemies, am compelled to look out for a powerful nation which will maintain and protect my land and subjects. With this object in view, I pray for and accept the protection of the Honourable United Netherlands East Indian Company in order that they protect me including the king of Zamorin, against all mischievous people and enemies of my state. And at the same time, I yield and surrender to the same Honourable Company my person, territory and subjects.

" The council of this defensive fleet, in view of the active desire and earnest perseverance of the Paljetter, Come Menone, chief of the island of Baypin and Chenotty, has agreed to place him under the protection of the United Netherlands East Indian Company with the approbation of His Excellency the Governor-General and Council of India, in so far only as the Honourable Company has power and opportunity with God's help to assist him, provided he assures us on his part, that neither he nor his legal successors shall ever make a contract or alliance with the Portuguese, either directly or indirectly, under such pain as is prescribed by law, and more especially of losing his territory, person, subjects and properties, belike as he has made surrender of these to us in a separate letter. On board ship, the *Muscaatboom*, 12th March 1661 (at the bottom of the page). With approbation of the Honourable members of the Council of India, (signed) Ryklof Van Goens (on the margin). The Honourable Company's seal and underneath this: By order of His Honour, signed (Mr. Huysman, sworn clerk)".

Cochin was captured by the Dutch in 1663, and the Muṭṭa Tāvaḷi, Prince Vīra Kērala Varma, was installed as Raja of Cochin. Three years after, on the 5th of April 1666, we see the Dutch Admiral entering into an engagement with Pāliyaṭṭ Atchen guaranteeing Dutch protection against aggressions by the Malabar powers. It says, "If any of the Rajas of Malabar were to do the slightest injustice to the Pāliyaṭṭ Atchen, his manager or any of his subordinates, such as do anything against the rules or do anything against the privileges granted by the ancient Rajas, the Commodor of the Company at Cochin shall order them to observe the rules and privileges. If, in spite of that, they were to do any further injustice, the Company itself will interfere in the matter to help the Atchen and redress his grievances."

The following letters will show in what estimation the Dutch held the Pāliyaṭṭ Atchen, and how ready they were to render all assistance to him, whenever wanted. They also throw considerable light on his power and status on the Coast at the time:

" To

" The Noble Lord,

" The Palyath in the kingdom of Cochin.

"We received two letters of your noble person of which we have seen the complaints regarding the injury and diminution, which your Excellency suffered in your honour and reputation. We ordered Mr. Flors Blom to repair there as our Commissary, and recommended him to do everything possible to please your noble personage, and have written to our new Commander Adrian Van Ommen to give your Excellency all possible pleasure. We further pray the Almighty to spare your Excellency for many years with health and prosperity, and with our cordial salutation,

"We are as the good friend of your nobility,

"(Signed) Neder Govoica,

"The Governor-General of India.

"Wiltun Van Outhorn.

"In the Fort of Batavia, 20th August, 1690.

"Agreed with original.

"(Signed) Paulus De Roo,

"Secretary."

"The Pāliyaṭṭ Atchens, being Chief Commander of and First Noble under, the Kingdom of Cochin and as such rendering faithful and ready service to its King did * * * testimony of his Praiseworthy Sacrifice through the Admiral Ryclof and considering we had not at that time become settled on the coast, did yet readily take from us an assurance. So wishing to renew our testimony in favour of the said Pāliyaṭṭ Atchens, the Commander and Council for the time being are recommended to favour the said Pāliyaṭṭ Family, should such be required, and to help them and defend them from their enemies because the Honourable Company are indebted to them and are therefore bound to defend them.

"On the Ship *Dregterland* lying at anchor in the Roads at Cochin:—

"23rd November 1691.

"(Signed) A. V. Reede.

"(L. S)

"By order of His Excellency.

"(Signed)

"Sea—Secretary."

A few years later, we come upon a further communication, which shows that the Dutch Government sought the aid of the Pāliyaṭṭ Atchen in dealing with certain country powers, and that the East India Company cherished the friendship of the Pāliyaṭṭ house.

" To

" His Excellency Paliyat, The first Minister and Administrator

" To the kingdom of Perumpadappil, (Cochin).

" The proposition made by your Excellency in your two letters of the 17th March of this year addressed to the Governor-General Joas Van Hoorn, and to the Extraordinary Councillor Henries Swar de Kroon, were read and contents noted. The Commander and the Councillors of Cochin obtain therefrom order anent the kings of Calicut, Ferok and Cochin. Your Excellency would be pleased to lend your aid to promote with efficacy and faithfulness agreeably to his request. The execution of the same would enable us to become friends with the house of Paliyat. May God grant you His Grace for the same. In the Fort of Batavia the 25th day of September 1708. By order of their nobilities, the Lord Governor-General and the Councillors of India.

" (Signed) Isaak Garsim,

" Secretary. "

Evidently, the house of Pāliyam was rapidly rising in power and importance. For the Dutch to have sought its aid in dealing with the Zamorin and the king of Ferok, Pāliyam should have attained at the time a commanding position on the coast of Malabar, and, from what our author says, we gather that he was a dangerous neighbour both to his own sovereign as well as to the Company. Pāliyam had its ancestral seat at Chēnnamangalam, the territory around which was subject to his rule. Besides this, the Atchen possessed vast estates throughout the kingdom, over some of which he was even the ruling chief. The island of Vypīn was and still is almost his, and he seems to have resided there at the time of the incident referred to by our author. The audacity of a member of the Pāliyam family in slaying one of the East India Company's merchants had to be left unnoticed, as the Company felt that it was no match for his superior power. His own sovereign did not, however, leave the incident unnoticed. We learn from the chronicles of the Cochin State that, during the reign of king Ravi Vaṙma who died in 1732—3, Pāliyaṭṭ Ikkēla Atchen, a junior member of the family, slew one Malapai, a rich Canarese merchant, and committed other atrocities, for which the Raja assumed all the Pāliyam estates lying outside Chēṅṅamangalam, and confined the Pāliyam family and its adherents to Chēṅṅamangalam. Many followers of the Pāliyam house were also slain. The Pāliyam faction caused considerable disturbance, and the country was much distracted, owing to the disturbances occasioned by Pāliyam and by the adherents of the Raja. But, before the Raja died, the differences were made up at the instance of Iṭṭuṇṇi Kumāran Atchen and Kuṅṅiṭṭuṇṇān Atchen. Pāliyam had to pay a heavy fine, and peace was restored in the country.

In spite of the check thus administered to his rising power by his suzerain, the Pāliyaṭṭ Atchen continued to prosper and to consolidate his authority. The Raja of Cochin soon came to be completely under the influence of the Atchens, and the Pāliyam estates spread far and wide throughout Cochin. The Dutch Government records of Cochin of the year 1743 say that "Pāliyaṭṭ Atchen, or free Raja, had a residence at Chenotta (Chēṅṅamangalam), close to Cṙānganūr, and was the *free-lord* of the island of Vypīn, and some time previously, he had become the ruling sovereign of Manakkōṭṭa and Muḷḷūrkkara, lying above Chēṙṙuvāye: also his rights extended over the old kingdom of Williar Wattata (Villār-vaṭṭam), an island, a little to the north from the town of Cochin, which he got, in ancient times, from the king of Cochin who had inherited the same from a Nayar chief." The territory of Muḷḷūrkkara covered an area of 26½ square miles. In 1743, it was a free-lordship possessed by the

Atchens of Manakkōte, which was but another branch of the house of Pāliyam. "It has since been rooted out, and hence it has now passed into the hands of the branch to which the present Pāliyaṭṭ Atchen belongs."[1] They held it till 1809, when, on Pāliyam rebelling against the British Government, it was assumed by the Raja and transferred to the Ṭalappilli Taluk of Cochin.

The Pāliyaṭṭ Atchen, as chief minister, continued to direct the affairs of Cochin, holding supreme power, and, at times, casting into the shade even the royal authority. In the year 1753, Pāliyaṭṭ Kōmi Atchen, who was a clever diplomatist, succeeded, from his confinement at Trivandrum, in bringing about amicable relations between the Rajas of Cochin and Travancore, much to the advantage of Cochin. It was about this time that the Zamorin made endeavours to allure the Raja of Cochin, promising to give up his hereditary feud with that State, if the Raja would only join the Zamorin in attacking Travancore. Looking to the recent events, the Raja was inclined to close with the bargain, but Kōmi Atchen felt the danger of the enterprise; he foresaw the disaster it would lead to, and wisely weaned his sovereign from evil counsels, with the result that it was not long before Cochin was able finally to drive the Zamorin out of Cochin territory with the active co-operation of Travancore. Of this Pāliyaṭṭ Atchen, the Dutch Governor Moens writes, "The last Paljetter and Prime Minister of the king of Cochin, who died on the 17th June in the year 1779, was a statesmanly man and always full of plans to reinstate his king."

The Pāliyaṭṭ Atchens retained their power till the year 1809, when the then Valia Atchen or senior member, in conjunction with Vēlu Ṭampy Ḍalava, minister of Travancore, incited a rebellion against the English, and endeavoured to murder Col. Macauly, the British

1. Moens' *Memorials*.

Resident. The Atchen was then deprived of all his dignities, and deported to Chingelpet, and his estates confiscated to the State. From that time, the Pāliyaṭṭ Atchens ceased to be hereditary ministers of Cochin, though they are even now reckoned the premier noblemen of the State. The exiled Atchen died at Chingelpet. The Pāliyam estates were, after some time, restored to the family, but the chief was shorn of many of his dignities. Still, the Pāliyam continued to command considerable influence in the country though not at court. Latterly, the Cochin Rajas have, in one way or other, managed to curtail the power and influence of the family. Large estates, which have been enjoyed tax-free from time immemorial, have been assessed to tax on the plea that the Pāliyam failed to prove the grant under rules passed by the State. The laws of escheat enforced by the revenue authorities, the jurisdiction of Civil Courts being taken away by special legislation, have also been the means of depriving them of the Manakkōte estate.[1] The power of interdiction from caste exercised by the Raja has also been the means of lowering the Pāliyaṭṭ house much in the estimation of the people, and the family had to make large sacrifices to obtain communion with caste members. The following letters show what power the Atchen wielded in the country at one time, and how his assistance was availed of by Col. Macauly in those troubulous times:

"INFORMATION.

"The Resident of the Court of Trivandrum has accepted the proposals made in the letter sent by Paliyat Achen through the hands of his man and also the verbal proposals delivered by the same message which will be without delay made known to Government until a favourable reply be obtained from Government. I have to say that the Resident of Trevedan is

1. This estate has been subsequently restored to them on payment of a heavy fine, but not rent-free as before.

acquainted that Pāliyaṭṭ Atchen feels great sorrow on account of the misdeeds he had committed and on account of what had passed in the Court of Trevedan. I do recommend herein Pāliyaṭṭ Atchen, as soon as he receives this letter, to write a letter signed and sealed by himself stating that he will break off his close friendship with the Diwan of Trevadancoat. That he will act agreeably to the orders of the Honourable Company, that he agrees to let the Company's forces come through the Territories of the King of Cochin. That he will supply those forces with provisions on receiving the value of such supplies from the Honourable Company and that he will afford every assistance to serve the avowed enemy of both countries in the manner the Government of Honourable Company may judge proper. The Resident of Trevadancoat gives also assurances that, agreeably to the former agreement, he will procure the Honourable Company's assistance for the King of Cochin, that he will cause the necessary respect to be paid, that *he will protect Paliyat Atchen, his property and his relations* and afford them sustenance, and that he will make proper inquiries and regulate matters. As for all other matters, the King of Cochin, Pāliyaṭṭ Atchen and the inhabitants must faithfully depend upon the goodwill of the British Government through the medium of the Resident of Trevedancoat since they are well acquainted with the laudable proceedings of that Government from a length of time.

"10th February, 1809
"Or
"27th Macarum, 984

"(Signed) C. MACAULY."

"To

"Colonel Macauly,
" &c. &c. &c.

"I have perused the letter you sent to me and have understood the contents of the same. Agreeably to the instructions contained in this letter, I have broken off the friendship which had till now existed between me and the Diwan of Tiruvidam Cotta. I will strictly abide by the orders of the Honourable Company, and I do also consent to the Honourable Company's forces to pass through the territories of the King of Cochin. I will send for the necessary provisions and supply the Honourable Company's forces *with them* for price. I will also afford my assistance to the Honourable Company in all the measures they may adopt against their enemies. As I have now agreed to all these terms in writing, I entreat that you will yourself procure every necessary assurance for the King of Cochin, for his Kingdom and *for myself*. I beg also to be favoured with a reply to this letter acquainting me that this letter has reached that place and treating about the assurance you may obtain for doing in such things after acquainting the Government with these circumstances.

"28th of the month of Tye of the year 984,

"(11th February 1809).

"The Signature and Seal of Pāliyaṭṭ Atchen."

23. **Customs observed at Deaths and at Coronations.** In this para, we have a clear account of what takes place on the death of the Raja, and the description is as true today as it was when it was written, or as the custom used to be for ages before. These observances are similar all over Malabar and are not confined to Cochin. The accounts of the death ceremonies in the family of the Zamorin of Calicut given by the Portuguese writers are almost the same. Barbosa, writing about 1503, says, "This king of Calicut, and so also the other kings of Malabar, when they die, are burned in the country with much sandal and aloe wood; and, at the burning, all the nephews and brothers and nearest relations collect together, and all the grandees of the realm and confidantes of the king, and they lament for him and burn him. And before burning

him, they keep him there for three days waiting for the assembling of the above-mentioned persons, that they may see him. if he died a natural death, or avenge his death, if any one killed him, as they are obliged to do in case of a violent death. And they observe this ceremony very rigidly.[1] After having burned him, all shave themselves from head to foot, excepting the eyelashes—from the prince, the heir to the throne, to the smallest child of the kingdom—that is, those who are gentiles; and they also clean their teeth, and universally leave off eating betel for 13 days from that time; and, if in this period they find anyone who eats it, his lips are cut off by the executioner. During these thirteen days, the prince does not rule, nor is he enthroned as king in order to see, if in this time any one will rise up to oppose; and when this time is accomplished, all the grandees and former governors make him swear to maintain all the laws of the late king, and to pay the debts which he owed, and to labour to recover that which other former kings had lost. And he takes this oath, holding a drawn sword in his left hand, and his right hand placed upon a chain lit up with many oil wicks, in the midst of which is a gold ring which he touches with his fingers, and then he swears to maintain everything with that sword When he has taken the oath, they sprinkle rice over his head with many ceremonies of prayer and adoration to the sun, and immediately after, certain Counts, whom they call Kaimals, along with all the others of the royal lineage and the grandees, swear to him, in the same manner to serve him, and to be loyal and true to him. During these thirteen days, one of the Kaimals governs and rules the State like the king himself: he is like an Accountant-General of the king and of all the affairs of

1. At present, cremation takes place as early as it can be arranged, in no instance going beyond 24 hours from death. Perhaps the custom of keeping the body longer than that has ceased along with the cessation of the reason for the same; for violent deaths seldom or ever occur in these days.

the kingdom. This office and dignity is by right and inheritance. This person is also the chief treasurer of the kingdom; without him, the king cannot open or see the treasury ; neither can the king take anything out of the treasury without a great necessity and by the consent of this person and several others, and all the laws and ordinances of the kingdom are in the keeping of this man. No one eats meat or fish in these thirteen days, nor may any one fish under pain of death.[1] During that period, large alms were given from the king's property, of food to many poor people, and to Brahmans, and, when the 13 days are ended, all eat what they please, except the new king who observes the same abstinence for one year; neither does he shave his beard, nor cut a hair of his head nor of his body nor his nails, and he says prayers for certain hours of the day, and does not eat more than once a day. And before he eats, he has to wash himself, and after washing, he must not drink anything until he has eaten."[2]

Varthema's account differs but little. He says, "On the death of the king, all the people of the kingdom shave their beards and their heads, with the exception of some part of the head, and also of the beard, according to the pleasure of each person. The fishermen also are not allowed to catch any fish for eight days." He adds, " As an act of devotion, the king does not sleep with women or eat betel for a whole year."[3]

The big feast at the end of the year is referred to as a great event by Purchas who says, " The year being ended, he observeth a kind of *Dirige* for his predecessor's soul, whereat are assembled 100,000 persons; at which time he giveth great alms, and then

1. So late as 1780, the king of Travancore ordered that the fishermen of Anjengo should not exercise their profession for a fixed number of days after the death of his mother. See Bartolomeo, p. 144.

2. P. 108.

3. P. 144.

is confirmed."[1] Of this feast, Varthema observes, "As soon as the year of the mourning is accomplished, he (the king) sends an invitation to all the principal Brahmans who are in his own kingdom, and he also invites some from other countries. And when they are arrived, they make great feasting for three days. Their food consists of rice dressed in various ways, the flesh of various hogs and a great deal of venison,[2] for they are great hunters.[3] At the end of three days, the said king gives to each of the principal Brahmans 3-4-5 pardu, and then every one returns home."[4]

With the above description may be compared the following account of the observances of the royal family in Travancore given by Mr. Mateer:—"*Sickness, death, and funeral ceremonies.*—In case of illness, famous native doctors are applied to for treatment, as well as the services of the English court physician. Difficulties arise from the confict of Hindu and caste usages with the particular diet or drugs that may be prescribed according to European medical science. Frequently, a fair and sufficient trial is not given to European skill and medicines.[5]

"Travelling for change of air and scene, and for pleasant bathing, is commonly resorted to with advantage. This is turned into, or combined with, a pilgrimage to shrines and sacred places, to which, sometimes, an improvement in health is attributed rather than to the fresh air and exercise, and the hopefulness inspired by the effort. One prince expended more than his income on gifts to the deities and temples in seeking to ward off death, and spent all his

1. P. 627.

2. Evidently, the traveller was misinformed with respect to this item of fare; for the Malabar Brahmans are and have always been strict vegetarians.

3. This may be true of the Nayars, but not of the Nambūṭiri Brahmans.

4. P. 175.

5. Not correct now at any rate.

time in repeating 'Rama, Rama,' employing a person to count the number of repetitions.

" Further superstitious measures are tried. The prasādam, or oblations of food, consecrated by dedication to the idol, and brought from the temple of Padmanābhan, are expected to exert a healing power. Special praises of the gods, sacrifices to conquer death, vows to noted temples, and other rites are performed by Brahman priests. Many Brahmans are fed with the most delicious articles of food, and endowed with liberal gift.

" Should sickness be prolonged and distressing, and appear to be mortal, it is supposed that the sins of the invalid hinder his peaceful departure. And, in any case, the burden of sin and the need of a sin-bearer cannot but be felt.

" The Ālingana Ḍānam—embrace gift—is now made, a most touching ceremony, which bears some resemblance to the Jewish institution of the scapegoat. A holy Brahman is found who is willing to undertake this responsibility in consideration of a large sum of money, rupees ten thousand ; he is brought in, and, after the performance of certain ceremonies by the Brahmans, closely embraces the dying man, and says, 'O King! I undertake to bear all your sins and diseases. May Your Highness live long and reign happily'. Thereby assuming the sins of the sufferer, the man is sent away from the country and never more allowed to return.

" Gifts of cows are also made to Brahmans to ensure the support of a cow in crossing the river of death. Gōmūlya Ḍānam, or gift to purchase cows, is a present of 45 fanams each, given in money, instead of the actual animals, to a thousand Brahmans, this being equal to the gift of a thousand cows. Śūdras, when ill, sometimes offer a cow, with silver decorations on the horns, to Brahmans for atonement of sin and recovery of health.

"To worship the cows, especially at the time of death, is a favourite one with the Hindus. Baka Bhai, widow of the last Raja of Nagpore, spent twelve hours daily in the adoration of cows, the ocimum plant (ṭulasi), the Sun, and her idols. When her end was at hand, five cows were introduced into the room where she lay, in order to be bestowed on Brahmans. The gift of the animal was accomplished by a further donation in money; and, as one after another they passed onward from the bedside, they were supposed to help the dying woman forward on her way to heaven. Among the last acts of her life was to call for a cow, and, having fallen at its feet, as far as her now fast waning strength would allow her, she offered it grass to eat, and addressed it by the venerated name of mother.

"When death is imminent, Kāla Ḍānam, or the death-gift, is made. A buffalo is brought; it is covered with valuable cloths, the neck and horns decked with jewels, and a little fire in a pot tied under its belly, but without touching it. A Brahman is called, who receives four parās of sesamum seed and a few rupees, and is then mounted on the buffalo and sent away.

"The dying person is laid on the ground upon soil brought from Āttingal, a last farewell taken of the members of the family, and disposition made of personal effects. Words of consolation and kind advices are also addressed, and reconcilations effected. All the rites and donations are completed, the sacred oblations of the household deity brought from the pagoda and applied to the eyes and forehead; and a Brahman repeats some manṭrams in the ears of the expiring Raja.

"The women connected with the palace, assembled in expectation of the solemn event, stand in two lines, ready to commence mourning. Immediately the death occurs, they begin a terrible wail, beating their breasts and unloosing their long hair. The cry is heard outside, and hundreds of women join in concert.

"Trumpeters are instantly sent round, whether it be day or night, to call in the whole of the Nayar Brigade, and the barrack bell is also rung. At dead of night, as on the last occasion, the melancholy sounds of the death-horn are sadly impressive.

"The household being polluted by the occurrence of death, none can partake of food, till the remains are disposed of. The body is, therefore, washed, rubbed with sacred ashes, and at once prepared for cremation. The funeral pile is quickly erected in a small yard outside the fort, the fuel of mango, with some cedar and sandalwood, being in readiness beforehand. A shed, ornamented with flowers, is put up to protect the pile from rain, and sufficiently high to be out of reach of the fire. The body is lavishly decked with bracelets, necklaces, and ear-rings of plain gold (no precious stones being allowed), all of which are burnt along with it, the melted gold becoming the perquisite of the priest and others. The body is also wrapped in a silk cloth and girdle bestowed by Paṭmanābhaswāmi on his servant, the king, as he also is accustomed to give the sere cloth for burial to his dependants. This cloth is brought from the temple in procession with music.

"Placed in the State palankeen, the mortal remains are closely covered up, the palankeen also being overspread with a rich silken pall, and decked with garlands of jasmine and other flowers. It is taken out of the palace through a breach in the wall, made for the purpose, to avoid pollution of the gate, and afterwards built up again, so that the departed spirit may not return through the gate to trouble the survivors. On the starting of the mournful procession, and during its progress, minute guns are fired, one for each year of age of the departed prince.

"The funeral procession much resembles that on the occasion of the Ārāṭṭu, or bathing of the god, and starts within a few hours after the decease. It is headed by the Maharaja's body-guard on foot, bareheaded, and leading their horses, followed by the band, with drums muffled and colours draped in black. The bandmen march bareheaded, playing the Dead March; the Brigade also bareheaded, their muskets reversed and flags furled; the English officers on foot in full uniform with strips of crape. Behind the band walk the great officers of State, then the Elaya Raja who is to succeed, next the princes in order. Behind these comes the palankeen with the royal remains borne by a caste called *Pounders* (Pōṇṭanmārs). It is surrounded by the domestics and favourite followers, and by hundreds of Śūdra women, with their hair dishevelled, wearing but a single cloth around the waist, and filling the air with their loud weeping and lamentations. All are in similar undress; even in the heaviest showers, not an umbrella is permitted, so that the risk is sometimes great to delicate constitutions from standing two or three hours in rain during the cremation. A vast multitude of men, women, and children, of various castes and creeds, follow the funeral procession to the burning-ground, but only the princes and chief officials are allowed to enter it. The ceremonies are performed under the direction of the Brahmans.

"Underneath the high outer shed, a small inner canopy, immediately over the pile, is very handsomely decorated with flowers, plantain trees, young cocoanuts, palmyra nuts, and many other ornaments. The fuel is piled on planks, and a mattress placed on the top. The remains are laid in the centre—the head southwards, the feet to the north—and completely covered with sandal-wood. As soon as the body reaches the place, it is borne round the pile three times, then placed on the pyre, and three volleys of musketry fired—the last salute to departed royalty. Then the brothers and nephews put a little rice and money in the mouth, and break the pots of water according to custom. Two lights are placed at the head and at the feet, and kept burning for five days and nights.

"Before lighting the pile, a manṭram is repeated, giving the elements of the body to the five elements—the eye to the sun, the breath to the wind, the limbs to the earth, the water, and the plants whence they had been derived. In accordance with the theory that each element must have a portion of the body at dissolution, it usually expires on the earth, is washed with water, burnt with fire, to set free the spiritual element from the superincumbent clay and complete the regenerative process; and the ashes are, in some cases, scattered in the air, in others, buried in the earth, or thrown into the rivers or the sea.

"Fire is applied to the pile by several of the neareat relatives, the chief mourners, who hold the torch behind their backs, reverently looking away from the remains. The military and band are now permitted to depart, but the princes and high officials remain for two or three hours, till the body is consumed. Fuel is added, and oil and butter poured on, with fragrant substances, till the body is fairly reduced to ashes. Then, more oil and ghee are supplied in order to raise the flame so as to ignite the sheds and their decorations. At intervals, the mourning women utter a loud wail, all in unison.

"The bereaved family now return to their palaces, bathe, and continue in deep mourning for eleven days, the pile being left to smoulder under charge of a guard of about fourteen sepoys, till the fire dies out in a day or two.

"After the funeral is over, Brahmans flock in and receive gratuities of three or four fanams each.

"A notification is at once issued by the Dewan announcing the demise, the consequent closing of all public offices and institutions, and suspension of all business for three days, and other customary marks of mourning. All shops are closed, and work dropped throughout the kingdom. Umbrellas also are not allowed to enter the fort. For eleven days, the palace women and all Nayars have to go mourning with hair loose and without wearing new cloths or rubbing sacred ashes. For the same period, mourning is observed by the Nayar Brigade, the men shaving off their moustaches and hair, excepting the Kudumi which hangs loose, and going about bare-headed, without their turbans.

* * * *

"In Alleppey, as soon as the sad intelligence is known, the Commercial Agent orders all the shops in the town to be closed, and the national standard hoisted half mast from the flagstaff.

"For a full year, it is forbidden to celebrate marriages, or other occasions, with the usual music or display.

"It is customary to give a chuckram to each Sirkar official present at the burning, which he is supposed to place in the mouth of the deceased. The surviving relatives, therefore, for some days after, always enclose a chuckram in letters to officials whom they may have occasion to address.

"After the cremation, the royal palankeen is again brought, morning and evening, for five days in procession to the burning-ground, accompanied by a Brahman priest, sepoys, and attendants, and mourning women, who cry as before. It is carried round the ashes thrice, and then taken back.

"On the fifth day, by which time relatives who live at a distance will have arrived, a new prince goes as before, bare-headed and bare-footed, and wearing only a single cloth, in procession with music, wailing women, &c., to collect the ashes and the remains of bones still unconsumed. After a Brahman called the Kakkāṭṭu Pōṯṯi has performed certain ceremonies, the bones are gathered, and part placed in a pot to be sent to the Ganges at Benares in charge of a Brahman, who receives two thousand rupees for this service, and is also regarded as degrading himself by such an office. The remainder is put with many ceremonies in another urn, and buried under a jack tree in some compound in the neighbourhood. Over this grave is placed a stone with the name and age of the deceased, and the owners of the garden receive, for the perpetual guardianship of the tomb, a daily grant of two measures of rice, and half a nāli of cocoanut oil for constantly burning at night in a lamp over the grave.

"The ashes of junior members of the royal family are buried at the burning-place, and a jack tree planted over each.

"The melted gold is divided into three or four parts, and distributed to the officiating priest, the temple, the palankeen bearers, and the mourning women.

"On the twelfth day, Puṇyāham, or cleansing from pollution, is celebrated by the Pōṯṯies, after which the new ruler can take possession. Into a quantity of water in a vessel, they throw sacred flowers, then prayers are recited; the holy water is sprinkled over the person and the house to be purified. Presents are again made to Brahmans.

"Sixteen days after the cremation, the Śrāḍḍha, oblation to the manes for the repose of the soul, is celebrated, and this is continued daily in the palace itself for some time It consists in the offering of piṇḍams, or rice balls, and oblations of water to the deceased ancesṭors and the gods, with the feeding of Brahmans ṛequired in all ceremonies.

* * * *

"As the new sovereign cannot, through press of offcial duties, observe all the mourning ceremonial, it is customary for the next heir, the Elaya Raja, to conduct these: he willingly remains in mourning and unshaven for the twelve months, during which the Śrāḍḍhās are frequently repeated.

"On the first anniversary of the Maharaja's death, and, commencing some days before that date, the Ṭirumāsam, or annual Śrāḍḍha is observed. Many thousands of people are then amply fed, and largesses freely distributed for four days amongst the Brahmans, the first day at the rate of one rupee each, on succeeding days one fanam each, and five rupees per head to Nambūri Brahmans. The royal party and *suite* visit in procession the temple of Paraśu Rāma at Ṭiruvellam, near Trivandrum, where further rites are performed, and gifts presented to Brahmans. The Elaya Raja is now relieved from mourning observances. The temple at Neyyāṭṭinkara is also visited in State, and offerings presented there.

"Śrāḍḍhās are repeated annually as long as there are relatives to take an interest in the ancestors and remember the anniversary of their deaths. At Paḍmanābhapuram, and Śuchīnḍram, a ceremony of long-standing usage is annually observed in grand style—the feeding of some hundreds of Nambūri Brahmans for the good of the departed spirits of some Rajas of bygone days.

"A palace in which the sovereign dies is left vacant, and preserved, with all its furniture and contents intact for one or two generations before it is again opened and re-occupied; as in Central Africa, everything belonging to the deceased king is preserved with the greatest reverence. Care is taken, if possible, that younger members of the house die in some unoccupied palace, that can conveniently be spared from ordinary use."[1]

"**Accession to the Musnad, or Throne.** During the eleven days of mourning for the deceased Raja, the

1. Pp. 135-142.

new king lives a life of seclusion, attends the funeral ceremonies and mourning, and receives expressions of sympathy in his bereavement, and of submission to himself as the incoming ruler. On the second day after the obsequies, all the officers of State visit his palace, in mourning attire, to condole with the young Raja. And on the sixth day, the native officers of the Brigade visit the new ruler, when each offers a present of a piece of silk cloth. The new king is not, however, proclaimed for thirteen days. The usual guard of honour attends upon the prince anyhow in the meantime. Until formally installed, he is addressed by his previous title.

"A new Governor-General having arrived in India in the interregnum between the death of the late, and the accession of the present Maharaja, the usual official intimation had to be addressed to the Rāṇi. The letter was in English, accompanied by a translation in Persian, beautifully written on paper powdered with silver, and enclosed in a rich satin bag, covered with white net.

"The days of mourning for the deceased ruler being ended, purification is made on the twelfth day, and, on the thirteenth day, the new Raja visits the pagoda of Paḍmanābhan for the native ceremonial answering to a coronation. The whole kingdom having been bestowed by Raja Mārttāṇḍa Varma on this deity, in 1750, in perpetual endowment, the crown can only be received from him through the Brahmans. The ceremony is called Paṭiyēttam, receiving the subsistence allowance, and is the clearest possible acknowledgment of entire subservience to the god and his only representatives, the priests. The Rāṇīs, being regarded as the custodians of the keys of the temple, while the god is absent from it at the Āraṭṭu procession, receive for this service a small allowance of rice; the new Raja, likewise, attends the temple for his instructions, and allowances of food and clothing and for investment with office, and with the first of his official titles, *Sree Padmanabha Dasa*, the servant, or slave, of the holy Paḍmanābhan.

"The royal house of Orissa, in like manner, 'has for centuries performed menial offices before the image of Jagannath; and, as the sweeper caste is the lowest in the Hindu commonwealth, so the kings of Orissa have reached the climax of religious humility in their most cherished title of "Hereditary Sweeper of Jagannath."'[1]

"Ascending the temple steps with due acts of homage to the presiding deity, the Maharajah receives from him an allowance of rice and cloth, in token of administering the kingdom as his tenant and vicegerent. The head-accountant of the temple reads from the ritual the rules originally prescribed for observance on the accession of a new sovereign. Offerings are then presented, and various acts of adoration performed, such as Pṙaḍakṣhiṇa, circumambulating the pagoda, and Sāṣhtāngam, prostration of the whole body. The Maharajah is anointed (Abhiṣhēkam) with consecrated water, and the whole is concluded by the high priest handing to His Highness the sword of State and the belt (which are supposed to belong to Paḍmanābhan, and have been kept in the temple from the demise of the late king), the Pṙasāḍam (sandal-wood powder given from the temple as a mark of the god's favour), the ration of a cocoanut, and one and a half eḍungaĪys of rice, which the Rajah has boiled, and eats. The eight Yōgakkārs (Brahmans who are the members of the ruling council of the temple) give the ṅīṭ, or grant of the regal office. On receiving the sword, the Maharajah says, 'I will keep this sword until the uncle who has gone to Mecca returns'[2]. "Finally, marching round

1. Hunter's *Orissa*, p. 115.

2. This is not a correct statement. No such declaration is made. State Manual, Vol. I, p. 225.

the pagoda, he returns to take possession of the palace and to sign his first order. This, in case of the present sovereign, was a grant of an additional five thousand rupees per annum for the repairs of temples, which caused a profound sensation throughout the country in favour of idolatry. So, also, on the arrival of the new Diwan, his first official act was to sign an order for the punctual feeding of the Brahmans.

"On the day of the native installation, special pūjās and offerings for the Raja's health and prosperity are made at the temple in the fort, and at all other pagodas throughout the kingdom. European officials and friends now congratulate him on his accession.

"As soon as convenient, a Darbar, or *levee* is held for the public recognition and installation by the British Government. Till this comes off, there is a sort of interregnum, the reign of each Rajah being officially dated from this day. The old Audience Hall in the fort is still preferred, on account of its historical associations, to the Durbar Hall in the new public buildings. The British sepoys from Quilon, with their English officers, are invited to be present, and all Europeans resident in the country; while multitudes of the native population flock into the capital for a holiday, to witness the pageant and join in the general rejoicings. The houses are gaily decorated with floral arches and fruiting stems of the plantain, and festoons of foliage, bright-coloured flowers, and palm-leaf ornaments are strung across the roads from tree to tree.

"The Durbar Hall is a long, narrow, upper room, handsomely furnished with carpets, sofas, large mirrors and lamps, paintings of former Rajahs and distinguished British officers, and other furniture in western style. Outside, in the great square, the troops are drawn up under arms in imposing array; the State elephants, richly caparisoned, and with bells about their necks, bear costly howdahs, though rarely, or never used for riding purposes; and crowds of the people assemble in honour of the occasion.

"The royal party, officers, and retinue being in readiness a little beforehand, the British Resident is received on his arrival, with the usual salute from the artillery and troops, takes the Maharajah's arm, and is placed on a seat immediately on his right. The Commanding Officer of the Nayar Brigade, who also bears Her Majesty's commission, sits on the other side; and the princes and English officials or guests, with their respective wives, take their seats on either side of the room, the whole forming a brilliant and impressive scene.

"The ivory throne at the head of the hall is adorned with cushions, shield, and weapons, and a glittering canopy supported on pillars of silver. Beside it stand the Prime Minister and favoured officers in appropriate costume.

"The Maharajah is now placed upon the throne by the Resident and the Commanding Officer, when the Resident also presents the insignia of sovereignty—what may be called the crown—a plumed and jewelled turban worn by each ruler in succession, with drooping feathers of birds of Paradise, aigrette of diamonds and emeralds, and two large pendent pearls. The new Rajah, in turn, resigning the turban that appertains to the heir-apparent, hands it over to the next heir, who thus becomes Elaya Rajah. It cannot but be deeply touching to those who may have known and entertained personal affection for the ruler so recently departed, to witness his crown thus solemnly handed over to his successor. A proclamation by the Governor of Madras is then read, proclaiming the new king, and 'requiring and directing all the subjects of the Travancore Sirkar to acknowledge and obey His Highness as their Maharajah and sovereign.'

BP.

"The reading of this proclamation is followed by a royal salute and a *feu de joie*. A translation of the same in Malayalam, accompanied by a proclamation from the new ruler, is read to the people outside, the Rajah, Resident, and assembled company standing in the long verandah in front of the Hall; another salute being fired, a number of unfortunate criminal convicts, corresponding to the years of the Maharajah's age, and previously selected as the fittest objects of his clemency are liberated down below from their chains to commemorate the auspicious day. Throughout the ceremonial, the company politely rise and stand whenever His Highness does so, or sit when he does. After further congratulations, a speech by the Rajah expressing his sentiments on the occasion, and the principles on which he intends to govern, is read. On the installation of the present Maharajah (1883), this was a most remarkable document, such, it was observed, as few of the native princes of India could prepare or deliver. Another royal salute, and the assemblage is dismissed with distribution of garlands and bouquets of jasmine flowers, and the fragrant leaves of the artemisia; rose water is sprinkled, and each visitor shakes hands with the Maharajah on retiring.

"After this Durbar, attended by Europeans and the representatives of the British Government, is over, the Rajah resumes his seat on the musnad; and another *levee* is held for the reception of the native officers of position in the service of the State, who have all been ordered in from their posts throughout the country in order to pay homage by offering the usual tribute of money, each according to his rank and grade. The amount formerly presented was one-tenth of a month's salary—now a much smaller sum.

"About 3 o'clock P. M., the Rajah goes in public procession for Paṭṭaṇapṛavēsam, entering the city, in his State palankeen, every one but himself marching on foot; even a little son will walk holding on by a corner of the royal palankeen for assistance. They go round the principal streets of the Fort, escorted by the Body Guard and Brigade, and attended by the Diwan and native officials, and a vast concourse of the people. All being obliged to walk, and no umbrellas allowed by etiquette to the highest or the feeblest, this is a very exhausting ceremony in the hot sun. A royal salute and three volleys of musketry are fired on His Highness appearing after his return on the upper terrace of the palace. Provisions are afterwards distributed to the Brahmans under the superintendence of the sepoys out of uniform.

" In the evening, a State dinner is given at the Residency; and next day, the Maharajah honours the British Resident with a visit, coming in full procession of cavalry and led horses, Brigade brass bands and native musicians with strange flutes and other instruments, the State elephants and carriages, attendants strewing green leaves on the ground, the sword and emblems of State, and two curious gold stands for a kind of incense sticks always borne burning before the Rajah in State procession."[1]

The coronation ceremony in Cochin is almost the same, so far as the British Resident's Durbar is concerned. As to the religious ceremony, there are local variations.

24. **Kankanoer.** This is Kaṇayannūr, a place close to Ṭṛppūṇiṭṭura, where the Rajas of old used to live. The deceased Rajas of Cochin are generally referred to as the Raja who died at Trichur or the Raja who died at Irinjalakkuda, etc.

25. **Vanneri.** This is a place near Velianköṭe in the Chowghat Taluk of British Malabar. It is not far from the celebrated Vishṇu shrine of Guruvāyūr. The tradition is that the Cochin family had its origin in Vaṅṅēri. The Cochin chronicles say that, at Vaṅṅēri,

1. Mateer's *Life in Travancore*, pp., 119—23.

the five branches into which the family was originally divided had each a separate residence and properties attached to it. The place now belongs to the British and it is said that the Cochin Rajas are debarred from wearing their crown, as they could do so only after performing certain ceremonies at Chiṭṭṛakūṭam in Vaṅṅēri, which they cannot now do, as the place is beyond their territory. There is still a piece of ground in this locality which goes by the name of Perumpaṭappu, which is the dynastic name of the Cochin Rajas. Traces of the Chiṭṭṛakūṭam palace still exist. There is a temple of some importance near it, which is now under the management of the Cochin State.

Books referred to in the preparation of this work.

A.

Abidas—Historia Certaminis Apostolici.

Ameer Ali, Sir Seyed, the Rt. Hon.—Muhammadan Law.

American Anthropologist, N. S. 1905.

Anantakrishna Iyer, L. K.—Castes and Tribes of Cochin, Government Press, Cochin.

Antiquary, The Indian.

Arthur, Lieut. Report—Selections from the Records of Travancore.

Asher—The Itinerary of Rabbi Benjamin.

Asiatic Journal, Selections from 2 Volumes.

Asiatic Researches.

Assemani, Joseph Simonius—Bibliotheca Orientalis De Syris Nestorianis.

Astley—A New Collection of Voyages.

Augur—Church History of Travancore.

B.

Barbosa, Duarte—Description of the Coasts of Africa and Malabar in the beginning of the 16th Century.

Bartolomeo, Fra Paolino da S—A Voyage to the East Indies.

Bengal, Journal of the Asiatic Society of.

Bhandarkar, Dr. R. G.—Early History of the Dekhan.

Biddulph, Col.—The Pirates of Malabar, etc.

Bilhana—Vikramakavya.

Birdwood, Sir George—Report on the old Records of the India Office.

Blavetsky, Madam—Isis Unvieled.

Buchanan—Canara and Malabar.

Buchanan, Claudius, D. D.—Christian Researches in Asia.

Buchanan, Hamilton, Dr.—Account of the Kingdom of Nepal.

Burnell, Dr. A. C.—Elements of South Indian Palaeography.

Burton, Captain R. F.—Goa and the Blue Mountains.

C.

Caldwell, Right Rev. Bishop—Comparative Grammar of the Dravidian Languages.

Do. Do—History of Tinnevelly.

Camoens—The Lusiad—Mickles' Translation.

Census Report, of Travancore.

C.—*cont.*

Churchill—Collection of Voyages and Travels.

Coleridge, Fra—Life and Letters of St. Francis Xavier.

Collection, of Early Voyages—Voyage of Albuquerque.

Collins, Revd. Richard—Missionary Enterprise in the East.

Cornill—Atlas.

Correa, Gasper Lendas—The Three Voyages of Vasco da Gama.

Cunningham, General—Geography of Ancient India.

D.

D'Albuquerque, Alfonso—Commentaries. Haklyut Society's Publication.

Danvers, F. C.—Report on the Portuguese Records.

Do. The Portuguese in Asia.

Day, Dr. Francis—Land of the Perumals.

Dillon, M.—The East Indies.

D'Orsey, The Rev. Alexand. J. D—Portuguese Discoveries, Dependencies and Missions.

Drury, Major Heber—Life and Sport in South India.

Dubois, Abbe J.—Manners and Customs of the People of India, Edited by Mr. Beauchamp.

Dutt, R. C.—Ancient India.

E.

East India Company, Letter Book of.

Edge—Description of the Sea-ports of Malabar.

Elliot, Sir H. M.—The History of India as told by its own Historians.

Ellis—Mirasi Papers.

Encyclopaedia Britanica, Vols. V—9th Edn.

Ensubius—Ecclesiastical History, Translated by Mr. Parker, 3rd Edn.

Epigraphia Indica.

Esoteric Hinduism.

F.

Faria Y Sousa, Manoel—The Portuguese Asia.

Fawcett—Bulletin on the People of Malabar.

Ferguson, James, D. C. L.; F. R. S.—History of Indian and Eastern Architecture.

Fitch, Ralph—England's Pioneer to India, by J. Horton Ryley, 1899.

Fleet, Dr.—Sanskrit and Old Canarese Inscriptions.

Forbes, James—Oriental Memoirs.

Forest—Cities of India.

Foulks—Geography of Travancore.

Foulkes, Rev. Mr.—Manual of the Salem District.

F—*cont.*

Frazer—The Golden Bough.

Fryer, Dr. J.— A New Account of the East India and Persia.

G.

Geddes—History of the Malabar Church.

Geological Survey of India, Records of ; Memoirs of.

Gibbon—Decline and Fall of the Roman Empire.

Giuseppe, Fr.—Second Expedition of Fr. Sebastioni India Oriental.

Gollenesse, Von—Memorials—Dutch Records.

Gopala Panikkar, C.—Malabar and its Folk.

Green—Short History of the English People.

Grose, John Henry—A Voyage to the East Indies.

Gundhert, Dr.—Malayalam Dictionary.

H.

Hakluyt's Voyages.

Hamilton, Captain Alexander—A New Account of the East Indies.

Do. W.—Account of the East Indies.

Do. Walter—Hindustan.

Heber's Journal, 2 Vols.

Horsley, Lieutenant—Memoirs of Travancore.

Horton, Ryley—Ralph Fitch, England's Pioneer to India.

Hough, Rev. James—Reply to the Letters of the Abbe Du Bois

Do. History of Christianity in India.

Hunt, Mr. Justice J. F. R.—Judgment in the Kottayam Cheriapally Case.

Hunter, Sir William—Short History of the Indian People.

Do. do. The Indian Empire.

Do. do. The History of British India.

Do. do. Orissa.

I.

Ibn Batuta—The Travels of—Lee's Translation.

Indian Review—From Madras.

Ives, Edward—Voyages.

J.

Johnson—Early Relations of the most Famous Kingdoms of the World (1611)

Do. Keith—Royal Atlas.

Jones, Sir William—Works of.

Jordanus, Friar—Wonders of the East (Mirabila Descripta Hak : Soc.)

Journal of Literature and Science, Madras.

Do. the Bengal Asiatic Society,

Do. Bombay do.

Do. Royal do.

K.

Kanakasabhai Pillai—The Tamils, Eighteen Hundred Years Ago.
Keye, Sir W.—Christianity in India.
Keralamahatmyam
Keralapazhama.
Keralavisesha Mahatmyam
Keralolpatti.
Kerr's Voyages.
King—Records of the Geological Survey of India for 1882.
Kirkpatrick Col.—Account of Nepal.
Kottayam, College Magazine.
Kunju Raman Nayar, Mr. Justice—Memo on the Land Tenures of Travancore.

L.

La Croze, M. V.—Hist. du Christianisme des Indes.
Lake, Mr. Philip—Geology of South Malabar.
Lang, Mr. Andrew—Customs and Myths.
La Roque—Voyage to Arabia the Happy.
Lassen—Ind. Alterthumskunde.
Laterneau—The Evolution of Marriage.
Lawson, Sir Charles—British and Native Cochin.
Layard—Nineveh and its Remains.
Lee, Rev.—The Churches in Southern India.
Logan, William—A Manual of the Malabar District.
Lubbock, Sir John—Origin of Civilization.
Lucena—Life of St. Francis Xavier.
Luigard—History of England.

M.

Mackenzie's Roman Law.
Maclean, Dr.—Standing Information regarding the Administration of the Madras Presidency.
Maclenan—Primitive Marriage.
Madras Review.
Mahabharata.
Maine, Sir Henry—Early Law and Custom.
Do. do. —Village Communities of India.
Major—India in the Fifteenth Century.
Malabar Gazetteer by Messrs. Evans, Todhunter and Cotton.
Malabar Law Reports.
Malabar Quarterly Review.
Manning, Mrs.—Ancient and Mediaeval India.
Manu Smriti.
Manual of the Geology of India.
Marco Polo's Kingdom of Eli.

M.—*cont.*

Mateer, Rev. S.—Native Life in Travancore.
Max Muller—Chips from a German Workshop.
Do. Sacred Books of the East, Vol. 36.
Mayne, J. D.—Hindu Law.
Mc Crindle, J. W.—Ancient India as described by Ktesias.
Do. do. do. Megasthenes.
Do. do. do. Ptolemy.
Do. Photios' abridgment of Ktesias.
Do. The Periplus.
Medlycott, Right Rev. Bishop—St. Thomas and India.
Middleton, Life of Bishop.
Mill, James—History of India.
Milne, Rae—The Syrian Church in India.
Moens, Van Adrian—Memorial. Dutch Government Records.
Montaigne—Essays.
Muir—Sanskrit Texts.

N.

Nagam Aiya—State Manual of Travancore.
Neale, Rev. J. M. D. D.—Patriarchate of Antioch.
Nieuhof, John—Remarkable Voyages and Travels into the best Provinces of the West and East Indies.
Nierenberg—Natural History.

O.

Oldham, Major—The Sun and the Serpent.
Oppert, Dr. Gustave—A Lecture on the Ancient Commerce of India.
Do.—On the Weapons, Army Organisation and Political Maxims of the Ancient Hindus.
Orme, Robert—The Works of.

P.

Pantaneus—Ecclesiastical History. Translated by Mr. Parker.
Pharos—Gazetteer of S. India.
Pinkerton—Collection of Voyages and Travels.
Pliny—Natural History.
Prananath Saraswati, Pandit—The Hindu Law of Endowments.
Pratt, Archdeacon—Scripture and Science not at Variance.
Purchas, Samuel—His Pilgrims.

R.

Ragozine, Zenaide A.— Vedic India.
Rajendra Lala Mitra, Dr.—Beef in Ancient India.
Ramraz—Essay on the Architecture of the Hindus.
Rangachariar, Professor M.—On the Yugas.
Raulin, Fr.—A Voyage to the East Indies.

R.—*cont.*

Raynal, Abbe W. F.—Histoire Philosophique et Politique (Edition de la Haye 1774—5).
Do. do. History of Settlements and Trades in the East Indies.
Reclus, Elie M.—Primitive Folk.
Do. do. Universal Geography.
Reinaud—Memoire Geographique Historique et Scientifique Sur l' Inde.
Renadot—Translation of 'The Travels of Two Muhammadans into India and China in the 9th Century.'
Report, Archaeological Survey.
Do. of the Malabar Marriage Commission.
Do. of the Travancore State Geologists.
Do. on the Administration of Travancore for 1881.
Do. The Fifth Report of the Select Committee of the House of Commons on the Affairs of the East India Company 1812.
Robertson, Dr.—Ancient India.
Do. Historical Disquisition concerning Ancient India.
Roulandson, Lieut—Tohfut-ul-Mujahideen—Translation of.

S.

Sankara Menon—Census Report of Cochin.
Sankara Smriti.
Schott, Fr.—Physica Curiosa.
Schroeder, Dr.—Prehistoric Antiquities of the Aryan People.
Sewell, Robert—A Forgotten Empire.
Do. do. Archaeological Survey of S. India.
Do. do. List of Antiquities in S. India.
Do. do. Sketches of Dynasties of S. India.
Shungunny Menon, P.—A History of Travancore.
Smith, Bosworth—Carthage and the Carthagenians.
Solyman—Chaine de Chroniques.
Sonnerat—Voyage to the East Indies, 1774 and 1781.
Starke, Herr—The Primitive Family, Its Rise and Development
Stavorinus, John Splinter—Voyages to the East Indies.
Stead, W. T.—Review of Reviews.
Stephen, Morse—Albequerque—Rulers of India series.
Subrahmanya Ayyar, Dr.—Census Report of Travancore.
Sundram Pillay, P—Early Sovereigns of Travancore.
Swaarder Kroon—Memorial on the Malabar Coast.
Syncellus—Chronographia.

T.

Tavernier, Jean Baptiste—Travels of—Balls' Edition.
Taylor—Primitive Culture.
Taylor, Rev. William—Translation of Oriental Historical MSS.

T—*cont.*

Theosophist.

Theosophic Thinker.

Thornton—Gazetteer of S. India.

Thurston, Dr. Edgar—Castes and Tribes of S. India.

Do. do. Ethnological Notes.

Tillemont—Ecclesiastical History of the First Six Ages.

Transactions of the Bombay Society, selections from.

U.

Upham—Mahavamsa.

V.

Varahamihira—Brihatsamhita.

Varthema, Lodovico di—The Travels of

Vasco de Gama, Roteiro de.

Venkasami Row—Manual of the Tanjore District.

W.

Walker, Major—Report on the Land Tenures of Malabar.

Ward and Conor—Memoir of the Survey of Travancore and Cochin.

Weber—History of Sanskrit Literature.

Welsh, Col. James—Military Reminiscences.

Westermarck—History of Human Marriage.

Wheeler, Talboys—The History of India.

Whitehouse—Historical Notices of Cochin.

Do. Lingerings of Light in a Dark Land.

Whiteway—Rise of the Portuguese Power in India.

Wigram—Malabar Law and Custom.

Wilkes, Col.—Mysore.

Wilkins—Hindu Mythology.

Williams, Prof. Monier—Hinduism.

Do. Lectures on Indian Epic Poetry.

Do. Religious Thought and Life in India.

Do. Descriptive Catalogue of the Mackenzie Collection.

Wilson—History of India.

Do. Rig Veda.

Do. Vishnu Purana.

Y.

Yoga-Vasishta.

Yule—Cathay and the Way Thither.

Do. The New Marco Polo.

Yule—The Wonders of the East—Friar Jordanus.

Yule and Burnell—Hobson—Jobson. A Dictionary of Angle-Indian Terms.

The Transliteration Table followed in the printing of this work.

The Press has accented letters only for 12 point capitals and lower case letters ; and, even among these, the sets are not complete.

In spite of great care, a few mistakes have crept in to mar the uniformity attempted to be maintained in spelling the names of places and of persons. For this, the Editor craves the pardon of the reader.

This Press owns no letters of the Nagara alphabet, and so Malayalam characters have to be used.

അ	a	ഖ	kha	പ	pa
ആ	ā	ഗ	ga	ഫ	pha
ഇ	i	ഘ	gha	ബ	ba
ഈ	ī	ങ	nga	ഭ	bha
ഉ	u	ച	cha	മ	ma
ഊ	ū	ഛ	chha	യ	ya
ഋ	ṛ	ജ	ja	ര	ra
ൠ	ṝ	ഝ	jha	ല	la
ഌ	ḷ	ഞ	ña	വ	va
ൡ	ḹ	ട	ṭa	ശ	śa
എ	e	ഠ	ṭha	ഷ	ṣha
ഏ	ē	ഡ	ḍa	സ	sa
ഐ	ai	ഢ	ḍha	ഹ	ha
ഒ	o	ണ	ṇa	ള	l̇a
ഓ	ō	ത	ţa	ക്ഷ	kṣha
ഔ	au	ഥ	ţha	റ	ṙa
അം	aṃ	ദ	ḑa	ഴ	l̈a
അഃ	aḥ	ധ	ḑha	റ്റ	ťťa
ക	ka	ന	ṅa	ന്റ	ńťa

INDEX TO THE NOTES.

A.

B.

BR.

B.—*cont.*

C.

C—*cont.*

D.

E.

E—*cont.*

I.

J.

K.

K—*cont.*

L.

M.

M.—*cont.*

M.—*cont.*

N.

O.

P.

P.—*cont.*

P.—*cont.*

Q.

R.

S.

S.—*cont.*

T.

U.

V.

W.

X.

Y.

Z.

E.